Lives and Legacies:
An Encyclopedia of People Who Changed the World

Artists, Writers, and Musicians

Edited by Michel-André Bossy, Thomas Brothers,
and John C. McEnroe

Writers

Kim Domenico

Steve Goldberg

James Manheim

John C. McEnroe

Deborah Pokinski

Sasha Watson

ORYX PRESS
2001

The rare Arabian Oryx is believed to have inspired the myth of the unicorn. This desert antelope became virtually extinct in the early 1960s. At that time several groups of international conservationists arranged to have 9 animals sent to the Phoenix Zoo to be the nucleus of a captive breeding herd. Today the Oryx population is over 1,000, and over 500 have been returned to the Middle East.

© 2001 by The Oryx Press
An imprint of Greenwood Publishing Group
88 Post Road West, Westport, Connecticut 06881

Produced by The Moschovitis Group, Inc.
339 Fifth Avenue, New York, New York 10016
www.mosgroup.com

Publisher: Valerie Tomaselli
Executive Editor: Hilary Poole
Design and Layout: Annemarie Redmond
Original Illustrations: TurnStyle Imaging
Editorial Coordinator: Sonja Matanovic
Line Editing: Stephanie Schreiber, Drew Silver
Copyediting: Carole Campbell
Fact Checking: Colleen Sullivan
Proofreading: Joseph Reilly
Editorial Assistants: Matt Doyle, Colleen Sullivan
Index: AEIOU, Inc.

Published simultaneously in Canada
Printed and Bound in the United States of America

ISBN 1-57356-154-1

Library of Congress Cataloging-in Publication Data

Table of Contents

Listing of Biographies

Achebe, Chinua
Ailey, Alvin
Alberti, Leon Battista
Anderson, Marian
Angelou, Maya
Anguissola, Sofonisba
Arbus, Diane
Armstrong, Louis
Austen, Jane
Bach, Johann Sebastian
Baldwin, James
Balanchine, George
Bashō
Basquiat, Jean-Michel
Baudelaire, Charles-Pierre
Beckett, Samuel
Beethoven, Ludwig van
Berlin, Irving
Bernini, Gian Lorenzo
Bernstein, Leonard
Blake, William
Borges, Jorge Luis
Bosch, Hieronymus
Botticelli, Sandro
Bourke-White, Margaret
Brahms, Johannes
Brecht, Bertolt
Brontë, Charlotte
Brown, James
Büchner, Georg
Cage, John
Camões, Luíz Vaz de
Caravaggio
Cassatt, Mary
Cervantes, Miguel de
Césaire, Aimé-Fernand
Cézanne, Paul
Chaucer, Geoffrey
Chekhov, Anton
Chopin, Fryderyk
Coltrane, John
Conrad, Joseph
Copland, Aaron
Cruz, Celia
Cruz, Sor Juana Inés de la
Cunningham, Merce
Dalí, Salvador
Dante
Davis, Miles
Debussy, Claude

Degas, Edgar
Diaghilev, Serge
Dickens, Charles
Dickinson, Emily
Disney, Walt
Dorsey, Thomas A.
Dostoyevsky, Fyodor
Duchamp, Marcel
Duncan, Isadora
Duras, Marguerite
Dürer, Albrecht
Dylan, Bob
Eakins, Thomas
Eliot, George
Ellington, Duke
Faulkner, William
Fela
Flaubert, Gustave
Franklin, Aretha
Frost, Robert
García Márquez, Gabriel
Gentileschi, Artemisia
Gershwin, George
Giotto
Goethe, Johann Wolfgang von
Goya, Francisco
Graham, Martha
Gregory I, Pope
Griffith, D. W.
Guo Xi
Handel, George Frideric
Haydn, Franz Joseph
Hendrix, Jimi
Hiroshige
Hitchcock, Alfred
Holiday, Billie
Homer
Homer, Winslow
Hugo, Victor-Marie
Ibsen, Henrik
Jackson, Mahalia
Jāmi
Jobim, Antonio Carlos
Johnson, Robert
Joplin, Scott
Josquin des Prez
Joyce, James
Kafka, Franz
Kahlo, Frida
Kalthum, Umm

Keats, John
Kern, Jerome
Khan, Nusrat Fateh Ali
Kōetsu
Kurosawa Akira
Lawrence, Jacob
Lennon, John and Paul McCartney
Leonardo da Vinci
Lin, Maya
Liszt, Franz
Lorca, Federico García
Lynn, Loretta
Makeba, Miriam
Manet, Edouard
Mann, Thomas
Marley, Bob
Matisse, Henri
Melville, Herman
Michelangelo
Mies van der Rohe, Ludwig
Milton, John
Modersohn-Becker, Paula
Molière
Moloney, Paddy
Mondrian, Piet
Monet, Claude
Monteverdi, Claudio
Moore, Henry
Morrison, Toni
Mozart, Wolfgang Amadeus
Murasaki Shikibu
Nadar
Neruda, Pablo
Ni Zan
O'Keeffe, Georgia
Orwell, George
Ovid
Paik, Nam June
Palestrina, Giovanni Pierluigi da
Palladio
Parker, Charlie
Paz, Octavio
Piaf, Edith
Piazzolla, Astor
Picasso, Pablo
Pollock, Jackson
Pound, Ezra
Presley, Elvis
Proust, Marcel
Pushkin, Aleksandr

Raphael
Rauschenberg, Robert
Reich, Steve
Rembrandt
Renoir, Pierre-Auguste
Rilke, Rainer Maria
Ringgold, Faith
Rivera, Diego
Rockwell, Norman
Rodin, Auguste
Rubens, Peter Paul
Sappho
Schoenberg, Arnold
Schumann, Robert
Sesshū
Shakespeare, William
Shankar, Ravi
Shen Zhou
Smith, Bessie
Sophocles
Stravinsky, Igor
Swift, Jonathan
Tagore, Rabindranath
Tanner, Henry Ossawa
Tchaikovsky, Peter Ilich
Tharp, Twyla
Titian
Tolstoy, Leo
Truffaut, François
Ts'ao Hsüeh-ch'in
Tu Fu
Twain, Mark
Tyagaraja
Van Eyck, Jan
Van Gogh, Vincent
Varèse, Edgard
Velázquez, Diego
Verdi, Giuseppe
Virgil
Wagner, Richard
Warhol, Andy
Welles, Orson
Whitman, Walt
Williams, Hank
Williams, Tennessee
Woolf, Virginia
Wordsworth, William
Wright, Frank Lloyd
Yeats, William Butler
Zeami Motokiyo

Introduction

As part of the *Lives and Legacies* series, this volume aims to link the work of individual writers, artists, and musicians to the influence they have had on their discipline and on our lives. All these individuals, in their own ways, are impressive for the extent to which their work influenced and guided contemporary and future generations, shaped the thinking about their craft, and addressed the sensibilities of their audience.

The most challenging aspect of producing this book was surely the initial phase—selecting 200 men and women out of many thousands of visual artists, musicians, and authors. We have tried to span the breadth of history and genres to identify individuals from various cultures and perspectives who influenced the shape of our present world. By necessity, we have left out some individuals of note, but we hope the reader will forgive such omissions.

In this introduction, we have attempted to outline major historical trends in visual art, music, and literature in order to offer a context for the way we selected the individuals in the book and for how we assessed their contributions.

Visual Art

Few questions elicit more heated responses than "What is Art?" Part of the difficulty in the question lies in the enormous diversity of images people have made. Human beings have been making visual images for over 25,000 years. Across the globe, images are essential to religion, politics, and cultural identity. Images can make our most abstract conceptions concrete. We can use images to visualize the future or to commemorate the past. They can embody our highest aspirations or our deepest fears. Visual images not only address issues of "truth and beauty," but have also involved lies and ugliness. Throughout history visual stereotypes, for example, have been used to justify racism, xenophobia, and anti-Semitism, enabling the dominant elements of societies to maintain power over those who were in some way different. For good or for evil, visual images are indispensable components of human society. Given that vast diversity of images, it is difficult to find a single description that suits them all.

Even more problematic is the fact that the vast majority of the visual images made in the past were not "art" in the way that we generally use the term today, nor were they made by individuals who regarded themselves as "artists." Our conceptions of art and artist are relatively recent phenomena and are limited to our own Western culture.

Today the word *artist* conjures up a particular image: the specially gifted, but isolated genius suffering for the sake of art and self-expression. Only in the years around 1500 did this notion of the artist as creative genius begin. Previously "creativity" was a power accorded only to God. With artists like Michelangelo—called *il Divino*, "the Divine," by his admirers—the concept shifted. Michelangelo was credited with the God-given gift of creative power. Interestingly, the earliest biographies of artists, particularly those by the Italian painter and writer Giorgio Vasari, were introduced at about the same moment in history. These two phenomena were linked. Like the concept of creativity and genius, biographies located the source of originality in the individual. From Italy, this new notion of the artist, as opposed to medieval craftmaker, slowly spread throughout Europe.

If the concept of the artist began only in the Renaissance, the concept of art is even more recent, going back only to the late eighteenth century. For Immanuel Kant and other philosophers of the Enlightenment, "Art" (with a capital A) was something that transcended the mundane realities of daily life. Rather than serving some religious, social, or practical purpose, true Art was "Art for art's sake"—intended primarily for aesthetic appreciation by people of taste.

This definition of art had distinct qualitative implications. It implied that a work of art is somehow superior to a mere craft because art addresses a higher level of human sensibilities. Earlier visual images, a cave painting, for example, or a Renaissance painting of the Madonna, or a portrait of a king, might be regarded as art only to the extent that they rose above their other, more immediate functions.

Through the nineteenth century, the concepts of art and artist continued to evolve. The Romantic movement of the mid-nineteenth century saw the artist as a heroic figure. The Romantics emphasized the importance of individual experience, feelings, and emotions. To them, reason and logic were only partial guides to the human condition and the artist-genius—the visual artist, musician, or writer—rather than the scientist was seen as the person best able to directly access and express the deepest realms of human experience.

During the twentieth century the idea of art was often problematized by artists themselves: When Marcel Duchamp fastened a bicycle wheel to the top of a wooden stool and submitted it for exhibition, he was presenting a direct challenge to the conventional idea of art. Why was this odd combination of ordinary mass-produced objects "art"? In one move Duchamp had jettisoned traditional expectations of craftsmanship and aesthetic quality. To him it was primarily the artist's conception—the idea rather than the object—that mattered.

Duchamp set the stage for much of the art of the second half of the twentieth century. In the 1970s Earth Art, Performance Art, Video Art, and Conceptual Art expanded the concept of art beyond the traditional frameworks of painting, sculpture, and architecture. Some artists rebelled against the notion of the art object as a commercial commodity. Conversely, at about the same time the Pop Art of artists like Andy Warhol reveled in commercialization. Warhol blurred the boundaries between art and mass culture and challenged the elitism of the traditional idea of art. Just as Warhol imagined a world in which everyone would be famous for 15 minutes, so too in his world everything might be art.

By the 1980s a new wave of artists committed to social issues such as the politics of race, gender, and sexual orientation questioned the presumed disinterestedness of "Art for art's sake." Contrary to what the philosophers of the Enlightenment had believed—no

work of art, they asserted, could be completely detached from its social context—all images, particularly those that claimed the elitist designation "art," had political implications.

This outraged conservative critics such as Hilton Kramer: To them, these so-called Post-Modern challenges to the traditional ideas of "Art" are generally seen as either political correctness run amok or as a nihilistic attempt to undermine the basic idea of quality. Many saw Pop Art as equally insidious: to say everything was art was to say that nothing was art.

Today the question "What is Art?" continues to elicit emotionally charged responses from artists, critics, and students precisely because the question is entangled in these complex issues. When we attempt to address the question, we are entering into a conversation that has been gradually evolving and transforming itself for more than two centuries. There is no simple answer. However, to dismiss the term as meaningless would be to miss out on something important. If we look at some of the works made by the visual artists considered in this book—a painting by Rembrandt, a film by Orson Welles, a sculpture by Auguste Rodin, as examples—we will come to the understanding that visual artists have often managed to express ideas, feelings, and experiences that could not be expressed in any other way.

John C. McEnroe
July 2001

Music

Music floats through the air, available to anyone to make of it what he or she wishes. The individual experience of music ranges from the intensely personal to the boldly political. A composer may sit at his desk and invent music that has tremendous influence, much like the discovery of a scientist. The direct impact of a singer or an instrumentalist on an audience may extend long past the immediate duration of the sounds, depending on how the music merges with social activities of various kinds. In this regard, the power of music increased dramatically during the twentieth century, because of a series of technological innovations involving the distribution of recorded sound. In the music entries for *Lives and Legacies*, we have tried to present a diverse selection of musicians who made their marks in various ways. For the purpose of introducing the entries, it may be useful to speak of three groups, "classical" composers in the European tradition, major innovators outside of this tradition, and twentieth-century "popular" musicians, with special emphasis on African Americans.

The word *classical* implies permanent values that transcend the particulars of time and place. That is hardly an accurate way to think about any kind of music, which is always conditioned by relative values that change over time and through different cultures. Yet there are good reasons for the fact that European music in the high art tradition achieved a special status, and one of the main reasons has to do with the way that it was transmitted. Early in the Middle Ages, musical notation came to be favored as a way to make the melodies of plainchant (religious music in the medieval church) permanent and unchangeable. A legend credited Pope Gregory I (Gregory the Great) with creating the chants through the inspiration of the Holy Spirit. Musical notation quickly spread throughout the European monasteries as the best way to fix the content of these melodies. Gregory may not have composed a single one, but the huge repertory of Gregorian chant was the legacy that the medieval Church assigned to him. Gregorian chant did not lose its place in Roman Catholic churches until the 1960s—well over a thousand years after being written down.

With musical notation, the composer gained increasing status; as a result, the European high art tradition developed differently from high art traditions in other parts of the world. We have included entries for several important early composers. Compositions by Josquin des Prez were studied by everyone in the sixteenth century who aspired to be a composer. He rose to fame just when music printing started to be profitable, around 1500. Following him, Giovanni Pierluigi da Palestrina became the first composer whose music for the church continued to be performed for many centuries. At the end of the sixteenth century stands Claudio Monteverdi, a towering figure who is especially important for having created the first great operas; they are still performed today. We have included several more recent and better-known musicians who were also important for their innovations in opera, including

Wolfgang Amadeus Mozart, Richard Wagner, and Giuseppe Verdi.

The legacy of a classical composer may have as much to do with the continuing presence of his music as with any single innovation with which he was credited. Johann Sebastian Bach is perhaps the first composer who contributed to what stands today as the classical canon—that is, an unofficially collected body of recognized masterpieces, known intimately by professionals and by serious lovers of the tradition. Bach was hardly the most famous composer of his lifetime, and when he died he was isolated from current musical fashions. But it did not take long for the depth of his achievement to be appreciated by the masters of the late eighteenth century. Mozart studied his music—and also the music of George Frideric Handel, Bach's contemporary—just as he studied Franz Joseph Haydn, his older colleague. Ludwig van Beethoven absorbed the legacies of all of these. This process was intensified in the nineteenth century, and in this way the legacy of each of these masters extends far beyond what he ever could have imagined. Of course, the classical repertoire of the eighteenth and nineteenth centuries still has a large presence in concert halls. Thus, the legacies of Fryderyk Chopin, Robert Schumann, Franz Liszt, Johannes Brahms, and Peter Ilich Tchaikovsky, in addition to all the composers just mentioned, are all very present in the lives of concert goers, in addition to whatever influence they might have on professional composers today. Furthermore, most of these masters were innovative. Liszt, for example, extended the boundaries of piano virtuosity, while Brahms was a great innovator in harmony.

The classical tradition is a living one, and concert goers know well the much-loved masterpieces of composers like Aaron Copland and Leonard Bernstein. Composers of ragtime, popular songs, and musicals were just a step away from the classical tradition; Scott Joplin, Irving Berlin, George Gershwin, Jerome Kern, and Duke Ellington each had a huge impact on the American musical scene. Around 1900, trends in classical music emerged that took it outside of mainstream concert halls and had much to do with avant-garde Modernism in the other arts. Claude Debussy straddled the two worlds, the avant-garde and the concert-going public, as did Igor Stravinsky.

Arnold Schoenberg created dissonant music that is not easily accessible. His place in this volume is not dictated by his status in the concert hall but by his innovative modern style. He was followed in this regard by Edgard Varèse, who experimented with artificial sounds, by John Cage, who experimented with random sounds, and by Steve Reich, who experimented with Minimalism.

Musical traditions that flourish independently of musical notation leave less certainty about who was responsible for innovations, but many figures still stand out. Zeami Motokiyo helped to form Noh drama in Japan, around 1400. Tyagaraja, a pioneer in South India from around 1800, composed songs that are still well known. Umm Kalthun is widely thought to be the Arab world's greatest musician of the twentieth century. Several relatively recent figures have been important in bringing traditional music to the world stage. Nusrat Fateh Ali Khan played a central role in both preserving the traditional music of Sufi Pakistan and, at the same time, modernizing that tradition. Paddy Moloney did something similar for Irish "folk" music, through the band known as The Chieftains. Astor Piazzolla worked with the traditional music of Argentina to form a compositional tradition based on the tango, and Antonio Carlos Jobim did something similar in Brazil with the tango. Ravi Shankar became famous as a practitioner of high-art music from northern India, performing as a virtuoso sitarist. Celia Cruz from Cuba brought salsa to international attention. Edith Piaf and Hank Williams played prominent roles in the traditions of French music hall and American country music, respectively.

Through recorded sound, music that was not created or distributed in writing could achieve a lasting presence comparable to what the great European classical composers had achieved through notation. Twentieth-century innovations in musical technology exploded alongside tumultuous politics, allowing music to play a highly noticeable role in social change. In colonial Africa and in Jamaica, Miriam Makeba, Fela, and Bob Marley established powerful voices for social change. Elvis Presley, Bob Dylan, John Lennon and Paul McCartney, and Jimi Hendrix were central to youth movements during the 1950s and 1960s. Loretta Lynn brought to the fore in country music a women's perspective.

One goal of *Lives and Legacies* is to draw attention to the achievements of people who have overcome great difficulties. Many important African-American musicians have left a stunning and broadly influential musical legacy. In blues, there is the important work of Bessie Smith and Robert Johnson, and in jazz, Louis Armstrong, Billie Holiday, Charlie Parker, Miles Davis, and John Coltrane. In religious music, Thomas A. Dorsey left a compositional legacy and Mahalia Jackson left a vocal performance legacy; secularized religious music offers Aretha Franklin and James Brown. On the concert stage, Marian Anderson broke the color barrier with a voice that many felt was unparalleled.

This is also the place to mention our entries for important figures in the history of dance. Isadora Duncan was a pioneer in modern dance around the beginning of the twentieth century, and Twyla Tharp at the end of that same century. Martha Graham collaborated with Copland, Serge Diaghilev with Stravinsky and Merce Cunningham with Cage to produce landmark events in musical-dance collaborations. George Balanchine brought the Russian tradition to New York. And Alvin Ailey pioneered a dance tradition in which African-American techniques merged with ballet.

Thomas Brothers
July 2001

Literature

Literature shares certain affinities with music and with visual art. As its basic materials are words, literature employs *sound* as its primary medium. In most civilizations, in fact, melody and poetry first arose in unison, in the form of songs. Poets of all ages and nations have recalled this ancient bond of kinship between their art and music—see, for example, Virgil, William Shakespeare, Johann Wolfgang von Goethe, William Blake, Victor-Marie Hugo, Rainer Maria Rilke, and William Butler Yeats. Literature, like music, can be preserved and passed on from one generation to the next by human memory alone, without the aid of paper, clay tablets, or any other writing material or technological instrument. Poems and stories transmitted in this unwritten way are often referred to as *oral literature*. Masterpieces of oral literature are generally anonymous, so their creators remain outside the purview of this collection of biographies. (One exception is the legendary Homer, whose name has come down to us, even though his life is not documented in any way.)

Yet the word *literature* comes from the Latin noun *littera*, meaning a written sign, a letter of the alphabet. That etymology reminds us how closely literature in script-using civilizations is intertwined with the images that preserve it. Poetry becomes inseparable from the shapes of its written signs, especially when the culture's alphabet is logogrammatic (every word represented by a separate sign). In such cultures poetry is fused to calligraphy, the visual art of writing, as exemplified by Tu Fu and Bashō. In the West, Blake also stands out as a creator who was simultaneously a poet, graphic artist, and painter.

Speaking more generally, we observe that literature uses words to conjure images in our mind's eye. As listeners or readers, we come to *envision* scenes, situations, and characters. Creative writers are often said to "paint" with words—Simonides of Keos stated around 500 B.C.E. that "poetry is a speaking picture, painting a silent poetry." Moreover, throughout the history of Western literature many thinkers have enjoined writers to *depict* life accurately and to *portray* believable characters. In their literary treatises, Aristotle and Horace propagated the view that poetry and painting were both imitative arts. Aristotle's immensely influential *Poetics* stressed in particular that poetry and tragic drama (as exemplified by Sophocles) should "mirror" life in a representational way. According to Aristotle, the purpose of literary art was to provide a *mimesis* (or imitation) of reality that would bring into relief its universal characteristics. This mimetic doctrine became the foundation of Western Neoclassicism and profoundly influenced narrative poets and playwrights from the late Middle Ages until the eighteenth century, including Dante, Geoffrey Chaucer, William Shakespeare, John Milton, and Molière. It also played a major role in the development of the novel, with its search for ever-sharper verisimilitude, from Miguel de Cervantes to nineteenth-century authors like Jane Austen, Charlotte Brönte, George Eliot, Charles Dickens, and Gustave Flaubert.

Mimetic forms of literature presume a firm distinction between subject and object. In this "realistic" perspective the individual self stands apart from the objective world that it perceives and that it represents and reproduces in the form of art. Many writers, however, have questioned this simple dichotomy between self and object, or between the knower and what it knows. For them, as for Homer, there is no split between knowing subject and known object, and no boundary between the creative imagination and what it envisions. For some of these writers inner vision intrinsically surpasses outer perceptions—for example, in Europe romantic poets such as the young Goethe, William Wordsworth, and John Keats; in Asia, such poets as Jāmi and Rabidranath Tagore. For other writers, such as Charles-Pierre Baudelaire, Fyodor Dostoyevsky, and Joseph Conrad, inner vision is a creative act that must be strenuously undertaken against the repressive weight of society. Certain creators embrace both positions by juxtaposing a spontaneous and unmediated vision of innocence with a bitterly hard-won vision of experience (Blake and Yeats, for example).

During the past century Modernist writers spearheaded the opposition to complacent mimetic literary doctrines and practices in the West. Their ranks included certain authors whose aesthetic views and techniques were avant-garde while their social politics were fairly middle-of-the-road, such as Thomas Mann, James Joyce, Franz Kafka, and Samuel Beckett; some could be characterized as conservative, including William Faulkner and Jorge Luis Borges, or on the extreme right, including Ezra Pound. Other twentieth-century writers, however, moved in progressive or even strongly radical ideological directions, in support of large-scale social and political changes. Such writers include Federico García Lorca, Virginia Woolf, Bertolt Brecht, George Orwell, Pablo Neruda, Aimé-Fernand Césaire, Octavio Paz, James Baldwin, and Chinua Achebe. Post-Modernists too vary in their politics. In their works they subvert the continuity of history and the concept of objective truth even more extensively than did the Modernists, and to that end they employ techniques of extreme fantasy, stylistic eclecticism, and self-parody. Joyce, Gabriel García Márquez, Maguerite Duras, and Toni Morrison represent this trend.

During the past two centuries many leading writers have been fascinated by the contingency of literary forms and conventions. This acute aesthetic consciousness has often been accompanied by a desire to invert conventions and draw forms into new configurations. New literary vogues and movements have followed on each other's heels at a quickening rate. To achieve an effect of novelty, writers disinter older forms that have fallen into disuse; the refurbished forms then become elements of creative parody. Literature reinvigorates itself by scavenging through its own half-forgotten attic treasures. At the same time, however, literature still revitalizes itself by borrowing heavily from the other arts—especially popular music, film, and video. Music and visual art remain literature's close companions in contemporary culture.

Michel-Andre Bossy
July 2001

The
Biographies

Achebe, Chinua

Novelist
1930–

Life and Work

Chinua Achebe is one of Africa's most influential and widely published writers.

He was born Chinualumogu Albert Achebe, in Ogidi, what is today Anambra State in Nigeria, on November 16, 1930. His parents were evangelical Anglican Protestants, who raised him in both Christian and Nigerian Ibo tradition.

Achebe attended Government College in Umuahia and then went on to earn his undergraduate degree from University College in Ibadan in 1953. He studied English philology, history, and theology and later studied broadcasting at the BBC in London.

His first and best-known novel, *Things Fall Apart*, was published in 1958. The story of an Ibo leader who is banished when he accidentally kills a member of his community is set in the 1890s, when colonial government and Christian missionaries were first attempting to change Ibo culture. The novel illustrates the complex African battle with colonialism.

Achebe's career has been both political and academic. He worked in the Biafran government service during the Nigerian Civil War from 1967 to 1970. In 1967 he also founded a publishing house with a poet, Christopher Okigbo. Soon after, he began teaching literature at the University of Nigeria. Other teaching positions followed, including posts at the University of Massachusetts at Amherst, Connecticut College, and Bard College, among others. Since 1971 Achebe has edited *Okike*, the leading journal of Nigerian new writing. He has also been instrumental in introducing the work of many African writers to the larger English-speaking world as the founding editor of and chief editorial advisor to the African Writers Series of the British publisher Heinemann.

In his 21 novels, short stories, and collections of poetry, Achebe has often returned to the themes of traditional Ibo life in conflict with colonial society. His work has been widely acclaimed and his novels, including *No Longer At Ease* (1960), *Arrow of God* (1964), and *Anthills of the Savannah* (1987), have won international awards.

A repressive series of Nigerian dictatorships have caused Achebe to live primarily outside of the country since the 1970s. A serious car accident in 1990 left Achebe paralyzed from the waist down. He continues to teach, to write, and to be an active force in politics.

Legacy

Chinua Achebe's satirical prose, written in the rhythms of spoken language, and his articulate political engagement have made him one of the most highly esteemed African writers in English.

Achebe was one of the founders of a new Nigerian literature in the 1950s. During this time of social upheaval, many young writers used the turmoil of the society around them and the African oral tradition in their work. Achebe was widely considered a leader of these writers, and his work quickly became internationally known.

Achebe has adapted the novel, originally a European form, blending its narrative structure with those of African tradition. African experience informs the content, the rhythm, and the aesthetic of his novels, with portraits of African communal life often taking the place of the traditional European portraits of individual character. Achebe was among the first African writers to use the conventions of the novel to convey the historical and social conditions of African life.

Achebe has ensured that politics are deeply embedded in Nigerian literature, declaring that all art should have a message and a purpose. His novels often describe the effects of Western customs and values on traditional African society, and his essays, collected in the volumes *Morning Yet on Creation Day* (1975), *The Trouble With Nigeria* (1983), *Hopes and Impediments* (1988), and *Home and Exile* (2000), are often directly and vigorously political. Achebe has frequently attacked critics who refused to look at African literature on its own terms.

Watson

WORLD EVENTS	ACHEBE'S LIFE
Great Depression 1929–39	
1930	Chinua Achebe is born
World War II 1939–45	
Communist China 1949 is established	
Korean War 1950–53	
1953	Achebe graduates from college
African independence 1957 movement begins	
1958	Achebe publishes *Things Fall Apart*
1967	Achebe founds publishing house
1971	Achebe starts *Okike*
Vietnam War ends 1975	
1987	Achebe publishes *Anthills of the Savannah*
1990	Achebe is paralyzed in car accident
Dissolution of 1991 Soviet Union	

For Further Reading

Ezenwa-Ohaeto. *Chinua Achebe: A Biography.* Bloomington: Indiana University Press, 1997.

Wren, Robert M. *Achebe's World: The Historical and Cultural Context of the Novels of Chinua Achebe.* Washington, D.C.: Three Continents Press, 1980.

Ailey, Alvin

Dance Pioneer
1931–1989

Life and Work

A choreographer who led a dance company of worldwide renown, Alvin Ailey brought together the worlds of concert dance and African-American artistic expression.

Ailey was born in Rogers, Texas, on January 5, 1931. As a child, he picked cotton and did laundry with his mother, who had split up with his father when Alvin was six months old. Ailey's Baptist upbringing manifested itself in his later work. His mother moved him to Los Angeles when he was 12. First a school field trip to see the Russian Ballet of Monte Carlo and then a performance by the Katherine Dunham Dance Company stirred his interest in dance. He began to dance himself, taking classes with Lester Horton, the creator of per-

WORLD EVENTS	AILEY'S LIFE
Great Depression 1929–39	
	1931 Alvin Ailey is born
World War II 1939–45	
Communist China 1949	
is established	
Korean War 1950–53	
	1953 Ailey leads Lester Horton Dance Theater
	1954 Ailey moves to New York City
African independence 1957	
movement begins	
	1958 Ailey establishes Alvin Ailey American Dance Theater
	1960 Ailey choreographs *Revelations*
	1963 Ailey integrates his dance company
	1969 Ailey founds own dance school
Vietnam War ends 1975	
	1989 Ailey dies
Dissolution of 1991	
Soviet Union	

haps the first racially integrated dance company in the United States.

When Horton died in 1953, the 22-year-old Ailey took over the Lester Horton Dance Theater and began to create dances of his own. He gave up that position to move to New York the following year, dancing in the Broadway musical *House of Flowers* and studying with several major figures of modern dance, including MARTHA GRAHAM and Doris Humphrey. He founded the Alvin Ailey American Dance Theater in 1958.

In its early years Ailey's company was comprised solely of black dancers; several of his major ballets from those years treated aspects of the African-American experience. *Revelations*, a 1960 work danced to black spirituals, drew on the religious experiences of Ailey's own youth. Ailey would continue to turn to African-American music and subject matter for the rest of his life, often choreographing works based on jazz (*The River*, a 1970 work, featured music by DUKE ELLINGTON). He integrated his company in 1963 and addressed a wide variety of music and material in his 79 ballets. He also contributed choreography to non-ballet stage works, including LEONARD BERNSTEIN's ambitiously ecumenical *Mass*. Ailey's works merged elements of modern dance, classical ballet, jazz, other African-American dance, and world dance traditions.

A dance educator committed to reproducing the opportunities that he himself had enjoyed, Ailey founded a dance school, the Alvin Ailey American Dance Center, in 1969, and worked to bring dance to schools and summer education programs. Ailey died of the rare blood disease dyscrasia in New York on December 1, 1989.

Legacy

A lvin Ailey's dances represented American culture at its eclectic and inclusive best. He spread his vision of a truly American dance all over the world; the Alvin Ailey American Dance Theater had performed in 68 countries on six continents as of 1999.

All the institutions he put in place continued to flourish after his death. The dance company championed the work of innovative and emerging dancers and choreographers; by 1999 it had offered exposure to 67 choreographers. Ailey's American Dance Center, begun with 125 students, expanded to an interna-

tional student body of 3,500, many of whom would emerge with a commitment to Ailey's idealistic goals of cultural bridge building. His youth education efforts blossomed into the Ailey Camps, which offered low-income youngsters summer days full of creative activities and arts-oriented field trips. Clearly the artistic impulses Ailey set in motion transcended his own personal leadership.

Ailey's impact as an African-American dancer was immense. Growing up in poverty in the segregated, pre-civil-rights-era South to become the leader of an innovative, internationally recognized, and widely popular dance company, he increased exponentially the presence of black dancers in the world of the formal stage. Popular touring companies of the 1990s such as the Dance Theater of Harlem owed their existence to Ailey's work with young black artists.

In a wider sense, Ailey spoke in motion with an idealistic, humanistic voice that helped to transform dance from an elite art to a vital component of American popular culture. The dances he choreographed were often humorous and touching, reflecting a wide range of human emotions and interactions. He emphasized the universality of his art, despite criticism from 1960s militants for his integrationist views. Ailey insisted on the right of black dance artists to work with materials that originated outside African-American culture, and the immensely popular *Harlem Nutcracker* must be seen as part of his legacy. Drawing on African-American cultural wellsprings, Alvin Ailey invigorated the world of dance.

Manheim

For Further Reading

Ailey, Alvin. *Revelations: The Autobiography of Alvin Ailey*. Secaucus, N.J.: Carol Publishing, 1995.

Dunning, Jennifer. *Alvin Ailey: A Life in Dance*. Reading, Mass.: Addison-Wesley, 1996.

Alberti, Leon Battista

Architect, Sculptor, and
Theoretician
1404–1472

Life and Work

Although known today chiefly as an architect, Leon Battista Alberti produced theoretical work that substantially promoted the social and intellectual status of artists in Renaissance Italy.

Alberti was born in Genoa in 1404, where his family lived in exile, having fled from Florence in 1402. He attended the University of Bologna, receiving a doctorate in canon law in 1428. Earning his living primarily as an advisor to princes and popes, he was able to extend his architectural influence well beyond the buildings he designed. A Renaissance humanist, Alberti had read *De Architectura* by the Roman architect Vitruvius and also studied ancient buildings; these experiences gave him a thorough understanding of Roman architecture.

In 1434, Alberti returned to Florence, where he became acquainted with the new generation of innovative Florentine artists: Tommaso Masaccio, Donato Donatello, and Filippo Brunelleschi. He dedicated his treatise *De Pictura* (*On Painting*), completed in 1435, to his friend Brunelleschi.

When Sigismondo Malatesta, the despotic ruler of the city of Rimini, commissioned him to design the exterior for the Church of San Francesco, Alberti was able to give his classical ideas worldly form. With this design, and another in 1470 for the Church of Sant' Andrea in Mantua, he sought to update existing medieval churches with architectural forms derived from Roman antiquity and organized according to simple mathematical proportions.

Alberti also designed the facade for the Palazzo Rucellai in Florence, which he began in the mid-1450s. This building became the model for many later Florentine palaces.

Alberti wrote several works in Latin, ranging from poetry to a treatise on how to conduct family life (though he remained a bachelor) called *On the Family*. He also wrote an autobiography. The treatises on painting (*De Pictura*) and sculpture (*De Statua*) explained the underlying principles of these art forms. His ideas on architecture, such as his preference for centralized plans, his close study of the true proportions of the classical orders, and his ideas on facade design, had a great impact on Renaissance architecture.

After spending his final years in Rome, Alberti died in 1472.

Legacy

Leon Battista Alberti's writing provided the first theoretical descriptions of the new Renaissance style. Although others had developed aspects of the theory (Brunelleschi introduced scientific perspective), Alberti was the first to systematize and publish it, thus providing the first organized explanation of the revolutionary developments in the works of contemporary Florentine artists.

His works on architecture, painting, and sculpture were soon translated into the vernacular Italian, making them available to artists and patrons. Such broad accessibility ensured their status as the most influential books written on art during the Renaissance. In providing a popular theoretical basis for the new movement in art, Alberti helped move the visual arts from the realm of medieval manual crafts to an intellectual enterprise.

Alberti's impact extended into later Renaissance architecture. He promoted a centralized plan for church structures based on the ideal shape of the circle, which, in its balanced harmony, would reveal divinity. Although he never actually built such a "Christian temple," the centralized plan established the trend for architecture in the High Renaissance (1495–1520). In addition to his pursuit of mathematical ideals, Alberti was also an expert on Roman architecture. His buildings represent the quintessential fusion of ancient forms with fifteenth-century building types that became the paradigm of the Renaissance style.

Today, Alberti fulfills the ideal of *l'uomo universale* ("universal man") through his humanist interests, broad learning and capabilities, love of beauty, and hope for enduring fame.

Domenico

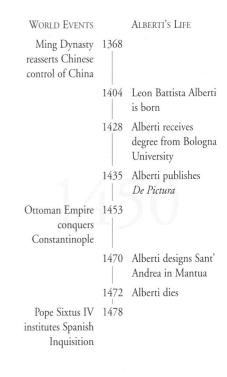

WORLD EVENTS		ALBERTI'S LIFE
Ming Dynasty reasserts Chinese control of China	1368	
	1404	Leon Battista Alberti is born
	1428	Alberti receives degree from Bologna University
	1435	Alberti publishes *De Pictura*
Ottoman Empire conquers Constantinople	1453	
	1470	Alberti designs Sant' Andrea in Mantua
	1472	Alberti dies
Pope Sixtus IV institutes Spanish Inquisition	1478	

For Further Reading

Alberti, Leon Battista. *On Painting and On Sculpture: The Latin Texts of "De Pictura" and "De Sculptura."* Translated and edited by C. Grayson. London: Phaidon, 1972.

Gadol, Joan. *Leon Battista Alberti: Universal Man of the Early Renaissance.* Chicago: University of Chicago Press, 1969.

Grafton, Anthony. *Leon Battista Alberti: Master Builder of the Italian Renaissance.* New York: Hill and Wang, 2000.

Anderson, Marian

Vocalist
1897–1993

World Events		Anderson's Life
Germany is united	1871	
	1897	Marian Anderson is born
Spanish-American War	1898	
World War I	1914–18	
Russian Revolution	1917	
	1925	Anderson wins New York Philharmonic vocal contest
	1929	Anderson travels to Europe
Great Depression	1929–39	
	1935	Anderson signs with promoter Sol Hurok
	1939	Anderson denied access to Constitution Hall
World War II	1939–45	
Communist China is established	1949	
Korean War	1950–53	
	1955	Anderson sings at Metropolitan Opera
African independence movement begins	1957	
	1961	Anderson sings at Kennedy inauguration
Vietnam War ends	1975	
Dissolution of Soviet Union	1991	
	1993	Anderson dies
South Africa dismantles apartheid	1994	

Life and Work

In the course of a career that immeasurably advanced the prospects of African Americans in the field of classical music, Marian Anderson emerged triumphant from one of the civil rights movement's great milestone confrontations.

Anderson was born in Philadelphia on February 17, 1897. Her voice received its initial challenges when she joined the junior choir of the Union Baptist Church at the age of six. Both Anderson's parents died when she was in her teens, but church members took up a collection to finance her voice lessons with a local operatic tenor, Giuseppe Boghetti; she had had trouble finding a teacher willing to take on a black protegée.

In 1925 she won a contest organized by the New York Philharmonic and appeared with that orchestra at an outdoor concert. Four years later she went to Europe, and her concerts there earned growing critical praise. The legendary Italian conductor Arturo Toscanini told her that "a voice like yours is heard only once in a hundred years." Back in the United States in 1935, Anderson signed with the promoter Sol Hurok and made an acclaimed appearance at New York's Town Hall.

In 1939 Hurok tried to book Anderson into Washington, D.C.'s Constitution Hall, a building owned by the Daughters of the American Revolution (D. A. R.). When the D. A. R., for purely racial reasons, refused the booking, massive protests erupted. Anderson won the support of First Lady Eleanor Roosevelt, who resigned from the D. A. R. in protest. Roosevelt arranged a concert by Anderson at the Lincoln Memorial on Easter Sunday, April 9, 1939. An audience of 75,000 in Washington was augmented by millions of radio listeners, many of whom learned a great deal about the self-effacing Anderson's long, quiet struggle against racial discrimination.

In 1955 Anderson became the first African American to take the stage at New York's Metropolitan Opera; although she was past her prime as a singer, the inspiration she had given younger artists made her a natural choice. Anderson sang at the inaugurations of Presidents Eisenhower and Kennedy; she retired in 1965. She died in Portland, Oregon, on April 8, 1993.

Legacy

Marian Anderson remains best known for the Constitution Hall controversy, but she herself generally shunned the role of political activist. The influence of her music, however, was substantial.

African Americans have been fairly well represented on world operatic and concert stages, and in large measure it was Anderson's career that paved the way. Vocal stars Leontyne Price, Jessye Norman, Shirley Verrett, and Kathleen Battle have all named Anderson as an impetus for their own performing ambitions. Anderson herself took an active interest in the education of younger singers; awarded a large cash prize in 1939 by the National Association for the Advancement of Colored People (NAACP), she used the money to establish a scholarship fund for aspiring vocal students. When Anderson sang for and met with heads of state and even European royalty (she sang at various times for the kings of Sweden, England, and Denmark), the impression she made on an African-American citizenry just beginning to struggle out of poverty was profound.

Anderson's artistry had a power all its own; the singers who followed her often recalled the beauty of her voice as an inspiration beyond her status as a leader and role model. "I listened, thinking, 'This can't be just a voice, so rich, so beautiful,'" Jessye Norman was quoted as saying in Anderson's *New York Times* obituary. "It was a revelation. And I wept." Anderson had a big voice, partly forged, like that of many other African-American performers, in the black church. But what she brought to classical vocal artistry was power tempered by technique.

Her recitals encompassed an impressive range of music from stirring spirituals to intimate German art songs, and the mix of materials she brought to the stage, so successful in making a connection with audiences, has been imitated by other vocalists, not all of them African American. A supremely talented and persistent artist, Marian Anderson broke down political and musical barriers.

Manheim

For Further Reading
Anderson, Marian. *My Lord, What a Morning*. New York: Viking, 1956.
Tedards, Anne. *Marian Anderson*. Philadelphia: Chelsea House, 1988.

Angelou, Maya

Poet and Autobiographer
1928–

Life and Work

Maya Angelou, an important poet and autobiographer, has brought the experience of African-American women and a message of strength and love to popular American literature.

Angelou was born April 4, 1928, as Marguerite Johnson in St. Louis, Missouri, and was raised by her paternal grandparents in segregated rural Arkansas. She had a troubled childhood and adolescence, and gave birth to a son at the age of 17. She received no formal education beyond high school but has said that her education continued through her travel, political activities, and life experience.

As a young mother, Angelou worked as a cook, a dancer, a dishwasher, a barmaid, and, as she wrote in one of her autobiographies, a prostitute. In the 1950s, she became active in the civil rights movement, working for Martin Luther King, Jr.'s Southern Christian Leadership Conference (SCLC).

Married to a South African political exile, Angelou moved to Cairo, Egypt, in 1961. There she worked as an editor of the newspaper *The Arab Observer*. After her divorce in 1963, she moved to Ghana, where she worked as a teacher and editor of *The African Review*. She returned to the United States in 1966. The first of her series of five autobiographical

works, *I Know Why the Caged Bird Sings*, was published in 1970 to immediate acclaim.

In addition to the four autobiographical narratives that have followed, Angelou has published eight volumes of poetry, including *Just Give Me a Cool Drink of Water 'Fore I Diiie* (1971), *And Still I Rise* (1978), *Oh, Pray My Wings Are Gonna Fit Me Well* (1975), and *I Shall Not Be Moved* (1990). The *Complete Collected Poems* of Maya Angelou was published in 1994. In 1997 she brought out a collection of essays, *Even the Stars Look Lonesome*. Angelou has also continued her performing career and has directed several films.

Angelou was appointed by President Gerald Ford to the Bicentennial Commission in 1976 and by President Jimmy Carter to the National Commission on the Observance of International Women's Year in 1977. In 1981 she became a special professor of American Studies at Wake Forest University. In 1993, Angelou became the second American poet to read a poem at a presidential inauguration. She has been awarded over 50 honorary degrees.

Legacy

Maya Angelou's account of her life in her five-book autobiographical narrative has deeply affected many readers. *I Know Why the Caged Bird Sings* was the first book by an African-American woman to reach the *New York Times* bestseller list and her books that followed have also been extraordinarily successful.

Angelou was one of a group of African-American women, including Alice Walker, TONI MORRISON, and Toni Cade Bambara, who gained widespread recognition in the 1970s. With these women, Angelou helped to open the field of African-American literature by speaking openly and honestly about her own experiences as an African-American woman, mother, feminist, and political activist. Angelou brought this fraught experience into popular American consciousness, thus making way for others to accept and to recognize their own experiences as an integral part of American history, and to write about them.

Angelou's accessible work with its message of common humanity and the importance and power of love has found a large audience. She has broken new ground for African-American women in film and television as well as in literature. She has written and produced several prize-winning documentaries, including *Afro-*

Americans in the Arts, a PBS special for which she received the Golden Eagle Award. Her screenplay *Georgia, Georgia* was the first by a black woman to be filmed, and she was nominated for an Emmy Award for her acting in *Roots*, the television version of the novel by Alex Haley.

Watson

WORLD EVENTS		ANGELOU'S LIFE
Russian Revolution	1917	
	1928	Maya Angelou is born
Great Depression	1929–39	
World War II	1939–45	
Communist China is established	1949	
Korean War	1950–53	
African independence movement begins	1957	
	1961	Angelou moves to Egypt
	1963	Angelou moves to Ghana
	1966	Angelou returns to the United States
	1970	Angelou publishes *I Know Why the Caged Bird Sings*
	1971	Angelou is nominated for Pulitzer Prize for *Just Give Me A Cool Drink of Water 'Fore I Diiie*
Vietnam War ends	1975	
Dissolution of Soviet Union	1991	
	1993	Angelou reads at President Clinton's inauguration
South Africa dismantles apartheid	1994	

For Further Reading

McPherson, Dolly. *Order Out of Chaos: The Autobiographical Works of Maya Angelou*. New York: Peter Lang, 1990.
Shuker, Nancy. *Maya Angelou*. Englewood Cliffs, N.J.: Silver Burdett Press, 1990.

Anguissola, Sofonisba

Painter

c. 1535–1625

Life and Work

Sofonisba Anguissola was the first woman painter to achieve international fame.

Anguissola was born in Cremona in northern Italy around 1535. Her father, an impoverished and landless aristocrat, nevertheless had his six daughters educated as sixteenth-century noblewomen, including tutoring in the fine arts—music, literature, and painting. When Sofonisba, the eldest of the sisters, was in her early teens she continued her serious art training with an apprenticeship with a local painter. Although almost unprecedented for a young woman, an apprenticeship was the only way to gain the training necessary to become a professional artist at the time. Usually, the only women to have this opportunity were the daughters of artists.

Anguissola became so skillful that one of her drawings came to the attention of Michelangelo, who admired and critiqued her work. He even sent back a follow-up challenge for the young artist: to paint a crying child. Her very realistic drawing of her brother, *Boy Bitten by a Crab* (before 1559), was the successful result.

Although she received professional training, Anguissola still faced restrictions as a woman and as an aristocrat. She was not allowed to formally study anatomy or the human figure, and she probably did most of her work at home using herself and members of her family as subjects. Like her teacher, Anguissola's first specialty was portrait painting. She gained a considerable reputation around Cremona and her many self-portraits became collectors' items.

In 1559, probably through her father's connections with the court of Philip II of Spain, Anguissola was invited to Madrid to become the painting instructor for Philip's new young queen, Isabel of Valois. This was not only an honor and an acknowledgement of her reputation, it was also an acceptable solution for the dilemma of marriage for Anguissola. Her father's lack of money meant there would be no dowries for any of his daughters and therefore no likely marriages. But, in Madrid, Anguissola would be a lady-in-waiting to the queen and a member of the royal court.

Anguissola remained in Spain for nearly 20 years. During that time she painted scores of portraits; her subjects included the queen, the king's sisters, other members of the court, and even the king himself. She also took up the challenge of larger, multifigured religious subjects. When Isabel of Valois died in 1568, the king, according to the queen's last wishes, arranged a marriage for Anguissola. In 1573, she married Don Fabrizio de Moncada, an aristocrat from Sicily, and returned with him to his home. After her husband's death, Anguissola met a Genoese nobleman, Orazio Lomellini, whom she married shortly afterward. She remained in Genoa and continued to paint until her death in 1625, at nearly 90 years of age.

Legacy

Because she was one of the first highly successful women artists, Sofonisba Anguissola was also one of the most well-known artists of her time, partly because female artists were so rare.

Giorgio Vasari, the first art historian, helped guarantee Anguissola's fame when he visited her while she was still a young painter in Cremona and included her in his book, *Lives of the Artists* (1550). PETER PAUL RUBENS and later Anthony Van Dyke both visited her when she lived in Genoa. Van Dyke recorded his visit with a small sketch of Anguissola in his journal.

Because of her fame, Anguissola became a role model for many of the women artists who were to follow her. Baroque painter ARTEMISIA GENTILESCHI certainly knew of her. Anguissola raised the level of recognition and respect given to women artists. As a well-born lady who always presented herself with dignity and poise, she commanded respect. Her example set the standard by which other women artists were regarded. Her frequent self-portraits also served as prototypes for later women artists, particularly sixteenth century Italian painter Lavinia Fontana. Anguissola's most significant contribution in this regard was her *Self-Portrait at the Easel* (1556), in which she emphatically depicted herself as a professional artist at work.

Anguissola contributed a more informal and personal approach to sixteenth-century portraiture. Many of her subjects were well known to her—family and friends—rather than formal commissions. Thus she gave their images believable personalities and genuine human qualities. In her early work, many of the paintings of her sisters and brother showed them in ordinary situations, playing games, laughing, or behaving like children rather than as small adults dressed up for formal pictures. Anguissola was one of the first to develop this unusual type of portraiture.

Anguissola continued to be well known and written about during the seventeenth and eighteenth centuries. In the nineteenth century she, like many women artists, was ignored and then forgotten by art historians. Today her work has been revived and recognized by art historians who regard her as a path breaking artist.

Pokinski

World Events		Anguissola's Life
Protestant Reformation begins	1517	
	c. 1535	Sofonisba Anguissola is born
	1549	Anguissola joins court of Philip II of Spain
Ottoman dominance of Mediterranean ends	1571	
Thirty Years' War in Europe	1618–48	
	1625	Anguissola dies
Glorious Revolution in England	1688	

For Further Reading

Ferino Pagden, Sylvia. *Sofonisba Anguissola: A Renaissance Woman*. Exhibition catalogue. Washington, D.C.: National Museum of Women in the Arts, 1995.

Perlingier, Ilya Sandra. *Sofonisba Anguissola: First Great Woman of the Renaissance*. New York: Rizzoli, 1992.

Arbus, Diane

Photographer
1923–1971

Life and Work

With her brutally frank portraits of people on the fringes of society, Diane Arbus stretched the boundaries of documentary photography and captured the uneasy mood of America in the late 1960s.

Diane Arbus was born Diane Nemerov in New York in 1923 into a privileged and sheltered life. Her father owned a department store on Fifth Avenue and the family lived in luxurious apartments with numerous servants. Her brother, Howard Nemerov, became a significant poet.

At age 18, she married Allan Arbus and quickly began to share his interest in photography. In 1946 the couple opened a fashion photography business, initially producing advertisements for her father's store, but soon taking on assignments for *Glamour*, *Vogue*, and *Seventeen*.

From 1955 to 1957 Arbus studied with the Austrian photographer Lisette Model and began to take her art more seriously. While she continued to create portraits of famous figures like writers Norman Mailer, W. H. Auden, and Susan Sontag for *Harper's* and *Esquire*, she became increasingly fascinated with making disturbing images of people who lived on the margins of society: side-show freaks, transvestites, Siamese twins, midgets, mentally handicapped people, and middle-aged nudists. In ruthlessly frank photographs the subject typically faces the camera directly, caught in the center of the square frame and lit by the unnatural light of the flash. The photographs placed both the photographer and the viewer in the uncomfortable position of voyeur, taking guilty delight in the spectacle of the subject's oddity. Even Arbus's photographs of people on the street uncovered the freakishness within the most ordinary of them. Her new work was the antithesis of her early work for fashion magazines.

Arbus quickly received critical acclaim. She was awarded two Guggenheim Fellowships. In 1971, at the height of her career, Arbus committed suicide. In 1972, her work was included in an important exhibition of the Museum of Modern Art.

Legacy

Immediately after her death, Diane Arbus became a cult figure. In 1972 she was selected as the first American photographer to represent the United States in the Venice Biennale, an exhibition of modern art featuring artists from around the world. In the same year, the Museum of Modern Art in New York mounted a retrospective show of her work that traveled across the country. In 1973 a Japanese retrospective of her work traveled through Europe and the Pacific.

At first Arbus's images were regarded as controversial. Many of her photographs seemed cruel, invasive, and cynical. These unsettling images are often presumed to have been a factor in her suicide—perhaps she had walked too close to the fire in her pursuit of the bizarre. Nevertheless, her images captured an important part of the deeply disturbed atmosphere of the era of Richard Nixon, the Vietnam War, and the protest movement. Her photographs of pro-war demonstrators or the image of a boy grimacing into the camera after pulling the pin from a toy hand grenade embodied the rage of an entire generation.

Arbus challenged the limitations of what was considered tasteful or acceptable. She took the apparently realistic style of documentary photographers like MARGARET BOURKE-WHITE and Dorothea Lange and stripped it of its romanticized nobility. Arbus's images were obsessive, pitiless, and grotesque; they continue to unsettle viewers today.

Contemporary photographers continue to be influenced by Arbus's direct, confrontational style, and have adopted her rejection of the formal poses and beautiful composition typical of traditional photography. Photographers like Duane Michels have imitated her look of spontaneity, and others have emulated her attempts to enter into her subjects most private realms. Her use of the flash to magnify the grossness of the flesh has become widespread. Today we see reflections of Arbus's work in the portrait photography of photographers like Richard Avedon, in the new genre of street photography, and even in advertising.

McEnroe

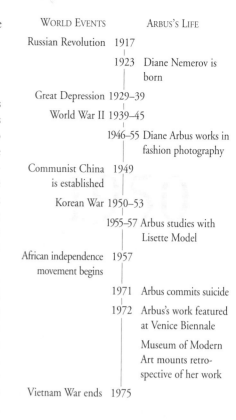

World Events		Arbus's Life
Russian Revolution	1917	
	1923	Diane Nemerov is born
Great Depression	1929–39	
World War II	1939–45	
	1946–55	Diane Arbus works in fashion photography
Communist China is established	1949	
Korean War	1950–53	
	1955–57	Arbus studies with Lisette Model
African independence movement begins	1957	
	1971	Arbus commits suicide
	1972	Arbus's work featured at Venice Biennale
		Museum of Modern Art mounts retrospective of her work
Vietnam War ends	1975	

For Further Reading

Arbus, Diane. *Diane Arbus*. Millerton, N.Y.: Aperture Books, 1972.

———. *Diane Arbus, Magazine Work*. Millerton, N.Y.: Aperture Books, 1984.

———. *Untitled*. Millerton, N.Y.: Aperture Books, 1995.

Bosworth, Patricia. *Diane Arbus: A Biography*. New York: Knopf, 1984.

Armstrong, Louis

Trumpeter
1901–1971

Life and Work

Among the most important of all jazz musicians, Louis "Satchmo" Armstrong virtually created the idea of jazz as a music that rested on the improvisatory talents of individual soloists.

Armstrong was born into dire poverty in New Orleans, Louisiana, on August 4, 1901. As a youth, he sang in a street-corner quartet that exposed him to musical harmony. Armstrong ended up in an orphanage, where he was given a cornet and played in a band. Determined to become a musician, he began to mix with players of the new music called jazz. In the late 1910s he also performed on Mississippi riverboats—a job that probably required him to become proficient at reading musical notation—and in 1918 he won a place in a band led by trombonist Edward "Kid" Ory.

Present when jazz was taking shape in New Orleans, Armstrong subsequently traveled to the new music's other two major centers. He joined King Oliver's Creole Jazz Band in Chicago in 1922, and in 1924 moved to New York to work with the more controlled Fletcher Henderson Orchestra; Henderson's musicians recognized and encouraged his growing skill as an improviser and his subtle control over the syncopated rhythms that would become known as swing. In 1925 Armstrong returned to Chicago and organized a group, the Hot Five.

The recordings Armstrong made between 1925 and 1928 with the Hot Five (and the associated Hot Seven) are milestones in jazz history. In them, Armstrong switched to the trumpet and stepped to the fore as a soloist, forging complex musical utterances in which he might relate solos musically to one another or engage in dialogue with the rest of the band. In 1929 Armstrong again moved to New York, appearing in the Fats Waller musical *Hot Chocolates*.

Through the 1930s and 1940s he worked equally prominently as a vocalist; his characteristic gravelly voice became nearly universally known to Americans. Armstrong achieved considerable pop success, becoming the first black performer to host his own advertiser-driven radio show. In later years he toured the world as an American "goodwill ambassador" under the auspices of the U.S. State Department. He died in New York on July 6, 1971.

Legacy

A maxim attributed to trumpeter MILES DAVIS holds that "there's nothing you can play on that horn that Louis didn't play first." The formulation is an apt one, for it recognizes not only Louis Armstrong's role as a jazz pioneer, but also the range of his musical imagination and his preeminence as a jazz soloist.

Armstrong was one of those rare musicians who was both innovator and master. Jazz had its beginnings as an ensemble music, but after Armstrong, jazz musicians became individual artists first and foremost. Even when bandleaders such as DUKE ELLINGTON and Benny Goodman turned again to the ensemble ideal, they had to incorporate the individual musical personality into the structures they created. Jazz soloists of the 1930s on various instruments often seemed to be working out ideas Armstrong had introduced; among the careers to which Armstrong's own bands gave birth was that of pianist Earl Hines, with whom Armstrong recorded a fascinating duet, "Weather Bird," in 1928. In its rhythmic freedom and sophistication of dialogue, this piece looked decades forward into the future of jazz.

Indeed, many of Armstrong's prime performances of the late 1920s are so daring rhythmically and harmonically that the jazz modernism of bebop, the radical style born in the 1940s, seems almost historically preordained. "West End Blues," recorded in 1928, is one of those Armstrong performances that influenced jazz soloists for decades to come; its powerful internal logic propels the listener from a complex, melodically wide-ranging introduction toward a final chorus in which Armstrong unexpectedly sustains a single long note. Another example is a striking passage in 1927's "Hotter Than That": Armstrong in one "scat" vocal solo launches into a sustained two-against-three pattern of unparalleled rhythmic virtuosity. Armstrong was a pioneer of the scat technique of vocally imitating an instrument, and his relaxed vocal treatment of rhythm became quite influential on its own, affecting the styles of Bing Crosby, Frank Sinatra, and others. As an instrumentalist, he was quite simply a giant.

Manheim

World Events		Armstrong's Life
Spanish-American War	1898	
	1901	Louis Armstrong is born
World War I	1914–18	
Russian Revolution	1917	
	1918	Armstrong wins place in Kid Ory's band
	1922	Armstrong joins King Oliver's Creole Jazz Band
	1924	Armstrong moves to New York
	1925	Armstrong organizes Hot Five in Chicago
	1928	Armstrong records "Weather Bird"
	1929	Armstrong appears in musical *Hot Chocolates*
Great Depression	1929–39	
World War II	1939–45	
Communist China is established	1949	
Korean War	1950–53	
African independence movement begins	1957	
	1971	Armstrong dies
Vietnam War ends	1975	

For Further Reading

Armstrong, Louis. *Louis Armstrong, In His Own Words*. Edited and with an introduction by Thomas Brothers. New York: Oxford University Press, 1999.

Bergreen, Laurence. *Louis Armstrong: An Extrravagant Life*. New York: Broadway Books, 1997.

Giddins, Gary. *Satchmo*. New York: Doubleday, 1988.

Austen, Jane

Novelist

1775–1817

Life and Work

Jane Austen, one of the best-loved authors in the English canon today, wrote only six novels.

Austen was born on December 16, 1775, in the village of Steventon, England, the seventh of eight children. Although she received only one year of formal education, her family read avidly, and she was encouraged in her love of both reading and writing from a young age.

In her early twenties, Austen took an enthusiastic part in the life that she would eventually describe with such precision in her novels. She attended balls, visited friends, and went for long walks in the Hampshire countryside. It was at this time that she wrote the early versions of her first three novels. In 1797 Austen's father sent *First Impressions*, the first version of *Pride and Prejudice*, to a London publisher, who declined to read it.

In 1801, Austen moved with her parents and her sister to the city of Bath, whose urban environment she found stifling. It wasn't until her return to Hampshire in 1809 that she began to write again. In the next seven and a half years, she revised and published *Sense and Sensibility* (1811), *Pride and Prejudice* (1813), and *Mansfield Park* (1814).

During her lifetime, Austen anonymously signed her books as "A Lady." The work was widely read and well received, and the Prince Regent, later George IV, was among her most loyal fans. It was to him that Austen "respectfully dedicated" *Emma* in 1815.

In 1816 Austen became ill with what appears to have been Addison's disease, a tubercular disease of the kidneys. She died in the arms of her sister Cassandra in Winchester on July 18, 1817, at the age of 41, and was buried in Winchester Cathedral.

After her death, Henry Austen, her brother, announced her authorship of the novels and supervised the posthumous publication of *Northanger Abbey* (1817) and *Persuasion* (1817).

Legacy

Stepping away from the sentimental and romantic traditions of her day, Jane Austen brought a combination of perceptive wit and acute emotional and historical observation of everyday life to the arena of English literature; she is often credited with adding a modern sensibility to the novel.

Before the 1920s, Austen's novels were admired intensely by a small public, but they did not sell widely. At a time when the novel was considered a low art next to the more elevated forms of poetry and drama, they did not receive critical acclaim.

In the middle of the twentieth century, however, academics and critics joined an increasingly devoted public in praising Austen's six novels. The enduring appeal of Austen's work is often attributed to its quizzical humor, its acute, though never moralizing, ethical perception, and the wisdom and playfulness of its insight into characters' sentiments and thoughts.

Austen's arch irony and elegantly structured stories and dialogue opened up the world of the novel to include the examination of the everyday. Readers and writers after her would rarely think of the English countryside, or any other familiar territory, as too homely a setting for a novel.

Elizabeth Bennett and Mr. Darcy, the spirited protagonists of *Pride and Prejudice*, who first clash and then work their way toward mutual understanding, have won the sympathy of an enormous public. In recent years, that public has expanded even further with popular productions of several film versions of Austen's books. Perhaps surprisingly, Austen's romantic sensibilities have also appealed to audiences in modernized adaptations of her works, such as *Clueless* (1995), a very loose adaptation of *Emma*, and *Bridget Jones's Diary*, (novel, 1998; film, 2001) which owes a spiritual debt to *Pride and Prejudice*.

Watson

World Events		Austen's Life
Glorious Revolution in England	1688	
	1775	Jane Austen is born
United States declares independence	1776	
French Revolution begins	1789	
	1795–98	Austen writes early versions of *Northanger Abbey*, *Sense and Sensibility*, and *Pride and Prejudice*
	1797	Austen's *First Impressions* is rejected by London publisher
Latin American independence movement begins	1811	Austen's *Sense and Sensibility* is published
	1813	Austen publishes *Pride and Prejudice*
	1814	Austen publishes *Mansfield Park*
Congress of Vienna reorganizes Europe	1815	
	1817	Austen dies; Austen's *Northanger Abbey* and *Persuasion* are published posthumously
Revolutions in Austria, France, Germany, and Italy	1848	

For Further Reading

Copeland, Edward, and Juliet McMaster, eds. *The Cambridge Companion to Jane Austen*. Cambridge: Cambridge University Press, 1997.

Tanner, Tony. *Jane Austen*. Cambridge, Mass.: Harvard University Press, 1986.

Bach, Johann Sebastian

Composer
1685–1750

WORLD EVENTS		BACH'S LIFE
Thirty Years' War in Europe	1618–48	
	1685	Johann Sebastian Bach is born in Eisenach, Germany
Glorious Revolution in England	1688	
	1703	Bach obtains his first post in Arnstadt
	1708	Bach assumes directorship of ducal chapel in Weimar
	1717	Bach becomes court music director in Köthen
	1722	Bach writes first book of the *Well-Tempered Clavier*
	1729	Bach writes *St. Matthew Passion*
	1747	Bach plays for Frederick the Great
	1750	Bach dies
United States declares independence	1776	

Life and Work

Johann Sebastian Bach was one of the towering geniuses of Western musical culture, but his life was notable for its lack of outward drama.

Born in Eisenach, Germany, on March 21, 1685, Bach worked for most of his life in central Germany. He came from a musical family, and several of his sons would become well-known composers after his death. From 1700 to 1702 he studied music in Lüneburg, where he encountered some of northern Germany's great organ players; after he got his first job in 1703, as a church organist in the small town of Arnstadt, he went north again, traveling 200 miles on foot to hear the greatest North German organist of all, Dietrich Buxtehude. Bach, who never suffered fools gladly, revealed the first signs of his characteristic stubbornness when he overstayed the leave his employer had given him for this journey by more than two months.

Nevertheless, his compositions and his formidable organ skills propelled his career forward. He worked as a church organist in Mühlhausen in 1707 and 1708; there he began to master the cantata, a Lutheran church genre that mixed simple, often moralistic choruses with emotional, quasi-operatic solo expressions of religious fervor. He then moved on to the ducal court at Weimar, where he wrote some of his greatest organ music. In Köthen, where Bach became court music director in 1717, he was responsible for instrumental music, composing his famous *Brandenburg Concertos* among other works. In 1723 Bach became cantor of the St. Thomas School in Leipzig and the director of musical activities in the city. Required to supply large quantities of church music, he wrote five full annual cycles of cantatas for Sunday services; one of his great choral settings of the biblical accounts of Christ's life, the *St. Matthew Passion*, dates from the Leipzig years, probably from 1729.

Bach quarreled occasionally with the Leipzig authorities and thought of moving again, but he remained in Leipzig. His fame spread; in 1747 Bach had an audience with Frederick the Great and improvised on a theme the king had given him. This improvisation became the basis for the *Musical Offering*, which, in its density and rigor, was characteristic of Bach's later work. Bach died in Leipzig on July 28, 1750.

Legacy

Johann Sebastian Bach worked at the end of the Baroque era in music, which lasted from about 1600 to 1750. His style inspired almost none of his immediate successors directly (though both WOLFGANG AMADEUS MOZART and LUDWIG VAN BEETHOVEN knew his music). His work, however, remains central to the Western classical tradition.

Although he did not advance music's stylistic frontiers, Bach exhaustively explored every genre he took up. Many of his hundreds of harmonizations of Lutheran chorale tunes remain mainstays of Protestant hymnals today. His large body of organ music lies at the core of the repertoire for that instrument; his sets of preludes and fugues that he published under the title *The Well-Tempered Clavier* continue to serve as exemplars of those forms for listeners and performers. His more than 200 extant cantatas realize every possibility of the form. Bach provided musicians avenues to display their skills; his works for solo violin and cello, profoundly difficult, often sound as though two or three instruments are playing at once. Counterpoint—the learned art of combining independent musical lines—is the foundation of Bach's writing in every genre and gives his music its richness, density, and emotional and intellectual depth.

When Bach's music was rediscovered in the nineteenth century, musicians and pedagogues realized that his treatments of the forms in which he composed were so thorough that his work could be used in the training of young musicians, essentially as a core of classical music. Even today students learn the classical system of harmony by studying Bach's chorale harmonizations and trying to emulate them and learn counterpoint by doing the same with Bach's *Two-* and *Three-Part Inventions* for keyboard. The goal is not to make them into compositional clones of Bach, but to provide models of intellectual discipline, balance, and human understanding that have never since been equaled.

Manheim

For Further Reading

Boyd, Malcolm. *Bach*. New York: Schirmer, 1997.

David, Hans T., and Arthur Mendel. Revised and enlarged by Christoph Wolff. *The New Bach Reader: A Life of Johann Sebastian Bach in Letters and Documents*. New York: W. W. Norton, 1998.

Balanchine, George

Choreographer and Dancer
1904–1983

Life and Work

The co-founder and longtime chief chorographer of the New York City Ballet, George Balanchine was a prolific creative figure, a Russian emigré who shaped ballet in the United States and around the world.

George Balanchine was born Georgi Melitonovich Balanchivadze in St. Petersburg, Russia, on January 22, 1904. His studies at St. Petersburg's Imperial Ballet Academy were interrupted by the Russian Revolution of 1917 and 1918, which eventually drove the young choreographer to immigrate to France in 1924, after his early works were criticized for their experimental styles.

Altering his name to Georges Balanchine, he danced and served as company choreographer for the Ballets Russes (Russian Ballet) company of SERGE DIAGHILEV, an icon of Russian modernism who had brought IGOR STRAVINSKY's groundbreaking works to the Parisian public over the previous decade. Balanchine remained with the Ballets Russes until Diaghilev's death in 1929; in the early 1930s, he created new works for other European companies.

Balanchine anglicized his first name to George when he moved to the United States in 1933. He came at the invitation of impresario Lincoln Kirstein, who for many years would be his collaborator and partner in bringing ballet

to the American public. Together Balanchine and Kirstein founded the School of American Ballet (1934), a touring company called the Ballet Caravan (1936), and, most important, the New York City Ballet, which took its present name and form in 1948. Balanchine's works, which included more than 100 full-length ballets, had roots in classial Russian ballet, but also included modern elements. Many of them (the 1967 work *Jewels* is a good example) eliminated or de-emphasized a plot in favor of abstract motion and pattern.

In addition to ballets, Balanchine choreographed operatic and musical theater and film productions, including the Richard Rodgers musicals *On Your Toes* of 1936 and *The Boys from Syracuse* of 1938, and the 1938 film *The Goldwyn Follies*, which included music by GEORGE GERSHWIN. He had a knack for good public relations, helping to attract attention to innovative artists through such moves as devising choreography for a group of 50 elephants to accompany a performance of Stravinsky's *Circus Polka*, commissioned by the Ringling Brothers and first performed in 1944.

Active until the very end of his long life, Balanchine died in New York on April 30, 1983.

Legacy

George Balanchine was influential as a choreographer, but equally as much or more so as an exemplar of creativity whose energetic endeavors founded a dance tradition where only fragments of one had existed previously.

Ballet's prominence in the United States is attributable largely to his initiative and his inexhaustible invention; as a company leader, he focused both on training dancers and on widening the creative world in which they performed. A broad swath of twentieth-century dance works are modern in their exploration of the expressive powers of motion itself but classical in the clarity and technique they demand. Such "neoclassic" works owe their existence to Balanchine's example. More generally, the Russian tinge in American ballet was absorbed directly from him.

Beyond his personal style, Balanchine was expert at putting himself and his art across to audiences, and he gave dance an immediacy in American culture that resonated in various ways in the middle of the century. In addition to his New York City Ballet productions, which often numbered half a dozen or more per year, Balanchine lent his art to theatrical, film, and

television productions that brought ordinary Americans into contact with the power of dance. The elaborate dances that were components of 1940s and 1950s movie musicals took off from Balanchine's example.

An effective popularizer, Balanchine often turned his choreographic efforts to difficult contemporary music compositions; his dances to music by ARNOLD SCHOENBERG, Anton von Webern, and Charles Ives gained listeners for those composers' works. The many dancers' careers Balanchine made possible, and the modern dance schools they wove into the fabric of American life, constitute his greatest legacy.

Manheim

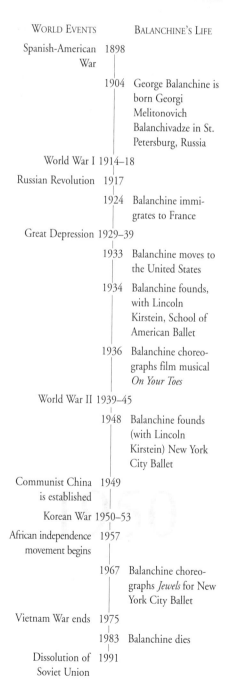

WORLD EVENTS		BALANCHINE'S LIFE
Spanish-American War	1898	
	1904	George Balanchine is born Georgi Melitonovich Balanchivadze in St. Petersburg, Russia
World War I	1914–18	
Russian Revolution	1917	
	1924	Balanchine immigrates to France
Great Depression	1929–39	
	1933	Balanchine moves to the United States
	1934	Balanchine founds, with Lincoln Kirstein, School of American Ballet
	1936	Balanchine choreographs film musical *On Your Toes*
World War II	1939–45	
	1948	Balanchine founds (with Lincoln Kirstein) New York City Ballet
Communist China is established	1949	
Korean War	1950–53	
African independence movement begins	1957	
	1967	Balanchine choreographs *Jewels* for New York City Ballet
Vietnam War ends	1975	
	1983	Balanchine dies
Dissolution of Soviet Union	1991	

For Further Reading

McDonagh, Don. *George Balanchine*. Boston: Twayne Publishers, 1983.

Taper, Bernard. *Balanchine: A Biography*. Berkeley: University of California Press, 1996.

Baldwin, James

Novelist and Dramatist
1924–1987

Life and Work

James Arthur Baldwin brought the densely lyrical voices of gospel music, spirituals, and religious preaching to experimental writing that addressed questions of racial identity.

Baldwin was born in Harlem, in New York City, on August 2, 1924, and was raised in a large family with a stepfather who was a Pentecostal preacher. His mother was a domestic worker and Baldwin, as the oldest of nine children, took on much of the responsibility of raising his younger siblings. In junior high school, he was encouraged in his writing by his teacher, the poet Countee Cullen. Baldwin was converted to Pentecostal Christianity at the age of 14, and preached in a storefront church, the Fireside Pentecostal Assembly Church, throughout his high school years.

In Paris, where he moved in 1948 and lived most of his life, Baldwin became friends with the older African-American novelist, Richard Wright. Baldwin completed his first novel, *Go Tell It on the Mountain*, in 1953. One of his recurring themes was the search for love. Baldwin was criticized for the openly homosexual nature of his later novel, *Giovanni's Room* (1956), while *Another Country* (1962) was controversial for its candid sexuality.

During the 1960s Baldwin was considered one of the leading spokesmen of the civil rights movement. He supported the militant movements of both Malcolm X and Stokely Carmichael. In the late 1960s and early 1970s he considered his fiction, including a collection of stories, *Going to Meet the Man* (1965), and a novel, *Tell Me How Long the Train's Been Gone* (1968), to be attempts to influence the day-to-day lives of African Americans and the civil rights movement.

Baldwin's nonfiction works also focused on racial inequality. His collection of essays *Notes of a Native Son* was published in 1955. *The Fire Next Time* (1963), a book about the Black Muslim separatist movement, was widely read as a plea for racial harmony and a manifesto for black liberation.

Baldwin was also one of the few African-American authors of the 1960s to have had more than one play open on Broadway. Both *Blues for Mister Charlie* in 1964 and *The Amen Corner* in 1965 had successful runs and revivals on stage.

Baldwin died of stomach cancer in the south of France on December 1, 1987. At the time of his death he was at work on a biography of Martin Luther King, Jr.

Legacy

James Baldwin set a precedent for the literary activists of the 1960s and beyond with his insistent and tolerant treatment of racial and sexual difference. In his novels and essays, he explored controversial issues of identity, challenging readers to confront the differences among people in American society and to resolve them with tolerance and love.

Baldwin refused to be defined simply as a black writer. He emphasized that he was an American writer drawing from his own experience, which included but was not limited to his race. However, as his career progressed, he became more and more embroiled in the American race struggle. With his book of essays *Nobody Knows My Name* (1961) and *The Fire Next Time*, his passionate and inflammatory arguments against racial inequality positioned him as a leader in the racial struggle.

Baldwin is not only one of the important literary figures of the civil rights movement but is also as a predecessor of the gay liberation movement. His open portrayals of homosexual love and relationships in his work were among the earliest to make their way into American literature. Contemporaries, including Norman Mailer and Truman Capote, both friends of Baldwin's, were influenced by this frankness and responded to it in their own works. His advocacy of love and tolerance of difference also preceded the talk of acceptance of self that would, in the 1960s, become part of common parlance.

Baldwin had great influence as a writer and as a social critic. His belief that relations between blacks and whites could one day be peaceful caused a rift with more militant exponents of black power, including Eldridge Cleaver, the leader of the Black Panthers. His literary descendants include poet MAYA ANGELOU, novelist TONI MORRISON, and poet and writer Amiri Baraka, all of whom spoke at his funeral.

Watson

World Events		Baldwin's Life
Russian Revolution	1917	
	1924	James Baldwin is born
Great Depression	1929–39	
	1938–41	Baldwin preaches at the Fireside Pentacostal Assembly church in Harlem
World War II	1939–45	
	1948	Baldwin moves to Paris
Communist China is established	1949	
Korean War	1950–53	
	1953	Baldwin publishes *Go Tell It on the Mountain*
	1955	Baldwin publishes *Notes of a Native Son*
	1956	Baldwin publishes *Giovanni's Room*
African independence movement begins	1957	
	1964	*Blues For Mister Charlie* opens on Broadway
	1965	Baldwin publishes *Going to Meet the Man*
Vietnam War ends	1975	
	1987	Baldwin dies
Dissolution of Soviet Union	1991	

For Further Reading

Leeming, David Adams. *James Baldwin: A Biography.* New York: Knopf, 1994.

Pratt, Louis H., and Fred L. Standley, eds. *Conversations with James Baldwin.* Jackson: University Press of Mississippi, 1978.

Bashō, Matsuo

Poet
1644–1694

Life and Work

Matsuo Bashō, commonly known as Bashō, was Japan's first great haiku poet. He established a tradition of reflective verse that persists to this day.

Bashō was born in Ueno in Iga Province in 1644. As a young man he served an aristocratic master and became a samurai, taking the warrior name Matsuo Munefusa. He began writing during this time and by 1664 several of his haiku appeared in a Kyoto verse anthology.

Two years later Bashō went to Kyoto to study philosophy, poetry, and calligraphy. He quickly became known as one of the city's finest poets and had his work anthologized in a number of verse collections. In 1672 Bashō compiled an anthology, *The Seashell Game*, to which 30 poets contributed. Soon after its completion he moved to Edo. His reputation grew while he continued to write verse, judge contests, publish small volumes of work, and teach students of his own. Bashō took his literary name in 1680, when his students built him a small house with a *bashō* (banana) tree outside. Bashō lived a meditative life, studying and practicing Zen Buddhism.

Bashō traveled a great deal in the second half of his life, making long journeys on foot, which he described in a series of travel journals. One of the best known of these, *The Records of a Travel-Worn Satchel*, describes a 1687 trip from Edo to Akashi. In 1691 he and several of his students compiled a haiku anthology called *The Monkey's Raincoat*, which is considered the peak of the Bashō style of haiku. At that time haiku was considered a trivial art to be used for word games and jokes, not unlike today's limerick. Bashō, however, used the 17-syllable form to express complex ideas about life and the environment, incorporating Zen Buddhist philosophy and the teachings of the Taoist sage, Chuang-Tzu.

Bashō died of a stomach illness after one of his long journeys in Osaka on November 28, 1694.

Legacy

As Matsuo Bashō gave lasting poetic life to the haiku, he also developed the theme of human spiritual identification with nature that would come to characterize Japanese poetry.

The renku, an academic form written by several poets collaboratively, was preferred by serious poets before Bashō, while the humorous haiku with its discussion of the lighter sides of life was considered less important. The change that Bashō brought to the form and therefore to Japanese poetry brought him wide acclaim during his lifetime. He taught a generation of younger poets his new conception of the haiku, establishing the form as one of the most vital of Japanese arts.

Bashō deepened the humorous and light-hearted haiku form, attaching importance to the role of thought and spiritual growth in his poems. His dramatic expressions of humor, depression, happiness, or confusion evoked human nature and reminded readers of the scale of humanity within the vastness of nature.

Bashō's poetic diaries and travel journals are some of the most lyrical in the tradition of Japanese prose literature. He based much of his writing on the concept of sabi, the idea that humans attain spiritual peace by immersing themselves in the impersonal life of nature. The identification of the self with nature became an idea central to Japanese poetry.

Bashō's major contribution to Japanese literature was his emphasis on the subtler nuances of a work, in which he insisted upon a poetic cohesion throughout a poem, rather than relying simply on the word games and verbal tricks that were popular at the time.

Watson

WORLD EVENTS	BASHŌ'S LIFE
Thirty Years' War 1618–48 in Europe	
1644	Matsuo Bashō is born
1666	Bashō goes to Kyoto to study
1672	Bashō publishes *The Seashell Game*
1687	Bashō publishes *The Records of a Travel-Worn Satchel*
Glorious Revolution 1688 in England	
1691	Bashō publishes *The Monkey's Raincoat*
1694	Bashō dies
United States declares 1776 independence	

For Further Reading
Bashō, Matsuo. *The Essential Bashō*. Translated by Sam Hamill. Boston: Shambhala Press, 1999.
Usda, Makoto. *Matsuo Basho*. Tokyo; New York: Kodansha International, 1982.

Basquiat, Jean-Michel

Painter and Graffiti Artist
1960–1988

World Events		Basquiat's Life
African independence movement begins	1957	
	1960	Jean-Michel Basquiat is born
Vietnam War ends	1975	
	1978	*Village Voice* article features Basquiat's art
	1981	Basquiat has first public exhibition at Times Square Show
	1982	Basquiat has first one-person show; Basquiat completes *K*
	1984	Basquiat completes *Flexible*
	1988	Basquiat dies
Dissolution of Soviet Union	1991	

Life and Work

American graffiti artist, painter, and sculptor, Jean-Michel Basquiat achieved great success and celebrity in the New York art world of the 1980s.

Born in New York City in 1960, Basquiat's early interest in art was cultivated by his parents, particularly his mother, who took him to New York City art museums. Basquiat was raised in an Afro-Caribbean family (Haitian and Puerto Rican) and had a solidly upper-middle-class childhood in Brooklyn.

A true eclectic, Basquiat drew artistic energy from a variety of sources: the Spanish–Caribbean culture of his mother; his own prolific reading; jazz and blues; and black heroes, ranging from American boxer Joe Walcott to Toussaint-Louverture, the liberator of Haiti. He studied comic book drawings and the paintings of abstract expressionists Franz Kline and Cy Twombley. His reading of *Gray's Anatomy*, the classic illustrated guide to the human body, when he was eight, reportedly led to his interest in depicting body parts in his work.

Basquiat, while attending high school from 1976 to 1978, began to experiment in the underground New York graffiti art movement (which is now recognized along with break dancing as the beginnings of hip-hop culture). His work, which was signed typically "SAMO" (Same Old Shit), gained its first mass exposure in a 1978 *Village Voice* article.

In the late 1970s, Basquiat was a regular at various artists' and musicians' clubs and hangouts, where he became acquainted with art dealers and collectors. Basquiat's first public exhibition was in 1981 at the Times Square Show; in 1982, he had his first one-person show. His mixed media works reflected the influences of art history, autobiography, black history, politics, and pop culture. He used personal signs and symbols and words and phrases that appeared to be nonsense but commented on contemporary urban culture. Among his recurring motifs were the three-pointed crown in *K* (1982) and the transparent man in *Flexible* (1984).

During his later years, Basquiat formed a close relationship with pop artist ANDY WARHOL, with whom he collaborated on a number of projects.

Basquiat died of a heroin overdose in 1988 at the age of 27. A prolific painter, he left 95 paintings and 900 works on paper at the time of his death.

Legacy

One of the key figures in the art world of the 1980s, Jean-Michel Basquiat merged the traditions of street life and clubs, graffiti, and fine art.

Basquiat's raw energy and candid social commentary stood as a stark contrast to the dispassionate conceptual and minimalist work in vogue in the major galleries. For a while, he was widely popular with critics and gallery owners, based partly upon his genuine talent and partly perhaps to fulfill a need in the white art world for a "Negro pet," a term used by the African-American writer Zora Neale Hurston. Basquiat's meteoric rise was regarded by some critics as evidence of the art world's fascination with novelty and the dilettante collectors' search for a hot new prospect rather than of the intrinsic merit of his work.

Interest in Basquiat continues to grow, however. He was the subject of a 1996 feature film directed by Julian Schnabel, another one of the hot artists of the1980s. While being an entertaining depiction of Basquiat's life that remains true to the facts, the film fails to ask deeper questions about the social factors, including racism, that led to his early death.

Basquiat helped to change the narrow and elitist art establishment, just as rap and hip-hop changed the face of American music. He blurred the lines between street art and the "high" art of the galleries and museums. By tapping the vigor of multicultural New York City, he breathed new life into the art world.

Domenico

For Further Reading

Geldzahler, Henry. *Making It New: Essays, Interviews, and Talks.* New York: Turtle Point Press, 1994.

Hoban, Phoebe. *Basquiat: A Quick Killing in Art.* New York: Penguin Books, 1999.

Baudelaire, Charles

Poet, Translator, and Critic
1821–1867

Life and Work

Charles Baudelaire, one of the most influential poets of the nineteenth century, brought vice to poetry, Edgar Allan Poe's work to France, and the prose poem to literature.

Baudelaire was born in Paris on April 9, 1821. His father, whose interest in literature and painting he shared with his young son, died when Baudelaire was six. His mother remarried a year later and the family moved from Paris.

After high school Baudelaire returned to Paris and enrolled in law school. However, Baudelaire spent his time meeting with friends in the bohemian Latin Quarter, becoming addicted to opium and hashish, and acquiring the syphilis that would eventually kill him.

In June 1841, his stepfather, in an attempt to curb Baudelaire's dissolute lifestyle, sent him on a two-year trip to India. Baudelaire chose not to complete the trip but spent time in Mauritius—the scenery of which was to furnish much of the lush, exotic imagery that later filled his poems—before returning to France.

In 1842, Baudelaire received an inheritance from his father's estate, which he squandered; two years later his mother had him legally restrained and put on a monthly allowance. From that point on he lived in poverty, accumulating debt that he would never be able to repay.

In 1847, a turning point for Baudelaire and for French literature, he discovered the American writer Edgar Allan Poe, who had died only a few years before. Baudelaire began translating Poe in 1852; he identified strongly with the disasterous course of Poe's life, feeling that the writer's drug addiction and destitution mirrored his own. Baudelaire recognized his own aesthetic and artistic beliefs in Poe's work. These beliefs in the purity of art, the potential for beauty in the most sordid of circumstances, and the absolute importance of technical perfection in writing would be borne out in his own poetry.

Baudelaire was able to publish his first collection of poetry, *Les Fleurs du mal* (*The Flowers of Evil*), in 1857. Although the book caused a scandal—he, his publisher, and his printers were immediately prosecuted for obscenity and blasphemy—it was nonetheless a failure.

Baudelaire went even more deeply into debt but continued to write art criticism and the prose poems that would make up his posthumous book of poetry, *Le Spleen de Paris* (*Paris Spleen*; 1869); he was greatly disappointed by the failure of *The Flowers of Evil*.

In 1866, his syphilis paralyzed him and in 1867 Baudelaire died in his mother's arms in Paris.

Legacy

Though he died impoverished, his work largely forgotten and much of it unpublished, Charles Baudelaire had established the foundation on which the next great movement in French poetry would be built.

The Symbolist poets, beginning with Stéphane Mallarmé, Paul Verlaine, Arthur Rimbaud, and Paul Claudel, drew on Baudelaire's evocative analysis of urban life and decay, erotic love, and personal despair when they wrote poetry that evoked emotional response through suggestion rather than with traditional description.

The innovative style of the prose poems of *Spleen* was to have a great influence on all of these poets, and is particularly evident in the experimental style of Rimbaud's famously hallucinatory poem, *Le Bateau ivre* (*The Drunken Boat*). The prose poem also proved to be an important form for twentieth-century poets in French, English, and other languages.

In the twentieth century, critics paid equal attention to Baudelaire's poetry and his critical writings. Baudelaire believed that the two were interdependent, criticism allowing for the necessary deep contemplation of art, while concepts outlined in criticism were only truly rendered in a work of art.

Writers including T. S. Eliot and WILLIAM BUTLER YEATS also recognized in Baudelaire the beginnings of their own efforts to express meaning through symbol, though they would go on to examine critically and expand upon Symbolist assumptions about poetry. Eliot called Baudelaire "the greatest exemplar of modern poetry in any language."

Baudelaire carried along the intensity of emotion of the Romantics in his exploration of the city and his questioning of religion, without departing, in *The Flowers of Evil*, from traditional form. Mallarmé would continue where Baudelaire left off, developing the book of poetry as a form of its own.

Watson

WORLD EVENTS		BAUDELAIRE'S LIFE
Congress of Vienna reorganizes Europe	1815	
	1821	Charles Baudelaire is born
	1841	Baudelaire travels to Mauritius
Revolutions in Austria, France, Germany, and Italy	1848	
	1852	Baudelaire begins translations of Edgar Allan Poe
	1857	Baudelaire publishes *The Flowers of Evil*
U.S. Civil War	1861–65	
	1867	Baudelaire dies
	1869	*Paris Spleen* is published posthumously
Germany is united	1871	

For Further Reading

Babuts, Nicolae. *Baudelaire: At the Limits and Beyond*. Newark, Del.: University of Delaware Press, 1997.

Baudelaire, Charles. *Charles Baudelaire: Complete Poems*. Translated by Walter Martin. Concord, Mass.: Paul & Company Publishing Consortium, 1998.

———. *Flowers of Evil*. Translated by Geoffrey Wagner. Norfolk, Conn.: New Directions, 1946.

Carter, A. E. *Charles Baudelaire*. Boston: Twayne Publishers, 1977.

Beckett, Samuel

Playwright, Poet, and Novelist
1906–1989

Life and Work

Samuel Beckett, one of the most influential voices in twentieth-century theater and literature, explored fundamental questions of existence in novels, short stories, poems, and scripts for radio, television, and film.

Beckett was born to Protestant Anglo-Irish parents on April 13, 1906, in Foxrock, Ireland, near Dublin. He attended Trinity College in Dublin, graduating first in his class in 1927. He was invited to spend two years lecturing at the renowned École Normale Supérieure in Paris.

In Paris Beckett met and became a protégé of JAMES JOYCE helping him to research and type the manuscript of *Finnegans Wake*. Over the next 10 years Beckett moved from place to place, reading and continuing his studies in literature, philosophy, and theology.

In 1940, Beckett joined one of the first underground Resistance groups to form in Nazi-occupied France. When it was betrayed in 1942 Beckett was forced to flee Paris. After the war he was awarded both the Croix de Guerre and the Médaille de la Résistance.

Between 1946 and 1950, Beckett wrote his trilogy of interior monologue novels, *Molloy* (1951), *Malone Dies* (1951), and *The Unnamable* (1953)—powerful examples of stream-of-consciousness prose. His play *Waiting for Godot*, (in French as *En Attendant Godot*) opened at the tiny Théâtre de Babylone in Paris in 1952 and was an instant and overwhelming success.

Vladimir and Estragon, two men who wait by the side of the road for the mysterious Godot, who never arrives, introduced the bleak, minimalist atmosphere that characterizes much of Beckett's work. Beckett continued to develop the themes of the inevitability of human loneliness and death with increasing levels of absurdity in works like *Endgame* in 1957, *Krapp's Last Tape* in 1959, and *Happy Days* in 1961.

In the late 1940s Beckett began writing solely in French, often translating his own work into English. As he grew older, his dialogues became briefer and denser until in *Breath* (1970), a 35-second play, there was no dialogue but only an amplified cry and a breath.

Beckett was awarded the Nobel Prize for Literature in 1969. Always an extremely reserved man who avoided personal publicity of any kind, he accepted the award but did not attend the ceremony.

Beckett died in Paris in December 1989 at the age of 83.

WORLD EVENTS		BECKETT'S LIFE
Spanish-American War	1898	
	1906	Samuel Beckett is born
World War I	1914–18	
Russian Revolution	1917	
	1927	Beckett graduates from Trinity College
Great Depression	1929–39	
World War II	1939–45	
	1942	Beckett flees Nazi-occupied Paris
	1945	Beckett is awarded Croix de Guerre
Communist China is established	1949	
Korean War	1950–53	
	1952	Beckett's *Waiting for Godot* opens in Paris
African independence movement begins	1957	
	1969	Beckett is awarded Nobel Prize for Literature
Vietnam War ends	1975	
	1989	Beckett dies in Paris
Dissolution of Soviet Union	1991	

Legacy

The bleak outlook, absurdist sensibility, and minimalist means characteristic of Samuel Beckett's work altered the possibilities for literature in general and for theater in particular.

Although Beckett shared a certain mixture of darkness and bitter humor with other second-generation Modernists of the like Vladimir Nabokov, WILLIAM FAULKNER, Henry Miller, and Nathanael West, his work was unique. Its uncompromising bleakness was the starting point for a new conception of what was possible in theater.

With their austere settings and increasingly sparse dialogue, Beckett's plays completely rejected the naturalist theater that preceded them. This minimalism was in stark contrast to the psychological realism being popularized by Lee Strasberg and others in the United States at the time.

Echoes of Beckett's spare and unpredictable dialogue, his preoccupation with degeneration and isolation, his minimal plots, and his combination of misery and comedy can be heard quite clearly in the works of many playwrights who came after him. Among those who claim him as a conscious influence are Harold Pinter, Edward Albee, Tom Stoppard, David Mamet, and Athol Fugard.

Although Beckett's major plays, particularly *Waiting for Godot*, are now cornerstones of contemporary theater, Beckett's work has affected all literature. His influence may be found in every artistic medium.

Watson

For Further Reading

Cronin, Anthony. *Samuel Beckett: The Last Modernist.* New York: HarperCollins, 1997.

Knowlson, James. *Damned to Fame: The Life of Samuel Beckett.* London: Bloomsbury, 1996.

Beethoven, Ludwig van

Composer
1770–1827

Life and Work

A giant among composers in the European classical tradition, Ludwig van Beethoven created works of passionate expression in which every detail was in perfect balance with its surroundings, pieces of music that crashed through existing boundaries yet were governed by a powerful formal logic.

Beethoven was born in Bonn, Germany, on December 17, 1770. His alcoholic father, determined to make him into a child prodigy like WOLFGANG AMADEUS MOZART, forced him to practice the piano in marathon sessions. The young Beethoven indeed became a fearsome keyboard virtuoso. He soon outgrew Bonn's musical scene and moved to Vienna, Austria, at the time Europe's musical capital, where he took composition lessons from FRANZ JOSEPH HAYDN. Beethoven's early masterpieces, such as the Piano Sonata No. 8 (*Pathéthique*) and the Symphony No. 1, both of 1799, overflowed with an energy at odds with the graceful style of late-eighteenth-century music.

In 1802, beginning to recognize that his encroaching deafness was incurable, he poured out his fears and creative hopes in an unmailed letter to his brother, which became known as the *Heiligenstadt Testament*. Nearly all the symphonies, piano sonatas, and string quartets of the following years broke vast new artistic ground. They often seemed to communicate some intense conflict that in the end was triumphantly resolved. Beethoven's sweeping Symphony No. 3 (*Eroica*, 1803) was initially dedicated to the French general Napoléon Bonaparte, but Beethoven, disillusioned when Napoléon assumed dictatorial powers, removed the dedication. The Symphony No. 5 of 1808, with its first movement woven tightly out of its famous initial motif of three short notes and one long one, at once demonstrates the thrilling sense of struggle in Beethoven's music and the iron rigor of its design.

Beethoven in his later years was a famous public figure, but one beset by family troubles,

romantic rejection (he never married), and deteriorating health. Despite his troubles, his late music seemed to bespeak acceptance and even ecstasy. His Symphony No. 9 (1825) was unprecedented in that it introduced a chorus for its vast "Ode to Joy" finale. Beethoven died near Vienna on March 26, 1827.

Legacy

Every composer who followed Ludwig van Beethoven in the European classical tradition has felt the inspiration and the weight of his example; even outside that tradition his influence has been vast. Embodying his personal struggles in music, Beethoven achieved something universal: he redefined the nature of the creative musical endeavor.

Nineteenth-century composers tried to match Beethoven's achievements in various areas. JOHANNES BRAHMS brooded over Beethoven's nine symphonies for years before taking up the genre in middle age and producing four of his own. The representations of nature in Beethoven's Symphony No. 6 (*Pastoral*) became the foundation for a century of "program music" based on extramusical subjects. RICHARD WAGNER saw in the chorus-and-orchestra breakthrough of the Symphony No. 9 the beginning of a path that would lead to his gigantic operas and to his efforts to bring together multiple media to create a "total work of art."

In smaller forms, too, Beethoven paved the way for the future. With *An die Ferne Geliebte* (1816), he invented the song cycle, a connected group of songs expressing a sequence of events in the life of a poetic protagonist; the language of the piano, a young instrument when Beethoven first came to it, was fundamentally shaped at his hands.

Beethoven's formal influences dominated subsequent music, but his influence in the most basic realms of the human spirit perhaps looms even larger. Beethoven transformed what it meant to write a piece of music. For him a composition was something more than a work of beauty or a piece of perfect workmanship: it was an expression of individual experience, a triumph over adversity. He himself wrote in the *Heiligenstadt Testament* that "I would have ended my life—it was only my art that held me back."

It is often said that Beethoven brought to a culmination the Classic style of the eigh-

teenth century and laid the groundwork for the Romanticism of the nineteenth. We might further think of him, although his interest in politics was only intermittent, as the musical champion of the individual's irreducible significance.

Manheim

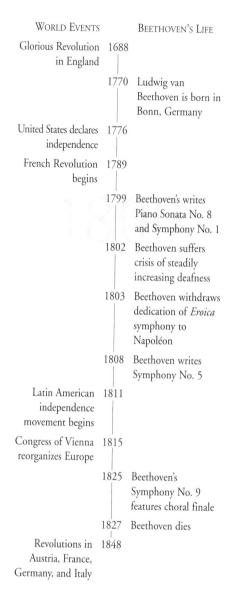

WORLD EVENTS		BEETHOVEN'S LIFE
Glorious Revolution in England	1688	
	1770	Ludwig van Beethoven is born in Bonn, Germany
United States declares independence	1776	
French Revolution begins	1789	
	1799	Beethoven's writes Piano Sonata No. 8 and Symphony No. 1
	1802	Beethoven suffers crisis of steadily increasing deafness
	1803	Beethoven withdraws dedication of *Eroica* symphony to Napoléon
	1808	Beethoven writes Symphony No. 5
Latin American independence movement begins	1811	
Congress of Vienna reorganizes Europe	1815	
	1825	Beethoven's Symphony No. 9 features choral finale
	1827	Beethoven dies
Revolutions in Austria, France, Germany, and Italy	1848	

For Further Reading

Arnold, Denis, and Nigel Fortune, eds. *The Beethoven Companion*. London: Faber & Faber, 1971.

Solomon, Maynard. *Beethoven*. New York: Schirmer Books, 1977.

Berlin, Irving

Songwriter
1888–1989

Life and Work

A prolific creative artist whose career spanned seven decades, Irving Berlin is universally acclaimed as one of America's greatestsongwriters.

WORLD EVENTS		BERLIN'S LIFE
Germany is united	1871	
	1888	Irving Berlin is born Israel Baline in Temun, Russia
Spanish-American War	1898	
	1905	Berlin promotes songs for publisher von Tilzer
	1907	Berlin's "Marie from Sunny Italy" is published
	1911	Berlin's "Alexander's Ragtime Band" becomes a hit
World War I	1914–18	
Russian Revolution	1917	
	1927	Berlin writes "Blue Skies"
Great Depression	1929–39	
	1935	Berlin's musical *Top Hat* includes "Cheek to Cheek"
	1938	Kate Smith introduces Berlin's "God Bless America"
World War II	1939–45	
	1942	Berlin writes "White Christmas"
	1946	Berlin writes musical *Annie Get Your Gun*
Communist China is established	1949	
Korean War	1950–53	
African independence movement begins	1957	
Vietnam War ends	1975	
	1989	Berlin dies at age 101
Dissolution of Soviet Union	1991	

Berlin was born Israel Baline in the Siberian city of Temun, Russia, on May 11, 1888. His family fled persecution and settled in New York when he was four. After his father's death he sang for a time on the streets, but by 1905 he was singing in theaters for Harry von Tilzer, a songwriter and the leading music publisher of the day. He also worked as a singing waiter in a Chinatown restaurant, and between these two jobs was inspired to create songs of his own.

When "Marie from Sunny Italy" was published in 1907, his last name was misspelled as "Berlin" on the cover of the sheet music, and he kept the new name. Berlin hit it big with "Alexander's Ragtime Band" in 1911, and over the next four years he wrote more than 180 songs. Unlike most of his contemporaries, he wrote both music and lyrics. After a stint in the U.S. Army during World War I, Berlin resumed his former productivity. The year 1919 brought "A Pretty Girl Is Like a Melody" among many others. Most of Berlin's songs during this period were written for stage revues. The exquisitely simple ballads Berlin wrote in the 1920s, including 1927's "Blue Skies," may have had emotional roots in the composer's relationship with his future wife, Ellin Mackay, a Catholic who had been forbidden by her father to marry Berlin.

Berlin could not read or write musical notation, and since he could play the piano only in one key he had his instrument outfitted with a contraption that would shift the strings and automatically transpose the music. Yet songs such as "Puttin' On the Ritz" had a musical sophistication that kept them interesting after many hearings, and his romantic ballads relied on distinctive, beautifully crafted melodies rather than on singsong rhymes and cheap sentiments.

His talents proved adaptable to stage and film musicals, with "Cheek to Cheek" helping to popularize the 1935 Fred Astaire vehicle *Top Hat* and 1942's *Holiday Inn* introducing "White Christmas." "God Bless America" was introduced by radio singer Kate Smith on November 11, 1938. *Annie Get Your Gun*, from 1946, is widely considered Berlin's best stage musical. Berlin's creative life continued into the 1960s. For the last three decades of his life he settled into a secluded retirement. He died in New York on September 22, 1989, at the age of 101.

Legacy

The most naturally talented of the immigrant Jews who shaped American entertainment in the early years of the twentieth century, Berlin played a unique role in the development of the modern popular song.

American musical theater grew out of both operetta and vaudeville; some of its practitioners early in the twentieth century were trained composers, while others were rapid-fire popular songsmiths. Berlin was essentially a creature of the latter camp, but his musical craft was nevertheless superb. Irving Berlin proved that true musical art could grow from the streets.

Beyond that, he gave back to the citizenry into which he immigrated a body of song that became part of the American mind. The most familiar of Berlin's compositions, including "White Christmas" and "God Bless America," had by the time of his death assumed the status of folk songs that seemed less the product of a creative act and more the actual substance of American cultural identity. Relatively few Americans could identify their composer, but fewer still would fail at the task of singing at least their opening lines.

Other Berlin songs have survived and caught the imagination of contemporary performers like few others of their era; Willie Nelson's 1978 recording of "Blue Skies" is a modern reading that shows the timelessness of Berlin's music. An immigrant like so many other Americans, Berlin became perhaps the quintessential American songwriter.

Manheim

For Further Reading

Bergreen, Laurence. *As Thousands Cheer: The Life of Irving Berlin.* New York: Viking, 1990.
Furia, Philip. *Irving Berlin: A Life in Song.* New York: Schirmer Books, 1998.
Jablonski, Edward. *Irving Berlin: American Troubador.* New York: Henry Holt, 1999.

Bernini, Gianlorenzo

Sculptor, Architect, and Painter
1598–1680

Life and Work

Baroque painter, sculptor, and architect, Gianlorenzo Bernini was the most successful artist in seventeenth-century Italy.

Born in Naples in 1598, Bernini moved to Rome in 1605 with his family and his sculptor father, Pietro Bernini. His father's work for Pope Paul V's chapel in Santa Maria Maggiore prompted the promising start of the younger Bernini's career when Gianlorenzo was brought to the attention of the Pope and Cardinal Scipione Borghese. Until 1624, he worked in the cardinal's service, specializing in sculptures depicting dramatic mythological and religious figures. Notable among these were *Apollo and Daphne* (1622–25) and the emotionally intense *David* (1623). The latter exemplifies the energetic quality expressive of the Baroque spirit. Unlike MICHELANGELO's *David*, standing tense but still, Bernini's *David* is caught in mid-action, arching his torso as he prepares to heave the stone at Goliath. Unlike statues of the earlier Renaissance, Bernini's *David* seems to exist in physical space with its implication of the presence of the giant just off stage.

With the accession of Pope Urban III to the papacy, Bernini increasingly began to be assigned important work. After 1624, he was almost exclusively engaged in religious work. In 1629, he was appointed architect of St. Peter's Basilica at the Vatican. Although he was also in great demand as a portrait sculpturist in the 1620s, his religious commissions took up most of his time.

As architect of St. Peter's, Bernini made many additions to the structure, including the lavish *Baldacchino* (1624–33) located above the main altar under the cathedral's dome; the *Cathedra Petri* (1656–66), a dramatic altar in the apse; and the loggia (begun in 1656), a curving colonnade that encircles visitors in the basilica's immense courtyard.

One of the best examples of Bernini's work is the Cornaro Chapel (1645–52) at the Church of Santa Maria Della Vittoria in Rome. Here, architecture, sculpture, and painting are combined in the effectively staged depiction of the dramatic sculpture of St. Teresa receiving the dart of divine love in *The Ecstasy of St. Teresa of Avila.*

Although accomplished in many areas, Bernini, like Michelangelo, considered himself to be primarily a sculptor of marble. Unlike the reclusive Michelangelo, the aristocratic Bernini was an outgoing man of charm and conviviality. His work for the Popes Paul V, Urban III, and Innocent X included tombs, statues, chapels, churches, fountains, and monuments, as well as the square of St. Peter's. He continued to work until the end of his very long life in 1680.

Legacy

As Michelangelo did a century earlier, Gianlorenzo Bernini achieved the status of universal genius through his talents as a painter, architect, and sculptor. He was greatly esteemed by the popes, artists, and prominent men of his time, and his style became influential throughout the Roman Catholic areas of Europe. Bernini's work for the papacy, combined with his own deep religious convictions, made him the ideal artist of the Counter-Reformation.

Bernini dominated the art of Rome for half a century. When he was put in charge of St. Peter's, in effect, he became the director of the arts' program for the entire city. No sculptor before him had ever worked on such a vast scale. He employed an entire corps of assistants who took care of the more physically demanding tasks, leaving the essential details to his own close supervision. The grandiose products of his workshop embodied the spirit of the Counter-Reformation.

Bernini's reputation waned as the power of the papacy diminished. By the late eighteenth century, Neoclassical critics began to disparage his work, seeing it as overly ornate and lacking in clarity and logic. In fact, the term "baroque," which was originally used to refer to distorted and exaggerated forms, was apparently coined with Bernini in mind. Bernini was held in low esteem throughout the nineteenth century.

In the twentieth century, however, scholars began to reexamine Bernini in the context of his own time. He is now widely regarded as one of the most brilliant and imaginative artists of the Baroque period.

Domenico

WORLD EVENTS		BERNINI'S LIFE
Ottoman dominance of Mediterranean ends	1571	
	1598	Gianlorenzo Bernini is born
	1605	Bernini moves to Rome
Thirty Years' War in Europe	1618–48	
	1629	Bernini is appointed architect of St. Peter's Basilica
	1645–52	Bernini designs Cornaro Chapel
	1680	Bernini dies
Glorious Revolution in England	1688	

For Further Reading

Avery, Charles. *Bernini: Genius of the Baroque.* London: Thames and Hudson, 1997.

Hibbard, Howard. *Bernini.* New York: Viking Penguin, 1991.

Lavin, Irving. *Bernini and the Unity of the Visual Arts.* New York: Pierpont Morgan Library and Oxford University Press, 1980.

Bernstein, Leonard

Composer and Conductor
1918–1990

Life and Work

Leonard Bernstein, composer of one of the most famous and innovative works of the American musical stage, was equally well known as the nation's leading symphony conductor, and, for a time, as a television personality who succeeded as few others have in making the world of classical music accessible to ordinary listeners.

He was born Louis Bernstein to immigrant Russian Jewish parents in the mill town of Lawrence, Massachusetts, on August 25, 1918; as a teenager, he changed his name to Leonard to set himself apart from other men named Louis in his family. He attended Boston's prestigious Latin School and became interested in music after his family bought a piano when he was 10. Bernstein's father wanted him to enter the family cosmetology-supply business, but he took to music lessons immediately. As an undergraduate at Harvard, he studied composition with Walter Piston and came in contact with his mentor, conductor Dimitri Mitropoulos.

His training in popular music began after college with a job as an arranger at the New York music publisher Harms-Remick. Becoming the assistant conductor of the New York Philharmonic in 1942, Bernstein received an unusually lucky break: he filled in for ailing guest conductor Bruno Walter in a nationally broadcast concert in November of 1943. The photogenic young pinch hitter wound up on the front pages of newspapers across the country.

Bernstein wrote his Symphony No. 1 ("Jeremiah") in 1944 and a second symphony (subtitled "The Age of Anxiety") in 1949. Several light operas, including 1952's *Trouble in Tahiti* and 1956's *Candide* (based on the Voltaire novel), paved the way for Bernstein's greatest stage success. *West Side Story* recast Shakespeare's story of Romeo and Juliet into a tragic romance that fell victim to gang violence; completed in 1957, it has since been a staple of American stages from Broadway to community and school theaters.

Bernstein followed up this success with one just as striking: in 1958 he became the first native-born American to assume the conductorship of the New York Philharmonic Orchestra, arguably the nation's flagship symphonic ensemble. Some critics objected to his flamboyant conducting style, but the warmth of personality that gave rise to it endeared Bernstein to the American public, and his televised "Young People's Concerts" and several other programs found success for many years.

Retiring from the Philharmonic in 1969 in favor of a prestigious schedule of European guest-conducting appearances, Bernstein was active as a conductor and composer until his death on October 14, 1990, in New York.

Legacy

A dynamic fixture of American musical life in the years following the twin triumphs of *West Side Story* and his New York Philharmonic appointment, Leonard Bernstein had a tremendous impact in all his various fields of endeavor.

Although preceded in its serious aspects by Rodgers and Hammerstein's *Carousel* (1945), *West Side Story* virtually transformed the musical with its story drawn from New York's increasingly violent streets. Suddenly the musi-

cal was an ambitious art form that could support complex stories, formal experimentation, and social commentary; chief among those who followed Bernstein's example in expanding the form's horizons was his *West Side Story* lyricist, Stephen Sondheim.

Bernstein's use of his Philharmonic post as a bully pulpit for classical music brought the genre to a high watermark of popularity, and when presenters later in the century attempted to recapture some of the popularity lost by Bernstein's successors, they turned again to his techniques of informality and demystification. Among his many purely musical legacies as a conductor was his introduction of the music of Gustav Mahler to American audiences.

Bernstein focused with equal intensity on classical and popular music, and he mixed the two with particular success in *Mass*, a sprawling, ecumenically minded setting of the Roman Catholic mass written in 1971. At the twentieth century's end, it seemed likely that Bernstein's eclecticism and his insistence on simply disregarding the boundaries between classical and popular music would constitute his deepest legacy. In the 1960s Bernstein had stood nearly alone among leading classical composers in avoiding the difficult, abstract compositional system known as serialism, but by the 1990s many composers (some no doubt raised on Bernstein's generous-spirited television broadcasts) had discarded serialism and were incorporating into their works a broad mixture of influences that ranged from popular music to non-Western to religious. The ramifications of Bernstein's inclusive vision of American music are still unfolding.

Manheim

World Events		Bernstein's Life
Russian Revolution	1917	
	1918	Leonard Bernstein is born Louis Bernstein
Great Depression	1929–39	
World War II	1939–45	
	1942	Bernstein becomes assistant conductor of New York Philharmonic
	1943	Bernstein gains national publicity in substitute slot
Communist China is established	1949	
Korean War	1950–53	
African independence movement begins	1957	Bernstein writes *West Side Story*
	1958	Bernstein becomes New York Philharmonic conductor
	1969	Bernstein retires from the Philharmonic
	1971	Bernstein composes *Mass*
Vietnam War ends	1975	
	1990	Bernstein dies
Dissolution of Soviet Union	1991	

For Further Reading

Peyser, Joan. *Bernstein: A Biography.* New York: Billboard Books, 1998.

Secrest, Meryle. *Bernstein: A Life.* New York: Alfred A. Knopf, 1994.

Blake, William

Poet

1757–1827

Life and Work

William Blake's unique combination of mythical prophecy, poetry, and illustration created some of England's most compelling and inspiring poetry.

Blake was born on November 28, 1757, in London. He attended drawing school at age 10 and, in 1772, became an apprentice to an engraver. He later studied engraving at the Royal Academy of Arts. As a young boy, he had mystical visions of God and angels, which would later make their way into his poetry. He published his first collection of verse, *Poetical Sketches*, in 1783. As the proprietor of a print shop, Blake invented the technique of illuminated printing and used that method to print his own bound works of poetry and drawings. His rare and beautiful illuminated books had individually hand-colored engravings.

In 1788 he printed his first two books, *There Is No Natural Religion* and *All Religions Are One*. He soon published some of his most famous works, including *Songs of Innocence* (1789), *The Marriage of Heaven and Hell* (1793), and *Songs of Innocence and Experience* (1794).

Blake's active admireration of the French Revolution brought him into contact with such radical thinkers as Thomas Paine and Mary Wollstonecraft. Blake's political ideals became important elements of his poetry. He also believed his divine mission was to express the spiritual superiority of the imagination over the force of reason. While much of his work expresses deep pain and prophetic anger, he was also capable of treating serious subjects in a lighthearted way, using the forms of popular ballads and children's rhymes.

Blake also wrote narrative poetry: *The Book of Thel* in 1789 and a series of prophetic books, including *America, A Prophecy* in 1793. *The Song of Los*, written in 1795, illustrates an epic battle between the forces of reason and the imagination. His epic poems include *The Four Zoas* (c. 1796), *Milton* (c. 1804), and *Jerusalem* (c. 1804).

Blake used his own complicated mythological structures in all his work, drawing on the Bible, JOHN MILTON, and DANTE. He treated such subjects as religion, morality, art, and politics in the context of these spiritual beliefs.

Blake supported himself by making commissioned engravings. Near the end of his life, he was hired to paint watercolor illustrations for Dante's *Divine Comedy*, a project that he left incomplete at his death in 1827.

Legacy

William Blake, an extremely individual poet and a radical thinker, is considered to be one of the greatest English Romantics.

Blake opened poetry to new and less restrictive forms, anticipating much of the English poetic innovation of the nineteenth and even the twentieth century. The formal changes that he brought to poetry included the elimination of the end-rhyme. He used the repetition of words and phrases to create a rhythmic unity.

During his life, Blake was better known for his engravings and art than for his poetry. The visions and prophecies that he spoke and wrote about gained him a reputation as a lunatic, and his work was not taken seriously, though he was greatly respected by his fellow Romantic poets Samuel Taylor Coleridge and Charles Lamb.

An 1863 biography by Alexander Gilchrist brought serious critical attention to Blake for the first time. Gilchrist argued that Blake's supposed madness was actually an eccentric imagination at work. A renewed interest in Blake and his work resulted in critical evaluations by the English poets Dante Gabriel Rossetti and Algernon Charles Swinburne.

In the late 1890s, WILLIAM BUTLER YEATS, who was also a spiritualist poet, edited a collection of Blake's poems and wrote commentary on *The Four Zoas* and *The Marriage of Heaven and Hell*, examining their mythology and symbolic systems.

Studies on Blake continued to grow into the twentieth century with work by critics including S. Foster Damon, Northrop Frye, and Harold Bloom. Frye wrote a study in 1947, *Fearful Symmetry: A Study of William Blake*, that formed the foundation for much of the current critical work on Blake.

Innumerable poets have been influenced by Blake's unique vision. One of the most recently prominent of these is Allen Ginsberg, the Beat poet who was a great proponent of Blake's work and used pieces of it in his own poetry and performances from the 1960s until his death in 1998.

Watson

WORLD EVENTS		BLAKE'S LIFE
Glorious Revolution in England	1688	
	1757	William Blake is born
	1772	Blake is apprenticed to engraver
United States declares independence	1776	
	1783	Blake publishes first book of poetry
French Revolution begins	1789	Blake publishes *Songs of Innocence* and *The Book of Thel*
	1793	Blake publishes *The Marriage of Heaven and Hell*
	1794	Blake publishes *Songs of Innocence and Experience*
	1795	Blake publishes *The Song of Los*
Latin American independence movement begins	1811	
Congress of Vienna reorganizes Europe	1815	
	1827	Blake dies
Revolutions in Austria, France, Germany, and Italy	1848	

For Further Reading

Erdman, David V. *Blake: Prophet Against Empire*. New York: Dover, 1991.

Frye, Northrop. *Fearful Symmetry: A Study of William Blake*. Boston: Beacon Press, 1962.

Gilchrist, Alexander. *The Life of William Blake*. New York: E. P. Dutton, 1942.

Borges, Jorge Luis

Short Story Writer, Poet,
and Essayist
1899–1986

Life and Work

Jorge Luis Borges wrote innovative and experimental fiction that changed the direction of Latin American literature and influenced literature worldwide.

Borges was born on August 24, 1899, in Buenos Aires. He attended school in Geneva and afterward spent time in Spain with the Ultraists, a group interested in expanding artistic expression beyond traditional boundaries of form and narrative. When he returned to Buenos Aires in 1921, he established the Ultraist movement in Argentina. He published

poems, essays, criticism, and the first Spanish translations of sections of JAMES JOYCE's *Ulysses*, and founded three literary magazines. With the publication of his first books of poetry, *Fervor de Buenos Aires* in 1923 and *Luna de enfrente* in 1925, he became known as one of Argentina's most gifted writers.

In the 1930s and early 1940s, Borges worked in a library in Buenos Aires and wrote the short stories that would be collected in *Ficciones* (*Fictions*), published in 1944, and *El Aleph* (*The Aleph*), published in 1949. In these works he mingled fiction, nonfiction, and poetry, employing both imaginary worlds and scholarly techniques to ask metaphysical questions in a fictional context and often spoofing established forms.

When Juan Perón came to power in Argentina in 1946, Borges spoke out against the dictatorship. In retaliation, Perón dismissed him from his library post and made him national poultry inspector. Borges supported himself by giving lectures, selling his writings, and working as an editor. In 1952 he published *Otras inquisiciones*, (*Other Inquisitions*, 1937–52). After Perón's fall in 1955, Borges was appointed director of the national library and professor of English and American literature at the University of Buenos Aires.

Borges was nearly blind by the early 1950s and, partly as a result, he began dictating short texts, including the parables of his later years. Many of these are collected in *El Hacedor* (*Dreamtigers*), published in 1960, and *Manuel de zoologia fantastica* (*The Book of Imaginary Beings*) published in 1967. In 1961 Borges was awarded, along with SAMUEL BECKETT, the Formentor Prize.

Borges continued writing until the end of his life. He died of cancer on June 14, 1986.

Legacy

Jorge Luis Borges opened the way for a Latin American literature of imagination, dream, philosophy, and enigmas that explored metaphysical questions of time and reality.

Borges created a new fictional world for Latin American literature, one that, in its mingling of fantasy and reality, addressed the actual experience and tradition of Latin American life.

As a defender of fantasy literature's capacity to address actual concerns, Borges ushered in a generation of Latin American writers who, in their attempts to experiment with form and narrative, relinquished traditional European realism for a more fantastical treatment of themes of time and loss, often returning to myth for inspiration and structure. The writers of the Latin American Boom, a period of immense literary productivity that began in the late 1950s, adopted Borges's ease of movement between the real and the unreal, treating the fantastic as an inherent aspect of modern life. Alejo Carpentier, Mario Vargas Llosa, Lezama Lima, Carlos Fuentes, and Julio Cortazar have all continued this tradition; Borges's influence is clear in the myth, history, and magic of GABRIEL GARCÍA MÁRQUEZ's *100 Years of Solitude* (1965), despite great differences in the politics and aesthetics of the two writers.

Borges was unknown outside of Latin America until the 1940s, when translations of his work began to be published around the world. His popularity grew quickly and he became the first Latin American writer to gain an international reputation. After he received the Formentor Prize in 1961, critics increasingly referred to his works as classics of twentieth-century literature, often comparing them to those of FRANZ KAFKA. His work exerted a strong influence on European and North American writers, particularly on the experimental writers of the 1960s and 1970s such as John Barth and John Updike, who both wrote extensively about Borges. Updike's early novel *The Centaur* (1963) told an allegorical story using characters based on mythical prototypes, techniques that find their origins in the work of Borges. Barth also interwove multiple plot lines using fantasy and myth in his experimental narratives.

Watson

WORLD EVENTS		BORGES'S LIFE
Spanish-American War	1898	
	1899	Jorge Luis Borges is born
World War I	1914–18	
Russian Revolution	1917	
	1923	Borges publishes first book of poetry, *Fervor de Buenos Aires*
Great Depression	1929–39	
World War II	1939–45	
	1944	Borges publishes *Fictions*
Communist China is established	1949	Borges publishes *The Aleph*
Korean War	1950–53	
	1952	Borges publishes *Other Inquisitions*
	1955	Borges is appointed director of national library
African independence movement begins	1957	
	1961	Borges shares the Formentor Prize with Samuel Beckett
Vietnam War ends	1975	
	1986	Borges dies
Dissolution of Soviet Union	1991	

For Further Reading

Alazraki, Jaime. *Jorge Luis Borges*. New York: Columbia University Press, 1971.
Lennon, Adrian, and Steven Samuels. *Jorge Luis Borges*. New York: Chelsea House, 1992.

Bosch, Hieronymus

Painter

1453–1517

Life and Work

The fantastic, allegorical, and often nightmarish paintings of Hieronymus Bosch reflect the artist's perceptions of the pessimistic, fear-filled time in which he lived.

Bosch's life and career remain in some ways as mysterious as his work. Little is known of his early life, except that he was born in 1453 in 's Hertogenbosch, an affluent town in what is now the Netherlands. A third-generation painter, it is likely that he was taught by his father. Neither his themes nor his style reflected those employed by contemporary Flemish painters, with their use of chiaroscuro, natural light, and sculptural forms. Instead, Bosch used a flat style and painted directly onto the canvas to produce what appear to be graphically presented moral sermons. The individuality of his work in style and theme may be attributable to his financial independence. Tax records from the time show that he achieved a sizable sum through the sale of a portion of his wife's property.

Bosch's *Temptation of St. Anthony* (1500–05) reflects the extreme spiritual pessimism of the age. The saint is portrayed as a Christ-like hero able to resist both worldly goods and sexual enticement. This triptych is a thorough account of all the fears and convictions of medieval society: it includes demons, astrological beliefs that link evil influences to the position of the planets, and themes relating to the Seven Deadly Sins and the Antichrist.

Painted between 1505 and 1510, *The Garden of Earthly Delights* is considered to be the apex of Bosch's fantastic, imaginative, and personal works. The left panel of the triptych shows the creation of Eve in the Garden of Eden, but in this view of paradise, evil lurks in the form of ravens and an owl, symbolic references to witchcraft and sorcery. The central panel, which depicts a swarm of nude men and women overwhelmed by the need for sensual gratification, portrays the consequences of unredeemed original sin. The right panel shows Hell and the hideous torments of the damned.

The Garden of Earthly Delights, in its visual references to magic and alchemy, reflects Bosch's thematic sources in medieval bestiaries, Flemish proverbs, and dream books. There is disagreement in its interpretation: the picture may be a sermonic narrative or, as some suggest, an allegory showing the four stages of the alchemical distillation process through which individuals are transformed from their base existence on Earth to an eternal union with God. Although the artist's precise intentions may never be known, the painting reflects the millennialist fears and deep spiritual unrest that swept through Europe in the years around 1500.

Bosch died in 1517.

Legacy

Hieronymus Bosch's artistic vision serves as the antithesis of the optimistic humanism of the contemporaneous Italian Renaissance. His neo-medieval style exposes an unstable world run by swindlers, sinners, and idiots.

Although Bosch maintained a shop in his hometown of 's Hertogenbosch, he had a reputation that went far beyond its boundaries. Many of his works were engraved by Alart du Hameel and widely imitated. By the early sixteenth century, his works were collected as far away as Italy and Prague; Philip II of Spain was an avid collector of his works. Bosch's reputation remained alive in Spain through the eighteenth century, while elsewhere he was largely forgotten.

Bosch was "rediscovered" near the end of the nineteenth century, when he came to be regarded as a painter of fantasy. Later, he was admired and imitated by twentieth-century Surrealist painters such as SALVADOR DALÍ.

Over the past several decades, art historians have begun to unravel Bosch's ties to fifteenth-century religious reform, witchcraft, and folktales, providing a more accurate picture of the painter. His subjective, highly individualistic work is appreciated today for its fantastic imagery hinting at malevolent forces and serves as a forerunner to modern comic book artists like R. Crumb and Frank Miller. However, art historians view him primarily as a moralist, rather than purely as an inventor of fantasy.

Domenico

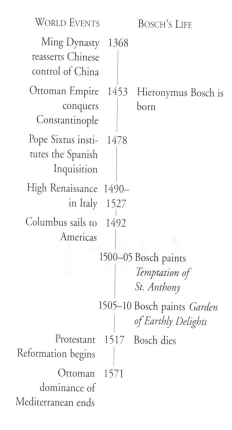

WORLD EVENTS		BOSCH'S LIFE
Ming Dynasty reasserts Chinese control of China	1368	
Ottoman Empire conquers Constantinople	1453	Hieronymus Bosch is born
Pope Sixtus institutes the Spanish Inquisition	1478	
High Renaissance in Italy	1490–1527	
Columbus sails to Americas	1492	
	1500–05	Bosch paints *Temptation of St. Anthony*
	1505–10	Bosch paints *Garden of Earthly Delights*
Protestant Reformation begins	1517	Bosch dies
Ottoman dominance of Mediterranean ends	1571	

For Further Reading

Gibson, Walter S. *Hieronymus Bosch.* London: Thames and Hudson, 1985.

Snyder, James. *Bosch in Perspective.* Englewood Cliffs, N.J.: Prentice Hall, 1973.

Botticelli, Sandro

Painter
1445–1510

Life and Work

Sandro Botticelli was a Florentine painter who produced most of his work in the last quarter of the fifteenth century. His highly per-sonal work reflected the humanist interest in ancient mythology fused with Christian faith.

Botticelli was born Alessandro di Mariano Filipepi in 1445. His first teacher was the painter Fra Filippo Lippi. Later, he studied under Andrea del Verocchio, who also taught the young LEONARDO DA VINCI. Although competent in the methods and styles of con-temporary Renaissance painters, (monumen-tality, attention to atmosphere, and scientific approach), Botticelli's style—more decorative and linear—was original. His clear-edged bod-ies seemed to float weightlessly, their mass smooth and unmuscular, but solid.

One of the favorite painters of the Medicis, Botticelli incorporated classical mythology into his work, which reflected the humanist atmosphere of their cultivated circle. In these devotional paintings, a classical figure such as Venus could be represented as the source of divine love interchangeable with the Virgin Mary. During the medieval period, such an image would have been denounced as pagan, but within the Medici circle of influence, Neoplatonic mysticism opened its followers up to alternative images of the divine.

Painted to honor the marriage of Lorenzo di Pierfrancesco de' Medici, Botticelli's *Primavera*, completed around 1482, was placed outside the nuptial chamber in his palace. Filled with mythological references, many elements in the painting appear to refer to the Medici family also. *The Birth of Venus* (1484–85), also painted for Lorenzo di Pierfrancesco, treats respectfully the classical subject matter of the birth from the sea of the goddess Venus, transforming the myth into an allegory of the human soul. The heavenly Venus represents the soul in its origi-nal perfection and beauty, prior to its descent (birth) into the body.

The religious reform movement in Florence of the 1490s led by the monk Girolamo Savonarola attacked the "cult of paganism" of the city's ruling class. The Florentine artists lost their major source of patronage when the Medicis and other nobility were banished from the city by Savonarola's followers. Botticelli became a follower of the reform movement and was influenced by the surrounding politi-cal and religious turmoil. His later paintings, such as the *Mystical Nativity* (1500), reflect this personal change in their use of traditional religious subject matter.

During the final 10 years of his life, Botticelli apparently withdrew from the art world. According to Giorgio Vasari, his six-teenth-century biographer, Botticelli aged pre-maturely and walked with two canes. He died in 1510.

Legacy

Before his religious conversion, Sandro Botticelli's paintings combined the human-istic scholarship of the Renaissance with the highly decorative, artificial style of the late Middle Ages.

Throughout the greater part of his career, Botticelli was one of the most admired painters of his generation. He received commissions from extremely prominent families in Florence, as well as an important commission from the Pope, and was known by art patrons through-out Italy.

Toward the end of his life, however, Botticelli's works were regarded as hopelessly outdated. Around 1500, a new style emerged. Da Vinci, MICHELANGELO, and RAPHAEL, whose work exemplified the Renaissance prin-ciples of monumentality and science-based realism, received the major commissions, while Botticelli's more poetic, personal, and linear style diminished in popularity.

Botticelli's reputation was obscured by his more celebrated contemporaries for more than 300 years. In the nineteenth century, artists of the Pre-Raphaelite movement rediscovered his work. They appreciated its innocent simplicity, which stood in contrast to the pomposity of the academic tradition of the Royal Academy in Britain, which had long been centered on Raphael's style.

Today, Botticelli's *Primavera* and *Birth of Venus* are among the most familiar of Renaissance paintings. They are loved by the public for their accessible, delicate imagery, even though their original symbolic meaning has been largely forgotten. To scholars, Botticelli embodies the combination of medieval Christian traditions and a revived interest in classical subjects that defined the Renaissance.

Domenico

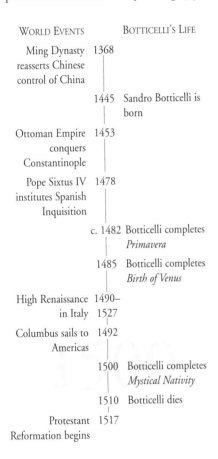

World Events		Botticelli's Life
Ming Dynasty reasserts Chinese control of China	1368	
	1445	Sandro Botticelli is born
Ottoman Empire conquers Constantinople	1453	
Pope Sixtus IV institutes Spanish Inquisition	1478	
	c. 1482	Botticelli completes *Primavera*
	1485	Botticelli completes *Birth of Venus*
High Renaissance in Italy	1490– 1527	
Columbus sails to Americas	1492	
	1500	Botticelli completes *Mystical Nativity*
	1510	Botticelli dies
Protestant Reformation begins	1517	

For Further Reading

Cheney, Liana. *Quattrocento Neoplatonism and Medici Humanism in Botticelli's Mythological Paintings*. Potomac, Md.: Scripta Humanistica, 1993.

Lightbrown, Ronald. *Sandro Botticelli: Life and Work*. 2 vols. Berkeley: University of California Press, 1989.

Wind, Edgar. *Pagan Mysteries in the Renaissance*. New Haven, Conn.: Yale University Press, 1958.

Bourke-White, Margaret

Photojournalist
1904–1971

Life and Work

Margaret Bourke-White helped establish the field of photojournalism and produced many of the key images of world events in the mid-twentieth century.

Bourke-White was born in 1904 in the Bronx, New York, and grew up in Bound Brook, New Jersey. She was the daughter of Minnie Bourke and Joseph White, an engineer and inventor. Bourke-White entered Rutgers University in New Jersey in 1921, planning to study biology. Over the next few years she changed schools several times, finally graduating from Cornell University in New York in 1927. She developed a serious interest in photography while attending Columbia University (1921–22) and studying with the prominent photographer Clarence White.

In 1927 Bourke-White moved to Cleveland, Ohio, and established the Bourke-White Studio, specializing in architectural and industrial photography. Her photographs of the Otis Steel Mill caught the attention of the magazine publisher Henry R. Luce. In 1929 Luce asked her to become the staff photographer for his new magazine, *Fortune*. While working for

Fortune, Bourke-White developed her characteristic format, the photo-essay.

Bourke-White worked on an increasingly varied series of projects. In 1930 she became the first American photographer to work in the Soviet Union, where she photographed a variety of subjects and eventually produced the book *Eyes on Russia* (1931), a rare look inside the Soviet Union. She collaborated with the novelist, Erskine Caldwell on three books: *You Have Seen Their Faces* (1937), about the ravaging effects of poverty in dust bowl America; *North of the Danube* (1937), a chronicle of life in Czechoslovakia before the Nazi takeover; and *Say Is This the USA* (1941), about life in America prior to World War II.

Bourke-White's career underwent a major change in 1936 when Henry Luce decided to establish a new magazine, called *Life*, in which the photographs rather than the text would tell the story. Bourke-White became one of four staff photographers: her photo of the Fort Peck Dam appeared on the cover of the first issue. For the next several years, Bourke-White traveled the globe on assignments for *Life* and produced many of the quintessential images of her generation.

During World War II, she spent four years as a war correspondent in North Africa, Western Europe, and the Soviet Union, often traveling in military planes on bombing missions. Her shocking photographs of Nazi death camps exposed the horrors of the Holocaust to the entire world. After the war, Bourke-White continued her adventurous career, providing images of Mahatma Gandhi's India, South Africa during apartheid, and the Korean War. Her famous photographs from these years include *Mahatma Gandhi Spinning* and a series on the diamond mines in South Africa.

In 1956 Bourke-White was diagnosed with Parkinson's disease. Her career in photography slowed, though she continued to write. Her autobiography, *Portrait of Myself,* was published in 1963. Bourke-White died in 1971 from complications associated with Parkinson's.

Legacy

As one of the founders of the new medium of photojournalism, Margaret Bourke-White helped to define the image of the photojournalist in the popular imagination. She

was recognized around the world as the quintessential photographer–adventurer who would go to almost any extreme to capture her story.

During her career, Bourke-White assembled an impressive list of accomplishments: immediately after college she became the country's leading female industrial photographer; she helped to invent the photo-essay; she was the first American photographer to work in the Soviet Union; she shot the first cover of *Life*; she was the author of six books; she was the first officially recognized female war correspondent; and she was one of the first photographers to photograph the Nazi death camps. Her work helped to establish the photo-essay as a major form of art.

Bourke-White witnessed wars, drought, and genocide, and shared these experiences with the world through her photography. *Life* magazine, which she did so much to shape, provided Americans of her generation with the defining images of their lives.

McEnroe

WORLD EVENTS		BOURKE-WHITE'S LIFE
Spanish-American War	1898	
	1904	Margaret Bourke-White is born
World War I	1914–18	
Russian Revolution	1917	
	1927	Bourke-White graduates from Cornell University
Great Depression	1929–39	
	1929	Bourke-White becomes staff photographer for *Fortune* magazine
	1936	Bourke-White joins *Life* magazine
World War II	1939–45	
Communist China is established	1949	
Korean War	1950–53	
	1956	Bourke-White is diagnosed with Parkinson's disease
African independence movement begins	1957	
	1971	Bourke-White dies
Vietnam War ends	1975	

For Further Reading

Bourke-White, Margaret. *Portrait of Myself.* New York: Simon & Schuster, 1963.

Goldberg, Vicki. *Margaret Bourke-White: A Biography.* New York: Harper & Row, 1986.

Silverman, Jonathan. *For the World to See: The Life of Margaret Bourke-White.* New York: Viking Press, 1983.

Brahms, Johannes

Composer
1833–1897

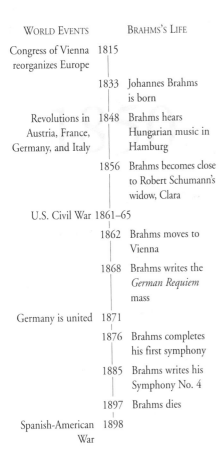

WORLD EVENTS		BRAHMS'S LIFE
Congress of Vienna reorganizes Europe	1815	
	1833	Johannes Brahms is born
Revolutions in Austria, France, Germany, and Italy	1848	Brahms hears Hungarian music in Hamburg
	1856	Brahms becomes close to Robert Schumann's widow, Clara
U.S. Civil War	1861–65	
	1862	Brahms moves to Vienna
	1868	Brahms writes the German Requiem mass
Germany is united	1871	
	1876	Brahms completes his first symphony
	1885	Brahms writes his Symphony No. 4
	1897	Brahms dies
Spanish-American War	1898	

Life and Work

Believers in a central, organically developing tradition of German classical music have long invoked the triumvirate of Bach, Beethoven, and Brahms in naming that tradition's finest representatives. Johannes Brahms is widely considered one of the greatest composers of the nineteenth century.

Brahms was born in Hamburg, Germany, on May 7, 1833. A sensational pianist by the time he was 10, he was recruited by an American promoter who wanted him to tour the United States as a new young prodigy. But he remained in Hamburg and began to compose, honing his skills by writing and arranging music for small ensembles of which his father was a part. Hungarian refugees from an 1848 uprising brought their music to Hamburg and inspired in Brahms a life long fascination with its rhythmic complexities.

In the early 1850s Brahms caught the attention of ROBERT SCHUMANN, the leading German composer of the day, and after Schumann's death in 1856, Brahms fell in love with Schumann's widow, Clara, a composer and renowned pianist in her own right. How far the relationship went is unclear, but these encounters stimulated Brahms's own compositional development.

In 1862 Brahms moved to Vienna. He hoped to move into a secure job as a conductor or composer, and to live, as he once wrote, "a decent, middle-class life." Success was slow to come, but Brahms made a major breakthrough with the German Requiem mass of 1868. This mass for the dead went beyond the music of Brahms's own time, incorporating the rich multipart choral textures of the religious music of the seventeenth and eighteenth centuries. In his four symphonies, too, Brahms confronted the musical models of a past master: reflecting on the influence of LUDWIG VAN BEETHOVEN, Brahms wrote, "You have no idea how someone like me feels when he hears such a giant marching behind him all the time."

Brahms completed his first symphony in 1876. Many of his later compositions were written for small ensembles. Complex and economical, they develop large yet tightly controlled structures from a simple kernel of music. Brahms died of liver cancer in Vienna on April 3, 1897.

Legacy

Johannes Brahms was at once the supreme conservative of nineteenth-century classical music and an inspiration to the compositional radicals who flourished decades after his death.

During Brahms's career many composers explored connections between music and the other arts. The "tone poems" of FRANZ LISZT and others were detailed musical representations of literary texts or actual exotic locales, and RICHARD WAGNER insisted on the primacy of opera as the one art form that could bring together music, drama, and visual elements. Others, however, resisted these trends, and in Brahms they found a standard-bearer for the idea that music should be its own message. Brahms wrote purely abstract symphonies, sonatas, concertos, and quartets. He never wrote an opera, and over the course of his career he incurred the wrath of Wagner, a gifted polemicist who several times attacked Brahms in print. The Viennese critic Eduard Hanslick was prominent among the composer's defenders.

Despite his conservative tendencies, Brahms thoroughly reworked the traditional forms and pursued their implications, and when the pendulum swung away from Romantic expressiveness in the first three decades of the twentieth century, composers admired Brahms for his compositional rigor and sought to emulate it.

Wagner had led the way in smashing the classical system of harmony, but Brahms's music (though he would never have aimed at anything of the sort) suggested new methods of making a composition hang together without it. The Viennese composer ARNOLD SCHOENBERG, who completely swept away the old harmonies and devised the new and entirely dissonant 12-tone system to replace them, studied Brahms's music closely and coined the term "developing variation" to describe the way Brahms could generate a large movement out of a small cell of music. Schoenberg and his contemporaries were particularly fascinated by the opening theme of Brahms's Symphony No. 4 of 1885, which used all 12 tones of the minor scale in succession. Brahms, then, explored music's past so thoroughly that he laid the groundwork for its future.

Manheim

For Further Reading
Geiringer, Karl. *Brahms: His Life and Work*. New York: Da Capo, 1982.
Swafford, Jan. *Johannes Brahms: A Biography*. New York: Alfred A. Knopf, 1997.

Brecht, Bertolt

Playwright and Director
1898–1956

Life and Work

Bertolt Brecht's revolutionary theater left convention behind as it turned drama into a rebellious forum for leftist causes and ideas.

Brecht was born Eugen Berthold Friedrich Brecht on February 10, 1898, in Augsburg, Bavaria, located in Germany. He published his first play, *The Bible*, in a school magazine in 1914 and began writing newspaper articles.

Brecht had friends among the Dadaists, a group of anarchistic artists who hoped to destroy traditional mimetic standards of art. He shared its strong anti-bourgeois sentiments and combined them with a newfound Marxist ideology, to which he became committed in the late 1920s.

Brecht produced his first play, *Baal*, in Bavaria in 1923 and gained public recognition when he received the prestigious Kleist Prize. By the time *In the Jungle of the Cities* was produced in late 1923, he had already risen to the highest ranks of contemporary German playwrights. In 1924 he left Bavaria and moved to Berlin. In 1928 he wrote *Die Dreigroschenoper* (*The Threepenny Opera*) with composer Kurt Weill. The opera, based on a play by John Gay, was a satire on bourgeois ethics, which proved enormously popular with the middle-class public.

In 1933 Brecht fled Nazi Germany, living first in Denmark, and then the United States.

While in the United States, Brecht worked on films with expatriate German director Fritz Lang and wrote many plays, essays, and poems. Among the most important of these plays are *Mutter Courage und Ihre Kinder* (*Mother Courage and Her Children*, 1941), *Der Gute Mensch von Setzuan* (*The Good Woman of Setzuan*, 1943), and *Der Aufhaltsame sufsteig des Arturo Ui* (*The Resistible Rise of Arturo Ui*, 1958), a play parodying Hitler's rise to power.

Brecht's theory of "epic theater" stated that the audience should not be lulled into believing that the events occurring onstage were truly occurring; instead, the spectators should be constantly reminded that those events were staged. In this way, alienated from the narrative, the audience would be aware of the art of the theater and would observe with critical detachment.

In 1947 Brecht was called before the House Un-American Activities Committee and accused of being a communist. He left the United States and moved to Switzerland. In 1949, Brecht returned to Berlin and formed The Berliner Ensemble, his own theater company. The work he produced with the group was always controversial, both praised and criticized for its continuing attack on bourgeois aesthetics and its Marxist and communist politics. In 1955 he was awarded the Stalin Peace Prize. Brecht died of a heart attack in East Berlin on August 14, 1956.

Legacy

Bertolt Brecht demystified the theater, bringing it physically and intellectually closer to audiences.

Brecht was well known in Germany throughout his career and his works began to be treated critically and to be increasingly performed outside of Germany in the 1960s. Since then, innumerable progressive theater groups have cited Brecht and his work as an influence. Among the most important of these are The San Francisco Mime Troupe, founded in 1959; The Teatro Campesino, founded in 1965 in California; and The Performance Group, founded in the early 1970s in New York. Although very different from one another, these groups share an experimental aesthetic that often includes the mixing and spoofing of genres; the joining of music, dance, and theater; and the use of strong political content.

Brecht had an enduring influence on plays—depicting characters as contradictory and changeable beings rather than as fixed representatives of one trait or emotion. More interested in the effect of a social situation on a character than in a character's individual psychology, Brecht shifted the focus in theater away from the individual and toward the working of the play's structure as a whole. Among the playwrights influenced by Brecht are: Peter Weiss, John Arden, Edward Bond, and David Hare.

Principles of stage design used by Brecht—including minimal, functional, and flexible sets; sparse staging with one object symbolizing a locale or a situation; and set changes that made these devices visible to the audience—are now widely used in contemporary theater.

The current work of directors Peter Brook, Giorgio Strehler, and Peter Stein reflects Brecht's style. These directors tend to encourage a group approach to theater, often expressing political and social views in an effort to transcend social and cultural boundaries on stage. Dancer-choreographer Pina Bausch, playwright and director Robert Wilson, and playwright Heiner Müller all create such questioning, multilayered performances that can be traced in part to Brecht's influence.

Watson

WORLD EVENTS		BRECHT'S LIFE
Germany is united	1871	
Spanish-American War	1898	Bertolt Brecht is born
World War I	1914–18	
Russian Revolution	1917	
	1923	Brecht produces first play, *Baal*
	1928	Brecht writes *The Threepenny Opera* with Kurt Weill
Great Depression	1929–39	
	1933	Brecht flees Nazi Germany
World War II	1939–45	
	1947	Brecht is called before U.S. House Un-American Activities Committee
Communist China is established	1949	Brecht forms The Berliner Ensemble
Korean War	1950–53	
	1955	Brecht receives Stalin Peace Prize
	1956	Brecht dies of heart attack
African independence movement begins	1957	

For Further Reading

Martin, Carol, and Henry Bial, eds. *Bertolt Brecht: A Critical Anthology.* New York: Routledge, 1999.

Brecht, Bertolt. *Brecht on Theatre.* Translated by John Willett. New York: Hill and Wang, 1990.

Brontë, Charlotte

Novelist
1816–1855

Life and Work

Charlotte Brontë was the first novelist to depict the psychological and social reality of a woman's struggle for power in novels that also vitally engaged the reader.

WORLD EVENTS		BRONTË'S LIFE
Congress of Vienna reorganizes Europe	1815	
	1816	Charlotte Brontë is born
	1846	Brontë publishes book of poems with her sisters, Anne and Emily
	1846	Brontë writes *The Professor*
	1847	Brontë publishes *Jane Eyre*
Revolutions in Austria, France, Germany, and Italy	1848	
	1849	Brontë publishes *Shirley*
	1853	Brontë publishes *Villette*
	1855	Brontë dies
	1857	Mrs. Gaskell publishes *The Life of Charlotte Brontë*
U.S. Civil War	1861–65	

Born in Yorkshire, England, on April 21, 1816, Charlotte Brontë was the third daughter in a family that included the writers Anne and Emily Brontë. The children were largely educated at home by their father, a clergyman who had them read widely—WILLIAM SHAKESPEARE, JOHN MILTON, John Bunyan, and others, as well as newspapers of the day. Eventually, Charlotte Brontë attended a private school at Roe Head, where she later returned to teach for a short time. She also worked as a governess in several different families, gaining experience that she would draw upon in her novels.

In 1846, Charlotte, Emily, and Anne Brontë published a volume of poetry under pseudonym, *Poems of Currer, Ellis, and Acton Bell*. That same year, Charlotte wrote her first novel, *The Professor*, which would not be published until after her death.

The following year she published her second novel, *Jane Eyre*, which met with immediate success among critics and readers. The heroine of the title is not the traditionally passive and submissive female protagonist of the Gothic fiction that Brontë was heir to. As an outwardly unattractive child, Jane is an outcast and a rebel, characterized by a fierce inner strength that she draws upon in her quest for spiritual freedom. Jane narrates the novel, which was published under the pretense of being an autobiography, and tells her story with an authority and conviction unusual in a female narrator.

In 1849, Brontë published a third novel, *Shirley*, which received a far cooler reception. A novel of social commentary, Shirley takes place in the midst of the industrial conflict of the English countryside and addresses the social failings that made it impossible for working-class women to exercise control over their own lives. Although Brontë's readers, eager for another tale of fiery romance, were disappointed, the novel has been placed alongside works by CHARLES DICKENS and Elizabeth Gaskell (Mrs. Gaskell) as an important contribution to the Victorian examination of industrial capitalism.

Villette, published in 1853, is Brontë's most complex and sophisticated work. The novel's main character, Lucy Snowe, a governess and teacher, casts a critical and ironic eye on the situations in which she finds herself and the other characters. The axis of the story is the protagonist's sense of longing and deep frustration with her position in society, which is limited both by her gender and her class. *Villette*, a study of a female psyche imprisoned by societal restrictions and self-doubt, gives a powerful portrait of her suffering.

Brontë died from complications of pregnancy on March 31, 1855. Her good friend, the author Elizabeth Gaskell, wrote a biography of Brontë called *The Life of Charlotte Brontë*, which was published in 1857. The book sold well and ensured that Brontë retained a presence in the literary world after her death.

Legacy

The power of Charlotte Brontë's work has not diminished and today it holds the attention of a wide variety of readers and academics.

The popularity of Brontë's work, great during her life, gained momentum following her death. Gaskell's biography brought readers closer to the writer, and the most devoted of those readers founded societies and a museum in her name, made pilgrimages to her home, and, of course, continued to buy and read her novels.

Brontë contributed a new psychological realism to the development of the novel as a genre, for she wrote about emotional repression and the female psyche. In light of the new depth and intensity that she brought to the treatment of character and motivation, she can be seen as a precursor to writers including GEORGE ELIOT, D. H. Lawrence, and Thomas Hardy, all of whom wrote novels with strong female protagonists.

The 1970s saw a renewed interest in Brontë's work and particularly in *Jane Eyre*, as feminist critics began to make a distinction between male and female writers' styles and subjects. These critics discussed *Jane Eyre* as an early example of a female author writing to women about the restrictions placed upon women's lives and minds. The book even inspired another work of fiction, *Wide Sargasso Sea* by Jean Rhys, which is a rewriting of the story from the point of view of the character Bertha, a madwoman locked in an attic and eventually killed in a fire.

Jane Eyre continues to be read and discussed in terms of Victorian literary studies and women's studies, and is undoubtedly one of the most readable and interesting novels of the Victorian era.

Watson

For Further Reading
Gaskell, Elizabeth. *The Life of Charlotte Bronte*. 1857. Reprint, New York: Penguin Books, 1998.
Gates, Barbara Timm, ed. *Critical Essays on Charlotte Brontë*. Boston: G. K. Hall, 1990.

Brown, James

Vocalist

c. 1933–

Life and Work

One of the leading creators of soul music in the 1960s and 1970s, James Brown developed a radical and extremely influential inflection of that style. Brown's musical innovations drew on the tremendous vocal and kinetic energy he displayed in performance.

Brown was born in Barnwell, South Carolina, around 1933. He grew up in dire poverty and was raised primarily in Augusta, Georgia, by a great-aunt. The manic, compelling quality of his stage performances as an adult may be traceable to his experiences singing and dancing on the streets as a child. At 16 Brown was convicted of breaking into a car and put in a youth work camp. Released early, Brown began singing in a quartet called the Gospel Starlighters.

This group switched to secular music in the early 1950s, becoming known first as the Flames and then as the Famous Flames. The group's debut recording, first cut at a Macon, Georgia radio station, was 1956's "Please Please Please"; a moderate success, the song gave the first hints of Brown's emotion-laden intensity. Other early releases on the Cincinnati, Ohio-based King Records failed to tap Brown's distinctive abilities, but 1960's "Think" inaugurated a string of Brown hits that remained unbroken through 1977.

Brown's *Live at the Apollo* album of 1963 spread the word about his live performances, in which individual songs were extended to staggering lengths through Brown's screams, whispers, and perfectly controlled dialogue with his audiences. With the 1964 single "Out of Sight" and its top-selling successor, "Papa's Got a Brand New Bag," Brown created a unique and extreme new style that integrated his vocal acrobatics into intense rhythmic patterns. Subsequent Brown singles such as 1967's "Cold Sweat" and 1970's "Sex Machine" honed the intensity of Brown's rhythmic world. His 1968 release "Say It Loud—I'm Black and Proud" was identified with black activism, but Brown's personal politics were somewhat conservative.

Brown formed a new band, the JBs, after signing with the Polydor label in 1971. In his mature recordings and performances, he and his backing ensemble essentially became a single unit, exploring, sometimes at great length, the possibilities of a specific rhythmic pattern. Brown's vocals and his instrumental arrangements were percussive in nature; the "rhythm section" of his band did not end with drums or even with a group of horns, but was composed of the entire group, including Brown himself.

The lush disco style of the late 1970s finally dented his popularity. Brown was imprisoned again in 1988 after resisting arrest in a car chase, but continued to perform and record after his release in 1991, his status as an American icon assured.

Legacy

Throughout the late twentieth century, James Brown's music never went out of date. It inspired first the funk style of the late 1970s and then, to some measure, the hip-hop revolution of the 1980s and 1990s; at the century's end, Brown seemed to be a pivotal figure in the establishment of a new and fundamentally rhythmic basis for African-American music.

Brown and Sylvester Stewart (leader of Sly and the Family Stone) may be viewed as funk's twin progenitors, and several veterans of Brown's bands in the 1970s were important figures in the genesis of the style. Bassist Bootsy Collins went on to form Bootsy's Rubber Band, one of the seminal funk ensembles; alto saxophone player Maceo Parker worked with leading funk bands Parliament and Funkadelic before beginning a long solo career.

Numerous hip-hop artists signaled their indebtedness to Brown's music by including "samples," or brief sonic excerpts, of his vocals in their own collage-like musical structures. The bass guitar patterns of Brown's 1960s bassist Clyde Stubblefield were often sampled as well, for they marked the first appearance in African-American music of the heavy, sharp yet relaxed bass lines that would become one of hip-hop's defining features.

Hip-hop has for ancestors a host of African and Afro-Caribbean genres that incorporated spoken text into music, but Brown and his funk successors influenced it at a deeper level. The percussive poetry of rap was just a brief step from improvisatory rants that were a benchmark of Brown's later work. "Sometimes I look back on my life and wonder just how one man could achieve all I've done," Brown once said. It might not be too much to say that he laid the rhythmic foundations for the music of the twenty-first century.

Manheim

WORLD EVENTS		BROWN'S LIFE
Great Depression	1929–39	
	1933	James Brown is born
World War II	1939–45	
Communist China is established	1949	
Korean War	1950–53	
	1956	Brown records "Please Please Please"
African independence movement begins	1957	
	1960	"Think" begins 17-year string of hits
	1963	Brown records *Live at the Apollo* LP
	1964	Brown pioneers new rhythm-dominated style with "Out of Sight" single
	1967	Brown records "Cold Sweat"
	1968	"Say It Loud—I'm Black and Proud" inspires black activists
Vietnam War ends	1975	
	1988	Brown is imprisoned on charges of resisting arrest
Dissolution of Soviet Union	1991	Brown is released

For Further Reading

Brown, James. *James Brown, The Godfather of Soul.* New York: Macmillan, 1986.

Guralnick, Peter. *Sweet Soul Music: Rhythm and Blues and the Southern Dream of Freedom.* New York: Harper & Row, 1986.

Büchner, Georg

Playwright
1813–1837

Life and Work

The author of only three plays and a novella in the early nineteenth century, Georg Büchner exerted one of the most powerful influences of any writer on modern theater.

Büchner was born in Goddelau, Hesse-Darmstadt, and raised in the duchy's nearby capital city, Darmstadt. Büchner's father, a doctor, was determined that his son should follow in his footsteps, while his mother endowed him with her love for literature and art. In 1831 he went to Strasbourg, France, to study medicine, and was exposed to then radical politics espoused by liberal German thinkers. He returned to Germany to study in Giessen in 1833, where he collaborated on a political pamphlet with a well-known revolutionary, Friedrich Ludwig Weidig. The pamphlet, called *The Hessian Messenger* (1834), advocated reform of the Hessian government on a French republican model and encouraged peasants to rise up against the aristocracy. Büchner fled to his parents' home when several of his friends were arrested for their political activity. There he wrote his first play, *Danton's Death* (1835), a work dramatizing the differences between the radical and moderate factions of the French Revolution.

In 1836 he returned to Strasbourg, fleeing the constant surveillance of the police to which he had been subjected since the publication of *The Hessian Messenger*. He ceased his political activities and continued his study of medicine and philosophy. He began work on *Lenz*, a novella based on the life of the Sturm und Drang dramatist Jakob Michael Reinhold Lenz. His next work was a play called *Leonce and Lena* (1836), a satirical romance written for entry in a romantic comedy competition. He wrote *Woyzeck* (published in 1879), a play about a peasant man who is manipulated by various authorities and in the end kills his lover, that same year.

In 1837, Büchner, who was teaching in Zurich, Switzerland, contracted typhus and died on February 19—he was 23 years old.

Many of Büchner's writings were in the possession of his fiancée, Wilhelmine Jaegle, and while she made the manuscripts of *Leonce and Lena* and *Lenz* available to his publisher, she later destroyed one of his diaries, a collection of letters, and possibly a completed version of his lost play *Pietro Aretino*.

Legacy

Georg Büchner's small literary output has had an impact on modern European theater out of all proportion to its size. Largely unrecognized for the 50 years following his death, Büchner's work found its voice at the end of the nineteenth century, when dramatists began to turn to his work for inspiration and to write critical praise of it. Gerhart Hauptmann, one of the most prominent German exponents of Naturalism (Naturalists believed that actions were determined by environment and heredity), first promoted Büchner's works in the late 1880s. He pointed to *Woyzeck* as an early example of a play with a lower-class hero who is tragically manipulated by forces outside his control. This theme would become important in modern theater. The attack on middle-class hypocrisy in *Woyzeck* also inspired Frank Wedekind's play *Spring Awakening* (1891).

German Expressionists of the early twentieth century, who attempted to portray inner psychological realities onstage rather than external "realistic" conditions, also turned to Büchner's work for the freshness of his language, which was very different from the formality of conventional theatrical language of the time, and for the strength and simplicity of his characters' moral and social positions. The Expressionists also imitated the structure of Büchner's plays, in which a series of unrelated episodes follow one another to create a coherent whole.

Among the later playwrights heavily influenced by Büchner was BERTOLT BRECHT, who was inspired by Büchner's departure from traditional narrative structure. Büchner's episodic storytelling technique seemed to him to be true to the random nature of reality. Brecht said that he drew artictic inspiration from Büchner's combination of humanitarian and revolutionary themes with realistic and surrealistic situations and vital poetic language.

Büchner was also a major intellectual influence in post–World War II France. The French Existentialist movement of the late 1940s and 50s, and those influenced by it, such as the creators of the Theater of the Absurd, read his work as an expression of existential fear and the absurdity of existence. Büchner's characters and those of his absurdist descendants frequently speak in a language that seems incapable of meaningful communication; they speak in clichés and seem unable to understand one another. Plays that reflect this influence include Arthur Admov's *The Parody* (1947), Ionesco's *The Bald Soprano* (1948), and SAMUEL BECKETT's *Waiting for Godot* (1952).

Büchner's plays have also been adapted to opera. Alban Berg made *Woyzeck* (1925), Gottfried von Einem, *Danton's Death* (1947), and Kurt Schwaen, *Leonce and Lena* (1960).

Watson

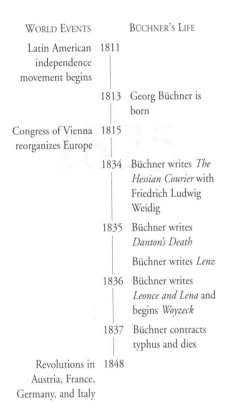

World Events		Büchner's Life
Latin American independence movement begins	1811	
	1813	Georg Büchner is born
Congress of Vienna reorganizes Europe	1815	
	1834	Büchner writes *The Hessian Courier* with Friedrich Ludwig Weidig
	1835	Büchner writes *Danton's Death*
		Büchner writes *Lenz*
	1836	Büchner writes *Leonce and Lena* and begins *Woyzeck*
	1837	Büchner contracts typhus and dies
Revolutions in Austria, France, Germany, and Italy	1848	

For Further Reading

Büchner, Georg. *Complete Works and Letters*. Vol. 28 of The German Library. Edited by Walter Hinderer and Henry J. Schmidt. Translated by Henry J. Schmidt. New York: Continuum Publishing, 1986.

Reddick, John. *Georg Büchner: The Shattered Whole*. Oxford: Oxford University Press, 1994.

Cage, John

Composer
1912–1992

Life and Work

John Cage was an American composer who pushed the boundaries of experimental music to the limit. One of his most famous pieces, *4'33"*, features a performer who takes the stage and sits silently for that length of time, compelling the audience to listen to the ambient sounds of the venue.

Cage was born on September 5, 1912, in Los Angeles. The son of an inventor, he enrolled at the prestigious Pomona College, but took off for Europe and North Africa in 1930 before graduating. Cage devised his own numerical system of composition, and, upon his return he worked with the Austrian composer ARNOLD SCHOENBERG, then recently arrived in California. He also studied with Henry Cowell, whose physical experiments with the piano would prove to be a stronger influence. In 1936 Cage moved to Seattle, where he met the choreographer MERCE CUNNINGHAM, a life-long associate, and began to write for percussion ensemble.

The strands of Cage's education came together in 1938, when he was asked to furnish music for a dance piece called *Bacchanale*. Space limitations frustrated his plans for a percussion ensemble, but he improvised by placing objects inside a piano so that it could produce percussive effects. In his early years Cage was best known for this "prepared piano," for which he wrote the *Sonatas and Interludes* between 1946 and 1948.

In the late 1940s Cage became interested in Zen Buddhism and other forms of Eastern philosophy, and he began to look for ways to renounce control over the materials of music. The 1951 *Music of Changes* was based on the Chinese *I Ching* (*Book of Changes*), a book of geometrical diagrams that embodies chance operations and is used in making predictions. *4'33"* followed in 1952, and in the mid-1950s Cage wrote several pieces for radios that in the course of a performance might pick up anything from music to static. In *Fontana Mix* (1958), Cage incorporated electronic sounds; while working on that piece in a studio in Italy, he put to use his encyclopedic knowledge of mushrooms when he appeared on an Italian television quiz show and won a large cash prize.

Performances of Cage's works often outraged audiences, but even critics and cynics had to concede his utter originality. Cage continued to explore chance procedures, and later in his life he became something of an elder statesman to American artistic freethinkers. He died in New York on August 12, 1992.

Legacy

An iconoclastic thinker, John Cage had a seminal influence on the American creative avant-garde in the second half of the twentieth century.

His work certainly displays parallels with that of artist JACKSON POLLOCK, who dripped paint on canvas in semirandom patterns, but he also played a role comparable to that of the poet Allen Ginsberg—he was among the cultural figures, several of them of a mystical bent, who paved the way for the alternative consciousness of the Vietnam War era. In his insistence that "everything we do is music," that art and life needed no dividing boundary, Cage offered an idea that resonated with the counterculture of the 1960s and 1970s. He both inspired and participated in the "happenings" of the late 1960s, large multi-media events that featured simultaneous performances of various kinds of music and works in other media; *HPSCHD* (1969) was a happening-like work to which he contributed. "Here we are. Let us say Yes to our presence together in Chaos," Cage said in one of his widely heard lectures.

Cage's idea of incorporating chance into the structure of a musical composition was taken up by many younger figures, including the Europeans Karlheinz Stockhausen and Witold Lutoslawski. Composers such as Earle Brown and Morton Feldman took as a point of departure Cage's actual musical scores, which might consist of anything from a few verbal directions to a group of small modules of music that might be ordered however the performers chose.

Cage's sheer adventurousness often placed him well ahead of new creative trends. One time he realized a piece in performance by slicing some vegetables, putting them in a blender, and drinking the resulting smoothie; many performance artists who flourished two decades later acknowledged their debt to endeavors of this kind. If the arts of the later twentieth century often took the attitude that "anything goes," it was John Cage who first opened the door to such total liberation.

Manheim

For Further Reading
Kostelanetz, Richard. *John Cage (Ex)plain(ed)*. New York: Schirmer Books, 1996.
Pritchett, James. *The Music of John Cage*. Cambridge: Cambridge University Press, 1993.
Revill, David. *The Roaring Silence: John Cage, A Life*. London: Bloomsbury, 1992.

WORLD EVENTS	CAGE'S LIFE
	1912 John Cage is born
World War I 1914–18	
Russian Revolution 1917	
Great Depression 1929–39	
	1930 Cage travels to Europe and North Africa
	1938 Cage first uses "prepared piano"
World War II 1939–45	
	1946 Cage begins *Sonatas and Interludes*
Communist China is established 1949	
Korean War 1950–53	
	1951 Cage composes *Music of Changes*
	1952 Cage composes *4'33"*
African independence movement begins 1957	
	1958 Cage uses electronic sounds in *Fontana Mix*
	1969 Cage contributes to *HPSCHD*
Vietnam War ends 1975	
Dissolution of Soviet Union 1991	
	1992 Cage dies
South Africa dismantles apartheid 1994	

Camões, Luíz Vaz de

Poet
1524/5–1580

World Events		Camões's Life
Protestant Reformation begins	1517	
	1524/25	Luíz Vaz de Camões is born
	1553	Camões embarks on travels throughout India and Africa
	1570	Camões returns to Portugal
Ottoman dominance of Mediterranean ends	1571	
	1572	Camões publishes *The Lusiads*
	1580	Camões dies of the plague
	1595	*Rimas* is published
Thirty Years' War in Europe	1618–48	

Life and Work

Luíz Vaz de Camões was the author of Portugal's great epic poem, *The Lusiads* (*Os Lusíadas*), the story of Vasco de Gama's discovery of the sea route to India and a celebration of Portugal at the height of its expansionist empire.

Little is known about Camões' life but it is fairly certain that he was born in Lisbon in 1524 or 1525, within a year of the death of the great Portuguese explorer Vasco de Gama. Camões was born into a noble family and most likely attended university, where his studies would have concentrated on Greek, Latin, mythology, and ancient history. He also read the literature of the modern languages, Spanish and Italian. These subjects were common to the Portuguese aristocracy of the time and his knowledge of them is evident in his poetry.

Camões left the world of the court behind when he departed for India with the Portuguese military. According to legend, he engaged in military action in India and then left the military to travel as a merchant and adventurer. He wrote the lyric verse that would make up his collection *Rimas* as well as *The Lusiads* during his 17 years of travel throughout India and Africa.

The Lusiads, an epic poem divided into 10 cantos, with a total of 1,102 stanzas, tells the story of de Gama's discovery of the sea route to India. This story is the vessel into which Camões, using Virgil's *Aeneid* as a model, poured the grand tale of Portugal's rise to power, invoking the gods of mythology to describe the war waged upon the ignorance of the non-Christian world. Using figures of pagan mythology to illustrate the glory of Christianity, Camões, like other great epic poets such as Dante, created one of the great examples of the use of poetic license.

After many adventures and the loss of his riches, Camões made his way back to Portugal in 1570. Dismayed by the state of the country, which had recently been devastated by the plague, Camões wrote a dedicatory prologue and epilogue to the king, requesting publication of *The Lusiads*. It was passed by the royal censor and published in 1572.

None of Camões' other writings were published during his lifetime. He died of the plague in Lisbon on June 10, 1580. *Rimas* was published in 1595. In the centuries that followed, many poems have been added to the collection and then removed again by scholars, that it is not always clear which were actually written by Camões. In 1880, remains believed to be his were interred beside those of Vasco de Gama in a church in Belem devoted to the discovery of the sea route to India.

Legacy

Luíz Vaz de Camões' epic work, *The Lusiads*, combined poetic vision, historical documentation, patriotic zeal, and classical learning to create one of the most powerful examples of epic poetry in history. The excitement of the era's new sophistication, exemplified by scientific discoveries as well as exploration and expansion, is present in the poem.

The Lusiads still stands as Portugal's great epic poem, chronicling not only the history of its empire but also the spirit of Europe at that time, with its grand quests for expansion of both territory and Christianity. During this time the face of the globe changed dramatically, and the poem's lyrical interpretation of and tribute to the greatness of Portugal and its people transformed poetry. Camões used the ancient form of the epic to express his modern reality, simultaneously celebrating what he saw as a race of divinely inspired heroes and providing a detailed record of the experience of travel and exploration of the time. *The Lusiads* is invaluable both as an epic poem and as a historical document.

Camões mingled classical techniques and a lighthearted, often ironic subject matter in his lyric poems, which were collected in *Rimas*. These have left no doubt that he was Portugal's finest lyric poet.

Watson

For Further Reading

Camões, Luíz Vaz de. *The Lusiads*. Translated by William C. Atkinson. New York: Penguin Books, 1952.

Manteiro, George. *The Presence of Camões: Influences on the Literature of England, America, and Southern Africa.* Lexington: University Press of Kentucky, 1996.

Caravaggio

Painter
1571–1610

Life and Work

Caravaggio, with his individualistic brand of naturalism, rebelled against Renaissance idealism and established one of the major styles of Baroque painting.

Born in 1571, Michelangelo Merisi was born in Caravaggio (near Milan), Italy, and became known by that name. LEONARDO DA VINCI, working 100 years earlier, continued to be a strong influence in the area around Milan. The ambitious Caravaggio began his career in art in 1592, after moving to Rome. Although descended from minor aristocracy, he arrived in Rome destitute. Initially he earned a living by painting small portraits, but also produced pictures of lowlifes and street urchins for sophisticated patrons. It may have been this experience on the streets that accounted for his unique and unidealized renderings of religious themes, as well as for his rejection of Renaissance ideals of beauty. The most accomplished in his series of paintings of seductive boys is *Bacchus* (1595).

Threatened by the growing power of Protestantism, Rome functioned as a theocratic state during the Counter-Reformation. From 1597 on, Caravaggio's painting showed a new kind of immediacy: the realism, simplicity, and piety of his work suited the taste of the Roman Catholic authorities who commissioned him to produce religious scenes. In *The Calling of St. Matthew* (1597–98), painted for the church of San Luigi dei Francesi, he depicted the traditional scene of Christ choosing Matthew, a wealthy tax collector, to become a disciple. Christ's divinity is indicated only by the radiant beam of sunlight illuminating his face. Such an unconventional representation of divine revelation, characterized as an inward experience available to all, appealed to Protestants as well as to the Roman Catholics who had commissioned the work. The painting shows the heightened realism employed by Caravaggio and displays his *tenebroso* technique: figures emerge from dark, shadowy backgrounds with faces and gestures theatrically spotlighted. Ironically, the lack of idealism in Caravaggio's religious work shocked the common people for whom it was intended but was admired by artists and connoisseurs. The popular desire was for the idealized classicism of traditional religious art.

Throughout his life, Caravaggio had trouble with the law and was arrested several times for various violent offenses and assaults. This culminated in a murder charge in 1606 that forced him to flee from Rome. In the four remaining years of his life, he lived as a fugitive. Nevertheless, he continued to develop his art while living in Malta, Naples, and Sicily. He died of malaria in 1610 at Porto Ercole in the north of Rome.

Legacy

Although Caravaggio's unbridled naturalism was startling, even shocking, to many of his contemporary viewers, he nevertheless had a large following in Italy. His sometimes violent, dramatic tableaus were the most exciting works of their time.

Caravaggio's style was widely imitated immediately after his death. Baroque painters Domenichino and ARTEMISIA GENTILESCHI were indebted to his dramatic subjects and style. Soon "Caravaggism" spread to France, as reflected in the work of Georges de la Tour. In Spain Caravaggio's influence is seen in the work of DIEGO VELÁZQUEZ. The Dutch Caravaggisti, such as Frans Hals and REMBRANDT, brought Caravaggio's style to the Netherlands. During the first half of the seventeenth century, Caravaggio may have been the most influential artist in Europe.

To the following generation of Baroque painters, however, Caravaggio seemed to be an artless painter: he appeared to have no sense of the ideals of beauty; rather, he seemed to record the mere appearance of things. This is what the French painter Nicolas Poussin remarked: Caravaggio had "come into the world to destroy painting," and the common people he painted seemed crude. Poussin's generation thought that art should be grander than life and should provide the viewer with an elevating experience, not just visual stimulation.

Not until the twentieth century was Caravaggio again admired. A major exhibition of his works in Milan in 1951 helped to revive his reputation. Today biographical accounts of this unconventional, uncompromising, and rebellious artist, including the 1986 movie *Caravaggio* by Derek Jarman, continue to engage new admirers.

Domenico

WORLD EVENTS		CARAVAGGIO'S LIFE
Ottoman dominance of Mediterranean ends	1571	Caravaggio is born
	1592	Caravaggio moves to Rome
	1595	Caravaggio completes *Bacchus*
	1597–98	Caravaggio works on *The Calling of St. Matthew*
	1606	Caravaggio is charged with murder
	1606–10	Caravaggio spends his last years as a fugitive
	1610	Caravaggio dies
Thirty Years' War in Europe	1618–48	

For Further Reading

The Age of Caravaggio. Exhibition catalogue. New York: Metropolitan Museum of Art and Electa/Rizzoli, 1985.

Hibbard, Howard. *Caravaggio.* New York: Harper & Row, 1983; later edition, 1985.

Puglisi, Catherine R. *Caravaggio.* London: Phaidon, 1998.

Cassatt, Mary

Painter and Printmaker
1844–1926

Life and Work

Mary Stevenson Cassatt was the only American participant in the avant-garde French Impressionist movement at the end of the nineteenth century and one of the first painters to depict modern women as a primary subject.

Cassatt was born on May 22, 1844, in Allegheny City, now a suburb of Pittsburgh, Pennsylvania. She was the fourth of five children of socially prominent parents. In 1860, at the age of 16 she enrolled at the Pennsylvania Academy of Fine Arts, one of the oldest and most prestigious art schools in the country. She studied the standard curriculum, which included anatomy, drawing, modeling, and painting. Before leaving the academy, Cassatt informed her family that she was serious about becoming an artist and wanted to continue her studies in Europe, despite her father's disapproval.

In 1866 Cassatt moved to Paris, the center of the nineteenth-century art world. She spent three years taking classes, painting, and hoping for recognition at the annual Paris Salon exhibitions. Cassatt's first exhibited work, *The Mandolin Player*, was included in the Salon in 1868.

In 1871, one year after returning home, Cassatt received a commission from the archbishop of Pittsburgh to make copies of the famous frescoes of Renaissance painter Antonio Correggio in Parma, Italy. Cassatt spent nearly a year in Italy completing the commission, traveled to Spain and the Netherlands, and finally returned to Paris in 1874.

Ambitious and increasingly confident, Cassatt decided to remain in Paris, which was the center of cultural activity. Even more unusual for a young, single American woman, she also decided to turn her back on conventional art and the traditional paths to artistic success. At the moment when she began her mature professional life, Cassatt made the risky decision to align herself with the independent and controversial artists associated with the Impressionist movement, such as EDOUARD MANET, EDGAR DEGAS, and Berthe Morisot. In 1877, Degas, with whom she had developed a relationship of mutual admiration, invited her to join the group, and, in 1879, she made her debut at the fourth Impressionist Exhibition. It was a great success and established her reputation overnight.

Like her colleagues from the Impressionist movement, Cassatt painted images and themes from modern life. For Cassatt this involved the people and experiences she knew firsthand as an upper-middle-class woman of the late nineteenth century. Cassatt's family became the familiar subjects for her paintings of modern life in such works as *The Loge* (1877–78), *Five O'Clock Tea* (1879–80), and *Lydia at a Tapestry Loom* (1880–81).

Cassatt remained in France for the rest of her life, returning to the United States only a few times. She painted until cataracts caused her eyesight to fail. In 1926 she died at her home in Beaufresne, north of Paris, at age 82.

Legacy

Mary Cassatt was an important participant—and the only American—in the avant-garde movement that ushered in the era of modern art.

In her print series of the 1890s, Cassatt perfected formal innovations that furthered the modern move away from traditional illusionistic techniques such as modeling and perspective. She replaced these with elegant contour lines, unmodulated color washes, and changes in pattern to define form and space. Together with her close friend Degas, Cassatt revitalized and modernized the art of printmaking.

Through her painting, Cassatt provided important insights into the social and cultural realities of women during the emerging modern era. Her images from the 1870s and 1880s of women attending the theater, reading or having tea at home, boating, or caring for children were never sentimentalized or idealized.

Cassatt, often surrounded by her young nieces and nephews, became interested in painting children and the ways they interact with adults. She brought to the subject the same objective, unsentimental perspective she used on her depictions of women. In this regard she modernized the portrayal of children and gained great respect for her ability to capture their individuality. Early-twentieth century-critics were the first to recognize this unique gift and to celebrate her acute insights.

Cassatt was also extremely influential as promoter of the new styles in art and advised many of her wealthy American friends to buy Degas, CLAUDE MONET, and PIERRE-AUGUSTE RENOIR paintings when they visited Paris. As a result, American collectors were among the first to acquire important Impressionist paintings, and today American museums such as the Metropolitan Museum in New York, the Institute of Fine Arts in Chicago, and the National Gallery in Washington, D.C., possess some of the finest collections of Impressionist art in the world.

Since the rise of the feminist movement in the 1970s, Cassatt's reputation has continued to grow.

Pokinski

WORLD EVENTS		CASSATT'S LIFE
Congress of Vienna reorganizes Europe	1815	
	1844	Mary Cassatt is born
Revolutions in Austria, France, Germany, and Italy	1848	
	1860	Cassatt enrolls at Philadelphia Academy of Fine Arts
U.S. Civil War	1861–65	
	1868	Cassatt's *The Mandolin Player* is exhibited in Paris Salon
Germany is united	1871	
	1879	Cassatt participates in Impressionist Exhibition
Spanish-American War	1898	
World War I	1914–18	
Russian Revolution	1917	
	1926	Cassatt dies
Great Depression	1929–39	

For Further Reading

Gouveia, Georgette. *The Essential Mary Cassatt*. New York and London: Harry N. Abrams, 2000.

Mathews, Nancy Mowll. *Mary Cassatt: A Life*. New Haven, Conn.: Yale University Press, 1994.

Pollock, Griselda. *Mary Cassatt: Painter of Modern Women*. New York: Thames & Hudson, 1998.

Cervantes, Miguel de

Poet and Novelist

1547–1616

Life and Work

Miguel de Cervantes Saavedra was born in October 1547 in Alcalá de Hénares, a university town outside Madrid. The exact date of his birth is unknown but he was baptized on October 9 in the church of Alcalá. He moved around Spain with his family as a child, living in Valladolid, Seville, and Madrid. He began studying with Juan López de Hoyo, a celebrated teacher and priest from Madrid around 1568. López compiled an official act of homage for Queen Isabella in 1569, which contained four poems by Cervantes, his earliest known verse.

Possibly to avoid prosecution for having wounded a man in a duel, Cervantes went to Rome in 1569, where he became a chamberlain for Cardinal Giulio Acquaviva. He left the position in 1571 to become a soldier in the war against the Muslim Turks. He fought in the Battle of Lepanto in 1571 and lost his left hand. He returned to military duty in 1572 and took part in the campaigns of Corfu, Navarino, and Tunis before boarding a ship to return to Spain in 1575. The ship was captured by pirates and Cervantes, along with the rest of the ship's crew, was sold into slavery in Algiers, where he was held for ransom for five years. He made several attempts to escape and was jailed for much of that time. In 1580 his family was finally able to pay his ransom. Some of his experiences as a prisoner are described in his plays *Los Tratos de Argel* (*Life in Algiers,* 1615) and *Los Baños de Argel* (*The Bagnios of Algiers*, 1615) as well as in a section of *Don Quixote* called "The Captive's Tale".

Cervantes spent the next six years in Madrid, where he wrote a number of plays, including *La Numancia* (1583), a historical drama based on the Numantians' resistence to Roman invasion. He also began his novel *La Galatea*, an idyllic pastoral romance about an Arcadian shepherdess. He published the first part of the novel in 1585.

Cervantes was poor for most of his adult life. He held minor government positions in which he moved around Spain, providing food and goods for the Spanish Armada under Philip II. In 1605 he published the first part of *Don Quixote*, a parody of a chivalric romance in which an elderly country gentleman, under the influence of his reading of medieval romances, acts as a knight. The novel was an immediate success. It was followed by *Exemplary Tales* in 1613, *Journey to Parnassus* in 1614, and *Ocho comedias y ocho entremeses* (*Eight Plays and Eight Interludes*) in 1615. While he was working on the second volume of *Don Quixote* (1615), a forged second volume was published by Alonso Fernández de Avellaneda in 1614.

After completing *Don Quixote*, Cervantes spent the rest of his life writing *Los Trabajos de Persiles y Sigismunda* (*The Trials of Persiles and Sigismunda*, 1617), a Byzantine novel that has never received the admiration given to *Don Quixote*. He died on April 22, 1616, and was buried in Madrid.

Legacy

Don Quixote was immediately successful, was reprinted five times in Miguel de Cervantes's lifetime, and was translated into English and French. Nevertheless, Cervantes was not universally considered a serious author. Among his contemporaries, both the playwright Lope de Vega and the poet Luis de Góngora thought him a poor poet and a sensational novelist. Within a century of Cervantes's death, however, *Don Quixote* had become known internationally, exerting its comedic influence on world literature, including that of Spanish America.

Don Quixote, with its satiric questioning of literary authority, became a model for the comic novel the world over. The German Romantics of the nineteenth century saw the novel as a truly important work; they saw the character of *Don Quixote* not as a clown, but as a tragic hero. Modern critical interpretation has seen the work as an important step in the creation of the modern novel. It has given rise to countless imitations. In the eighteenth century Henry Fielding wrote *Don Quixote* in England in 1729, and his *Joseph Andrews* (1742) was an acknowledged imitation. The Irish satirist JONATHAN SWIFT, referred to *Don Quixote* in *A Tale of a Tub* (1704). Many of the great novelists of the nineteenth century were influenced by *Don Quixote*, including CHARLES DICKENS, GUSTAVE FLAUBERT, HERMAN MELVILLE, and FYODOR DOSTOYEVSKY.

Versions of *Don Quixote* have been staged in theater, dance, and opera, and it has been put to music countless times; William Hogarth, FRANCISCO GOYA, and PABLO PICASSO are among the artists who have created visual works based upon it.

Don Quixote's influence has extended into the twentieth century. JAMES JOYCE acknowledged it—*Ulysses* might be described as the greatest picaresque novel since Cervantes—and JORGE LUIS BORGES made it the focal point of one of his greatest stories, "Pierre Menard, Author of *The Quixote*."

Watson

For Further Reading

Cervantes, Miguel de. *Don Quijote: A New Translation, Backgrounds and Contexts, Criticism.* Edited by Diana de Armas Wilson. Translated by Burton Raffel. New York: W. W. Norton, 1999.

McRory, Donald P. *No Ordinary Man: The Life and Times of Miguel de Cervantes.* London: Peter Owen, 2001.

Nabokov, Vladimir. *Lectures on Don Quixote.* San Diego: Harcourt Brace, 1983.

WORLD EVENTS		CERVANTES'S LIFE
Protestant Reformation begins	1517	
	1547	Miguel de Cervantes Saavedra is born
	1569	Cervantes's poems are published in memorial to Queen Isabella
Ottoman dominance of Mediterranean ends	1571	
	1575	Cervantes is captured by Turks and sold into slavery
	1580	Cervantes is ransomed and returns to Spain
	1585	Cervantes publishes first part of *La Galatea*
	1605	Cervantes publishes first part of *Don Quixote*
	1615	Cervantes publishes second part of *Don Quixote*
	1616	Cervantes dies
Thirty Years' War in Europe	1618–48	

Césaire, Aimé-Fernand

Poet, Dramatist, and Essayist
1913–

Life and Work

Aimé-Fernand Césaire was one of the founding poets of negritude, an artistic movement whose surrealist writing and impassioned political-poetic outcries called upon black Africans to embrace black heritage and to unite against colonialism.

Césaire was born on June 25, 1913, in Basse-Pointe, Martinique, at that time a French colony. He left Martinique as a young man to study in Paris, at the prestigious Ecole Normale Superieure. There he met Léopold Senghor, poet and future president of Senegal, and Léon Damas, a poet from French Guinea. In the late 1930s the three published the review *l'Etudiant*

WORLD EVENTS		CÉSAIRE'S LIFE
Spanish-American War	1898	
	1913	Aimé-Fernand Césaire is born in Martinique
World War I	1914–18	
Russian Revolution	1917	
Great Depression	1929–39	
	1930s	Césaire founds *l'Etudiant Noir*
World War II	1939–45	
	1946	Césaire elected one of Martinique's three deputies to French Parliament
		Césaire publishes *Notebook of a Return to the Native Land*
Communist China is established	1949	
Korean War	1950–53	
African independence movement begins	1957	
	1963	Césaire writes *The Tragedy of King Christophe*
Vietnam War ends	1975	
Dissolution of Soviet Union	1991	
South Africa dismantles apartheid	1994	

Noir, in which they began the discussion of the common heritage of blacks; this dialogue resulted in the influential negritude movement.

Césaire returned to Martinique in 1939 and became an active advocate for the independence of the West Indies colonies. In 1945 he was elected mayor of Fort-de-France and in 1946 he became one of the island's three deputies to the French Parliament.

In Martinique, Césaire founded *Tropiques*, a political and cultural review that was one of the main proponents of Surrealism outside of France and that, unlike Surrealist publications within France, published primarily black writers.

In 1946 Césaire published his long poem, *Cahiers d'un retour au pays natal* (*Notebook of a Return to the Native Land*), in which he coined the term negritude and which is widely considered to be his greatest work. The poem, divided into three parts, uses Surrealist devices first to describe the devastating effect of French colonialism in Martinique, then to demonstrate Césaire's own efforts to remove himself from the French cultural history in which he was educated, and finally to celebrate his race and heritage.

As a dramatist, Césaire veered away from Surrealism, preferring to make his plays accessible to the general public. In his plays, such as *La Tragédie du Roi Christophe* (*The Tragedy of King Christophe*, 1963), he dramatized his political ideals, expressing these ideas in more uncompromising terms as time went on. In *Une tempete* (*A Tempest*, 1969), an adaptation of WILLIAM SHAKESPEARE's *The Tempest*, Césaire portrayed the magician Prospero, the enslaver of the creature Caliban in Shakespeare's version, as a colonizer ruling over slaves. He discussed racial politics in his powerful *Une saison au Congo* (*A Season in the Congo*, 1966), a play about the 1960 rebellion in the Congo.

Legacy

Aimé-Fernand Césaire's originality began with his use of the French language—widely considered the province of a European literary elite—to describe an experience that was not itself European. Using the fractured phrases and images of Surrealism, Césaire staked a claim to the French language for colonial identity and created a place in its literature for black African populations of the colonies. *Notebook of a Return to the Native Land* used Surrealist techniques in combination

with powerful political beliefs, personal emotional experience, and traditional African oral tradition's insistent rhythm and repetition. Césaire's use of a highly polished French to express a non-European point of view allowed it to be a vehicle for non-Western thought for the first time. He and his fellow negritude writers began a cultural renaissance that would influence generations of writers around the world as they opened up the language to new themes, sensibilities, and styles.

Césaire was much admired by many of the important French thinkers and writers of his day. André Breton, the founder of French Surrealism, was one of the major admirers of his work, publishing and publicizing him throughout the 1950s. Jean-Paul Sartre wrote an important essay on negritude, *Black Orpheus*, in 1948, in which he recognized that the poet had taken the French language and transformed it into a means of communication for black African authors.

An abundance of North African literature with roots in negritude and in Césaire's work has been written in French. Writers well known in both North Africa and France as well as outside of the French-speaking world include Henri Kréa, Jean Amrouche, Mohamed Dib, Albert Memmi, and Kateb Yacine.

The concept of negritude has spread beyond francophone culture. Literature that holds issues of race and language at its core remains indebted to this groundbreaking work. Americans who have cited Césaire's work as an influence include Richard Wright, JAMES BALDWIN, and Amiri Baraka.

Watson

For Further Reading

Arnold, James A. *Modernism and Négritude: The Poetry and Poetics of Aimé Césaire*. Cambridge, Mass.: Harvard University Press, 1981.

Césaire, Aimé. *The Collected Poetry*. Translated by Clayton Eshleman and Annette Smith. Berkeley: University of California Press, 1983.

Cézanne, Paul

Painter

1839–1906

Life and Work

The Post-Impressionist painter Paul Cézanne was the precursor of several of the most radical art styles of the early twentieth century, such as Cubism and Fauvism.

Cézanne was born in 1839 in Aix-en-Provence, France. After studying law from 1859 to 1861, he shifted his attention to painting. His earliest works were emotionally charged paintings modeled after the dark, brooding chiaroscuro of the Romantic tradition. Several pieces, like *A Modern Olympia* (1869–70), combined his misogynist sexual obsession with his desire to experiment in the avant-garde style introduced in EDOUARD MANET's *Olympia* in 1865. Cézanne's first submission to the official Salon of 1863 was rejected, as were each of the works that he continued to submit for the next 19 years.

A turning point in Cézanne's career came in 1872 when he began to study with the Impressionist painter Camille Pissarro. Through the influence of the Impressionists, Cézanne gave up his interest in emotionally expressive painting and began to concentrate on the purely optical effects of painting. Cézanne exhibited with the Impressionists in 1874 and again in 1877, but even in his earliest Impressionist paintings, such as *The House of the Hanged Man* (1874), Cézanne was moving quickly toward the development of his unique style. Of all the Impressionists, he was the painter who most boldly rejected the polished drawing and idealism of the academic tradition.

After the 1877 exhibition, Cézanne left Paris and returned to his native Provence. Isolated from the Impressionist mainstream, his works became increasingly individualistic. Although he continued to embrace the detached, analytical approach of CLAUDE MONET and his colleagues, Cézanne rejected what he regarded as the superficial, ephemeral nature of Impressionism. His aim was not to record the momentary effects of light, but to make substantial, monumental paintings that defined their own reality. One of the favorite subjects in

his later paintings was Mont Sainte-Victoire, a huge mountain that loomed over the countryside near his house. In his many paintings of the mountain, Cézanne created bold patchworks of gold and green in paintings that were, in their own way, as monumental as the mountain itself. His numerous still lifes from that period, such as *Still Life with Apples* (c. 1895–98), were even more radical in their willingness to reject traditional one-point perspective and to reassemble the natural forms into compositionally coherent paintings.

Among Cézanne's later work was a series of monumental paintings of bathers, including the *Large Bathers* (1900–06). In these works Cézanne applied the same autonomous brushwork that he employed in landscapes and still lifes to classical nudes in the grand tradition of TITIAN and PETER PAUL RUBENS.

Cézanne died in 1906.

Legacy

Paul Cézanne almost certainly had more of an impact on the direction of twentieth-century art than any other nineteenth-century painter.

Few of his generation would have anticipated his future significance. For most of his life, Cézanne was a little-known figure. A cantankerous person, he intentionally removed himself from the main centers of the art world and rarely exhibited his work. An exhibition organized by the dealer Amboise Vollard in 1895 introduced his work to a younger generation of artists, and, late in life, Cézanne began to acquire the reputation of the quintessential artistic rebel.

In 1907, the year after his death, an exhibition of his work at the Salon d'Automne influenced several later styles of art. His *Bathers* series not only encouraged the experimentations of HENRI MATISSE and Fauvist art, but also was also a point of departure for PABLO PICASSO's *Les Demoiselles d'Avignon* (1907) and his subsequent Cubist works. Cézanne's *Large Bathers* also affected later artists such as HENRY MOORE. Cézanne can be seen as an important forerunner of several Modernist styles.

Cézanne's most important contribution to Modernism was his rejection of the traditional role of painting as the illusionistic process of representing outside reality. For him, the goal

of painting was not to represent; rather, the painting was first and foremost a material entity unto itself with its own independent reality. Cézanne's concept of the autonomy of painting serves as the basis for much of the abstract art of the twentieth century.

McEnroe

WORLD EVENTS		CÉZANNE'S LIFE:
Congress of Vienna reorganizes Europe	1815	
	1839	Paul Cézanne is born
Revolutions in Austria, France, Germany, and Italy	1848	
	1859–61	Cézanne studies law
U.S. Civil War	1861–65	
	1869–70	Cézanne completes *A Modern Olympia*
Germany is united	1871	
	1874	Cézanne participates in Impressionist show
	1895	Cézanne begins to gain recognition for his work
Spanish-American War	1898	
	1900–06	Cézanne works on *Large Bathers*
	1906	Cézanne dies
World War I	1914–18	

For Further Reading

Gowing, Lawrence. *Cézanne: The Early Years, 1859–1872*. Exhibition catalogue. Washington and New York: National Gallery of Art in association with Harry N. Abrams, 1988.

Lindsay, Jack. *Cézanne: His Life and Art*. New York: Harper & Row, 1972.

Weschler, Judith, ed. *Cézanne in Perspective*. Englewood Cliffs, N.J.: Prentice-Hall, 1975.

Chaucer, Geoffrey

Poet

c. 1340–1400

Life and Work

Geoffrey Chaucer, poet, government official, and diplomat, is widely regarded as the founder of English literature and as its most important figure before WILLIAM SHAKESPEARE.

Born around 1340 in London, Chaucer was what a later age would call middle class and upwardly mobile. His father was a prosperous winemaker. Although we know little of Chaucer's education, he clearly knew several languages and was well read. Cultivating con-

nections with England's royal family, Chaucer worked as a page in the household of King Edward III's son. He joined Edward's army and was taken prisoner by the French in 1359, but was ransomed—a testament to his rising status. In the late 1360s Chaucer was sent on diplomatic missions to Spain, France, and elsewhere. His first major poem was the *Book of the Duchess* (1369–70), a long lament on the death from plague of the duchess of Lancaster, wife of his patron John of Gaunt. This and other early works were influenced by contemporary French poetry on themes of love. He also translated several Latin and French works into English.

Chaucer flourished in the 1370s and early 1380s; he was appointed to a powerful customs post in 1374, and later became a justice of the peace and briefly a member of Parliament. He continued to undertake diplomatic missions, and familiarizing himself with an ever-widening variety of Continental literature and thought. His narrative poem *Troilus and Criseyde*, based on the military exploits and romantic tragedy of the mythical Trojan warrior Troilus, skillfully combined ideas drawn from a variety of philosophical sources. Another noted work of this period is the Valentine's Day poem *The Parlement of Foules* (*The Parliament of Fowls*), a humorous but not unphilosophical work influenced by the Italian storyteller Bocaccio.

Though Chaucer's political situation worsened temporarily in the late 1380s, he seems to have turned ill fortune into an opportunity. After 1387 he began work on *The Canterbury Tales*, his greatest work; it remained unfinished at his death. Structured as a collection of stories told in an inn near London by a group of pilgrims headed for Canterbury Cathedral, *The Canterbury Tales* collectively offer a vivid portrait of medieval England. With an abundance of humor, charm, and insight, Chaucer depicted people from all walks of English life.

Chaucer died in London on October 25, 1400.

Legacy

Around Geoffrey Chaucer's crypt in Westminster Abbey grew a "Poets' Corner" in which other great English writers were buried—a reflection of Chaucer's centrality in the British literary tradition.

Like Shakespeare, Chaucer influenced the development of the English language. To read his works today requires some immersion in the Middle English of Chaucer's time; the sounds and forms of English began a major shift in the century after his death. Chaucer almost singlehandedly established a set of conventions for literary English, however, and some of the basic forms of poetry that he established are still commonplace. An example is the "heroic couplet"—a rhyming pair of lines in iambic pentameter, with each line including five pairs of two syllables each. As a poetic stylist, Chaucer was praised by contemporaries and successors alike.

The great medieval poets of the Continent, such as DANTE in Italy and the composer-poet Guillaume de Machaut in France, were erudite men. Their lengthy works created miniature worlds, synthesizing storytelling with religion, history, science, philosophy, and other fields of human knowledge. In Chaucer, for the first time, the isolated British Isles had a figure of letters who could stand comparison with them. The realism and vivid characterization of *The Canterbury Tales* anticipated the future not only of poetry but also of drama.

The Canterbury Tales, which synthesized everything Chaucer had learned and looked forward to a new humanism, first placed English literature on the world stage, from which it has never departed. Shakespeare, especially in his use of humor, showed Chaucer's influence, and John Dryden called him "the father of English poetry."

Manheim

WORLD EVENTS		CHAUCER'S LIFE
Hundred Years' War begins	1337	
	c. 1340	Geoffrey Chaucer is born in London
	1359	Chaucer is taken prisoner by French
	1360s	Chaucer is active as diplomat
Ming Dynasty reasserts Chinese control of China	1368	
	1369–70	Chaucer writes *Book of the Duchess*
	1374	Chaucer obtains customs post
	c. 1387	Chaucer begins *The Canterbury Tales*
	1400	Chaucer dies
Ottoman Empire conquers Constantinople	1453	

For Further Reading

Brewer, Derek. *Chaucer and His World*. New York: Dodd, Mead, 1977.

Howard, Donald R. *Chaucer: His Life, His Works, His World*. New York: Duttton, 1987.

Chekhov, Anton

Short Story Writer and Dramatist
1860–1904

Life and Work

Anton Pavlovich Chekhov, a doctor and a writer, helped to redefine Russian literature in an international context and gave new form and character to the short story.

Chekhov was born in the Russian seaport of Taganrog on January 17, 1860, the son of a former serf. He remained there until the age of 19, when he left to study medicine at Moscow University. While in Moscow, Chekhov sold satirical sketches and comedic stories to humor magazines to support himself and his family. He completed his first full-length play, *P'yessa bex nazvaniya* (*That Worthless Fellow Platanov*), in the early 1880s. In 1884 he finished his degree, established a medical practice, and published his first collection of short stories, *The Tales of Melpomene.* Other collections followed and as his reputation grew he became a regular contributor to the prestigious Moscow daily, *Novoye vremya.* In 1888 he was awarded the Pushkin Prize for Literature by the Academy of Sciences.

Chekhov's most famous play, *Chayka* (*The Sea Gull,* 1898), was performed by the newly formed Moscow Art Theater in 1898 to great acclaim. This was the beginning of a long relationship between the writer and this innovative theater, which used the image of a seagull as its emblem. It was here that the director Konstantin Sergeyevich Stanislavsky, a founder of the theater, developed his influential ideas and techniques of naturalistic acting. The theater would go on to perform Chekhov's *Tri sestry* (*The Three Sisters,* 1901) and *Vishnyovy sad* (*The Cherry Orchard,* 1904).

Chekhov wrote between 700 and 800 short stories during his career. With his lyric stories unified by mood and atmosphere rather than by a conventional plot, he has often been considered a literary heir to Ivan Turgenev. Chekhov's stories offer a panorama of Russian life with characters of varied social status struggling with the petty difficulties of daily life— the selfishness, disloyalty, dishonesty, and pretension that render his characters' lives unlivable. In Russia, a "Chekhovian mood" has come to be understood as a state of mind

in which no ideal or hope motivates the daily struggle with frustrating circumstances.

By 1900 Chekhov had risen to eminence in Russian letters. Ten volumes of his collected works were published between 1899 and 1901 and in 1900 both he and LEO TOLSTOY were elected honorary members of the newly created Section of Belles Lettres of the Academy of Sciences. In 1902 he resigned his membership in the academy as a protest against Maksim Gorky's exclusion because of his political beliefs.

Chekhov wrote his last short story, *Betrothed,* in 1903. His health made work impossible after that and on June 3, 1904, he died of tuberculosis at Badenweiler, a German health resort.

Legacy

Anton Chekhov was one of the great innovators of the short story and gave new direction to Russian drama, bringing it to an international audience.

Chekhov created a new theater, moving away from the conventional realism of Tolstoy and Aleksandr Nikolayevich Ostrovsky toward impressionistic drama. In his refusal to comply with dramatic tradition, he created plays without rigorous plot, central heroes, or clearly delineated relationships between characters. Instead he wrote about characters who embodied human weaknesses. The theatrical innovations used to express this type of life included symbols, like the seagull or the cherry orchard, highly suggestive sets, and offstage sounds.

This impressionistic theater, with its detailed observation and understanding of human behavior, was taken up by Stanislavsky, who used Chekhov's plays and the Moscow Art Theater to revolutionize the theater of the day. This collaboration invigorated Russian theater at a time when many of the plays performed in Moscow and Saint Petersburg were translations of plays by Western European writers.

Chekhov's fame only grew after his death, when his position at the center of the Silver Age of Russian literature (1890s to 1917) became increasingly secure. He created the tradition of the Russian short story, replacing the closed plots of traditional short stories with an open-ended narrative about everyday life, and drawing on epic, dramatic, and lyric techniques.

Russian literature changed direction with Chekhov's work. He and many of his contem-

poraries enabled Russian literature to be valued on the same terms as Western European writing. Major Russian writers of the twentieth century, including Yury Trifonov, Irina Grekova, Andrei Bitov, and Venedikt Erofeev, have returned to Chekhov's treatment of ordinary people and their petty human weaknesses. Moreover, Chekhov's atmospheric story has found imitators all over the world, and, indeed, literature's very concept of the short story was recast by the new form that he meticulously invented.

Watson

WORLD EVENTS		CHEKHOV'S LIFE
Revolutions in Austria, France, Germany, and Italy	1848	
	1860	Anton Chekhov is born
U.S. Civil War	1861–65	
Germany is united	1871	
	1879	Chekhov moves to Moscow to study
	1884	Chekhov publishes *The Tales of Melpomene*
	1888	Chekhov awarded Pushkin Prize for Literature
Spanish-American War	1898	Chekhov's play, *The Sea Gull,* has premiere
	1899–1901	Chekhov's collected works are published
	1900	Chekhov is elected honorary member of the Academy of Sciences
	1904	Chekhov dies
World War I	1914–18	

For Further Reading

Callow, Philip. *Chekhov: The Hidden Ground.* Chicago: Ivan R. Dee, 1998.
Rayfield, Donald. *Anton Chekhov: A Life.* New York: Henry Holt, 1997.

Chopin, Fryderyk

Composer
1810–1849

Life and Work

The creator of intense miniatures, sweeping quasi-improvisatory essays, and stirring pieces with a flavor of Polish nationalism, Fryderyk Chopin was a giant among nineteenth-century composers for the piano.

Chopin was born in the Polish village of Zelazowa Wola, near Warsaw, on March 1, 1810. A child prodigy almost on the order of

MOZART, he played his first public concert in February of 1818 at the age of seven; he had already published his first composition, a ceremonail dance called a *polonaise*, the previous year. He enrolled at the Warsaw Conservatory in 1826, where he made his way competently through a conventional musical education and flourished whenever he had the chance to play and compose for the piano. When the Italian violinist Niccolo Paganini visited Warsaw in 1829, Chopin got a taste of the new world of the traveling virtuoso star. Chopin gave a concert of his own in Vienna later that year, and his Polish-flavored piano music was enthusiastically received. He settled in Paris, the nerve center of Continental Romanticism, in 1831, and though he used the French form of his name, Frédéric, he continued to identify himself with Poland.

Chopin's output, almost exclusively for the piano, included *nocturnes* (night pieces) and short pieces based on dance rhythms: the Polish *mazurka*, the waltz, and others. He wrote preludes that explored the harmonic possibilities of all 24 musical scales, and *études* (studies) that breathed unprecedented musical interest into technical exercises; after hearing them, one is not surprised to learn that Chopin made a living as one of Paris's top piano teachers. He also wrote longer virtuoso showpieces (ballades, *scherzos*, sonatas, and two concertos for piano and orchestra), but generally left their performance to others. His Sonata in B-flat minor, composed between 1837 and 1839, includes a funeral march that has become part of common musical knowledge.

Chopin was a sharp, quick-witted person, a fine caricaturist on top of his musical gifts, who moved easily in Parisian aristocratic circles. From 1838 until the late 1840s he was the lover of the pioneering female novelist George Sand, whose real name was Aurore Dudevant. Chopin died of the tuberculosis that had long plagued him on October 17, 1849.

Legacy

Fryderyk Chopin virtually defined the image of Romantic piano music with his lyrical, graceful melodies and the harmonically complex accompaniments that brought to those melodies exquisite emotional shadings.

Before Chopin, the small piano piece was in general a much less significant genre. LUDWIG VAN BEETHOVEN and Franz Schubert made

their grand keyboard statements in weighty sonatas, but Chopin (and to a lesser extent Felix Mendelssohn) defined the piano as an instrument of intimate emotional haunts—expressive of nostalgia, quiet warmth, fleeting beauty. He created an array of new pianistic textures; some were marked by the use of the piano's sustaining pedal (the center pedal), which could be used to suffuse a passage of music with a harmonic color that would slowly fade away. Chopin's use of the piano directly influenced the compositions and playing of the great virtuoso of the century, FRANZ LISZT.

Some of Chopin's larger, more bravura pieces were seen as evocative of Polish patriotism, and although he spent most of his creative life in France, the Polishness of his music held important implications for the future. His mazurkas, based on a folk dance rhythm, were among the first examples of music based directly on national folk characteristics, a trend that would steadily gain importance, especially in Eastern Europe, for the rest of the nineteenth century.

His treatment of harmony was bold, and his set of Preludes codified Romantic harmony in much the same way as JOHANN SEBASTIAN BACH's Preludes and Fugues had done for the Baroque. They inspired a host of later sets by composers such as Aleksandr Scriabin (whose music in general owes much to Chopin's) and Dmitry Shostakovich. Though Liszt exceeded Chopin's accomplishments as a piano virtuoso who dazzled audiences with his own compositions, it was Chopin who made the piano the ultimate instrument of Romantic self-expression.

Manheim

WORLD EVENTS		CHOPIN'S LIFE
French Revolution begins	1789	
	1810	Fryderyk Chopin is born near Warsaw, Poland
Latin American independence movement begins	1811	
Congress of Vienna reorganizes Europe	1815	
	1818	Chopin plays his first public concert
	1826	Chopin enrolls at Warsaw Conservatory
	1829	Chopin hears Paganini in Warsaw
	1831	Chopin moves to Paris
	1838	Chopin becomes romantically involved with George Sand
	1839	Chopin completes Sonata in B flat minor with famous funeral march
Revolutions in Austria, France, Germany, and Italy	1848	
	1849	Chopin dies
U.S. Civil War	1861–65	

For Further Reading

Samson, Jim. *Chopin*. Oxford and New York: Oxford University Press, 1996.

Zamoyski, Adam. *Chopin: A New Biography*. Garden City, N.Y.: Doubleday, 1980.

Coltrane, John

Saxophonist
1926–1967

Life and Work

For many listeners the extreme, technically brilliant sound of John Coltrane's tenor saxophone epitomizes the adventurous and committed spirit of modern jazz.

Coltrane was born in rural Hamlet, North Carolina, on September 23, 1926. He took almost immediately to a saxophone his mother bought him, but was also influenced musically and spiritually by two grandfathers who were ministers. Coltrane studied music in Philadelphia and landed a gig with Eddie "Cleanhead" Vinson's band in 1947. For some years Coltrane applied his talents to a variety of styles, but when he joined trumpeter MILES DAVIS's seminal quintet in 1955, he began to train his musically exploratory mind upon individual songs, trying to explore and exhaust any possibility a song might offer.

Davis fired Coltrane from his band in 1957 because of drug and alcohol problems, but Coltrane bounced back. Discovering a partly Eastern-oriented spirituality later given expression on the 1964 album *A Love Supreme*, Coltrane overcame his addictions. He played with the band of the terse, offbeat pianist Thelonious Monk, and then returned to Davis, his technical skills at a new and surpassing level. Critics picked up the phrase

"sheets of sound" coined by one of their number to describe his playing.

In 1960 Coltrane, already acclaimed as the greatest jazz saxophonist since CHARLIE PARKER, formed his own band. The new direction he took was typified by his 1963 transformation of the *Sound of Music* hit "My Favorite Things" into an extended jam, rhapsodic and yet single-minded. The recording remained one of Coltrane's most famous, and showed Coltrane's ability to connect with popular balladry that persisted even amid radical experimentation.

In the 1960s Coltrane led jazz into unknown terrain. His nobly tragic 1963 track "Alabama" was inspired by the cadences of the black preachers who had nurtured the civil rights movement. In 1965 Coltrane released *Ascension*, one of several avant-garde recordings in which he almost completely abandoned melody and traditional harmony, leading his group in ecstatic, primordial free improvisations. He relentlessly pursued a deeper musical expression, reportedly practicing twelve hours a day even at the height of his fame, but he became ill and in his last days performed in great pain. When Coltrane died in New York on July 17, 1967, the cause was given as liver cancer.

Legacy

John Coltrane changed both the sound and the spirit of jazz, emerging as a giant influence on jazz of the turbulent 1960s and beyond.

Various musicians of the late 1950s worked to extend Charlie Parker's bebop revolution in their own directions, but it was Coltrane who made clear that the virtuosity and the sheer improvisatory freedom of the style would have to be pursued to their ultimate limits. He cultivated the tenor saxophone's repertoire of growls, shrieks, and strong tone colors in ways that have influenced nearly every later player of the instrument in some way.

Early in the 1960s his search for new instrumental sonorities led him to resurrect the soprano saxophone, a nearly forgotten member of the saxophone family with a piercing, unforgiving tone, and by the 1970s it had become part of the arsenal of many top jazz saxophonists.

As an avant-garde destroyer of tonality, Coltrane had been preceded by Pharoah Sanders, Ornette Coleman, and others, but

Coltrane's "free jazz" albums were the most successful in their own time and were the most influential for the generations that followed; it was perhaps the spiritual component in Coltrane's stylistic advances that made them so compelling for other musicians. The work of avant-garde groups like the Art Ensemble of Chicago and the ensembles of Sun Ra took off directly from Coltrane's conflation of expanding musical freedom with religious intensity, and the style has remained a vital one even as jazz fashions have shifted.

John Coltrane was a great jazz innovator, but his greatest legacy to the musical world was that he succeeded in making jazz into the deepest possible representation of a personal quest.

Manheim

WORLD EVENTS		COLTRANE'S LIFE
Russian Revolution	1917	
	1926	John Coltrane is born
Great Depression	1929–39	
World War II	1939–45	
	1947	Coltrane joins band of Eddie "Cleanhead" Vinson
Communist China is established	1949	
Korean War	1950–53	
	1955	Coltrane joins Miles Davis's quintet
African independence movement begins	1957	Coltrane is fired by Davis, but returns
	1960	Coltrane forms own band
	1963	Coltrane records "My Favorite Things"
	1965	Coltrane releases *Ascension* LP
	1967	Coltrane dies
Vietnam War ends	1975	

For Further Reading
Nisenson, Eric. *Ascension: John Coltrane and His Quest*. New York: St. Martin's Press, 1993.
Porter, Lewis. *John Coltrane: His Life and Music*. Ann Arbor: University of Michigan Press, 1998.

Conrad, Joseph

Novelist
1857–1924

World Events		Conrad's Life
Revolutions in Austria, France, Germany, and Italy	1848	
	1857	Józef Korzeniowski is born in Berdichev, Ukraine
U.S. Civil War	1861–65	
Germany is united	1871	
	1894	Conrad completes first novel, *Almayer's Folly*
Spanish-American War	1898	
	1900	Conrad publishes *Lord Jim*
	1902	Conrad writes "Heart of Darkness"
	1904	Conrad publishes *Nostromo*
	1910	Conrad suffers nervous breakdown
World War I	1914–18	
Russian Revolution	1917	
	1924	Conrad dies
Great Depression	1929–39	

Life and Work

Known for a series of novels and stories whose adventure-packed narratives led readers into shadowy moral worlds, Joseph Conrad was one of British literature's leading novelists of the early twentieth century.

The writer who created some of the most stylistically distinctive prose ever written in English barely spoke a word of the language until he was in his twenties. Joseph Conrad was born Józef Teodor Konrad Korzeniowski on December 3, 1857 into minor Polish nobility in Berdichev, in what is now Ukraine. His father was a writer and a Polish nationalist who was persecuted by Poland's Russian rulers and exiled with his family to frigid northern Russia, and Conrad's mother died of tuberculosis in 1865.

An uncle tried to provide for his orphaned nephew's education, but Conrad was set on a career at sea. Before he was 17, he headed for the French port of Marseilles and spent much of the next 20 years as a merchant ship's officer and finally captain, mostly on English ships. Conrad's first novel, *Almayer's Folly*, was published in 1895; it depicted the disintegration of the world of a British trader married to a Malay woman and anticipated the themes of his later work.

Perhaps his first masterpiece was the story "Heart of Darkness" (1902), the recollections of a riverboat captain, Marlow, who uncovers the depravities perpetrated by an insane white trader, Kurtz. *Lord Jim* (1900) concerns a ship's captain who abandons his sinking vessel after it hits a submerged hulk; *Nostromo* (1904) tells the story of a fictitious South American country whose fate is determined by colonialist political quarrels over a silver mine. *The Secret Agent* (1907), though it takes place on British soil, likewise inhabits a murky and exotic world, that of espionage. These and others among Conrad's works of the period depict characters cut loose from the moorings of conventional society and brought face to face with the evil of which humans, including themselves, are capable.

Conrad suffered a nervous breakdown in 1910; after that, his writings had a somewhat more traditional adventure-oriented character. He died in Canterbury, England, on August 3, 1924.

Legacy

Although never a self-conscious Modernist, Joseph Conrad anticipated some of the characteristic traits of Modernist fiction.

Chief among them is the sense of disorientation that pervades his tales. Conrad's protagonists face extreme situations, but they are not the conventional admirable heroes of the Victorian era, overcoming extremes through will and courage. Instead, through confusion, inertia, or ennui, they wander outside the familiar moral world into areas where chaos and evil proliferate. The ships that figure in so many of Conrad's stories are not simply devices for producing adventure but worlds in themselves, cut off from society, where human relationships come to the fore in primal form. Conrad's world is never divided into good and evil; instead it is a morally neutral place, in some ways not far from that of the Continental Existentialists, whose inhabitants define their own lives through often disastrous choices.

Conrad's work is sometimes difficult to read, because Conrad denies his readers any comfortable overview of the action. In his novels temporal flow is distorted or abandoned, and key facts are withheld from the reader as they are from the protagonists. Conrad anticipated the challenging modes of such otherwise very different writers as James Joyce and William Faulkner.

Conrad's experiences as he worked his way up through the galleys of British imperialism were also formative ones for twentieth-century fiction. Conrad's Third World was a dangerous place, it is true, but not much more so than the one defined by the impulses of many of his English characters, who range from venal to violently crazed. For Conrad, European empires were an open field for the growth of human evil, a message that resonated clearly in the late twentieth century. "Heart of Darkness," transferred to the jungles of Vietnam, served as the model for an epic film of the 1970s, *Apocalypse Now*. Conrad's work introduced a powerful and lasting note of pessimism into twentieth-century literature.

Manheim

For Further Reading

Gillon, Adam. *Joseph Conrad*. New York: Twayne Publishers, 1982.

Said, Edward W. *Joseph Conrad and the Fiction of Autobiography*. Cambridge, Mass.: Harvard University Press, 1966.

Watt, Ian. *Conrad in the Nineteenth Century*. Berkeley and Los Angeles: University of California Press, 1979.

Copland, Aaron

Composer
1900–1990

Life and Work

The creator of an enduring vision of America in music, Aaron Copland is generally considered to be one of the twentieth century's greatest classical composers. He is also perhaps the best loved.

On November 14, 1900, Copland was born in Brooklyn, New York, into a family of Russian-Jewish immigrants. Apart from a music-loving mother who encouraged piano playing as a hobby, little in his background impelled him toward music. Forced to study its fundamentals through a correspondence course, he persevered, and finally, in 1921, he was able to travel to France for summer music study. There he met Nadia Boulanger, a famed Parisian music teacher who would be a crucial formative influence in the lives of various American composers; Copland became her first American student.

Copland's success as a composer depended on his unfailing ability to sense which way the musical winds were blowing. In the mid-1920s he expressed a desire to compose in an American idiom, and gained recognition for such jazz-inflected works as the *Piano Concerto* of 1926. However, European composers such as IGOR STRAVINSKY and Darius Milhaud had already experimented with incorporating jazz into classical music, and when European fashion swung toward Stravinsky's dry "neo-classic" style

around 1930, Copland followed, producing the *Short Symphony of 1933* among other works.

As an aesthetic of simplicity gained ascendancy during the Great Depression, Copland returned to American themes with a series of assured works that were also his most distinctive. Several were ballet scores that drew on American folk music: 1938's *Billy the Kid* and 1944's *Appalachian Spring* have remained popular in concert presentations as well as on stage. *The Lincoln Portrait*, a 1942 work for speaker and orchestra that quotes from the Gettysburg Address, is part of many a patriotic celebration. Copland was also intrigued by Latin rhythms and explored them in such works as *El salón México* (1936).

After World War II Copland abandoned an overt Americanism in favor of the difficult 12-tone method of composition, an interwar invention by ARNOLD SCHOENBERG that seemed to be the wave of the future at the time. A popular elder statesman of American music, Copland lectured widely in his later years. Copland died in North Tarrytown, New York, on December 2, 1990.

Legacy

Aaron Copland's musical Americanism attracted listeners not only in his native country but also internationally. More than any of his other works, his evocations of American life connected with audiences and inspired later composers.

He created a musical language animated not by empty patriotism, but by the application of precise modern orchestral and harmonic effects to the representation of familiar physical and cultural landscapes. When Copland depicted the American West in *Billy the Kid* and *Rodeo*, he did it not simply by quoting folk and cowboy songs and rhythms, but also by forging sequences of unusual, widely spaced chords and airy coloristic effects that made the vastness of the mountain terrain seem palpable. His American nationalism affected contemporaries and successors such as Roy Harris and the conductor and composer LEONARD BERNSTEIN, who once called Copland his substitute father. Bernstein was influenced by Copland in his orchestral writing, and one may also hear echoes of Copland's diluted Latin sounds in Bernstein's musical *West Side Story*.

Outside of the realm of classical music, Copland's techniques had additional reso-

nance in the vast body of music written for movie and television soundtracks. His ability to suggest features of American culture and geography through finely drawn, economical musical statements amounted to a kind of compositional shorthand that commercially oriented composers have studied closely. When a film, for example, employs a passage of heroic or humorous soundtrack music in which potential sentimentality is blunted by the use of a modern idiom, it is likely that Copland is the stylistic source. American classical music came of age with Aaron Copland, and he molded many aspects of the country's still emergent national musical language.

Manheim

WORLD EVENTS		COPLAND'S LIFE
Spanish-American War	1898	
	1900	Aaron Copland is born
World War I	1914–18	
Russian Revolution	1917	
	1921	Copland travels to France for study
	1926	Copland writes jazz-influenced piano concerto
Great Depression	1929–39	
	1936	Copland writes *El salón México*
World War II	1939–45	
	1942	Copland writes *Lincoln Portrait*
	1944	Copland writes *Appalachian Spring*
	late 1940s	Copland adopts 12-tone method
Communist China is established	1949	
Korean War	1950–53	
African independence movement begins	1957	
Vietnam War ends	1975	
	1990	Copland dies
Dissolution of Soviet Union	1991	

For Further Reading

Butterworth, Neil. *The Music of Aaron Copland*. New York: Universe Books, 1986.

Pollack, Howard. *Aaron Copland: The Life and Work of an Uncommon Man*. New York: Henry Holt, 1999.

Cruz, Celia

Vocalist

c. 1924–

Life and Work

Celia Cruz is the preeminent vocal star of the Latin-Caribbean music known as salsa, which originated in her native Cuba. She is one of the key contributors to that music's rapidly expanding popularity.

Cruz has been reticent about her age, but she is thought to have been born on October 21, 1924, in Havana, Cuba. She impressed relatives early with her singing, but her father pushed her toward teaching. After winning a radio talent show, she began, with support from her mother, to think about a musical career. She gave more performances on the radio and, in 1947,

WORLD EVENTS		CRUZ'S LIFE
Russian Revolution	1917	
	c.1924	Celia Cruz is born
Great Depression	1929–39	
World War II	1939–45	
	1947	Cruz enrolls in Cuba's National Conservatory of Music
Communist China is established	1949	
	1950	Cruz becomes lead vocalist with La Sonora Matancera
Korean War	1950–53	
African independence movement begins	1957	
	1959	Cruz leaves Cuba
	1961	Cruz becomes a U.S. citizen
	1973	Cruz appears in Spanish version of *Tommy*
Vietnam War ends	1975	Cruz sings on successful Fania All Stars' live album
	1990	Cruz wins Grammy award
Dissolution of Soviet Union	1991	
	1992	Cruz appears in *The Mambo Kings Play Songs of Love*
South Africa dismantles apartheid	1994	

enrolled in Havana's National Conservatory of Music, where she gained a valuable understanding of musical fundamentals but vocally stuck close to her own Afro-Cuban style. A professor at the conservatory encouraged her to embark on a full-time singing career.

In 1950 Cruz became the lead vocalist for a big band called La Sonora Matancera, a mainstay of Havana's vibrant nightclub scene. She toured widely with this group and left Cuba with them when Fidel Castro came to power in 1959. In 1961 Cruz gained U.S. citizenship. Success was slow to come in her adopted country, but the ascendancy of salsa in the 1960s and 1970s put her back in the spotlight for good. Salsa, a mixture of jazz, Latin dance music, and Afro-Caribbean rhythms, proved an ideal medium for her talents; she was both a talented improviser (who sometimes imitated instruments vocally in a Latin equivalent of "scat" singing) and a rhythmically compelling singer with a hypnotic control over audiences.

Cruz appeared in a 1973 Spanish-language adaptation of the Who's rock opera *Tommy*, but it was probably her association with the pioneering New York salsa label Fania that did most to spread her fame beyond the Latin community; her work on the 1975 Fania All Stars' *Live at Yankee Stadium* album captured the excitement of her performances.

Film has also proved to be a congenial medium for this charismatic artist: she has appeared in *The Mambo Kings Play Songs of Love* (1992), *The Perez Family* (1995), and several other films. Among the honors she has accrued are a Grammy award (for the album *Ritmo en el corazón*, in 1990) and an honorary doctorate from Yale University. An opponent of the Cuban communist regime that denied her the chance to attend her mother's funeral, Cruz vowed in 1999 that she would not sing in her homeland again unless that regime collapsed.

Legacy

Equal in stature and in improvisatory skill to such U.S. jazz vocalists as Sarah Vaughan and Ella Fitzgerald, Celia Cruz played a role similar to theirs in bringing a vocal personality to a primarily instrumentally inspired music. As a result, she became one of the first Latin Americans to become a star on her own musical terms.

Like the American big-band jazz that influenced it, salsa is essentially dance music; its primary figures, most notably Tito Puente and Willie Colón, have been bandleaders and instrumental musicians. While jazz has evolved into a sophisticated art best appreciated by connoisseurs, salsa has flourished as a popular form. Cruz has been at least partly responsible for keeping salsa down to earth. The vigorous call-and-response patterns she sets up with audiences in performance puts her hearers in touch with the African roots of Cuban music in an immediate way. Her gift for improvising rhymed lyrics gained wide exposure just as the genre of rap music was beginning to grow, helping to give salsa currency with the young people who were embracing that style.

Cruz has become something of an emblem of cultural identity, not only for Cuban-Americans, but also for Puerto Ricans and other Americans of Latin descent. The evolution of her vocal personality coincided with a general rise in cultural self-awareness among U.S. Hispanics and Latin American peoples, and Cruz, with her regal head-to-toe stage garb, was an instantly identifiable figure. Even though she has resided in the United States since 1961, she has declined to record in English.

Celia Cruz, then, has been both a creative force and a star. Although Cruz herself never really sought out the Anglo-American market, Gloria Estefan and the other 1990s vocalists who have brought Latin music to the American mainstream owe Cruz a tremendous debt.

Manheim

For Further Reading

Boggs, Vernon W. *Salsiology: Afro-Cuban Music and the Evolution of Salsa in New York City.* New York: Excelsior Music Publishing, 1992.

Broughton, Simon, Mark Ellingham, David Muddyman, and Richard Trillo, eds. *World Music: The Rough Guide.* New York: Penguin, 1999.

Cruz, Sor Juana Inés de la

Poet
1651–1695

Life and Work

Sor Juana Inés de la Cruz was a Mexican nun, a child prodigy, a protofeminist, and one of the most remarkable poets of colonial Spanish America.

Cruz was born Juana de Asbaje y Ramírez in San Miguel Nepantla, Mexico, on November 12, 1651, the illegitimate daughter of a Spanish sailor and a Creole woman. Cruz displayed unusual intelligence early, learning to read in her grandfather's library at age three and writing her first dramatic poem at eight. As a young girl, Cruz was sent to live with an aunt in Mexico City, where she quickly became known as a prodigy. She had had no formal education other than 20 lessons in Latin. Cruz forced herself to quickly learn the language by cutting off her own hair when she made a mistake.

In 1662 she became a lady-in-waiting to the vicareina, wife of the viceroy, and moved to the royal palace, where she distinguished herself by her intelligence and beauty. Then in February 1669 Cruz left the court to become a nun in the convent of San Jerónimo. Her decision seems to have been influenced not only by piety, but also by an avowed distaste for marriage and a desire to continue her studies and writing in relative independence.

Cruz filled her cell at the San Jerónimo convent in Mexico City with over 4,000 books, creating the largest library in the city; with works of art; with musical and scientific instruments; and, on the nights when she held her salon, with the most important intellectuals and artists of the day. Over the course of her career, Cruz wrote more than 400 poems, 23 short plays, two full-length plays, and many prose works. She also conducted scientific experiments, composed music, and corresponded with people in Spain and the Americas.

The best known of Cruz's writings are *El Divino Narciso* (*The Divine Narcissus*), written in 1680, a religious play discussing the subject of physical and spiritual desire that runs through much of her work; *Primero sueño* (*First Dream*), a philosophical poem written in the Baroque style; and *Respuesta a Sor Filotea* (*Reply to Sister Filotea*), a defense of her literary career written in 1691.

In her writings she defended the rights of women, slaves, and South American Indians, as well as questioning and examining the roles of men and women in society. In the late 1680s a growing portion of the religious community began objecting to her writings and her position as an intellectual. Whether by force or by choice, Cruz sold her books and scientific instruments, gave the profits to the poor, and retired from intellectual life.

Three volumes of her works were published in Spain: the first *Inundación castálida* (*Flood From the Muses' Springs*), in 1689; *Segundo volumen de las obras de Sor Juana Inés de la Cruz* (*Second Volume of the Works of Sister Juana Inés de la Cruz*) in 1692; and, *Fama y obras póstumas de Fénix de México y Dézima Musa* (*Fame and Posthumous Works of the Mexican Phoenix and Tenth Muse*) in 1700.

Cruz died of the plague in 1695, after devoting herself to nursing victims of the epidemic.

Legacy

During her lifetime Sor Juana Inés de la Cruz was well known as the Monja de México (Nun of Mexico), or the tenth muse, throughout Mexico, Spain, and the rest of the Spanish-speaking world. Her portrait was painted by the artists Miguel Cabrera and Juan de Miranda, and she associated with the intellectual and social elites.

For two centuries after her death, however, her work was largely forgotten and it wasn't until 1910, when the poet Amado Nervo wrote a book called *Juana de Asbaje*, that interest in her work revived. Gabriela Mistral, a Chilean poet and the first Latin American writer to win the Nobel Prize in Literature, claimed her as an influence. Mexican poets of the 1950s read and discussed her poetry, among them Xavier Villaurrutia, Jorge Cuesta, and OCTAVIO PAZ. Between 1951 and 1957 Alfonso Méndez Plancarte gathered, edited, and published her complete works into four volumes of poetry, drama, and prose.

Cruz's life and work continue to fascinate artists and intellectuals today. Paz's 1988 biography, *Sor Juana: Or, The Trap of Faith*, has been followed by dozens of critical studies. She has been the subject of many dramas, and of more than one film, including *I, the Worst of All* by Argentinian director María Luisa Bemburg in 1990. She is a national figure of Mexico, where her portrait adorns the 200-peso bill.

Cruz is one of the earliest examples of a prominent female intellectual and the past 20 years have seen any number of feminist re-readings of her work. She has been credited as the "first feminist of the Americas" and her writing, in which she specifically considers the roles of men and women, is rich material for examination of a woman's position in a society intellectually and artistically dominated by men.

Manheim

WORLD EVENTS		DE LA CRUZ'S LIFE
Thirty Years' War in Europe	1618–48	
	1651	Sor Juana Inés de la Cruz is born
	1662	Cruz moves to royal palace
	1669	Cruz becomes a nun
	1680	Cruz writes *The Divine Narcissus*
Glorious Revolution in England	1688	
	1689	Cruz sees first volume of her works published in Spain
	1691	Cruz writes her *Reply*
	1692	Cruz has second volume of her works published
	1695	Cruz dies
	1700	Third volume of her works is published
United States declares independence	1776	

For Further Reading

Paz, Octavio. *Sor Juana: Or, The Trap of Faith*. Cambridge, Mass.: Harvard University Press, 1988.
A Sor Juana Anthology. Translated by Alan S. Trueblood. Cambridge, Mass.: Harvard University Press, 1988.

Cunningham, Merce

Choreographer
1919–

Life and Work

One of the truly groundbreaking choreographers of the twentieth century, Merce Cunningham found analogues in motion for great experimental ideas derived from music and visual art.

He was born Mercier Cunningham in Centralia, Washington, on April 16, 1919. Studying dance at Seattle's Cornish School in the late 1930s, he met composer JOHN CAGE when Cage was hired to provide music for the school's dance rehearsals. Cunningham moved on to Mills College in Oakland in 1938, studying with choreographer Lester Horton. The following year Cunningham caught the attention of MARTHA GRAHAM, then at the height of her

WORLD EVENTS		CUNNINGHAM'S LIFE
Russian Revolution	1917	
	1919	Merce (Mercier) Cunningham is born
Great Depression	1929–39	
	1938	Cunningham enrolls at Mills College
	1939	Cunningham joins Martha Graham's company
World War II	1939–45	
	1943	Cunningham begins to create his own dances
	1944	Cunningham begins working with John Cage
Communist China is established	1949	
Korean War	1950–53	
	1952	Cunningham creates choreography for electronic piece
	1953	Cunningham forms own dance company
African independence movement begins	1957	
Vietnam War ends	1975	
	1985	Cunningham wins MacArthur Foundation "genius grant"
Dissolution of Soviet Union	1991	

career as a modernist choreographer. She invited him to join her company as a dancer, and from 1939 to 1945, he created roles in new dances and helped realize many of Graham's ideas.

Cunningham began to create dances of his own in 1943. After leaving Graham's company he renewed his connection with Cage; in 1944, the two began working together. For many years their unusual endeavors attracted only the very forward-thinking, but they gave joint programs at least yearly in New York City. One of their early collaborations was 1947's *The Seasons*. Cage often allowed the structure of his compositions to be determined in part by chance or by ambient environment, and Cunningham, with his "choreography by chance," set out to do the same thing with dance. For example, dancers might use a coin toss to determine the order of a set of movements. In 1953 he formed his own group, the Merce Cunningham Dance Company, with Cage and his associate David Tudor as resident musicians.

Much as Cage and other composers used everyday sounds in their music, Cunningham broke down the barrier between dance-specific and ordinary movement, using everyday motions and gestures in such works as 1952's *Symphonie pour un homme seul* (also known as *Collage*). That work, performed to a composition of taped electronic sounds, illustrated Cunningham's interest in new media; beginning in 1974, he created a series of works for video, working with filmmaker Charles Atlas and others.

Indeed, Cunningham's experimental vision was never restricted to the relationship of dance and music. He also collaborated with abstract artists—radical experimenters such as ROBERT RAUSCHENBERG (*Summerspace*, 1958) and Jasper Johns (*Un Jour ou Deux* [*One Day or Two*], 1973) worked as designers on his productions, and his own art was entirely non-narrative. Cunningham's dancers were parts of abstract tableaux; they might be thought of as hosts for the work being presented, and often they would not even have heard the music to which they were dancing before a work's first performance.

Cunningham won a MacArthur Foundation "genius grant" in 1985 and through the 1990s he created new work.

Legacy

A rebellious spirit had bubbled under the surface of the dance world since the days

of ISADORA DUNCAN, but it was not until Merce Cunningham that dance would come under the sway of an experimentalist aesthetic comparable to that of music and art.

Cunningham's creative relationship with Cage carried forward an important process that had begun with the Russian impresario-composer pair of SERGE DIAGHILEV and IGOR STRAVINSKY: the emergence of dance as an equal participant in the expansion of the frontiers of creative expression.

Just as Cage seemed to push music to a point at which its very basis was called into question, so Cunningham did the same for dance. His influence on the choreographers and dancers who came after him must be seen in terms of the general liberation he brought to the art of dance as well as in the cool, limb-oriented "Cunningham technique" that is still widely taught. For the many dancers who were part of his prolifically generated creations (by the end of the twentieth century he had choreographed more than 150 works with his own company alone), nearly any innovation was permissible, and probably desirable.

Among the dancers who studied with Cunningham were Paul Taylor and TWYLA THARP; Tharp shared Cunningham's willingness to take dance out of the theater and into whatever venue seemed to suit it, be that a gymnasium, a museum, or a train station. Cunningham, then, epitomized in motion the untrammeled creatisve freedom so characteristic of the arts in the twentieth century.

Manheim

For Further Reading
Cunningham, Merce. *The Dancer and the Dance.* New York: M. Boyars, 1985.
Vaughan, David. *Merce Cunningham: Fifty Years.* New York: Aperture, 1997.

Dalí, Salvador

Artist

1904–1989

Life and Work

A native of Catalonian Spain, Salvador Dalí was one of the most prolific artists of the twentieth century. He was a painter, draftsman, illustrator, sculptor, writer and filmmaker who was most famous for his association with Surrealism.

Dalí was born in 1904 in Figueres, Spain. As a child, he studied art with Ramon Pichot, an Impressionist who had once worked with PABLO PICASSO. In 1921, Dalí entered the Academy of Fine Arts in Madrid; during his years of study, he admired nineteenth-century painters such as Jean Millet and Arnold Bocklin, as well as the modern work of Giorgio de Chirico and Carlo Carrà. Dalí discovered Sigmund Freud, whose influential writings on dreams and the unconscious helped explain to him some of the mental torments that he had suffered since childhood. During the same period, he befriended the poet FEDERICO GARCÍA LORCA. Between 1925 and 1927, Dalí experimented with Cubism, Neoclassicism, and a highly detailed form of Realism.

In 1928, Dalí achieved international renown when three of his paintings were included in the third annual Carnegie International exhibition. The following year, Dalí made a film with Luis Buñuel called *Un Chien Andalou*, an intentionally disturbing film that portrayed dreamlike conditions. The reputation achieved by that film led to Dalí's association with André Breton and the French Surrealists. At that time, Dalí formulated the theoretical basis for his work, calling it "paranoiac-critical." Drawing on the theories of Jaques Lacan and Freud, Dalí, a virtuoso draftsman, produced paintings that were fantastic and dreamlike executed in a realistic style. *Illumined Pleasures* (1929) reflects the influence of de Chirico and Yves Tanguy but contrasts with them in its portrayal of pervasive violence. *The Persistence of Memory* (1931) uses a intricately detailed technique reminiscent of fifteenth-century Flemish art; its limp watches have become synonymous with Surrealist imagery.

Partly because of Dalí 's lack of sincere political commitment, he was expelled from the Surrealist group in 1934. In the late 1930s, Dalí moved away from Surrealism and toward Renaissance classicism. In 1940, he moved to the United States, where he became a familiar figure in post–World War II America. He continued to turn out an impressive number of paintings. He also contributed to films by ALFRED HITCHCOCK and WALT DISNEY and created designs for the theater, periodicals, jewelry, and advertisements.

Dalí returned to Spain in 1948. His paintings after 1950 showed an increasing concern with Roman Catholicism (*The Last Supper*, 1955). In 1974 he founded the Teatre-Museo Dalí in Figueres, Spain, as a museum for his works; he taught classes there until late in his life. Dalí died in 1989.

Legacy

One of the most controversial artists of his day, Salvador Dalí's work ranged from the intellectual world of Surrealism to the glamorous world of show business.

Throughout his life, Dalí's painting was inseparable from his flamboyant personal style. Dalí was such a gifted and meticulous draftsman that to many it appeared that his paintings did not spring from his unconscious but were carefully constructed fictions. Other Surrealists thought that Dalí lacked sincerity and commitment to the movement.

Much of the European art world regarded Dalí skeptically; however, he was hugely successful in the United States. His works were avidly collected, and his carefully stylized personal image made him an international celebrity; he was a familiar face in magazines, newspapers, and television.

In 1941, soon after Dalí arrived in the United States, the Museum of Modern Art in New York held an important retrospective show. His critical reputation began to diminish as the new style, Abstract Expressionism, began to develop. From the late 1940s through the 1970s, American art critics consistently promoted abstract art as the standard of "high" art and the culminating style of the Modernist movement. By such criteria, Dalí's seemingly effortless and superficial late works simply did not qualify as "high" art. In addition, because of his commercial ventures, the majority of

established art critics continued to regard Dalí as a superficial self-promoter rather than as a serious artist. Much of the American public, however, disagreed. In 1995 the Salvador Dalí Museum opened in St. Petersburg, Florida.

Despite his marginalization by many critics, Dalí's technically impressive surreal images have had a profound effect on American visual culture. Much of the popular art associated with the psychedelic 1960s was rooted in the style of Dalí. In fact, it is hard to imagine record album covers, MTV videos, or the flamboyant posturing of Pop artists such as ANDY WARHOL without Dalí's example. Today it appears that Dalí's impact on popular culture almost outweighs his effect on the history of painting.

Domenico

WORLD EVENTS		DALÍ 'S LIFE
Spanish-American War	1898	
	1904	Salvador Dalí is born
World War I	1914–18	
Russian Revolution	1917	
	1921	Dalí enters the Academy of Fine Arts in Madrid
	1929	Dalí collaborates with Luis Buñuel on *Un Chien Andalou*
Great Depression	1929–39	
	1931	Dalí completes *The Persistence of Memory*
World War II	1939–45	
	1940–48	Dalí lives in United States
	1941	Museum of Modern Art mounts retrospective of Dalí's work
Communist China is established	1949	
Korean War	1950–53	
African independence movement begins	1957	
Vietnam War ends	1975	
	1989	Dalí dies
Dissolution of Soviet Union	1991	

For Further Reading

Ades, Dawn. *Dali*. Rev. ed. New York: Thames and Hudson, 1998.

Descharnes, Robert. *The World of Salvador Dali*. New York: Viking Press, 1968.

Secrest, Meryle. *Salvador Dali*. New York: Dutton, 1986.

Dante

Poet
1265–1321

Life and Work

In his epic poem, *La Divina commedia* (*The Divine Comedy*), Dante set humanity in the face of its eternal destiny, creating a modern myth that addresses universal human concerns in some of the most beautiful poetry ever written.

Dante Alighieri was born in Florence in 1265, and, as his poetry informs us, under the sign of Gemini, which places the exact date sometime between mid-May and mid-June.

World Events		Dante's Life
Mongol conquest of China	1215	
	1265	Dante Alighieri is born
	1293	Dante publishes *La Vita nuova*
	1302	Dante is exiled from Florence
	1308–20	Dante writes *The Divine Comedy*
	1321	Dante dies in Ravenna
Hundred Years' War begins	1337	

Little is known of Dante's early life and studies but, in the tradition of the time, they were doubtlessly based on the Bible and the writings of Aristotle, Cicero, Seneca, and other classical authors, especially VIRGIL and OVID.

The poet's earliest known works are sonnets written when he was 18 years old. Dante's first published collection of poetry, *La Vita nuova*, was completed around 1293.

During the 1290s, Dante studied philosophy and became active in Florentine politics. The Ghibelline imperial forces and the Guelf papal forces fought for control of Florence throughout the late 1200s before the Guelfs drove the Ghibellines out in 1266. Florence grew as a political power and as an intellectual center under the Guelfs, which split into two factions called Black and White. The White Guelfs, of which Dante was a vocal member, exiled the Black Guelfs. But in 1302, while he was traveling as an ambassador to Pope Boniface VIII, whose policies he disliked, Florence was again occupied by the Black Guelfs. Dante was sentenced to death in the city of his birth and thus began the exile that he would dramatize in *The Divine Comedy*.

In the first years of his exile, around 1304, Dante began compiling the *Convivio*, his second collection of poetry, which consists of poems and prose commentary. The collection is a series of philosophical instructions examining the moral and political questions of the day.

During his travels between 1308 and 1321, Dante wrote *The Divine Comedy*. The poem follows its narrator as he is led through hell and purgatory by Virgil and then into paradise by his muse, Beatrice. Dante used his own exile to represent the troubles of Italy, and, ultimately, the Judeo-Christian story of the fall of humankind. *The Inferno* begins with an allegorical representation of the death of Christ as Dante leaves the world, moving on to *Purgatorio* where Dante sees his own flaws in order to rise, like Christ, to a new understanding of human life in the *Paradisio*. Dante's distaste for the political and religious corruption in the world around him is pointedly expressed in the journey from hell to paradise.

Dante died in Ravenna in 1321.

Legacy

Dante incorporated important political, philosophical, and religious themes in *The Divine Comedy*, bringing a profound moral wisdom and stylistic artistry to bear on his creation of universal types from his contemporary.

The importance of Dante's great work was quickly recognized. In the century that followed his death *The Divine Comedy* became an emblem of Italian civilization. Many commentaries on it were written; Giovanni Boccaccio, the Italian poet and author of the *Decameron* (c. 1350), wrote the first biography of Dante and delivered a series of lectures on *The Divine Comedy*.

One of the great changes in literary history brought about by *The Divine Comedy* was to the language in which it was written. Latin was the prevalent literary mode of the day but Dante chose to write in the Italian vernacular, giving a literary voice to the common people of Italy for the first time. Dante's masterpiece caused Italian to become the prevailing literary language of Western Europe for several centuries following its publication.

Since Dante's era, readers and writers have found a reflection of their own times in his work. His profound vision of hell has never flagged in its ability to inspire writers from all ages. Among the great poets who have referred to his work are GEOFFREY CHAUCER, JOHN MILTON, RAINER RILKE, Stefan George, WILLIAM BUTLER YEATS, T. S. Eliot, and Eugenio Montale. Musical works referring to motifs from the *Inferno* include FRANZ LISZT's *Dane Symphony*, and PETER ILICH TCHAIKOVSKY's *Fantasia Francesca da Rimini*. Artists including SANDRO BOTTICELLI, MICHELANGELO, Eugène Delacroix, Jean-Auguste-Dominique Ingres, WILLIAM BLAKE, and Gustave Doré all painted images inspired by the work.

Important translations of *The Divine Comedy* into French and English revived interest in it by the Romantic poets. Samuel Taylor Coleridge, Percy Bysshe Shelley, and Lord Byron were influenced by what they considered Dante's romantic idea of the power of love. Francois-René de Chateaubriand and VICTOR-MARIE HUGO both reacted to the medieval religiosity of the poem. Philosophers, including Friedrich Wilhelm Joseph von Schelling and Georg Wilhelm Friedrich Hegel, also wrote extensively on the work. Most recently, Robert Pinsky, the current poet laureate of the United States, translated the *Inferno* into English.

Watson

For Further Reading

Dante Alighieri. *The Inferno of Dante*. Translated by Robert Pinsky New York: Farrar, Straus & Giroux, 1994.

Jacoff, Rachel, ed. *The Cambridge Companion to Dante*. Cambridge: Cambridge University Press, 1993.

Davis, Miles

Trumpeter
1926–1991

Life and Work

Miles Davis is one of the towering figures of late-twentieth century jazz; no other jazz musician of any period was so innovative for so long.

Davis was born in Alton, Illinois, near St. Louis, on May 25, 1926. Unlike most African-American youngsters of the time, Davis was raised in comfortable circumstances; his father was an oral surgeon who gave him a trumpet for his thirteenth birthday. In just two years he was playing jazz in St. Louis clubs and was a member of the musicians' union. Davis moved to New York City in 1944, agreeing to his parents' request that he study classical music at the Juilliard School. But, at the height of the revolutionary jazz style known as bebop, there was no keeping him away from jazz. Davis broke into jazz's elite circle when he recorded with legendary bebop saxophonist CHARLIE PARKER between 1945 and 1948.

Striking out on his own in 1948, Davis led a nine-piece band that moderated the relentless drive and speed of bebop and aimed at a more relaxed, yet still precise, sophistication. However, Davis became addicted to heroin in the early 1950s, and his music suffered. A proud man who brooked no disrespect from the police, he suffered the first of several arrests.

Davis broke out of his lethargy with the formation of the New Miles Davis Quintet in 1955; the group included saxophonist JOHN COLTRANE and a top-notch rhythm section. Among their recordings was 1955's *Round About Midnight*. Some of Davis's other recordings from this period were collected on an LP whose title, *Birth of the Cool*, recognized Davis's position as the founder of "cool jazz."

In 1957 Davis began to work intensely with composer and arranger Gil Evans, whose subtle orchestral palette perfectly matched his own restrained but questing trumpet style. Several Davis–Evans collaborations, including their 1958 version of GEORGE GERSHWIN's opera *Porgy and Bess* and 1959's *Sketches of Spain* LP, have been hailed as among the greatest jazz recordings of all time.

Inspired in part by his encounter with the work of guitarist JIMI HENDRIX, in the 1960s Davis once again moved in a new direction, embracing rock music even as most jazz musicians ignored it. Davis's "fusion" albums, including 1969's *Bitches Brew*, brought him rock listeners and even commercial success. Ill health slowed him in the 1970s, but he continued to record, experimenting with non-Western styles and black popular music, through the 1980s. He died in Santa Monica, California, on September 28, 1991.

Legacy

Miles Davis had the independence to swim against the prevailing jazz currents for nearly his entire career; often when he struck out in a new direction, his vision was compelling enough that legions of musicians followed. The musicians who have passed through Davis's own bands by themselves form a pantheon of jazz all-stars.

In an era when bebop fired the jazz world with revolutionary excitement, Davis's *Birth of the Cool* sessions went instead in a contemplative direction. They launched several careers, including that of John Lewis (later the founder of the classical-leaning Modern Jazz Quartet), and spawned a whole new West Coast–based "cool jazz" scene. Davis's small-group recordings of the late 1950s brought several careers to new levels, most crucially those of saxophonists Sonny Rollins and the world-shaking John Coltrane, whose work on Davis's near-perfect *Kind of Blue* album in 1959 foreshadowed the impressive trajectory of his own solo career.

It was Davis's rock-influenced music of the late 1960s that proved most outwardly influential of all his work. Thirty years later fusion was still an extraordinarily popular style, and the list of musicians Davis enlisted in his efforts reads like a Who's Who of modern jazz: guitarist John McLaughlin, pianists Keith Jarrett and Chick Corea, keyboardist Joe Zawinul, and percussionist Jack DeJohnette, to name just a few.

Beyond all these specific influences, Davis proved to his fellow musicians and to the world that jazz meant staying true to one's own artistic vision and instincts. He was one of the most original musicians ever to play jazz, but he was never really part of a conscious avant-garde, and his innovations always connected with listeners, drawing on music's past as they created its future.

Manheim

WORLD EVENTS		DAVIS'S LIFE
Russian Revolution	1917	
	1926	Miles Davis is born
Great Depression	1929–39	
World War II	1939–45	
	1944	Davis moves to New York City
	1945	Davis makes first recordings with Charlie Parker
	1948	Davis forms own band
Communist China is established	1949	
Korean War	1950–53	
	1955	Davis forms New Miles Davis Quintet
African independence movement begins	1957	Davis begins to work with Gil Evans
	1969	Davis releases fusion-oriented *Bitches Brew* LP
Vietnam War ends	1975	
Dissolution of Soviet Union	1991	Davis dies

For Further Reading

Carr, Ian. *Miles Davis: The Definitive Biography.* London: HarperCollins, 1998.

Davis, Miles. *Miles: The Autobiography.* New York: Simon–Schuster, 1989.

Debussy, Claude

Composer
1862–1918

Life and Work

An innovator whose entirely original language pointed toward and influenced much music of the twentieth century, Claude Debussy is widely regarded as France's greatest composer of the modern era.

Debussy was born in St.-Germain-en-Laye, near Paris, on August 22, 1862. His family's difficult financial circumstances turned even worse when his father was thrown in prison during the revolutionary Paris Commune of 1871, but the following year Debussy began piano studies with the mother-in-law of the poet Paul Verlaine. She recognized his talent and in 1872 she directed him toward the Paris Conservatory, the top French music school of the time. After winning the Prix de Rome (a major composition prize) in 1884, Debussy

seemed to be headed for a prestigious career. Instead, he went his own way, living on a shoestring with his girlfriend Gabrielle Dupont from about 1888 to 1897 and taking time to develop his unique musical ideas. His personal life would always be scandal-ridden: first Dupont and later Debussy's first wife, Rosalie, would attempt suicide after being abandoned by the composer in favor of other women.

His first masterstroke was the *Prelude to the Afternoon of a Faun*, from 1894. His only opera, 1902's *Pelléas et Mélisande*, was widely recognized as fundamentally new and divergent from RICHARD WAGNER's larger-than-life style. The orchestral *Nocturnes* (*Night Pieces*, 1899) and *La Mer* (*The Sea*, 1905) immediately became concert favorites, as did the piano collections entitled *Images and Préludes*. Debussy's music has often been termed Impressionist, and certainly its blurred, atmospheric outlines and its engagement with nature recall the Impressionist paintings of the 1870s. In the realm of harmony Debussy was among the first to use the whole-tone scale (which can be produced by playing every other note on a piano keyboard). Such devices reduced the sense of movement toward a tonal center in Debussy's music, putting the focus instead on local effects. His characteristic layered textures and freely moving rhythms may have been influenced by the sound of the Javanese gamelan, an orchestra of metal keyboards and gongs, that Debussy heard in Paris in 1889.

The early symptoms of rectal cancer began to trouble the composer in 1909, and in the following years his health steadily declined. During World War I Debussy composed mostly for piano or for small groups of instrumentalists. He died in Paris on March 25, 1918.

Legacy

Claude Debussy's free yet exquisitely subtle works, many of which represented the natural world, found favor with audiences even as they broke new musical ground. Many have remained standards in the repertory of classical music.

Although Debussy was never without detractors, both among musical conservatives and among revolutionary firebrands, he gradually became an icon of French modern music. His music, again like the paintings of the Impressionists, was easy to imitate in its exter-

nal details but elusive in its creative essence, and although he had no desire whatsoever to be the founder of a new style, that was what he to some extent became. For several decades after the peak of his career, concert stages resounded with evocative depictions of places and natural phenomena; such popular works as Ottorino Respighi's *The Pines of Rome* took Debussy's music as a clear point of departure.

Others looked more deeply into Debussy's music and saw the ways in which he had pushed at the boundaries of his own sound world. He had laid down a variety of examples for them to follow. His treatment of the orchestra, in which each instrument contributed clearly to a palette of subtle colors, impressed a range of twentieth-century composers, including IGOR STRAVINSKY and Bela Bartók. For Antonio Webern and other later composers who made timbre or tone quality into an important primary building block of music, Debussy's explorations were fundamental. EDGARD VARÈSE pursued Debussy's shifting rhythms first into a world of pure percussion music and then into musical electronics. Nor should a catalogue of his influences neglect his sense of humor and the attention he paid to popular musical trends, both on display in the piano piece *Golliwog's Cakewalk*, from the *Children's Corner* collection of 1908.

A broader and more general inspiration still was Debussy's insistence on developing a musical language of his own. He was the first of the twentieth century's characteristically individual voices.

Manheim

WORLD EVENTS	DEBUSSY'S LIFE
U.S. Civil War 1861–65	
	1862 Claude Debussy is born
Germany is united 1871	
	1872 Debussy enrolls at Paris Conservatory
	1884 Debussy wins Prix de Rome composition prize
	1894 *Prelude to the Afternoon of a Faun* first performed
Spanish-American War 1898	
	1899 Debussy composes *Nocturnes* for orchestra
	1902 *Pelléas et Mélisande*, Debussy's only opera, is first performed
	1905 *La Mer* is first performed
	1909 Debussy is stricken with cancer
World War I 1914–18	
Russian Revolution 1917	
	1918 Debussy dies
Great Depression 1929–39	

For Further Reading

Nectoux, Jean M., et al. *The New Grove Twentieth-Century Masters.* New York: Norton, 1986.

Parks, Richard S. *The Music of Claude Debussy.* New Haven, Conn.: Yale University Press, 1989.

Wenk, Arthur B. *Claude Debussy and Twentieth-Century Music.* Boston: Twayne, 1983.

Degas, Edgar

Painter

1834–1917

Life and Work

Edgar Degas was one of the key figures associated with the Impressionist movement that revolutionized art in the late nineteenth century.

Degas was born Hilaire Germain Edgar Degas in 1834, the son of an aristocratic Parisian banker. He received traditional academic training, first with Louis Lamothe, and then at the École des Beaux Arts. In addition, he traveled extensively in Italy, studying the works of Renaissance and Baroque painters and, in Paris, made copies of paintings in the Louvre. Throughout his life, Degas, more than any of his colleagues, continued to rely upon the solid drawing skills he developed during years of training.

However, Degas did not remain a part of the academic tradition. In 1862 he met EDOUARD MANET and the two quickly became friends. Degas shared Manet's interest in creating a form of art appropriate to the emerging modern age. Rather than painting the grand historical narratives that still predominated in the official Salons, Degas began to focus on painting scenes of contemporary Parisian social life. He chose his subjects from the ballet, music halls, and racecourses that were so much a part of the flourishing world of upper-middle-class Paris. By 1866, Degas was an important member of the group of artists, later to be called the Impressionists, that met at the Cafe Guerbois to discuss their experimental new styles and their discontent with the restrictive atmosphere of the Salons. When the group decided to organize its own independent exhibition in 1874 in Paris, Degas participated.

Over the next several years, Degas contributed to seven of the eight Impressionist exhibitions. He became especially closely associated with the American Impressionist painter MARY CASSATT. Nevertheless, Degas resisted being labeled an Impressionist himself, preferring instead to be called a Realist. Indeed, his work differs significantly from Impressionism as practiced by painters such as CLAUDE MONET and Camille Pissarro.

Unlike the Impressionists, Degas did not specialize in *plein-air* (open air) landscapes, preferring instead to paint interior scenes with dramatic artificial lighting. In *Rehearsal on the Stage* (1874), the viewer looks down on a stage full of young ballet dancers and their dance master lit by floodlights from below. At first the asymmetrical composition looks almost accidental. As in photography, which Degas studied assiduously, the viewing angle seems informal, and the figures appear to be accidentally cropped from the sides of the picture. In the foreground looms the silhouette of the top of a cello, a spatial device that Degas learned from Japanese prints. Only the open brushwork and the abrupt juxtaposition of unmodulated hues connect the image with Impressionism.

As Degas's eyesight began to fail, he turned to pastels and sculpture. During his lifetime, he exhibited only one sculpture, *Little Fourteen Year-old Dancer* (1881). A painstakingly realistic wax figure of a ballerina wearing a real tutu shown at the Impressionist exhibition of 1881, it was criticized as disturbingly ugly. More than 150 clay figures that Degas had apparently made as studies were found in his studio after his death in 1917.

Legacy

Despite his ambivalent attitude toward Impressionism, Edgar Degas was a crucial figure in this revolutionary group of artists. His aristocratic manner and financial independence, which came from family money, allowed him immediate access to the most important figures in the art world. He opened the social doors for artists such as Cassatt and established collegial relationships that encouraged mutual stylistic developments in prints and pastels.

Toward the end of the nineteenth century many artists began to turn from the surface effects of Impressionism toward an art that dealt with three-dimensional forms. Degas's carefully modeled late works proved particularly important to painters like PIERRE-AUGUSTE RENOIR.

Degas was not only an important painter, he was also an important collector of Modernist art. He had intended to establish a museum to display his vast collection, but financial problems late in his life made this impossible. After his death, his heirs sold the collection, but in 1998 much of it was brought together again for a major exhibition.

Degas's painting continues to generate new interpretations and reevaluations. A major retrospective of his work was held in 1988–89 and traveled to Paris, Ottawa, and New York. Today Degas's reputation is secure as one of the primary figures in the development of Modernism.

McEnroe

WORLD EVENTS		DEGAS' LIFE
Congress of Vienna reorganizes Europe	1815	
	1834	Edgar Degas is born
Revolutions in Austria, France, Germany, and Italy	1848	
U.S. Civil War	1861–65	
Germany is united	1871	
	1874	Degas participates in first Impressionist exhibition
	1881	Degas completes wax sculpture *Little Fourteen Year-old Dancer*
Spanish-American War	1898	
World War I	1914–18	
Russian Revolution	1917	Degas dies
Great Depression	1929–39	

For Further Reading

Reff, Theodore, *Degas: The Artist's Mind.* Cambridge, Mass.: Belknap Press of Harvard University Press, 1987.

Sutton, Denys. *Edgar Degas: Life and Work.* New York: Rizzoli, 1986

Diaghilev, Serge

Dance Impresario
1872–1929

Life and Work

The creator and manager of the Ballets Russes, the daring Russian dance company that took Paris and the rest of the world by storm in the early twentieth century, Serge Diaghilev was one of the dance world's great masterminds. Through the creative figures he

WORLD EVENTS		DIAGHILEV'S LIFE
Germany is united	1871	
	1872	Serge Diaghilev is born
	1890	Diaghilev begins study of law
Spanish-American War	1898	
	1899	Diaghilev founds art journal
	1906	Diaghilev curates Russian art exhibit in Paris
	1909	Diaghilev forms Ballets Russes
	1911	The Ballets Russes perform *Petrushka*
	1913	Igor Stravinsky's *The Rite of Spring* causes audience riot
World War I	1914–18	
Russian Revolution	1917	
	1924	Diaghilev discovers George Balanchine
	1929	Diaghilev dies
Great Depression	1929–39	

brought together, he stood at the center of a revolution in the arts.

Born Sergei Pavlovich Diaghilev in Novgorod, Russia, on March 31, 1872, he was the son of a military officer. He went to St. Petersburg to study law in 1890, but he found that he preferred the company of painters and musicians. Diaghilev flirted with a career as a composer, but soon he realized that he was gifted with an instinct for identifying talent and his calling was to be an artistic organizer—an impresario. He began in the visual arts, founding a journal called *World of Art* in 1899 and, after he moved to Paris in 1906, organizing an exhibition of contemporary Russian art there. He then turned to music, introducing the Russian operatic bass Fyodor Chaliapin to French audiences.

When Diaghilev formed the Ballets Russes (Russian Ballet) in 1909, he envisioned it as a medium that would bring dance, music, and art together in a new synthesis. Influenced in this ambitious ideal by the revolutionary American dancer ISADORA DUNCAN, Diaghilev realized it by bringing together a creative team that included the dancer and choreographer Vaslav Nijinsky and the composer IGOR STRAVINSKY, whose kinetic, propulsive early ballet scores were perfectly suited to Diaghilev's aims. No mere promoter, Diaghilev was directly responsible for the creation of *Petrushka*, a 1911 work that remains among Stravinsky's most popular. The 1913 premiere of *The Rite of Spring*, with music by Stravinsky and choreography by Nijinsky, occasioned riot-like tumult in the audience.

The controversy, of course, established Diaghilev's reputation, and for the rest of his life he led the Ballets Russes on highly influential tours of Europe and the Americas. The company offered a season of performances every year until its creator's death from diabetes on August 19, 1929, while he was vacationing in Venice.

Legacy

Serge Diaghilev was a key figure in advancing modernist ideas, not only in dance, but also in music and the visual arts.

He brought the adventurous spirit of the twentieth century into the dance world; as a result, he was credited after his death with revitalizing the tradition of ballet in the West. Ironically, the Ballets Russes never performed

in Russia. Yet ever since Diaghilev's time, the art of ballet has been identified with Russia and with Russian artists. The list of dancers and choreographers who were associated with Diaghilev at one time or another makes clear the depth of his influence; in addition to Nijinsky, they included the dancer Anna Pavlova and the choreographers Michel Fokine, Léonide Massine, and, toward the end of Diaghilev's career, GEORGE BALANCHINE, whom Diaghilev discovered in 1924. Balanchine immigrated to the United States in the 1930s, bringing with him an inexhaustible creative and promotional energy that he learned directly from Diaghilev.

As an incubator of creative talent Diaghilev's influence extended beyond the world of dance. His most famous protégé was Stravinsky, who even after his shocking early works, continued to write with the ballet in mind, collaborating with Balanchine among others. Diaghilev's ballets also helped to popularize the music of other forward-looking composers, including CLAUDE DEBUSSY (who called him "a wonderful, terrible man who could make even the stones dance"), Erik Satie, and Serge Prokofiev. He also worked with the French poet Jean Cocteau, likewise a figure whose influence crossed genre lines. Léonide Massine would extend Diaghilev's idea of a synthesis between art and dance by working with artists of the highest stature, including PABLO PICASSO.

Although his name is not universally known outside the dance world, Diaghilev left an indelible imprint on the expressive culture of the twentieth century.

Manheim

For Further Reading

Drummond, John. *Speaking of Diaghilev*. London: Faber & Faber, 1997.

Garafola, Lynn. *Diaghilev's Ballets Russes*. New York: Oxford University Press, 1979.

Dickens, Charles

Novelist
1812–1870

Life and Work

Charles Dickens was born in Portsmouth, England, on February 7, 1812, but spent most of his childhood in London. His father, a minor government official, was sent to debtors' prison, forcing the young Dickens to work in a factory, a traumatic experience that would appear in his novels.

He worked as a court reporter, and then as a journalist, using the pseudonym Boz. His first book, *Sketches by Boz*, was published in 1836. He then began writing and serially publishing the immensely popular comic narrative *Posthumous Papers of the Pickwick Club*, which gained him a celebrity unprecedented for an author.

Dickens continued to publish his novels serially throughout his career. His early novels, *Oliver Twist* (1838), *The Life and Adventures of Nicholas Nickleby* (1839), and *The Old Curiosity Shop* (1841), had readers waiting for hours before each new chapter arrived in the stores. Dickens's radical condemnation of British institutions and of the conditions of industrial life are evident in these novels; for example *Oliver Twist* addressed the plights of orphans and pickpockets on the streets of London.

Dickens wrote *A Christmas Carol*, the story of Ebenezer Scrooge's transformation from a cruel miser into a loving and generous spirit, in 1843. The character of Scrooge has entered the vocabulary of nearly every English speaker.

The Personal History of David Copperfield, published in 1850, is a semi-autobiographical novel, *A Tale of Two Cities*, published in 1859 tells the story of the French Revolution; and *Great Expectations* of 1861 discusses the negative power of wealth and greed, an issue close to Dickens's' heart. He also described London, its geography, its populations, and its social conditions, with great accuracy.

In the 1850s and 1860s Dickens embarked on extremely popular reading tours throughout England and the United States. He collapsed during one of these tours in 1869. He died on June 9, 1870, leaving unfinished his novel *The Mystery of Edwin Drood*.

Legacy

Throughout his career, Charles Dickens was extremely popular with readers and listeners of all social classes and levels of education. His appeal came from his comedic genius and the power of his indictments of social evils, as well as from his skill at documenting contemporary London life and creating fantastically unique characters.

Dickens largely defined Victorian literature, and addressed Victorian concerns about the effects of the Industrial Revolution and the need for social and political reform. Dickens's critical portraits of hypocritical governments and church leaders became a part of the public imagination of his time and have formed the impression of that era (1837–1901) for posterity.

Among his contemporaries, writers including Ralph Waldo Emerson, MARK TWAIN, (who credited Dickens for being the superior entertainer at their shared public readings and comedic performances), Edgar Allan Poe, and William Thackeray praised Dickens's work.

Despite his popularity with the public, Dickens was largely ignored by critics for some time after his death. Not until the early twentieth century would G. K. Chesterton, George Bernard Shaw, and Aldous Huxley write critical praise of his work; Shaw placed him alongside WILLIAM SHAKESPEARE as one of the greatest of English writers.

Dickens has come to be recognized as one of the most important contributors to the development of the social criticism novel. Both GEORGE ORWELL, who followed in his footsteps as a social satirist, and Edmund Wilson praised him as a great social critic.

Not only have the political stances of his novels maintained their popularity but his engaging prose and sharp, funny characterizations have kept his novels on bookshelves and on school reading lists for the past 150 years.

Watson

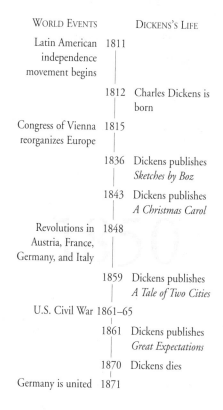

WORLD EVENTS		DICKENS'S LIFE
Latin American independence movement begins	1811	
	1812	Charles Dickens is born
Congress of Vienna reorganizes Europe	1815	
	1836	Dickens publishes *Sketches by Boz*
	1843	Dickens publishes *A Christmas Carol*
Revolutions in Austria, France, Germany, and Italy	1848	
	1859	Dickens publishes *A Tale of Two Cities*
U.S. Civil War	1861–65	
	1861	Dickens publishes *Great Expectations*
	1870	Dickens dies
Germany is united	1871	

For Further Reading

Bloom, Harold, ed. *Dickens*. Modern Critical Views. New York: Chelsea House, 1990.
Smith, Graham. *Charles Dickens: A Literary Life*. New York: St. Martin's Press, 1996.

Dickinson, Emily

Poet
1830–1886

Life and Work

Considered one of the greatest, most innovative poets of modern times, Emily Dickinson had a unique and intensely personal poetics, which continues to defy clear interpretation.

Dickinson was born on December 10, 1830, in Amherst, Massachusetts. Her father was a treasurer of Amherst College. She attended Amherst Academy (1840–47), Mount Holyoke Female Seminary (1847–48), and continued her education with a tutor. Around 1850 Dickinson began to write poetry at the encouragement of this tutor. Dickinson was a great letter writer; one of her correspondents, Samuel Bowles, editor of *The Springfield Republican*, a local newspaper, published the seven poems that were printed during her lifetime. In 1858 she began binding her own poems into handcrafted books.

Dickinson, an eccentric recluse, dressed entirely in white and for the last 20 years of her life did not leave her family property. She wrote more than 1,700 poems, and nearly as many letters.

Dickinson's poems—short, lyric works, experimental in form and intensely intimate in tone and subject matter—discuss nature, death, love, and immortality, and are rarely titled.

Dickinson died in May of 1886 of Bright's disease, a kidney disorder. Her sister Lavinia, with whom she was extremely close, discovered her poetry after her death and had some of it published in a collection, *Poems by Emily Dickinson*, in 1890. Further collections were published between 1891 and 1957. In 1955 her complete poems were collected and published for the first time.

Legacy

Emily Dickinson's experiments with rhyme, assonance, consonance, and tonal harmony defied all poetic conventions of the time. Her innovative use of meter and rhyme,

startling imagery and vocabulary, epigrammatic, elliptical style, and her use of dashes as punctuation make her poetic work a body unto itself, spectacularly different from the mainstream poetry of her day.

Initial critical responses to *Poems by Emily Dickinson* were negative but the collection sold well, with 11 editions in two years. Dickinson's work found limited fame throughout the beginning of the twentieth century but came to true public and critical attention with the publication of her collected works in 1955. The collected poems sparked a large variety of critical work on Dickinson, which closely analyzed her poetic structure, her grammar, and her language and style. These works also addressed her treatment of religion and her femininity, as well as her responses to the Romantic and Transcendental work that was popular at the time.

A number of poets—Hart Crane, Louise Bogan, Adrienne Rich, and Susan Howe among them—have drawn from Dickinson's works, referring to her technical innovation and emotional depth. Howe's creative critical work, *My Emily Dickinson*, precipitated a new wave of appreciation and analysis by contemporary American experimental poets.

Watson

For Further Reading
Bloom, Harold, ed. *Emily Dickinson*. Bloom's Major Poets. New York: Chelsea House, 1999.
Howe, Susan. *My Emily Dickinson*. Berkeley, Calif.: North Atlantic Books, 1985.

Disney, Walt

Cartoonist, Filmmaker, and
Entrepreneur
1901–1966

Life and Work

W alt Disney, a pioneer of animated films, created such legendary characters as Mickey Mouse, Donald Duck, and Pluto.

Born in Chicago, Illinois, in 1901, Disney moved while still an infant to rural Missouri. A few years later, the family moved to Kansas City, Missouri, where Disney first began to study cartooning, a form for which he had shown an early aptitude. At 14 Disney began taking classes at the Kansas City Art Institute and School of Design. In 1917, the family returned to Chicago, where Disney attended high school and continued to study cartooning with the idea of becoming a newspaper cartoonist. At age 16 he volunteered as a truck driver for the American Red Cross in Europe during the last days of World War I. Upon returning to Kansas City in 1919, he went to work for a commercial art studio where he formed a friendship with Ub Iwerks. Together they began to produce short animated features, the beginning of a life-long collaboration.

Forming their own company, the two began making short one- and two-minute advertising films and other animation projects. When it went bankrupt, Disney left Kansas City to join his brother Roy in Los Angeles. Roy became his brother's business manager, and Iwerks joined him in drawing cartoons. In 1928, the brothers produced a cartoon, *Steamboat Willie,* featuring their new character Mickey Mouse and the innovative technology that was adding sound to motion pictures. It was a huge success.

One year later, Disney produced a film called *The Skeleton Dance* as part of his animated musical series *Silly Symphonies,* in which a skeleton rises from the grave and dances to the classical strains of Camille Saint-Saens's *Danse Macabre.* Spurred on by the popularity of Minnie and Mickey Mouse, the Disney group developed other animal characters, including Donald Duck, Goofy, and Pluto.

In 1935, Disney, in order to expand the earning potential of the cartoon, started working on one of the first feature-length animated films, *Snow White and the Seven Dwarfs* (1937). Previously, cartoons had almost exclusively featured animal characters; Disney introduced realistic human characters and thus enlarged the possibilities of animated film. The success of *Snow White* (which others in the industry had called "Disney's folly") led to more feature-length animated films: *Pinocchio* (1940), *Dumbo* (1941), and *Bambi* (1942). Another innovative Disney venture, *Fantasia* (1941), was an episodic feature-length animated film in which cartoon figures moved and acted to classical music.

The Disney studio diversified in the 1940s and began producing nonanimated films for theaters and, later, for television. Popular nature-based series that used voice-over narration and first-rate wildlife photography included *Seal Island* (1948) and *The Living Desert* (1953). Disney live-action films of the period included *The Shaggy Dog* (1959), *The Absent-Minded Professor* (1961), and *Mary Poppins* (1964). For television, the Disney studio produced popular series such as *Zorro* (1957–59) and *Davy Crockett* (beginning in 1950), and shows such as the *Mickey Mouse Club* (1955–59) and *The Wonderful World of Color* (beginning in 1961).

In 1955, Disney opened the theme park Disneyland, in Anaheim, California, which became a worldwide tourist attraction. Disney World followed, in Orlando, Florida, and was completed in 1971. Disney died in 1966.

Legacy

W alt Disney's meteoric success in animated films resulted from his experimentation with new technologies, such as sound, color, and more intricate movement in cartoons, as well as the broad appeal of his energetic characters. His style set the benchmark against which other leading animators of the 1940s and 1950s, such as Bill Hanna, Joe Barbera, and Walter Lantz, responded to with their sharper-edged and less sentimental cartoons.

During the 1930s and 1940s the Disney studios became a source of tremendous technical innovation. *The Skeleton Dance* (1929) and the *Silly Symphonies* that followed introduced the use of a prerecorded music track. His animated short *Flowers and Trees* (1932) was the first cartoon to employ the new three-strip Technicolor process. The studio also developed and pioneered the use of the multi-plane camera, which brought greater depth, perspective, and more intricate action to animation. Disney was also a pioneer in the marketing of movie-related merchandise and in the development of theme parks.

Since Disney's death in 1966, the Disney Company has continued to successfully produce motion pictures and animated films. The Disney Company produced the first feature-length computer animated cartoon, *Toy Story,* in 1995.

Perhaps Disney's enduring influence on the culture can best be seen in the continued popularity of his cartoon creations: Mickey Mouse, Donald Duck, Goofy, Pluto, and the rest, images familiar to generations of children and their parents. In Disney's work, commerce meets art. Through toys, T-shirts, movies, and mugs, his art continues to reach people around the world.

Domenico

WORLD EVENTS		DISNEY'S LIFE
Spanish-American War	1898	
	1901	Walt Disney is born
World War I	1914–18	
Russian Revolution	1917	
	1928	Disney produces *Steamboat Willie*
Great Depression	1929–39	
	1937	Disney produces *Snow White and the Seven Dwarfs*
World War II	1939–45	
Communist China is established	1949	
Korean War	1950–53	
	1955	Disney opens theme park, Disneyland
African independence movement begins	1957	
	1966	Disney dies
Vietnam War ends	1975	

For Further Reading

Bright, Randy. *Disneyland: Inside Story.* New York: H. N. Abrams, 1987.

Finch, Christopher. *The Art of Walt Disney: From Mickey Mouse to the Magic Kingdoms.* New York: Abradale Press, 1983.

Watts, Steven. *The Magic Kingdom: Walt Disney and the American Way of Life.* Boston: Houghton Mifflin, 1997.

Dorsey, Thomas A.

Composer
1899–1993

World Events		Dorsey's Life
Spanish-American War	1898	
	1899	Thomas A. Dorsey is born
World War I	1914–18	
	1916	Dorsey moves to Chicago
Russian Revolution	1917	
	1924	Dorsey becomes "Ma" Rainey's musical director
	1928	Dorsey forms Georgia Tom and Tampa Red duo
Great Depression	1929–39	
	1932	Dorsey renounces secular music
	1933	Dorsey co-founds National Convention of Gospel Choirs and Choruses
	1939	Dorsey hires Mahalia Jackson
World War II	1939–45	
Communist China is established	1949	
Korean War	1950–53	
African independence movement begins	1957	
Vietnam War ends	1975	
Dissolution of Soviet Union	1991	
	1993	Dorsey dies
South Africa dismantles apartheid	1994	

Life and Work

Known as the "Father of Gospel Music," Thomas A. Dorsey was also an important figure in the history of the blues, paradoxically as the creator of some of the genre's most memorable sexual double entendres. But it was gospel that inspired his best known and most heartfelt compositions, "Precious Lord, Take My Hand" and "Peace in the Valley."

The son of a traveling preacher father and a church organist mother, Dorsey was born in rural Villa Rica, Georgia, on July 1, 1899. The family moved to Atlanta, and as a youth Dorsey encountered a large range of music, from spirituals to notated "shape note" hymns that helped him learn to read music; by the time he was 12 he had become a fine pianist. As a teenager he heard performances by the legendary blues singers "Ma" Rainey and BESSIE SMITH, both in the early stages of their own careers. Dorsey attended Morehouse College for a short time and then moved to Chicago in 1916.

He continued to hone his musical skills at Chicago's College of Composition and Arranging, and soon he followed successfully in the steps of composer W. C. Handy, arranging the southern blues with which he had grown up for small theatrical ensembles. Dorsey published his first song in 1920; he encountered gospel music the following year when he attended the National Baptist Convention. Powerfully drawn to gospel, he nevertheless remained primarily a secular musician for over a decade. He became Rainey's musical director in 1924, and in 1928 he teamed with guitarist Hudson Whitaker to form Georgia Tom and Tampa Red. This duo's "hokum" blues recordings often featured sexually suggestive lyrics; their hits included "Somebody's Been Using That Thing" and "It's Tight Like That."

In 1932, after his wife's death, Dorsey abandoned secular music; he is said to have composed "Precious Lord, Take My Hand" in his initial grief. In 1933 he co-founded the National Convention of Gospel Choirs and Choruses (he remained its president until 1973), and through the decade and beyond he energetically organized new ensembles. An indefatigable composer, he employed a succession of female vocalists to introduce his new hymns; the most famous of these was MAHALIA JACKSON, who joined Dorsey in 1939. Over his long career he composed more than 1,000 songs, and he remained active as a promoter and administrator. Dorsey died in Chicago on January 23, 1993.

Legacy

Thomas Dorsey's influence as a gospel composer was immense. His style provided the template against which those of Jackson and other great gospel vocalists evolved, and his work became widely known among Americans of all races.

During black gospel music's classical age in the 1940s and 1950s, Dorsey's music dominated the field. His noble yet personal hymns have become lasting documents of evangelical Protestantism in their African-American inflection, and his compositions provided the vehicles through which young singers expanded their powers: such major figures as Sister Rosetta Tharpe and the vocal groups the Dixie Hummingbirds and the Soul Stirrers all had gospel hits with Dorsey pieces early in their careers.

Further, the very concept of a gospel hit itself, and the presence of black gospel music as a commercial entity, came about largely through Dorsey's promotional efforts. His songs helped to expand the reach of African-American religious music beyond the realm of the black church. "Peace in the Valley" gained massive success in recordings by ELVIS PRESLEY and country singer Red Foley, and Dorsey's compositions remain well represented in the country gospel repertoire.

A commonplace observation among observers of African-American music is that it is marked by the interpenetration of sacred and secular. What is less widely recognized is that this condition of mutual influence is to some substantial degree Dorsey's work. His dual careers in gospel and blues are contradictory only on the surface, for his gospel songs incorporated the rhythmic freedom and the personal intensity of the blues into their structures. Vocalists from Sam Cooke to ARETHA FRANKLIN and beyond could migrate easily from gospel to pop because Dorsey had gone before them and sensed the commonality of the two genres in African-American thinking and musical expression. Hardly one of the most celebrated musicians of twentieth-century America, he nevertheless was a pivotal figure.

Manheim

For Further Reading

Harris, Michael W. *The Rise of Gospel Blues: The Music of Thomas Andrew Dorsey in the Urban Church.* New York: Oxford University Press, 1992.

Heilbut, Anthony. *The Gospel Sound: Good News and Bad Times.* New York: Limelight Editions, 1985.

Dostoyevsky, Fyodor

Novelist

1821–1881

Life and Work

Fyodor Dostoyevsky made the neurotic, the criminal, and the mystic central figures of twentieth-century fiction.

Dostoyevsky was born into an aristocratic family in Moscow in 1821. He attended boarding school in Moscow and later graduated from the St. Petersburg School of Military Engineers. He spent a year in the corps of engineers before leaving to pursue a career as a writer.

Bednyye lyudi (*Poor Folk*), Dostoyevsky's first novel, was published in 1846 and was an immediate success. However, his literary career came to a temporary halt when, in 1849, he was arrested for socialist activity and sentenced to death—later commuted to four years of hard labor in Siberia. After completing his sentence, Dostoyevsky joined the military, spending a total of 10 years in Siberia before returning to St. Petersburg.

In 1864 Dostoyevsky published *Zapiski iz podpolya* (*Notes from Underground*), the first of his philosophical works. *Prestupleniye i nakazaniye* (*Crime and Punishment*) followed two years later. Dostoyevsky's portrait of Raskolnikov, an intellectual who tries to justify his murder of a female pawnbroker, was published serially in *The Russian Herald* from 1866 to 1867.

Dostoyevsky, a compulsive gambler, was deeply in debt for much of his life. He wrote several of his greatest novels while fleeing creditors, living in Germany, Italy, Switzerland, and Austria. He finished *Idiot* (*The Idiot*) in 1869 and *Besy* (*The Possessed*) in 1872. He returned to Russia in the early 1870s to become editor of the conservative weekly paper *The Citizen*.

Bratya Karamazovy (*The Brothers Karamazov*), widely considered to be his greatest work, was written during 1879–80, appearing serially in *The Russian Herald*. The work, heavy with Christian symbolism and references to the Russian religious consciousness, has the strongest literary subtext of any of his novels, drawing heavily on the Bible and many literary giants from various Western cultures.

Each of Dostoyevsky's novels, particularly *The Brothers Karamazov*, presents a philosophical argument through story and allegorical subtext, often making use of a Christian image of an all-forgiving Christ and referring to Christianity as a religion of divine love and self-sacrifice.

On June 8, 1880 Dostoyevsky delivered a speech at the unveiling of a monument to ALEKSANDR PUSHKIN. This famous text, called *Discourse on Pushkin*, solidified Pushkin's place as Russia's national poet.

Dostoyevsky died of a pulmonary hemorrhage in St. Petersburg in 1881.

Legacy

Fyodor Dostoyevsky's work, which has been called visionary, proto-Freudian, and existentialist, continues to be explored and analyzed with new dimensions constantly being revealed.

Although not considered an important writer in his lifetime, Dostoyevsky has come to be considered, along with Ivan Turgenev and Aleksey Pisemsky, as one of the last great Russian Realist novelists. Dostoyevsky was a well-known figure and his work was widely read, but he had few admirers among important contemporary Russian thinkers.

In the late 1800s, the poet Alexander Blok and the writer Andrei Bely both claimed Dostoyevsky as an important influence. In 1929, Mikhail Bakhtin wrote his *Problems of Dostoyevsky's Oeuvre*, naming Dostoyevsky as one of the great Russian novelists, and declaring that his works should be read as complex texts

written in multiple voices. The writer Vsevolod Ivanov published another critical essay in 1932. His interpretation of Dostoyevsky's work as multilayered and symbolic, along with Bakhtin's study, formed the starting point for the Russian and international critical study of Dostoyevsky that continues to this day.

Notes from Underground, in which an anti-hero is unable to accept the absolute truth of logic and reality but insists on asserting his free will in spite of his suffering, helped to form the basis of twentieth-century Existential philosophy. The philosophers Albert Camus and Jean-Paul Sartre both discussed Dostoyevsky in their works and his ideas have often been placed alongside those of Søren Kierkegaard and Friedrich Nietzsche.

In addition to Existentialist, Dostoyevsky's work has also often been considered to be anticipatory of the principles of Freudian psychoanalysis and of the ideas of Oswald Spengler. The Symbolist poets Arthur Rimbaud, Paul Valéry, and Jean Moréas considered him a religious visionary, and this reputation has persisted, offering yet another reading of his work.

Watson

WORLD EVENTS		DOSTOYEVSKY'S LIFE
Congress of Vienna reorganizes Europe	1815	
	1821	Fyodor Dostoyevsky is born
	1846	Dostoyevsky publishes *Poor Folk*
Revolutions in Austria, France, Germany, and Italy	1848	
	1849	Dostoyevsky sentenced to hard labor in Siberia
U.S. Civil War	1861–65	
	1864	Dostoyevsky publishes *Notes from Underground*
	1866	Dostoyevsky publishes *Crime and Punishment*
	1869	Dostoyevsky publishes *The Idiot*
Germany is united	1871	
	1879–80	Dostoyevsky publishes *The Brothers Karamazov*
	1881	Dostoyevsky dies
Spanish-American War	1898	

For Further Reading

Bakhtin, Mikhail. *Problems of Dostoyevsky's Poetics.* Reprint. Minneapolis: Universtiy of Minnesota Press, 1990.

Frank, Joseph. *Dostoyevsky: The Miraculous Years, 1865–1871.* Princeton, N.J.: Princeton University Press, 1997.

Mochulsky, Konstantin. *Dostoyevsky: His Life and Work.* Princeton, N.J.: Princeton University Press, 1972.

Duchamp, Marcel

Artist
1887–1968

Life and Work

Forerunner to the movements of Futurism, Dadaism, and Surrealism, as well as Pop art and minimalism, Marcel Duchamp was one of the most influential artists of the modern era.

Born in 1887 in Normandy, France, Duchamp began painting at age 15. After com-pleting his schooling, Duchamp joined his older brothers in Paris to pursue a career as an artist. An undistinguished student at the Academie Julian, he frequently sketched every-day scenes and earned money selling his car-toons during his early years in Paris. In 1909, his paintings were exhibited at the Salon des Independents and Salon d'Automne in Paris, as well as in Rouen, France.

The influence of PAUL CÉZANNE was appar-ent in his early work, although Duchamp's work contained more intense color. In the gar-den of his brother's home in suburban Paris, Duchamp mingled with avant-garde artists and writers, among them Guillaume Apollinaire, Albert Gleizes, and Fernand Leger, whose influence led him to increased experi-mentation with his art.

Nude Descending A Staircase No. 2 (1912), Duchamp's best-known work, combined Cubist themes with sequencing techniques used in photography. Withdrawn from submission to the Salon des Independents because its nontra-ditional subject was regarded as inappropriate for Cubism, it was eventually shown at the 1913 New York Armory show, where it became a scandalous sensation and brought Duchamp international celebrity. After dis-carding the conventions of Cubism with *Nude Descending*, Duchamp created the first "ready-made," or found object, called *Bicycle Wheel* (1913), which challenged the very notion of what constituted art.

In 1915 during World War I, Duchamp moved to New York City and became the cen-tral figure in the avant-garde community, which included other American and European exiles. His most complex work, *The Bride Stripped Bare by Her Bachelors, Even* (1915–23), better known as *Large Glass*, was con-structed during this period. He also continued to work on ready-mades. In 1917, he submit-ted a piece called *Fountain*, a urinal turned on its side and signed with the fictitious name "R. Mutt," to the first exhibition of the Society of Independent Artists. *Fountain* was refused on the basis that it was not a work of art.

In 1923, Duchamp returned to France, where he became very active in professional chess and began a study of perspective and optics, resulting in works such as *Rotary Demisphere* (1925).

He fled to the United States again during the Nazi occupation of Paris in 1942. Here, he worked intermittently over the next 20 years on *Given: 1 The Waterfall: 2 The Illuminating Glass* (1946–66), a large three-dimensional tableau. Duchamp died in 1968.

Legacy

Marcel Duchamp's consistent defiance of established standards and practices in art, his refusal to repeat himself, and his hos-tility to the commercialization of art have pro-foundly influenced later artists.

Duchamp's influence was particularly strong among his circle of close friends—Man Ray, Francis Picabia, John Crotti, Joseph Stella, and John Coverta. He was instrumental in the evo-lution of a New York school of Dadaism. Duchamp's influence was also strong in Surrealism. However, although both the Dadaists and Surrealists benefited from his support of their ideas, his own idiosyncratic style clearly stood apart from both.

Through Duchamp's influence, a major strand of modern art—more conceptual than formal—evolved. Beginning in 1913, he effectively abandoned the traditional methods of painting and moved art away from the visual to the realm of ideas. His sculpture, *Bicycle Wheel*, introduced two major innova-tions to twentieth-century art: the mobile, or sculpture that actually moves, and the "ready-made," a work made from existing, usually commonplace, objects. His conception of the ready-made challenged the basic definition of art.

In the last decade of his life, Duchamp became a cult figure among avant-garde artists in the United States and Europe. Among the artists of the 1950s and 1960s who were influ-enced by his work were the composer JOHN CAGE, Jasper Johns, Robert Morris, ROBERT RAUSCHENBERG, and ANDY WARHOL. Thus, Duchamp was instrumental in the Pop, Minimalist, and Conceptual art of the 1960s and 1970s.

In 1963, a retrospective of his work was held at the Pasadena (California) Museum of Art. Since his death, major exhibitions of his work have been held at prominent museums in the United States, Paris, and Venice.

Domenico

WORLD EVENTS		DUCHAMP'S LIFE
Germany is united	1871	
	1887	Marcel Duchamp is born
Spanish-American War	1898	
	1913	*Nude Descending a Staircase No. 2* is exhibited at Armory show in New York
		Duchamp creates first ready-made, *Bicycle Wheel*
World War I	1914–18	
	1915	Duchamp moves to New York
Russian Revolution	1917	Fountain rejected for exhibition by Society of Independent Artists
	1923	Duchamp returns to France
Great Depression	1929–39	
World War II	1939–45	
	1942	Duchamp returns to New York
Communist China is established	1949	
Korean War	1950–53	
African independence movement begins	1957	
	1968	Duchamp dies
Vietnam War ends	1975	

For Further Reading

D'Harrancourt, Ann, and K. McShine, eds. *Marcel Duchamp*. Exhibition catalogue. New York: Museum of Modern Art, 1973.

Schwarz, Arturo. *The Complete Works of Marcel Duchamp*. New York: H. N. Abrams, 1969.

Tomkins, Calvin. *The Bride & the Bachelors: The Heretical Courtship in Modern Art*. New York: Viking Press, 1965.

Duncan, Isadora

Dance Pioneer
1877–1927

Life and Work

Rejecting her artistic inheritance more thoroughly than almost any other creative artist of any era, Isadora Duncan virtually created a new art form. Modern dance is a fixture of the cultural scene today, but almost nothing like it existed before Duncan's time.

Isadora Duncan was born Angela I. Duncan in San Francisco, California, on May 26, 1877. She may have studied ballet briefly as a child, but in the main her conception of dance was her own creation, formed when she was still in her youth. It was a radical conception indeed. Duncan totally discarded the rules and ways of classical ballet, feeling that they restricted her creative spirit. Instead of wearing ballet slippers, she appeared on stage barefoot. She exalted the natural, and sometimes would dance without illumination from spotlights, preferring the plain ambient light of the hall. Duncan rejected the ballerina's traditional tight-fitting clothing in favor of drape-like coverings that amplified her own expressive motions. These garments, and Duncan's repertoire of gestures, drew on the ideals of ancient Greek art.

Duncan danced with several companies early in her career, but it soon became clear that she could best put her ideas across as a soloist. An 1899 recital in Chicago was poorly received, but in 1900 she went to Paris and gave a series of solo performances there. Instead of the square, steady-beat music previously written for the ballet, Duncan danced to the serious, independent instrumental music of classical composers—LUDWIG VAN BEETHOVEN and FRYDERYK CHOPIN, among them. Initially she was criticized for this, but European audiences took to her innovations; by 1904, Duncan was well established enough to give a performance at the Bayreuth Festival, the seat of power for the followers of the influential nineteenth-century composer RICHARD WAGNER. That year Duncan established in Berlin the first of a series of schools for children designed to perpetuate her ideas. An outspoken writer and commentator on social as well as choreographic issues, Duncan toured Russia several times, first in 1905; she returned there in 1921 and married a young poet named Sergey Esenin who spoke no English (her own Russian was minimal).

Duncan died by strangulation in Nice, France, on September 14, 1927, when her scarf got tangled in the wheel of a car.

Legacy

Appearing alone on stage, Isadora Duncan embodied the idea of individual expression. In a broad sense the whole field of modern dance may be viewed as her legacy, but in particular the concept of dance as a realization of individual feeling, so commonplace today, traces its origins directly to Duncan's career.

When Duncan sought the approval of Parisian audiences, she became one of the first American dancers (and one of the first American fine artists in any field) to gain fame in Europe. Modern dance was one of the first manifestations of a radical American creativity in the arts, and Duncan's utter individualism inspired both American and European dancers to create innovations parallel to hers. The choreographer Loïe Fuller, in whose company Duncan danced as a young woman and who, like Duncan, traveled to France, both influenced and was inspired by Duncan to forge connections between dance and the other arts; Fuller's novel stage lighting effects allied dance with elements of theatrical design.

Duncan's rethinking of the relationship between dance and music liberated her successors from the confinement of rigid musical accompaniments, opening up a whole range of new possibilities. After Duncan, a dancer might express her feelings about a great piece of music, comment on some aspect of it, even satirize it; henceforth, dance would take music as an equal partner. The great and mutually beneficial creative partnerships between twentieth-century choreographers and composers, for example, between MARTHA GRAHAM and AARON COPLAND and between MERCE CUNNINGHAM and JOHN CAGE, would have been impossible without the groundwork Duncan laid.

One of the century's true trailblazers, Isadora Duncan came to grips with the very foundations of her chosen creative medium and upon them built something wholly new.

Manheim

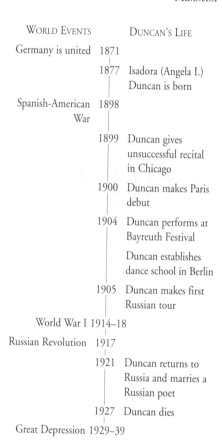

WORLD EVENTS		DUNCAN'S LIFE
Germany is united	1871	
	1877	Isadora (Angela I.) Duncan is born
Spanish-American War	1898	
	1899	Duncan gives unsuccessful recital in Chicago
	1900	Duncan makes Paris debut
	1904	Duncan performs at Bayreuth Festival
		Duncan establishes dance school in Berlin
	1905	Duncan makes first Russian tour
World War I	1914–18	
Russian Revolution	1917	
	1921	Duncan returns to Russia and marries a Russian poet
	1927	Duncan dies
Great Depression	1929–39	

For Further Reading

Blair, Frederika. *Isadora: Portrait of the Artist as a Woman.* New York: McGraw-Hill, 1986.

Duncan, Isadora. *My Life.* New York: Boni & Liveright, 1927.

Duras, Marguerite

Novelist, Dramatist, Filmmaker, Short Story Writer, and Journalist
1914–1996

WORLD EVENTS	DURAS'S LIFE
World War I 1914–18	
	1914 Marguerite Duras is born in French Indochina
Russian Revolution 1917	
Great Depression 1929–39	
	1932 Duras moves to Paris
World War II 1939–45	
Communist China 1949 is established	
	1950 Duras publishes *The Sea Wall* to critical acclaim
Korean War 1950–53	
African independence 1957 movement begins	
	1959 Duras writes script for *Hiroshima, Mon Amour*
Vietnam War ends 1975	Duras writes and directs *India Song*
	1984 Duras publishes *The Lover* and wins Prix Goncourt
Dissolution of 1991 Soviet Union	
South Africa 1994 dismantles apartheid	
	1996 Duras dies

Life and Work

Marguerite Duras breathed emotional and erotic life into the sometimes sterile air of the French novel of the 1960s.

Born Marguerite Donnadieu in 1914 in a small town outside Saigon in what was then French Indochina; she and her two brothers grew up poor, speaking fluent Vietnamese. In 1932, at the age of 17, she moved to France, where she studied law and politics at the Sorbonne in Paris.

Duras started writing when she was quite young and had completed two autobiographical novels before the success of her third, *Un barrage contre le Pacifique* (*The Sea Wall*), in 1950. The novel, set in Indochina, included close observation and pointed criticism of French colonialism and addressed the issues of culture and social injustice that interested Duras throughout her career.

During World War II Duras took part in the French Resistance. Her husband, Robert Antelme, was captured and sent to a concentration camp; Duras wrote of his return in *La Douleur*, published in English as *The War*. She later joined the Communist Party for a brief time. While her leftist politics are evident in her work, Duras focused on the emotional lives of individual characters, not the political movements themselves.

Her first work to gain international recognition was the script she wrote in 1959 for the film *Hiroshima, Mon Amour*, directed by Alain Resnais. The film employs many of the techniques found throughout Duras's later work: dialogue imbued with emotion, pain, and a sense of isolation, and a minimal plot. In 1975 she adapted her play *India Song* for a film that she then directed herself.

In 1984 *L'Amant* (*The Lover*) was published, for which Duras received the Prix Goncourt, a prestigious annual award for French fiction. This semiautobiographical novel about a 15-year-old girl's love affair with a Vietnamese man in his twenties was her most commercially successful novel.

Duras started as a realistic writer using traditional narrative structures; over time, her work became more and more abstract, bringing emotionally paralyzed characters into contact with the destructive powers of love and desire.

Duras, who struggled with alcoholism and illness throughout her life, died in Paris in 1996.

Legacy

Marguerite Duras took part in the birth of the French Nouveau Roman (New Novel) in the 1950s and 1960s, while maintaining her own distinct and impassioned prose style.

Writers associated with the Nouveau Roman, such as Nathalie Sarraute, Michel Butor, and Alain Robbe-Grillet, developed techniques that removed the French novel from its traditional descriptive-narrative format, employing highly stylized narrative and little plot. While Duras brought a similarly spare, occasionally clinical narrative style to novels like *The Square* (1955), she combined it with the intense physicality of her own characteristic prose.

Although carefully crafted, Duras's style was often rough and ungrammatical in its stream-of-consciousness directness. Taking the French literary world by surprise—in part, because she was a woman—she brought a new vitality to the language of the novel. She used fragmented imagery and ideas, juxtaposed images, and used nonchronological structure, consciously seeking to break down the barriers between literature, theater, and film.

Duras played almost as important a role in experimental film as in literature, and she was an innovator in the theater as well. She shared with SAMUEL BECKETT a tendency toward minimalism, as her broken, enigmatic dialogue became briefer and more densely packed with emotion, edging, as she grew older, toward silence and the void.

Watson

For Further Reading

Adler, Laure. *Marguerite Duras: A Life*. Translated by Anne-Marie Glasheen. Chicago: University of Chicago Press, 2000.
Vircondelet, Alain. *Duras: A Biography*. Translated by Thomas Buckley. McLean, Ill.: Dalkey Archive Press, 1994.

Dürer, Albrecht

Painter, Printmaker, and Theoretician
1471–1528

Life and Work

As painter, printmaker, and theoretician, Albrecht Dürer was the greatest German artist of the Renaissance and the first artist to attempt to establish Italian Renaissance ideas in northern Europe.

Born in 1471 in Nuremberg, Germany, Dürer received early training in goldsmithing from his father. The boy was precocious and self-confident, producing a silverpoint self-portrait at the age of 13 that already evidenced his mastery of drawing. Dürer was apprenticed in 1486 to Michael Wolgemut's studio, where he probably worked on illustrations for the famous *Nuremberg Chronicle*, an elaborately illustrated history of the world.

Dürer traveled around Europe from 1490 to 1494, continuing his studies and spending time in Basel and the Netherlands. In 1495, he traveled to Italy to study and later returned for a year in 1505. Dürer's copying of the engravings of Andrea Mantegna gave him familiarity with the Italian style before his Italian trip; upon his return his work united, for the first time, Italian large-scale, idealized forms with northern love of naturalistic detail.

Accomplished in the traditional areas of religious paintings, portraits, and self-portraits,

Dürer achieved his greatest success in print-making, a popular art form that emerged after the introduction of the printing press and the rise of the book publishing industry. A prolific woodcutter and engraver, he became rich through the sale of his work.

The *Apocalypse* (1498) series of woodcut prints based on the Book of Revelation was an early success. Although traditionally Gothic in its complex detail and vigorous action, the prints showed the influence of the Renaissance in the more sculptural figures. Dürer's adoption of Italian Renaissance theory and the impact of his own anatomical studies were apparent in the classically rendered figures of Adam and Eve in *The Fall of Man* (1504). In typical Renaissance fashion, the biblical subject matter of the engraving is infused with ideas from Neoplatonism, such as the symbolic representation of the four humors: cat (choleric), elk (melancholic), rabbit (sanguine), and ox (phlegmatic).

Dürer is regarded as the first great Protestant painter, and the influence of Lutheranism imbued his final works, such as *Last Supper* (1523, woodcut), *Portrait of Melanchthon* (1526, engraving), and *Four Apostles* (1526, painting), with a studied simplicity. Dürer wrote two art theory books, *Instruction of Measurement* (1525) and the first volume of *Four Books on Human Proportion* (1528), leaving other volumes unfinished at his death in 1528.

Legacy

Albrecht Dürer combined Italian theory with northern naturalism to form a distinct, new style, introducing the concept of the "artist" to northern Europe, and elevating the visual arts to a new status. His work was highly regarded by both German humanists and Italian scholars.

His talent as a printmaker elevated the craft to a new level in the visual arts. Furthermore, he was the first northern artist to make himself a celebrity to later generations through self-portraits, diary entries, and correspondence.

Although his work briefly went out of style in the mid-sixteenth century, the popularity of Dürer's prints continued even after his death. Between 1570 and 1630 interest in Dürer's work rose dramatically, producing a phenome-

non known as the "Dürer Renaissance." So many copies and imitations were produced during this period that experts still have considerable difficulty in distinguishing some of the copies from Dürer's originals.

In Italy, Dürer's work was studied by important artists, including CARAVAGGIO. Dürer's religious works were sought out by the devout as well as by connoisseurs. Many pieces, especially *Small Passion* (1510–11), were reproduced as devotional images.

In the eighteenth century, German intellectuals began to regard Dürer as a founder of German art. A scholarly catalogue of Dürer's works was published in 1778. In Germany, his name became increasingly associated with growing national pride

Like LEONARDO DA VINCI, Dürer believed that artistic genius brought the artist closer to the creative power of God, which gave religious significance to his work regardless of the subject. Today, Dürer is widely regarded as the greatest artist in German history.

Domenico

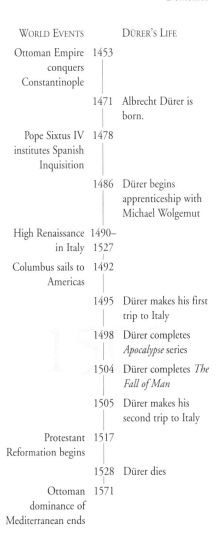

WORLD EVENTS		DÜRER'S LIFE
Ottoman Empire conquers Constantinople	1453	
	1471	Albrecht Dürer is born.
Pope Sixtus IV institutes Spanish Inquisition	1478	
	1486	Dürer begins apprenticeship with Michael Wolgemut
High Renaissance in Italy	1490–1527	
Columbus sails to Americas	1492	
	1495	Dürer makes his first trip to Italy
	1498	Dürer completes *Apocalypse* series
	1504	Dürer completes *The Fall of Man*
	1505	Dürer makes his second trip to Italy
Protestant Reformation begins	1517	
	1528	Dürer dies
Ottoman dominance of Mediterranean ends	1571	

For Further Reading

Anzelewsky, F. *Dürer: His Art and Life*. London: G. Fraser, 1982.

Hutchison, Jane Campbell. *Albrecht Dürer: A Biography*. Princeton, N.J.: Princeton University Press, 1990.

Panofsky, E. *Life and Art of Albrecht Dürer*. Princeton, N.J.: Princeton University Press, 1955.

Dylan, Bob

Singer-Songwriter
1941–

Life and Work

Emerging from the revival of folk music that flourished in American cities in the early 1960s, Bob Dylan became one of the most influential figures in the history of rock and roll.

Dylan was born Robert Allen Zimmerman on May 24, 1941, in Duluth, Minnesota; the son of a furniture store owner, he grew up in the small, mining-oriented city of Hibbing. He enrolled at the University of Minnesota in 1959, planning to study art. But the city's

WORLD EVENTS	DYLAN'S LIFE
World War II 1939–45	
1941	Bob Dylan is born Robert Allen Zimmerman
Communist China 1949 is established	
Korean War 1950–53	
African independence 1957 movement begins	
1959	Dylan enrolls at University of Minnesota
1961	Dylan moves to New York's Greenwich Village
1962	Dylan releases debut album, *Bob Dylan*
1965	Dylan performs with electric accompaniment at Newport Folk Festival
1969	Dylan releases *Nashville Skyline* LP
Vietnam War ends 1975	
1979	Dylan turns to Christian themes with *Slow Train Coming* LP
Dissolution of 1991 Soviet Union	
South Africa dis- 1994 mantles apartheid	
1998	Dylan releases *Time out of Mind* album

growing folk coffeehouse scene drew his attention, and he started performing under the name Bob Dylan, taking the name from the poet Dylan Thomas. A 1960 encounter with bluesman Jesse Fuller led to the infusion of blues into Dylan's music; he also modeled his attitude and gravelly vocals after those of folksinger Woody Guthrie.

In 1961 Dylan moved his base of operations to New York's Greenwich Village and visited the dying Guthrie in the hospital. The legendary talent scout John Hammond signed him to Columbia Records; his first album, 1962's *Bob Dylan*, offered folk and blues standards. In 1963 *The Freewheelin' Bob Dylan* served notice that Dylan was a major songwriting force; that album's "Blowin' in the Wind" was recorded by the folk group Peter, Paul & Mary and became an almost universally known anthem of the turbulent 1960s.

By 1964 Dylan had begun to develop a more consciously literary style. He reached the apex of his popularity after his performance at the 1965 Newport Folk Festival, where, to the dismay of folk partisans, he sang to the accompaniment of amplified electric instruments. The single release "Like a Rolling Stone" showed off the new sound and shattered pop conventions. His albums of this period, including *Highway 61 Revisited* and *Blonde on Blonde*, are considered rock classics.

Injured in a 1966 motorcycle accident whose severity has been debated, Dylan emerged in the late 1960s with a quieter, more folk-oriented sound, and recorded the country-tinged *Nashville Skyline* in 1969. Through the following decades Dylan was never creatively silent for long and continued to explore new genres. *Slow Train Coming* (1979) inaugurated a series of Christian-themed works. His 1998 release *Time out of Mind* recaptured the intensity of his early recordings, and through the 1990s he performed to reliably large and enthusiastic crowds.

Legacy

More than any other individual, Bob Dylan defined rock as an art form with serious intentions, and no rock subgenre remains untouched by his impact.

Early on, Dylan inaugurated a new era in popular music simply through the sound of his voice, a nasal rasp that was as far as could be imagined from the smooth standards of pop, and even from the raw energy of early rock and

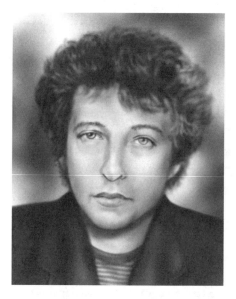

roll. Dylan was one of the first "singer-songwriters"; under his influence popular music fans would come to value honest representation of personal experience as much as beautiful or powerful singing.

When Dylan did turn to rock, he made one innovation after another. Inspired in his electric experiment by the reinvigoration of rock and roll at the hands of the so-called British Invasion bands, Dylan in the 1960s wielded an influence notable for its trans-Atlantic reach. The Byrds' recording of Dylan's "Mr. Tambourine Man" set British music on a path that reflected his poetic ambitions, and many British songwriters, including JOHN LENNON, Van Morrison, and T. Rex's Marc Bolan, would at times adopt a bristly, confessional tone that showed marks of their encounters with Dylan's work.

The genre of folk-rock flowed from Dylan's early electric albums, and the long effort to merge country and rock, an idea that was still resounding in the 1990s, was partly set in motion by *Nashville Skyline* and by its predecessor, *John Wesley Harding*. Bruce Springsteen, another John Hammond discovery who was perhaps American rock and roll's biggest star of the late 1970s and 1980s, made his name with a narrative style and a grandiose populism profoundly indebted to Dylan; although a singer of much greater gifts, Springsteen also imitated Dylan vocally. As evidence of Dylan's influence continued to accumulate in the 1990s, it seemed clear that he had altered the path of a genre's development in a way that few other musicians of any epoch or culture had done.

Manheim

For Further Reading

Shelton, Robert. *No Direction Home: The Life and Music of Bob Dylan.* New York: W. Morrow Beech Tree, 1986.
Spitz, Bob. *Dylan: A Biography.* New York: McGraw-Hill, 1989.

Eakins, Thomas

Painter and Photographer
1844–1916

Life and Work

Painter, photographer, and teacher, Thomas Eakins was the leading American Realist of the late nineteenth century.

Born into a working-class family in Philadelphia in 1844, Eakins may have acquired his interest in art from his father, an amateur artist. Although he studied at the Pennsylvania Academy of the Fine Arts, he was primarily influenced by his experience at the Ecole des Beaux Arts in Paris from 1866 to 1870, when he studied under the prominent artist Jean-Leon Gérome. While in Spain, his study of the works of DIEGO VELÁZQUEZ and José Ribera provided Eakins with a precise approach to painting and an unwavering devotion to depicting real life in his work.

Eakins returned to Philadelphia in 1870 and launched his career with his father's financial support. An early work, *Max Schmitt in a Single Scull* (1871), depicting an amateur rower resting in his boat on the Schuylkill River, demonstrates his brilliance as a painter. Its dramatic light and exacting approach typifies his work. *The Gross Clinic* (1875), his most famous painting, portrays a famous surgeon presiding over an operation at Jefferson Medical College in Philadelphia. Its unsparing accuracy in depicting such stark subject matter shocked viewers and stirred a controversy that led to its rejection

by the jury for the Centennial Exhibition for which it had been painted.

His commitment to realism led Eakins to experiment with photography, and he often incorporated photographic effects into his painting, for example, *The Swimming Hole* (1883). Eakins was hired as a teacher at the Pennsylvania Academy of the Fine Arts and became director of instruction there in 1882, instituting a curriculum that placed the study of the human figure at its core. His insistence on the use of nude models, even in coed classes, led to his dismissal in 1886.

Late in 1886 Eakins traveled west to the Dakota territory and soon after met the poet WALT WHITMAN, with whom he developed a friendship. His portrait of Whitman (*Walt Whitman*, 1887), with its somber light and deep insight into character, demonstrates why his portraiture is often compared to REMBRANDT's work. *Mrs. Edith Mahon* (1904), which shows its subject alone and grieving, demonstrates the sadness that pervades much of Eakins's portrait work after 1887.

After Eakins's death in 1916, memorial exhibitions in New York in 1917 and in Philadelphia in 1918 increased public enthusiasm for his work.

Legacy

Primarily a portrait painter, Thomas Eakins was known for the utter honesty with which he represented his subjects. Previously, portrait artists had flattered their subjects by depicting them with their social status intact or falsely endowing them with beauty or dignity. Eakins emphatically broke with this tradition by presenting people in a more candid manner that revealed their inner truth, sadness, and strength.

In his quest for realism, Eakins was among the first American artists to experiment with photographic images of the human figure, including the figure in motion, and among the first to incorporate photographic studies (often of his students) into his paintings.

Under his directorship, the Pennsylvania Academy of Fine Arts became established as an important center for the study of figure drawing, yet few of his students directly imitated his style.

Like American painter WINSLOW HOMER, Eakins never received the recognition that he believed he deserved. Today, however, he is regarded as one of the most important painters

of the nineteenth century. Perhaps even more than Homer, Eakins stands as a representative of a distinctly American form of Realism: frank, insightful, pragmatic, and unconcerned with sentimentality or superficial beauty. Eakins marks the moment in American history when the visual arts, like literature, began to find a distinctly American expression. Eakins did not introduce a new style, but he did give shape to a new attitude. His brand of Realism transformed the role of portraiture from an idealizer of beauty and status to a conveyor of psychological depth.

Domenico

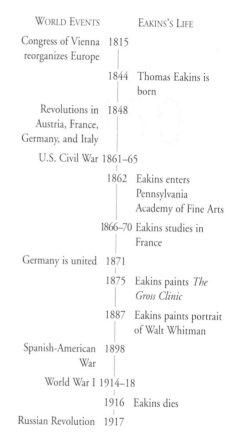

WORLD EVENTS		EAKINS'S LIFE
Congress of Vienna reorganizes Europe	1815	
	1844	Thomas Eakins is born
Revolutions in Austria, France, Germany, and Italy	1848	
U.S. Civil War	1861–65	
	1862	Eakins enters Pennsylvania Academy of Fine Arts
	1866–70	Eakins studies in France
Germany is united	1871	
	1875	Eakins paints *The Gross Clinic*
	1887	Eakins paints portrait of Walt Whitman
Spanish-American War	1898	
World War I	1914–18	
	1916	Eakins dies
Russian Revolution	1917	

For Further Reading

Homer, William Innes. *Thomas Eakins: His Life and Art*. New York: Abbeville Press, 1992

Johns, Elizabeth. *Thomas Eakins: The Heroism of Modern Life*. Princeton, N.J.: Princeton University Press, 1983.

Eliot, George

(Mary Ann Evans)

Novelist

1819–1880

Life and Work

"George Eliot" was the pseudonym of Mary Ann (or Marian) Evans, one of the most influential British novelists of the nineteenth century.

Mary Ann Evans defied convention as she found the path to a creative life. She was born November 22, 1819, on an estate where her father worked, in England's Warwickshire district. Her boarding school teachers led her toward evangelical religion. After her mother's death in 1836, Evans managed her father's household. In 1841, the family moved to Foleshill, near Coventry, where Eliot became friends with Charles Bray, a factory owner and radical activist. Bray's brother-in-law Charles Hennell had written a book questioning the validity of the Christian faith, which focused her own growing religious doubts. Her intellectual activities were a major source of friction with her conservative, conventional father. For a time, to her father's dismay, she stopped going to church.

After her father's death in 1849, Evans traveled and studied in Switzerland. In 1851 she moved to London to try to make a living as a writer and editor. She participated in the literary and intellectual life of London; among the literary figures she met was George Lewes, a writer trapped in a crumbling marriage. Lewes and Evans fell in love, and in 1854—alienating her family—they moved in together.

Lewes encouraged her to write fiction; when she published her first short story she did so under the pen name "George Eliot" to shield herself from public controversy over her personal life. ("George" was in honor of Lewes.)

Eliot's first major novel, *Adam Bede* (1859), is a realistic tale of rural tragedy that was a major success, with eight printings in a year. Its title character may have been based on Eliot's father. Several other of her novels, including *The Mill on the Floss* (1860) and *Silas Marner* (1861), are also rooted in the English countryside. Most ambitious was *Middlemarch* (1871–72), which Henry James once called "a treasure-house of detail." The novel interweaves a basic story of a woman's unhappiness in her small-town life and marriage with a multitude of other plot lines that involved every level of British society. Eliot's last novel, *Daniel Deronda* (1876), assailed anti-Semitism.

In 1880, after Lewes's death, Eliot married her business manager John Cross, who was more than 20 years her junior. Seven months later, on December 22, 1880, she died in London.

Legacy

George Eliot wrote fiction on a grand scale that attempted to encompass both the inner lives of individuals and the fabric of society. She wrote not of great deeds but of people who "lived faithfully a hidden life and rest in unvisited tombs," as she put it in *Middlemarch*.

Sometimes compared to the panorama-creating Russian novelist LEO TOLSTOY, Eliot,

especially in her later novels, captured in prose the relationship of individual to larger society more profoundly than any other English writer of her time. Despite her freethinking ways, Eliot was not a conscious innovator; she worked in well-established forms, taking as her underlying subject the emerging content of modernity. She wrote romantic tragedies, but they were studies of inner lives, not Gothic grotesqueries. She was capable of highly detailed realism, but her characters were never mere social types.

Eliot was forgotten for a time after her death but has been greatly admired in the twentieth century for her insight and sophistication "It was really George Eliot who started it all," wrote the twentieth-century British novelist D. H. Lawrence. "It was she started putting action inside." Lawrence meant that her fiction was among the first to focus on the psychology of her characters. For all the sprawling detail of *Middlemarch*, at its center lie the inner feelings of its heroine, Dorothea Brooke.

Eliot drew on her own life in her fiction, on the confining situations she had escaped; while her work is not overtly protofeminist, her novels are especially insightful in their treatment of women. Eliot was praised by the twentieth-century novelist VIRGINIA WOOLF, who wrote in 1919 that *Middlemarch* was "one of the few English novels written for grown-up people." Indeed, with Eliot, the English novel became an intellectually serious and ambitious form of writing.

Manheim

WORLD EVENTS		ELIOT'S LIFE
Congress of Vienna reorganizes Europe	1815	
	1819	Mary Ann Evans is born
Revolutions in Austria, France, Germany, and Italy	1848	
	1851	Evans moves to London
	1854	Evans begins living with George Lewes
	1859	Eliot publishes *Adam Bede*
	1860	Eliot publishes *The Mill on the Floss*
	1861	Eliot publishes *Silas Marner*
U.S. Civil War	1861–65	
Germany is united	1871	
	1871–72	*Middlemarch*, Eliot's masterwork, is published
	1876	Eliot publishes *Daniel Deronda*
	1880	Eliot dies
Spanish-American War	1898	

For Further Reading

Dodd, Valerie. *George Eliot: An Intellectual Life*. New York: St. Martin's Press, 1990.

Ermarth, Elizabeth Deeds. *George Eliot*. Boston: Twayne Publishers, 1985.

Karl, Frederick R. *George Eliot, Voice of a Century: A Biography*. New York: W. W. Norton, 1995.

Ellington, Duke

Composer and Bandleader
1899–1974

Life and Work

Duke Ellington's works held the arts of composition and improvisation in delicate balance. He is considered one of the most significant figures in the history of jazz and one of the greatest composers of the twentieth century generally.

The son of a butler, he was born Edward Kennedy Ellington on April 29, 1899, in Washington, D.C. Initially he studied the piano with classical music in mind, but ragtime piano music won him over; his first known composition was the "Soda Fountain Rag" of 1914.

Moving to New York in 1923, he organized a band that gained recognition as it acquired distinctive soloists and as Ellington's compositional reach grew. With the "East St. Louis Toodle-Oo" of 1926 and the "Black and Tan Fantasy" of the following year, Ellington hit on a distinctive style that led to his group's installation as house band at Harlem's famed Cotton Club.

At the Cotton Club, Ellington's band grew to include some of the players who would help him realize his signature style and who would accompany him into the realm of worldwide fame after the smash success of 1930's "Mood Indigo." Ellington left the Cotton Club in 1931; for the rest of the decade and much of the rest of his life he profitably led his band on tours of the United States and Europe. In the 1930s and 1940s

Ellington's orchestral palette seemed to take on new shades with every piece he composed.

Ellington's accomplishments rested on three main innovations. First, he deepened his ability to integrate improvised jazz solos into a composed piece. The 1940 *Concerto for Cootie*, written with the skills of trumpeter Cootie Williams in mind, was one of many pieces that seemed to transcend the duality of improvisation and composition. Second, instead of simply setting up contrasts between groups of instruments, Ellington combined individual instruments to form unique orchestral colors, in the manner of a classical symphonic composer. Finally, Ellington broadened the jazz form to include large, abstract structures, beginning with the *Crescendo and Diminuendo in Blue* of 1937. Ellington's most famous recording was 1941's "Take the 'A' Train," a sprightly piece in pure swing style composed by pianist Billy Strayhorn.

Later in life Ellington wrote a number of works that were almost jazz symphonies; one of the first, 1943's *Black, Brown and Beige*, had a mixed reception at its premiere, but is now considered one of his greatest works. Ellington died in New York on May 24, 1974.

Legacy

Duke Ellington's finely crafted ensemble works had a profound impact on the future of jazz, over both the short term and the span of generations.

In the 1930s Ellington was first the progenitor and later one of the chief practitioners of the big band movement in jazz. When he appeared on the scene, the small combos of New Orleans and Chicago had begun to make a strong impact on New York's jazz scene, and powerful soloists such as LOUIS ARMSTRONG seemed to represent the future of jazz. Building on the contributions of bandleader Fletcher Henderson, Ellington gave new weight to the roles of the bandleader, composer, and arranger, all of which he filled himself; in the late 1930s swing bands of Benny Goodman, Tommy Dorsey, and their contemporaries, these functions might be divided among several individuals.

Ellington's own skills as a pianist have sometimes been underestimated. In truth, he possessed a strong sense of how to decorate a melody both distinctively and with restraint, and he influenced the style of the economical and iconoclastic Thelonious Monk, among others.

Ellington's long-range impact lay beyond swing, beyond the piano, beyond even his miniature masterpieces of the 1930s and 1940s. By elevating the role and range of jazz composition, Ellington expanded the creative realm of jazz to encompass the full sweep of human experience. Ellington's influence resounded not only in MILES DAVIS's ambitious collaborations with composer Gil Evans, but in such large, jazz-based dramatic works of the 1980s and 1990s as Anthony Davis's *X*, (a 1986 work that dealt with the life of black leader Malcolm X) and the various album-length compositions of trumpeter Wynton Marsalis. Jazz has had its share of individual geniuses, but as an art form it came of age with Duke Ellington.

Manheim

WORLD EVENTS		ELLINGTON'S LIFE
Spanish-American War	1898	
	1899	Edward Kennedy Ellington is born
	1914	Ellington composes his first known piece
World War I 1914–18		
Russian Revolution	1917	
	1923	Ellington moves to New York City
	1927	Ellington releases "Black and Tan Fantasy"
Great Depression 1929–39		
	1930	Ellington releases "Mood Indigo"
	1931	Ellington leaves Cotton Club and begins touring
	1937	Ellington releases *Crescendo and Diminuendo in Blue*
World War II 1939–45		
	1941	Ellington records "Take the 'A' Train"
	1943	Ellington's symphonic piece *Black, Brown, and Beige* premieres
Communist China 1949 is established		
Korean War 1950–53		
African independence movement begins	1957	
	1974	Ellington dies
Vietnam War ends	1975	

For Further Reading

Collier, James Lincoln. *Duke Ellington*. New York: Oxford University Press, 1987.

Ellington, Duke. *Music Is My Mistress*. Garden City, N.Y.: Doubleday, 1973.

Hasse, John Edward. *Beyond Category: The Life and Genius of Duke Ellington*. New York: Simon & Schuster, 1993.

Faulkner, William

Novelist

1897–1962

Life and Work

William Faulkner, the most prominent writer of southern fiction, and a writer of dense and experimental modernist works, expressed the universal struggles of human existence in a distinctly American context.

WORLD EVENTS		FAULKNER'S LIFE
Germany is united	1871	
	1897	William Faulkner is born
Spanish-American War	1898	
World War I	1914–18	
Russian Revolution	1917	
	1924	Faulkner publishes collection of poetry, *The Marble Faun*
Great Depression	1929–39	
	1929	Faulkner publishes *Sartoris* and *The Sound and the Fury*
	1931	Faulkner publishes *Sanctuary*
World War II	1939–45	
Communist China is established	1949	Faulkner is awarded the Nobel Prize for Literature
Korean War	1950–53	
African independence movement begins	1957	
	1962	Faulkner dies
Vietnam War ends	1975	

Faulkner was born on September 25, 1897, in New Albany, Mississippi. He dropped out of high school but continued his education on his own, by reading extensively. After spending some time in the military, he returned home and began publishing poems and short stories in local magazines.

His first published book was a collection of poetry, *The Marble Faun* (1924). His first novel, *Soldier's Pay,* came soon after in 1926. In 1929 he published the two novels that first gained him critical attention, *Sartoris* and *The Sound and the Fury.* The latter used an experimental and innovative narrative—four different points of view in which past and present events overlap. Faulkner's main themes, the disintegration of family and the struggle to endure, are present in both novels.

His next novel, *Sanctuary* (1931), was a portrait of the evil of humanity. The graphic violence and the depravity of the characters caused some controversy upon its publication and increased public interest; it became one of his best-selling novels.

In the 1930s Faulkner published *As I Lay Dying* (1930), *Light in August* (1932), and *Absalom, Absalom!* (1936). All of these works used increasingly experimental narrative techniques, including the methodical revelation of characters and events through shifting points of view and the use of flashback. They also address the issues of southern race relations and connection to the land that mark Faulkner's work as distinctly of the American South. His final novels, grouped together as the *Snopes Trilogy,* include *The Hamlet* (1940), *The Town* (1957), and *The Mansion* (1959).

Faulkner also wrote screenplays and short stories—and his short stories were often set in the same fictional Yoknapatawpha County as his novels. One short story collection, *Go Down, Moses* (1942), is noted as one of his major works and is particularly widely read. The historical development of the county and its inhabitants can be followed over decades throughout his work.

Faulkner was awarded the Nobel Prize for Literature in 1949. In the 1950s he traveled and lectured at universities in the United States and Europe. His health declined as he grew older, due in part to his alcoholism, and he died of a heart attack on July 6, 1962.

Legacy

William Faulkner's technical innovations and the density of his stories and complex characterization made his work some of the most innovative and difficult of any American writer of the twentieth century.

Influenced by T. S. Eliot, Sherwood Anderson, and JAMES JOYCE, Faulkner moved into new areas with his technical sophistication, narrative experimentation, complex stylistic and thematic patterning, and focused attention on the insular life of the South.

Along with Joyce's *Ulysses,* Faulkner's *The Sound and the Fury* was key in integrating the use of so-called stream-of-consciousness prose into literature. He influenced many writers, notably the Beat writer Jack Kerouac. Faulkner's many narrative innovations continue to have a lasting effect on experimental American writers. Thomas Pynchon, Don DeLillo, and David Foster Wallace have all drawn on his multi-layered, ambiguously narrated work in their own experimental fiction. Latin American authors Carlos Fuentes and GABRIEL GARCÍA MÁRQUEZ have also been influenced by Faulkner. Márquez's *One Hundred Years of Solitude* is a novel that, like Faulkner's Yoknapatawpha County stories, traces the life of a fictional community, Macondo. The tradition of southern writing has been carried on by writers including Alice Walker and TONI MORRISON.

Watson

For Further Reading

Honnighausen, Lothar. *Faulkner: Masks and Metaphors.* Jackson: University Press of Mississippi, 1997.

Weinstein, Philip M., ed. *Faulkner.* Cambridge Companions to Literature. Cambridge: Cambridge University Press, 1995.

Fela

Songwriter and Vocalist
1938–1997

Life and Work

An innovator whose antiauthoritarian music stirred resistance to the military regime of the West African nation of Nigeria, Fela Anikulapo Kuti created a new fusion of African and Western music.

A member of the Yoruba ethnic group, Fela (widely known by that name alone) was born October 15, 1938, in the town of Abeokuta, Nigeria. His mother was an activist who worked toward Nigeria's independence from England (achieved in 1960); his father was a priest and teacher. Fela was sent to London to finish his education and soon enrolled at Trinity College of Music, studying classical piano and, on the side, leading an African jazz band called Koola Lobitos. Fela brought the band to the United States in 1969; they had little success, but Fela met with and absorbed the thinking of the black radical activists Angela Davis and Stokely Carmichael.

Fela became one of the most famous musicians in Africa in the early 1970s. His concerts were Dionysian affairs in which the performance of a single song might extend an hour or more. A single performance number often included a spoken passage on a political theme; it might be broken down to a short slogan that would be tossed back and forth in call and response by Fela and his background singers or the audience.

The sweep of his performances, and his skill in creating large structures in which different musical elements were matched with different ways of addressing an audience, came through only imperfectly on the more than 50 albums he released. His songs included African, Caribbean, and American elements in a mixture he dubbed "Afrobeat." They mocked the rich and powerful, taking particular aim at Nigeria's dictatorship; his 1976 hit "Zombie" attacked the military mindset.

In 1977 soldiers burned Fela's compound to the ground, throwing his mother out of a window and inflicting upon her what would turn out to be fatal injuries; Fela later responded by traveling with his 27 wives to the ruling party's headquarters and placing his mother's coffin on the steps of the building. He continued to tangle with authorities for the rest of his life; Fela served a prison term in 1984 and 1985 after a dubious currency-smuggling arrest. He died from heart failure related to AIDS in Lagos, Nigeria on August 2, 1997.

Legacy

At the peak of Fela's influence in the 1970s and 1980s, he harnessed music and politics with a potency few other artists have equaled.

In both realms the figure he cut was sharp, outrageous, and unprecedented. His mix of Western and African elements in his music was unique and attracted listeners of various musical backgrounds. Fela developed a strong following among progressive young West Africans; his burial drew an estimated one million mourners. Even after his death, as Nigeria struggled toward a democratic form of government at the end of the 1990s, his ideas and his mistreatment at the hands of the military emerged as national issues.

Fela is perhaps rivaled only by Jamaican reggae star BOB MARLEY as an artist whose words had direct and widespread political impact. His music's themes differed in some respects from Marley's, whose lyric message was couched in general terms of confrontation, uplift, and redemption, whereas Fela was often pointed and specific. He could exhort his audiences with indignant or inspirational lyrics, but often his message was delivered with humor, which made it even more dangerous to the authorities. Ultimately, Fela was one of the great satirical minds of twentieth-century music, and he sharpened his verbal assault with a supremely intelligent musical language.

In another way, too, Fela may be compared with Marley: both musicians, though deeply rooted in their own cultures and times, developed an international appeal that outlasted their lifetimes. Fela, nearly as much as Marley, became something of a hero among idealistic young people in the United States and Europe, and his 1980s collaborations with British rock musician Peter Gabriel not only brought him new listeners but also did much to establish an interest in African music in progressive rock circles. At the turn of the century Fela's legacy was being carried forward by his son Femi Kuti, who has also demonstrated an appeal to Western audiences.

Manheim

WORLD EVENTS		FELA'S LIFE
Great Depression	1929–39	
	1938	Fela Anikulapo Kuti is born in Abeokuta, Nigeria
World War II	1939–45	
Communist China is established	1949	
Korean War	1950–53	
African independence movement begins	1957	
	1969	Fela and his band visit United States
Vietnam War ends	1975	
	1976	Fela satirizes Nigerian military with "Zombie"
	1977	Fela's home is burned by Nigerian soldiers
	1984	Fela is imprisoned on questionable smuggling charges
Dissolution of Soviet Union	1991	
South Africa dismantles apartheid	1994	
	1997	Fela dies

For Further Reading

Broughton, Simon, Mark Ellingham, David Muddyman, and Richard Trillo, eds. *World Music: The Rough Guide.* New York: Penguin, 1999.

Stewart, Gary. *Breakout: Profiles in African Rhythm.* Chicago: University of Chicago Press, 1992.

Flaubert, Gustave

Novelist and Short Story Writer
1821–1880

World Events		Flaubert's Life
Congress of Vienna reorganizes Europe	1815	
	1821	Gustave Flaubert is born
	1844	Flaubert returns to Croisset from Paris
Revolutions in Austria, France, Germany, and Italy	1848	
	1849	Flaubert completes *The Temptation of Saint Anthony*
	1857	Flaubert publishes *Madame Bovary* and is prosecuted for and acquitted of blasphemy
U.S. Civil War	1861–65	
	1862	Flaubert publishes *Salammbo*
	1869	Flaubert publishes *A Sentimental Education*
Germany is united	1871	
	1877	Flaubert publishes *Three Stories*
	1880	Flaubert dies
Spanish-American War	1898	

Life and Work

Gustave Flaubert, with his acerbic wit, keen psychological observation, and painstaking stylistic precision, introduced an unprecedented emotional distance to the relationship between author and character.

Flaubert was born in Rouen in 1821, the son of a successful surgeon. As a young man, he studied law in Paris, but in 1844 he became ill with a nervous disorder similar to epilepsy. He returned to his parents' home in Croisset, a small town outside of Rouen, to devote himself to writing.

Flaubert's early novel *La Tentation de Saint Antoine* (*The Temptation of Saint Anthony*, completed in 1849) was inspired by his ambition to write a French Faust story, a story of a man who sells his soul to the Devil. When friends didn't like the novel, he put it in a drawer and began what would be his most celebrated work, *Madame Bovary*.

Madame Bovary (1857) is a detailed portrait of a young woman unhappy with her dull marriage, who commits adultery in a search for passion. Through this subject, which Flaubert himself called "vulgar," he created a biting satire of bourgeois life, narrated dispassionately and analytically, which distanced him from his characters. Nevertheless, he conveyed a strong empathy for the young woman, trapped by small-town social values, reserving the depth of his contempt for an oppressive and hypocritical society instead.

When the novel was published, Flaubert, his publisher, and the printers were prosecuted for blasphemy and immorality. Flaubert and the others went before the same board that Charles-Pierre Baudelaire would appear before only a few months later on similar charges, but, unlike Baudelaire, they were acquitted.

None of Flaubert's later works garnered the popular acclaim that *Madame Bovary* did in the wake of its obscenity trial, but he produced several more plays, the historical novel *Salammbo* (1862), and a revised edition of the novel *L'Education sentimentale* (*A Sentimental Education*, 1869), begun early in his career. The late work that has received the most critical attention is the volume *Trois contes: "Un coeur simple," "La Legende du Saint Julien l'Hospitalier," et "Héroidas"* (*Three Stories: A Simple Heart, The Legend of St. Julian the Hospitaler, and Herodias*), published in 1877. These stories are widely considered to be among the best short fiction in French literature.

Bouvard and Pécuchet, the novel that Flaubert left unfinished, tells the story of two simple men attempting to master all of human knowledge. As they do, they encounter, embody, and discuss every kind of prejudice and bit of misinformation that might exist. Both this book and Flaubert's *Dictionary of Received Ideas* mock the clichés of popular culture and contain sharp attacks on bourgeois culture and social attitudes.

Flaubert died of a brain hemorrhage in 1880.

Legacy

Gustave Flaubert is often hailed as the father of the Realist movement that developed soon after he published *Madame Bovary*.

Flaubert's friends, including writers George Sand, Ivan Turgenev, and Henry James, were all affected by his acute psychological portraiture. The Realists who followed, notably Emile Zola, Guy de Maupassant—who was a protégé of Flaubert's—and Anatole France, all hailed his work as an important predecessor of their own.

Flaubert created a form of the novel as a tightly constructed work of art in which he used narrative and structural systems to convey meaning. Emma Bovary's boredom and inability to communicate with the other inhabitants of her small town are expressed through repeated symbols, the novels in which she immerses herself, and the banality of the objects and people around her, instead of direct description by an emotionally involved narrator.

This new novel of Flaubert's was strikingly different from those of the Romantics who preceded him. His narrative dissociation can be seen as an early step towards the sense of alienation that filled the works of many of the Modernist writers of the early twentieth century, and it certainly opened the form to any number of innovations by these writers. Marcel Proust, André Gide, Jean-Paul Sartre, and Vladimir Nabokov were all great admirers of Flaubert's art.

Flaubert drew meaning out of a chaotic universe of conflicting information; his belief in the power of art to create beauty and perfection from this universe was behind the meticulous style and structure of his greatest works.

Watson

For Further Reading

DeMan, Paul, ed. *Madame Bovary: Backgrounds and Sources, Essays in Criticism.* New York: W. W. Norton, 1990.
Porter, Lawrence M. *Critical Essays on Gustave Flaubert.* Indianapolis, Ind.: Macmillan, 1986.

Franklin, Aretha

Vocalist
1942–

Life and Work

Aretha Franklin's informal title, the "Queen of Soul," is well merited, for she has been by far soul music's most prominent female vocalist.

Franklin was raised in the bosom of the Baptist church's African-American branch; her father, C. L. Franklin, was a preacher with a wide reputation. She was born in Memphis on March 25, 1942, but lived in Detroit from the age of two. Her father's church played host to such giants of gospel singing as Clara Ward and MAHALIA JACKSON, who was a major stylistic influence.

Franklin began recording gospel music in 1956. Inspired by the crossover success of gospel star Sam Cooke, she began to dream of a pop career. In 1960 she was signed to the Columbia label and recorded a dozen albums between 1960 and 1966. These releases, many of which backed Franklin with a subdued accompaniment, failed to tap her powers fully.

As was also true of Wilson Pickett and other soul artists, Franklin's creative breakthrough came when she returned briefly to the South. Signing with Atlantic in 1966, she was sent by label head Jerry Wexler to record at the Fame Studios in Muscle Shoals, Alabama, the site of many key soul recordings. The session crackled with creative tensions, but yielded "I Never Loved a Man (The Way I Love You)," a mag-

nificent recording that brought Franklin's gospel piano to the fore and set the tone for a string of hits over the next five years. Many of them, including 1967's "Respect" (from the *I Never Loved a Man* album) and 1968's "Think," are considered classics of soul music.

Over the next three decades Franklin was treated by concert audiences as a living legend. She began recording for Arista in 1980 and had some success working in the label's upbeat dance pop style; the 1985 LP *Who's Zoomin' Who* was particularly successful commercially. The dimensions of Franklin's vocal gifts were made startlingly apparent when she substituted for the ailing tenor Luciano Pavarotti and sang the Puccini opera aria "Nessun dorma" on the 1998 Grammy awards program.

Legacy

At her peak in the late 1960s and early 1970s, Aretha Franklin's vocal art displayed a triad of virtues rarely brought together by the same singer: sheer virtuosity, down-to-earth emotional intensity, and a gospel-based sense of moral authority and power. No singer during the following decades could reassemble the same constellation of vocal powers, and Franklin stands as arguably the greatest vocalist of the twentieth century's second half.

Franklin had few direct followers; her voice was really one of a kind, and less emotionally raw genres have overtaken soul in popularity. Nevertheless, she established a benchmark against which subsequent vocalists had to measure themselves. Black secular vocals had always been rooted in the church, but after Franklin, gospel-based, ecstatic virtuosity became pervasive in the genre known as r&b, or rhythm and blues.

Aspects of her vocal technique and personality shaped the approaches of younger singers, from the self-assured sass and exclamatory, multi-octave vocal embellishments of Chaka Khan in the 1970s to the sheer athleticism of the divas of the 1990s. Her album, *I Never Loved a Man (The Way I Love You)*, has remained in print continuously since its release.

Franklin's legacy goes beyond mere technique and continuing chart popularity. Her music seemed to represent strength and dignity in a way that took it beyond the realm of entertainment; Franklin herself had a powerful physical presence, a regal quality, that affected African-

American female vocalists as fundamentally as had BESSIE SMITH half a century earlier. Her music, like that of JAMES BROWN, has been linked with the civil rights movement and the long shift in consciousness it represented; indeed, "Respect," something of a civil rights anthem in its day, became one for the feminist movement as well. Franklin was and is a force, both vocally and personally. Not a songwriter nor a creative artist in the conventional sense, she did what few pure vocal stylists have done—she changed the way people think.

Manheim

WORLD EVENTS		FRANKLIN'S LIFE
World War II	1939–45	
	1942	Aretha Franklin is born
Communist China is established	1949	
Korean War	1950–53	
	1956	Franklin makes first recordings
African independence movement begins	1957	
	1960	Franklin signs with Columbia label
	1966	Franklin moves to Atlantic label
	1967	Franklin releases *I Never Loved a Man (The Way I Love You)* LP
Vietnam War ends	1975	
	1980	Franklin signs with Arista label
	1985	Franklin releases *Who's Zoomin' Who* LP
Dissolution of Soviet Union	1991	
South Africa dismantles apartheid	1994	
	1998	Franklin sings opera on Grammy awards program

For Further Reading

Bego, Mark. *Aretha Franklin: The Queen of Soul.* New York: St. Martin's Press, 1989.
Franklin, Aretha, with David Ritz. *Aretha: From These Roots.* New York: Villard, 1999.

Frost, Robert

Poet
1874–1963

Life and Work

With ordinary American speech for its medium and rural New England for much of its subject matter, Robert Frost's poetry earned the love of a wide public as well as the ongoing scrutiny of critics and scholars fascinated by the craft it showed.

Irascible and not always as affectionately regarded by his acquaintances as he was by the public, Frost possessed a stubbornness that stood him in good stead in his long struggle to live a poet's life. He was born in San Francisco on March 26, 1874; his mother, a teacher who placed stern demands on her own children, moved the family back to its ancestral New England home in 1885 after the death of his father. Frost graduated as co-valedictorian of his high school class in 1892; he shared the title with Elinor White, whom he married three years later.

Frost attended Dartmouth College and Harvard University for a time, but chafed at the rituals of college life and in 1900 moved his growing family to a poultry farm in Derry, New Hampshire. Failing to find publishers for his poetry, he moved to England in 1912. English audiences responded immediately to the originality of the almost 40-year-old poet, and his first book, *A Boy's Will*, was published in 1913. The following year *North of Boston* became an American bestseller and set the tone for his future work. When he returned to the United States in 1915, he did so as a literary celebrity. For the next several decades Frost augmented his writing income by "barding around," as he called it, from one university lectureship to another. He won the Pulitzer Prize four times, for *New Hampshire* (1923), *Collected Poems* (1930), *A Further Range* (1936), and *A Witness Tree* (1942).

Frost's poems often deal with questions of meaning in the absence of a given or divine order; some of his poetic speakers look to the heavens or to the seas in search of signs. Other poems, such as the famous semidramatic "The Death of the Hired Man" (1914), depict isolated individuals in rural New England, wringing from them views of the bedrock of human relationships. Natural phenomena, too, serve as signs of deeper truths, an effect only heightened by the care and precision with which Frost might depict a New England winter or a stone ledge once raked by glaciers.

An honored statesman of American literature in his old age, Frost read his poem "A Gift Outright" at the inauguration of President John F. Kennedy in 1961. He died in Boston on January 29, 1963.

Legacy

In an era when to be "modern" often meant to dissociate oneself from a general audience, Robert Frost found a middle way: he became something of a Modernist-regionalist.

In its pervasive sense of doubt and of the neutrality or even malevolence of the natural world, Frost's poetry was very much of the twentieth century. In "Design" (1936), the poet encounters a white moth, trapped in the web of a white spider that rests on a white flower—"Assorted characters of death and blight/Mixed ready to begin the morning right." The mixture of horror and amusement here is distant indeed from the spiritual immersion in nature so prized by the nineteenth-century Romantics. Frost, along with T. S. Eliot and EZRA POUND and largely in advance of them, helped bring American poetry into the modern age, finding a uniquely American language for the pessimistic message he shared with many of his contemporaries. The poetry of such later figures as Theodore Roethke, in which nature seems to merge into an individual cry of pain, seems inconceivable without Frost's influence.

Frost was no bleak philosopher or rarefied prophet of doom, however. His poems crowd schoolbooks because readers find them real and rooted in the experiences of ordinary people. An often overlooked aspect of his work is its frequent humor. Frost's New England is a place that builds character, even if of a rather gloomy kind; "Mending Wall" (1914) has bequeathed to the English language the maxim "good fences make good neighbors," even if the wall the two neighbors build is at the mercy of the freeze-thaw cycle and ultimately meaningless.

Perhaps Frost's most influential creation was the dry New England voice from which his poems are inseparable. The language of one of his most famous poems, "Stopping By Woods on a Snowy Evening," is that of Everyman, although the poem hints at death or suicide. Frost affirmed that the American vernacular could carry messages of fundamental import, and thus helped to bring American poetry, to use a phrase from one of his own works, "to earthward."

Manheim

For Further Reading
Gerber, Philip L. *Robert Frost*. Rev. ed. New York: Twayne Publishers, 1982.
Pritchard, William H. *Frost: A Literary Life Reconsidered*. New York: Oxford University Press, 1984.

García Márquez, Gabriel

Novelist and Journalist
1928–

Life and Work

Gabriel García Márquez is a major contributor to the literary movement known as magical realism.

García Márquez was born on March 6, 1928, in Aracataca, a small town in northern Colombia. He was raised by his maternal grandparents in a house full of family members and the ghosts that inhabited the stories told by his grandmother.

After finishing high school, he went on to study law in Bogotá. He preferred poetry and novels to law, however, and began reading contemporary authors. Important among his discoveries was FRANZ KAFKA's *The Metamorphosis*, which he has credited with inspiring him to write. He abandoned law and began to study journalism and to write for several left-wing newspapers. In 1946 he published his first short story, "The Third Resignation."

In the years that followed, he wrote for a number of newspapers and wrote short fiction. García Márquez began his uncomfortable relations with political powers early in his career, writing articles that were so frowned upon by the Colombian government that his newspaper sent him to Europe in 1955 as a foreign correspondent to protect him. From 1959 to 1961 he worked for the news agency *La Prensa* in Havana, Cuba, and in New York City, where his anti-American and pro-Castro politics made him unwelcome. After he left New York in 1960, he was not allowed back to the United States until 1979.

García Márquez lived in Mexico City with his family in the 1960s, mostly unemployed and poor. In 1965, he began to write *Cien años de soledad* (*One Hundred Years of Solitude,* 1967). The first chapter came to him fully formed, he has said, and he had only to type it. He wanted to tell the story of a Colombian family as his grandmother would have told it, incorporating the supernatural in an entirely natural manner.

During the 1970s he continued his political work and writing. He helped found the Colombian political party Firmes and HABEAS, a human rights organization. He also supported leftist causes in Colombia, Venezuela, Nicaragua, Argentina, and Angola. In 1981 he was forced to flee Colombia when the government accused him of funding leftist guerrillas. He was welcomed back, however, the following year when he was awarded the Nobel Prize for Literature.

Today García Márquez lives and writes in Mexico City.

Legacy

Gabriel García Márquez brought together in his work Modernism, his grandmother's ghost stories, and the political upheaval that surrounded him.

García Márquez was recognized early in his career when, upon publication of *The Third Resignation*, the press hailed him as one of a "boom" of new Latin American writers linked by the influence of the Argentine writer JORGE LUIS BORGES. Others in this group included the Cuban Alejo Carpentier, the Mexican Carlos Fuentes, and the Peruvian Mario Vargas Llosa. García Márquez lived in poverty, however, until the overwhelming reception of *One Hundred Years of Solitude*, which sold over a million copies in the three years following its publication. The book's first printing sold out immediately, it has since been translated into over two dozen languages, and has received worldwide acclaim.

With *One Hundred Years of Solitude*, García Márquez set the standard for the new style of magical realism, which combines realistic description of Latin American life with fantastical stories of ghosts and of magic. These elements confronted Western literature's reliance upon rationality, asserting the validity of Latin American myths, stories, and traditions. He has continued with this style in his later works, and other writers have adopted and expanded it. The common themes are those of political oppression and strong family ties in Latin American life along with the complementary magic of strong religious and supernatural beliefs.

García Márquez's overwhelming success brought him recognition as one of the great writers of the twentieth century. Among his best-known titles are *El Coronel no tiene quien le escriba* (*No One Writes to the Colonel,* 1961), *Innocent Eréndira* (1972), *Crónica de una muerte anunciada* (*Chronicle of a Death Foretold,* 1981), *Amor en los tiempos de cólera* (*Love in the Time of Cholera,* 1985), and *El General en su Laberinto* (*The General in His Labyrinth,* 1989).

Watson

WORLD EVENTS		GARCÍA MÁRQUEZ'S LIFE
Russian Revolution	1917	
	1928	Gabriel García Márquez is born
Great Depression	1929–39	
World War II	1939–45	
	1946	García Márquez publishes "The Third Resignation"
Communist China is established	1949	
Korean War	1950–53	
African independence movement begins	1957	
	1967	García Márquez publishes *One Hundred Years of Solitude*
Vietnam War ends	1975	
	1981	García Márquez flees Colombia
	1982	García Márquez receives Nobel Prize
	1989	García Márquez publishes *The General in His Labyrinth*
Dissolution of Soviet Union	1991	

For Further Reading

Bell, Michael. *Gabriel García Márquez: Solitude and Solidarity.* New York: St. Martin's Press, 1993.

Bell-Villada, Gene H. *García Márquez: The Man and His Work.* Chapel Hill: University of North Carolina Press, 1990.

McGuirk, Bernard, and Richard Cardwell, eds. *Gabriel García Márquez: New Readings.* Cambridge and New York: Cambridge University Press, 1987.

Oberhelman, Harley D. *Gabriel García Márquez: A Study of the Short Fiction.* Boston: Twayne, 1991.

Gentileschi, Artemisia

Painter
1593–1652

World Events		Gentileschi's Life	
Ottoman dominance of Mediterranean ends	1571		
	1593	Artemisia Gentileschi is born	
	1610	Gentileschi completes *Susanna and the Elders*	
	1611–12	Gentileschi completes *Judith Decapitating Holofernes*	
	1612	Gentileschi is raped and testifies at trial	
Thirty Years' War in Europe	1618–48		
	c. 1620 –30	Gentileschi lives in Rome	
	1638–41	Gentileschi works in London	
	1652	Gentileschi dies	
Glorious Revolution in England	1688		

Life and Work

Artemisia Gentileschi was the first woman artist to become a successful painter of important large-scale figure compositions. She was particularly famous for her depictions of heroic women from history and the Bible.

Gentileschi was born in Rome, on July 8, 1593. Her father was the painter Orazio Gentileschi. She was the eldest of four children and the only daughter. More important for her father, she was the only one of his children who demonstrated any talent for art and so, at about age 12, she became his apprentice. At the time, would-be artists received their training with a professional master and it was common for painters to train their own children, usually the sons. Occasionally, daughters also received training, particularly if they were talented. Prior to the nineteenth century, this would have been the only way for most women to become artists.

Gentileschi was a gifted student and by age 17 had produced her first mature work, *Susanna and the Elders* (1610), depicting a heroine of the Old Testament. In 1612, she was raped by a young painter who was working with her father. Her trauma was intensified by the public scandal of a trial and, according to the legal customs of the day, by her subjection to a form of torture to prove she was telling the truth about the rape. Nevertheless, during the period of the trial, she completed *Judith Decapitating Holofernes* (c.1611–12), the first in a series of paintings of Judith, another Old Testament heroine. In 1612, soon after the trial ended, Gentileschi moved to Florence and began her independent career.

Between about 1620 and 1630, Gentileschi was again living and working in Rome. During that decade she painted other versions of Judith and Holofernes. Between 1638 and 1641 she spent time in London collaborating with her father on a fresco for King Charles I. Her father died there in 1639 and Artemisia completed their work. She then moved to Naples, where she worked continuously on commissions until she died in 1652.

Legacy

Artemesia Gentileschi was one of the most well-known artists of her day and an important inspiration to later generations of women artists.

Gentileschi painted strong female figures with original interpretations of many standard themes. Images of heroic women such as Judith, Susanna, and Lucretia were well known in the seventeenth century and were represented by many artists. But Gentileschi's versions were unique—her portrayals were realistic both physically and psychologically. For example, not only did her Judith seem strong enough to cut off the enemy's head, she also appeared to know how to do it. Her images depicted mature, expressive women rather than women who were simply beautiful. Additionally, her dynamic compositions of these women enhanced the strong sense of drama and emotional tension that was typical of her work. Other artists, including Van Dyke, PETER PAUL RUBENS, and REMBRANDT adapted both compositional and thematic elements from Gentileschi's work.

Gentileschi also possessed a unique understanding of the female nude. Her father's training established her mastery of anatomical drawing. But, as a woman, she probably had an unusual number of female models willing to pose nude for her. Gentileschi's nudes, such as Susanna and Cleopatra, were robust and natural, unlike the idealized pale and smooth, and sometimes anatomically curious nudes of many of her male contemporaries. Rubens and Rembrandt were the only artists to match the realistic representations of her female nudes.

For a number of years, especially during most of the twentieth century, art historians tended to focus on famous male painters of the past and overlooked the work of Gentileschi. Today aspects of her reputation have been revived, and she is recognized as one of the most original and powerful practitioners of the dramatic style developed by CARAVAGGIO, who was a mentor to her father. Unfortunately, many of her works have been lost or are misidentified; currently only about 34 paintings are definitely attributable to her.

Pokinski

For Further Reading

Bissell, R. Ward. *Artemisia Gentileschi and the Authority of Art: Critical Reading and Catalogue Raisonné*. University Park: Pennsylvania State University Press, 1998.

Garrard, Mary D. *Artemisia Gentileschi: The Image of the Female Hero in Italian Baroque Art*. Princeton, N.J.: Princeton University Press, 1989.

Gershwin, George

Songwriter and Composer
1898–1937

Life and Work

One of the great songwriters of the American musical stage, George Gershwin was a figure of protean creativity whose talents led him in the direction of classical music as well as musical theater.

Gershwin was born Jacob Gershvin in Brooklyn, New York, on September 26, 1898. His parents were Russian Jews who had arrived in New York in the early 1890s; they scraped together a living, moving 22 times between 1895 and 1917. The family bought a piano in 1910, and George took to it rapidly.

His piano teacher introduced him to classical music; the popular side of his musical education began when he dropped out of school in 1914 to work as a salesman for the Remick music publishing firm. This job let Gershwin rub elbows with songwriters and Broadway entrepreneurs; a fine pianist, he was also keenly attuned to the new "stride" style emerging in Harlem. He began writing songs and had his first hit in 1920 when the crowd-pleasing vocalist Al Jolson recorded "Swanee."

Gershwin began to work with his lyricist brother Ira, who devised lyrics that matched George's increasingly daring rhythmic complexities. By 1924 the pair had scored a major success with the musical *Lady, Be Good*, from which the title track and the song "Fascinating Rhythm" have endured as classics.

That same year Gershwin broke through to national renown with the *Rhapsody in Blue*. This work for piano and small orchestra had the outward trappings of a classical concerto, but incorporated jazz elements; its irrepressible melodicism has made it a perennial concert favorite. Gershwin followed it up with other orchestral works; 1928's *An American in Paris* crystallized impressions Gershwin had gathered during his own trip to the City of Light. Gershwin's 1935 opera *Porgy and Bess*, based on the DuBose Heyward novel about an African-American neighborhood in South Carolina, is perhaps his masterpiece; its many famous songs, "Summertime" among them, drew on their composer's long familiarity with black music.

The Gershwins continued to write for the musical stage; 1930's *Girl Crazy*, which included "I Got Rhythm," was among their most successful shows. They signed a contract with the RKO film studio in 1936. Amid the whirl of life in Hollywood, the symptoms of George Gershwin's growing brain tumor were misdiagnosed as stress-related. He died in Hollywood on July 11, 1937.

Legacy

George Gershwin crossed musical boundaries, creating a series of works that bridged the divides between popular music, classical music, and jazz.

His work was influential in all three genres. As a pop composer, Gershwin was especially notable for having created a rhythmic idiom that bore deep marks of his exposure to jazz and its African-American musical predecessors. A song like "I Got Rhythm," structurally built on the simultaneous sounding of contrasting rhythms, testified to a deeper encounter with jazz than any of Gershwin's contemporaries managed; jazz musicians returned the homage by making the song the basis for countless improvisations of their own.

Despite the lukewarm critical reception first accorded the *Rhapsody in Blue*, Gershwin's classical compositions offered a new approach to the problem of how to forge a uniquely American classical style. They were admired not only in America, but also by a number of leading European composers, including the extremely modernist Austrians Alban Berg and ARNOLD SCHOENBERG, Gershwin's occasional tennis partner in Hollywood. In the United States, Gershwin's orchestral pieces are concert standards, and the later twentieth century saw the revival of his small piano pieces as well. With the inclusion of the *Rhapsody in Blue* in the Disney studios' *Fantasia 2000,* a reprise of the pioneering 1941 fusion of classical music and animation, Gershwin's reputation seemed ready for the twenty-first century.

Perhaps even greater than Gershwin's considerable significance in the histories of both classical and pop was the example he set by following his creative impulses into both fields. For a successor in this regard he had LEONARD BERNSTEIN, who excelled as a classical composer and conductor while maintaining a musical theater career that culminated in *West Side Story* (1957).

Later in the twentieth century, classical and pop traditions drew farther apart, but Gershwin's accomplishment seemed all the more compelling. Classical composer John Adams predicted in 1999 that "something else is going to evolve in the next 100 years that will be a mixture of what we now call pop music and what we now call contemporary music." He might have been describing the music of George Gershwin.

Manheim

For Further Reading
Jablonsky, Edward. *Gershwin.* New York: Doubleday, 1987.
Peyser, Joan. *The Memory of All That: The Life of George Gershwin.* New York: Billboard Books, 1998.
Rosenberg, Deena. *Fascinating Rhythm: The Collaboration of George and Ira Gershwin.* Ann Arbor: University of Michigan Press, 1997.

WORLD EVENTS		GERSHWIN'S LIFE
Spanish-American War	1898	George Gershwin is born Jacob Gershvin
	1914	Gershwin takes sales job with Remick music publishing firm
World War I 1914–18		
Russian Revolution	1917	
	1920	Al Jolson records Gershwin's "Swanee"
	1924	Gershwin composes *Rhapsody in Blue*
	1928	Gershwin composes *An American in Paris*
Great Depression 1929–39		
	1935	Gershwin composes the opera *Porgy and Bess*
	1936	George and Ira Gershwin sign film-music contract
	1937	Gershwin dies
World War II 1939–45		

Giotto

(Giotto di Bondone)

Painter

c. 1267–1337

WORLD EVENTS		GIOTTO'S LIFE:
Mongol conquest of China	1215	
	c. 1267	Giotto is born
	c. 1306 –10	Giotto paints the Arena Chapel at Padua
	1334	Giotto is appointed *capomaestro* at Florence
Hundred Years' War begins	1337	Giotto dies
Ming Dynasty reasserts Chinese control of China	1368	

Life and Work

Giotto was an innovative painter who broke with the rigid medieval tradition of Byzantine art and foreshadowed the achievements of the Renaissance.

Although Giotto was one of the leading painters of his era, and the model for later generations of Italian artists, remarkably little is known about his life. The information available has been pieced together from a handful of legal documents preserved in governmental archives and the much later, largely fictional, account of his life by the sixteenth-century biographer Giorgio Vasari. He was probably born around 1267. Legend has it that when Giotto was a poor shepherd boy, he was discovered by the Florentine painter Cimabue while making drawings of sheep on a rock. Cimabue took the young Giotto into his workshop and provided him with traditional training. By around 1300, Giotto seems to have established himself as an independent painter. One of the earliest works attributed to him is the large *Crucifix* in the church of Santa Maria Novella in Florence.

In 1306 Giotto was given a commission to paint a series of frescoes in the Arena Chapel in Padua. These frescoes, representing the lives of the Virgin and of Christ, were revolutionary; in his massive, carefully modeled forms, human figures have a new sense of three-dimensional substance and weight. Giotto also introduced a new form of linear perspective to provide his figures with a stage-like spatial setting.

But perhaps most important, Giotto was a superb dramatist who captured both the physical reality of his characters, and their emotional reality. For example, by repeating the pose of Mary holding the baby Jesus in the scene of Mary mourning Jesus' dead body, Giotto underscored the human tragedy of the event. Giotto's expression of dramatic human narratives distinguished his work from the static conventions of the Byzantine tradition.

In the 1320s Giotto painted two other monumental fresco cycles for the Bardi and Peruzzi chapels in the church of Santa Croce in Florence. He also traveled to Naples, where he became closely associated with King Robert.

In 1334, Giotto returned to Florence and was appointed *capomaestro* (headmaster) of all public works sponsored by the city and by the cathedral. Ordinarily reserved for a prominent architect, this prestigious position was a great honor for a painter.

Giotto died in 1337.

Legacy

Giotto was one of the most innovative artists in European history. By 1310 he was described in DANTE's *Divine Comedy* as the leading painter of his generation.

His stylistic innovations, however, had only a rather limited effect on painters of the following generation. Some, like Bernardo Daddi, turned toward a more decorative, ornamental style. Others, such as Andrea Orcagna, perhaps in reaction to the Black Death that devastated Florence in 1348, returned to the heightened spirituality of the medieval tradition. Only Taddeo Gaddi, Giotto's foster son, attempted to follow Giotto's interest in the human figure and human drama.

To later generations, however, Giotto was regarded as the founder of Italian Renaissance art; his name was revered through the Renaissance. Generations of Italian artists, including Masaccio and MICHELANGELO, honed their drawing skill by copying Giotto's frescoes in Santa Croce. Giotto's rise from traditional craftsman to illustrious artist and administrator was seen to anticipate the Renaissance struggle to have the visual arts accepted as liberal arts.

For several centuries, Giotto's art was eclipsed by enthusiasm for the more elaborated, "realistic" works of the later Renaissance. As a taste for the Italian "primitives" of the earlier period developed in the late nineteenth century, however, Giotto became once again a focus of attention. In the twentieth century, artists such as HENRY MOORE saw in his bold, simple forms something relevant to the new abstract art.

Today, Giotto is seen as a key figure on the cusp between the Middle Ages and the Renaissance. He introduced a style of spaciousness, solidity, and human drama that laid the groundwork for the aesthetics of the High Renaissance.

McEnroe

For Further Reading

Cole, Bruce. *Giotto and Florentine Painting.* New York: Harper & Row, 1976.

Stubblebine, James. *Assisi and the Rise of Vernacular Art.* New York: Harper & Row, 1985.

Goethe, Johann Wolfgang von

Poet, Novelist, Dramatist
1749–1832

Life and Work

Johann Wolfgang von Goethe, widely recognized as the greatest writer of the German tradition, was not only a lyric poet, novelist, and dramatist, but also a scientist who wrote on geology, botany, and physics, as well as a literary and art critic and theorist. The German cultural period of the late-eighteenth and early-nineteenth century, including both Neoclassic and Romantic literary trends, is often referred to as the age of Goethe.

Goethe was born in Frankfurt in 1749. As a young boy, he wrote stories and novellas and later, as a student at the university in Leipzig, he began the breadth of study that characterized him as a writer. He studied law, drawing, music, science, alchemy, and chemistry. He went on to the University of Strasbourg in France, where he studied WILLIAM SHAKESPEARE, German folk songs, and HOMER and other classical authors, all of which would resonate in his early poetic and dramatic works.

Goethe published his first novel, *Der Leiden des Jungen Werthers* (*The Sorrows of Young Werther*), in 1774. The story, inspired by events in his life, was that of a young artist who falls in love with a married woman and eventually commits suicide. It was the primary instigator

of Sturm und Drang, a literary movement that incorporated a strong critique of classicism, a sense of nationalistic patriotism, an interest in folk culture and art, and was characterized by romantic and emotional extremes, that favored inspiration over logic in art.

Soon after the publication of *The Sorrows of Young Werther*, Goethe went to Weimar, where he became a minister of state for the next 25 years, serving as the court poet and director of the ducal theater. Goethe traveled in Italy in 1786 and during this time wrote the poems of *Römische Elegien* (*Roman Elegies*) and *Hermann und Dorothea*. He also published several scientific works on botany, optics, and physics.

In the 1790s Goethe was head of the university at Jena, where the German Romantic movement developed. In 1795, Goethe published *Wilhelm Meister's Lehrjahre* (*Wilhelm Meister's Apprenticeship*). It was with this novel that Goethe helped to invent the bildungsroman, a German coming-of-age novel depicting a young man's search for meaning.

Goethe began work on his great drama, *Faust*, while still a student; he published the first version in 1790. The completed version of the first section of the work, *Faust I*, appeared in 1808 while the second part, *Faust II*, did not appear until 1832—after Goethe's death. Goethe's version of the medieval story of a man who sells his soul to the Devil is considered one of the greatest examples of the European Romantic movement and is worthy of being placed alongside the works of DANTE and Shakespeare.

Goethe continued writing and received visits and honors from writers and artists around the world. It was in this role of literary sage that he produced the mystical works of his later years, including the collection of poetry *West-Östlicher Divan* (*West-Easterly Divan*, 1819), and the novels *Wilhelm Meisters Wanderjahre* (*Wilhelm Meister's Travels*, 1821) and *Die Wahlverwandtshaften* (*Elective Affinities*, 1809). He died of heart disease on March 22, 1832.

Legacy

Johann Wolfgang von Goethe raised German literature from a position of little international importance to that of the most vital and respected in Europe.

Goethe spearheaded the Sturm und Drang movement in its reaction against the rational art of the Enlightenment and the Neoclassical movement. *The Sorrows of Young Werther* was so startling in its exploration of passion and despair that it not only was widely read, it also provoked a string of imitation suicides throughout Europe.

The bildungsroman, a type of novel that Goethe helped to establish as a form, quickly became a staple of German literature. One of the best-known examples of the form is *The Magic Mountain* by THOMAS MANN.

Faust is considered one of the greatest monuments of nineteenth-century Romanticism. Friedrich and Wilhelm von Schlegel, leaders of the younger Romantic movement in Jena, were particularly influenced by *Wilhelm Meister*, and the German Romantic poet Novalis praised and drew upon Goethe's work. As the Romantic movement spread across Europe, Samuel Taylor Coleridge, WILLIAM WORDSWORTH, JOHN KEATS, Percy Shelley, Lord Byron, and Sir Walter Scott in England all made references to the work. Mann's *Doctor Faustus* is a famous literary heir to the drama. Composers, including RICHARD WAGNER, Hector Berlioz, ROBERT SCHUMANN, and FRANZ LISZT, have all based works on Goethe's interpretation of the Faust legend.

Watson

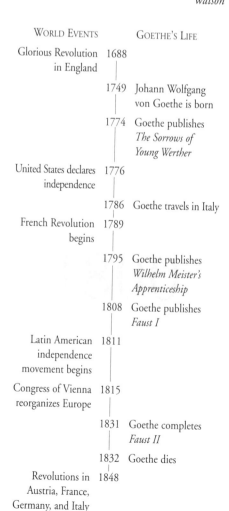

WORLD EVENTS		GOETHE'S LIFE
Glorious Revolution in England	1688	
	1749	Johann Wolfgang von Goethe is born
	1774	Goethe publishes *The Sorrows of Young Werther*
United States declares independence	1776	
	1786	Goethe travels in Italy
French Revolution begins	1789	
	1795	Goethe publishes *Wilhelm Meister's Apprenticeship*
	1808	Goethe publishes *Faust I*
Latin American independence movement begins	1811	
Congress of Vienna reorganizes Europe	1815	
	1831	Goethe completes *Faust II*
	1832	Goethe dies
Revolutions in Austria, France, Germany, and Italy	1848	

For Further Reading

O'Connell, David, ed. *Goethe.* Twayne's World Authors Series. New York: Twayne Publishers, 1998.

Williams, John R. *The Life of Goethe: A Critical Biography.* Oxford: Blackwell Publishers, 1998.

Goya, Francisco

Painter
1746–1828

Life and Work

Francisco José de Goya y Lucientes was the most prominent Spanish painter of his generation and a harbinger of Modernist art.

Goya was born in the town of Fuentetodos in 1746. At 14 he was apprenticed to the painter José Luzan Martinez and learned to

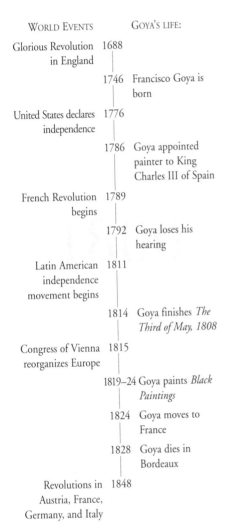

WORLD EVENTS		GOYA'S LIFE:
Glorious Revolution in England	1688	
	1746	Francisco Goya is born
United States declares independence	1776	
	1786	Goya appointed painter to King Charles III of Spain
French Revolution begins	1789	
	1792	Goya loses his hearing
Latin American independence movement begins	1811	
	1814	Goya finishes *The Third of May, 1808*
Congress of Vienna reorganizes Europe	1815	
	1819–24	Goya paints *Black Paintings*
	1824	Goya moves to France
	1828	Goya dies in Bordeaux
Revolutions in Austria, France, Germany, and Italy	1848	

paint in the Rococo style. By the 1780s Goya began to specialize in portraits. In 1786 he was made a court painter to King Charles III and, in 1799, was appointed principal painter to King Charles IV.

Although Goya spent much of his career associated with the royal court, he was an independent political thinker, deeply concerned with the major issues of his day. Some critics have even suggested that Goya's large, extremely unflattering painting *The Family of Charles IV* (1800) was intended to show the royal family as a group of inept bumblers. Although in retrospect that sort of direct insult seems unlikely, it is true that Goya preferred the more liberal policies of Charles III to the reactionary policies of Charles IV.

Goya was deeply critical of Spanish society. He began a series of some 80 etchings called *Los Caprichos* (*The Caprices*, 1796–98) with a print entitled *The Sleep of Reason Produces Monsters*, showing a sleeping man from whose unconscious bursts a stream of bats, owls and monsters. The rest of the series reveals the range of follies that promised to overtake Spanish society unless it turned to the life of reason and logic.

Goya's best known painting, *The Third of May, 1808*, was painted in 1814. It depicts an incident in the Napoleonic Wars (1803–15; in Spain, 1808–14). A group of Spanish guerrilla fighters had killed some French soldiers. In retaliation, on the following night the French rounded up hundreds of Spanish civilians and executed them. Goya's painting shows a faceless French firing squad shooting into a disorganized group of Spanish peasants who react with horror, disbelief, and fruitless resistance.

Goya's most disturbing works are the so-called *Black Paintings* that he painted on the wall of his house between 1819 and 1824. Goya had lost his hearing in 1792 and had become increasingly isolated. In these enigmatic works the dark forces of unreason rise again. In one mythological scene, the god Saturn is shown as a giant eating one of his own children.

In 1824 Goya moved to France, where he died four years later.

Legacy

Francisco Goya had little immediate impact on the course of Spanish painting. He had

few students, and his individualistic style and deeply emotional approach was ill-suited to the more conservative world of Spanish court painting. His *Black Paintings* were regarded as monstrous.

Goya's reputation fared better in France, where his etchings, particularly *Los Caprichos*, enjoyed wide circulation. The Romantic movement was just getting under way, and painters such as Delacroix began to investigate the realm of feeling and emotion that Goya had depicted. In the latter half of the nineteenth century, a new generation of artists began to reconsider Goya's art. PIERRE-AUGUSTE RENOIR, PAUL CÉZANNE, VINCENT VAN GOGH and especially EDOUARD MANET studied his prints. Manet even traveled to Spain to see his paintings. Goya's painterly style and rejection of idealized beauty seemed to foreshadow their own avant-garde works.

Goya's career marks the transition between two world orders: the static, aristocratic order of the old royal courts and the new world of individuality and personal expression. His paintings stand at the beginning of the Romantic movement in which human emotions and feeling came to be valued as much as the traditional academies had prized classical form. In Romanticism, the artist-genius was the person who could provide access to the world of the human unconscious.

Today, along with DIEGO VELÁZQUEZ and PABLO PICASSO, Goya is regarded as one of the most important artists in the history of Spanish art.

McEnroe

For Further Reading

Gassier, P., and J. Wilson. *The Life and Complete Works of Francisco Goya*, 2nd ed. New York: Harrison House, 1981.

Licht, Fred. *Goya: The Origins of the Modern Temper in Art*. New York: Universe Books, 1979.

———. *Goya in Perspective*. Englewood Cliffs, N.J.: Prentice-Hall, 1973.

Graham, Martha

Choreographer
1894–1991

Life and Work

Widely regarded as one of the twentieth century's greatest choreographers, Martha Graham brought psychological depth and, often, tragic power to modern dance.

Born in rural Pennsylvania on May 11, 1894, Graham spent her childhood in the South but moved with her family as a teenager to Santa Barbara, California. The West Coast was the birthplace of American modern dance, and in 1916 Graham became a dancer and student at Denishawn, the pioneering company and school founded by dancers Ruth St. Denis and Ted Shawn. She gained insight there into the power dance held in many cultures of the world; although she rejected the company's exoticism, many of her early works had a ritualistic aspect.

Graham moved to New York City and made her debut as an independent artist in 1926. One of her most important early works was 1931's *Primitive Mysteries*, a piece inspired by the Native American Catholicism of the Southwest. Setting a pattern she would repeat for much of her career, Graham both danced in this work and created movements for other dancers; her choreography was in a sense an extension of her own dancing.

Collaboration with set designers, notably the Japanese-American sculptor Isamu Noguchi, was integral to Graham's vision; she first worked with Noguchi in 1935 on *Frontier*, the first of several American-themed works she created. However, Graham conceived of dance as a basic form of expression, not as an accompaniment to music or any other art; her works were developed independently of the music that was written for them, even in the case of 1944's *Appalachian Spring*, which, thanks to its beloved score by composer AARON COPLAND, became one of her most famous pieces.

In the works of her maturity of the 1940s and 1950s Graham often turned to Greek mythology in search of the elemental insights into the human condition that she aimed for in her own work; 1947's *Errand into the Maze*

evoked the legend of the Minotaur as part of its examination of the subconscious. Graham often turned to biblical subjects as well and created two works about Judith, the warrior decapitator of Holofernes. Graham retired as a dancer in 1970, but her roughly 200 dances spanned her entire life, until just before her death in 1991 at the age of 96.

Legacy

Martha Graham's work was of definitive importance for modern dance, both technically and in the realm of expression.

Graham's approach to movement, which relied on sharp contrasts of tension and release, stood in distinct contrast to the flowing motion of classical ballet and enabled her to produce psychologically influenced images of humans in the grip of inner drives. In place of the controlled set of possibilities open to a dancer schooled in nineteenth-century techniques, Graham drew on a choreographic palette that involved the entire body (the physical regime she required of dancers was exacting in the extreme) and a range of motion from the exuberant to the driven to the abrupt. Graham's transformation of dance from an art of beauty to one of profound expression opened the door for a plethora of further innovations in modern dance.

She created, in the celebrated phrase of critic Eric Bentley, a "dance of anxiety." Her use of the body, particularly of characteristic pelvic contractions, gave her works an unprecedented undercurrent of sexual tension; more generally, the look of her dances was disharmonious and intense. Graham was an energetic teacher; she and her followers codified her techniques, which are still widely taught. The many dancers who passed through her company would go on to create works that were more daring in their representations of the sense of dislocation that was such a prominent feature of twentieth-century cultural expression; the most notable one among them was the experimentalist choreographer MERCE CUNNINGHAM, who was one of Graham's leading dancers during the years surrounding World War II. But all of them owed to Graham the sense that a dance audience should be stirred, challenged, unsettled at the recognition of their deepest impulses and fears.

Manheim

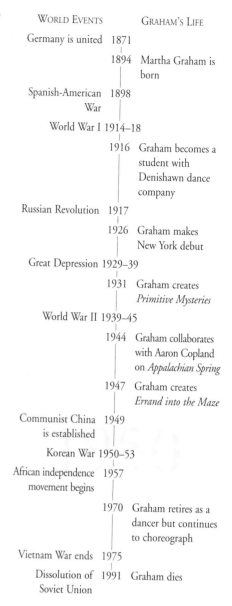

WORLD EVENTS		GRAHAM'S LIFE
Germany is united	1871	
	1894	Martha Graham is born
Spanish-American War	1898	
World War I	1914–18	
	1916	Graham becomes a student with Denishawn dance company
Russian Revolution	1917	
	1926	Graham makes New York debut
Great Depression	1929–39	
	1931	Graham creates *Primitive Mysteries*
World War II	1939–45	
	1944	Graham collaborates with Aaron Copland on *Appalachian Spring*
	1947	Graham creates *Errand into the Maze*
Communist China is established	1949	
Korean War	1950–53	
African independence movement begins	1957	
	1970	Graham retires as a dancer but continues to choreograph
Vietnam War ends	1975	
Dissolution of Soviet Union	1991	Graham dies

For Further Reading

Freedman, Russell. *Martha Graham: A Dancer's Life*. New York: Clarion Books, 1998.

Graham, Martha. *Blood Memory*. New York: Doubleday, 1991.

Gregory I, Pope

(Gregory the Great)

Musically Influential Church Leader
c. 540–604

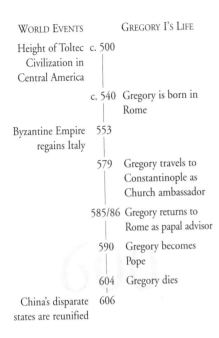

World Events		Gregory I's Life
Height of Toltec Civilization in Central America	c. 500	
	c. 540	Gregory is born in Rome
Byzantine Empire regains Italy	553	
	579	Gregory travels to Constantinople as Church ambassador
	585/86	Gregory returns to Rome as papal advisor
	590	Gregory becomes Pope
	604	Gregory dies
China's disparate states are reunified	606	

Life and Work

A legend that lasted for centuries held that Pope Gregory I (Gregory the Great) personally, under divine inspiration, composed the body of unison musical church song that even today is called Gregorian chant. In reality, the thousands of chants of the early Christian church evolved over a period of several centuries, and no one person could have composed them all. Yet the legend of Pope Gregory, as legends often do, contained a grain of truth.

Descended from the old noble class that had slowly fallen into ruin following the removal of the last Roman emperor in 476 C.E., Gregory was born in Rome around 540. He was the great-grandson of Pope Felix III (r. 483–492). In 579 he was made a Church ambassador and traveled to Constantinople (now Istanbul, Turkey), the capital of the old empire's eastern half and the center of the Church's activities in the Near East. There he encountered a culture that, although Christian in religion, was linguistically Greek and looked back to the glories of the ancient world. In 585 or 586 he returned to Rome as an advisor to Pope Pelagius II and reluctantly accepted election to the papacy in 590 after Pelagius's death.

Gregory was among the Popes who succeeded in expanding the Church's influence after the disappearance of the Roman Empire. He centralized power in Rome, bringing the Christian churches of Spain under Roman influence and, farther afield, beginning to win over the Anglo-Saxon tribes of England to Christianity. At a distance of 1,400 years it is difficult to be certain about Gregory's specifically musical activities. He established or reconfigured the Schola Cantorum, a music school that trained boys and men as church singers; he took an interest in the Church's musical order of service, permitting new kinds of chant derived from the Byzantine worship he had known in Constantinople, but forbidding deacons from performing other chants. As chant in the days before musical notation was transmitted by ear, and thus was a repertory to which singers added constantly, it is indeed possible that Gregory composed new chants himself. The important point, however, is that his efforts toward centralization and standardization of worship extended to music.

Gregory died in Rome on March 12, 604.

Legacy

Chant was the music that knit European society together during the medieval era. Even after the advent of polyphonic (multipart) music, chant lay at the center of European composition for hundreds of years. If the legend of Gregory I the musician was a fanciful one, created by medieval church musicians intent on linking their own activities to the name of one of history's greatest popes, it was nevertheless of critical importance for Western music.

For the modern observer, the image of monks intoning in unison the peaceful, graceful melodies of Gregorian chant suggests a static and timeless faith. Yet chant as it developed reflected centuries of musical and even political change. The crucial event in its development, and one of the milestones of European history, was the advent of musical notation. The earliest surviving examples of written-down music date from more than two centuries after Gregory's papacy, but notation evolved in response to the requirements he helped to develop: it was a means of standardizing what was sung in churches dispersed over a wide geographical area. Of the medieval leaders who drew on Gregory's administrative lessons, the great Frankish ruler Charlemagne was perhaps the most important.

Once the idea of "Gregorian" chant was in place, it laid the foundation for a tradition of music that endured for centuries, and indeed formed part of Roman Catholic church services until the Vatican II reforms of the 1960s. Notation preserved for posterity the glorious Alleluia and Gradual chants, sweeping "melismatic" pieces in which each syllable of text might have its own long flourish of sung notes; these chants likely predated Gregory—perhaps even forming a musical link with the Church's Middle Eastern origins.

Pictorial representations from medieval times show Gregory receiving the chants from a white dove representing the Holy Spirit, with a scribe hovering in the background to write them down. This image of the birth of European music may have originated as a kind of propaganda, but it reflected the fundamental significance in Western culture of the great tradition of music that Pope Gregory had helped to set in motion.

Manheim

For Further Reading

Markus, R. A. *Gregory the Great and His World.* Cambridge and New York: Cambridge University Press, 1997.

Richards, Jeffrey. *Consul of God: The Life and Times of Gregory the Great.* London and Boston: Routledge and Kegan Paul, 1980.

Griffith, D. W.

Filmmaker
1875–1948

Life and Work

D. W. Griffith, American actor, writer and filmmaker, was a key figure in the birth of the American movie industry.

Griffith's childhood was a significant influence in many of his later films. He was born in 1875 outside Louisville, Kentucky, the son of a former officer in the Confederate army. The family struggled financially through the Reconstruction era, clinging to memories of better days in the antebellum South.

Griffith had little formal education. He began his career in drama by acting in local theaters in Louisville. In 1906 he got a job acting and writing scripts for the Biograph film company in New York, and soon began directing. Between 1908 and 1913, he turned out more than 400 mostly one-reel films.

Griffith's first major film, *The Birth of a Nation*, opened in 1915. In it Griffith set out to create an epic on the scale of the grandest works of painting and sculpture. Everything about the film was grandiose. Its initial run in New York, where it was accompanied by a full orchestra and chorus, lasted 44 weeks. The film was a technical tour de force and set new records for ticket sales.

The Birth of a Nation was also one of the most controversial films ever made. Based on Thomas

Dixon's popular 1905 novel *The Clansman*, it is a melodrama about the Civil War and Reconstruction told from a Confederate point of view. Griffith, following Dixon (and popular myth), portrayed the anarchy and poverty that allegedly resulted from allowing "greedy carpetbaggers" and "incompetent" African Americans to participate in government—a situation that called for the heroic intervention of the Ku Klux Klan.

The film was severely criticized for its blatant racism and simplistic stereotypes. Even after several of its most overtly racist scenes were cut, the film was banned in several states.

Griffith seems to have been both surprised and hurt that his masterpiece had been seen as racist. In response, he decided to make another epic film, *Intolerance*, in 1916. In this film, Griffith explored the topics of prejudice and censorship during four different historical periods. An elaborate costume drama, *Intolerance* brought the scholarly look of academic paintings to the movies. Although a financial failure, *Intolerance* has come to be regarded as an artistic high point of the silent film era, as well as an important link between moving pictures and fine art.

Griffith continued to make films through the 1920s; although he was widely regarded as an important force in the film industry, few of his later films were commercially successful.

Griffith died poor and virtually forgotten in Hollywood in 1948.

Legacy

D. W. Griffith was a key figure in establishing Hollywood as the moviemaking capital of the world. In 1919 he became one of the founders of United Artists. This innovative company aimed to ensure complete artistic freedom for filmmakers by allowing them control over both production and distribution, circumventing the existing Hollywood studio system.

Griffith left a mixed legacy. In *The Birth of a Nation*, he introduced several techniques that would become standard in later films: the panoramic shot; flashbacks; the contracting and expanding "iris" signaling a change of scenes; even color tinting of individual frames. His complex editing techniques, including the use of the close up and the fadeout, inspired European avant-garde filmmakers of the next generation, including Sergei Eisenstein.

On the other hand, *The Birth of a Nation* contributed to the revival of the Ku Klux Klan across the United States, which used the film for recruitment as recently as the 1960s.

Although he was a commanding figure in the film industry, Griffith's unbridled egotism and fundamentally nineteenth-century attitudes increasingly isolated him from the Hollywood mainstream. Nevertheless, he is regarded today as perhaps the most influential person in the history of American film. Perhaps more than any other filmmaker, Griffith transformed the cinema from an amusing novelty into a medium for artistic expression.

McEnroe

WORLD EVENTS		GRIFFITH'S LIFE
Germany is united	1871	
	1875	D. W. Griffith is born
Spanish-American War	1898	
	1908	Griffith becomes a director for Biograph
World War I	1914–18	
	1915	Griffith directs *Birth of a Nation*
	1916	Griffith makes *Intolerance*
Russian Revolution	1917	
Great Depression	1929–39	
	1931	Griffith directs his final film, *The Struggle*
World War II	1939–45	
	1948	Griffith dies
Communist China is established	1949	

For Further Reading

Schickel, Richard. *D. W. Griffith: An American Life.* New York: Simon and Schuster, 1984.

Simmon, Scott. *The Films of D. W. Griffith.* New York: Cambridge University Press, 1993.

Williams, Martin T. *Griffith, First Artist of the Movies.* New York: Oxford University Press, 1980.

Guo Xi

(Kuo Hsi)

Painter and Theoretician
c. 1000–c. 1090

Life and Work

Guo Xi, also known as Kuo Hsi, was the leading landscape painter in the Imperial Painting Academy at the court of the Northern Song dynasty (960–1127) in the second half of the eleventh century.

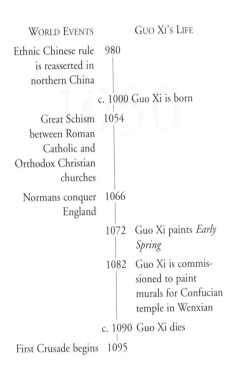

World Events		Guo Xi's Life
Ethnic Chinese rule is reasserted in northern China	980	
	c. 1000	Guo Xi is born
Great Schism between Roman Catholic and Orthodox Christian churches	1054	
Normans conquer England	1066	
	1072	Guo Xi paints *Early Spring*
	1082	Guo Xi is commissioned to paint murals for Confucian temple in Wenxian
	c. 1090	Guo Xi dies
First Crusade begins	1095	

Guo Xi was born around 1000 in Wenxian (Wen district) in northern Henan Province, China. According to Guo Roxu's *Experiences in Painting*, an eleventh-century history of Chinese painting, Guo Xi was known for his "landscapes with wintry forests," and studied and followed Li Cheng (919–967), the foremost landscape painter of the mid-tenth century.

Guo Xi was already a mature painter when he was recruited as a court painter in 1068. His seasonal landscape paintings commissioned for various palace halls were greatly appreciated by Emperor Shenzong (r. 1068–85). In 1082 Guo Xi was commissioned to paint what he regarded as his ultimate achievement—the four murals of landscapes and eroded rocks, for the Confucian temple of his native Wenxian. The screen panels and murals did not survive.

Submitted to the Song Emperor Shenzong around 1118, *Lofty Ambition in Forests and Springs*, a collection of essays edited by his son, Guo Si, offers Guo Xi's comprehensive theory on the monumental style of landscape painting of the Northern Song dynasty. He describes such concepts as the "three types of distances" for achieving a believable perception of nature during a visual journey through the landscape, as well as the "host-guest" relationship between mountain peaks and pine trees, which serves as a visual correlative for the proper reciprocal relations between ruler and subjects.

Guo Xi carefully observed and depicted the transformational changes of nature during the cycle of the seasons. This can be seen in his monumental hanging scroll, *Zaochun*, or *Early Spring* (1072), in which Guo Xi captures nature in that critical moment of transformation from a state of decline in the depths of winter to its renewal in early spring. The ultimate significance of the work lies in the disclosure of the patterns of relations in nature and their orderly change. This provided the basis upon which the orderly relations of social community may be ethically established. *Early Spring* might thus be understood as a metaphor for the success of the emperor and his policies.

Legacy

Although Guo Xi's art was greatly admired by Emperor Shenzong, his work fell out of favor with Emperor Huizong (r. 1100–25). Nevertheless, the paintings of Guo Xi and his mentor, Li Cheng, came to form the dominant school of landscape painting in northern China after the fall of the capital and conquest of the north by the invading Jurchen tribes from Mongolia in 1127.

The subsequent Yuan dynasty (1279–1368) revived Guo Xi's style. One of the prominent features associated with Guo Xi and Li Cheng and imitated by artists of the Yuan dynasty were the tall pines with "crab-claw" endings to their branches and twigs, and gnarled smaller trees below them. In Cao Zhibo's *Two Pine Trees* (1329), the nobility of pines standing out against a bleak landscape is considered to be a comment on the harsh conditions Confucian scholars had to endure during the Mongol-dominated Yuan dynasty.

The restoration of Chinese rule in the Ming dynasty (1368–1644) saw the codification of the style of Guo Xi as an official imperial manner. For instance, *Visiting Pang Degong* [undated] by Ni Duan (active first half of thirteenth century) and *Mountain Villa and Lofty Recluse* [undated] by the fifteenth-century court painter Li Zai are both painted in the style of Guo Xi. They represent attempts by early Ming court painters to reestablish a sense of continuity for the Ming regime with the imperial court in the Song dynasty after the disruption of the intervening Yuan dynasty.

To the monumental composition of Guo Xi's *Early Spring*, the Ming court painters added numerous human figures as narrative comes to play an increasingly important role in landscape paintings. The cloud-shaped mountain peaks and tree motifs of Ni Duan and Li Zai are strongly sculpted and sharply delineated as readability takes precedence over the articulation of spatial relations by subtle transitions in the saturation of ink. The revival of the imperial manner of Guo Xi's style and its association with the court continued well into the sixteenth century.

Goldberg

For Further Reading

Bush, Susan, and Hsio-yen Shih, eds. *Early Chinese Texts on Painting*. Cambridge, Mass.: Harvard University Press, 1985.

Fong, Wen, and James C. Y. Watt, et al. *Possessing the Past: Treasures from the National Palace Museum, Taipei*. Exhibition catalogue. New York: The Metropolitan Museum of Art, 1996.

Guo Roxu's "*Experiences in Painting*" (*Tuhua jianwen zhi*): *An Eleventh Century History of Chinese Painting Together with the Chinese Text in Facsimile*. Translated and annotated by Alexander C. Soper. Washington, D.C.: American Council of Learned Societies, 1951.

Handel, George Frideric

Composer
1685–1759

Life and Work

The composer of some of the most beloved choral music in the classical tradition, George Frideric Handel was also a master of eighteenth-century opera.

Handel was born in Halle, Germany, on February 23, 1685. He was the son of a barber who had planned a career as a lawyer for him. Forbidden to play music, the young Handel sneaked a small keyboard instrument into his attic. His efforts paid off when his organ playing attracted notice from the Duke of Saxe-Weissenfels on a family visit to the court. He moved back to Halle to go to the university in 1702, but left for Hamburg, northern Germany's opera center, the following year.

Handel's notoriously sharp temper flared in 1704 when he fought a duel with the composer Mattheson over the proper accompaniment for the latter's opera *Cleopatra*. His own earliest surviving composition was the opera *Almira* of 1705. In Hamburg, Handel's music once again pleased a powerful patron, the Italian duke Ferdinando de' Medici, and he spent the next several years in Italy soaking up new music. His 1709 opera *Agrippina* was a sensational success during the Carnival season

in Venice, and the young German composer was on his way.

Handel moved briefly back to Germany, but he had his sights set on England and its growing vogue for Italian opera. The move was facilitated by the ascension of his German employer, the Elector of Hannover, to the English throne (as George I) in 1714, thanks to intermarriages between the English and Hannoverian royal families. Handel's 1711 opera *Rinaldo* had already been a hit on the London stage, and Italian operas would make him England's reigning composer. His *Water Music* of 1717, a small-orchestra composition designed for a royal boat outing, was as well-loved as his vocal works. Many of Handel's operas, such as 1724's *Giulio Cesare*, had serious plots set in Greek and Roman times.

In his later years Handel turned to the oratorio, a concert (not for church) work for chorus, soloists, and orchestra that often told a biblical story. The most famous of Handel's many brilliant oratorios was *Messiah* (1742), an Easter tale of Christ's death and resurrection that thanks to its joyous Hallelujah chorus is now inseparable from the Christmas holiday. Handel died in London on April 14, 1759.

Legacy

George Frideric Handel's impact on the world of classical music is more tangible than that of most other composers, coming into evidence with every small-town performance of *Messiah*.

In the mid-eighteenth century, Handel's impact came at least as much from his operas as from his oratorios. He was one of the most important practitioners of the late Baroque *opera seria* (serious opera), an Italian-language style that featured heroic, often moralizing stories punctuated by beautifully melodic, fiery yet balanced arias written for talented individual soloists. Although Handel in his own surroundings faced stiff competition from lighter English-language operas, his operatic works held center stage in England for three decades, and Continental productions carried them back to Germany and Italy, where Handel's operatic style had first taken shape.

By the century's end it was the oratorios that were remembered most—*Messiah* above all, but also *Judas Maccabeus, Israel in Egypt*, and others. WOLFGANG AMADEUS MOZART

made an orchestration of *Messiah*, and Handel's work became the foundation of a long series of grandiose works for large chorus that included FRANZ JOSEPH HAYDN's *The Creation*, the oratorios of Isaac Mendelssohn, and FRANZ LISZT's *Christus*.

In the United States *Messiah* was popularized in part by performances organized by the Handel and Haydn Society of Boston, a large community-based chorus formed in 1815 and still in existence. It remains one of the most widely performed pieces in the entire classical repertoire, but unfortunately it rarely inspires its performers to investigate the other works by its composer.

Manheim

WORLD EVENTS		HANDEL'S LIFE
Thirty Years' War in Europe	1618–48	
	1685	George Frideric Handel is born in Halle, Germany
Glorious Revolution in England	1688	
	1703	Handel moves to Hamburg, a major musical center
	1705	Handel writes opera *Almira*, his earliest surviving composition
	1711	Handel succeeds in London with opera *Rinaldo*
	1717	Handel writes *Water Music*
	1724	Handel writes *Giulio Cesare*
	1742	Handel's *Messiah* is first performed
	1759	Handel dies
United States declares independence	1776	

For Further Reading
Burrows, Donald. *Handel.* New York: Oxford University Press, 1994.
Keates, Jonathan. *Handel: The Man and His Music.* New York: St. Martin's Press, 1985.

Haydn, Franz Joseph

Composer
1732–1809

Life and Work

Austrian composer Franz Joseph Haydn did not invent the symphony and the string quartet single-handedly, but he brought them to prominence in European music.

Haydn was born in the village of Rohrau, Austria, on March 31, 1732. A gifted singer as a child, he joined the choir of the grand St. Stephen's Cathedral in Vienna when he was eight. Leaving the choir after his voice changed in 1749, for several years he eked out a living giving music lessons that barely paid the rent

on an attic room. His fortunes began to improve when some illustrious pupils came his way; in 1761 Haydn was named music director for the aristocratic Eszterházy family. He would spend most of his life composing music and arranging performances at the family's palace in Hungary.

His employers required from him various kinds of music, ranging from opera to trios featuring the baryton, an archaic stringed instrument played by Prince Eszterházy himself. Haydn attracted the most outside attention for his 107 symphonies and 69 string quartets. Both genres were in their infancy when Haydn took them up, and over the course of his career he standardized the four-movement makeup of the symphony and worked out a quartet style that gave equal weight to the ensemble's four instruments.

In 1790 and 1794 Haydn, by then famous all over Europe, made two trips to London, writing 12 symphonies for performances there. These perennially successful works included the "Surprise" symphony (No. 94) of 1791, with its crashing chord that jolted audiences lulled by a seemingly uneventful slow-movement tune. On the way back to Austria in 1792, Haydn stopped in Bonn, Germany and agreed to accept the young LUDWIG VAN BEETHOVEN as a student.

In his own time as in ours, Haydn was known as the master of musical humor, carving out a permanent place in classical music for what the British critic Charles Burney called "learning lightly worn." Other masterpieces of Haydn's later years included two oratorios, *The Creation* (1796–98) and *The Seasons* (1799–1801); these grand works drew on the tradition of *Messiah* and the other oratorios of GEORGE FRIDERIC HANDEL. Haydn died in Vienna on May 31, 1809.

Legacy

The formal coherence and elegance for which music of the Classic period (1750–1825) is known were largely due to Franz Joseph Haydn's shaping of these instrumental music genres.

He exerted a strong influence upon his younger contemporary, WOLFGANG AMADEUS MOZART, with whom he enjoyed a relationship of deep mutual respect and admiration—perhaps not untinged with a bit of rivalry. Haydn's *Opus 20* string quartets, published in

1772, were the set in which he took the greatest strides toward creating the feeling of a conversation between the four instruments; after the teenaged Mozart heard these works, his own compositions would henceforth be imbued with greater depth and weight. Mozart in the 1780s would in turn dedicate a set of six quartets to Haydn. The two composers, the greatest of the age, continued to inspire each other until Mozart's death in 1791.

By the 1780s and 1790s Haydn's name and compositions were known all over Europe, and many composers were writing music in the genres Haydn had perfected. The extent of his influence on his last great composition pupil, Beethoven, is a fascinating open question. The relationship between the two was a prickly one, perhaps complicated by Beethoven's experiences with his alcoholic and frequently absent father and his subsequent mistrust of authority figures. Yet Beethoven dedicated his first set of piano sonatas to Haydn when they were published in 1795, and Beethoven's style in some respects bears the mark of Haydn's in its reliance on spinning an ongoing drama out of a single musical theme and in its bent toward the unexpected. In a way, Beethoven turned Haydn's penchant for comedy into the raw materials of musical drama.

In a sense, Haydn lived long enough to reap the benefits of his own innovations. Late in life he composed a series of masterpieces well loved for their sense of humor, and that sense of humor derived in large part from the way they frustrated the expectations that his own earlier works had done much to set in place.

Manheim

World Events		Haydn's Life
Glorious Revolution in England	1688	
	1732	Franz Joseph Haydn is born in Rohrau, Austria
	1749	Haydn leaves choir of St. Stephen's Cathedral, gives music lessons
	1761	Haydn is named music director at Eszterházy court in Hungary
	1772	Haydn publishes influential *Opus 20* string quartets
United States declares independence	1776	
French Revolution begins	1789	
	1791	Haydn writes "Surprise" symphony
	1792	Haydn accepts Ludwig van Beethoven as student
	1796–98	Haydn writes *The Creation*
	1809	Haydn dies
Latin American independence movement begins	1811	

For Further Reading

Geiringer, Karl. *Haydn: A Creative Life in Music*. Berkeley: University of California Press, 1982.
Landon, H. C. Robbins, and David Wyn Jones. *Haydn: His Life and Music*. Bloomington: Indiana University Press, 1988.

Hendrix, Jimi

Guitarist
1942–1970

Life and Work

Widely considered to be the greatest instrumentalist in the history of rock music, Jimi Hendrix invented a completely new sound for the electric guitar over a period of just a few years.

Born James Marshall Hendrix in Seattle, Washington, on November 27, 1942, he played in a band in high school and became acquainted with the harmonically daring music of 1940s jazz guitarist Charlie Christian. As a U.S. army paratrooper stationed in Kentucky, he heard country blues musicians from nearby southern states; upon his discharge in 1961 he went to Nashville, where he met soul music guitarist Steve Cropper.

Hired as a backup guitarist by the frenetic rock-and-roll vocalist Little Richard in 1963, he was befriended by the virtuoso blues guitarist Albert King while on a tour of the South. His reputation as a session and touring-band player began to spread among black musicians. He toured with Ike and Tina Turner, Solomon Burke, B. B. King, the Isley Brothers, and many other leading acts, developing a flashy solo style that included such tricks as playing the guitar while holding it behind his back.

Hendrix's great breakthrough came when he melded this virtuosity with the experimental spirit of rock music as it was evolving in the major urban centers of the United States and Britain. He moved to New York's Greenwich Village in 1965, coming under the influence, both in terms of songwriting and of general experimental spirit, of BOB DYLAN and other rising rock and folk figures. While in England in 1966, he formed The Jimi Hendrix Experience with two British musicians; the following year the release of the album *Are You Experienced?* showed the spectacular results of Hendrix's long and complex apprenticeship. Such songs as "Purple Haze" featured dense textures in which the basic guitar chords were overlaid with distortion, feedback, pedal effects, and other utterly unprecedented guitar sounds.

Two 1968 albums, *Axis: Bold as Love* and the double LP *Electric Ladyland* (which included a version of Dylan's "All Along the Watchtower") extended Hendrix's technique even further, and that technique became indelibly ingrained in the popular musical consciousness with his chaotic performance of the American national anthem at the Woodstock festival in 1969. The final album released during Hendrix's lifetime was 1970's live *Band of Gypsys*; that year, on September 18, he died in London after an apparently accidental drug overdose.

Legacy

Jimi Hendrix's music has been required listening for rock guitarists ever since it was created; he transformed rock guitar playing into a virtuoso art.

Hendrix's basic style was rooted in the blues, but with the speed and volume of his playing, and with the new sounds that came from his guitar, he pushed blues music to its limit and finally departed from it. Although his live performances were justifiably famous, Hendrix came up with his real innovations in the studio, in collaboration with recording engineers; after Hendrix, an album by Jeff Beck or one of rock's other "guitar gods" would require some months of studio work to assemble. This purely electronic aspect of his music perhaps had little to do with the blues, but in the way he thought about musical space he was much more closely tied to the blues tradition; a Hendrix recording was an extreme and exhaustive exploration of a single musical idea, different in result but not in kind from the vast, ambitious solos of bluesman Muddy Waters, whom Hendrix observed closely at Chicago's Chess Records studios in the early 1960s.

Although Hendrix inspired many guitarists, among whom Stevie Ray Vaughan achieved particular prominence in the 1980s and 1990s, his own style was so personal and idiosyncratic that it could not really be imitated. The end result of all his technical experimentation was that, as much as Dylan or the Rolling Stones, Hendrix gave musical voice to the creative and social rebellion of the 1960s. The disunity of that decade, and perhaps even that of the twentieth-century artistic consciousness itself, seemed made manifest as the tune of the "Star-Spangled Banner" disappeared into a barrage of noise.

Manheim

WORLD EVENTS		HENDRIX'S LIFE
World War II 1939–45		
	1942	James Marshall (Jimi) Hendrix is born
Communist China is established	1949	
Korean War	1950–53	
African independence movement begins	1957	
	1963	Hendrix plays guitar in Little Richard's band
	1965	Hendrix moves to Greenwich Village
	1966	In England, Hendrix forms The Jimi Hendrix Experience
	1967	Hendrix releases *Are You Experienced?* LP
	1968	Hendrix releases *Electric Ladyland*
	1969	Hendrix performs at Woodstock festival
	1970	Hendrix dies
Vietnam War ends	1975	

For Further Reading

Hendrix, James A., as told to Jas Obrecht. *My Son Jimi.* Seattle: AlJas Enterprises, 1999.

Shapiro, Harry. *Jimi Hendrix, Electric Gypsy.* New York: St. Martin's Press, 1995.

Ward, Ed, Geoffrey Stokes, and Ken Tucker. *Rock of Ages: The Rolling Stone History of Rock & Roll.* New York: Rolling Stone Press, 1986.

Hiroshige

Printmaker
1797–1858

Life and Work

Hiroshige was the last great master of the theme of landscapes in the *ukiyo-e* tradition of woodblock prints.

WORLD EVENTS		HIROSHIGE'S LIFE
French Revolution begins	1789	
	1797	Hiroshige is born
	1809	Hiroshige becomes disciple of Utagawa Toyohiro
Latin American independence movement begins	1811	
Congress of Vienna reorganizes Europe	1815	
	1833–34	Hiroshige produces *Fifty-three Stations of the Tokaido*
Revolutions in Austria, France, Germany, and Italy	1848	
	1858	Hiroshige dies
U.S. Civil War	1861–65	

Hiroshige (Ando Hiroshige in full) was born in 1797, the son of a fire warden in Edo, Japan. With the tragic death of his parents in 1809, Hiroshige, at age 12, became heir to his father's official position and the family inheritance. Seeking a career in the arts, Hiroshige became a disciple of the *ukiyo-e* woodblock-print master Utagawa Toyohiro (1774–1829) that same year. Hiroshige also trained in the Kano School of decorative screen paintings with Okajima Rinsai and *bunjinga,* or literati painting, with Ooka Umpo. He also demonstrated an interest in the use of Western representational techniques as found in the paintings of the Shijo School.

In 1830 Hiroshige finally turned to the genre for which he would become best known, landscape woodblock prints. *Ukiyo-e* woodblock prints were mechanically reproduced art that catered to the popular tastes of the merchant class that was becoming increasingly affluent in Edo, the new administrative center of Japan. Among the themes typically represented in *ukiyo-e* ("art of the floating world") were images of geisha and their life in the pleasure quarters of the Yoshiwara district, as well as portraits of actors in the popular Kabuki theater.

Hiroshige was profoundly influenced by the work of Katsushika Hokusai (1760–1849), who introduced scenes of the Japanese landscape in such series of prints as the *Thirty-six Views of Mount Fuji,* begun in 1823 and completed around 1831.

With the publication of the series, *Fifty-three Stations of the Tokaido* (1833–34), Hiroshige emerged as the most famous and popular printmaker of the Tokugawa period. This series was based on Hiroshige's experiences when he accompanied a group traveling to Kyoto along the main highway known as Tokaido, or Eastern Sea Route. Each scene captures the ambience and local activities of those living at the various post stations along the road connecting Edo with Kyoto. Hiroshige introduces a seasonal element and vivid atmospheric effects signifying the different weather conditions. For example, *Sudden Shower at Shonon* portrays villagers on a road running for shelter from the sudden downpour. The roofs of the village can be seen below, as the artist masterfully captures row after row of trees progressively receding through gray veils of rain and mist. Hiroshige also developed new compositional arrangements that present an aerial view, or a low vantage point and level perspective into the distance. This series quickly established Hiroshige as the most popular printmaker of his day.

Hiroshige went on to develop another series based on the inland highway known as Kisokaido, as well as local scenic spots around the important cities of Edo and Kyoto. He was active up until the end of his life. In 1858, at the age of 61, he died when a cholera epidemic swept through the city of Edo.

Legacy

Hiroshige's works would come to exert a powerful influence on late nineteenth-century French Impressionist painters.

A year after Hiroshige's death, his 13-year-old adopted daughter, Otatsu, married one of his disciples, Shigensobu (1826–69), who would go on to adopt the family name Ando and the title Hiroshige II. He made a large number of prints in Hiroshige's style, such as the series *One Hundred Views of Celebrated Places in Various Provinces,* published between 1859 and 1861. In 1865, not long after Hiroshige II left his master's house, Otatsu married another one of her father's disciples, Shigetora (also known as Shigemasa), who would eventually come to be known as Hiroshige III. His landscape prints in the tradition of Hiroshige were among the works sent by Japanese officials to the Paris Universal Exposition in 1867. In the twentieth century, the prints of Kawase Hasui (1883–1957) are perhaps most closely identified with the Hiroshige style.

Hiroshige's influence was perhaps most importantly felt in Europe. Japanese woodblock prints are believed to have first entered Paris when they were used to wrap Japanese ceramic export ware. The influence of these prints can be found in the works of EDOUARD MANET, VINCENT VAN GOGH, and Paul Gauguin. Van Gogh was especially influenced by the rich color and flat planar design of Hiroshige's prints. He made several paintings based on Hiroshige's images of delicate plum blossoms, as well as an actual copy in oil paint of Hiroshige's *Rain Shower on Ohashi Bridge,* a print from a series executed in his last years, *One Hundred Views of Famous Places in Edo* (1856–58).

Goldberg

For Further Reading

Hiroshige. *One Hundred Famous Views of Edo.* New York: George Braziller, 1986.

Michner, James A. *Japanese Prints: From the Early Masters to the Modern.* Rutland, Vt., and Tokyo: Charles E. Tuttle Publishers, 1959.

Stern, Harold P. *Master Prints of Japan: Ukiyo-e Hanga.* Exhibition catalogue. New York: Harry N. Abrams, 1969.

Hitchcock, Alfred

Filmmaker
1899–1980

Life and Work

Alfred Hitchcock, the English-born film director, gained worldwide popular and critical renown for the many suspense thrillers he made during a 51-year career that began during the silent era in England and ended in postwar America.

Born in 1899, the son of a grocer, Hitchcock studied engineering at the University of London, and subsequently took a position in the advertising department of a telegraph and cable company. His first film job, in 1920, was designing title cards for the Famous Players-Lasky Corporation, an American company. He made his directorial debut in 1925 with *The Pleasure Garden*. Hitchcock's second film, *The Lodger* (1926), about a man suspected of being Jack the Ripper, was a success, and introduced a theme he was to revisit many times in his career—a protagonist is falsely accused of a crime and becomes involved in a web of intrigue in his efforts to prove his innocence.

Hitchcock went on to make *The Man Who Knew Too Much* (1934), *The Thirty-Nine Steps* (1935), *Sabotage* (1936, adapted from JOSEPH CONRAD's *The Secret Agent*), and *The Lady Vanishes* (1938). He made his last film in England, *Jamaica Inn* (1939), the same year he immigrated to the United States.

Hitchcock's American work began successfully with the Oscar-winning feature *Rebecca* (1940), which, like *Jamaica Inn*, was based on a novel by Daphne du Maurier. Working within a highly commercialized industry whose intent was to produce formulaic features for mass consumption, Hitchcock, along with a handful of other directors, managed to develop a recognizable personal style.

One of the most popular American filmmakers of his time, Hitchcock has become one of the most written about and critically lauded. While the public flocked to his films for the delicious experience of being manipulated by a masterful entertainer, critics admired his meticulous technique and disturbing insight into the evil that lurked just below the surface of everyday normality. Among the highlights of his output in the 1940s were *Suspicion* (1941), *Shadow of a Doubt* (1943), *Spellbound* (1945), and *Notorious* (1946).

Hitchcock meticulously planed every shot, including lighting and camera angles. His reputation as the master craftsman rests most securely on the series of big-budget classics of the 1950s, including most notably *Strangers on a Train* (1951), *Rear Window* (1955), *Vertigo* (1958), and *North by Northwest* (1959).

This period of brilliant productivity concluded with the release of *Psycho* (1960), his most famous and perhaps most frightening film. It shocked audiences of its time with its uncommonly graphic violence, in particular its famed shower scene—a tour de force of editing and shot selection—and with its breaking of film convention: the murder of a protagonist early in the film

Hitchcock continued to amplify and explore his favorite themes in successful thrillers and espionage films that included *The Birds* (1960) and his final film, *Family Plot* (1976). During the 1950s and 1960s, Hitchcock also produced and hosted two successful television mystery series. He received the American Film Institute's Lifetime Achievement Award in 1979, and was knighted by Queen Elizabeth II shortly before his death in April of 1980.

Legacy

Universally acknowledged as the master of cinematic suspense, Alfred Hitchcock virtually invented the thriller genre. His theory of suspense was based on the idea that the film must let the audience in on information that

its threatened protagonists were not privy to. His films, which involved a subtle blend of sex, humor and suspense, shamelessly manipulated the emotions and minds of his audience.

Hitchcock has a well-deserved reputation as a master of efficiency in filmmaking. The bulk of his editing took place before a film was made and was reflected in his careful scripting of every aspect of every shot. His style combined, as has no one's before or since, a fluency in all the visual aspects of filming: framing a shot, camera movement, and cutting from one scene to another. Thus he became the greatest visual artist in American film.

Hitchcock's high rank among international film directors is unquestionable. The degree of influence he has had on younger directors can be seen in the fact that so many of them have chosen to write about him: FRANÇOIS TRUFFAUT, Peter Bogdanovich, Claude Chabrol, and Eric Rohmer have all written books on his work. For the critics of the French New Wave, who held him in reverence, he exemplified their auteur theory of the cinema. His immensely popular films are instantly recognizable as the distinctive work of an original artist; they are "Hitchcock films."

Domenico

WORLD EVENTS		HITCHCOCK'S LIFE
Spanish-American War	1898	
	1899	Alfred Hitchcock is born
World War I	1914–18	
Russian Revolution	1917	
	1925	Hitchcock directs his first film
Great Depression	1929–39	
	1934–39	Hitchcock directs a series of thrillers in Britain
World War II	1939–45	
	1939	Hitchcock moves to the United States
Communist China is established	1949	
Korean War	1950–53	
African independence movement begins	1957	
	1960	Hitchcock directs *Psycho*
Vietnam War ends	1975	
	1980	Hitchcock dies
Dissolution of Soviet Union	1991	

For Further Reading
Phillips, Gene D. *Alfred Hitchcock*. Boston: Twayne Publishers, 1984.
Rothman, William. *Hitchcock: The Murderous Gaze*. Cambridge, Mass.: Harvard University Press, 1982.
Spoto, Donald. *The Dark Side of Genius: The Life of Alfred Hitchcock*. Boston: Little, Brown, 1983.

Holiday, Billie

Vocalist
1915–1959

Life and Work

Widely recognized as jazz's greatest vocalist, Billie Holiday was different from that music's other acclaimed singers. Instead of dazzling audiences with virtuosity and power, she created a quiet, personal style that seemed rooted in the tragic events of her own life.

Dubbed "Lady Day" by her creative partner, saxophonist Lester Young, Holiday was born Eleanora Fagan on April 17, 1915, in Baltimore, Maryland. Her childhood left her with psychic scars that troubled her for all of her short life: she was abandoned by her father, Clarence Holiday, a traveling jazz guitarist, and apparently was forced to turn to a life of prostitution while in her early teens.

It was in a brothel that she first encountered jazz recordings by LOUIS ARMSTRONG and BESSIE SMITH, each of whom influenced her profoundly. From Armstrong she learned that the voice could transform and elaborate a melody line as surely as any instrument could. From Smith, Holiday inherited a mixture of sharp pride and melancholy vulnerability; in her own work, the combination seemed emotionally stretched to the breaking point.

Holiday made her vocal debut at a Harlem nightclub in 1931; two years later Columbia talent agent John Hammond heard her singing and arranged for her to record with bandleader Benny Goodman. In 1935 Holiday had her first artistic successes on recordings made with a band led by pianist Teddy Wilson. In 1938 she toured with the group of white bandleader Artie Shaw, challenging the show business segregation that was the norm at the time.

Never a runaway popular success, she gained favor with progressive audiences, especially in New York City, and secured it with 1939's brilliant "Strange Fruit," a powerful anti-lynching song. One of the few jazz vocalists to contribute original compositions to the repertoire, Holiday co-wrote the much-covered "God Bless the Child," a chillingly wry reflection on the childhood poverty she knew so well.

In the 1940s Holiday became addicted to heroin and alcohol; she was jailed for much of 1947 on drug charges. Although later albums such as 1958's *Lady in Satin* revealed no diminution of her expressiveness, her voice suffered. On her deathbed in 1959 she faced police who were investigating her drug use. She died in New York on July 17 of that year.

Legacy

As the African-American social critic Amiri Baraka once trenchantly observed, Billie Holiday expressed "a black landscape of need." She has been remembered not only for her vocal abilities but also for how she made her art and life seem one and the same.

Preeminent among jazz vocalists in her subtlety of technique, she was named by Frank Sinatra, a singer of a completely different personality, as the greatest single influence on his own style. Extending the accomplishments of her mentors, she virtually created the art of modern jazz singing with her light, flexible style that seemed to dance around the beat and traverse a range of moods within the scope of a single musical phrase.

Not a powerful singer like Smith, Holiday was an artist of the microphone, which kept her voice at a conversational level and heightened the personal quality of her singing. Ultimately that personal quality has been Holiday's greatest legacy, setting her apart among creators in an art form that has often valued pure technique. Holiday sang from the heart and said herself that she drew on her own life in her singing.

"Strange Fruit" spawned a tradition of political jazz songs that could be heard several decades later in the work of such vocalists as Abbey Lincoln and Nina Simone. Yet even Holiday's more political work seemed to emanate from her own victimization. In Billie Holiday, the hard life of African Americans was transformed into tragic vocal art.

Manheim

For Further Reading

Clarke, Donald. *Wishing on the Moon: The Life and Times of Billie Holiday.* London and New York: Viking, 1994.

Holiday, Billie. *Lady Sings the Blues.* New York: Avon, 1976.

O'Meally, Robert G. *Lady Day: The Many Faces of Billie Holiday.* New York: Arcade, 1991

Homer

Poet

c. Eighth Century B.C.E.

Life and Work

The *Iliad* and the *Odyssey*, two epic poems about the Trojan War attributed to a singer of tales named Homer, are cornerstones of Western literature.

Homer may have been an actual individual—or more than one. Some scholars contend that the two epics were composed by two different poets. Above all, though, Homer is a legend, an idea. Beyond what can be speculatively inferred from the language and descriptions in the *Iliad* and the *Odyssey*, nothing is known about when and where he might have lived. The poems themselves tell stories set in a distant past: the *Iliad* depicts the exploits of the Greek hero of the Trojan War, Achilles, and the *Odyssey* describes the eventful return home from the war of a king, Odysseus.

Greece at the time the poems originated had no writing system; the syllabic writing of the Mycenaean culture of around the twelfth century B.C.E. had disappeared, and the diffusion of what became the classical Greek alphabet lay in the future. The epics were first written down in the late seventh century B.C.E. after having been passed on orally for a length of time, during which any actual recollections about a possible historical Homer were lost. The creator(s) of the poems clearly knew the geography around Troy that forms their backdrop, spoke a language that suggests the poems were composed after 900 B.C.E. but before 700, and refer to certain cultural details that point to the latter part of that time span. Beyond that, Homer remains a cipher.

Nevertheless, the knowledge that Homer was an oral poet, a bard rather than a writer, tells us something about the two great poems themselves and about their creation. The *Iliad* is over 16,000 lines long, but we know from observing oral poets in other, more recent cultures that its maker did not commit every word of the text to memory. Instead the poem is constructed through the use of formulas of various kinds—stock descriptions, story elements, rhetorical blocks that begin and conclude sections of text, for example—that the poet might vary according to inspiration or the needs of a specific performance. The *Odyssey* includes an episode in which a blind poet sings heroic tales at a feast; some scholars believe that Homer offered the interlude as a kind of self-portrait.

Legacy

Homer's legacy rests on the monumentality and the compelling grip of his two great poems. Even today, at a distance of almost 3,000 years, there is little diminution in the enjoyment that students of literature find when encountering them.

Even if not composed by the same person, the action-packed *Iliad* and the adventure-rich *Odyssey* form a compelling pair—as the later Greeks themselves recognized. Aristotle speculated that the *Odyssey* was a work of Homer's old age. His supposition was but one of a whole host of stories about Homer that the Greeks fabricated out of whole cloth, clearly demonstrating the extent to which the ideals of heroism and quest exemplified by the two epics informed the entire tradition of Greek literature and drama. The great epic of ancient Rome, VIRGIL's *Aeneid*, though it was a written-out work, took Homer's works as models, and the elevated language and idealism of that work in turn influenced European literature for centuries. JAMES JOYCE built, in *Ulysses*, a structure elaborately parallel to that of the *Odyssey*, secure in the knowledge that educated readers would enjoy discovering the relationship between the two texts. Homer is immediately comprehensible, then, in part because his influence lives on today.

The ways in which the *Iliad* and *Odyssey* are different from other epics are at least as important as the similarities mentioned above. While the epics of Scandinavia or the Balkans that have come down to modern times may last for several hours when spoken, they are dwarfed by the Homeric poems, which must have required several sessions to be performed in full. The *Iliad* and the *Odyssey* are novelistic in scope, with numerous characters, including gods and monsters, whose paths cross and whose motivations conflict. They present not simply warriors but fully formed human beings in dramatic interactions. They are, in short, not tribal tales but Western culture's first works of art and in large measure the inspiration for all the others that followed.

Manheim

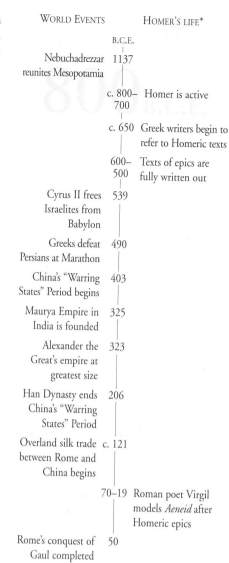

WORLD EVENTS		HOMER'S LIFE*
	B.C.E.	
Nebuchadrezzar reunites Mesopotamia	1137	
	c. 800–700	Homer is active
	c. 650	Greek writers begin to refer to Homeric texts
	600–500	Texts of epics are fully written out
Cyrus II frees Israelites from Babylon	539	
Greeks defeat Persians at Marathon	490	
China's "Warring States" Period begins	403	
Maurya Empire in India is founded	325	
Alexander the Great's empire at greatest size	323	
Han Dynasty ends China's "Warring States" Period	206	
Overland silk trade between Rome and China begins	c. 121	
	70–19	Roman poet Virgil models *Aeneid* after Homeric epics
Rome's conquest of Gaul completed	50	

Scholars cannot date the specific events in Homer's life with accuracy.

For Further Reading

Beye, Charles Rowan. *Ancient Epic Poetry*. Ithaca, N.Y.: Cornell University Press, 1993.

Camps, W. A. *An Introduction to Homer*. Oxford: Oxford University Press, 1980.

Griffin, Jasper. *Homer on Life and Death*. Oxford: Oxford University Press, 1980.

Homer, Winslow

Painter, Printmaker, and Illustrator
1836–1910

WORLD EVENTS		HOMER'S LIFE:
Congress of Vienna reorganizes Europe	1815	
	1836	Winslow Homer is born
Revolutions in Austria, France, Germany, and Italy	1848	
	1859	Homer begins working as an illustrator for *Harper's Weekly*
U.S. Civil War	1861–65	
	1866	Homer is influenced by French painters
Germany is united	1871	
	1873	Homer begins to paint in watercolors
	1883	Homer moves to Prout's Neck, Maine
Spanish-American War	1898	
	1910	Homer dies
World War I	1914–18	

Life and Work

Winslow Homer, regarded as America's greatest watercolorist, explored in his work the complex relations between humankind and the natural world.

Born in Boston in 1836, Homer was the son of a father who was a hardware importer and a mother who was an amateur painter. His early interest in art led to an apprenticeship at age 19 to a lithographer in Boston. He began working as a freelance illustrator in 1857, and in 1859 he was hired as an illustrator by *Harper's Weekly*, for which he worked on and off for the next 28 years.

Traveling with the Union armies during the Civil War, Homer sent back drawings of military life for *Harper's*. During this period, he began to work in oils. One of the best known of his early works in oil, *Prisoners from the Front* (1866), is a moving depiction of war.

During a 10-month stay in France beginning in 1866, Homer was profoundly influenced by the realistic style of the Barbizon School of painters. On his return to the United States, he began to focus on outdoor scenes as his primary subject, completing *Snap the Whip* (1872) and *Game of Croquet* (1866). In subject matter, these paintings belonged to the genre tradition but avoided the sentimentalism that characterized the work of earlier genre artists. A turning point in Homer's career came in 1873 when he took up watercolor painting, which was to become his signature medium.

During a two-year stay on the coast of England, Homer worked almost exclusively in watercolor, perfecting his technique. His subject matter gradually shifted from lighthearted genre scenes to the struggle between humankind and nature. *The Lifeline* (1884) is a good example of Homer's dramatic work. In it, an unconscious woman and a heroic rescue worker make their way from a sinking ship to a rescue boat, precariously suspended by cables over a violent sea.

Returning to America, Homer built a studio in 1883 on the coast of Maine. He continued to focus on the relationship between humans and the sea, producing such early classic paintings as *The Fog Warning* (1885) and *Eight Bells* (1886).

In later works, such as *The Northeaster* (1895), humans began to fade from his pictures as Homer turned his attention to the power of the sea. Over the course of his career, he moved away from the carefully crafted studio oils of the 1860s to the spontaneous expression of watercolors painted on site. This change imbued his work with a sensuality that his oils lacked. Although he traveled widely, his subject was invariably the world of nature that he loved. Homer died in 1910.

Legacy

Regarded in his later years as America's greatest painter, Winslow Homer received many awards and honors but was never financially successful. The public of his time preferred sentimental narrative scenes to Homer's realism.

Homer is often compared to his contemporaries, the French Impressionists. Like them, he preferred painting out-of-doors, focused on middle-class subject matter, and had a more painterly interest in color than did the linear stylists of the Academy.

However, Homer was an individualist. Unlike the Impressionists, he did not blur the distinction between foreground and background. While light is important in Homer's work, he did not organize his paintings centrally around the concerns of light and color. Finally, and increasingly in his later works, he was influenced by the scientific age then emerging: he sought to investigate the relation between humans and nature. Whether intentionally or not, his paintings of humans set amidst an untamed and indifferent nature appeared to reflect the controversy raging in America between Darwinian natural selection and biblical manifest or revealed truth.

Today Homer is regarded as a uniquely American painter who helped nineteenth-century American painting emerge from the shadows of French art and who captured America's enthusiasm for the outdoors. His watercolors, in particular, have influenced artists as diverse as John La Farge, John Marin, and Andrew Wyeth.

Domenico

For Further Reading

Grossman, Julian. *Echo of a Distant Drum: Winslow Homer and the Civil War.* New York: Harry N. Abrams, 1974.

Hendricks, Gordon. *The Life and Work of Winslow Homer.* New York: Harry N. Abrams, 1979.

Kushner, Marilyn S. *Winslow Homer: Illustrating America.* New York: George Braziller, 2000.

Hugo, Victor-Marie

Novelist, Poet, Dramatist, and Critic
1802–1885

Life and Work

Victor-Marie Hugo, prolific writer, political reformer, and lover of life, became a symbol of French culture within his lifetime. His vital presence continues today in the realms of literature and, perhaps surprisingly, musical theater.

Hugo was born in Besançon, France, into a military family in 1802. He traveled widely throughout his childhood until, at 12, he and his mother settled in Paris. When he was about 17, Hugo founded a literary review, *Le Conservateur littéraire* and published *Odes et poésies*, his first volume of poetry. Hugo wrote and published a succession of novels and poems while also writing plays and advocating a new kind of dramatic art. In an introduction to his play *Cromwell* (1827), he demanded that modern drama abandon the strictures of classical tragedy in favor of a form that would mingle the grotesque and the sublime to create emotionally appealing and historically realistic drama.

In 1831 Hugo published his novel *Notre Dame de Paris* (*The Hunchback of Notre Dame*) to immediate international acclaim. The novel tells a romantic story of great breadth and emotional power that revolves around Hugo's political convictions. The novel demonstrates that the poor function as scapegoats for bourgeois society and makes demands for greater rights.

Hugo was elected to the Académie Française in 1841 and his literary production lessened as he became more involved in politics. He wrote *Les Chatiments* (1853) as a political indictment of Napoléon and his repressively dictatorial policies.

His next work, *Les Contemplations* (1856), was a spiritual autobiography discussing the nature of life and death. *Les Misérables*, his epic novel about the battle of good and evil among the poor and the rich of Paris, was published in 1862 and continues to be his most widely read work.

Hugo died in Paris in 1885 and was buried with great honor in the Panthéon, along with other prominent French citizens, such as Voltaire and Jean-Jacques Rousseau. According to his last request, his body was carried to burial in a poor man's hearse; it was followed by a parade of mourners through the streets of Paris.

Legacy

Victor-Marie Hugo was a national hero in his lifetime; people around the world celebrated his poetry, attended his plays, and read his novels. His work survived the century following his death with its emotional intensity and dramatic potential intact.

The Symbolist movement that came after Hugo's death was greatly influenced by the metaphysical ruminations of *Les Contemplations*. The important poets of that movement, particularly Stéphane Mallarmé, examined the use of symbol and metaphor in the often obscure language of Hugo's spiritual autobiography, considering it as important as CHARLES-PIERRE BAUDELAIRE's *Les Fleurs du mal* (1857).

Hugo's poems, novels, and plays have all inspired musical and theatrical reworkings over the years. Hungarian composer FRANZ LISZT began the tradition with his *Mazeppa*, a symphonic poem inspired by *La Légende des siécles*. Louis-Hector Berlioz hoped to make *The Hunchback of Notre Dame* into an opera but Hugo declined. The greatest example of this trend is, of course, the musical theater version of *Les Misérables*, which opened in the early 1980s in London and has continued with unabated popularity ever since. Film versions of a number of Hugo's works have been made over the years, including the famous *The Hunchback of Notre Dame*, starring Lon Chaney, in 1924; *Ruy Blas*, adapted and directed by Jean Cocteau in 1947; and a cartoon version of *The Hunchback of Notre Dame*, made by Walt Disney Pictures in 1996.

Watson

WORLD EVENTS		HUGO'S LIFE
French Revolution begins	1789	
	1802	Victor Hugo is born
Latin American independence movement begins	1811	
Congress of Vienna reorganizes Europe	1815	
	1819	Hugo founds *Le Conservateur littéraire*
	1831	Hugo publishes *The Hunchback of Notre Dame*
	1841	Hugo is elected to Académie Française
Revolutions in Austria, France, Germany, and Italy	1848	
U.S. Civil War	1861–65	
	1862	Hugo publishes *Les Misérables*
Germany is united	1871	
	1885	Hugo dies
Spanish-American War	1898	

For Further Reading

Houston, John Porter. *Victor Hugo*. Indianapolis, Ind.: MacMillan Publishing, 1988.
Robb, Graham. *Victor Hugo: A Biography*. New York: W. W. Norton, 1998.

Ibsen, Henrik

Playwright and Poet
1828–1906

Life and Work

Henrik Ibsen created a national theater for Norway and changed the direction of nineteenth-century theater with his realistic plays depicting the defects of society.

Ibsen was born into a wealthy family in Skien, Norway, on March 20, 1828. He was 22 when his first play, *The Burial Mound*, was staged at the Christiana Theater. In 1851 he became the assistant stage manager in the Norwegian Theater in Bergen, where one of his duties was to write and produce one play each year. His verse plays of the period were largely based on Norse sagas and traditional Scandinavian folk songs and stories.

When the Norwegian Theater went bankrupt in the early 1860s, Ibsen left Norway to live and travel in Germany, Italy, and Denmark. While abroad, Ibsen kept his distance from the surrounding people and cultures as he focused on writing realistic dramas portraying Norwegian culture and character. These early plays, including *Brand* (1866) and *Peer Gynt* (1867), introduced themes that would reappear throughout much of his work: the duty of the individual to be true to his own convictions and the role of the individual in society. *Peer Gynt* was harshly critical of the Norwegian national character.

Between 1877 and 1882, Ibsen published the four realistic social plays that caught the public's attention: *Samfundets Støtter* (*The Pillars of Society*, 1877), *Et dukkehjem* (*A Doll's House*, 1879), *Gengangere* (*Ghosts*, 1881), and *En folkefiende* (*An Enemy of the People*, 1882). The plays' subjects, which included marriage, adultery, and religion, challenged a middle-class value system that Ibsen saw as standing in the way of individual freedom.

Nora, Ibsen's most famous rebel and the protagonist of his most controversial play, *A Doll's House*, recognizes that her marriage is based on false assumptions about her identity and desires. Nora eventually leaves her husband and her young children, liberating herself from her society's traditional institutions and authority.

Ibsen's dramatic confrontations with the values of bourgeois society made his work the subject of censorship, controversy, and immense popularity throughout Europe. The English playwright George Bernard Shaw was among several celebrated defenders of the plays.

Plays written during the 1880s and 1890s like *Vildanden* (*The Wild Duck*, 1884) and *Hedda Gabler* (1890) continued to address the relationship between the individual and society while using complex symbolic elements such as the wild duck, a child's pet that comes to represent a variety of the forces at work in the play. In 1891 Ibsen returned to Norway and wrote several important plays, *Bygmester Solness* (*The Master Builder*, 1892), *Lille Eyolf* (*Little Eyolf*, 1894), and *Naar vi døde vaagner* (*When We Dead Awaken*, 1899) among them. These later plays increasingly portrayed the individual as isolated from society rather than battling it.

Ibsen suffered a series of strokes after the completion of *When We Dead Awaken*. He died on May 23, 1906.

Legacy

With what is referred to as his "social problem play," Henrik Ibsen turned the theater into a socially relevant forum in which to engage the problems and fears of a people.

Much of late nineteenth-century theater was light comedy that sought only to entertain, drew on the emotions of Romanticism, and refused to reflect upon the drastic changes taking place in a newly industrialized society. Ibsen's plays flew in the face of these outdated concepts and defied the Romantic idea that art's single purpose was to represent the beautiful and the ideal. Instead, his plays focused on the most painful and degraded sides of social life. Their realistic depiction of social ills struck a chord with audiences, first in Norway and, soon, all over Europe. *A Doll's House* was received enthusiastically by contemporary feminist thinkers and with outrage by those who stood for more traditional values. Nora's decision to leave her husband, and thus the play's advocacy of a woman's right to choose the direction of her life, has been pointed to as a starting point of the women's movement of the turn of the century.

Ibsen's work was important to the Modernist writers who, following on his heels, gave him credit for freeing the drama from its trivial role as a mirror of bourgeois life and allowing it to reveal the deeper human forces behind the social world. JAMES JOYCE and VIRGINIA WOOLF both wrote of Ibsen's transformation of the play into a potent commentary upon modern life and society.

The influence of Ibsen's social problem play continues to be apparent in modern drama that tackles difficult and controversial subjects. Like *A Doll's House*, Arthur Miller's *The Crucible* (1953) allegorically discussed a larger social issue (in Miller's case, McCarthyism in the United States) in the context of a small community.

Watson

WORLD EVENTS		IBSEN'S LIFE
Congress of Vienna reorganizes Europe	1815	
	1828	Henrik Ibsen is born
Revolutions in Austria, France, Germany, and Italy	1848	
	1850	Ibsen's *The Burial Mound* is staged
U.S. Civil War	1861–65	
	1867	Ibsen writes *Peer Gynt*
Germany is united	1871	
	1879	Ibsen writes *A Doll's House*
	1891	Ibsen returns to Norway
Spanish-American War	1898	
	1899	Ibsen writes his final play, *When We Dead Awaken*
	1906	Ibsen dies
World War I	1914–18	

For Further Reading
Ibsen: The Complete Major Prose Plays. Translated by Rolf Fjelde. New York: Penguin Books, 1965.
McFarlane, James, ed. *The Cambridge Companion to Ibsen.* Cambridge: Cambridge University Press, 1994.

Jackson, Mahalia

Vocalist

1911–1972

Life and Work

Widely acclaimed as the greatest black gospel vocalist of them all, Mahalia Jackson had a contralto voice of a sheer power that seemed to match the exalted subject matter about which she sang.

Jackson was born into profound poverty in New Orleans on October 26, 1911. The family had to use cornmeal to filter the water pumped to its small shack. Both her parents were devout Baptists, and Jackson was singing in church by the time she was four. Her vocal education came partly in church choirs, but as a young woman she also absorbed the deliberate, powerful blues of BESSIE SMITH. In addition, Jackson learned from the unrestrained emotionalism of black sanctified churches, effectively fusing it with her own majestic style.

After moving to Chicago in 1927, she worked as a domestic servant. She made a recording in 1934, but success would not come until after she spent five years (1939 to 1944) touring as a song demonstrator with the renowned gospel composer THOMAS A. DORSEY. Dorsey's slow, intense hymns provided space for Jackson's towering musical trajectories; he is said to have written his famous "Peace in the Valley" with her in mind. In 1946, Jackson broke through with a recording on the Apollo label, "Move On Up a Little Higher." This and its successors spread Jackson's fame far and wide in black churches. Jackson began to reach white audiences as well with a 1950 Carnegie Hall concert, and in 1954 she was given a Sunday evening gospel show on the CBS radio network.

Appearing on the *Ed Sullivan Show* in 1956, she moved toward a musical sound shaped by white string orchestra and small combo arrangers, but refused to record secular music or appear in club venues despite all the offers that resulted from her massive popularity. Her performance of a funeral hymn in the 1959 film *Imitation of Life* gave the flavor of her appearances in person. Instead of crossing over to pop, Jackson tried to spread the gospel music and message as widely as she could. She toured Europe several times, and sang "I've Been 'Buked and I've Been Scorned" before Dr. Martin Luther King, Jr. delivered his famous "I Have a Dream" speech; some observers have claimed that she urged King to "tell them about your dream." After a bitter divorce and several years of ill health, Jackson died near Chicago on January 27, 1972.

Legacy

The porous nature of the boundary between sacred and secular in African-American music is illustrated well by Mahalia Jackson's career and its later resonances. Although she resolutely stuck to gospel, she built her style on the blues and shaped the vocals of several generations of secular female vocalists who came after her.

Looming large among those who felt her influence was ARETHA FRANKLIN, a gospel-drenched vocalist who in her early recordings for the Columbia label in many ways stepped into the pop shoes that had been offered to Jackson. Franklin's classic recordings for Atlantic, more touched by southern soul and gospel, further revealed her indebtedness to Jackson: songs such as "I Never Loved a Man (The Way I Love You)" drew on Jackson's sense of the architecture of a slow blues-inflected piece, on her explosive vocal inflections, and on the characteristic piano accompaniment of her Apollo recordings. Franklin herself named Jackson as her favorite singer.

Beyond Franklin, the list of vocalists who Jackson influenced is a long one. It has become commonplace to speak of the influence of black gospel on contemporary rhythm-and-blues music, but not so commonly recognized is the fact that the influence comes primarily in the vocal realm, and to a significant degree from Jackson. In musical texture, harmony, and form, black popular music diverges considerably from its sacred counterpart, but in the area of vocal style the transition from youthful singing in church to adult pop activity has been an easy one for performers to make. Jackson's ability to produce a soaring, long-breathed sound from deep in her chest was emulated by such vocal stars as Gladys Knight, Martha Reeves, and Etta James, to name just a few.

Mahalia Jackson's commitment to the gospel message was unwavering, but she enjoyed an influence that extended even beyond the genre she brought to perfection.

Manheim

WORLD EVENTS		JACKSON'S LIFE
Spanish-American War	1898	
	1911	Mahalia Jackson is born
World War I	1914–18	
Russian Revolution	1917	
	1927	Jackson moves to Chicago
Great Depression	1929–39	
	1934	Jackson makes first recording
	1939	Jackson begins touring with composer Thomas A. Dorsey
World War II	1939–45	
	1946	Jackson records "Move On Up a Little Higher"
Communist China is established	1949	
	1950	Jackson appears at Carnegie Hall
Korean War	1950–53	
	1954	Jackson is given show on CBS radio
African independence movement begins	1957	
	1959	Jackson appears in film *Imitation of Life*
	1972	Jackson dies
Vietnam War ends	1975	

For Further Reading

Goreau, Laurraine. *Just Mahalia, Baby.* Waco, Tex.: Word Books, 1975.

Jackson, Mahalia, and Evan McLeod Wylie. *Movin' On Up.* New York: Hawthorn Books, 1966.

Jāmi

(Mowlana Nur Ad-Din 'Abd
ar-Rahman Ibn Ahmad)

Poet
1414–1492

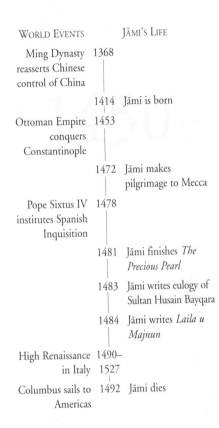

WORLD EVENTS		JĀMI'S LIFE
Ming Dynasty reasserts Chinese control of China	1368	
	1414	Jāmi is born
Ottoman Empire conquers Constantinople	1453	
	1472	Jāmi makes pilgrimage to Mecca
Pope Sixtus IV institutes Spanish Inquisition	1478	
	1481	Jāmi finishes *The Precious Pearl*
	1483	Jāmi writes eulogy of Sultan Husain Bayqara
	1484	Jāmi writes *Laila u Majnun*
High Renaissance in Italy	1490–1527	
Columbus sails to Americas	1492	Jāmi dies

Life and Work

Jāmi was one of the greatest classical poets of the golden age of medieval Persian poetry, helping to create the tradition of Sufic mystical poetry.

Mowlana Nur Ad-Din 'Abd ar-Rahman Ibn Ahmad was born on November 7, 1414, in the small town of Kharjird in Iran. He attended school in Herat, where he excelled in the study of rhetoric. He was exposed to Sufism for the first time when his father took him to see a Sufic saint on his way to Mecca. Jāmi then moved to Samarkand, where he studied astronomy. Legend has it that he won a debate with a famous teacher and suggested brilliant improvements upon literary works as a young man, thus gaining a reputation as a genius.

Jāmi was initiated into the Naqshbandi order of Sufi mystics as an adult. Sufism is an Islamic form of mysticism in which the believer rejects the material world and achieves a state of mystical union with God and with the Prophet Muhammad. There is a strong tradition of mystical literature within Sufism. Other medieval Persian poets include Omar Khayyam, Rumi, Saadi, Sanai, Attar, and Hafez. Like these poets, Jāmi combined religious and secular themes as he celebrated the beauty of the world in poems about love, pleasure, and poetry itself. He used these subjects to ask searching questions about wisdom, mortality, salvation, and the search for enlightenment. Jāmi was considered the last of the "seven masters" in Persian literature. In one of his great works, *Haft Aurang* (*The Seven Thrones*), he wrote an imitation of the poet Nexami's series of five epic poems, the *Khamseh*, enlarging it into seven parts.

Jāmi returned to Herat and joined the court of Sultan Husain Bayqara, who surrounded himself with scholars, poets, and artists. In 1472 Jāmi made a pilgrimage to Mecca. By this time he was already famous for his mystical poetry. He was invited by the Ottoman Sultan Muhammed II to join his court in Istanbul but declined, preferring a life of meditation and poetry. Muhammed II later asked him to write a poem comparing theologians, philosophers, and Sufis. Jāmi responded by writing *al Durrah al-Fakhirah* (*The Precious Pearl*, 1847). In it he asks a series of questions about the nature of God and discusses the positions of the three groups. Jāmi presents the Sufis as superior to the first two because it reconciles their opposing views.

In 1483, Jāmi wrote a eulogy of Sultan Husain Baiqara, which became the most well known of his poems. It is a romantic and mystical story of Joseph and Potiphar's wife from Sura XII in the Koran that has been widely imitated by Persian and Turkish writers. In 1484 Jāmi wrote *Laila u Majnun*, a work that combines a love story with a message of spiritual seeking; it was widely adapted by other poets.

Jāmi died in Herat in 1492.

Legacy

In Herat, the last great center of Islamic art during the golden age, Jāmi was one of the most important mystical poets.

During his lifetime, Jāmi was widely honored and celebrated by scholars and royalty throughout Persia and Turkey. His works continued to be widely read and commented upon after his death. *The Precious Pearl* generated a number of commentaries, one of the most famous by Abd al-Ghafur al-Lari, who also wrote a biography of Jāmi.

In his ghazals, traditional Persian lyrics, Jāmi juxtaposed devotional, satirical, mystical, and didactic subjects. His elaborate verse and beautiful imagery had a strong influence on the work of Persian-language poets who followed him in Iran, Turkey, and northern India.

One of Jāmi's prose works, the *Nafahat al-Uns*, a compendium of biographies of Muslim saints, has long been a source of historical information on Sufic mysticism. In the mid-nineteenth century there was a resurgence of scholarly interest in Jāmi's lyric poetry. Much of it was translated at that time, particularly by German and English scholars. In 1879 Jacobus Ecker completed a Latin translation of *The Precious Pearl*.

Jāmi's work was the subject of commentaries and critical studies in the twentieth century as well. In 1942 respected scholar Ali Asghar Hikmat wrote a monograph on Jāmi in which he stated that Jāmi was one of the greatest prose writers and poets of Islamic culture.

Watson

For Further Reading

De Bruijn, J. T. P. *Persian Sufi Poetry: An Introduction to the Mystical Use of Classical Persian Poems.* Richmond, England: Curzon Press, 1997.

Schimmel, Annemarie. *A Two-Colored Brocade: The Imagery of Persian Poetry.* Chapel Hill: University of North Carolina Press, 1992.

Jobim, Antonio Carlos

Musician
1927–1994

Life and Work

Brazil's most prominent and successful musical ambassador, the composer and pianist Antonio Carlos Jobim was one of the creators of bossa nova, a quiet style of jazz song that has often lent a Latin tinge to North American popular music.

Jobim (pronounced zho-BEEM) was born in Rio de Janeiro on January 25, 1927; he grew up in the city's Ipanema neighborhood, which would later lend its name to his most famous composition. A middle-class son of a diplomat–poet, Jobim studied several instruments with a German music teacher, but also grew to love the samba music that emanated from Rio's hillside slums.

Dropping out of architecture school to try to make a living in music, he at first played the piano in bars he called "little hells." In 1952 he broke into the recording business and rose quickly as an arranger and producer. His own creativity was fired by a 1956 collaboration with the British-educated Brazilian poet Vinícius de Morais on a stage production that retold the Greek Orpheus legend, setting it among Brazil's poor. Jobim's music became part of the internationally acclaimed film version, entitled *Black Orpheus*.

Gaining fluency as a songwriter, Jobim in 1958 embarked on another crucial collaboration when he met the guitarist and singer João Gilberto. Gilberto's low-key vocals and smooth guitar stylings fit perfectly with Jobim's romantic songs, which to North Americans would represent ideal evocations of tropical life. The new style the two created became known as bossa nova (in English "new wave"); the American jazz saxophonist Stan Getz was the first to realize its international potential. Getz included a version of Jobim's "Desafinado" ("Out of Tune") on his *Jazz Samba* album of 1962 (recorded with guitarist Charlie Byrd), and soon recorded his "The Girl from Ipanema" with Jobim and Gilberto themselves (Morais wrote the lyrics), featuring Gilberto's wife Astrud on vocals. This top 1964 hit inspired an American bossa nova craze; it succeeded in part because of the smooth translation of its text into English, a process Jobim supervised closely.

Jobim made his own U.S. recording debut in 1963, and among his many LP successes was a 1967 duet with an admirer, *Francis Albert Sinatra and Antonio Carlos Jobim*. His work from the 1970s on increasingly had classical orchestral elements; in this enterprise he had yet another important collaborator, the arranger Claus Ogerman. Jobim died in New York on December 8, 1994.

Legacy

Sometimes called the GEORGE GERSHWIN of Brazil, Antonio Carlos Jobim is a comparable figure: a composer-pianist whose work touched each leg of the twentieth-century musical triad of pop, jazz, and classical styles.

The parallel may be extended even further, for each composer succeeded in transplanting the music he had created onto another continent, where it flourished—Gershwin did much to spread American jazz and popular song in Europe, while Jobim left a lasting imprint on North American music. When he was at the peak of his fame in the 1960s, Jobim's bossa nova had numerous followers in pop and jazz.

Jobim's influence as a jazzman began with a 1962 concert at New York's Carnegie Hall in which he performed with Getz, Byrd, and the American dean of Latin jazz, trumpeter Dizzy Gillespie. It continued through Brazilian-influenced albums by many of the leading jazz stars of the later twentieth century; two perennially popular vocal examples were Sarah

Vaughan's *I Love Brazil* of 1977 and Ella Fitzgerald's 1980 *Ella Abraca Jobim*. Several of Jobim's compositions, such as the "One-Note Samba," became jazz standards.

Such bands as Sergio Mendes and Brasil '66 offered a smoothed-out version of bossa nova that enjoyed wide success and carved out a Brazilian niche in American pop. The bossa nova craze waxed and waned quickly, but Jobim's reputation as a songwriter never suffered; by the 1990s, when there was a strong revival of interest in sophisticated and adventurous popular songs from earlier eras, collectors and historians began to seek out his work, only a small percentage of which has been translated into English. An enduring presence in music as a result of such songs as "The Girl from Ipanema," "Desafinado," and "Quiet Nights of Quiet Stars," Jobim at the century's end seemed one of those musicians whose output would continue to yield hidden treasures.

Manheim

WORLD EVENTS		JOBIM'S LIFE
Russian Revolution	1917	
	1927	Antonio Carlos Jobim is born
Great Depression	1929–39	
World War II	1939–45	
Communist China is established	1949	
Korean War	1950–53	
	1952	Jobim breaks into Brazilian recording business as arranger
	1956	Jobim collaborates with Vinicius de Morais on *Orpheus* play
African independence movement begins	1957	
	1958	Jobim meets João Gilberto
	1962	Jobim performs at Carnegie Hall in New York
	1963	Jobim makes first U.S. recordings
	1964	"The Girl from Ipanema" becomes a hit
	1967	Jobim records with Frank Sinatra
Vietnam War ends	1975	
Dissolution of Soviet Union	1991	
South Africa dismantles apartheid	1994	Jobim dies

For Further Reading

McGowan, Chris, and Ricardo Pessanha. *The Brazilian Sound: Samba, Bossa Nova, and the Popular Music of Brazil.* Philadelphia: Temple University Press, 1998.

Schnabel, Tom. *Rhythm Planet.* New York: Universe Publishing, 1998.

Johnson, Robert

Musician
1911–1938

WORLD EVENTS		JOHNSON'S LIFE
Spanish-American War	1898	
	1911	Robert Johnson is born
World War I	1914–18	
Russian Revolution	1917	
Great Depression	1929–39	
	c. 1930	Johnson leaves the Mississippi Delta and later returns
	early 1930s	Johnson gains reputation as performer in Mississippi Delta region
	1936	Johnson recommended to ARC label by talent scout
		Johnson records in San Antonio
	1938	Johnson dies
World War II	1939–45	
Korean War	1950–53	
African independence movement begins	1957	
	1961	First LP reissue of Johnson's recordings
	1970	Second volume of Johnson's recordings reissued
Vietnam War ends	1975	

Life and Work

A shadowy figure known mostly through a few recordings and a large accumulation of legends, Robert Johnson was a force in transforming the blues from a shared folk music into an individualistic art form.

Johnson, a wandering musician who played in "juke joints" and other gathering places of his native Mississippi Delta, left only scant traces for later chroniclers. He seems to have been born on a plantation near Hazlehurst, Mississippi, on May 8, 1911. Bluesman Son House, who knew Johnson and likely influenced him stylistically, recalled the teenage Johnson's playing as an annoyance. Around 1930 Johnson left the Delta for some months, perhaps because of the death of his first wife. After he returned to Mississippi, the improvement in his skills was dramatic enough to inspire the story that Johnson had sold his soul to the Devil in exchange for mastery of the guitar. He may have been tutored by a never-recorded bluesman named Ike Zinnerman, and he also paid attention to the eerie music of Skip James, whose "22-20 Blues" Johnson reworked as the "32-20 Blues."

In 1936 a Jackson, Mississippi, music store owner and talent agent, H. C. Speir, recommended Johnson to the ARC record label, and in November of that year he went to San Antonio, Texas, and recorded 16 songs. One of them, "Terraplane Blues," sold reasonably well, and in June 1937 he recorded 13 more numbers. Accompanied only by his own guitar, he was just one of the many Delta blues singers recorded during the 1920s and 1930s, but each of his records was an unnerving and utterly distinct masterpiece. Johnson's songs were fearsomely complex rhythmically, instantly setting a dangerous-seeming level of tension. His lyrics, not all of them marked by the existential dread of his famous "Crossroads Blues" and "Hellhound on My Trail," were unified wholes, not strings of recalled verses like the lyrics of earlier folk blues performers.

Johnson's life ended near Greenwood, Mississippi, on August 16, 1938. He was most likely poisoned by the jealous husband of a woman he had flirted with at a performance a few days before.

Legacy

"The King of the Delta Blues Singers" was little known outside the Mississippi delta during his own lifetime, but since Robert Johnson's death his music has resounded in successive waves of influence. By the century's end he was considered the most celebrated figure of the country blues genre and one of the giants of blues in general.

Even in Johnson's own day, serious white blues aficionados were aware of his originality; when he died, Columbia Records impresario and BOB DYLAN discoverer John Hammond was trying to track him down to arrange a performance at a Carnegie Hall concert of 1938.

Although Johnson's music never really caught on with the record-buying public ("Terraplane Blues" was his sole success), it did not escape the notice of his fellow Delta musicians. Many of them were on the verge of moving north to Chicago, where they would create a new, urban form of the blues—by the 1950s played mostly by bands with electric instruments. Although Johnson played only an acoustic guitar, his music marked that of the next blues generation: Muddy Waters, Elmore James, and Jimmy Reed were a few of the musicians who were influenced by Johnson. The complex rhythms of Johnson's music impressed the Chicago bluesmen, and Johnson's virtuosity was a more general inspiration. After Johnson, the blues became a more individual, intentional form.

In the 1960s and 1970s, some of the young rock and roll guitarists who immersed themselves in Chicago blues began to investigate the music of the man who had inspired Waters and other urban bluesmen and spawned the inexhaustibly various versions of "Sweet Home Chicago." Johnson's recordings were reissued on two LP records (1961 and 1970), and finally his music became more widely known. Guitarist Eric Clapton recorded the "Crossroads Blues" with the British blues-rock group Cream, and there were many other rock versions of Johnson's songs. By the 1990s, after sumptuous boxed sets, biographical attempts, and dramatizations of Johnson's life, his place in history was secure.

Manheim

For Further Reading

Charters, Samuel. *Robert Johnson*. New York: Oak Publications, 1973.

Davis, Francis. *The History of the Blues*. New York: Hyperion, 1995.

Joplin, Scott

Pianist and Composer
1868–1917

Life and Work

One of the creators of piano ragtime, Scott Joplin wrote the "Maple Leaf Rag," the most famous and familiar rag of them all. He turned a barroom style of piano music into a genre of well-wrought composition that, he insisted, could stand comparison to the European classics.

Joplin was born on November 24, 1868, near the Texas–Louisiana border, and grew up in the town of Texarkana, which straddles Texas and Arkansas. Joplin sang in quartets and studied harmony with a local German musician who introduced him to classical music. Between 1884 and 1888, he left home and made a living as a wandering musician, playing the piano in clubs and saloons of various degrees of respectability and ill repute. He played cornet in a band at the 1893 Columbian Exposition in Chicago, a world's fair that brought African-American musicians new and wide exposure.

In 1895 two of his songs were published, and the following year he landed in Sedalia, Missouri, where he studied music and found a backer, the publisher John Stark, who agreed to pay him royalties of one cent per copy of sheet music sold. It was an unusually fair contract for an African-American musician of the day, and it paid off for Joplin with the "Maple

Leaf Rag" of 1899: that piece eventually sold more than half a million copies.

One of the first piano rags issued as published sheet music, the "Maple Leaf Rag" elegantly incorporated varied textures and graceful pianistic gestures into the basic ragtime framework of march music invigorated by syncopated off-beat accents. Joplin followed it up with equally beautiful rags over the next two decades; such works as "Elite Syncopations," "The Entertainer" (a 1902 rag later featured in the 1973 film *The Sting*), and the 1907 "Gladiolus Rag" were meticulously composed wholes whose five sections flowed from one into another with clear musical logic.

Joplin believed that his rags were fine art, not simply barroom entertainment. Harmonically, they sometimes borrowed from the more advanced realms of classical music. He also attempted to compose in larger forms. The scores of an early ballet and opera have been lost, but in 1911 Joplin published *Treemonisha*, a theatrical work that blended ragtime, pop, and operatic elements. He was bitterly disappointed that he could not find backing to bring the work to the stage. Joplin died of syphilis in New York on April 1, 1917.

Legacy

The "Maple Leaf Rag" was the beginning of the twentieth century's first great musical craze, and Scott Joplin, with that composition and others, defined the ragtime genre.

Joplin's success inspired a host of imitators, many of them white, and the waltzes, marches, and minstrel melodies of an earlier day gave way to a new music more fundamentally marked by African-American rhythms. Ragtime became the sensation of the time, much loved but hotly attacked by musically conservative commentators. Thousands of rags were published between 1900 and 1920, and songs like IRVING BERLIN's "Alexander's Ragtime Band," with little actual ragtime rhythmic content, referred to the phenomenon.

Among the first African-American musicians to distill an unwritten tradition of piano music and fix it in notation that could be sold in sheet music form, Joplin brought the intoxicating ragtime style out of the bars and into the living rooms of ordinary Americans, who owned pianos if they could possibly afford to do so.

The artistry and ambition of Joplin's music likewise inspired serious pianists who came

after him; the "Maple Leaf Rag" and other Joplin works were well known to the performers at whose hands ragtime evolved into piano jazz. The ragtime pianist Eubie Blake and New York "stride" pianists such as James P. Johnson adopted and elaborated on both basic ragtime rhythms and Joplin's ability to exploit contrasts in register and musical texture.

Beyond these specific stylistic influences, Joplin set a more general example with his confident assertion of the musical value of his works. With Joplin the African-American musician emerged as an independent artistic creator, as something other than an entertainer or a participant in a folk tradition. The self-aware creator of unique and distinct musical compositions, Joplin paved the way for the twentieth century's most complex African-American art form, jazz.

Manheim

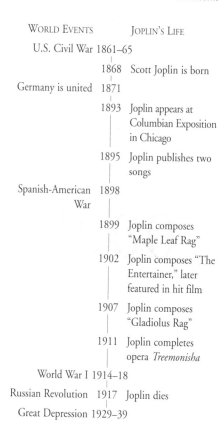

WORLD EVENTS	JOPLIN'S LIFE
U.S. Civil War 1861–65	
	1868 Scott Joplin is born
Germany is united 1871	
	1893 Joplin appears at Columbian Exposition in Chicago
	1895 Joplin publishes two songs
Spanish-American War 1898	
	1899 Joplin composes "Maple Leaf Rag"
	1902 Joplin composes "The Entertainer," later featured in hit film
	1907 Joplin composes "Gladiolus Rag"
	1911 Joplin completes opera *Treemonisha*
World War I 1914–18	
Russian Revolution 1917	Joplin dies
Great Depression 1929–39	

For Further Reading
Berlin, Edward A. *King of Ragtime: Scott Joplin and His Era*. New York: Oxford University Press, 1994.
Curtis, Susan. *Dancing to a Black Man's Tune: A Life of Scott Joplin*. Columbia: University of Missouri Press, 1994.

Josquin des Prez

Composer

c.1455–1521

Life and Work

"He is master of the notes," wrote the founder of Protestantism, Martin Luther. Josquin des Prez towered above other composers of the Renaissance era.

One of a series of Renaissance composers from northern France, Josquin (generally known by his given name alone) was probably born around 1455. The earliest records of his employment place him at the court of René of Anjou. This may have been followed by a brief stay at the royal court of Louis XI in the early 1480s. During the Renaissance, the great courts and churches of Italy competed among themselves to hire the top musical talent from northern Europe. Josquin was the cream of the crop, and in 1484 he was hired by the powerful Cardinal Ascanio Sforza, who was based in Milan and Rome. Special dispensations had to be made, because Josquin was not, at this time, a priest. In the 1490s he entered the Papal Choir as a singer in the Sistine Chapel—his signature was recently discovered on one of the choir stalls.

As was common in the Renaissance, much of Josquin's music was written for unaccompanied groups of singers. Many of his 20 masses feature complex manipulations of a *cantus firmus,* a pre-existing tune that served as a basis for an entire composition. A piece might entail some kind of puzzle: for example, the proportional repetitions of the *cantus firmus* in the *Missa di dadi* (*Mass of Dice*) are indicated in the manuscripts with pictures of dice and relate to a game of the time. In his motets (settings of sacred texts drawn from outside the mass), Josquin developed a style in which such abstract devices gave way to a closer relationship between text and music. Each phrase might begin with its own "point of imitation" in which the melody would pass through each voice in turn. In the famous motet *Ave maria...virgo serena,* Josquin achieved a marvelously clear texture in which each vocal line seems to weave itself naturally into a song of praise to the Virgin Mary. Josquin also wrote secular songs (*chansons*), many of which carry the profound mixture of expression and sheer compositional skill that is at the heart of his music.

Josquin maintained ties with his French homeland, and, after a stint as choirmaster to Duke Ercole I of Ferrara, he began to find his way back home. He fled plague-ravaged Ferrara in 1505 and found employment as a provost at the Church of Notre Dame in Condé, where he died on August 27, 1521.

Legacy

One way to appreciate Josquin des Prez's work might be to compare it with the paintings of the German artist Albrecht Dürer (1471–1528), who also spent part of his life in Italy: both men grafted an expressive Italian style onto a foundation of extreme technical accomplishment characteristic of northern Europe and ultimately extended medieval procedures.

To an astonishing degree, Josquin's music reached both backward and forward from his own time. In the complexity of his contrapuntal writing—his ability to combine independent lines of music in interesting ways—he looked back to the Middle Ages. The mathematical devices and elegant solutions to compositional problems that abound, especially in his masses, can offer deep rewards to those willing to lay the groundwork necessary to become aware of them. Josquin clothed with the splendor of Renaissance Europe the preoccupation with number and numerology that animated medieval music and philosophy.

For composers who followed him in the sixteenth century, Josquin's influence was fundamental; for many decades they devoted themselves to working out the implications of his ideal of text expression. The point of imitation became nearly a cliché, and composers began to employ dissonances and splashes of harmonic color in search of heightened expressivity.

The idea that music and text should be married in a unique expressive whole was one of the great achievements of Renaissance culture, and the idea both received its impetus from Josquin and reached its first perfection in his works. The murky anguish of Josquin's motet *De profundis clamavi ad te* (*From the Depths I Cried to Thee*), to name only one of his masterly pieces, led over the centuries to a situation in which the union of music and text seemed a natural thing. In the realm of Western classical music, that union was initially Josquin's creation.

Manheim

For Further Reading

Brown, Howard Mayer. *Music in the Renaissance.* Englewood Cliffs, N.J.: Prentice Hall, 1976.

Reese, Gustave, et al. *The New Grove High Renaissance Masters: Josquin, Palestrina, Lassus, Byrd, Victoria.* New York: W. W. Norton, 1984.

Joyce, James

Novelist
1882–1941

Life and Work

James Joyce pushed the English language to its limit, and in so doing became the prime exponent of Modernist experimentation in the novel.

Joyce was born in Dublin on February 2, 1882. His father had a political patronage job, but the family's fortunes deteriorated during Joyce's youth; in his semiautobiographical novel *A Portrait of the Artist as a Young Man*, Joyce described a father figure as "a bankrupt and at present a praiser of his own past." Joyce attended Jesuit schools and University College, Dublin, but abandoned his family's Roman Catholic faith. When he was 18 he published an essay on the Norwegian playwright HENRIK IBSEN in a leading literary magazine and resolved to become a writer.

In 1904 Joyce left Ireland, settling in the Austro-Hungarian city of Trieste (now in Italy). His first major work was a set of short stories called *Dubliners* (1914). This collection of incisive character studies matches narrator to subject matter, with stories about childhood told through the eyes of children at the beginning and an extended Christmas story suffused with mortality, "The Dead," at the end.

A Portrait of the Artist as a Young Man was published in the United States in 1916 and

gained Joyce great acclaim. Forced to leave Trieste during World War I, Joyce went to neutral Switzerland; in 1920 he moved to Paris, where he spent much of the rest of his life.

His 1922 novel *Ulysses* follows a husband and wife, Leopold and Molly Bloom, through a single day in Dublin. Vast interior monologues are intercut with episodes in which the authorial voice and the nature of the book's language itself shift drastically according to what is being described, and the whole structure elegantly replicates that of the *Odyssey*. The book's frank sexual content led to its being banned in the United States until 1933, but the ban helped to increase Joyce's renown. He worked on *Finnegans Wake* from 1922 to 1939, producing a text that borders on incomprehensibility but fascinates readers with its sheer virtuosity. Like *Ulysses*, the book uses a short span of time as a lens for viewing a bewildering panorama of material.

Finding himself once again an enemy alien in a country at war, Joyce left Paris for Zurich in late 1940. He died there, of a perforated ulcer, on January 13, 1941.

Legacy

The experiments with form and narration that flowered in European and American fiction of the mid-twentieth century were in large part the product of James Joyce's influence.

One of his most significant innovations was given a name that has become part of everyday language: stream of consciousness. Ulysses, especially, incorporated long sequences of seemingly unedited thoughts of its characters, expressing by turns hopes and fears, beauty and ugliness, and proceeding in a realistically fitful and often self-contradictory way. Many writers before Joyce made use of individual inner monologues, but none had come close to letting characters spill apparently uncontrolled across the page in the way that Joyce did. Such monologues figure in the writings of various later twentieth-century figures; the most prominent is perhaps WILLIAM FAULKNER.

The sheer mind-expanding freedom of Joyce's manipulations of structure and language was influential in a more general way. Joyce was something of a counterculture figure of his day—he lived with Nora Barnacle from 1904

on, but out of anti-Catholic conviction refused to marry her until 1931—and the radical, experimental writers of the century's second half, like the novelists Thomas Pynchon and John Barth, had clearly studied Joyce's work. Marathon readings of *Ulysses* and *Finnegans Wake* took place on college campuses.

In the end it is the ambitions of Joyce's style that made him loom so large in the minds of his successors. For Joyce, style became more than the grounding of an authorial voice, more even than the display of virtuoso craft. The raw linguistic material of Joyce's novels becomes a way, not of imposing order on a blooming, confusing world, but of plunging headlong into it, attempting to encompass all of it. Thus Joyce became a central literary figure of a century in search of meaning.

Manheim

WORLD EVENTS		JOYCE'S LIFE
Germany is united	1871	
	1882	James Joyce is born in Dublin, Ireland
Spanish-American War	1898	
	1904	Joyce leaves Ireland
	1914	Joyce writes *Dubliners*
World War I	1914–18	
	1916	Joyce's novel *A Portrait of the Artist as a Young Man* is published
Russian Revolution	1917	
	1920	Joyce settles in Paris
	1922	Joyce's *Ulysses* is published
	1939	Joyce publishes *Finnegans Wake*
Great Depression	1929–39	
World War II	1939–45	
	1941	Joyce dies
Communist China is established	1949	

For Further Reading

Ellmann, Richard. *James Joyce.* Rev. ed. New York: Oxford University Press, 1982.

Fargnoli, A. Nicholas, and Michael Patrick Gillespie. *James Joyce A to Z: The Essential Reference to the Life and Work.* New York: Facts On File, 1995.

Rice, Thomas Jackson. *Joyce, Chaos, and Complexity.* Urbana: University of Illinois Press, 1996.

Kafka, Franz

Novelist and Short Story Writer
1883–1924

WORLD EVENTS		KAFKA'S LIFE
Germany is united	1871	
	1883	Franz Kafka is born
Spanish-American War	1898	
	1912	Kafka writes *The Judgment*
	1914	Kafka begins writing *The Trial*
World War I 1914–18		
	1915	Kafka publishes *The Metamorphosis*
Russian Revolution	1917	Kafka is diagnosed with tuberculosis
	1920	Kafka publishes short story collection, *The Country Doctor*
	1924	Kafka dies
Great Depression 1929–39		

Life and Work

Franz Kafka's fiction gave literary voice to social ills that would come to typify the twentieth century. Not long after his death, his name and the adjective "Kafkaesque" became synonymous with bureaucratic dehumanization and the alienation of the individual from modern society.

Kafka was born into a wealthy family in Prague in 1883. He had a difficult relationship with his authoritarian father that would be reflected in much of his writing. Two of the issues that would haunt him and inform his writing were present from his youth: the isolation inherent in being Jewish in a Christian city and his own conflicted feelings about the bourgeois luxury in which he was raised. In 1906 he earned a law degree at the German University in Prague and went to work in a government insurance office.

In 1912 Kafka began to produce what he considered his first mature works. These included *Das Urteil* (*The Judgment*, 1912) and *Die Verwandlung* (*The Metamorphosis*, 1915), both of which contained the psychological and physical brutality that characterized all of his work. *The Metamorphosis*, one of the great short stories of the century, tells of Gregor Samsa, a man who wakes up one day to find that he has turned into an insect. Themes of alienation and quasi-mystical transformation that are present in this story reappear in his later work. In 1914 he began writing *Der Prozess* (*The Trial*), one of his best-known novels.

Kafka wrote the majority of the works for which he is known after 1917, when he was diagnosed with tuberculosis. He left his job and spent the rest of his life in sanitariums. One of the few works published during his lifetime, *Ein Landarzt* (*The Country Doctor*), a short story collection, came out in 1920.

His major novels *The Trial* (1925), *Das Schloss* (*The Castle*, 1926), and *Amerika* (1927) were all left unfinished when he died on June 3, 1924. Although he had ordered that the manuscripts be destroyed, his friend Max Brod prepared them for publication. All are surreal, with a character on a frustrating and frightening quest, and all are characterized by a lucid writing style that often serves to heighten their nightmarish quality.

Kafka died of tuberculosis on June 3, 1924.

Legacy

Franz Kafka brought a new fictional universe into the world with his startlingly clear vision of a sterile and rigid authority, which expressed the repetitive futility of life in a world where beauty and art are replaced by the mechanical workings of bureaucracy.

He applied the scientific technique of one of his great influences, GUSTAVE FLAUBERT, to modernist writing. Like Flaubert, Kafka wrote in a detached and precise manner, using legal and scientific language to create works of lucid prose that appeared utterly removed from the author's own emotions or opinions. This style was distinct from that of T. S. Eliot, JAMES JOYCE, and VIRGINIA WOOLF, all of whom were writing at the same time about a society and psychology fractured by war. Kafka helped to define Modernism with his absurdist worldview and mixture of bleak seriousness and sharp humor. His fiction's distorted image of the world and his characters' acceptance of surreal situations—Gregor Samsa's lack of surprise when he wakes up as an insect, for example—all pointed out the irrationality at the roots of a supposedly rational world.

Kafka's characters are trapped in a system of laws and values that they have not chosen and never quite understand. All exhibit the self-hatred, guilt, and exhaustion that have come to be expected of a pawn of capitalist society who achieves success by obeying the rules and repressing his or her humanity. A great deal of fiction that followed, particularly science fiction was based on this premise. The authoritarian nightmare of GEORGE ORWELL's *1984*, published in 1949, as well as works by Ray Bradbury, Isaac Asimov, and many others can be traced to themes in *The Trial* and *The Castle*.

While Kafka's work has been analyzed in innumerable ways, called prophetic, mystical, Marxist, existentialist, and allegorical, what is certainly true is, as Russian novelist and critic Vladimir Nabokov said, that he was one of the greatest German-language writers of our time.

Watson

For Further Reading

Bloom, Harold, and William Golding, eds. *Franz Kafka: Modern Critical Views*. New York: Chelsea House, 1987.

Brod, Max. *Franz Kafka: A Biography*. New York: Schocken Books, 1960.

Unseld, Joachim. *Franz Kafka: A Writer's Life*. Riverside, Calif.: Ariadne Press, 1997.

Kahlo, Frida

Painter
1907–1954

Life and Work

During her short and tormented life, Frida Kahlo painted some of the twentieth century's most moving autobiographical paintings.

Born in 1907 in Mexico City, Kahlo was of European and Mexican Indian descent. In 1925, at age 18, she was severely injured in a bus accident. Despite a series of 30 operations, for the rest of her life Kahlo experienced serious physical pain and emotional distress over her inability to bear children.

Kahlo took up painting while recuperating from the accident, and in 1929 showed her work to the prominent Mexican mural painter DIEGO RIVERA, whom she married later that same year. Their passionate, tumultuous relationship would become the second major influence on Kahlo.

Kahlo shared Rivera's interest in traditional Mexican folk art and also shared his commitment to communism. Her style, however, was deeply personal and highly individual. Her 1939 painting *Two Fridas* refers in part to her temporary divorce from Rivera; they later remarried. The painting shows two self-portraits, one dressed in a white European dress, the other in brown and blue Mexican clothing. The two figures hold hands, and their exposed hearts are joined by a blood vessel that leaks blood onto the white dress.

The leader of the French Surrealist movement, André Breton, saw her work in 1939, and immediately connected the psychoanalytical nature of her paintings to Surrealism. Although Kahlo denied any real similarity, Breton was instrumental in having her work shown in Europe and America.

Kahlo maintained that her work came from her personal experiences, that it had little to do with the depiction of the unconscious that was the purported aim of artists like SALVADOR DALÍ. Her 1932 painting, *Henry Ford Hospital*, deals with one of her three miscarriages. She shows herself naked on a bloody hospital bed surrounded by images of a pelvis, a fetus, a womb, and a snail. In *Broken Column* (1944) Kahlo stares directly at the viewer, her nude torso cut away to reveal a shattered column in place of her spine; tears flow from her eyes and nails pierce her flesh.

The last year of her life was especially painful. In 1953 she had to have her right leg amputated because of gangrene. The following year, while suffering from pneumonia, she died, probably a suicide.

Legacy

During her lifetime, Frida Kahlo became a celebrity, partly because of her association with Diego Rivera and partly because of her many romantic affairs. She was closely associated with prominent intellectuals such as Breton, and with important political figures, including Leon Trotsky. Her status as a local and national hero was secured when her home was opened as the Frida Kahlo Museum in 1958.

As an artist, however, Kahlo had only three exhibitions during her lifetime, one in Paris, one in New York, and one in Mexico City. Her introspective, autobiographical art was too individualistic to exert direct influence on other painters of her generation.

For the next several decades, while Rivera was often described as the most important mural painter since Michelangelo, Kahlo was regarded as a marginal figure and was routinely omitted from most surveys of modern art.

Over the past two decades, however, her reputation has grown. The feminist movement encouraged art historians to search for figures who, like Kahlo, had been effectively written out of mainstream art history. At the same time, feminist art historians became increasingly interested in exploring the role women's life experiences play in shaping their art. Kahlo quickly emerged as a key figure. No one had more honestly and thoughtfully used art as a way of analyzing and thinking about issues that are both profoundly personal and universally human. Today it is she, rather than her famous husband, who is considered to be the crucial figure in the history of modern art.

McEnroe

WORLD EVENTS		KAHLO'S LIFE:
Spanish-American War	1898	
	1907	Frida Kahlo is born
World War I	1914–18	
Russian Revolution	1917	
	1925	Kahlo is injured in bus accident
Great Depression	1929–39	
	1929	Kahlo marries Diego Rivera
	1939	Kahlo paints *Two Fridas*
World War II	1939–45	
	1944	Kahlo paints *Broken Column*
Communist China is established	1949	
Korean War	1950–53	
	1954	Kahlo dies
African independence movement begins	1957	

For Further Reading

Herrera, Hayden. *Frida Kahlo*. New York: Rizzoli, 1992.

Kahlo, Frida. *The Diary of Frida Kahlo: An Intimate Self-Portrait*. Introduction by Carlos Fuentes; essay and commentaries by Sarah M. Lowe. New York: Harry N. Abrams, 1995.

Kalthum, Umm

Vocalist
c. 1904–1975

Life and Work

It has been said that there are only two things about which all Arabs agree: Allah and Umm Kalthum. Kalthum was an Egyptian singer, poised between the classical and popular realms, who is widely thought to be the Arab world's greatest musician of the twentieth century.

Kalthum was born in the Nile Delta village of Tammay al-Zahayrah, Egypt, probably on May 4, 1904. She grew up in small mud house, but her father was the imam at the local mosque, and she was able to attend religious schools.

Kalthum learned to sing from her father and sometimes filled in for her brother at local celebrations. Kalthum later attributed her vocal skills to her religious training, but she is also said to have recited verses at local cafes, sometimes dressing as a boy.

In 1923 Kalthum's family moved to the Egyptian capital of Cairo to further her career. She learned the nuances of refined Arabic speech and poetry from the writer Ahmed Ramy, who became the composer of 132 of the 286 songs she recorded. Kalthum was one of the leading vocalists in Cairo by 1928. In the 1930s her songs tended toward the romantic, with a European-inflected style that sometimes featured the cello and double bass.

Kalthum released recordings from the late 1920s until the end of her life. She made her debut on Egyptian National Radio in 1934 and in movies the following year. A quick-witted and strong-minded person who had the determination to control her career, Kalthum navigated the various problems faced by a woman in a largely male-dominated tradition.

She enjoyed a popularly acclaimed "golden age" in the 1940s and 1950s, when she gave up her romantic style in favor of a more indigenously Egyptian one. Her stage performances—in which she could draw out her improvisations on a love song to a length of over an hour—were legendary.

For the last three decades of her life she suffered from kidney and gall bladder problems, often traveling to France and the United States for treatment. She died on February 3, 1975.

Legacy

Umm Kalthum's funeral, attended by more than three million people, did not mark an end to her popularity. Her voice resounded from radios in Arab countries well into the 1990s.

Her personal charisma and stage presence were considerable, but Kalthum magnified her impact through her keen awareness of the power of new media. She was one of the first musicians from the Third World whose career grew exponentially and crossed national borders through the power of radio and film (and eventually television, on which she made her debut in 1960).

Kalthum was a true star, the first in the Middle East, who managed her image carefully, cultivating friendly journalists to whom she would grant exclusive interviews.

The Middle East is a region where, despite the power of cultural influences from the West, innovative new musics with traditional elements have flourished with greater vigor than in many other parts of the world. Kalthum was one of those musicians whose example set the music on that path.

Musically Kalthum forged a middle way between modernization and tradition. Both her modern romantic style of the 1930s and her later, more roots-oriented style were new developments in their own times; although from a modern perspective she is seen as part of the Egyptian classical tradition, she put in place the pillars of a vibrant popular music in Egypt.

Manheim

For Further Reading

Broughton, Simon, et al., eds. *World Music: The Rough Guide.* London: Rough Guides, 1994.

Danielson, Virginia Louise. *"The Voice of Egypt": Umm Kalthum, Arabic Song, and Egyptian Society in the Twentieth Century.* Chicago: University of Chicago Press, 1997.

Keats, John

Poet
1795–1821

Life and Work

John Keats wrote some of the most technically perfect and lushly sensual poetry in the English language.

Keats was born in London on October 31, 1795. He was the oldest of four children of a modest middle-class family in London. His father's death, when Keats was nine, eventually created severe financial problems for the family. He lived with his grandmother and, later, with his mother; he and his brothers attended a progressive school where he first read the poetry that would influence his later work.

In 1811, after the death of his mother, Keats was taken from school by the guardian who had been appointed for the Keats children and apprenticed to an apothecary. Four years later he began medical courses in London. In 1816 he passed examinations to become a surgeon, but rather than practice medicine he devoted the rest of his life to writing poetry.

In 1817 Keats published *Poems*, his first collection. This was followed in 1818 by *Endymion: A Poetic Romance,* an allegory in rhyming couplets, which tells the story of the goddess Diana's love for the shepherd Endymion, strongly emphasizing the Romantic theme of the search for ideal, transcendent love.

Keats was thus deeply implicated in the Romantic school from the beginning of his writing career. Along with the other English Romantics, who included his predecessors WILLIAM WORDSWORTH and Samuel Taylor Coleridge, and his contemporaries, Lord Byron and Percy Bysshe Shelley, Keats rejected the strict Classical and Neoclassical rules of poetry in fashion at the time and wrote poems in freer verse in which he expressed passionately subjective emotion.

Keats began showing signs of tuberculosis soon after *Endymion*'s publication; he then devoted himself to reading and writing. In 1820 he published his final collection, *Lamia, Isabella, The Eve of St. Agnes, and Other Poems.* This collection included the odes for which he is most admired: "On Indolence," "On a Grecian Urn," "To Psyche," "To a Nightingale," "On Melancholy," and "To Autumn."

In 1820 Keats traveled to Italy, where he hoped to recover from his worsening tuberculosis. He died soon after and was buried in Rome.

Legacy

John Keats's poetics was exemplified in his characteristic combination of technical perfection with deeply sensual imagery. In much of his work, and particularly in the odes, Keats focused on a single object, idea, or emotion in order to explore such themes as the discrepancy between art and life or the transcendent power of beauty and art. He made the stories of classical myth intimate and personal as he used them to express his ideas.

Keats was not widely recognized as a great poet during his life. Many of his contemporaries found his work overly emotional and his sensual imagery shocking. Moreover, Keats's social origins were held against him; *Endymion* received fiercely negative reviews from the leading literary journals of the day, which attacked the work, the Romantic school with which it was associated, and Keats himself. These articles set the tone for much of the criticism that followed, which found his work flowery and without intellectual merit.

While the contemporary critical reception was not glowing, Keats's fellow Romantic poets and writers admired him. Both Byron and Shelley wrote about him after his death. Shelley's *Adonais: An Elegy on the Death of the Poet John Keats* described Keats as a frail and sickly genius, a romantic portrait that continues to be widely accepted and that may have contributed to the trivializing of his work.

Interest in Keats grew during the nineteenth century. Richard Monckton Milnes's 1848 biography presented Keats's letters, many of which it reprinted, as evidence of the intellectual substance of his poems. In 1880 Matthew Arnold, an English poet and critic, published an essay in which he wrote that Keats was as great as WILLIAM SHAKESPEARE, thus fixing him as a major figure in English letters. The lyric poet Algernon Charles Swinburne was among the first to write extensively about the odes in 1882. Gerard Manley Hopkins, an English poet and Roman Catholic priest, was also greatly influenced by Keats.

While his reputation as an intellectual poet grew, Keats was still seen as a poet of sensual pleasure. Pre-Raphaelite poets and painters such as William Morris, Dante Gabriel Rossetti, and William Holman Hunt all drew upon this aspect of Keats's work. In general, though, it was not until the twentieth century that Keats was fully appreciated as a great, and serious, poet. Keats's aesthetics and imagery continue to interest contemporary critics, such as Harold Bloom and Helen Vendler, and his poetry continues to move ordinary readers.

Watson

WORLD EVENTS		KEATS'S LIFE
French Revolution begins	1789	
	1795	John Keats is born
Latin American independence movement begins	1811	
Congress of Vienna reorganizes Europe	1815	
	1816	Keats passes his medical exams
	1817	Keats publishes *Poems*
	1818	Keats publishes *Endymion: A Poetic Romance*
	1820	Keats publishes *Lamia, Isabella, The Eve of St. Agnes, and Other Poems*
	1821	Keats dies
Revolutions in Austria, France, Germany, and Italy	1848	

For Further Reading

Bate, Walter Jackson. *John Keats.* Cambridge, Mass.: Harvard University Press, 1963.
Motion, Andrew. *Keats.* New York: Farrar, Straus, & Giroux, 1997.
Ward, Aileen. *John Keats: The Making of a Poet.* Rev. ed. New York: Farrar, Straus & Giroux, 1986.

Kern, Jerome

Composer
1885–1945

Life and Work

One of the greatest composers of musicals, and certainly the genre's most important pathbreaker, Jerome Kern wrote songs that are known to almost all Americans. The most famous was "Ol' Man River," from Kern's musical, *Show Boat.*

Kern was born in New York City on January 27, 1885. Unlike such contemporaries as Irving Berlin, he studied music formally, taking classes in music theory and piano at the New York College of Music in 1902, and then traveling to Heidelberg, Germany, for further instruction.

Back in New York, he worked on Broadway as a "song plugger," a piano-playing pitchman who promoted songs from the catalogue of the publisher T. B. Harms for inclusion in vaudeville shows and performers' concerts. He began to write songs in 1904, Americanizing popular British operettas of the time by adding his own songs to them. Kern amassed a large song catalogue of his own by the time World War I broke out in 1914.

Nobody Home, from 1915, was Kern's first show of his own, and by 1918's *Oh Lady! Lady!* (with lyrics by comic novelist P. G. Wodehouse), he had begun to work out a new kind of musical. Where operetta presented fanciful stories with stock characters and revues and vaudeville shows offered song-and-dance numbers barely strung together with a plot, Kern began to forge effective musical plays, with realistic characters, in which song, dialogue, and story were all integrated and moved forward naturally.

Show Boat (1927), with text by Oscar Hammerstein II, was Kern's greatest musical; in addition to "Ol' Man River" its score included "Can't Help Lovin' Dat Man of Mine" and other standards. With its progressive tale of a biracial woman who is prohibited from performing on a Mississippi riverboat, it brought the musical to a new level of seriousness.

Kern continued to enjoy success in the 1930s and 1940s with musicals such as 1939's *Very Warm for May,* which included the ever-green "All the Things You Are." Later in life he wrote scores for film musicals. Kern died suddenly in New York on November 11, 1945.

Legacy

Jerome Kern's innovations defined the musical as a substantial art form, and no composer of musicals from his own time to the present has remained untouched by them.

His sophistication as a songwriter did much to set the transformation in motion: such pieces as "Bill," which appeared in *Show Boat* but had its origins in *Oh Lady! Lady!,* impressed Kern's younger contemporaries GEORGE GERSHWIN and Richard Rodgers, spurring them toward the harmonic complexity and controlled melodic elegance that became the hallmarks of the classic Broadway song of the 1930s through the 1950s.

The impact of *Show Boat* itself, for many theatergoers the greatest of all American musicals, must not be underestimated. In its grandly ambitious (if sometimes melodramatic) concept, and in its score that traversed the genres of the American musical past, it was the direct ancestor of every serious or semiserious musical play, from *Carousel* to *Les Miserables* and beyond.

Beyond his compositional skill, and beyond the changes he brought about in the form of the musical, Kern set a tone that lasted. The characters in *Show Boat* were instantly recognizable American types; they included riverboat gamblers, highborn Southern ladies, and, for the first time in a white-produced Broadway musical show, African Americans depicted in a manner that was something other than demeaning. They were colorful, larger than life, yet familiar, and the romantic plots of future American musicals (*Oklahoma!* was just one example) would be played out against the kind of backdrop Kern and Hammerstein first created. When Kern inherited the musical theater form, it was as much European as American. Thanks to his contributions, it became the voice of the American Everyman and Everywoman.

Manheim

For Further Reading
Bordman, Gerald Martin. *Jerome Kern: His Life and Music.* New York: Oxford University Press, 1980.
Freedland, Michael. *Jerome Kern.* New York: Stein and Day, 1981.

Khan, Nusrat Fateh Ali

Vocalist
1948–1997

Life and Work

The foremost modern exponent of *qawwali*, a music associated with the Sufi practice of the Islamic faith, Nusrat Fateh Ali Khan simultaneously reasserted the vitality of that centuries-old tradition and modernized it in ways that were unprecedented for a non-Western musical style.

Khan, commonly referred to as Nusrat, came from a long line of performers in the *qawwali* tradition, which features vocal settings of devotional poetry; *qawwali* songs, which almost seem to refer to secular love but instead carry ecstatic overtones of the divine, are accompanied by hand claps and a small harmonium. Khan was born in the town of Lyallpur, Pakistan (now Faisalabad), on July 12, 1948. His father, Ustad Fateh Ali Khan, trained him in the *qawwali* tradition, but encouraged his son to pursue a secular professional career. Khan decided to become a *qawwali* singer after his father's death in 1964, when he repeatedly dreamed that he was giving a performance at the shrine of a great spiritual figure.

By 1971 he had taken over the leadership of the Party, the family ensemble, and over the next two decades he became known as *Shahen-Shah-e-Qawwali*, the brightest star in *qawwali*. In 1979 he sang at the shrine of which he had

dreamed after his father's death. He was much admired for his powerful performances, which could last up to 10 hours.

The second phase of Khan's career began when he sought to meld *qawwali* with Western forms. A 1985 performance in Britain won him European admirers, and a 1989 appearance at New York's Brooklyn Academy of Music accomplished the same in the United States. Among those who followed his work closely was the British rock star Peter Gabriel, whose association with the Real World record label paved the way for Khan to make a series of recordings that fused *qawwali* with the electronic rhythm tracks of Western popular music.

Musicians from the Indian subcontinent had been performing in the West at least since RAVI SHANKAR's first appearances in the 1950s. But even when they collaborated with Western musicians, they did so in the belief that they were introducing Western audiences to a difficult and unfamiliar tradition, one such audiences might never grasp in the way a native listener would. Khan's encounter with the West was of a different kind: his appeal to Western audiences was a direct one. *Qawwali* is a simple, ecstatic music, with drumming and hand clapping from Khan's ensemble building to intense peaks. Khan believed that something of the power of *qawwali* might come through even with considerable dilution.

The 1990 album, *Mustt Mustt,* employed Western ambient techno styles, provoking accusations of a sellout from some of Khan's Pakistani devotees. But a remix of its title track by the British dance group Massive Attack became a hit, and Khan defended his experimentation. He gained wider appreciation in the United States in 1995 when he supplied music for the soundtrack of the film *Dead Man Walking,* performing with rock musician Eddie Vedder of the group Pearl Jam. A diabetes sufferer, Khan died on August 16, 1997.

Legacy

Nusrat Fateh Ali Khan was among the major progenitors of "world music," a genre that mixed Western dance rhythms and musical structures with non-Western traditional vocal and instrumental sounds layered on top of them. Such musicians as the Indo-British vocalist Sheila Chandra enjoyed success with similar fusions, but Khan's efforts carried the greatest spiritual charisma.

For American and British audiences, Khan became a new kind of non-Western musician, almost a popular success, and during the 1990s he showed that Western audiences could be induced to seek out the music of what had been considered an arcane religious tradition. Other world music performers of the 1990s, such as the Tuvan throat singers of Mongolia, sought the same kind of direct connection with Western hearers that Khan accomplished.

For Eastern as well as Western audiences Khan's music carried connotations of idealism and spiritual enlightenment. Widely revered in Hindu India as well as in Muslim Pakistan, he was a cultural bridge builder between the two countries, which had fought four wars over the five decades of their existence and which seemed perpetually on the brink of new hostilities. Although religious fundamentalists on each side protested his association with the audiences of the other, Khan persisted. At the end of the twentieth century his music seemed to be the beacon of a new, international spirituality that could exist within the framework of popular culture.

Manheim

WORLD EVENTS		KHAN'S LIFE
World War II	1939–45	
	1948	Nusrat Fateh Ali Khan is born in Lyallpur, Pakistan
Communist China is established	1949	
Korean War	1950–53	
African independence movement begins	1957	
	1971	Khan assumes leadership of family ensemble
Vietnam War ends	1975	
	1985	Khan gains fans with performance in Britain
	1989	Khan performs at Brooklyn Academy of Music
	1990	Khan records pop-influenced *Mustt Mustt* album
Dissolution of Soviet Union	1991	
South Africa dismantles apartheid	1994	
	1997	Khan dies

For Further Reading

Broughton, Simon, et al., eds. *World Music: The Rough Guide.* New York: Penguin, 1999.
Qureshi, Regula. *Sufi Music of India and Pakistan: Sound, Context and Meaning in Qawwali.* Cambridge: Cambridge University Press, 1986.

Kōetsu

Calligrapher and Potter
1558–1637

Life and Work

Hon'ami Kōetsu, more commonly known as Kōetsu, was the founder of Rimpa ("School of Gems"), a school of decorative Japanese art that flourished in Kyoto from the seventeenth to the nineteenth centuries. He was also one of the most important calligraphers of the Edo period (1603–1868).

Kōetsu was born in 1558 to a family that for generations had been engaged in cleaning, polishing, and judging swords. In the age of the samurai warrior, this service was deemed vitally important. As a member of a hereditary artisan class, Kōetsu was trained in his father's profession. However, he developed broader cultural interests, becoming an enthusiast of the No theater and the tea ceremony and engaging in the art of calligraphy, pottery, metalwork, and lacquerware.

In calligraphy, Kōetsu has been classed alongside Konoe Nobutada (1565–1614) and Shōkadō Shōjō (c. 1584–1639) as the *Kan'ei Sampitsu*, the Three [Great] Brushes of the Kan'ei Era (1624–44). Kōetsu studied calligraphy for two years with the imperial prince Soncho, head of the highly influential Shōren-in school of calligraphy. He also collected the works of many celebrated late-Heian calligraphers, including Ono no Michizane and KūKai, and was well versed in Chinese calligraphy.

Kōetsu collaborated with his younger colleague Sōtatsu (1600–40) on a number of poem scrolls with decorative underpaintings, such as *Flowers and Plants of the Four Seasons*. On paper specially decorated by Sōtatsu in stamped gold with silver patterns of grape-leaf and other floral motifs, Kōetsu inscribed *waka* poetry from the Fujiwara period (898–1185). Kōetsu's characters are written in a style of calligraphy known as *chirashi-gaki*, or "scattered writing," in which each line of characters is free to shift its direction in response to the rhythmic arrangement of a scroll's decorative designs. The Rimpa artists' references to the painting, calligraphy, and poetry of the Fujiwara period and *yamato-e* style of art represented an attempt to reaffirm the cultural identity and aristocratic taste and courtly refinement of Kyoto, which was threatened by the permanent movement of the nation's administrative center to Edo in eastern Japan.

Kōetsu also produced some of the most profound examples of rakuware, tea bowls specifically designed to be used in a Japanese tea ceremony. One of his most famous is a red raku tea bowl called *Seppo* (Snow-covered Peak), in the Hatakeyama Museum, Tokyo. The firing methods used to make raku produces accidental fissures in the glazed surface that enhance the irregularities in the shape of the bowl, creating a sense of impermanence, simplicity, and minimal articulation.

Kōetsu died in 1637 at Takagamine, a religious center and artists' colony he founded near Kyoto.

Legacy

Hon'ami Kōetsu was active in many artistic fields and was venerated as a cultural leader in his day.

Kōetsu had been granted a tract of land just north of Kyoto, the Imperial capital. While there, Kōetsu founded the first artist's colony (Rimpa School) in Japanese history. He invited the most skillful artists and artisans of the day to work collaboratively on art that represented a revival of the decorative style and themes of *yamato-e*, the indigenous tradition of Japanese art. Most prominent in this first generation was Sōtatsu, an artist who began as a painter and owner of the Tawaraya fan shop in Kyoto and came to be known for his exquisite large-scale, decorative screens and handscrolls.

The Rimpa School underwent a revival in the late seventeenth century and was brought to new heights by Ogata Korin (1658–1716) and his brother, Kenzan (1663–1743). Their decorative scrolls, painted screens, ceramic vessels, and lacquer boxes represent the embodiment and continuation of the aesthetic values, collaborative ideal, and multitalented artistry of their predecessors.

In time Korin had gained such prominence that by the late nineteenth century, historians credited Korin with originating the school. It was not until the latter half of the twentieth century that Kōetsu was once again recognized as the founder of what has come to be known as Rimpa.

Goldberg

For Further Reading

Mason, Penelope. *History of Japanese Art.* New York: Harry N. Abrams, 1993.

Shimizu, Yoshiaki, and John M. Rosenfield. *Masters of Japanese Calligraphy 8th–19th Century.* Exhibition catalogue. New York: The Asia Societies Galleries and Japan House Gallery, 1984.

Stern, Harold P. *Rimpa: Masterworks of the Japanese Decorative School.* Exhibition catalogue. New York: Japan Society, 1971.

Kurosawa, Akira

Filmmaker
1910–1998

Life and Work

Akira Kurosawa, director of such landmark films as *Rashomon* (1950), *Seven Samurai* (1954), *Dersu Uzala* (1975), and *Ran* (1985), was the first Japanese filmmaker to gain international recognition for bringing Japanese themes and sensibility to a previously Western-dominated medium.

Kurosawa, the son of a veteran army officer turned athletic instructor, was born in Tokyo on May 23, 1910. The younger brother of a film industry worker who did voiceovers for silent films, Kurosawa attended the cinema often as a youth. His work as an adult would reflect the silent cinema in its use of lighting and camera work to tell a story without words.

At 17 Kurosawa attended art school and showed enough promise to have a piece displayed in the prestigious Nika Society Exhibition when he was 18. After failing to make a living in commercial art, he responded in 1936 to a film studio advertisement seeking assistant directors. He worked with director Kajiro Yamamoto for several years, and by 1941 was writing and directing entire segments of Yamamoto's films.

He made his directorial debut in 1943, with the *Sugata Sanshiro*. As did American films of the same period, Kurosawa's second film, *The*

Most Beautiful* (1944), contributed to his country's war effort. However, his film focused on the lives of young people struggling through a difficult time, rather than on the war itself. *No Regrets for Our Youth* (1946) introduced a new type of character to the Japanese audience, a dignified woman who maintains her anti-militaristic stance through World War II. His 1948 *Drunken Angel* was a great success, and made a star of actor Toshiro Mifune.

Rashomon (1950), which won the top prize at the Venice Film Festival, brought Kurosawa into the international spotlight. Set in the tenth century, the film's tale of a rape and a murder as recollected differently by several witnesses conveys the subjective and ambiguous nature of perception and memory. Kurosawa continued with a string of hits in the 1950s and early 1960s that were both artistically and commercially successful: *The Idiot* (1951, based on FYODOR DOSTOYEVSKY's novel), *Ikiru* (1952), *Seven Samurai* (1954), *Throne of Blood* (1957, based on WILLIAM SHAKESPEARE's *Macbeth*), *Yojimbo* (1961), and *Red Beard* (1965). During this period Kurosawa emerged as a master craftsman, co-writing, editing, and directing films set in a wide variety of genres, places and time periods.

During the late 1960s, Kurosawa worked for 20th Century-Fox on *Tora! Tora! Tora!*, a film about the Japanese attack on Pearl Harbor in 1941. Fearing that Kurosawa's dedication to precise realism would lead to cost overruns, Fox released him from the project. In December 1971 Kurosawa attempted suicide. He resumed work in 1975 with *Dersu Uzala*, made jointly with a Soviet production company, which won that year's Oscar for Best Foreign Film.

His later work includes the epic productions *Kagemusha* (1980), with its unforgettable battle scenes, and *Ran* (1985), an adaptation of Shakespeare's *King Lear* set in sixteenth century Japan.

Kurosawa died in 1998.

Legacy

Akira Kurosawa's success as a filmmaker derived from his strength as a storyteller; his introspection and moral depth; and his skill as a visual artist. In America, he is influential as an action director, in Europe as a meditative artist, and in Asia as a maker of moralistic films with a social message.

When *Rashomon* was awarded the Grand Prix at the Venice Film Festival in 1950, it marked the entrance of Asia onto the international stage; Japanese studios began to pour more money into production and Japanese films won more international awards.

In the United States, where Kurosawa's major impact was as a maker of action movies, there have been a number of copies of Kurosawa's films. John Sturges's *The Magnificent Seven* (1960) was a remake of *Seven Samurai* in a Western setting. Sergio Leone's *A Fistful of Dollars* (1967) and its two sequels were recreations of *Yojimbo*, as was Walter Hill's *Last Man Standing* (1996).

Kurosawa's films continue to command serious attention in the West. They are considered unique for their combining of traditional Japanese elements such as subtlety of feeling and thought, brilliant visual artistry, and use of samurai and other traditional Japanese themes with American-style drama and action and a frequent use of Western stories.

Domenico

WORLD EVENTS		KUROSAWA'S LIFE:
Spanish-American War	1898	
	1910	Akira Kurosawa is born
World War I	1914–18	
Russian Revolution	1917	
Great Depression	1929–39	
World War II	1939–45	
	1943	Kurosawa directs his first film
Communist China is established	1949	
Korean War	1950–53	
	1950	Kurosawa wins top prize at Venice Film Festival for *Rashomon*
	1954	Kurosawa directs *Seven Samurai*
African independence movement begins	1957	
Vietnam War ends	1975	
Dissolution of Soviet Union	1991	
South Africa dismantles apartheid	1994	
	1998	Kurosawa dies

For Further Reading

Kurosawa, Akira. *Something Like an Autobiography*. Translated by Audie E. Bock. New York: Vintage Books, 1983.

Prince, Stephen. *The Warrior's Camera: The Cinema of Akira Kurosawa*. Princeton, N.J.: Princeton University Press, 1991.

Richie, Donald. *The Films of Akira Kurosawa*. Rev. ed. Berkeley: University of California Press, 1984.

Lawrence, Jacob

Painter
1917–2000

Life and Work

Jacob Lawrence was a groundbreaking African-American artist who pioneered an aesthetic based on his racial identity.

Lawrence was born in Atlantic City, New Jersey in 1917. When he was 12 he moved to Harlem with his mother. During the Depression (1928–39), he began to study art; he continued his studies at the Harlem Community Art Center with the sculptor Augusta Savage and from 1936 until 1940 held a scholarship at the American Artists' School.

WORLD EVENTS		LAWRENCE'S LIFE
World War I 1914–18		
Russian Revolution	1917	Jacob Lawrence is born
Great Depression 1929–39		
	1937	Lawrence paints 60 panel series, *Toussaint L'Ouverture*
World War II 1939–45		
	1940–41	Lawrence paints *Migration Series*
Communist China is established	1949	
Korean War 1950–53		
African independence movement begins	1957	
	1958–65	Lawrence teaches at Pratt Institute
	1970–83	Lawrence teaches at University of Washington
Vietnam War ends	1975	
Dissolution of Soviet Union	1991	
South Africa dismantles apartheid	1994	
	2000	Lawrence dies

Although by the 1930s the Harlem Renaissance was over, enthusiasm for African-American culture was still high, and Lawrence became acquainted with several of its leading proponents. He studied African-American history and African art with Charles Seifert. He met Alain Locke, a professor at Howard University, who in 1925 had written *The New Negro*, in which he called for the development of a specific "Negro aesthetic," a unique style capable of expressing the African-American experience.

Lawrence decided to focus specifically on making paintings that told the story of his people. In 1939, he exhibited his first major series of narrative paintings, *Toussaint L'Ouverture*, which celebrated that leader's role in the struggle against slavery in Haiti. The series of 60 panels was exhibited at the Baltimore Museum of Art and established Lawrence's reputation as a rising young artist. Over the next couple of years Lawrence turned out other series focusing on the lives of Harriet Tubman and Frederick Douglass.

Lawrence's best known work is the *Migration Series,* painted in 1940–41, when he was 23. The work, 60 panels in tempera and gouache, narrates the story of Lawrence's family during the Great Migration, the exodus of African Americans from the rural South to the urban North. From 1913 through the World War II, thousands of African Americans fled their homes in the hope of escaping poverty and segregation, only to find circumstances equally bad in the cities of the north.

The panels of the *Migration Series* were done in a style that Lawrence called "dynamic cubism," with figures rendered in broad, flat, angular planes. Patches of intensely saturated colors are rhythmically distributed across the panels, creating constantly shifting focal points. The broadly stylized figures resemble those of folk art.

The *Migration Series* was a great success. It was shown at Edith Halpert's Downtown Gallery in New York, and featured in *Fortune* magazine. Following the exhibition, the series was split between the Museum of Modern Art in New York and the Phillips Collection in Washington, D.C.

In addition to painting, Lawrence also had a long career as a teacher. From 1958 until 1965 he taught at Pratt Institute in Brooklyn. He

taught at the University of Washington from 1970 to 1983. Lawrence died June 9, 2000.

Legacy

Jacob Lawrence was one of the first artists to self-consciously address the African-American experience in order to develop a uniquely African-American style of art. His works bridged the worlds of traditional storytelling and intellectual history. His boldly simplified forms emphasize the universal human content of the specific historical events depicted.

Through the 1940s Lawrence's work was deeply admired by the foremost critics of the American avant-garde, including Alfred Barr, director of the Museum of Modern Art. In the 1950s and 1960s New York critics increasingly supported the emerging Abstract Expressionist movement being developed by JACKSON POLLOCK and others. The Abstract Expressionists were concerned more with formal than with social issues. Lawrence, however, never gave up his interest in narrative. For him, purely formal experiments in "art for art's sake" were not enough—social content was more important.

In the wake of the civil rights movement of the 1960s and the renewed interest in African-American studies, Lawrence has once again come to be respected as one of the pivotal figures in American art. He has become a role model to a younger generation of artists who, like him, are concerned with making art that engages important social issues.

McEnroe

For Further Reading

Turner, Elizabeth Hutton, ed. *Jacob Lawrence: The Migration Series.* Washington, D.C.: Rappahannock Press, in association with The Phillips Collection, 1993.

Wheat, Ellen Harkins. *Jacob Lawrence, American Painter.* Seattle: University of Washington Press, in association with the Seattle Art Museum, 1986.

Lennon, John; McCartney, Paul

Songwriters and Vocalists
1940–1980; 1942–

Life and Work

At the creative core of the monumentally successful group called the Beatles stood the dynamic tension between John Lennon and Paul McCartney.

Lennon (born October 9, 1940) and McCartney (born James Paul McCartney, June 18, 1942) were the founders of the group of working-class teenage musicians who joined forces in Liverpool, England, in 1956. The group went through several names, including the Silver Beetles; the final spelling came to Lennon in a dream.

By 1962 the group was comprised of the famous quartet: Lennon, McCartney, George Harrison, and Ringo Starr. That year the Beatles achieved their first British hit, "Love Me Do." Massive adulation from newly affluent teenage fans followed, and in 1964 the group rose to international fame with an appearance on U.S. television's *Ed Sullivan Show* and a simultaneous conquest of the five top spots on U.S. pop charts. With their mop-top haircuts and raffish ways, they seemed the very embodiment of a youth-culture fad, but observers of their music itself noticed that they were becoming much more than that. The sophistication of such top hits as "I Want to Hold Your Hand" showed that Lennon and McCartney were top-notch songwriters with a consciousness of their own originality.

Although Lennon and McCartney were credited as co-composers on all the Beatles songs they wrote, they usually did not collaborate on individual songs. After the Beatles moved into uncharted and ambitious creative territory, Lennon tended more toward poetic introspection (and sometimes toward raw emotional intensity), whereas McCartney remained a pop balladeer at heart; "Strawberry Fields Forever" was perhaps quintessential Beatles-era Lennon, and "Yesterday," one of the most popular songs of the late twentieth century by several measures, represented McCartney's style to perfection. Both contributed heavily as song-

writers to the landmark *Sgt. Pepper's Lonely Hearts Club Band* album of 1967.

After the Beatles broke up in 1970, both Lennon and McCartney had successful solo careers. Lennon, in partnership with his wife Yoko Ono, released albums marked by political and psychological concerns; until the end he tried to express personal feelings and beliefs in his music. He was killed by a mentally disturbed man in New York on December 8, 1980.

McCartney led the successful pop-rock band Wings in the 1970s and remained active through the rest of the century. The 1990s saw the release of three albums of classical music, such as 1999's *Working Classical*, in which McCartney's melodic ideas were orchestrated or arranged by academically trained composers.

Legacy

The Beatles stood at the creative summit of rock music in part because of the range of styles their music encompassed—from teen pop to circus music to Modernist electronic experiments and more.

That eclecticism resulted to some degree from the creative free-spiritedness of all four Beatles, but it was the particular consequence of the contrast and rivalry between Lennon and McCartney. In the late 1960s, pushing each other further with each new release, they helped to define rock and roll composition as a serious art. Aided in this respect by their collaboration with the classically trained producer George Martin, and rivaled only by the American songwriter BOB DYLAN, they forged albums that were creative wholes, incorporating aspects of each member's personality. Lennon gave voice to the drug-induced psychedelia of the era, while McCartney, in such songs as *Sgt. Pepper's* "When I'm Sixty-Four," delved into British pop music's past—and their divergent efforts, instead of creating the sensation of a meaningless pastiche, seemed to help rock music along the way toward becoming a mature art form, one that could express and encompass a great variety of human experiences.

Rock music could never quite recapture the creative balance that the Beatles achieved, but the imprint of their music has shown itself repeatedly. Lennon's attempt to break down emotional barriers through simple, elemental force, which appeared most strongly in his first solo albums after the Beatles'

breakup, resonated in the punk rock of the late 1970s, and McCartney remained an influential figure for mainstream rock figures from Elton John onward to the present time. If the essence of rock and roll was the concept of a group effort rather than an individual creative struggle, then the interaction of Lennon and McCartney was one of the twentieth century's definitive partnerships.

Manheim

World Events	Lennon and McCartney's Lives
World War II 1939–45	
1940	John Lennon is born
1942	Paul McCartney is born
Communist China is established 1949	
Korean War 1950–53	
1956	Lennon and McCartney begin playing together
African independence movement begins 1957	
1962	Final membership of Beatles is reached
1964	Beatles top U.S. charts
1967	Beatles record *Sgt. Pepper's Lonely Hearts Club Band*
1970	Beatles break up
Vietnam War ends 1975	
1980	Lennon is murdered in New York
Dissolution of Soviet Union 1991	
South Africa dismantles apartheid 1994	
1999	McCartney's *Working Classical* album is released

For Further Reading

Benson, Ross. *Paul McCartney: Behind the Myth.* London: Gollancz, 1992.

Davies, Hunter. *The Beatles.* New York: W. W. Norton, 1996.

Fawcett, Anthony. *John Lennon: One Day at a Time.* New York: Grove Press, 1980.

Leonardo da Vinci

Painter, Sculptor, and Scientist
1452–1519

Life and Work

Painter, engineer, biologist, botanist, astronomer, and courtier, Leonardo da Vinci was the quintessential "Renaissance man."

Leonardo was born in 1452 in Vinci, near Florence. About 1470 he began his training in the workshop of Andrea del Verrochio, and seems to have worked there for several years. By the late 1470s Leonardo was receiving his own commissions. The most important of these was *Adoration of the Magi*, commissioned by the monks of San Donato a Scoperto in 1481.

Before *Adoration of the Magi* could be completed, Leonardo left Florence for Milan, spending the next 20 years on a variety of projects for the duke of Milan. A skilled and famously charming courtier, Leonardo seems to have been a prominent figure in the duke's court.

During those years, Leonardo also painted. His *Last Supper* (c. 1495) for the church of Sta. Maria delle Grazie has since become perhaps the most famous picture in the world, with the possible exception of *Mona Lisa* (1503–06), also by Leonardo. The *Last Supper* is often regarded as marking the beginning of the High Renaissance style. His massive figures, unified composition, and concentration on human drama and psychology made earlier depictions of the scene look fussy and trivial in comparison. In this fresco painting Leonardo established a style of larger-than-life grandeur and idealism that would come to define the High Renaissance.

After 1495, Leonardo traveled throughout Italy, spending relatively little time in any one place. In 1501, he returned to Florence, where he was welcomed as a hero. He received a commission to do an altarpiece depicting the *Madonna and Child with Saint Anne* for the church of Santissima Annunziata. When the cartoon (full-scale drawing) for the painting was exhibited, it immediately became one of the most celebrated images in the city. The public flocked to see it, and artists, especially the young RAPHAEL, quickly began to imitate its style. It was probably during this stay in Florence that Leonardo painted the *Mona Lisa*, which is almost certainly a portrait of the wife of Francesco del Giocondo.

From 1508 until 1513 Leonardo was again in Milan. There he worked on some paintings, including the final version of *Madonna and Child with Saint Anne*, but after 1508 he devoted increasing time to his scientific studies. His voluminous notebooks show the broad range of his interests. They include anatomical and astronomical studies, military inventions and studies for flying machines.

In 1517, King Francis I of France invited Leonardo to spend his last years at the chateau of Cloux as a member of his court. Leonardo died there in 1519.

Legacy

Leonardo da Vinci was one of the most influential artists of the Renaissance. His *Last Supper* and the cartoon for *Madonna and Child with Saint Anne* introduced a new style of painting that was imitated in Florence by younger artists such as Raphael and Andrea del Sarto. Leonardo also seems to have influenced the development of High Renaissance painting in Venice. In Milan, the "Leonardesque" style was continued by lesser painters such as Bernardino Luini long after Leonardo's death.

Although Leonardo never served as architect for a building, his designs for centralized churches lie at the root of most High Renaissance innovations. Donato Bramante, with whom Leonardo was closely associated in Milan, used a variation of Leonardo's design in his plans for the new St. Peter's in Rome.

Leonardo's scientific drawings were not widely distributed, and therefore had little direct impact on the history of science. Nevertheless it is important to note Leonardo's advanced observations and understanding. His understanding of the circulation of blood, for example, anticipated that of William Harvey, more than a century later.

Today, Leonardo's *Last Supper* and *Mona Lisa* are probably the most famous paintings in the world. The *Mona Lisa*, in particular, has become almost an icon of art itself; she has become the foundation for an entire kitsch sub-industry, providing the inspiration for post cards, T-shirts, and socks.

McEnroe

WORLD EVENTS		LEONARDO'S LIFE
Ming Dynasty reasserts Chinese control of China	1368	
	1452	Leonardo da Vinci is born
Ottoman Empire conquers Constantinople	1453	
	c. 1470	Leonardo joins studio of Andrea del Verrocchio
Pope Sixtus IV institutes Spanish Inquisition	1478	
	1481– 1502	Leonardo moves to Milan
High Renaissance in Italy	1490– 1527	
Columbus sails to Americas	1492	
	c. 1495	Leonardo begins work on *Last Supper*
	1501	Cartoon of *Madonna and Child with St. Anne* is exhibited in Florence
	1503–06	Leonardo paints *Mona Lisa*
Protestant Reformation begins	1517	Leonardo is invited to live in France by King Francis I
	1519	Leonardo dies
Ottoman dominance of Mediterranean ends	1571	

For Further Reading

Clark, Kenneth. *Leonardo da Vinci.* Rev. ed. Baltimore, Md.: Penguin Books, 1967.

Kemp, Martin. *Leonardo da Vinci: The Marvelous Works of Nature and Man.* Cambridge, Mass.: Harvard University Press, 1981.

Turner, A. Richard. *Inventing Leonardo.* Berkeley: University of California Press, 1992.

Lin, Maya

Sculptor and Architect
1959–

Life and Work

Maya Lin is best known for her design for the Vietnam Veterans Memorial in Washington, D.C.

Lin was born in 1959 in Athens, Ohio, to Chinese immigrant parents. Her father was dean of fine arts and her mother a professor of literature at Ohio University. She grew up in a world of art and ideas.

Lin studied architecture at Yale University. She began working on her design for the Vietnam Veterans Memorial as a class project for a design course in 1980 while a 21-year-old undergraduate. The following year, she submitted her design (one of 1,400 submitted nationally) to the national design competition for the memorial, and her design was selected.

Lin's memorial design consisted of two partly submerged black granite walls, nearly 250 feet long, converging in a V-shape, and inscribed with the names of the 58,156 American soldiers who died in the war. In a city filled with memorials, the stark simplicity of Lin's monument was something new. Not quite architecture and not quite sculpture, her memorial was a place of quiet reflection: both literal reflection in the polished surfaces of the wall and contemplative reflection on the dead and the war.

As soon as Lin was awarded the commission, controversy erupted. Her design was described by critics as an ugly scar. Lin was personally attacked because of her age, sex, and race. A group of Vietnam veterans, outraged at the minimalist simplicity of the proposed memorial, demanded a monument showing heroic soldiers. Although Lin was disturbed by the controversy—she had hoped her memorial would provide an opportunity for healing—she refused to alter her design. In 1984 a compromise was reached and a more traditional monument by Frederick Hart depicting three soldiers and a flagpole was added, not to the apex of Lin's monument, where the veterans group had wanted it, but some distance away.

Commissions for other public monuments soon followed. In 1989, Lin created the Civil Rights Memorial in Montgomery, Alabama, in commemoration of those who had lost their lives in the struggle for civil rights. This monument, too, is one of understated simplicity. A sheet of water flows over a black granite table inscribed with a quote from Dr. Martin Luther King: "We are not satisfied and we will not be satisfied until justice rolls down like water, and righteousness like a mighty stream."

Lin has recently turned to other kinds of work, such as *Wave Field*, which she created in 1993 at the University of Michigan. Lin shaped a 90 foot square area into an undulating field of grass-covered waves that looks more like the result of some impossible act of nature than human design. *Wave Field* is mysterious, whimsical, and evocative.

Lin has received numerous awards, including honorary doctorates from Yale, Williams, and Smith Colleges. Today she runs a design studio in New York City.

Legacy

Maya Lin's Vietnam Veterans Memorial has become one of the most famous monuments in the country. Viewers find the memorial profoundly moving. Each year thousands of people visit it to pay tribute to those who died in the war. Taking rubbings of names and leaving behind mementos, the visitors become part of the memorial. In addition to the actual memorial in Washington, partial scale models tour the country and a virtual Vietnam Veterans Memorial has been built on the Internet.

The Vietnam Veterans Memorial has had two major effects. First, it has changed the fundamental nature of the commemorative monument. Traditional figurative war monuments that depict soldiers heroically struggling toward victory aim to elicit a relatively narrow range of responses, particularly pride and patriotism. That sort of simplistic nationalism would probably not have been appropriate for a war about which the country was so deeply ambivalent. Lin's memorial is much more open-ended. By avoiding a simple narrative program, Lin has created a place for contemplation where each viewer can come to his or her own understanding of the war. Many subsequent memorials, such as the one commemorating the victims of the 1995 bombing in Oklahoma City, have taken their inspiration from Lin's work.

Perhaps more important, the monument has had a profound effect on the country. Lin provided the nation with a means of addressing and acknowledging the mixed emotions of grief, anger, shame, and pride that surrounded the war. The Vietnam War tore the country apart, and Lin's memorial is still helping to heal the wounds.

McEnroe

WORLD EVENTS		LIN'S LIFE
African independence movement begins	1957	
	1959	Maya Lin is born
Vietnam War ends	1975	
	1981	Lin is awarded commission for Vietnam Veterans Memorial
	1989	Lin completes the Civil Rights Memorial in Montgomery
Dissolution of Soviet Union	1991	
	1993	Lin creates *Wave Field*
South Africa dismantles apartheid	1994	

For Further Reading

Lin, Maya Ying. *Boundaries.* New York: Simon & Schuster, 2000.

Mock, Freida May. *Maya Lin: A Strong Clear Vision.* Santa Monica, Calif.: Sanders & Mock Productions, 1994. Videorecording.

Liszt, Franz

Composer, Pianist, and Conductor
1811–1886

Life and Work

The foremost piano virtuoso of the nineteenth century, Franz Liszt dazzled audiences throughout Europe. As a composer, he was an innovator who generously championed the music of other progessive figures.

Liszt was born in Raiding, Hungary (now a part of Austria), on October 22, 1811. He was the son of a musician who earned a living herding sheep for the Esterházy family, formerly patrons of FRANZ JOSEPH HAYDN. In 1819 Liszt accompanied his father to Vienna, where the great pianist Carl Czerny agreed to give him lessons. The following year he made his concert debut, and in 1823 he moved to Paris with his father. In the next several years, they made concert tours of England, France, and Switzerland. In 1832 he heard a performance by the Italian violinist Niccolò Paganini, a showy virtuoso who pushed the violin to its absolute limit.

Liszt set out to bring the same kind of fireworks to the piano—among the fruits of his efforts were the *Transcendental Etudes* of 1837. These compositions pose deep challenges even for today's top-flight pianists, and in Liszt's time they were entirely unmatched. Until 1848, when he became music director at the ducal court in the city of Weimar, Liszt made a handsome living as a traveling concert virtuoso. He became a Hungarian national hero and composed a series of *Hungarian Rhapsodies* containing elements of Gypsy music. A flamboyant and even egocentric personality, Liszt entered into a series of notorious romantic attachments with aristocratic women.

Liszt's compositions had always married virtuosity to sound musical logic, and, in the 1850s, freed from the rigors of concertizing, he set out to produce even more substantial works. He wrote two symphonies (one, the *Faust* Symphony, appeared in 1854) and the first 12 of his 13 symphonic poems. Most of these works, like the symphonic poem *Hamlet*, were detailed musical representations of literary works, in which Liszt used melodies in service of characterization and narration in wholly new ways.

In the 1860s Liszt turned to a life of religious asceticism, living in a small cell in Rome, despite suggestions of insincerity. His late compositions were extremely experimental. Liszt died in Bayreuth, in Germany, on July 31, 1886.

Legacy

As a composer, Franz Liszt exerted enormous and often underestimated influence on the music of the second half of the nineteenth century.

Liszt was in some ways the first true musical superstar. The 1970s film *Lisztomania*, which depicts the composer as the object of adulation not unlike that enjoyed by a modern rock guitar hero, gives an exaggerated but oddly instructive impression of how he brought music into the public realm. It is important to remember that for nineteenth-century audiences, at least some genres of what is now called classical music were really the popular music of the day, not merely the province of the refined few. Liszt completed the transformation of the composer (begun by WOLFGANG AMADEUS MOZART and LUDWIG VAN BEETHOVEN) from aristocratic employee to fully public figure, supported by concerts attended by middle-class audiences.

The symphonic poem inspired by an extramusical story (or "program") was essentially Liszt's invention. An arch-Romantic conception that brought music into close intellectual contact with literature, Liszt's symphonic poems founded a tradition that resounded especially in Germany and in Liszt's native eastern Europe, where it became allied with nationalist feeling. Notable examples of works that expand on Lisztian musical narration are Bedrich Smetana's *Má Vlast* (*My Homeland*) a cycle composed between 1880 and 1894, and Richard Strauss's *Also Sprach Zarathustra* (*So Spoke Zarathustra*) of 1896, a work inspired by a philosophical tract of Friedrich Wilhelm Nietzsche. The use and transformation of themes in these works influenced the operas of RICHARD WAGNER (who married Liszt's daughter). Liszt's daring treatment of harmony may be seen to have initiated the long breakdown in the classical harmonic system that Wagner carried forward and ARNOLD SCHOENBERG, in the early twentieth century, completed.

Manheim

For Further Reading
Walker, Alan. *Franz Liszt.* New York: Knopf, 1983.
Williams, Adrian. *Portrait of Liszt: By Himself and His Contemporaries.* New York: Oxford University Press, 1990.

Lorca, Federico García

Poet and Playwright
1898–1936

Life and Work

Federico García Lorca, a prolific poet and playwright, was passionate about many traditional forms of art, including music, theater, puppetry, and poetry. With a great depth of emotion and love of the land and folk traditions of Spain, he engaged in these art forms, combining and revitalizing them for his contemporaries and those Spanish artists who came after him.

Lorca was born on June 5, 1898, in Granada in the Andalusian region of southern Spain. He grew up in a prosperous family, and as a child often wrote and staged plays for his family. A reluctant student of law at the University of Granada from 1915 to 1919, he spent most of his time writing poetry, discussing his ideas about art with intellectual friends, and reading Spanish writers.

In 1919 Lorca went to Madrid to study at the Residencia des Estudiantes, a liberal learning institution modeled after Cambridge and Oxford Universities. There he met the painter SALVADOR DALÍ, the filmmaker Luis Buñuel, and the poet Rafael Alberti, all of whom would be among his closest friends as well as some of the most influential artists of the Surrealist movement.

By 1928, Lorca had already written five collections of poetry: *Libro de poemas* (*Book of Poems*, 1921), *Poema del cante jondo* (*Poem of the Deep Song*, 1923), *Suites* (1926), *Canciones* (*Songs*, 1927), and *Romancero gitano* (*The Gypsy Ballads*, 1928). In much of this work he drew on the traditional forms of song and oral poetry of Spanish peasants and gypsies. He became known as a "gypsy poet," a definition that he later strove to refute with the complexity of the poems in his collection *Poeta en Nueva York* (*Poet in New York*, 1940).

In the 1930s, Lorca devoted himself to the theater in Spain. In 1931 he formed a traveling theater group, La Barraca, whose aim was to bring classical and innovative theater to rural Spain. Again he drew on folk tradition and history and explored what he considered to be the raw emotion of the countryside.

Spanish audiences were, meanwhile, receiving Lorca's own plays enthusiastically. His three tragedies about women and their relationships to passion and death, *Bodas de sangre* (*Blood Wedding*), which opened in Madrid in 1933, *Yerma* in 1934, and *La casa de Bernarda Alba* (*The House of Bernarda Alba*) in 1936, were all extremely successful and Lorca was soon considered among Spain's great dramatists.

In 1936 Civil War broke out in Spain with a military uprising led by General Francisco Franco. Lorca, a largely apolitical writer, was nonetheless identified with the liberal Spanish Republic. On August 16, 1936, he was taken from his parents' home in Granada. He was later executed and buried in an unmarked grave.

Legacy

Federico García Lorca's passionate raising up of the traditional arts of Spain to the level of avant-garde art, along with his conception of art as a vital part of everyday life, broadened the focus of Spanish poetry and theater.

After his death, Lorca's plays and poetry were suppressed in Franco's Spain. However, Antonio Machado, Pedro Salinas, and PABLO NERUDA were among the artists to decry Lorca's execution and to celebrate and continue the energy of his creative power in the years that followed.

Lorca was the most acclaimed of the literary group known as "The Generation of 1927," a group of young artists that included Rafael Alberti, Jorge Guillén, José Bergamín, Gerardo Diego, Damaso Alonso, and Juan Chabás, and his influence continued to be felt despite the repressive political climate.

Lorca had searched for and discovered new ways of fusing poetry and theater and can be seen as a predecessor to such theatrical experimenters as SAMUEL BECKETT, TENNESSEE WILLIAMS, and Harold Pinter. Through his influence and work with La Barraca, Lorca contributed to the flowering of local theater in Spain.

In the 1980s Spain saw a renewed burst of interest in Lorca's work. Many of the plays that had not been performed during his lifetime were produced, and unfinished volumes of poetry and collections of his correspondence were published. Lorca's plays, particularly the three tragedies, *Yerma, Blood Wedding*, and *The House of Bernardo Alba*, continue to be frequently produced both in Spain and elsewhere.

Watson

WORLD EVENTS		LORCA'S LIFE
Germany is united	1871	
Spanish-American War	1898	Federico García Lorca is born
World War I	1914–18	
	1915	Lorca enrolls at University of Granada
Russian Revolution	1917	
	1919	Lorca goes to study in Madrid
	1927	*Songs* is published
Great Depression	1929–39	
	1932	Lorca forms La Barraca
	1933	Lorca's tragedy, *Blood Wedding*, opens in Madrid
	1936	Lorca is executed
World War II	1939–45	

For Further Reading

Stainton, Leslie. *Lorca: A Dream of Life*. New York: Farrar, Straus, & Giroux. 1999.

García Lorca, Federico. *Selected Verse: Federico García Lorca*. Edited by Christopher Maurer. New York: Farrar, Straus, & Giroux, 1995.

Lynn, Loretta

Vocalist and Songwriter
1935–

Life and Work

A pioneering creative figure among women in country music, Loretta Lynn gave voice to the histories and emotional lives of American women of many different backgrounds.

Very much the "coal miner's daughter" she proclaimed herself in her 1970 hit recording of that name, Lynn was born Loretta Webb in the Appalachian Kentucky hamlet of Butcher Holler (or Hollow) on April 14, 1935. She married Mooney Lynn at the age of 13, a month after having met him, and had four children by the time she was 18. The couple moved to Washington state in search of work, and Lynn began to perform at a Grange hall.

She recorded for the Zero label in nearby Vancouver, Canada, in 1960. Lynn and her husband drove around the United States to promote her 45 rpm recording of "Honky Tonk Girl," personally visiting radio stations and buttonholing disc jockeys to encourage them to play the record. The success of this strategy in the highly centralized country music business was a measure of Lynn's talent and drive; the record rose to upper chart levels, and Lynn appeared on Nashville's *Grand Ole Opry* radio program. Once in Nashville, she impressed Patsy Cline and Doyle Wilburn, two of the leading performers of the day, and in 1962 she reached the country top ten with "Success," later covered by Irish rock superstar Sinead O'Connor.

Her debut LP, *Loretta Lynn*, was released on the Decca label in 1964; like much of her early work, it mined the vein of tremulous melancholy first opened up by 1950s vocalist Kitty Wells. In the middle 1960s, however, Lynn's songwriting came to the fore; she began to develop an assertive emotional vocabulary that addressed women's concerns. An example was 1966's "Don't Come Home a-Drinkin' (with Lovin' on Your Mind)," which sharply dramatized the revulsion many women felt at the sexual demands placed upon them by alcoholic partners. Lynn stirred controversy with the 1974 single "The Pill," an enthusiastic endorsement of that method of birth control, but enjoyed chart success through the 1970s, especially in a duet partnership with male vocalist Conway Twitty.

Lynn's autobiography *Coal Miner's Daughter* was a 1976 bestseller; it was equally successful as a 1980 film, with actress Sissy Spacek portraying Lynn. Lynn remained a strong concert draw through the 1980s and 1990s, and was preparing a second autobiography as the century neared its end.

Legacy

Country music, at mid-century almost an entirely male-dominated field, was by century's end offering more creative opportunities to women than any other American musical genre. Although she was not the sole instigator of this change, Loretta Lynn did more to bring it about than anyone.

Lynn redefined the role of women in country music primarily through her songwriting, fueled by a sense of women's rising dissatisfaction with their second-class status in American society. Nashville's music industry tended to divide the act of musical creation between songwriters and performers; Lynn was one of a group of 1960s songwriters (Merle Haggard was another) who reasserted the country song lyric as a vehicle for personal expression. Although she often performed and recorded songs by other writers, she was never merely a vessel for their ideas, and she maintained and managed her own creative personality—assertive, even confrontational when necessary, and often humorous—throughout her career. Country music grew as both female and male singers benefited from Lynn's self-assertion.

Younger singer–songwriters were quick to follow Lynn's example; Dolly Parton was the most prominent of those who moved into the niche Lynn created for a down-home common sense undergirded with powerful emotional perception. Beyond her immediate successors, though, Lynn's creative personality echoed through those of female performers for the rest of the century. Artists of the 1980s and 1990s, such as Reba McEntire, Patty Loveless, Mary Chapin Carpenter, and Wynonna Judd, pursued the ideal of an equal and independent female voice in country music and selected repertoire that represented women as free emotional agents unwilling to submit to victimization. For the core of their creative being, this group has Loretta Lynn to thank.

Manheim

WORLD EVENTS	LYNN'S LIFE
Great Depression 1929–39	
1935	Loretta Lynn is born Loretta Webb
World War II 1939–45	
Communist China 1949 is established	
Korean War 1950–53	
African independence 1957 movement begins	
1960	Lynn makes first recordings
1962	Lynn records top ten hit, "Success"
1964	Lynn's first LP is released
1966	Lynn records "Don't Come Home a-Drinkin' (with Lovin' on Your Mind)"
1974	Lynn creates controversy with recording "The Pill"
Vietnam War ends 1975	
1976	Lynn's best-selling autobiography is published
1980	Film *Coal Miner's Daughter* depicts Lynn's life
Dissolution of 1991 Soviet Union	

For Further Reading

Bufwack, Mary A. *Finding Her Voice: The Illustrated History of Women in Country Music.* New York: Henry Holt, 1995.

Lynn, Loretta, with George Vecsey. *Loretta Lynn: Coal Miner's Daughter.* Chicago: Regnery, 1976.

Makeba, Miriam

Vocalist
1932–

Life and Work

For many decades the chief musical spokesperson for the struggle against the apartheid system of racial segregation in South Africa, Miriam Makeba was also one of the first musicians who brought African sounds to the attention of the world and showed how they could be combined with other popular traditions.

Zensi Miriam Makeba was born in Johannesburg, South Africa, on March 4, 1932; she got an early taste of the country's police state, spending six months of her infancy in prison with her mother. As a teenager, Makeba worked as a maid, and she started singing in a church choir. Makeba emerged as a solo star in 1957, touring internationally as part of the African Jazz and Variety show.

She had an important part in the anti-apartheid documentary *Come Back, Africa*; when the film had its premiere in Venice, Italy, Makeba decided to stay away from South Africa—the revocation of her South African passport sealed her decision. In London Makeba met American entertainer Harry Belafonte, who had also campaigned against racial discrimination, and in 1959 Belafonte helped her launch her American career with an appearance on the Steve Allen television program and a performance at New York's Village Vanguard club.

In the early and middle 1960s, Makeba was a familiar musical figure in American progressive circles and found success with her jazz/African fusion American releases. Her American career took a downturn with her marriage to Black Panther leader Stokely Carmichael in 1968, but Makeba found in the rejection a chance to return to Africa: she and Carmichael moved to the West African nation of Guinea. They were later divorced, but Makeba continued to speak out and kept up a steady schedule of international appearances. In 1987 Makeba had a guest slot on Paul Simon's *Graceland* tour, making a historic visit to formerly white-ruled Zimbabwe; in 1990 she was allowed to return to South Africa as the apartheid system neared its inevitable end. Her full schedule of concerts in Africa and elsewhere through the 1990s included a 1995 performance at a Vatican Christmas concert and a private audience with Pope John Paul II.

Legacy

In an age when entertainers espouse political causes of all kinds, it is important to recognize the contributions of those, like Miriam Makeba, who first stepped out of the more restrictive entertainer's role of the past to try to influence the world for the better.

Although the impact of cultural leaders may be difficult to quantify, "Mother Africa," as Makeba was often called, plainly had an enormous role in the anti-apartheid movement as it grew over the five decades of her performing career. The South African government was terrified of her influence: Makeba was not even allowed to return to the country for her mother's funeral in 1960, and in 1963, all sales of her recordings were banned in South Africa. An exile from her own country who became one of popular music's first truly international figures, Makeba preceded BOB MARLEY, the Nigerian star FELA, and other musicians who addressed the struggles of their native lands and in so doing began to forge a more universal message of equality and justice.

As South Africa evolved into a multiracial democracy in the 1990s, another facet of Makeba's wide influence came more clearly into view. Makeba, on tour with Paul Simon in 1987, might have taken satisfaction in the fact that she had helped to make possible Simon's wildly successful mixture of African and Western pop styles. Her widely heard American recordings of the 1960s, including the Grammy-winning *An Evening with Belafonte/Makeba* of 1965 and the 1967 single "Pata Pata," introduced African popular music to wider audiences than it had ever enjoyed, and her infusion of indigenous musical materials into a jazz context presaged by some years even the work of her South African compatriot Abdullah Ibrahim, to say nothing of the wide sweep of 1990s music built on similar fusions. Miriam Makeba has been a powerful carrier of political and musical ideas.

Manheim

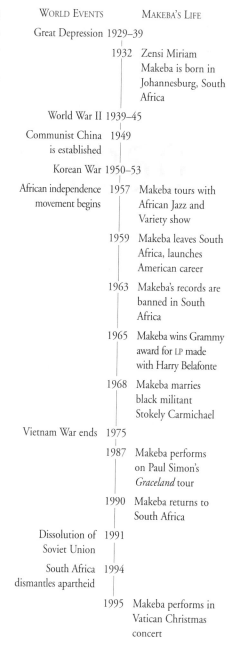

WORLD EVENTS	MAKEBA'S LIFE
Great Depression 1929–39	
	1932 Zensi Miriam Makeba is born in Johannesburg, South Africa
World War II 1939–45	
Communist China 1949 is established	
Korean War 1950–53	
African independence movement begins 1957	Makeba tours with African Jazz and Variety show
	1959 Makeba leaves South Africa, launches American career
	1963 Makeba's records are banned in South Africa
	1965 Makeba wins Grammy award for LP made with Harry Belafonte
	1968 Makeba marries black militant Stokely Carmichael
Vietnam War ends 1975	
	1987 Makeba performs on Paul Simon's *Graceland* tour
	1990 Makeba returns to South Africa
Dissolution of Soviet Union 1991	
South Africa dismantles apartheid 1994	
	1995 Makeba performs in Vatican Christmas concert

For Further Reading

Gwangwa, Jonas, and E. John Miller, Jr., eds., and Miriam Makeba, compiler. *The World of African Song*. Chicago: Quadrangle Books, 1971.

Makeba, Miriam, with James Hall. *Makeba: My Story*. New York: New American Library, 1988.

Manet, Edouard

Painter and Printmaker
1832–1883

Life and Work

Edouard Manet is one of the key figures in the development and philosophy of modern art.

Manet was born in Paris in 1832, at a time of profound change: industry, commerce, social life—even the city itself—were being radically transformed. The increasingly wealthy middle class took to the cafes, theaters, and streets of Paris in pursuit of pleasure. Manet's family wealth and his aristocratic demeanor allowed him to become both participant in and observer of the remarkable new times.

Manet's training was conventional. He worked for six years in the atelier of the academic painter Thomas Couture and closely studied the works of DIEGO VELÁZQUEZ, PETER PAUL RUBENS, and FRANCISCO GOYA in museums across Europe. Little in his background foretold the radical work he would do in the 1860s.

In 1863 Manet submitted his painting *Le Dejeuner sur l'Herbe* (*Luncheon on the Grass*) to the Salon, the annual exhibition of the Academy of Fine Arts. The judges rejected it, and Manet decided to exhibit at the Salon des Refusés, a private exhibition organized by the rejected artists. Even there the painting, which shows a nude woman sitting casually outdoors with two fashionably dressed young men while a second woman bathes in a pond, caused a scandal. Although Manet drew part of his inspiration from a Renaissance painting in the Louvre, the *Pastoral Concert* by Giorgione, viewers were disturbed both by its "indecent" subject matter and by the apparent carelessness of Manet's style.

Two years later, Manet's *Olympia* caused an even greater uproar. Basing his work on TITIAN's *Venus of Urbino*, Manet brought the painting up to date, by replacing the classical nude with the images of a real-life prostitute. The young woman looks directly at the viewer, while a black servant holds a bouquet of flowers that the Parisian viewer would have recognized as part of the transaction between prostitute and client. Once again, critics were outraged, both by the subject and by Manet's broad, flat painting style: neither belonged in a work of art.

These two works exemplify Manet's attempt to create a form of art appropriate for the modern world. For Manet, art should deal with modernity rather than classical myths and literary subjects. Modern painting should also reject the highly polished style of traditional paintings and should focus more on the actual process of painting than on creating an illusion of reality.

Because of his innovations, Manet became a celebrated figure among the Impressionst group of painters. His later works, such as *A Bar at the Folies-Bergère* (1882), come very close in style to the Impressionist works of PIERRE-AUGUSTE RENOIR and CLAUDE MONET. In subject, however, the superficial, vacuous barmaid/prostitute is rooted in the same view of modern Paris that Manet had portrayed in *Olympia* nearly 20 years earlier.

Manet died in 1883.

Legacy

Edouard Manet was one of the most influential artists of the nineteenth century. His stylistic innovations led directly to the development of Impressionism. Several of his students, including Berthe Morisot and Eva Gonzales, became prominent members of the Impressionist group. Although Manet chose not to exhibit with the Impressionists, he was an important voice in their frequent gatherings.

By referring directly to earlier paintings by old masters and intentionally subverting their forms, Manet was urging a rejection of the past and, at the same time, producing an art that was self-consciously about art. If the bourgeoisie found his paintings baffling, so much the better. For Manet, modern art, like modern life, should be difficult.

Manet's contributions have continued to be reevaluated over the last several decades. In the 1950s Clement Greenberg, the influential critic and chief proponent of Abstract Expressionism, pointed to Manet as the source of the Modernist movement. Modernism, according to Greenberg, involved each medium becoming conscious of its own inherent character. By rejecting traditional academic illusionism, Manet had initiated the process of formal experimentation that would achieve its ultimate expression in the purely abstract works of JACKSON POLLOCK nearly a century later.

While Manet did make important formal innovations, his primary contribution to the history of modern art may have been his daring rejection of the security of traditions and his embracing of the uncertain conditions of the modern world.

McEnroe

For Further Reading

Adler, Kathleen. *Manet.* Topsfield, Mass.: Salem House/Phaidon, 1986.

Clark, T. J. *The Painting of Modern Life: Paris in the Art of Manet and His Followers.* New York: Knopf, 1985.

Collins, Bradford R., ed. *12 Views of Manet's Bar.* Princeton, N.J.: Princeton University Press, 1996.

Mann, Thomas

Novelist

1875–1955

Life and Work

Thomas Mann's work joined consummate fiction writing to the sharpest political and cultural commentary, creating works that both embodied and examined a particular historical moment.

Mann was born on June 6, 1875, in Lübeck, Germany, a port city on the Baltic Sea. He grew up in a wealthy family and for much of his youth lived the comfortable life of the German bourgeoisie that he would describe in detail in *Buddenbrooks*, his first novel. Upon moving to Munich in 1894, Mann began writing and publishing short stories in local periodicals. In 1898 he published his first collection of stories, *Der kleine Herr Friedmann* (*Little Mister Friedemann*).

Mann began work on *Buddenbrooks* in 1897, completing the novel three years later. The story of the Buddenbrook family spans four generations and, with a nostalgic Romantic influence, recounts the fall of a successful merchant family.

Der Tod in Venedig (*Death in Venice*, 1912) is the story of a celebrated author, Gustav Aschenbach, who visits the plague-infested Italian city and, infatuated with a young boy he glimpses on the beach, remains and dies there. Through the realistic depiction of the artist's decline and death, Mann revealed artistic beauty to be merely an illusion.

In his novel *Der Zauberberg* (*The Magic Mountain*, 1924), Mann wrote about the loss of the past, which had been cut off from the present by the disaster of war. In this variation on the bildungsroman, or coming-of-age novel, he examined the Romantic German tradition and came to the conclusion that while a people without tradition lack identity, that tradition must be constantly reinterpreted if it is to continue to be meaningful. In 1929 Mann was awarded the Nobel Prize for Literature.

After leaving Germany and moving to Pacific Palisades, California, Mann wrote what some consider to be his greatest work: *Doktor Faustus* (*Doctor Faustus: The Life of the German Composer, Adrian Leverkühn, as Told by a Friend*, 1947). The novel is a reinterpretation of the Faust legend, the story of a man who sells his soul to the Devil, that originated in the Middle Ages and was most famously retold by JOHANN WOLFGANG VON GOETHE. Drawing on a wide variety of texts, including those of WILLIAM SHAKESPEARE, Friedrich Wilhelm Nietzsche, the German Romantics, LUDWIG VAN BEETHOVEN, ARNOLD SCHOENBERG, and newspaper and magazine articles, Mann made his protagonist representative of German culture as a whole. The novel is a farewell to that culture, whose fascist downfall is reflected in the decline of the syphilitic genius of the title, Leverkühn.

Mann left the United States in 1952 in response to McCarthyism. He himself had been attacked in the press, accused of being a communist sympathizer, and he saw Joseph McCarthy's anticommunism as a proto-fascist movement reminiscent of German Nazism. He spent his remaining years in Switzerland and died in Zurich on August 12, 1955.

Legacy

Thomas Mann chronicled the disappearance of the traditional European bourgeoisie and the entrance of Western Europe's new modern democratic ideals while establishing a tradition of intense intellectual examination and questioning in the novel.

Mann's first novel, *Buddenbrooks*, was not immediately successful. Its popularity grew with time, however, and within a few years more than 30,000 copies had been sold. In the 1920s his work was translated into nearly all of the European languages and Japanese. *The Magic Mountain*, a nostalgic description of the Europe that had been lost in the war, was immensely popular in Europe and the United States. After Mann's move to the United States he became as well known as a political figure as an author; as an intellectual and progressive artist, he came to represent what were considered the positive aspects of German culture.

Mann had much in common with his Modernist contemporaries, JAMES JOYCE, T. S. Eliot, and VIRGINIA WOOLF, all of whom wrote about a world whose stable foundations had been undermined by war. Yet, unlike these other Modernists, Mann maintained conventional literary forms and painstakingly revealed the essential isolation and alienation of his protagonists while examining questions of the artist's role in society and the nature of corruption. The searing political and cultural commentary in Mann's work defined a position within Modernism that relied more on intellectual questioning than on formal experimentation. *The Magic Mountain* was, however, more experimental than was widely acknowledged. The uneven flow of time in the novel, as well as its complex symbolism, link the novel to the work of his Modernist contemporaries.

Mann's influence on important writers of his time can be seen in his correspondences with the poet RAINER MARIA RILKE and Nobel Prize–winning novelist Hermann Hesse. Mann's vein of intellectual fiction has continued with writers including Susan Sontag, an American fiction writer and critic, who continues to apply his tradition of intellectual questioning in her analyses of modern culture and society.

Watson

WORLD EVENTS		MANN'S LIFE
Germany is united	1871	
	1875	Thomas Mann is born
Spanish-American War	1898	Mann publishes first collection of stories, *Little Mister Friedemann*
	1900	Mann completes *Buddenbrooks*
	1912	Mann writes *Death in Venice*
World War I	1914–18	
Russian Revolution	1917	
Great Depression	1929–39	
	1929	Mann is awarded Nobel Prize for Literature
World War II	1939–45	
Communist China is established	1949	
Korean War	1950–53	
	1952	Mann leaves the United States
	1955	Mann dies
African independence movement begins	1957	

For Further Reading

Heilbut, Anthony. *Thomas Mann: Eros and Literature.* Berkeley: University of California Press, 1997.

Winston, Richard and Clara, eds. and trans. *Letters of Thomas Mann 1889–1955.* Berkeley: University of California Press, 1970.

Marley, Bob

Musician and Bandleader
1945–1981

Life and Work

One of the creators of reggae music, Bob Marley over the course of his short life gave musical focus to the political struggles of black people in Jamaica and around the world.

World Events		Marley's Life
World War II	1939–45	
	1945	Bob Marley is born in St. Anns, Jamaica
Communist China is established	1949	
Korean War	1950–53	
African independence movement begins	1957	
	1963	Marley, Bunny Livingston and others form the Wailers
	1967	Marley begins to express Rastafarian ideas in songs
	1973	Marley records "I Shot the Sheriff"
Vietnam War ends	1975	
	1976	Marley survives assassination attempt
	1977	Marley records *Exodus* album
	1980	Marley performs in Zimbabwe
	1981	Marley dies
Dissolution of Soviet Union	1991	

Robert Nesta Marley was born in rural Nine Miles, St. Ann, Jamaica, on February 6, 1945. His mother, only 19 at the time, was the mistress of a white British land administrator; he married Marley's mother upon learning of the pregnancy but took little interest in his son's upbringing. Marley grew up mostly in the slums of Kingston, Jamaica, then, as now, among the world's most violent places. Looking to music as a way out, Marley and his friend Bunny Livingston (later Bunny Wailer) practiced playing guitars made from sardine cans and discarded wire. In 1963 Marley and Livingston joined singer Peter Tosh and three other musicians to form the Wailers.

Many of the group's early records were in the light, danceable ska style, but by 1967 they had begun to write songs expressing aspects of the Rastafarian faith and to lay the groundwork for a new style, later known as reggae, that featured complex rhythmic patterns over a foundation of heavy, hypnotic bass guitar. Rastafarianism and reggae became closely intertwined, expressing a message of peace and spirituality but warning ruling elites of resistance and ultimate judgment. Marley became the chief musical carrier of that message.

In the mid-1970s Marley became an international star, largely through his association with the internationally marketed, rock-oriented Island music label. His 1973 recording "I Shot the Sheriff" was covered by rock guitarist Eric Clapton, bringing the Wailers a large new audience, with each subsequent album eagerly awaited. Seeking to use his enormous influence in Jamaica to reduce the epidemic political violence there, Marley survived an assassination attempt in December of 1976. In the late 1970s he was troubled by a cancerous right toe. He refused to have it amputated and went to Europe for alternative treatment more in line with Rastafarianism, but the cancer spread to his lungs and brain. Marley died on May 11, 1981, in Miami.

Legacy

During his life and especially after his tragically early death, Bob Marley's songs brought Jamaican music from local popularity to a position of worldwide importance and familiarity.

Marley was not the only Jamaican artist to draw musical inspiration from the Rastafarian faith, but he was the only one who sensed the power its revolutionary ideals might have if they could be put before international audiences in musical form. Although Jamaican popular music shared (and continues to share) text subjects with other African-derived New World traditions, it is now widely defined by an image that includes spirituality, a peaceful exaltation of marijuana use, a mysterious patois full of Rastafarian concepts, the knotted strands of long hair known as dreadlocks, and a quiet but self-confident political radicalism that looks to the eventual overthrow of dominant elites. That image was spread in large part by Marley's massively popular 1970s albums, among them *Burnin'* (1973), *Rastaman Vibration* (1976), *Exodus* (1977), and *Survival* (1979). Its immediate impact was measurable by the success after Marley's death of numerous other reggae acts, including Marley's wife Rita and, in the late 1980s and early 1990s, his son Ziggy.

Beyond his success in communicating Jamaican musical and spiritual ideas, Marley was among the first musicians from anywhere in the Third World to achieve superstar status. He was widely popular in Africa, appearing before an audience of 40,000 in newly majority-ruled Zimbabwe shortly before his death in 1980 and introducing a reggae element into various traditions of African music. For listeners in much of the world he remained a well-remembered figure for decades after his death, but his music had its greatest resonance in what has been called the African diaspora. With Bob Marley, an emerging black spiritual and political sensibility found its voice.

Manheim

For Further Reading
Boot, Adrian. *Bob Marley: Songs of Freedom.* London: Bloomsbury, 1995.
White, Timothy. *Catch a Fire: The Life of Bob Marley.* New York: Holt, Rinehart and Winston, 1983.

Matisse, Henri

Painter and Sculptor
1869–1954

Life and Work

Henri Matisse was one of the leading avant-garde painters of the twentieth century.

Matisse was born in 1869 in Picardy, France. He had a traditional academic training, studying with William-Adolphe Bougereau at the Academie Julian and then with Gustave Moreau at the Ecole des Beaux Arts.

Between 1902 and 1905 Matisse became the leader of a group of painters that began experimenting with new forms of painting that built upon the boldly colored, emotionally charged paintings of VINCENT VAN GOGH and Paul Gaugin. Matisse and his colleagues aimed to further liberate color from its traditional role of describing the appearance of things and to make it instead a vehicle for direct emotional expression.

Matisse's *Portrait with a Green Stripe* (1905) was one of the boldest paintings in the new style. A simplified, strongly modeled portrait of his wife, the painting is disturbing in its abrupt juxtapositions of broad areas of clashing colors. One side of the face is yellow, divided by a green band from the other side, which is pink. A critic commenting on a 1905 exhibition referred to the group as "*les fauves*" —the wild beasts—a name, Fauvism, that was soon used to describe the style.

By 1908, Matisse had moved away from the sometimes disturbing effects of Fauvism toward an art that aimed to deal directly with visual pleasure. In his *Notes of a Painter,* published in 1908, he called for an art that would be "devoid of troubling or depressing subject matter . . . a mental comforter, something like a good armchair." In his *Dance* (1909), five nude female figures join hands to form a swirling wreath set against a background of intense blue and green. His joyous figures are the antithesis of the violent, confrontational nude women that PABLO PICASSO had depicted in his *Les Demoiselles d'Avignon* two years earlier.

Matisse continued to explore the rhythmic effects of line and color for the rest of his long career. He also worked extensively in small-scale bronze sculpture. In works such as *La Serpentine* (1909), he translated the undulating lines of *Dance* into three dimensions.

Late in life, with his eyesight failing, Matisse created a new technique for making images. He cut out large shapes of brightly colored paper and arranged them into boldly abstract compositions. One group of these images was published as a book entitled *Jazz* in 1947.

Matisse died in Nice in 1954.

Legacy

From a very early point in his career, Henri Matisse was widely regarded as one of the foremost avant-garde painters in Europe. Among his contemporaries, only his lifelong rival Picasso achieved greater success.

The Fauvist movement, which Matisse helped to initiate, was perhaps the first radically new painting style of the twentieth century. Although lasting only a brief time before its artists moved in different directions, Fauvism opened the door to numerous subsequent styles. Its interest in expressing emotions through the use of bold colors was a major source of inspiration for later Expressionist painters. Even Picasso, in paintings such as *Girl Before a Mirror* (1932), experimented with the bold planes of color and linear patterns he admired in the work of Matisse. Matisse's sculpture also had a significant influence on the following generation of sculptors, including Raymond Duchamp-Villon and Wilhelm Lehmbruck.

Later in the century, Matisse had a major effect on the American Abstract Expressionists, such as JACKSON POLLOCK and Mark Rothko, who saw his boldly abstract and rhythmically gestural works as a prelude to their own experimental works. The prominent critic Clement Greenberg, the foremost spokesperson for the Abstract Expressionists, described Matisse as the guiding force behind the movement.

Matisse's career spanned a half century of tumultuous change: two global wars, technological revolution, and a bewildering series of experimental art forms. Through it all he remained immersed in a world of pure visual pleasure.

McEnroe

WORLD EVENTS		MATISSE'S LIFE
U.S. Civil War	1861–65	
	1869	Henri Matisse is born
Germany is united	1871	
Spanish-American War	1898	
	1905	Matisse paints *Portrait with Green Stripe*
World War I	1914–18	
Russian Revolution	1917	
Great Depression	1929–39	
World War II	1939–45	
	1947	Matisse publishes *Jazz*
Communist China is established	1949	
Korean War	1950–53	
	1954	Matisse dies
African independence movement begins	1957	

For Further Reading

Elderfield, John. *Henri Matisse: A Retrospective.* New York: Museum of Modern Art, 1992.

Flam, Jack. *Matisse: The Man and His Art.* Ithaca, N.Y.: Cornell University Press, 1986.

Gowing, Lawrence. *Matisse.* New York: Oxford University Press, 1979.

Melville, Herman

Novelist, Short Story Writer, and Poet
1819–1891

Life and Work

Herman Melville wrote what many consider to be the supreme American novel, *Moby Dick*.

Melville was born in New York City on August 19, 1819. His father was a businessman and his childhood was comfortable until his father's business failure and subsequent death in 1832. At age 12 Melville left school and found work, beginning a process of self-education that would continue throughout his life.

The travel and adventure that Melville experienced early in life provided rich material for his later work. In 1839 he sailed for Liverpool on a merchant ship, which he would write about in his fourth novel, *Redburn: His First Voyage* (1849). After his return home he traveled to the West, making part of the journey on a Mississippi riverboat, an experience that would turn up in his short story, *The Confidence Man: His Masquerade* (1857).

Melville's next voyage was on the whaler *Acushnet*, where conditions proved so intolerable that he abandoned ship in the Polynesian islands. He and a companion were taken captive by a cannibalistic tribe and remained with them several months before escaping onto another whaling ship. Aboard this ship he joined a mutiny that led to his imprisonment in Tahiti. After his release he spent time in Hawaii and then, in 1844, finally returned to New York.

Melville's family and friends encouraged him to write about his unusual experiences. He did so in his first novel, *Typee: A Peep at Polynesian Life* (1846), and *Omoo: A Narrative of Adventures in the South Seas* (1847). These fictionalized versions of his adventures proved very popular.

Melville's third book, *Mardi: And a Voyage Thither* (1849), marks a change in style that led to the deeper symbolism of his later works. Although beginning as a realistic sailing adventure, it goes on to explore philosophical and metaphysical questions. This departure from the lighthearted adventure narrative of his first two books displeased his public and Melville's popularity began to wane.

Melville also began *Moby Dick* (1851), published in England as *The Whale*, as a mere adventure tale. Before long, however, the story of Ahab's quest for a white whale became a larger metaphysical exploration of good and evil. In his writing, Melville drew on the Bible, Edmund Spenser, WILLIAM SHAKESPEARE, JOHN MILTON, and personal correspondence with Nathaniel Hawthorne. Echoes of all of these can be heard in *Moby Dick;* in addition the novel's references to American folklore, Transcendentalist writers, and its fascination with the myth of the West make the work a deeply American piece of literature.

Melville published several collections of poetry, including *Battle-Pieces and Aspects of the War* (1866) and *John Marr and Other Sailors* (1888). After his retirement from his position in U.S. Customs, which he had held for 20 years, he began work on his last novel, *Billy Budd, Sailor,* a complex story of guilt and morality. *Billy Budd* was left among Melville's manuscripts when he died and was not published until 1924.

Melville died, largely unrecognized, in 1891

Legacy

Herman Melville's writings, unknown when he died, underwent a transformation of reputation that is unique in literary history.

Twenty years after his death, Melville was remembered primarily as a minor writer of sailing fiction. Wider interest in *Moby Dick* did not begin to grow until 1921, when Raymond Weaver published the first biography of Melville, *Herman Melville, Mariner and Mystic*. D. H. Lawrence followed suit, publishing critical discussions of *Typee, Omoo,* and *Moby Dick* in 1923. By the 1930s schools had begun teaching *Moby Dick* and the expansion of its reading public had begun.

Melville's combination of philosophical, scientific, and historical subject matter with the genres of drama, epic, and blank verse was ignored by an unprepared Victorian audience; in time, his writings found their audience. The fertile mixture of style and substance have made *Moby Dick* an abundant source of inspiration for later generations. Modernists in particular, whose sense of the darkness, destruction, and evil following World War I informed their own writing, appreciated the chaotic breadth of *Moby Dick*.

Melville's work was based on a uniquely American experience and society and inspired writers as varied as Jean-Paul Sartre, WILLIAM FAULKNER, and JORGE LUIS BORGES, among many others. All found rich material for their own critical and creative work in Melville's multilayered worlds of symbolism.

Three film versions of *Moby Dick* have been made, and artists of all media continue to draw from the novels—a recent work by performance artist Laurie Anderson was based on *Moby Dick*, and a movie, *Beau Travail,* by French filmmaker Claire Denis, was based on *Billy Budd*.

Watson

WORLD EVENTS		MELVILLE'S LIFE
Congress of Vienna reorganizes Europe	1815	
	1819	Herman Melville is born
	1839	Melville sails for Liverpool
Revolutions in Austria, France, Germany, and Italy	1848	
	1851	Melville publishes *Moby Dick*
U.S. Civil War	1861–65	
	1866	Melville publishes *Battle-Pieces and Aspects of the War*
Germany is united	1871	
	1888	Melville publishes *John Marr and Other Sailors*
	1891	Melville dies
Spanish-American War	1898	
World War I	1914–18	
	1917	
	1924	*Billy Budd, Sailor* is published
Great Depression	1929–39	

For Further Reading
Parker, Hershel. *Herman Melville: A Biography.* Baltimore, Md.: Johns Hopkins University Press, 1996.
Robertson-Lorant, Laurie. *Melville: A Biography.* New York: Clarkson Potter, 1996.

Michelangelo

(Michelangelo Buonarotti)

Sculptor, Painter, Architect,
and Poet
1475–1564

Life and Work

Michelangelo Buonarotti was born in the rural village of Caprese in 1475, and raised in the stonecutters' village of Settignano. At age 13 he was apprenticed to the Florentine painter Domenico del Ghirlandaio. The following year, the young Michelangelo came to the attention of Lorenzo de' Medici, the powerful ruler of the city of Florence, and was invited into the school Lorenzo had established for gifted craftsmen and artists. In the Medici household he was introduced to the scholars, poets, musicians, and writers of Florence.

During the extended political crisis following Lorenzo's death in 1492, Michelangelo traveled around Italy in search of commissions. In 1498 he was commissioned by a French cardinal to do the *Pietá,* now in St. Peter's. In its elaborate details, beautiful (and improbably young) Madonna, meticulously polished surfaces, and most of all, Michelangelo's proud signature on a band crossing the Virgin's chest, it is clear that Michelangelo intended the work to be a display of his technical ability. Other commissions soon followed.

In 1501 Michelangelo returned to Florence, where he was commissioned to carve the colossal *David* (1501–04). The project was grounded in Florentine politics. To celebrate the expulsion of the Medici family from Florence and the restoration of the Republic, city officials chose the figure of David, the quintessential underdog, and placed it in front of the town hall as an embodiment of the spirit of the Republic.

Michelangelo was called to Rome in 1505 by Pope Julius II to design the Pope's tomb, a project he never finished. Even in its unfinished state, the writhing nude male figures struggling against unseen bonds seem to parallel passages in Michelangelo's poetry that describe the human soul yearning to be released from the physical prison of the flesh.

In 1508, the Pope assigned Michelangelo to a new project, painting the ceiling of the Sistine Chapel. This colossal project, which took Michelangelo four years to complete, is considered to be one of the most significant works of European art.

Michelangelo spent the rest of his life moving between Rome and Florence. His major projects in Florence included a funerary chapel for the Medici family. In Rome he returned to the Sistine Chapel from 1536 until 1541 to paint the huge *Last Judgment* for Pope Paul III. Late in his career, Michelangelo increasingly concentrated on architecture. His design for the dome of St. Peter's is perhaps his best known architectural work.

Michelangelo died in 1564 at age 89, while working on a new version of the *Pietá.*

Legacy

In 1550, Giorgio Vasari wrote *Lives of the Most Excellent Italian Architects, Painters and Sculptors from Cimabue to Our Times,* often regarded as the first book of art history. Michelangelo was the only living artist included; he is also the great hero of the book, presented as the culmination of the process toward which earlier generations of artists had been leading.

The next generation of artists in Florence was deeply indebted to Michelangelo's style. His serpentine compositions provided the basis of Mannerist sculptures; painters imitated his highly polished human figures and love of complex allegory. In fact, Michelangelo's numerous imitators have since been criticized for making art that was drawn more from Michelangelo than from nature. Michelangelo continued to be an inspiration for the next 500 years—GIAN LORENZO BERNINI, AUGUSTE RODIN, and HENRY MOORE all studied his works closely.

Michelangelo changed the concept of an artist. Born at a time when artists were still regarded as craftsmen, he came to be revered as a genius whose creativity paralleled God's creativity. He not only redefined Renaissance art, but fundamentally changed the concept of "art" itself.

McEnroe

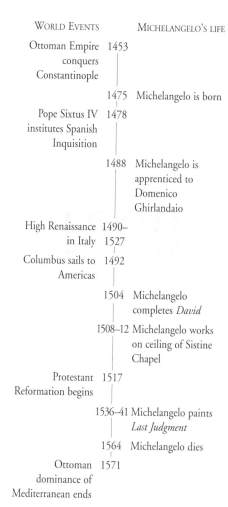

WORLD EVENTS		MICHELANGELO'S LIFE
Ottoman Empire conquers Constantinople	1453	
	1475	Michelangelo is born
Pope Sixtus IV institutes Spanish Inquisition	1478	
	1488	Michelangelo is apprenticed to Domenico Ghirlandaio
High Renaissance in Italy	1490–1527	
Columbus sails to Americas	1492	
	1504	Michelangelo completes *David*
	1508–12	Michelangelo works on ceiling of Sistine Chapel
Protestant Reformation begins	1517	
	1536–41	Michelangelo paints *Last Judgment*
	1564	Michelangelo dies
Ottoman dominance of Mediterranean ends	1571	

For Further Reading

Clements, Robert John. *The Poetry of Michelangelo.* New York: New York University Press, 1966.
Hartt, Frederick. *Michelangelo: The Complete Sculpture.* New York: Harry N. Abrams, 1968.
Hibbard, Howard. *Michelangelo: Painter, Sculptor, Architect.* New York: Vendome Press, 1978.

Mies van der Rohe, Ludwig

Architect and Educator
1886–1969

World Events		Mies's life
Germany is united	1871	
	1886	Ludwig Mies van der Rohe is born
Spanish-American War	1898	
World War I	1914–18	
Russian Revolution	1917	
	1920s	Mies experiments with "curtain-wall" construction
	1927	Mies directs Weissenhofseidlung exhibition in Stuttgart
	1929	Mies designs for International Exposition in Barcelona
Great Depression	1929–39	
	1930	Mies is appointed director of Bauhaus school
	1938	Mies moves to United States
World War II	1939–45	
Communist China is established	1949	
Korean War	1950–53	
African independence movement begins	1957	
	1958	Mies and Philip Johnson complete Seagram Building in New York
	1969	Mies dies
Vietnam War ends	1975	

Life and Work

Ludwig Mies van der Rohe may have been the most influential architect of the twentieth century.

Mies was born in 1886 in Aachen, Germany. Although he would later devote much of his career to educating students, Mies had no formal architectural training himself. At age 19 he went to work for the designer Bruno Paul and later for the architect Peter Behrens.

In the years immediately following World War I, architects across Europe began to experiment with radical new forms. For many, the war had signaled the complete collapse of the traditional world order. The aim of this new generation of architects was to reject traditional architecture and to find styles that would help to shape a new, democratic era.

In the 1920s Mies began experimenting with "curtain-wall" construction, which was being introduced simultaneously in Germany, in France, and in the Netherlands. In this type of construction, traditional load-bearing walls were replaced with light, thin (often glass) walls suspended from a steel framework; flat roofs took the place of traditional gables; and flexible industrial materials—steel, glass, and concrete—were valued over stone masonry with ornate sculpted decorations of traditional architecture.

In 1927 Mies became the director of the Weissenhofseidlung exhibition in Stuttgart, which brought together many of the leading architects of Europe; two years later, Mies designed the German Pavilion for the International Exposition in Barcelona. His long, low building composed of meticulously crafted and proportioned rectangular marble slabs was a masterpiece of the newly evolving International Style. Mies also designed the furniture for the Pavilion, including the famous steel-framed "Barcelona chair," which is still among the most famous examples of Modernist design.

In 1930, Mies was appointed director of the Bauhaus, the famous Weimar-era school of art and design whose teaching combined a Modernist industrial esthetic with a socialist political ethics. The school was closed by the Nazis in 1933.

In 1938 Mies moved to Chicago, where he became the head of the architecture program at the Armour Institute, which soon became part of the Illinois Institute of Technology (IIT). There he introduced the Modernist architectural movement to a new generation of American students. Over the next several decades, Mies designed some of the most important International Style buildings in the United States, including much of the IIT campus, the Farnsworth House (1945–50), and, with Philip Johnson, the elegant Seagram Building (1954–58). Each of his buildings was marked by his passion for order, simplicity, clarity, and attention to detail.

Mies died in 1969.

Legacy

Ludwig Mies van der Rohe's version of the International Style set the direction for the next generation of American architects and changed the face of American cities.

At IIT, he introduced a pedagogical approach based on the Bauhaus model and gave architects a new way of thinking about architecture. His oft-quoted phrase "less is more" referred to his desire to strip architecture of extraneous decoration and reduce it to its most basic essence.

His flat-topped skyscraper became the most common form of large urban structure in the booming post–World War II era. The form's popularity arose from the fact that it was inexpensive to imitate. Massive glass boxes sprang up in cities across the country.

While Mies's own architecture depended on subtlety of proportion, meticulous attention to details, and a respect for costly materials, derivatives of his style were often cheap, tasteless, and repetitive. By the 1970s and 1980s critics and architects such as Robert Venturi began to regard these derivatives as barren and dehumanizing. Mies was seen as having established the form of Modernism against which the new Postmodernist architecture reacted. In contrast to Mies's "less is more" dictum, Postmodernism revels in architectural pastiche, blending traditional motifs with elements from popular culture. In the Postmodern world of Las Vegas and the new Times Square, "more is more," and Mies's Utopian ideas seem increasingly remote.

McEnroe

For Further Reading

Blaser, Werner. *Mies van der Rohe: Less Is More.* Zürich and New York: Waser, 1986.

Carter, Peter. *Mies van der Rohe at Work.* London: Phaidon, 1974.

Schulze, Franze. *Mies van der Rohe: A Critical Biography.* Chicago: University of Chicago Press, 1985.

Milton, John

Poet and Essayist
1608–1674

Life and Work

Often considered the greatest writer in English after WILLIAM SHAKESPEARE, John Milton aspired to compose poetry the equal of the classics of the ancient world.

Milton was born in London on December 9, 1608, the son of a scrivener—a public clerk or notary. Milton was writing poetry in Latin by the time he was a teenager; he would work late into the night in a poorly lit room, which he later cited as the cause of his eventual blindness. Milton entered Cambridge University in 1625, and while there wrote three great short poems, "On the Morning of Christ's Nativity" (1629) and the paired "L'Allegro" and "Il Penseroso" (c. 1631). But the degree he earned in 1632 was not, in his own mind, the end of his education; he moved into his father's country house for several years of study and writing, and then traveled to Italy in 1638 and 1639.

Before his journey, Milton had written a poetic drama called *Comus* and several important poems; one of them, "Lycidas," an elegy for a classmate drowned in a shipwreck, took up the religious and philosophical themes to which he would later return. In the 1640s and 1650s, however, Milton mostly forsook poetry for the public sphere. He published pamphlets in support of Puritanism (the doctrine that the Church of England should purge itself of Roman Catholic rituals and hierarchies), and he argued in favor of press freedom, the right to divorce, and other progressive positions. Milton became an official in the revolutionary Commonwealth government of Oliver Cromwell; with the restoration of the monarchy in 1660 he was forced to go into hiding to avoid arrest.

By then completely blind, Milton returned to poetry and to the composition of an epic, first conceived years earlier, that he hoped would be as central to English literature as VIRGIL's *Aeneid* had been for ancient Rome, or HOMER's epics for the Greeks. For a time he had considered a topic from British history, but he settled on a blank verse (metrical but unrhymed) retelling of the biblical fall from Eden. The result was *Paradise Lost* (1667), his masterwork. It was followed by the sequel *Paradise Regained* (1671), which described Christ's sojourn and struggle with Satan in the wilderness, and *Samson Agonistes,* a semidramatic work based on the Book of Judges that was published with *Paradise Regained.* Milton died on November 8, 1674.

Legacy

John Milton was an intellectual titan of English poetry, and his meditations on sin, redemption, temptation, and free will, especially in his masterpiece *Paradise Lost,* are essential contributions to both Christian thought and English literature.

Paradise Lost, with its ambition to "justify the ways of God to man," stands at the center of his legacy, and has received attention from commentators, and, more important, other poets, in a measure that nearly rivals that given to Shakespeare. Almost every generation after Milton has found something new to admire in his poetry. His epic aims were recognized and emulated by later seventeenth-century poets such as John Dryden; the complex characterizations of the biblical figures in *Paradise Lost* allowed WILLIAM BLAKE and Percy Shelley to claim him as one of their own, reading Milton's seductive Satan as a kind of proto-Romantic rebel. One of Milton's champions in the twentieth century was the Christian novelist and critic C. S. Lewis, and one may perhaps detect a tinge of Miltonic ambition in his fantasy chronicles.

Milton's political philosophy appears not only in his prose writings, but also from time to time in his poetry. The Romantic WILLIAM WORDSWORTH admired and emulated Milton's defense of liberal ideals (and his long blank verse poems such as "Michael" show Milton's influence as well). T. S. Eliot and EZRA POUND, whose poetic practice encompassed terseness and compression, discounted Milton somewhat in the early twentieth century, but the experience of World War II, demonstrating the need for humane and enlightened leadership in the public sphere, helped to return his reputation to the summit. Milton's reputation remains secure as the author of one of the most significant bodies of poetry in the English language.

Manheim

WORLD EVENTS		MILTON'S LIFE
Ottoman dominance of Mediterranean ends	1571	
	1608	John Milton is born in London
Thirty Years' War in Europe	1618–48	
	1625	Milton enters Cambridge University
	1638	Milton travels to Italy
	1660	Milton goes into hiding
	1667	Milton publishes *Paradise Lost*
	1674	Milton dies
Glorious Revolution in England	1688	

For Further Reading
Danielson, Dennis, ed. *The Cambridge Companion to Milton.* Cambridge: Cambridge University Press, 1989.
Wilson, A. N. *The Life of John Milton.* Oxford: Oxford University Press, 1983.

Modersohn-Becker, Paula

Painter
1876–1907

Life and Work

Paula Modersohn-Becker was the first German artist to incorporate the innova-tions of French Post-Impressionist art into her own unique style.

Paula Becker was born in Dresden in 1876. At age 16, she began art lessons; after addi-tional studies in London and Berlin, in 1898 she joined the artists' colony at Worpswede, at the time a well-known artists' retreat. There she was influenced by the painters Fritz Mackensen and especially Otto Modersohn, whom she married in 1901.

The Worpswede painters were primarily concerned with painting realistic landscapes; Modersohn-Becker, however, became increas-ingly interested in the more advanced painting that was being done in France. She made sev-eral trips to Paris, learning about the Post-Impressionist art of Paul Gaugin, PAUL CÉZANNE, and VINCENT VAN GOGH.

While in Paris in 1906, Modersohn-Becker began to establish her own personal style. Her paintings increasingly concentrated on highly simplified, massive figures rendered in a lim-ited palette of pastel and earth tones that fur-ther emphasized their sculptural qualities. The bold masses of the figures were frequently set against a contrasting ornamental floral back-ground. Modersohn-Becker also began to con-centrate on the female nude. In paintings such as *Kneeling Mother and Child* (1907), the nude woman is presented as the archetype of all women, the source of the fertility that sur-rounds her in the symbolic form of fruits and plants. That many of Modersohn-Becker's images of nude women were self-portraits underscores her personal identification with the primordial Mother Goddess figure.

Modersohn-Becker's concern with the Mother Goddess theme proved to be tragically ironic. In 1907, shortly after giving birth to her daughter, she died.

WORLD EVENTS		MODERSOHN-BECKER'S LIFE
Germany is united	1871	
	1876	Paula Becker is born
Spanish-American War	1898	Becker moves to artists' colony in Worpswede
	1901	Becker marries Otto Modersohn
	1907	Modersohn-Becker paints *Kneeling Mother and Child*
		Modersohn-Becker dies
World War I 1914–18		

Legacy

Paula Modersohn-Becker was the first to bring turn-of-the-century French artistic ideas to Germany. Unfortunately, her career was shortened by her death at 31.

Her use of bold abstraction and simplified forms paralleled the ideas that PABLO PICASSO was experimenting with at the same time. But while Picasso's forms would lead to the purely formalistic art of Cubism, Modersohn-Becker never relinquished her concern with her subject.

Modersohn-Becker was one of the first artists to take a distinctly feminist approach to the depiction of the female nude. Since the time of classical Greece and the Renaissance, the female nude had traditionally been depicted as a passive object displayed for the (male) viewers' pleasure. For Modersohn-Becker, the female nude, often a self-portrait, became an examination of the essence of wom-anhood. It inspired self-reflection and medita-tion on the forces of nature. Before her work, the female body generally had been depicted in voyeuristic nudes by male artists; Modersohn-Becker helped to reclaim it as a subject for women. In this, her works are related to the works the French painter Suzanne Valadon.

Modersohn-Becker's reputation continued to grow after her death. Her works were col-lected by prominent intellectuals. When the Nazis began to mount organized attacks on modern art in 1937, Modersohn-Becker's works were among those they deemed to be "degenerate." Her frank, unidealized depic-tions of women in particular were considered to be subversive and immoral.

Since the 1970's, Modersohn-Becker has gained an even larger following among feminist artists and critics. She has come to be regarded as one of the key figures in early feminist art. Long after her death, her work helped to inspire a new generation of artists to reevaluate, again, the subject of the female nude. Modersohn-Becker became an icon to those of the new gen-eration of feminists who believed that there was a distinctly female approach to painting.

McEnroe

For Further Reading

Modersohn-Becker, Paula. *The Letters and Journals of Paula Modersohn-Becker.* Translated and annotated by J. Diane Radycki. Metuchen, N.J. : Scarecrow Press, 1980.

Perry, Gillian. *Paula Modersohn-Becker: Her Life and Work.* New York: Harper & Row, 1979.

Molière

(Jean-Baptiste Poquelin)

Playwright, Actor, and Director
1622–1673

Life and Work

With his irreverent dramas, Jean-Baptiste Poquelin, known by his stage name, Molière, satirized middle-class life for the entertainment of Louis XIV's court at Versailles. He comically illustrated the vices, pretensions, and moral and psychological flaws of the would-be nobles whose lives were ruled by money and class.

Molière was born in Paris on January 15, 1622, to a wealthy royal upholsterer in charge of arranging the king's bedchamber. He was educated at a Jesuit school where he studied classical literature, Latin, and plainsong. His interest in theater may have been sparked by the productions of Roman dramatists Terence, Plautus, and Seneca put on by the school.

His father hoped that he would succeed him as royal upholsterer, and for some time it seemed that he would; however, in 1643 Molière gave up his position to form the *Illustre Théatre* with the actress, playwright, and poet Madeleine Béjart. Molière wrote, directed, and acted with the troupe; after struggling for several years, the players began touring France and in 1653 were honored with a request to perform privately for the Prince de Conti.

In 1658 the troupe performed Molière's first important comedy, *Les Précieuses ridicules* (*The Affected Ladies*), for Louis XIV. The play was a satire of the literary affectations of the lesser salons of the day and is often considered to be the first comedy of manners written in France. The theater continued to perform at the Palais-Royal throughout the 1660s.

When *L'Ecole des femmes* (*The School for Wives*) was first performed in 1662, controversy arose over its supposed immorality. In response, Molière wrote *La Critique de l'ecole des femmes* (*The School for Wives Criticized*), in which a trio of buffoons debates the play's merits. This comic rebuttal to critics was performed along with the original play.

Tartuffe, written in 1664, is the story of a religious hypocrite who infiltrates a family, tricking the father into offering him his devotion, his daughter, and most of his possessions. The play's searing representation of a corrupt religious figure caused such outrage that Louis XIV forbade its performance.

In these plays and others, including *Le Misanthrope* (*The Misanthrope*), written in 1666, Molière moved away from the strict literary forms of the day, breaking the neoclassical rules that demanded that a five-act play be written in traditional alexandrine verse. At a time when tragedy was the more prestigious dramatic genre, Molière wrote farcical comedies based on the comic archetypes of the Italian *commedia dell'arte* (comedy of art).

Molière died in Paris on February 17, 1673, while performing in his last play, *Le Malade imaginaire* (*The Imaginary Invalid*).

Legacy

Molière saw ridicule as the best way of defining and correcting the vanities and foibles endemic to human nature. Above all, he wanted to entertain his audiences and therefore believed that no topic should be spared satiric examination.

Writing in simpler language than was customary for the theater, moving sometimes away from alexandrine verse to prose and a rhyming verse, Molière reshaped theatrical language and structure. Many of his plays had only one or three acts instead of five and he used fastpaced dialogue rather than long speeches. As a result he created a dramatic form that was intended to be spoken. The energetic and funny plays that came out of this style were successful, ener-

gizing the theater and making it relevant and accessible to a wider audience.

Many of Molière's characters were developments of the stylized comic archetypes that had been stock figures of the *commedia dell'arte*. He turned these traditional types, such as the pedant, the miser, the moral purist, the social climber, and the religious hypocrite, into multifaceted and more realistic characters. Using the mime, farce, buffoonery, and music of the *commedia dell'arte* as the basis for his comedy, Molière incorporated aspects of classical Roman comedy, creating a more profound comedic form than had existed previously and shaping the future development of French comedy.

Molière worked in the company of other great writers of the time, including Nicolus Boileau, Jean de La Fontaine, Claude Chapelle, and Jean Racine. His farces influenced the work of Eugène-Marin Labiche and Georges Feydeau in the nineteenth century as well as such varied playwrights as ANTON CHEKHOV in *The Bear* (1889) and *The Cook's Wedding* (1885); Oscar Wilde in his farce *The Importance of Being Earnest* (1899); and, more recently, the farcical writers Joe Orton, in *Loot* (1965) and *What the Butler Saw* (1969); and Tom Stoppard in *Real Inspector Hound* (1968).

Molière's humor has proven to be lasting and his plays, withstanding the tests of almost infinite adaptation, continue to be performed today in France and in translation all over the world. He played an important part in making satire the form that would be used by Voltaire, Percy Bysshe Shelley, JOHN KEATS, Nikolay Gogol, and many others, including playwright and screenwriter David Mamet, who writes contemporary satire today.

Watson

WORLD EVENTS	MOLIÈRE'S LIFE
Thirty Years' War 1618–48 in Europe	
1622	Molière is born
1643	Molière forms *Illustre Théatre* with Madeleine Béjart
1658	Molière performs *The Affected Ladies* for Louis XIV
1664	Molière writes *Tartuffe*
1666	Molière writes *The Misanthrope*
1673	Molière dies
Glorious Revolution 1688 in England	

For Further Reading

Molière. *Tartuffe and Other Plays*. Translated by Donald M. Frame. New York: Penguin Books, 1976.

Spingler, Michael, ed. *Molière Today*. Newark, N.J.: Gordon and Breach, 1998.

Moloney, Paddy

Musician

1938–

Life and Work

As the leader of the durable Irish band the Chieftains, Paddy Moloney is widely regarded as one of the twentieth century's most important creators in the field of folk and traditional music.

Patrick Moloney grew up in an environment suffused with traditional music. Born August 1, 1938, in Donnycarney, Ireland, near Dublin, he heard the bagpipe playing of his father, an Irish army sergeant, and his uncle, a renowned player. His mother, also musical, gave him a tin whistle when he was four, and soon he began taking lessons on the Irish uil-

leann pipes. In 1952, at 14, he emerged as the All-Ireland champion on the instrument.

In 1955 Moloney met Guinness beer heir Garech Browne, a folk music enthusiast who, although Irish traditional music was still generally thought of as a curiosity, founded the Claddagh label to promote its wider dissemination. The label would become the Chieftains' first musical home. Moloney's other major musical influence was the composer Seán Ó Riada—Moloney joined his ensemble, Ceoltóirí Cualann, in 1959. Ó Riada presented folk music in formal concerts, as if it were classical music; he inspired in the younger musician an awareness of how folk music's possibilities could be broadened through innovative, planned-out arrangements.

In 1963, several members of Ceoltóirí Cualann joined Moloney to form the Chieftains, at first something of an informal offshoot of Ó Riada's group. They started slowly, not releasing the LP *Chieftains 2* until 1969. By the middle 1970s, though, they had gained popularity, and in 1975 played a sold-out concert at the Albert Hall in London. That year, the Chieftains won an Academy Award for its soundtrack to Stanley Kubrick's film *Barry Lyndon*. Moloney generally has served both as the producer and as the main musical arranger for the Chieftains' many albums and is viewed as the group's mastermind. The range of his musical interests and imagination are responsible for the breadth of the Chieftains' work.

By the early 1980s the group's fame was international. In 1983 the Chieftains undertook a pioneering tour of the People's Republic of China, during which Moloney was impressed by parallels between Irish and Chinese traditional musics. The Chieftains' work of the 1980s and 1990s has been marked by collaborations with their musical admirers, who span the spectrum of musical genres from classical (they recorded in 1987 with flautist James Galway), to rock, to Latin-American; the group is also known to U.S. country music fans for its appearances on cable television's Nashville Network. In 1998 Moloney formed his own label, Wicklow, to further his innovative vision of traditional music.

Legacy

Among the original architects of the traditional music revival that gained momentum over the last half of the twentieth century, Paddy Moloney has also displayed a level of

musicianship and an ambitious spirit of adventure that have expanded the reach of Irish music in both its traditional and modernized forms.

Moloney was part of a small nucleus of tradition-minded musicians active in Ireland in the 1950s; although the whole realm of modern Irish folk music grew from the efforts of these musicians, Moloney was not the first to gain renown. The ground for the Chieftains' success in the United States, for example, was paved by the popularity of the Clancy Brothers among the folk revivalists of the 1960s. But Moloney took the musical materials he inherited in new directions that younger musicians were still exploring at the end of the twentieth century.

The Chieftains created a substantial market for virtuoso Irish instrumental playing where none had existed before and inspired a host of groups that rose to international prominence, Planxty and Altan among them. They inspired a similar boom in the French region of Brittany, a culturally Celtic area in whose music Moloney has remained vitally interested.

On the other side of the traditional–modern divide, the Chieftains' film scores and their several albums with orchestra gave rise to a growing genre that has been termed "Celtic fusion," with mainstream (Riverdance), pop (the Corrs), and various ambient and New Age manifestations. Moloney's vigorous musical exchanges with Séan Ó Riada in Ceoltóirí Cualann gave him the ability to create in the Chieftains' music a perfect balance between spontaneity and structured composition—a balance that few other musicians of the twentieth century achieved.

Manheim

WORLD EVENTS	MOLONEY'S LIFE
Great Depression 1929–39	
	1938 Patrick (Paddy) Moloney is born in Donnycarney, Ireland
World War II 1939–45	
Communist China 1949 is established	
Korean War 1950–53	
	1952 Moloney becomes All-Ireland piping champion
	1955 Moloney meets Guiness heir Garech Browne
African independence 1957 movement begins	
	1959 Moloney joins Ceoltóirí Cualann folk ensemble
	1963 Chieftains are formed
	1969 *Chieftains 2* album released
Vietnam War ends 1975	Chieftains play sold-out concert at Albert Hall
	1983 Chieftains tour People's Republic of China
Dissolution of 1991 Soviet Union	
South Africa 1994 dismantles apartheid	
	1998 Moloney forms Wicklow label

For Further Reading

Curtis, P. J. *Notes from the Heart: A Celebration of Irish Traditional Music.* Dublin: Torc, 1994.

Glatt, John. *The Chieftains: The Authorized Biography.* New York: St. Martin's Press, 1997.

Mondrian, Piet

Painter and Theorist
1872–1944

Life and Work

Piet Mondrian was an influential painter and theorist whose work embodies the Modernist desire to reduce each art form to its essence.

Born in 1872, Mondrian had a traditional academic training based on copying the works of the great masters. At age 20 he began to teach drawing, while continuing to develop his own art. From the 1890s on, Mondrian went through a rapid sequence of distinctly different styles. For a while he painted in an Impressionist mode, then turned to Symbolism, and after seeing a major exhibition of VINCENT VAN GOGH's work in Amsterdam in 1905, he experimented with simplified forms and intense, emotionally charged colors.

In 1912, Mondrian moved to Paris, where he became acquainted with a group of artists that included DIEGO RIVERA, Fernand Léger, and Georges Braque. For the next several years his works were closely related to Cubism. In works like *The Grey Tree* (1912), he reduced his formerly intense palette to almost monochromatic grays and browns and began to explore complexities of mass and space through the use of Cubist-like facets. By 1915, in works such as *Composition No. 10*, Mondrian reduced his style even further to a pattern of horizontal and vertical line segments.

Mondrian returned to the Netherlands just before the outbreak of World War I in 1914. There he met the artist Theo van Doesburg, and in 1917 they cofounded the art movement and the magazine they called *de Stijl* (*The Style*). Like those of the contemporary Bauhaus in Germany, the artists associated with the *de Stijl* group were concerned not only with painting, but with every aspect of visual and material culture, including architecture, furniture design, and graphic arts. Unlike the Bauhaus group, however, they were motivated not so much by the desire for social reform as by the pursuit of spiritual, even mystical, experience. Their method, of which Mondrian was the chief exponent and theorist, was known as Neo-Plasticism.

Mondrian left *de Stijl* in 1925 but continued to pursue the systematic purification of his art, in his idealistic search for a universal art form. He aimed to reduce painting to its essence, expressed in harmonious compositions of vertical lines, horizontal lines, and primary colors.

As the threat of war grew again, Mondrian fled, first to London and finally, in 1940, to New York. There he became deeply interested in jazz. In *Broadway Boogie Woogie* (1942–43) his geometric forms take on the energy and rhythms of the urban sounds.

Mondrian died in New York in 1944.

Legacy

Piet Mondrian was the principal figure in the founding of Geometric Abstraction during World War I and a quintessential purist.

While his mature painting style was imitated only by other members of *de Stijl*, indirectly Mondrian's art had a much broader effect on the visual culture of the twentieth century. Mondrian felt that painting should serve as a model for all the visual arts, and, like his contemporaries in the German Bauhaus, he felt that the aim of artists should be to address and reimagine all of visual and material culture.

When he moved to the United States, he was welcomed as an international celebrity. He had an important impact on the small but growing world of avant-garde art in this country. Late in his life, interest in his writings grew, and many of them were translated into English for the first time. A major retrospective of his work was held at the Museum of Modern Art in 1945.

Today, Mondrian is regarded as one of the fundamental figures in the history of non-representational art. His pursuit of absolute standards in art and desire to reduce art to its purest form had a deep effect on later generations of Geometrical Abstractionists such as Barnett Newman, Ad Reinhardt, and the Minimalists of the 1970s. Although his severely abstract paintings remain challenging to viewers, his resolute abstraction, visual clarity, and directness have profoundly influenced the look of the modern world.

McEnroe

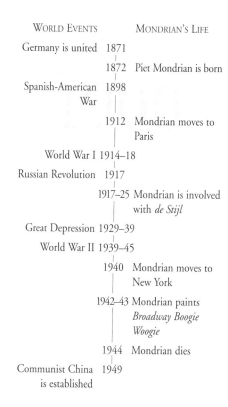

WORLD EVENTS		MONDRIAN'S LIFE
Germany is united	1871	
	1872	Piet Mondrian is born
Spanish-American War	1898	
	1912	Mondrian moves to Paris
World War I	1914–18	
Russian Revolution	1917	
	1917–25	Mondrian is involved with *de Stijl*
Great Depression	1929–39	
World War II	1939–45	
	1940	Mondrian moves to New York
	1942–43	Mondrian paints *Broadway Boogie Woogie*
	1944	Mondrian dies
Communist China is established	1949	

For Further Reading

Joosten, Joop M., and Robert P. Walsh. *Piet Mondrian: Catalogue Raisonné*. Munich and New York: Prestel, 1998.

Milner, John. *Mondrian*. New York: Abbeville, 1992.

Mondrian, Piet. *The New Art—The New Life: The Collected Writings of Piet Mondrian*. Edited and translated by Harry Holtzman and Martin S. James. Boston: G. K. Hall, 1986.

Monet, Claude

Painter
1840–1926

Life and Work

Claude Monet was the most prominent painter of the French Impressionist movement.

Monet (Oscar-Claude Monet) was born in Paris in 1840, the son of a grocer, and grew up

WORLD EVENTS		MONET'S LIFE
Congress of Vienna reorganizes Europe	1815	
	1840	Claude Monet is born
Revolutions in Austria, France, Germany, and Italy	1848	
U.S. Civil War	1861–65	
	1862	Monet joins Charles Gleyre's workshop
Germany is united	1871	
	1872	Monet paints *Impression, Sunrise*
	1874	First Impressionist exhibition
Spanish-American War	1898	
World War I	1914–18	
Russian Revolution	1917	
	1899	Monet begins *Waterlilies* series
	1926	Monet dies
Great Depression	1929–39	

in Le Havre in Normandy. He began to study art at an early age and pursued traditional academic training in Paris. In 1862 Monet began to study the works of the Barbizon group of landscape painters and their followers, including the Dutch painter Johann Barthold Jongkind, who encouraged Monet to take up *plein-air* landscape painting.

In the same year Monet joined the atelier of the academic painter Charles Gleyre in Paris. Gleyre's studio became the gathering place for a group of painters that included Frederick Bazille, Alfred Sisley, and PIERRE-AUGUSTE RENIOR, who shared Monet's interest in landscape painting. This group developed the style that came to be known as Impressionism.

Traditional academic painting demanded clarity of drawing and carefully modulated chiaroscuro in paintings that were meticulously finished; the Impressionists experimented with the application of highly saturated pigments directly on the canvas with little or no preliminary drawing. Painting outdoors, rather than in a studio, the Impressionists aimed to capture the sensuous effects of light on the surfaces of objects. To many academics, these new landscapes appeared to be unfinished sketches. As a result, Monet and his friends had difficulty in having their works accepted in the Salon exhibitions sponsored by the official French Academy.

Frustrated by this rejection, Monet encouraged his colleagues to establish their own independent artists' society and to hold their own exhibition. Their first exhibition was held in 1874 in the studio of the well-known photographer NADAR. Among the works exhibited was Monet's *Impression, Sunrise* (1872), the title of which inspired a critic to dub the entire group "Impressionists." Over the next 12 years, Monet and his friends organized seven more group exhibitions.

In the 1890s Monet became increasingly concerned with the problem of how to capture rapidly changing effects of light and turned to painting in series. Monet's last great set of paintings, which he worked on from 1899 to his death, were of the water lilies that grew in the pond in his garden in Giverny. As Monet's eyesight gradually failed these paintings became increasingly broadly painted. The late, wall-size, paintings are almost purely abstract surfaces of luscious blues and greens

that seem to immerse the viewer in a pond of sensuous experience.

Monet died in 1926.

Legacy

Claude Monet was the central figure of the Impressionist movement. He struggled early in his career, but his works did become profitable by the 1890s. Late in life, Monet was widely admired as a cultural hero, and his reputation continued to grow after his death. In May 1927, the Orangerie was built to display Monet's *Waterlilies*. Monet's house and garden at Giverny were opened to the public in 1980.

The style that Monet developed stood at the very beginning of the Modernist movement in art. Although Monet himself had few direct imitators, his style spread throughout Europe and the United States.

Perhaps even more important, Impressionism led directly to subsequent experimental styles, including the Post-Impressionism of PAUL CÉZANNE and VINCENT VAN GOGH, which in turn would lead to the development of Cubism and Expressionism. Decades later the critic Clement Greenberg recognized Monet's mural-size late paintings as a primary source for the Abstract Expressionist styles of JACKSON POLLOCK and Mark Rothko.

By loosening the rigid rules of art, Monet and his colleagues opened the door for all subsequent styles of Modernist painting.

McEnroe

For Further Reading

Stuckey, Charles. *Claude Monet 1840–1926*. New York: Thames and Hudson; Chicago: Art Institute of Chicago, 1995.

Tucker, Paul. *Claude Monet: Life and Art*. New Haven, Conn.: Yale University Press, 1995.

———. *Monet in the '90's: The Series Paintings*. Boston: Museum of Fine Arts; New Haven, Conn.: Yale University Press, 1989.

Monteverdi, Claudio

Composer
1567–1643

Life and Work

Although he was not the inventor of opera, Claudio Monteverdi was its first great figure. Largely unheralded today, he was one of Western art music's crucial innovators.

Monteverdi was baptized on May 15, 1567, in the Italian city of Cremona, where he studied with the composer Marc'Antonio Ingegneri. He was writing his own music while still a teenager, and the year 1587 saw the publication of his first book of madrigals—multipart settings of poetry, mostly on romantic themes.

About 1592 he took a job as a musician at the court of the Gonzaga family in Mantua; in the 1590s he was influenced by a radical group of composers who strove toward an extremely detailed musical representation of a piece's text. Monteverdi emerged as a leader of this group. In 1600 he was attacked in a pamphlet by the theorist Giovanni Maria Artusi, who claimed that Monteverdi's vivid musical effects violated compositional rules. In his famous response to Artusi, Monteverdi distinguished between a "first practice," in which text was subordinate to music, and a new "second practice," in which the text was paramount.

As he staked out this position, Monteverdi followed with interest the experiments of a group of Florentine intellectuals who were attempting to recreate the declamation of ancient Greek drama—from these experiments came the very first operas. In 1607 Monteverdi put opera on the map with *Orfeo*, a retelling of the Greek legend of Orpheus and Eurydice. It is the earliest opera that is still widely performed, and in its own time it was revolutionary and transformative. In place of the multipart textures of the Renaissance, Monteverdi offered songs and dramatic declamation supported by what we would now call harmony.

He followed *Orfeo* in 1608 with *L'Arianna*, of which only one scene survives. After a period of depression that followed these two enormous and path-breaking works, Monteverdi emerged with a great sacred piece, the *Vespers of 1610*, which applied aspects of the new operatic style to religious texts.

Monteverdi became music director of St. Mark's Cathedral in Venice in 1613 but continued to compose secular music for his former employers and for other noble houses. As he eased toward retirement in 1637, a new opera house was opened in Venice, and he capped his career with three great works; one of the two that survive, 1643's *The Coronation of Poppea*, is still widely performed. Monteverdi died in Venice on November 29, 1643.

Legacy

Perhaps more than any other single composer, Claudio Monteverdi laid the foundation of the world of classical music as it is known today. He was the most important among the early composers of opera, and from opera grew many of classical music's expressive ideals and stylistic innovations.

When the first operas were written around 1600, they consisted mainly of what in later operas would be called *recitative* (ress-it-a-TEEVE): sung dialogue that stuck close to the rhythms of speech rather than setting the text to a tune (an aria). From this dry exercise, Monteverdi created a new art form; from mere declamation, he created music drama by adding a variety of contrasting elements. A gigantic work in five acts, *Orfeo* used a large orchestra and many dramatic roles; the opera included songs of various kinds, instrumental interludes, virtuoso vocal displays, and spectacular dramatic scenes in addition to recitative-like dialogue. Over the course of the seventeenth century, opera spread through Italy's major cities and then through Europe. Later composers of opera streamlined Monteverdi's contrasts between lyric song and dramatic action. But it was Monteverdi who set opera composition in motion.

Later in his career Monteverdi developed and put into practice new ideas about the relationship between music and drama, fundamentally shaping the art of opera. In his later madrigals, which were almost like operatic excerpts, and in his dramatic works, he embraced a doctrine of realism, including representations of nature and of war that began to develop classical music's vocabulary for the depiction of external events. Some of these works were accompanied by groups of stringed instruments, the ancestors of the string section of the modern orchestra; in Monteverdi's 1624 work, *The Combat of Tancredi and Clorinda*, the sound of plucked strings expresses the clashing of swords in battle.

Monteverdi's final operas permanently established the role of music in dramatic character development; the lasting power of *The Coronation of Poppea* derives from the unprecedented realism of its characters and its cohesion as a drama. If we think today of music in part as an expression of human drama, we ultimately have Monteverdi to thank.

Manheim

WORLD EVENTS		MONTEVERDI'S LIFE
Protestant Reformation begins	1517	
	1567	Claudio Monteverdi is born in Cremona, Italy
Ottoman dominance of Mediterranean ends	1571	
	1587	Monteverdi's first book of madrigals is published
	c. 1592	Monteverdi is hired by the Gonzaga family
	1600	Monteverdi is attacked by the theorist Artusi
	1607	Monteverdi composes the opera *Orfeo*
	1613	Monteverdi becomes music director at St. Mark's cathedral
Thirty Years' War in Europe	1618–48	
	1624	Monteverdi composes *The Combat of Tancredi and Clorinda*
	1643	Monteverdi dies
Glorious Revolution in England	1688	

For Further Reading

Arnold, Denis. *Monteverdi*. London: J. M. Dent, 1990.

Schrade, Leo. *Monteverdi: Creator of Modern Music*. New York: W. W. Norton, 1969.

Moore, Henry

Sculptor
1898–1986

World Events		Moore's life
Spanish-American War	1898	Henry Moore is born
World War I	1914–18	
Russian Revolution	1917	
	1919	Moore begins study at Leeds School
	1924	Moore is appointed instructor at Royal College of Art
	1929	Moore completes *Reclining Figure*
Great Depression	1929–39	
World War II	1939–45	
Communist China is established	1949	
Korean War	1950–53	
African independence movement begins	1957	
	1963–65	Moore works on *Bronze Reclining Figure*
Vietnam War ends	1975	
	1986	Moore dies
Dissolution of Soviet Union	1991	

Life and Work

Henry Moore is generally acknowledged to be the most important British sculptor of the twentieth century.

Moore was born to a working-class family in Castleford, Yorkshire, in 1898. After a brief stint in the army, Moore studied art, first at the Leeds School of Art and then at the Royal College of Art in London, where he became an instructor in sculpture in 1924.

Moore soon began to develop an interest in art that was then outside the academic mainstream—the so-called "primitive" African and pre-Columbian art that had begun to interest Western artists and intellectuals in the decades before World War I. At the same time, Moore retained his interest in pre-Classical and Classical Greek sculpture, and throughout his career would make works in which he attempted to combine the monumentality of Classical art with the directness and immediacy of non-Western art. For example, his *Reclining Figure* (1929), which merges the pose of the Toltec–Maya warrior-priest with the Classical figures of the Parthenon frieze (Elgin Marbles) in the British Museum.

In the 1920s Moore traveled throughout Europe. In Italy he became interested in the work of GIOTTO and MICHELANGELO, while in France he was attracted to the work of PAUL CÉZANNE and HENRI MATISSE.

By the 1930s Moore became particularly interested in the work of PABLO PICASSO and Alberto Giacometti. His work, such as *Four-Piece Composition: Reclining Figure* (1936), became increasingly abstract, revealing affinities with the Surrealists, with whom Moore exhibited in 1936.

In the 1950s Moore drew inspiration from natural objects such as shells, pebbles, and bones—even the most abstract of his organic, undulating, and hollowed-out forms were often derived from his close inspection of, for example, the opening in a bleached animal pelvis.

Many of Moore's later sculptures, such as *Bronze Reclining Figure* (1963–65) for Lincoln Center in New York, were done in a new grand scale. For much of his career, Moore's interest in the reclining figure was related to his desire to associate the curvilinear masses of the human form with the undulating hills and valleys of landscape. The vast scale of his late works reasserted his belief in metaphorical unity of the organic forms of nature.

Moore died in 1986.

Legacy

By the end of his life, Henry Moore was widely recognized as one of the most prominent British artists in history and perhaps the most important sculptor of the twentieth century. A number of other artists, particularly his British colleague Barbara Hepworth, were directly influenced by his style. From the 1940s on, he was one of the central figures in the world of British avant-garde intellectuals.

Throughout his career, Moore's work focused on a limited number of recurring themes: the reclining figure, the mother and child, and the relation of internal and external form. He aimed at creating a harmonious synthesis of human figure and landscape, past and present, abstraction and nature.

Moore's abiding interest in the human form connects him with the grand tradition of Greek sculpture, with Michelangelo, and with AUGUSTE RODIN. Partly because of the representational element in his work, Moore came to be regarded as a conservative, establishment figure by younger, more radical British artists and critics.

Nevertheless, Moore continued to receive wide public recognition in the 1970s, which saw five major exhibitions of his work. In 1974 the Henry Moore Sculpture Center in the Art Gallery of Ontario opened in Toronto; in 1977, the Henry Moore Foundation was established in Much Hadham, England, where Moore lived after 1940.

McEnroe

For Further Reading

Hall, Donald. *Henry Moore: The Life and Work of a Great Sculptor*. New York: Harper & Row, 1966.

Moore, Henry. *Henry Moore: My Ideas, Inspiration and Life as an Artist*. London: Ebury Press; San Francisco: Chronicle Books, 1986.

Morrison, Toni

Novelist and Critic
1931–

Life and Work

In her lyrically innovative novels Toni Morrison discusses the conflict inherent in the lives of African Americans who inhabit a society dominated by white culture and values.

Morrison was born Chloe Anthony Wofford on February 18, 1931, in Lorain, Ohio, and her childhood was spent in this small African-American community. Her literary beginnings were in the ghost stories, myths, and folktales that she heard from friends and family, and in the novels of JANE AUSTEN, GUSTAVE FLAUBERT, and Russian authors. She received her bachelor of arts from Howard University in 1953 and her master of arts from Cornell in 1955, where she wrote her thesis on WILLIAM FAULKNER and VIRGINIA WOOLF. She then worked as an editor at Random House, where she was instrumental in publishing works by African, Caribbean, and African-American writers, including Toni Cade Bambara, Henry Dumas, and Gayl Jones.

The Bluest Eye, Morrison's first novel, was published in 1970; it tells the story of a young black girl, Pecola Breedlove, whose dream of having blue eyes survives her rape, her victimization, and her eventual insanity. The book examines the difficulty of reconciling African-

American cultural identity with white American cultural values, particularly those involving standards of physical beauty.

Morrison's third novel, *Song of Solomon,* won the National Book Critics Circle Award in 1977 and is credited with bringing Morrison and her work to the attention of mainstream audiences. In a story that chronicles the spiritual transformation of her protagonist, Milkman Dead, Morrison uses the myth and folktales of her youth to tell the story of a man in a racist society.

Perhaps Morrison's most widely read novel, *Beloved* is the story is of a runaway slave who, believing she will be returned to slavery, kills her young daughter to prevent her from also being enslaved. The daughter returns from the dead to exact revenge for her murder, awakening memories of the humiliations and violence of slave life. Morrison won the Pulitzer Prize for fiction in 1988 for *Beloved.*

In 1992 Morrison delivered a series of lectures at Harvard University that were eventually published as *Playing in the Dark: Whiteness and the Literary Imagination* (1992) in which she examined the racial assumptions of literary criticism.

Morrison was awarded the Nobel Prize for Literature in 1993. She has taught at Yale University, Bard College, and Princeton University.

Legacy

Toni Morrison has changed both American literature and American racial identity with her potent subject matter and formal experimentation.

Morrison's work has not only been lauded by the intellectual community, it has experienced more popularity than that of any other African-American woman author in American history. Along with her contemporaries—Alice Walker, Gloria Naylor, Jamaica Kincaid, and Terry McMillan—she has been read, translated, and discussed by a varied international readership. She has broken other racial barriers as well: a 1981 *Newsweek* cover photo made her the first African-American woman to appear on the cover of a national magazine since Zora Neale Hurston in 1943; her novel *Song of Solomon,* published in 1977, was the first Book-of-the-Month selection by an

African-American author since Richard Wright's *Native Son* in 1940; nearly all of her books have appeared on the best seller list.

In her widely read novels, Morrison furthered the examination of the role of race in American society. The experience of African-American life within the context of African-American culture and community has been largely ignored in American literature, which, as Morrison points out in her critical works, tends to treat these issues from the perspective of a culture dominated by white experience.

Her work, like that of William Faulkner and GABRIEL GARCÍA MÁRQUEZ, has blurred the lines between fantasy and reality. Her use of unconventional narrative structures, poetic language, myth, and folklore to discuss the emotional and social effects of racial and sexual oppression has resulted in what has been called an American magical-realism, the style associated with Latin American writers, JORGE LUIS BORGES and García Márquez.

Watson

WORLD EVENTS	MORRISON'S LIFE
Great Depression 1929–39	
	1931 Toni Morrison is born
World War II 1939–45	
Communist China 1949 is established	
Korean War 1950–53	
African independence 1957 movement begins	
	1970 Morrison publishes *The Bluest Eye*
Vietnam War ends 1975	
	1977 Morrison's *Song of Solomon* wins National Book Critics Circle Award
	1988 Morrison wins Pulitzer Prize for *Beloved*
Dissolution of 1991 Soviet Union	
	1992 Morrison delivers lectures eventually published as *Playing in the Dark*
	1993 Morrison wins Nobel Prize for Literature
South Africa 1994 dismantles apartheid	

For Further Reading

Gates, Henry Louis, Jr., and K. A. Appiah, eds. *Toni Morrison: Critical Perspectives Past and Present.* New York: Amistad Press, 1993.

Middleton, David L., ed. *Toni Morrison's Fiction: Contemporary Criticism.* New York: Garland Publishing, 1997.

Taylor-Guthrie, Danille, ed. *Conversations with Toni Morrison.* Jackson: University Press of Mississippi, 1994.

Mozart, Wolfgang Amadeus

Composer
1756–1791

Life and Work

Few would dissent from the consensus that Wolfgang Amadeus Mozart was one of the most brilliant composers in the history of Western classical music. His universally popular works are unexcelled for sheer lyrical beauty.

Born in Salzburg in what is now Austria on January 27, 1756, Mozart was music's most famous child prodigy. He was playing the harpsichord when he was three; at the age of five he was composing music, and throughout his childhood it was his astonishing musical recall that impressed observers the most. Mozart's father, Leopold, took him on a tour of Europe's capitals to show off his talents, and in 1769 the family made the first of three visits to Italy.

Mozart became music director for the archbishop of Salzburg, but chafed under the restricted musical life he led in that remote mountain capital. He continued to travel, visiting Mannheim, home to a renowned orchestra, in 1777, and Paris the following year. But no per-

manent position materialized, and he returned to Salzburg. Fresh on the heels of the success of his opera *Idomeneo* in Munich in 1781, Mozart got into a heated argument with the archbishop in Vienna and quit his Salzburg job.

Always searching for stable employment, Mozart for some time did well on his own. Many of his 27 piano concertos came from the Vienna years, and he never lost the ability to please a crowd as a performer. His operatic composition reached its high point with *The Marriage of Figaro* in 1786 and *Don Giovanni* the following year, and several Viennese patrons appreciated his complex string quartets and other chamber works. In 1789 Mozart composed his last three symphonies (Nos. 39, 40, and 41); more ambitious than any previous works in the genre, they do not seem to have been written for any specific occasion. Living beyond his means, Mozart ran into financial trouble. 1791 brought promising opportunities: a fellow Freemason composed the libretto for an odd, semipopular opera called *The Magic Flute,* and an anonymous commission came in for a requiem mass—a mass for the dead. On December 5, 1791, however, Mozart died after a short illness.

Legacy

Two images of Wolfgang Amadeus Mozart share space in the public imagination, and together they offer a definition of his legacy. On one hand, he was a boy genius, a natural font of melody whose early death proved that only the good die young. On the other—and this was the attitude of many of his contemporaries—Mozart was the creator of dense, difficult music with a subversive intensity, music said to have caused the Austrian emperor Joseph II, after a performance of a Mozart opera, to complain in bewilderment that there were "too many notes."

Mozart was not primarily a compositional innovator; it was his fervent admirer FRANZ JOSEPH HAYDN who helped create the major musical forms of the late eighteenth century. Rather, Mozart worked easily in all the styles of his day: Italian comic and serious opera, German opera of various kinds, the Viennese symphony and string quartet, and various other instrumental styles from Austria, Germany, and France. No matter what kind of music he was writing, he showed an uncanny ability to distill it to an elegant set of essentials and to make it sound inevitable. Mozart was, indeed, from a very early age, a creator of memorable melodies with a sublime hint of pathos, but their beauty always rests

on a sense of proportion born of Mozart's effortless absorption of the musical models he encountered. The melodic richness of Mozart's works has ensured their continual presence on classical concert programs.

The idea of sheer genius does seem to find an example in Mozart's music. This was the Romantic view of Mozart: as a rather childlike creator with supreme powers, cruelly neglected by an indifferent world. Yet Mozart was more than just a savant. His two greatest operas, *The Marriage of Figaro* and *Don Giovanni,* though outwardly comedies, crackle with sexual and class antagonisms of a kind that still seem modern; 30 years after *The Marriage of Figaro* came Gioacchino Antonio Rossini's perennially successful *The Barber of Seville,* based upon another play of the trilogy from which Mozart took his own *Figaro* story, and the mocking of the nobility that had been sharply satirical in Mozart's work was for Rossini almost mainstream. Mozart's three final symphonies and many of his other broadly scaled works were studied closely by nineteenth-century composers of instrumental music; LUDWIG VAN BEETHOVEN's first symphony was clearly modeled on and shadowed by Mozart's breathtaking *Jupiter* symphony.

Mozart is historically notable as one of the first composers to attempt to make a living as a musical freelancer, outside the long-standing system of noble and ecclesiastical patronage. But he was less than fully successful. Modern hearers seduced by Mozart's seemingly easy perfection may find it hard to believe that the composer's contemporaries could have failed to appreciate that perfection, but the explanation lies in the dual nature of Mozart's genius: he was both prodigy and creator.

Manheim

World Events		Mozart's Life
Glorious Revolution in England	1688	
	1756	Wolfgang Amadeus Mozart is born in Salzburg, Austria
	1769	Mozart and his family visit Italy
United States declares independence	1776	
	1778	Mozart visits Paris, but returns to Salzburg
	1781	Mozart quits Salzburg post
	1786	Mozart composes *The Marriage of Figaro*
	1787	Mozart composes *Don Giovanni*
French Revolution begins	1789	Mozart composes three symphonic masterpieces without apparent commission
	1791	Mozart dies
Latin American independence movement begins	1811	

For Further Reading

Gay, Peter. *Mozart.* New York: Penguin, 1999.

Hildesheimer, Wolfgang. *Mozart.* Translated by M. Faber. New York: Vintage Books, 1983.

Murasaki Shikibu

Novelist

c. 978–c. 1014

Life and Work

"Murasaki Shikibu" is the author of *The Tale of Genji* (*Genji Monogotari*), considered by many to be the world's first true novel. The coherence of Genji's narrative and the psychological depth of its characters were unprecedented in a fictional work of its length.

The author's real name remains unknown, as do most details of her life. "Murasaki" is the name of the main female character in *The Tale of Genji*; "Shikibu" is an honorary title roughly equivalent to the English "Lady." Some key facts have been gleaned from a diary—identified as hers by references to *Genji*—that Murasaki kept for several years and from documents written by contemporaries. She was born in Kyoto into a minor branch of the politically powerful Fujiwara family between 970 and 979. Her father was a classical scholar and a member of the emperor's court, who educated her beyond what was considered appropriate for girls; for instance, she knew Chinese (the language of the Japanese court) and was well read in the Chinese literature then available. As a member of the very small aristocratic class of the Heian period (794–1192), Murasaki lived a life circumscribed by rigid social conventions and ritual requirements.

In 996 Murasaki traveled with her father to Echizen province, and in 999 married a nobleman and distant relative named Fujiwara no Nobutaka, who died in a plague after only two years of marriage, leaving her with a daughter. Scholars believe that she wrote much of *The Tale of Genji* in the years immediately following his death.

The Tale of Genji is primarily the story of Prince Genji and the women with whom he conducted his many love affairs. Murasaki gives a detailed portrait of court life, its aesthetic ideals, and the importance attributed to poetry, music, calligraphy, and love, as well as the difficult and inferior position of its women. The story incorporates elements of Shinto belief and ritual as well as Buddhism. (Genji, the "Shining One" or "Shining Prince," has been read as a Bodhisattva figure, an "enlightened being" who has put off entering Nirvana as long as suffering creatures remain in the world.)

In approximately 1005 Murasaki joined the court of Empress Akiko; the diary she kept there for several years describes her daily life and is the source of most of what we know about her—it ends in 1010. She is also thought to be the author of a series of poems written between 1010 and 1014. Murasaki died in approximately 1014.

Legacy

The Tale of Genji is often referred to as the greatest work of Japanese literature; it has influenced all subsequnet Japanese literature and art.

For it, Murasaki Shikibu adapted the *monogatari*, a traditional Japanese prose form comprising a series of short, discrete episodes about characters drawn from myth and legend. While the novel's structure is episodic, as in a traditional *monogatari*, the episodes are linked and integrated in a unitary narrative. It was the first Japanese literary work to treat daily life (even if in an extraordinary setting) through realistic characters motivated by human emotion, rather than legendary heroes manipulated by fate and the will of the gods.

There is evidence that *Genji* was very widely read during Murasaki's life, and it soon became the subject of widespread literary analysis and critique. By the beginning of the fourteenth century, however, the Japanese language had changed enough to make the work difficult for most readers. Scholars of the medieval period compiled dictionaries of words used in *Genji* and wrote even more extensive commentaries explaining the plot. They developed complex textual theories and waged intellectual battles to defend them. Plot summaries were widely sold throughout this period, the most famous of which is called *Genji: A Small Mirror* (c. 1425). This critical activity has not abated—today it is estimated that at least 10,000 books have been written about *The Tale of Genji*.

Motoori Norinaga, an important scholar of eighteenth-century Japan, wrote a nine-volume interpretation of the novel. He rebutted the two prevalent interpretations—the Buddhist one, which held that *Genji* was about the impermanence of the material world, and the Confucian, that it was a series of instructional depictions of enlightened women. Motoori wrote that the novel was not an illustration of any theory or philosophy but a realistic portrayal of court life as well as a meditation on the nature of human goodness and the sorrow of existence. This quickly became the accepted interpretation.

The influence of the work in Japan has been immense. References to it are found across the history of Japanese poetry. Countless paintings have illustrated its 54 episodes. Its stories, images, and characters are deeply embedded in Japanese culture; the only thing comparable to it in Western culture is perhaps Greek and Roman mythology.

Genji has been translated into modern Japanese several times in the twentieth century, notably by Yosano Akiko in 1912 and by Tanizaki Junichiro in 1965. Late in the nineteenth century some of it was translated into English. The first substantial English translation, was published in several volumes between 1925 and 1933 and is still in print. In 1976 Edward Seidensticker published a new translation that is now the standard English version.

Watson

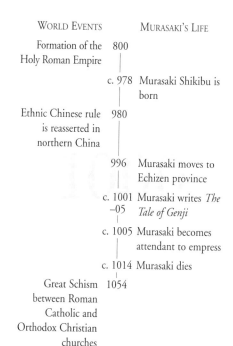

World Events		Murasaki's Life
Formation of the Holy Roman Empire	800	
		c. 978 Murasaki Shikibu is born
Ethnic Chinese rule is reasserted in northern China	980	
	996	Murasaki moves to Echizen province
	c. 1001 –05	Murasaki writes *The Tale of Genji*
	c. 1005	Murasaki becomes attendant to empress
	c. 1014	Murasaki dies
Great Schism between Roman Catholic and Orthodox Christian churches	1054	

For Further Reading

Bowring, Richard. *Murasaki Shikibu: The Tale of Genji*. Cambridge: Cambridge University Press, 1988.

Puette, William J. *The Tale of Genji: A Reader's Guide*. Rutland, Vt. and Tokyo: Charles E. Tuttle, 1983.

Nadar

(Gaspard-Félix Tournachon)

Caricaturist and Photographer
1820–1910

World Events		Nadar's Life
Congress of Vienna reorganizes Europe	1815	
	1820	Nadar (Gaspard-Félix Tournachon) is born
Revolutions in Austria, France, Germany, and Italy	1848	
	1853	Nadar establishes photography studio for his brother
	1858	Nadar takes first aerial photograph
U.S. Civil War	1861–65	
Germany is united	1871	
	1874	Nadar helps to organize first Impressionist Exhibition in his studio
Spanish-American War	1898	
	1910	Nadar dies
World War I	1914–18	

Life and Work

Nadar was the quintessential Bohemian of mid-nineteenth century France and a pioneer in the new art of photography.

Nadar was born Gaspard-Félix Tournachon in Paris in 1820. His father was a printer sympathetic to radical politics. The young Tournachon received a typical middle-class education. After his father's death, he began a career as a drama critic for a newspaper in Lyon.

Having established himself as a journalist, Tournachon returned to Paris and threw himself into the exciting world of the Bohemian intelligentsia. He took on a series of odd jobs and continued to write articles, reviews, and essays for the press. In 1848, a year of liberal uprisings against feudal and restoration regimes all over Europe, Tournachon enlisted with a group that called itself the Polish Legion, who planned to invade and liberate Poland from the Russian Empire. That misadventure ended with his arrest and return to France.

Back in Paris, he began to make caricatures of politicians for satirical magazines, which he signed with the pseudonym "Nadar." A brief stint in debtor's prison suggests that he was not an immediate financial success, but his ambitions grew. He planned a major project, the *Pantheon Nadar*, which was to have included caricatures of a thousand of the most famous personalities of the day. Although never completed, the project established Nadar as a celebrity.

Nadar may have become involved with photography while working on the caricatures. By 1853 he had set up a photography studio for his younger brother, and a few years later took it over himself. Although Nadar was only involved with photography for about 10 years, he quickly became one of the most successful and innovative practitioners in the new medium. Nadar specialized in portraits of intellectuals and celebrities. His photographs provide a virtual *Who's Who* of French intellectual and social life; his subjects included Charles-Pierre Baudelaire, Alexandre Dumas, Victor-Marie Hugo, George Sand, and Sarah Bernhardt. Typically Nadar depicted his sitters in a casual three-quarter pose, using soft lighting to subtly capture their often imposing personalities.

In the 1860s Nadar's interests moved from photography to aeronautics. He became an enthusiastic balloonist and, with Jules Verne, an early proponent of experimentation with heavier-than-air flight. But he retained his connections with the art world. In 1874 the first Impressionist Exhibition, featuring the works of Claude Monet, Edgar Degas, and Peirre-Auguste Renoir, took place in Nadar's studio.

Nadar died in 1910.

Legacy

Nadar is remembered today chiefly for his role in the early history of photography. During his relatively brief involvement in that field, Nadar introduced a number of important technical innovations. For example, in 1858 he produced the first successful aerial photographs, which he took from a balloon.

Nadar was also the first to use artificial lighting for photography, taking magnesium flares into the catacombs of Paris for a series of photographs in 1861. His last major project anticipated the development of photojournalism. Entitled *The Art of Living for 100 Years*, the project combined his interview with the chemist Michel Chevreul with a series of photographs shot by Nadar's son.

Nadar became a key figure in the larger Parisian art world. His studio was an important gathering place for artists, writers, and other intellectuals. Nadar also fought vigorously for official recognition of photography as a form of art. One of his cartoons depicts an animated camera beating furiously on the door to the official Salon, demanding to be admitted.

Nadar's key contribution to photography was his popularization of celebrity photographs. While other photographers attempted to legitimize photography as an art by making photographs that followed the traditional genres of painting (landscape, still life, and historical narratives), Nadar chose the celebrity image, a form that remains vigorous today.

Recently art historians and critics have begun to recognize the significance of Nadar's work. In 1995 a major retrospective of his work was held at the Metropolitan Museum of Art in New York. In 1999 the J. Paul Getty Museum organized a show called *Nadar/Warhol: Paris/New York* which explored the striking similarities between Nadar's work and that of Andy Warhol.

McEnroe

For Further Reading

Baldwin, Gordon. *Nadar/Warhol: Paris/New York*. Los Angeles: J. Paul Getty Trust, 1999.

Gosling, Nigel. *Nadar*. London: Secker & Warburg, 1976.

Hambourg, Maria Morris. *Nadar*. New York: Metropolitan Museum of Art, 1995.

Neruda, Pablo

Poet
1904–1973

Life and Work

Pablo Neruda, one of the most important and prolific Latin American poets of the twentieth century, wrote more than 30 books of poetry, two of prose, and a book of recipes.

Neruda was born Neftalí Reyes on July 12, 1904, in Parral, an agricultural region of southern Chile. Neruda often said that he was a poet by the age of 10. His first poems were published when he was 15, and at 17 the Student Federation of Chile awarded him a prize for his poem "La canción de la fiesta" and published it in the magazine *Juventud*. This poem and the collection that followed it, *Crepúsculario* (1923), were heavily influenced by Symbolist poetry and the work of WALT WHITMAN and the Nicaraguan poet Rubén Darío.

Neruda went to Santiago to study poetry at the University of Chile in 1921. Three years later his third collection of poetry, *Veinte poemas de amor y una canción desesperada* (*Twenty Love Poems and a Song of Despair*), was published. The collection established Neruda's reputation as a love poet. Neruda abandoned traditional form with his next collection of poetry, *Tentativa del hombre infinito* (*Venture of the Infinite Man*, 1925), one of the many radical shifts in style that characterized his career.

In 1927 Neruda was appointed Chilean consul to Burma. There he began his *Residencia en la tierra* (*Residence on Earth and Other Poems*, 1933), the first volume in a long work that employed innovative techniques, including interior monologue, dense language, and complex structure, which were important contributions to modern poetry all over the world.

Neruda's diplomatic career in the 1930s took him to Buenos Aires, Argentina, where he became friends with the poet FEDERICO GARCÍA LORCA, and then to Spain, where he established friendships with the poets of the literary group "the Generation of 1927"—Pedro Salinas, Rafael Alberti, and Vicente Aleixandre.

In 1943, after being dismissed from his government position for his socialist politics, Neruda traveled to France to organize a congress of artists against fascism and to aid refugees of the Spanish Civil War. He published the first part of his *Canto general de Chile* (1943), a collection of poems about Chilean history and politics with drawings by muralists DIEGO RIVERA and David Alfaro Siqueiros. Neruda then renounced all of his work written before 1937 as overly literary and elitist, asserting that he would write for the common people from that point on.

Neruda joined the Communist Party in 1945, and in 1949 he was forced to flee Chile after he accused Chile's president, Gabriel González Videla, of deliberately sabotaging the country's interests. When he gained international attention as the winner of the Stalin Prize for Literature and the Lenin Peace Prize in 1953, the Chilean government was embarrassed into inviting him to return. Neruda was awarded the Nobel Prize for Literature in 1971. He died of cancer in 1973.

Legacy

Pablo Neruda, whose long artistic career was characterized by change, helped shape contemporary Latin American poetry. In the 1920s he brought the region's poetry to international attention with his recurring themes of love, nature, and justice in Latin America.

Moving away from what had become clichés of Modernist and Romantic poetry, Neruda's *Twenty Love Poems and a Song of Despair* was one of the first truly modern collections of Spanish poetry. He focused not only on love but also on sex, rejecting Spanish Modernism's treatment of love as a sacred subject. He treated women as real physical beings in his poetry, rather than ethereal ideals, and he celebrated love in a Spanish that was conversational rather than elevated. These innovations, along with the poems' forthright expressions of desire, made finding a publisher difficult. Once published, however, *Twenty Love Poems and a Song of Despair* quickly became the most popular collection of love poems written in Spanish and even today people all over the Spanish-speaking world can recite them from memory.

Residence on Earth renewed Spanish-language poetry with a wealth of images that invited comparisons to European Surrealist works. Later in his career, Neruda would leave behind the lyrical symbolism of *Twenty Love Poems* and the Surrealistic style of *Residence on Earth* to write political poems and poems about mundane topics. In all of his work's incarnations Neruda created a new Spanish poetry, one that reflected and became a part of the everyday lives of readers.

Neruda's identification of his own personal life with his creative art produced a poetry drawn from direct experience. He thus formed a branch of Spanish poetry that continues to flourish in Latin America alongside the very different and far more abstract work of OCTAVIO PAZ.

Watson

WORLD EVENTS		NERUDA' LIFE
Spanish-American War	1898	
	1904	Pablo Neruda is born
World War I	1914–18	
Russian Revolution	1917	
	1923	Neruda publishes *Crepúsculario*
	1924	Neruda publishes *Twenty Love Poems and a Song of Despair*
	1927	Neruda travels to Burma as consul of Chile
	1929–39	
Great Depression	1939–45	
World War II	1945	Neruda joins Communist Party
Communist China is established	1949	
Korean War	1950–53	
	1953	Neruda receives Lenin Peace Prize and Stalin Prize for Literature
African independence movement begins	1957	
	1971	Neruda receives Nobel Prize for Literature
	1973	Neruda dies of cancer
Vietnam War ends	1975	

For Further Reading
Neruda, Pablo. *Pablo Neruda: Selected Poems*. Edited by Nathaniel Tarn. New York: Houghton Mifflin, 1990.
Roman, Joseph. *Pablo Neruda*. New York: Chelsea House, 1991.

Ni Zan

Painter and Scholar
1301–1374

World Events		Ni Zan's life	
Mongol conquest of China	1215		
	1301	Ni Zan is born	
	1328	Ni Zan inherits family fortune	
Hundred Years' War begins	1337		
	1352	Ni Zan is forced to sell family estate	
Ming Dynasty reasserts Chinese control of China	1368		
	1372	Ni Zan paints *Rongxi Studio*	
	1374	Ni Zan dies	
Ottoman Empire conquers Constantinople	1453		

Life and Work

Along with Wu Zhen (1280–1354), Huang Gongwang (1269–1313), and Wang Meng (1308–85), Ni Zan was one of the Four Great Masters of the Yuan dynasty (1279–1368).

Ni Zan was born in 1301 into a wealthy family in Wuxi, just north of Taihu, in Jiangsu Province. After the death of an older brother in 1328, he became heir to the family fortune. He erected a library, the *Qingbige* (Pure and Secluded Pavilion) on the estate where he housed his extensive collection of rare books, paintings, calligraphy, ancient bronze vessels, and *qin* (zithers).

As a member of the scholar-gentry class, Ni Zen was heir to a tradition of literati painting (*wenrenhua*) inaugurated in the late eleventh century among a small circle of scholar-officials. An important feature of literati painting is the use of the expressive calligraphic brushwork and natural scenery. There are many anecdotes about Ni Zan's obsession with cleanliness and his avoidance of contact with people he considered unclean or vulgar. It is said that he even had the *wutong* trees in his garden washed daily by his servants.

Ni Zan's life changed dramatically with the imposition of exorbitant land taxes by the Mongol government. In 1352 he dispersed or sold his property to relatives and acquaintances. In the last decades of his life, Ni Zan wandered with his wife in a houseboat throughout Taihu and its surroundings, visiting with friends or residing at Buddhist monasteries until his death in 1374.

Ni Zan is considered to be the quintessential Yuan scholar-painter. His landscape paintings exemplify what has come to be known as "landscapes of the mind." They typically depict a pavilion beside rocks, trees, and occasionally bamboo, on a riverbank, separated by the river from distant hills, and are noted for the absence of a human subject. Ni Zan's paintings, such as the *Rongxi Studio* (1372), are distinguished by the remarkable degree of subtlety in the nuances of movement and accents of pressure applied to the brush, qualities similar to those that appear in the thin, spiky calligraphy style of his accompanying poetic inscriptions. His painted worlds have a detached, remote, fragile quality often interpreted as expressing a sense of alienation from the harsh realities of life in China under Mongol rule.

Legacy

Ni Zan has come to be seen as the ideal embodiment of the *sanjue*, or "Three Perfections," of the scholar-artist: painting, poetry, and calligraphy.

His art is not only venerated for the supreme refinement of its execution, indicative of his attainment of the highest degree of self-cultivation, it is also accorded canonical status within the tradition of the scholar-artist, exemplifying the proper ways to present oneself when living under historical conditions similar to those Ni Zan experienced.

Throughout the Ming dynasty (1367–1644), Ni Zan's style was creatively appropriated by later scholar-painters as they attempted to represent themselves during the peaceful conditions in China after the overthrow of the Mongol regime.

In the early years of the Qing dynasty (1644–1911), Hongren (1610–64) and the Anhui School of literati painting invoked Ni Zan's style in order to address the Manchu conquest of China. Huangshan, a mountain range in southern Anhui province, was thematized in their work as a vehicle for reasserting regional and cultural identity—an act of resistance against the Manchu invaders.

Today, the Ni Zan legacy is sustained in the "mindscapes" of the traditional painter C. C. Wang of New York.

Goldberg

For Further Reading

Cahill, James. *Hills Beyond a River: Chinese Painting of the Yuan Dynasty, 1279–1368.* New York and Tokyo: Weatherhill, 1976.

Fong, Wen, and James C. Y. Watt, et al. *Possessing the Past: Treasures from the National Palace Museum, Taipei.* Exhibition catalogue. New York: Metropolitan Museum of Art, 1996.

Loehr, Max. *The Great Painters of China.* Oxford: Phaidon, 1980.

O'Keeffe, Georgia

Painter
1887–1986

Life and Work

Georgia O'Keeffe was an American Modernist painter whose paintings achieved a unique balance between representation and abstraction.

O'Keeffe was born in Sun Prairie, Wisconsin, in 1887. From 1905 to 1907 she studied art at the School of the Art Institute of Chicago and at the Art Students League in New York. After completing her studies, she worked for a while as a commercial artist and taught art at several schools in the southern United States.

O'Keeffe returned to New York in 1914 to teach at Columbia University Teachers College. At this time one of the important gathering places for the New York art world was 291, a gallery operated by the photographer Alfred Stieglitz. Stieglitz was one of the first people to bring the work of avant-garde European artists such as PABLO PICASSO and Georges Braque to the United States. Stieglitz was one of the most important promoters of the new style, and the central figure in a group of American artists. In 1916 O'Keeffe submitted some of her abstract drawings to Stieglitz for review, and he immediately offered her an exhibition. In 1919 O'Keeffe moved in with Stieglitz, and in 1924 they were married.

O'Keeffe may have been influenced by some of the photographers in Stieglitz circle when she painted *Petunia No. 2,* her first close-up flower picture, in 1924. By magnifying the forms and composing the image in broad, bold planes, O'Keeffe created a unique formal balance between the representation of natural forms and geometric abstraction.

Her place as a woman artist among an otherwise all-male avant-garde was a topic of major discussion in the 1920s. Many of her simplified close-up images of flowers and other natural forms were likened to stylized images of female genitalia. Other artists associated with the Stieglitz circle, including even Stieglitz himself, praised her works as the quintessence of "feminine" art. O'Keeffe adamantly resisted the notion that her works had anything to do with vaginal imagery or the implied female essence. She insisted that her abstracted forms transcended gender.

O'Keeffe spent much of her time outside the city in order to keep in touch with the natural forms that inspired her paintings. From 1929 on, she spent her summers in New Mexico, where she painted works such as *Black Cross, New Mexico* (1929). She moved permanently to Albiquiu, New Mexico, in 1949, not long after Stieglitz's death. There, she continued to paint highly abstracted images of the Western landscape, sky, and other elemental natural forms well into her old age.

O'Keeffe died in 1986 at the age of 98.

Legacy

Georgia O'Keeffe was one of the pioneer Modernists in American painting. She established her unique style, distinct from that of the European Modernists who exhibited at the Stieglitz gallery.

O'Keeffe's style can be tied to several later developments. At least in retrospect, her broad, flat organic abstractions appear to be similar to the Color Field painting done by artists such as Helen Frankenthaler beginning in the 1960s. Similarly, despite O'Keeffe's own explanations of the stylized flower and clamshell paintings, these images are frequently cited as the inspiration for the vaginal imagery of feminist artists such as Judy Chicago. In addition, O'Keeffe's reputation helped to establish Santa Fe as one of the most

important artists' colonies in America, and her paintings of New Mexico established a thriving subgenre of Western art.

O'Keeffe has become increasingly associated with feminist issues. A retrospective of her work at the Whitney Museum in 1970 introduced her to a new generation that was involved with the emerging "second-wave" feminist movement. O'Keeffe has since come to be revered as one of the matriarchs of modern art.

In 1997, the Georgia O'Keeffe Museum opened in Santa Fe, containing the world's largest public collection of her work. O'Keeffe is now regarded as one of the genuinely unique figures in the Modernist movement.

McEnroe

WORLD EVENTS		O'KEEFFE'S LIFE
Germany is united	1871	
	1887	Georgia O'Keeffe is born
Spanish-American War	1898	
	1905–07	O'Keeffe attends Art Institute of Chicago and Art Students League, New York
World War I	1914–18	
	1916	O'Keeffe has first major exhibition at Gallery 291
Russian Revolution	1917	
	1924	O'Keeffe paints *Petunia No. 2*
Great Depression	1929–39	
World War II	1939–45	
Communist China is established	1949	O'Keeffe moves to New Mexico
Korean War	1950–53	
African independence movement begins	1957	
Vietnam War ends	1975	
	1986	O'Keeffe dies
Dissolution of Soviet Union	1991	

For Further Reading

Eldredge, Charles C. *Georgia O'Keeffe.* New York: Harry N. Abrams in association with the National Museum of American Art, Smithsonian Institution, 1991.

Lisle, Laurie. *Portrait of an Artist: A Biography of Georgia O'Keeffe.* Albuquerque: University of New Mexico Press, 1986.

Robinson, Roxanna. *Georgia O'Keeffe: A Life.* New York: Harper & Row, 1989.

Orwell, George

(Eric Arthur Blair)

Journalist, Novelist, and Essayist
1903–1950

Life and Work

"George Orwell" was the pseudonym of Eric Arthur Blair, author of two of the most famous satirical novels of the twentieth century, and an important social critic, political journalist, and essayist.

Orwell was born on June 25, 1903, in Mothari, Bengal; his father was a minor official in the British Indian Civil Service. He attended Eton College, the British public (private) school, on a scholarship from 1917 to 1921. He did not go on to university; in 1922, he joined the Indian Imperial Police, spending five years in Burma as an assistant district superintendent. It was there that he expressed his discomfort with social inequality and the cynicism of power, as recorded in his essay "Shooting an Elephant" (1936).

Orwell's political convictions and working-class sympathies were always integral to his writing. His first published book was *Down and Out in Paris and London* (1933), a slightly fictionalized account of the several years he spent living among the poor of those cities. In 1936 he was commissioned to research life among the unemployed in the north of England; this led to his book *The Road to Wigan Pier* (1937). Late in 1936 he went to Spain to write about the Spanish Civil War; so aroused was his political passion that he joined a militia sponsored by a leading left-wing political party. He was seriously wounded and returned to England in 1937. His memoir *Homage to Catalonia*, recording his experiences and political insights, was published in 1938.

During World War II he headed the Indian service of the BBC until 1943, when he became literary editor of *The Tribune*, a left-wing socialist paper. Over the next several years, he wrote much of his serious journalism, many reviews, and a large body of literary criticism, much of it concerned with Englishness and the nature of English patriotism.

Orwell completed *Animal Farm*, a political fable of an egalitarian farmyard society that becomes a dictatorship of pigs, in 1944. Several publishers, including T. S. Eliot at Faber and Faber, rejected it. The book was published in 1945 and its immediate success was a surprise to both the publisher and Orwell.

In 1946 Orwell moved to the Scots island of Jura in the Hebrides. There he wrote much of his next novel, *Nineteen Eighty-Four* (1949), a tale of a society of the near future in which privacy, intellectual freedom, personal friendship, and individual liberty are all eliminated.

On January 21, 1950, believing that he was recovering from the tuberculosis that had plagued him for years, Orwell died of a sudden lung hemorrhage in a London hospital.

Legacy

George Orwell wrote some of the most powerful political literature of the twentieth century and has influenced writers of every generation since. A writer of moral integrity and independence, he was both a serious political thinker and a craftsman of language who brought political literature into the arena of literary art.

Nineteen Eighty-Four, probably his best-known work, reflects the atmosphere of insecurity that followed World War II. Orwell's projection of a bleak future of totalitarian social control based on the dictatorships of the 1930s resembled the worst imaginings of the Depression and war years and struck a chord at the time of its publication. In the earliest years of the Cold War the book assumed the status of a classic. It sold over 400,000 copies in its first year in print and over 11 million by the year of its title.

Nineteen Eighty-Four and *Animal Farm*, a satire about Stalinism, both left traces in the language. Phrases like "All animals are equal, but some are more equal than others" and "Big Brother is watching you" have become commonplace idioms in the political vocabulary with which we speak about government and other oppressive bureaucracies.

Orwell defined his literary career somewhat in opposition to the literary movements taking place in his lifetime. Rather than experimenting with language and narrative style, as did his Modernist contemporaries and predecessors, he used a traditional "plain" style to tell linear narratives. Whether in autobiography, essay, fiction or political fable, Orwell saw writers as having a distinct social responsibility. His goal was to use his writing to discern and clarify moral values and thereby influence the political thinking of society.

Orwell's example has influenced many, and his legacy has been fought over for decades by those on the left and the right who see themselves as his legitimate heirs.

Watson

World Events		Orwell's Life
Spanish-American War	1898	
	1903	Eric Arthur Blair is born
World War I	1914–18	
Russian Revolution	1917	
	1922	Blair joins Indian Imperial Police in Burma
Great Depression	1929–39	
	1933	Orwell publishes *Down and Out in Paris and London*
	1936	Orwell writes "Shooting an Elephant"; Orwell joins Republican militia in Spain
	1937	Orwell publishes *Road to Wigan Pier*
	1938	Orwell publishes *Homage to Catalonia*
World War II	1939–45	
	1945	Orwell publishes *Animal Farm*
Communist China is established	1949	Orwell publishes *Nineteen Eighty-Four*
	1950	Orwell dies
Korean War	1950–53	

For Further Reading

Crick, Bernard. *George Orwell: A Life*. New York: Viking Penguin, 1980.

Fowler, Roger. *The Language of George Orwell*. New York: St. Martin's Press, 1996.

Stansky, Peter. *The Unknown Orwell*. Palo Alto, Calif.: Stanford University Press, 1972.

Ovid

(Publius Ovidius Naso)

Poet

43 B.C.E.–c. 18 C.E.

Life and Work

The Roman poet Ovid is known for the passion and humanity with which he infused myth and history in his great poem the *Metamorphoses*.

Ovid was born into an upper-class family in central Italy on March 20, 43 B.C.E., one year after the death of Julius Caesar. As a young man, Ovid studied law and politics in Rome, but after serving in a series of minor government positions, he chose not to pursue a public career. He became a protege of Marcus Valerius Messalla Corvinus, a general, statesman, and patron of the arts, and devoted himself to writing poetry, becoming a part of a group of poets that included Propertius, Tibullus, and Horace.

Ovid published several collections of love poetry: the first was *Amores*, published in five volumes in 20 B.C.E., which tells a love story in the first person in a series of elegies; in his next collection, the *Heroides*, the poems are written as love letters of women from Greek myth, including Penelope, Medea, and Dido. Ovid's *Ars amatoria,* a guide to seduction, was published around 1 B.C.E. The book's erotic content caused a scandal in the tight moral atmosphere of Augustan Rome. All of Ovid's works were popular and widely read.

The emperor Augustus banished Ovid from Rome in 8 C.E., at the height of the poet's popularity. Ovid himself says only that he committed an "error" that he may not discuss, and that this, combined with the resentment over *Ars amatoria,* caused Augustus to exile him. He was sent to Tomis, a small city on the western shore of the Black Sea near present-day Constanza, Romania, then a dangerous frontier of the Roman Empire.

Shortly before he was exiled Ovid completed the majority of the *Metamorphoses*, universally considered his greatest work. The epic poem, which contains 15 books all written in hexameter verse, is a series of stories—many of them love stories—all unified by the theme of trans-formation. The book begins with a description of the initial transformation of chaos into order and ends with the death of Julius Caesar. Ovid used the stories of Greek myth as well as Roman and Mesopotamian lore. His poem is one of the primary sources by which these stories have entered Western culture.

After completing the *Metamorphoses*, Ovid began the *Fasti* (*Festivals*), a work that documents the calendar of Roman religious festivals. Never completed, it has nevertheless provided a great deal of information about Roman religion and culture. Ovid was able to finish only the first six books, covering six months of the year. Ovid also wrote the *Tristia* (*Sorrows*), a series of elegiac letters, the *Ibis*, and the *Epistulae ex Ponto* (*Letters from the Black Sea*), while in exile.

Ovid remained in Tomis until his death in 17 or 18 C.E.

Legacy

While Ovid's technical innovations of elegiac couplets and hexameter verse profoundly affected subsequent Latin poetry, they do not compare to the influence his mythical subject matter and passionate tone had on the history of Western poetry.

Ovid presented the stories of the gods in human terms, focusing on their affairs of love, jealousy, and anger. He thus made mythology integral to poetry and art. His exile and the subsequent removal of his books from Roman libraries did not prevent people from reading his work, and his style and subject matter were widely imitated by the generation of poets immediately following his. Ovid's work has continued to serve as a rich source of material for others.

Until the Renaissance, critics of his work dismissed it as frivolous, claiming that its stories of love could not be considered serious literature. Thereafter, however, the *Metamorphoses* was the most popular of the classical texts, and by the fourteenth century it had become part of the education of most literate people. GEOFFREY CHAUCER, John Gower, and WILLIAM SHAKESPEARE read Ovid and made reference to his work in their own. In the fourth book of the *Inferno*, the Italian poet DANTE names Ovid along with VIRGIL, HOMER, Horace, and Lucan as the greatest pre-Christian poets.

Ovid's work was mined for stories and allegories by the troubadours, early French poets who developed the poetry of courtly love, considered the beginning of French poetry. Chrétien de Troyes referred to Ovid in his romance *Tristan and Iseult.*

In 1567 the complete *Metamorphoses* was translated into English; it had already been translated into Italian, Byzantine Greek, German, French, and Spanish. Ovid had a particular appeal to English poets of the mid-eighteenth century—known as Augustans—who found inspiration in his light touch and formal versification. English writers who have translated Ovid over the years include Christopher Marlowe, John Dryden, Alexander Pope, and Joseph Addison, and more recently, the English poet Ted Hughes.

Watson

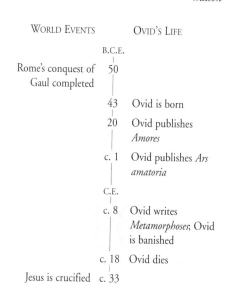

WORLD EVENTS		OVID'S LIFE
	B.C.E.	
Rome's conquest of Gaul completed	50	
	43	Ovid is born
	20	Ovid publishes *Amores*
	c. 1	Ovid publishes *Ars amatoria*
	C.E.	
	c. 8	Ovid writes *Metamorphoses*; Ovid is banished
	c. 18	Ovid dies
Jesus is crucified	c. 33	

For Further Reading

Syme, Ronald. *History in Ovid.* New York: Oxford University Press, 1978.

Thibault, John C. *The Mystery of Ovid's Exile.* Berkeley: University of California Press, 1964.

Williams, Gordon. *Change and Decline: Roman Literature in the Early Empire.* Berkeley: University of California Press, 1978.

Paik, Nam June

Musician, Sculptor, and
Performance and Video Artist
1932–

World Events	Paik's life
Great Depression 1929–39	
	1932 Nam June Paik is born in Seoul
World War II 1939–45	
Communist China 1949 is established	
Korean War 1950–53	
	1952 Paik begins studies at University of Tokyo
	1956 Paik moves to Germany
African independence 1957 movement begins	
	1963 Paik makes his first video art
	1964 Paik moves to New York
	1967 Paik and Charlotte Moorman collaborate on *Opera Sextronique*
Vietnam War ends 1975	
	1982 Paik retrospective is held at Whitney Museum, New York
	1986 Paik constructs *Family of Robots*
Dissolution of 1991 Soviet Union	

Life and Work

Nam June Paik is a performance artist, musician, and video artist whose work explores the complex relations between modern technology and the human imagination.

Paik was born in Seoul, Korea, in 1932. When he was 17, his family fled from the Korean War, moving first to Hong Kong, then to Tokyo. From 1952 to 1956, Paik studied art history and music at the University of Tokyo. In 1956, Paik moved to Germany to continue his studies.

In Germany, Paik became involved with a new movement known as Fluxus. Like the Dada artists in the early part of the century, Fluxus aimed to challenge the parameters of "high art" in a series of anarchic performances, treatises, and musical events. Paik participated in performances, experimented with new music, and made "anti-films"—in one case a film without images. At the same time, Paik became acquainted with the American avant-garde composer JOHN CAGE, who was to have an important influence on his work. Paik began to experiment with television sets in 1959. His first one-person show in 1963, *Exposition of Music—Electronic Music,* is often regarded as the first work of video art, an art whose character and assumptions are the antithesis of those of commercial television.

Paik moved to New York in 1964. The following year, he bought the first of the Sony Portapack video recorders to arrive in the United States. He reportedly made his first video recording with the camera on the way home in a taxi. The video, which featured the visiting Pope's entourage caught in a traffic jam, was shown that evening at the Café à Go Go. In the same period Paik began to collaborate with Charlotte Moorman, a cellist and promoter of new music. During one of their early works, *Opera Sextronique* (1967), Paik and Moorman, who was performing topless, were arrested for indecency.

Paik became extraordinarily prolific in New York. His works varied from electronically manipulated imagery (*Magnet TV,* 1965) to sculptural installations. For *Family of Robots* (1986), Paik constructed three generations of robots from old TV sets whose screens flickered with tapes celebrating human diversity. His 1982 installation *Tricolor Video* at the Centre Georges Pompidou in Paris was a landscape formed from a thousand TV sets.

Crippled by a stroke, Paik does little video art now, but continues to experiment with music.

Legacy

Nam June Paik is widely regarded as the father of video art. His joyous enthusiasm for the new medium opened the field for many younger artists. Paik's work was honored by a major retrospective at the Whitney Museum of American Art in 1982 and was featured at the Guggenheim Museum in 2000.

Paik was responsible for a number of important technical innovations. He experimented with the inner circuitry of televisions and developed new ways of manipulating the signal. With the engineer Shuya Abe he invented the Paik/Abe synthesizer, which became the first color synthesizer to be used by commercial broadcasters. Paik introduced new forms of quick editing that have had a profound effect on popular commercial art forms such as music videos. He also experimented with various forms of interactive installations in which the actions of viewers triggered effects in the videos.

Paik has challenged the traditional primacy of painting and sculpture as media, predicting that the cathode ray tube would replace the canvas. Yet for all his involvement with technology, Paik is not the prophet of a Brave New World of utopian technology—quite the opposite. Paik approaches high-tech art in a playful, mischievously low-tech way. His sculptural contraptions formed from old TVs are precariously patched together. In works like *TV Bra for Living Sculpture* (1969), which featured Charlotte Moorman with tiny TVs clamped to her breasts, Paik makes technology look ridiculous. Paik's work has less to do with technology than with the human spirit. In his world, the playful, imaginative anarchist always triumphs over the machine.

McEnroe

For Further Reading
Hanhardt, John G. *The Worlds of Nam June Paik.* New York: Guggenheim Museum, 2000.
Hanhardt, John G., ed. *Nam June Paik.* New York: Whitney Museum of American Art, 1982.

Palestrina, Giovanni Pierluigi da

Composer
1525 or 1526–1594

Life and Work

When in the sixteenth century Protestants broke away from Roman Catholicism to form new denominations, the Roman Catholic church reacted with a series of reforms that included musical restrictions. This conservative, self-purifying effort was known as the Counter-Reformation, and its greatest musical representative was Giovanni Pierluigi da Palestrina.

Palestrina took his name from a small town in the hills outside Rome that was home to his family; he was probably born there in 1525 or 1526. He learned about singing and musical composition as a choirboy in Rome; in 1551, he was appointed a choir director at St. Peter's church. Palestrina's chief backer, the bishop of Palestrina, had been elected Pope Julius III the previous year, and the young composer's career ascended rapidly.

His first book of masses was published in 1554, and in 1555 he won a prized spot in the Pope's own Sistine Chapel Choir. He soon had to resign from the choir because he was married, and one of the early Counter-Reformation reforms demanded that only celibate men be permitted among the chapel's personnel.

Despite this setback, Palestrina's reputation was already established. He moved on to influential posts at the magnificent St. John Lateran and Santa Maria Maggiore churches in Rome, and in 1568 turned down an offer from the Austrian emperor Maximilian II to come to Vienna. In 1571 Palestrina returned to St. Peter's, where he spent the last 23 years of his life. His music was in demand both in the church and in the private chapels of Italy's noble families.

What made Palestrina so successful was the way he reconciled the Roman Catholic church's new demands for simplicity and text intelligibility with the complex polyphony, or motion in independent voice parts, of Renaissance music. Palestrina's masses and other religious pieces were rich and sumptuous, yet they seemed crystal clear, and listeners could understand the sacred texts. Palestrina died in Rome on February 2, 1594.

Legacy

The control and harmonious flow of Giovanni Pierluigi da Palestrina's music made it influential not only for his direct successors, but also for composers in the classical tradition down to the present day, whose training often still requires study and mastery of his style.

Legend has it that Palestrina singlehandedly dissuaded the Roman Catholic church from abandoning polyphony altogether and going back to a musical diet of pure Gregorian chant. In fact the *Pope Marcellus Mass,* which was thought to have accomplished this reversal, was probably composed in 1562—several years before the church conclave at which the issue of music was being discussed. However the tale highlights the importance of Palestrina's role in forming the music of the new Roman Catholicism. Of the next generation of Roman Catholic composers who came under Palestrina's influence, the most significant was Spain's Tomás Luis de Victoria, who adopted but darkened Palestrina's style to create a deeply serious sacred music.

Other composers of the Renaissance were long forgotten and have been rediscovered only by modern musical scholars, but Palestrina's name never faded. In addition to the sheer beauty of his music, his reputation has rested on its consistent technique, on its

homogeneous sound world that excluded any jarring, out-of-place elements. Later musical theorists, beginning with Johann Joseph Fux in the eighteenth century and continuing to the present, analyzed Palestrina's style and distilled it into a set of rules for musical counterpoint—for the proper combination of individual musical lines. "Palestrina counterpoint" is still part of the curriculum of many music schools, and Palestrina's compositions themselves are timeless emblems of the sacred in music, exquisitely refined.

Manheim

WORLD EVENTS		PALESTRINA'S LIFE
Protestant Reformation begins	1517	
	1525 or 1526	Giovanni Pierluigi da Palestrina is born
	1551	Palestrina is appointed choir director at St. Peter's in Rome
	1554	Palestrina's publishes first book of masses
	1555	Palestrina joins Sistine Chapel Choir, but is forced to resign
	c. 1562	Palestrina composes influential *Pope Marcellus Mass*
	1568	Palestrina refuses offer to move to Vienna
Ottoman dominance of Mediterranean ends	1571	Palestrina returns to St. Peter's
	1594	Palestrina dies
Thirty Years' War in Europe	1618–48	

For Further Reading

King, Ethel M. *Palestrina: The Prince of Music.* Brooklyn, N.Y.: Gaus, 1965.

Reese, Gustave, et al. *The New Grove High Renaissance Masters: Josquin, Palestrina, Lassus, Byrd, Victoria.* London: Macmillan, 1984.

Palladio, Andrea

Architect and Theoretician
1508–1580

Life and Work

Andrea Palladio was an important architect in sixteenth century Venice and became the most influential architect in European history.

WORLD EVENTS		PALLADIO'S LIFE
Columbus sails to Americas	1492	
	1508	Andrea di Pietro (Palladio) is born
Protestant Reformation begins	1517	
	1537–42	Palladio completes his first independent work, Villa Godi-Malinverni
	1556–70	Palladio builds Villa Rotunda
Ottoman dominance of Mediterranean ends	1571	
	1580	Palladio dies
Thirty Years' War in Europe	1618–48	

Born Andrea di Pietro in Padua in 1508, Andrea began working as a stonemason's apprentice at age 13. Three years later he became a member of the guild of stonemasons and carvers in Vicenza.

The young Andrea became associated with the academy of Giangiorgio Trissino. Trissino gave him the nickname "Palladio" (after Pallas Athena, Greek goddess of wisdom) and introduced him to the world of Renaissance humanism. During five trips to Rome, Palladio made meticulous studies of the remains of ancient Roman buildings as well as the High Renaissance buildings of Bramante. Through them he learned not only the forms of classical architecture, but more important, the principles of classical design.

At the same time, Palladio began to study the architectural treatises of the first-century B.C.E. Roman architect Vitruvius, as well as *De Re Aedificatoria* of the fifteenth-century Florentine architect LEON BATTISTA ALBERTI. Soon Palladio began to write treatises of his own, including *L'antichità di Roma* (1554) and *I quattro libri dell'architettura* (*The Four Books on Architecture*; 1570).

Palladio is best known for the series of villas he built in the Veneto, the countryside around Venice. The villa was a new kind of architecture in Italy. Inspired in part by references to classical villas in ancient literature, these grand estates derived also from dramatic changes in the local economy. The formerly great Venetian maritime empire was in rapid decline. Wealthy Venetians fled the city, invested their fortunes in agriculture, and adopted the leisurely lives of gentleman-farmers.

Many of Palladio's villas, such as the grand Villa Barbaro (1549–58), were working farms. A large central pavilion inspired by the colonnaded facades of Classical temples was flanked by porticoes that connected with utilitarian wings on each end. Inside the main pavilion were large halls for entertaining, decorated with playful trompe l'oeil frescoes by Paolo Veronese.

Palladio designed two important churches in Venice, Il Redentore (1576/7–80) and San Giorgio Maggiore (1564–80). They were landmarks in the history of classical design.

Palladio returned to Vicenza in 1579 to design the Teatro Olimpico. He died the following year.

Legacy

Rising from an apprentice stonecutter to the lofty humanist circles of Vicenza and Venice, Andrea Palladio had an extraordinary career. Although profoundly influential, he remained poor until his latest years. After Palladio's death, because of the work of his follower Vincenzo Scamozzi and later imitators, Palladian villas became increasingly common in Italy.

Over the next two centuries, Palladio's designs and Palladian forms spread throughout Europe and eventually to the United States. Palladian designs became especially important in those regions, like England and the American South, where the wealthy chose to live in the country rather than in cities.

"Palladianism" was brought to England in the seventeenth century by the architect Inigo Jones. *The Four Books on Architecture* was translated into English in 1717. In England, Palladio's villas became the models for numerous country houses; these massive buildings and the estates that sustained them fundamentally altered the appearance and the economy of the English countryside. In the United States, Thomas Jefferson and others looked to Palladian models for their own country houses. Palladian forms characterize dozens of plantations of the antebellum South.

The Palladian villa style was rooted in an anti-urban philosophical program: cities were the centers of crime, corruption, and immorality; the country was safe, clean, and moral. Like their predecessors in the Veneto, these aristocratic and gentlemanly English and American builders were the beneficiaries of a social order founded on cheap or slave labor. Their villas were private utopias where wealthy landowners could conveniently ignore the sometimes bitter social and economic realities to which they owed their positions.

Over the past two decades Palladian windows and other motifs have become increasingly popular devices in expensive postmodern houses in suburbs across America. Developers of these suburban estates tend to emphasize their safety, cleanliness, and connection with "family values"—the latest version of the Jeffersonian anti-urbanism that has done much to shape the modern American built environment.

McEnroe

For Further Reading

Ackerman, James. *Palladio: The Architect and Society.* Harmondsworth, England: Penguin, 1966.

Boucher, Bruce. *Andrea Palladio: The Architect in His Time.* New York: Abbeville Press, 1994.

Palladio, Andrea. *The Four Books on Architecture.* With a new introduction by Adolf Placzek. New York: Dover, 1965.

Parker, Charlie

Saxophonist
1920–1955

Life and Work

At once an innovator and a dazzling virtuoso, saxophonist Charlie "Bird" Parker is generally acclaimed as one of the most important soloists in jazz history.

Parker was born in Kansas City, Kansas, on August 29, 1920, and in 1927 moved across the river with his family to Kansas City, Missouri, an important jazz center in the years before World War II. By 1933 he was playing the alto saxophone, and through the late 1930s he honed his craft with various Kansas City bands. In 1939 he went to New York, where he played in small groups with other experimental-minded musicians and observed more advanced players: at one point he is said to have worked as a dishwasher so that he could repeatedly hear the playing of pianist Art Tatum.

In 1940 Parker made his first recordings as part of small combo led by Jay McShann, for whom he had played intermittently for several years. He toured the country with McShann until 1942, and then joined a band led by pianist Earl Hines, since the late 1920s an iconoclastic, questing figure. This band included trumpeter Dizzy Gillespie, who would soon become a key partner in Parker's innovative efforts. In 1943 and 1944 Parker

and Gillespie took giant steps forward stylistically in late-night performances at New York clubs such as Minton's Playhouse. A few of these were recorded by a patron on portable tape equipment—but he tended to skip Parker's solos, thinking them inferior.

Parker formed a band of his own in 1945, by which time the style known onomatopoetically as bebop had fully taken shape; in addition to abrupt, irregularly accented rhythms, Parker's music was characterized by extensions of traditional jazz harmony. His improvisations were often based on blues and (usually renamed) popular songs, but instead of simply ornamenting the melody, he explored hitherto unrealized implications of a piece's harmonic structure. Parker's tempos were fast and his playing punishingly complex, but he was a physically and intellectually precise performer, and his ideas emerged with startling clarity.

Such postwar Parker recordings as "Anthropology," "Scrapple from the Apple," and "Embraceable You" are considered essential jazz classics. But Parker suffered personally as he triumphed artistically, undergoing a hospitalization for heroin and alcohol abuse in 1946 and beginning a serious decline after his visits to Europe in 1949 and 1950. He tried twice to commit suicide in 1954, and died on March 12, 1955, in New York.

Legacy

Charlie Parker, along with Dizzy Gillespie, defined the musical language of bebop, which in turn became the foundation of modern jazz.

He spurred the experiments of the saxophone radicals who came after him in the 1950s and 1960s, such as JOHN COLTRANE and Ornette Coleman, both of whom began their careers playing music strongly in the Parker mold. Coltrane carried the sheer speed and intensity of Parker's playing to even greater extremes; for both these musicians and others, Parker's melodic flights were critical steps toward a "free jazz" unbound by any model. Trumpeter MILES DAVIS (who worked with Parker beginning in 1947) and the iconoclastic pianist Thelonious Monk also showed Parker's influence even as they discarded the fast tempos and uncompromising aesthetic of bebop in favor of a sparser and more restrained sound:

"cool jazz" players unpacked Parker's dense musical structures and etched new layers into the spaces thus created.

Beyond his impact on the boundary-shattering jazz of the 1950s and 1960s, Parker attained a classic and even mythic status. Musically, bebop's durability has been astonishing; over half a century after Parker's pioneering postwar recordings, bebop flourishes as a jazz mainstream, while its more radical successors remain on the fringe. Jazz musicians study Parker's style and learn to play, essentially, like he did; playing in small groups they hold forth in smoky clubs and attempt to impress their audiences with the intensity of their musical elaborations and with the variety and surprise of their musical quotations—a Parker specialty. Parker's aloof personality, his intellectual, nonconformist social stance, and his long, laborious devotion to the acquisition of perfect technique all still seem exemplary for aspiring jazz players. In his life as well as in his music Charlie Parker defined what it meant to be committed to the art of jazz in the second half of the twentieth century.

Manheim

WORLD EVENTS		PARKER'S LIFE
Russian Revolution	1917	
	1920	Charlie Parker is born
Great Depression	1929–39	
World War II	1939–45	
	1939	Parker moves to New York City
	1940	Parker records with Jay McShann
	1943	Parker plays with Dizzy Gillespie at Minton's
	1945	Parker forms own band
	1946	Parker is hospitalized for substance abuse
Communist China is established	1949	Parker makes first visit to Europe
Korean War	1950–53	
	1954	Parker attempts suicide twice
	1955	Parker dies
African independence movement begins	1957	

For Further Reading

Giddins, Gary. *Celebrating Bird: The Life of Charlie Parker.* New York: Da Capo, 1998.

Koch, Lawrence O. *Yardbird Suite : A Compendium of the Music and Life of Charlie Parker.* Boston: Northeastern University Press, 1999.

Russell, Ross. *Bird Lives: The High Life and Hard Times of Charlie (Yardbird) Parker.* New York: Da Capo, 1996.

Paz, Octavio

Poet, Essayist, and Journalist
1914–1998

Life and Work

Octavio Paz united intense political and social awareness, intimate emotion, spiritual expression, and abstract language in his writing and profoundly influenced twentieth-century poetry.

Paz was born in Mexico City, Mexico, in March 1914, the son of an eminent lawyer who had defended the peasant revolutionary leader Emiliano Zapata. His family lost its wealth in the Mexican Civil War and he grew up poor, studying at a Roman Catholic school

WORLD EVENTS		PAZ'S LIFE
Spanish-American War	1898	
World War I	1914–18	
	1914	Octavio Paz is born
Russian Revolution	1917	
Great Depression	1929–39	
	1931	Paz founds literary magazine, *Barrandal*
	1933	Paz publishes first volume of poetry
	1937	Paz travels to Paris for Writers' Congress
World War II	1939–45	
	1943	Paz receives Guggenheim grant
Communist China is established	1949	
Korean War	1950–53	
	1950	Paz publishes *The Labyrinth of Solitude*
African independence movement begins	1957	
Vietnam War ends	1975	
	1990	Paz receives Nobel Prize for Literature
Dissolution of Soviet Union	1991	
South Africa dismantles apartheid	1994	
	1998	Paz dies

and then at the University of Mexico. He founded a literary magazine, *Barrandal*, that published avant-garde poetry in 1931 and his first volume of poetry, *Luna silvestre* (*Forest Moon*), was published in 1933.

In 1937 Paz was invited by PABLO NERUDA to join the Writers' Congress against fascism in Paris. He was profoundly affected by the politics of the congress as well as by his exposure to Parisian Surrealism, an art and literary movement that, unlike traditional Realism, used contrasting imagery and automatic writing to convey the real experience of thought. Paz subsequently became one of the main introducers of Surrealism to Mexico.

The history and character of Mexico were central to Paz's poetry and prose. In his early poetry he experimented with form, using Surrealist techniques to renew and refresh the Spanish language as he wrote about political and social issues. The collection *Aguila o sol?* (*Eagle or Sun?*, 1951) consisted of a sequence of visionary prose poems about the past, present, and future of Mexico. *Piedra de sol* (*Sun Stone*, 1957) used the structure of the Aztec calendar and blended myth, social and political commentary, and history and personal experience. In *El Laberinto de la soledad* (*The Labyrinth of Solitude*, 1950) he discussed Mexican history, mythology, and social behavior, examining Mexican identity with its mixed Indian and Spanish heritage and how it interacted with the United States. Much of his work was also strongly influenced by Eastern philosophy, as seen in his haiku works and in his collection of poetry *Ladera este* (*East Slope*, 1971), based on concepts of Hindu mysticism.

Paz's work in literary theory, criticism, and history included a broad history of modern poetry, *Los Hijos del limo: del romanticismo a la vanguardia* (*Children of the Mire: Modern Poetry from Romanticism to the Avant-Garde,* 1974) as well as *Sor Juana, o las trampas de la fe* (*Sor Juana: Or, The Trap of Faith*, 1982), a scholarly work on SOR JUANA INÉS DE LA CRUZ, the Mexican nun, scholar, and poet of the 1600s.

In 1943 Paz was awarded a Guggenheim grant in the United States. He served as the Mexican ambassador to India from 1962 to 1968, and later he taught at several American universities. In 1990 Paz was awarded the Nobel Prize for Literature, the first Mexican writer to be so honored. He died on April 20, 1998.

Legacy

Octavio Paz in his poetry and essays on esthetics, politics, Surrealist art, cultural anthropology, Mexican identity, and Eastern philosophy adopted a wide array of techniques and influences to create a uniquely abstract poetic tradition for Latin America.

Paz's work, with its Eastern influence and abstract meditations, had more in common with that of JORGE LUIS BORGES than with that of his fellow poet, Pablo Neruda. Rather than constructing the poem as a direct expression of his own emotion and experience as Neruda did, Paz saw a need for the poet to transcend the limitations of the self. Similar to Borges, Paz sought a universal poetic language that, like philosophical language, would be capable of addressing the enormity of the world's diversity. His abstract language and his blend of myth and intimate personal emotion, so unlike Neruda's populist poetry, have had a profound effect on twentieth-century art.

Paz redefined the avant-garde in Latin American literature, drawing on the works of Arthur Rimbaud, Stéphane Mallarmé, and EZRA POUND, and uniting Surrealist techniques with Mexican history and character. He endowed the experimental with a deeply personal emotional weight as he asserted that language and love could create meaning and wholeness out of the chaos of life.

With his close attention to language, Paz rejected the ornate and cliched rhetoric of the avant-garde at the beginning of the twentieth century, and brought a direct, vernacular diction into Spanish poetry. Paz was not alone in his attempt to revitalize the language. Short story writer Julio Cortázar, novelists GABRIEL GARCÍA MÁRQUEZ and Enrique Molina, and poets Mario Benedetti, Jaime Sabines, and José Emilio Pacheco all followed Paz and continued this effort, together creating a new mythic language in which to recount the stories and emotions of Latin America.

Paz's work treated specifically Mexican concerns as well as the universal themes of human isolation and love. His work was widely recognized both in and out of Latin America; in the United States his poems were translated by the poets William Carlos Williams and Muriel Rukeyser.

Watson

For Further Reading

Quiroga, José. *Understanding Octavio Paz.* Columbia: University of South Carolina Press, 1998.
Weinberger, Eliot, ed. *The Collected Poems of Octavio Paz 1957–1987.* New York: New Directions Books, 1987.

Piaf, Edith

Vocalist

1915–1963

Life and Work

One of the most popular French singers of the twentieth century, Edith Piaf gained international acclaim, even reaching audiences with no understanding of the French language.

Piaf was born Edith Giovanna Gassion in Paris on December 19, 1915. The daughter of a traveling acrobat and a young carnival worker, she had a childhood of extreme deprivation and instability. Piaf's maternal grandmother gave her wine to make her sleep; she would struggle with addiction for her entire life. By age 15 she was living a precarious existence on and off the streets of Paris with a friend. A daughter she bore in 1933 died in infancy.

Dressed in rags, she was discovered singing on the street in 1935 by Paris nightclub owner Louis Leplée. He gave her the name Piaf—Parisian slang for "sparrow"—because of her small stature. Her first commercial performance was praised by Maurice Chevalier, the leading French vocalist of the period.

Leplée was murdered in 1936, and press accounts placed Piaf under suspicion of the crime. But she overcame the scandal, making her radio debut that year and appearing in Paris's leading music halls. She scored a success in 1937 with "Mon Légionnaire" ("My Legionnaire"), perhaps the first of many songs

in which she took up the theme of abandonment. Piaf's profile rose in Paris's music halls in the late 1930s. During World War II she sang for French prisoners of war, and is said to have helped some of them escape confinement by bringing them forged documents.

Piaf rose to international stardom after the war, thanks partly to the strong sales of her 1946 hit "La Vie en Rose" ("Life in the Color Rose"), which she co-wrote. Singing mostly in French in the notoriously monolingual United States, she nevertheless enjoyed considerable success. She was one of those very few vocalists in whose performances singer and song seem indissoluble, whose art seems to directly reflect their lives. The waif-like Piaf on stage, clothed in a plain black dress, was a figure of almost existential loneliness.

Several automobile accidents in the 1950s left Piaf addicted to morphine and her health deteriorated. She achieved two of her biggest hits with 1954s "La Goulante de Pauvre Jean" (known in English as "The Poor People of Paris") and 1960s "Non, Je Ne Regrette Rien" ("No, I Regret Nothing"). She died on October 10, 1963, in Plascassier, France.

Legacy

Edith Piaf's instantly recognizable voice, honed to its bleakly passionate edge by a lifetime of tragedy, compelled identification at a level beyond words.

The international reach she enjoyed during and after her life eclipsed that of other French performers, whose popularity has proven difficult to transplant to foreign countries. "La Vie en Rose" and other songs were well known in the United States in the 1950s, with cover versions of her hits attempted by acts as varied as Lawrence Welk and the country vocal group The Browns.

Piaf's lasting popularity, however, has extended beyond the songs she made famous. As much as any of her American pop counterparts, she was an archetype of the torch singer. "Piaf was not the only singer to destroy herself as she sang of the destruction of love," wrote her biographer Margaret Crosland, comparing Piaf with such ill-fated contemporaries as BILLIE HOLIDAY and Judy Garland. Like the other members of that elite sisterhood, Piaf lived her life in the glare of publicity, and, like them, she came of age as a singer in tumultuous times. She tapped a deep stratum of dis-

satisfaction that ran through the lives of those who heard her songs.

Piaf remained widely known in Europe and America for decades after her death. When female musical artists such as Janis Joplin began to embrace a romantic self-destructiveness in the tradition of males, they found that Piaf had already blazed the way.

With several film appearances to her credit, Piaf became the subject of various documentaries and fictional treatments after her death, including the 1993 full-length stage work *Piaf*. The younger performers who continued to discover her work were also a diverse group, ranging from dance queen Grace Jones, who recorded "La Vie en Rose" in 1985, to the assortment of artists who contributed to the 1995 CD *Tribute: Edith Piaf*. One of the last great vocalists to emerge from the French music hall, Piaf had few direct successors, but the depth with which she expressed herself in song may well prove timeless.

Manheim

World Events	Piaf's Life
World War I 1914–18	
1915	Edith Piaf is born
Russian Revolution 1917	
Great Depression 1929–39	
1935	Piaf is discovered singing on streets of Paris
1937	Piaf scores success with recording "Mon Legionnaire"
World War II 1939–45	
1946	Piaf records "La Vie en Rose"
Communist China 1949 is established	
Korean War 1950–53	
1954	Piaf records "La Goulante de Pauvre Jean"
African independence 1957 movement begins	
1963	Piaf dies
Vietnam War ends 1975	

For Further Reading

Bret, David. *The Piaf Legend*. London: Robson, 1989.

Crosland, Margaret. *Piaf*. New York: Putnam, 1985.

Piazzolla, Astor

Composer
1921–1992

Life and Work

Among audiences worldwide, the name most identified with the tango, modern-day Argentina's national musical emblem, has been Astor Piazzolla.

Piazzolla (Pia-SOL-a) was born in Mar del Plata, Argentina, on March 11, 1921. When he was young, his family moved to New York's Little Italy neighborhood, and he grew up hearing American jazz and pop music; the compositions of DUKE ELLINGTON and GEORGE GERSHWIN in particular would influence his own attitudes. But his father gave him a *bandoneón*, a large Argentine accordion, as a musical memento of the family's homeland, and he also studied classical music. From these mixed seeds would grow Piazzolla's unique musical personality.

In 1934 he made a recording with the Argentine tango pioneer Carlos Gardel. Returning to Argentina, he played the *bandoneón* in a Buenos Aires tango orchestra from 1936 to 1944, but dreamed of a classical career. A chance meeting with pianist Arthur Rubinstein led to an introduction to Alberto Ginastera, Argentina's leading composer, and to several years of classical study. Piazzolla's first major piece fusing classical and homegrown Argentine influences, the *Sinfonia Buenos Aires,* gained international acclaim but was poorly received in Piazzolla's home country.

In 1954, Piazzolla went to Paris to extend his classical studies, working with the most famous composition teacher of the time, Nadia Boulanger. Paradoxically, however, the experience led him to reconnect with the tango; Boulanger, after hearing him play one of his tango pieces on the piano, told him never to abandon the tango. The *nuevo tango* (new tango) music that Piazzolla created upon returning to Argentina broke sharply with that music's traditional sound, and once again antagonized the music's Argentine partisans, one of whom even threatened him with a gun on one occasion. Often written for his Quinteto Tango Nuevo, the group he formed in 1960 that featured violin, guitar, piano, bass, and *bandoneón,* Piazzolla's more than 750 tango compositions included complex harmonies drawn from the world of modern concert music.

The 1968 stage work *Maria de Buenos Aires: A Tango-Operita,* inspired by Gershwin's *Porgy and Bess,* finally won over tango traditionalists, and for the last two decades of his life Piazzolla was considered an Argentine hero. Internationally, his reputation with both popular and specialized audiences continued to grow; his compositions became part of the 1986 U.S. musical *Tango Argentina* and also attracted progressive musicians, such as the members of the Kronos Quartet, who recorded Piazzolla's *Five Tango Sensations* of 1989. He died in Buenos Aires on July 5, 1992.

Legacy

Piazzolla was one of the twentieth century's great creative border crossers, blurring the increasingly strict line between popular and classical music.

"For me," Piazzolla once said, "tango was always for the ear rather than the feet." Piazzolla breathed new life into the tango itself, a dance music that emerged early in the twentieth century from the taverns and bordellos of Buenos Aires to become an international craze. By the latter part of the century the tango was under siege even within Argentina by more contemporary forms, but Piazzolla reawakened interest in the music, and the international exposure given his works touched off a series of tango films, stage productions, and recordings. The tango became part of the revival of ballroom dance that flourished toward the century's end, and most North American cities featured organizations of tango enthusiasts. The key to Piazzolla's popularity was that no matter how much he experimented with the musical materials of tango, he never lost touch with its sensual yet despairing emotional essence.

Piazzolla's unique blend of tango, classical music, and jazz stimulated new fusions that kept the tango alive and vibrant in Argentina, notably the *tango rokéro* (tango rock) of the 1970s. After his death the stylistic mixture he pioneered continued to resonate, and the dimensions of his accomplishment became clear. Jazz musicians, such as guitarists Al DiMeola and Charlie Byrd and the vibraphonist Gary Burton, have used Piazzolla's music as a point of departure.

The classical market saw the release of several compact discs of Piazzolla's music at the end of the 1990s, with performances by the Latvian violin virtuoso Gidon Kremer proving that despite its association with the *bandoneón,* Piazzolla's music could be effectively transferred to other instruments. At the turn of the century, Piazzolla seemed likely to take his place in musical history along with the very few other musicians who bridged the twentieth century's great divide between high art and popular culture.

Manheim

World Events		Piazzolla's Life	
Russian Revolution	1917		
	1921	Astor Piazzolla is born in Mar del Plata, Argentina	
Great Depression	1929–39		
	1934	Piazzolla records with Carlos Gardel	
	1936	Piazzolla begins performing with tango orchestra in Buenos Aires	
World War II	1939–45		
Communist China is established	1949		
Korean War	1950–53		
	1954	Piazzolla studies in Paris with Nadia Boulanger	
African independence movement begins	1957		
	1960	Piazzolla forms Quinteto Tango Nuevo	
	1968	Piazzolla composes *Maria de Buenos Aires*	
Vietnam War ends	1975		
	1986	Piazzolla's compositions are included in musical *Tango Argentina*	
	1989	Kronos Quartet stimulates Piazzolla revival with recording	
Dissolution of Soviet Union	1991		
	1992	Piazzolla dies	
South Africa dismantles apartheid	1994		

For Further Reading

Azzi, Maria Susana, and Simon Collier. *Le Grand Tango: A Biography of Astor Piazzolla.* New York: Oxford University Press, 2000.
Muñoz, Isabel. *Tango.* New York: Stewart, Tabori, and Chang, 1997.
Schnabel, Tom. *Rhythm Planet: The Great World Music Makers.* New York: Universe Publishing, 1998.

Picasso, Pablo

Painter and Sculptor

1881–1973

Life and Work

For much of the twentieth century, Pablo Picasso was the most famous artist in the world and was an innovator in many modern forms.

Picasso was born in 1881 in Malaga, Spain. The son of an art teacher, the young Picasso quickly established himself as a child prodigy. As a teenager, he studied in the Barcelona Academy and the Academy in Madrid, where he mastered the techniques of academic painting.

In 1900, Picasso traveled to Paris, where he was introduced to the Post-Impressionist avant-garde art of PAUL CÉZANNE and Paul Gaugin. In 1904 Picasso moved to Paris and began to experiment with new styles of painting. In his so-called Blue Period (1901–05), he painted images of people on the margins of French society in a somber blue palette. In his subsequent Rose Period, Picasso continued to explore human figures, but in a lighter, less morose manner.

Between 1905 and 1907 Picasso's style changed dramatically. He became deeply interested in so-called "primitive" art, particularly African masks and the archaic sculpture of his native Spain. His revolutionary painting *Les Demoiselles d'Avignon* (1907) drew on both sources. Starting with a traditional academic subject, a group of female nudes in a harem-like setting, Picasso created a brutally confrontational image of five prostitutes—the title refers to Avignon Street, the red-light district of Barcelona—aggressively confronting the viewer. The bodies of the women have been broken into the broad planes of Iberian sculpture and two of the faces are rendered as African masks.

Picasso's experiments with form soon led him, along with his colleague Georges Braque, to the development of Cubism, the most radical style of the new century. To some extent, Cubism can be seen as a continuation of Cézanne's attempts to reconfigure the three-dimensional forms of the objects he painted into geometrical shapes suited to his two-dimensional canvas. In paintings such as *Ma Jolie* (1911–12), Picasso went even further, breaking down the image of a young woman playing a guitar into its component parts and reassembling them as a pattern of rectilinear facets.

In 1937, during the Spanish Civil War, Picasso was commissioned by the Spanish government to create a painting for the Spanish Pavilion at the World's Fair in Paris. Earlier that year German pilots, in support of the fascists commanded by the future dictator Francisco Franco, had bombed the town of Guernica, killing hundreds of civilians. In his monumental painting *Guernica* (1937), a tangled pile of anguished and broken figures represent the brutality of war.

Picasso remained an international celebrity throughout his long life. He died in 1973 at the age of 92.

Legacy

An extraordinarily successful self-promoter, Pablo Picasso was the most famous artist of the twentieth century. He not only influenced virtually every major art movement of the century, but also epitomized the popular image of the modern artist as a creative, hyper-masculine, extroverted bohemian.

Cubism, the movement Picasso launched with Braque, became the model for subsequent formal revolutions like Italian Futurism, Russian Constuctivism, French Orphism, and British Vorticism. In the 1920s and 1930s Picasso's work was also tied to Surrealism.

When the American art world began to grow rapidly in the years after World War II, Picasso was the world's leading avant-garde artist. The artists of the Abstract Expressionist generation all educated themselves in Picasso's work, some to the point of obsession, and related to him as a powerful father figure. New York School artists such as JACKSON POLLOCK, Arshile Gorky, David Smith, and Willem de Kooning both incorporated and reacted against his achievement in their own work.

In more recent years, interest in Picasso has produced a sizeable industry. In 1985, the *Musée Picasso* opened in Paris. Picasso has been the subject of popular and scholarly biographies, innumerable academic studies, large-scale retrospectives, and ongoing critical reevaluations. Lately, there has been a growing interest in examining his often stormy relationships with the many women in his life. Picasso's exaggerated sense of masculinity is seen not only in his personal life but in his work.

Picasso's familiar imagery has been appropriated for use in all sorts of mass-produced artifacts, from shopping bags to T-shirts, and his name has become a sort of cultural talisman to be invoked by anyone who needs a shorthand term for "modern art."

McEnroe

WORLD EVENTS		PICASSO'S LIFE
Germany is united	1871	
	1881	Pablo Picasso is born
Spanish-American War	1898	
	1901–05	Picasso's Blue Period
	1907	Picasso paints *Les Demoiselles d'Avignon*
World War I	1914–18	
Russian Revolution	1917	
Great Depression	1929–39	
	1937	Picasso paints *Guernica*
World War II	1939–45	
Communist China is established	1949	
Korean War	1950–53	
African independence movement begins	1957	
	1973	Picasso dies
Vietnam War ends	1975	

For Further Reading

Huffington, Arianna Stassinopoulos. *Picasso: Creator and Destroyer.* New York: Simon & Schuster, 1988.

McCully, Marilyn, ed. *Picasso: The Early Years, 1892–1906.* Washington, D.C.: National Gallery of Art, 1997.

Richardson, John. *A Life of Picasso.* Vol. 1, *1881–1906.* Vol. 2: *1907–1917: The Painter of Modern Life.* With the collaboration of Marilyn McCully. New York: Random House, 1991; 1996.

Pollock, Jackson

Painter

1912–1956

Life and Work

Jackson Pollock created a unique form of Abstract Expressionism and was a key figure in the surge of interest in avant-garde art in post–World War II America.

Pollock was born in Cody, Wyoming, in 1912 and remained proud of his individualist Western heritage throughout his life. He began his study of art in Los Angeles in 1928 and moved to New York two years later to study with the muralist Thomas Hart Benton.

Like many artists during the Great Depression, Pollock was employed by the WPA Federal Arts project, painting murals and panels in a social realist style similar to Benton's. Later, when he had developed his own style, Pollock would refer to the domineering Benton as a good person to react against.

WORLD EVENTS		POLLOCK'S LIFE
Spanish-American War	1898	
	1912	Jackson Pollock is born
World War I	1914–18	
Russian Revolution	1917	
Great Depression	1929–39	
	1930	Pollock moves to New York
	1938	Pollock is treated for alcoholism
World War II	1939–45	
	1943	Pollock's first one-person show
	1946	Pollock begins "drip" paintings
Communist China is established	1949	
Korean War	1950–53	
	1956	Pollock dies
African independence movement begins	1957	

In 1939 Pollock saw PABLO PICASSO's *Guernica* at the Valentine Gallery in New York. *Guernica* opened his eyes to the potential of avant-garde painting. Soon Pollock began to experiment with Surrealist "automatism." In this technique, akin to stream-of-consciousness writing, the artist's subconscious is assumed to guide the painting process directly, unmediated and unfettered by rational planning or control. Pollock connected this technique with the Jungian analysis he had begun in 1938 to treat his alcoholism.

Pollock met the painter Lee Krasner in 1942, and they married in 1945. Krasner introduced Pollock to the major figures of the New York art world. His first one-person show was held at Peggy Guggenheim's Art of this Century gallery in 1943. Clement Greenberg, who would emerge as the most influential critic of the Abstract Expressionist movement, saw the show and from that point on remained Pollock's unfailing supporter.

In 1946 Pollock began painting in a new studio in Long Island where he developed the "drip" paintings for which he is best known. To make these paintings, Pollock laid large sheets of canvas on the floor and, moving around them as if in an energetic trance, dripped and threw paint on them with brushes, sticks and turkey basters, or poured directly from cans. The critic Harold Rosenberg characterized this process as "action painting"—painting as a record of the artist's existential interaction with the canvas.

By 1949, Pollock was widely recognized as the most radical of the new generation of avant-garde painters. That year, a cover story in *Life* magazine asked: "Is Jackson Pollock the Greatest Living Painter in the United States?"

Despite his fame, Pollock never achieved great wealth from his work. His alcoholism grew worse, and in 1956 he drove his car into a tree, killing himself and a female passenger.

Legacy

The *Life* magazine article made Jackson Pollock notorious, a frequent subject of sarcasm and satire in popular media catering to a mass public bewildered by modern art; *Time* magazine dubbed him "Jack the Dripper."

Today, Pollock is regarded as one of the pivotal figures in the history of modern art. His

career stands between the traditional styles of American art in the first half of the twentieth century and the abstraction that dominated American art in the second half of that century. His career also coincided with the postwar international ascendancy of the United States and of New York as the major center of modern art in the world. Pollock's international reputation grew as Abstract Expressionism was promoted via State Department–sponsored shows of American painting in Europe. In the early Cold War atmosphere, vigorous, individualistic—and nonpolitical—Abstract Expressionist paintings were presented as the embodiment of American virtues, in contrast both to European and to Soviet-style ideas about culture. New York had surpassed Paris as the cultural center of the postwar world, and Pollock was the quintessential American hero, a kind of art cowboy.

Today there is growing appreciation of Pollock. He has been the subject of at least three biographies. A massive retrospective was mounted at the Museum of Modern Art in New York in 1998, and in 2000 a Hollywood film about Pollock's life was released. Pollock's popular image, like that of James Dean, remains that of the rebellious, unfettered individualist—a tragic hero who struggled against conformity and the middle-class sentimentalities of artists such as NORMAN ROCKWELL. A disturbed alcoholic during his brief life, Pollock has become an icon of popular culture as well as one of the heroes of modern art.

McEnroe

For Further Reading

Landau, Ellen G. *Jackson Pollock.* New York: Harry N. Abrams, 1989.

Naifeh, Steven W., and Gregory White Smith. *Jackson Pollock: An American Saga.* New York: Harper Perennial, 1991.

O'Connor, Francis V., and E. V. Thaw. *Jackson Pollock: A Catalogue Raisonné of Paintings, Drawings and Other Works.* 4 vols. New Haven, Conn.: Yale University Press, 1978.

Pound, Ezra

Poet

1885–1972

Life and Work

Ezra Pound is regarded as an important progenitor of Modernism in poetry. His life was more controversial than his works; during World War II he made radio broadcasts on behalf of Italy's fascist rulers and was subsequently imprisoned by the U.S. government.

Ezra Loomis Pound was born in Hailey, Idaho, on October 30, 1885; his family moved to suburban Philadelphia after his father landed a job at the U.S. Mint. As a young man, Pound expressed a grand ambition to learn more about poetry than anyone else in the world. Pound attended the University of Pennsylvania and Hamilton College in upstate New York, graduating from the latter in 1905. He then enrolled in graduate school at the University of Pennsylvania; by the time he left for Europe two years later, with $80 in his pocket, he had mastered eight languages, including Latin and ancient Greek.

Landing in England after various travels, Pound found admirers and quickly published several books of poetry. He befriended other innovative writers, including JAMES JOYCE, ROBERT FROST, and T. S. Eliot, arranging for publication of their works and even rounding up financial support; he served for a time as WILLIAM BUTLER YEATS's secretary and influenced the older poet as well. In the 1910s he was associated with a group of poets known as Imagists, who cultivated a sparse style based on the brief, intense depiction of specific images or moments.

Pound moved to Paris in 1921 and to Italy in 1924; by 1930 he had completed *A Draft of XXX Cantos,* the first version of his major work, *The Cantos.* It is a series of fragmentary verses written in an extremely dense and allusive poetic language. Pound continued to add sections to this work for the rest of his life. (A single-volume version was published in 1969.)

When World War II began, Pound, who admired Italian dictator Benito Mussolini, remained in Italy; beginning in 1941, he made anti-American radio broadcasts that included anti-Semitic elements. At the war's end he was seized by American troops, charged with treason, and kept for several months in an outdoor cage. Returned to the United States in 1945, he was declared insane in lieu of a trial and confined to a mental hospital in Washington, D.C.

In the hospital, Pound wrote prolifically and was more or less free to receive visitors and conduct interviews with the press. In 1958, a campaign led by a number of well-known writers and critics, including, most influentially, Frost, succeeded in getting him released. Pound returned to Italy and died in Venice on November 1, 1972.

Legacy

Ezra Pound's legacy is sometimes thought to have resided as much in his energetic promotion of Modernist trends in the arts as in his own sometimes bewildering poetry. His writings themselves were influential in several respects, however.

Pound's influence was strong on the works of a few of his contemporaries. Eliot, especially, owed major features of his overall stance as a poet to Pound—both poets sought to integrate experimental manipulation of the technical elements of poetry into a dense universe of traditional erudition, and both tried to use the abbreviated, elliptical language of Modernism to achieve a dignified, classical melancholy. Eliot's long poem *The Waste Land,* which Pound edited, to its great benefit, and which is dedicated to him, rivaled Pound's own work in the density of its historical and classical references.

Another aspect of Pound's work that proved influential later in the century was his interest in poets of other languages. He translated classical Latin, medieval French, and Italian, and Chinese poetry, Japanese *Noh* dramas, and, late in life, ancient Egyptian poetry. Pound seemed at times to be trying to define the place of the arts in human existence, and this led him to a viewpoint that encompassed the artistic expressions of other cultures long before it was in vogue.

Pound's belief in the centrality of the arts might be seen as having contributed to the negative aspect of Pound's legacy. Frustrated with the impersonality of modern life, assuming the superior wisdom of poets and artists and believing that they should hold prominent places in society, he allowed his interest in politics and economics to lead him into the advocacy of antidemocratic panaceas, including, ultimately, fascism. It was a tragic conclusion to the life of a man whom his contemporaries considered generous and inspirational.

Manheim

WORLD EVENTS		POUND'S LIFE
Germany is united	1871	
	1885	Ezra Pound is born in Hailey, Idaho
Spanish-American War	1898	
	1908	Pound leaves the United States for Europe
World War I	1914–18	
Russian Revolution	1917	
	1924	Pound settles in Italy
Great Depression	1929–39	
	1930	Pound completes *A Draft of XXX Cantos*
World War II	1939–45	
	1941	Pound makes anti-U.S. broadcasts on Italian radio
	1945	Pound is confined to a mental hospital
Communist China is established	1949	
Korean War	1950–53	
African independence movement begins	1957	
	1958	Pound is released from hospital
	1972	Pound dies
Vietnam War ends	1975	

For Further Reading

Alexander, Michael. *The Poetic Achievement of Ezra Pound.* Berkeley: University of California Press, 1979.

Casillo, Robert. *The Genealogy of Demons: Anti-Semitism, Fascism, and the Myths of Ezra Pound.* Evanston, Ill.: Northwestern University Press, 1988.

Kenner, Hugh. *The Pound Era.* Berkeley: University of California Press, 1971.

Wilhelm, James J. *Ezra Pound: The Tragic Years, 1925–1972.* State College: Pennsylvania State University Press, 1994.

Presley, Elvis

Vocalist

1935–1977

Life and Work

More than any other musician, Elvis Presley is identified with rock and roll music, and, as such, he stands as the icon of an American art form that is still vital nearly a half century later.

Presley was born in Tupelo, Mississippi, on January 8, 1935. His family moved to Memphis in 1948, and beyond a somewhat rebellious personal style and an immersion in gospel music both black and white, little about Presley's youth hinted at what was to come.

Sun Records owner Sam Phillips saw in Presley an explosive performer who could merge the country and rhythm-and-blues styles. Presley quit his truck-driving job and began to tour as "The Hillbilly Cat"; his debut Sun recordings in 1954 and 1955, most

notably "That's All Right Mama" and "Mystery Train," sold well and grabbed the attention of various talent watchers. Presley's loose-legged, semierotic stage moves stirred controversy and invaluable publicity, and he was signed to the RCA record label. His first RCA single, "Heartbreak Hotel," was released early in 1956 and spent eight weeks as the country's number one song.

Such giant hits as "Don't Be Cruel" and "Hound Dog" soon made Presley the dominant figure of the fast-advancing rock-and-roll genre. Those records set the pattern for much of Presley's music in the 1950s; rooted vocally in black rhythm and blues, they featured smooth harmonizations from the vocal group the Jordanaires. Presley continued to top the charts even after his 1958 induction into the U.S. Army. His music veered in a pop direction with 1960's "Are You Lonesome Tonight?" (a remake of an Al Jolson recitation number) and "It's Now or Never." Presley also made a string of light musical-themed movies that were poorly received by critics.

A 1968 comeback was launched with a television performance in which Presley seemed to recapture his rock-and-roll roots. He again topped the charts with "In the Ghetto" and "Suspicious Minds." In total Presley placed over 100 records in the Top Forty, and he is said to have sold over a billion recordings worldwide.

Presley's weight ballooned in the 1970s, and he became primarily identified with performances in Las Vegas-style nightclubs. His death came at his Memphis mansion, Graceland, on August 16, 1977; while heart failure was listed as the cause, it was widely speculated that his use of prescription medications and other drugs was a factor.

Legacy

It is commonly said that Elvis Presley fused white country music with black rhythm and blues to create rock and roll. In fact white vocalists had been experimenting with black popular styles for decades, some of them quite successfully, and musical interaction between white and black Southerners was as old as American slavery. Presley was, however, a path breaker of a different kind.

Presley changed American music not just by being a white performer who had "the Negro

feel," as Sam Phillips put it, but by being musically protean enough to make the mixture work in many different contexts, including that of a controlled and carefully produced major studio popular sound. The two halves of his vocal personality give a clue to his versatility: Presley was both a screamer and a crooner, and in each song he sang he was able to combine the two inventively. To some extent, he helped to create the rock-and-roll phenomenon, but he also helped the music industry tame it.

A great deal of rock-and-roll music from 1956 through the Beatles-led British invasion of 1964 was patterned after Presley's recordings, but that music imitated the flawlessly promoted Presley of RCA Victor rather than the rockabilly artist of untrammeled passion who had recorded for Sun.

Except in the field of country music, where his bluesy crooning influenced performers such as Ronnie Milsap, Presley had few direct musical followers. So extraordinary were his personality and vocal style that any trace of them in another performer's act had to devolve into parody, or simply into the Elvis imitations practiced profitably by thousands of small-time performers for decades after Presley's death.

Presley's most lasting influence has been as a symbol—of a new popular music fundamentally influenced by black culture and of an emerging liberated sexuality. During his life, Presley succeeded musically in part by trying to be all things to all people. In his death the meanings the American public attached to his life and music only continued to multiply.

Manheim

For Further Reading

Brown, Peter H. *Down at the End of Lonely Street: The Life and Death of Elvis Presley*. New York: Dutton, 1997.
Guralnick, Peter. *Careless Love: The Unmaking of Elvis Presley*. Boston: Little, Brown, 1999.
———. *Last Train to Memphis: The Rise of Elvis Presley*. Boston: Little, Brown, 1994.

WORLD EVENTS	PRESLEY'S LIFE
Great Depression 1929–39	
1935	Elvis Presley is born in Tupelo, Mississippi
World War II 1939–45	
1948	Presley moves with his family to Memphis
Communist China 1949 is established	
Korean War 1950–53	
1954	Presley begins recording for Sun label
1955	Presley is signed to RCA label
1956	Presley releases "Heartbreak Hotel"
African independence 1957 movement begins	
1958	Presley is inducted into the U.S. Army
1960	Presley turns toward pop with "It's Now or Never"
1968	Presley launches comeback with television special
Vietnam War ends 1975	
1977	Presley dies
Dissolution of 1991 Soviet Union	

Proust, Marcel

Novelist

1871–1922

Life and Work

On the basis of a single monumental novel, *A la recherche du temps perdu* (*In Search of Lost Time;* in English, *Remembrance of Things Past*), Marcel Proust is considered to be the most significant French novelist of the twentieth century.

Proust was born near Paris on July 10, 1871. He was the son of a prominent doctor and grew up in a privileged environment, attending the private schools and frequenting the resorts and salons of the very wealthy. He suffered his first asthma attack at age nine, and for the rest of his life his health was precarious. In later years he insisted on living in a cork-lined, soundproofed room. Proust's mother was Jewish, and in the famous Dreyfus Affair of 1897–99, Proust emerged as one of the Jewish army officer's notable defenders. Proust's homosexuality, camouflaged by several love affairs with women, led to a duel fought with a critic who had insinuated the truth, but he emerged unhurt.

After finishing a university degrees in law and literature, Proust published a group of short stories, *Les Plaisirs et les jours* (*Pleasures and Days*), in 1896. An unfinished autobiographical novel, *Jean Santeuil* (1895–99), was in some respects a first draft for his magnum opus, but he set the book aside after discovering the writings of the British art critic John Ruskin, some of which he undertook to translate. Ruskin's essays renewed artistic interest in France's towering cathedrals of the medieval era; Proust himself likened the structure of his great work to that of a Gothic cathedral. Proust began *Remembrance of Things Past* in 1909; its first, mostly self-sufficient volume, *Du côté de chez Swann* (*Swann's Way*), was published in 1913. The novel grew to seven volumes, of which the last three remained unfinished at Proust's death. Modern editions run to over 3,000 pages. Near the beginning of the novel is a scene in which the unnamed narrator is flooded with childhood memories after eating a small cake called a *madeleine;* the novel as a whole weaves an enormous variety of subplots around events of profound significance in the narrator's life.

As subsequent volumes of the novel appeared, Proust's fame grew. In 1922 Proust contracted pneumonia, perhaps brought on by the combination of asthma and caffeine abuse, and died on November 8 of that year.

Legacy

For many reasons, *Remembrance of Things Past* has reverberated in readers' memories, both in France and beyond. Monumental in a way that few later novels have been, it delves deeply into history and social structure, music, art, politics, the natural world, and many other aspects of life. Particularly compelling in recent years, however, have been its emphasis on psychology, its pioneering treatment of homosexuality, and the complex relationship between the author and his creation.

Marcel Proust's characters emerge in pages-long paragraphs, packed with cascades of thoughts and images, not in the seemingly helter-skelter stream of consciousness of JAMES JOYCE but exquisitely balanced in an almost musical flow. The *madeleine* episode is but one of many in the novel that exploit a modern understanding of what we would call psychology. Since Proust, popular fiction, film, and television drama have often used similar devices to reveal their characters' memories to their audiences.

Proust's psychological insights were nowhere keener than in the area of human sexuality, of which he was really the first modern fictional investigator. Troubled by guilt over his own homosexuality, he was in no way a crusader for gay rights; the primary gay character in *Remembrance of Things Past* is unsympathetically treated and comes to a tragic end. Nevertheless, the fact that Proust avoided the destruction experienced by the homosexual British playwright Oscar Wilde and went on to introduce homosexuality as an important plot element at several points in his masterwork is regarded as a milestone in the emergence of a gay subculture into the larger culture.

Although it is told entirely in a realistic mode and rooted in nineteenth-century French fiction in many respects, *Remembrance of Things Past* treated the slippery and challenging relationship between artist and creation in an entirely original way. The novel's narrator is not outwardly a confessional Proust, but after all its convolutions, the story the novel tells is the story of its own genesis—another device that has been widely adopted. Its narrator, revealed toward the end to be named Marcel, begins writing a book—the very book that has just absorbed the reader for over 3,000 pages. Thus Proust takes his place among and helps to inspire the many twentieth-century novelists who make the storyteller part of the story.

Manheim

WORLD EVENTS		PROUST'S LIFE
U.S. Civil War	1861–65	
Germany is united	1871	Marcel Proust is born near Paris
	1893	Proust earns law degree
	1895	Proust earns literature degree
Spanish-American War	1898	
	1909	Proust begins writing *Remembrance of Things Past*
	1913	Proust publishes first volume of *Remembrance of Things Past, Swann's Way*
World War I	1914–18	
Russian Revolution	1917	
	1919–22	Proust works on last three volumes of *Remembrance of Things Past*
	1922	Proust dies
Great Depression	1929–39	

For Further Reading

Rivers, J. E. *Proust and the Art of Love: The Aesthetics of Sexuality and the Life, Times & Art of Marcel Proust.* New York: Columbia University Press, 1980.

Painter, George D. *Proust: The Early Years.* Boston: Atlantic-Little, Brown, 1959.

———. *Proust: The Later Years.* Boston: Atlantic-Little, Brown, 1965.

Shattuck, Roger. *Marcel Proust.* New York: Viking, 1974.

Pushkin, Aleksandr

Poet, Novelist, and Critic
1799–1837

Life and Work

Aleksandr Pushkin led the Golden Age of Russian poetry, leaving a literary heritage comparable in richness and breadth to that of WILLIAM SHAKESPEARE.

Pushkin was born in Moscow on May 26, 1799. He was descended from Russian nobility and, on his mother's side, from an Ethiopian prince who fought with Peter I (Peter the Great). At age twelve, he began attending the Lyceum, a school in St. Petersburg for sons of the nobility. He began writing poetry as a child and had his first poem published in 1814. By the time he finished school in 1817 he had been invited to join Arzamas, a group of leading Russian writers that supported Westernized language reforms.

While at the Lyceum, Pushkin began work on his first major poem, *Ruslan i Lyudmila* (*Ruslan and Ludmila*), a fairy story in verse that was published in 1820. He went to work for the College of Foreign Affairs after finishing school but his involvement in a subversive political group and his political poetry soon attracted the attention

of the Russian authorities. In 1820 he was banished to southern Russia.

Living in exile, Pushkin began writing verse epics in the style of Lord Byron. He soon became the leading figure of the Russian Romantic movement, though he preferred to call himself a classicist. His elegy, *To Ovid*, written in 1821, is considered to be one of his greatest works.

Pushkin began work on *Yevgeny Onegin* (*Eugene Onegin*), his masterpiece, in 1823. This verse work, published in 1833, provides a portrait of the poet's search for identity, world order, and a mythological heritage. While he was writing this poem, Tsar Nicholas granted him a complete pardon and he returned to St. Petersburg in 1826.

Pushkin was a great technical craftsman and could adapt his poetic style to any subject. *Medny Vsadnak* (*The Bronze Horseman*), a novel in verse published in 1833, provides a history of modern Russia; in the early 1830s he contributed to Russian theater with the plays *Skupoy Rytsar* (*The Avaricious Knight*, 1836), *Motsart i Salyeri* (*Mozart and Salieri*, 1831), *Kamenny Gost* (*The Stone Guest*, 1839), and *Pir Vo Vremya Chumy* (*The Feast in Time of the Plague*, 1832); and in the late 1830s he wrote a series of poems in the style of the Russian folk tale. He published *Boris Gudnov*, his great historical tragedy based on the reign of the tsar of Russia, in 1831.

In the late 1830s Pushkin began concentrating on fiction and journalism. He started a journal, *The Contemporary*, which was a financial failure, and completed his novel, *Kapitanskaya Dochka* (*The Captain's Daughter*, 1836).

On January 27, 1837, Pushkin was killed in a duel with a French officer whom he suspected, perhaps unjustly, of having seduced his wife.

Legacy

Aleksandr Pushkin provided a model of poetic craftsmanship, historical fiction writing, and pure artistry for his literary successors.

Pushkin gained great respect early in his career with the publication of *Ruslan and Ludmila*. He went on to dominate what is known as the Golden Age of Russian poetry (1820–35) when poetry was at the forefront of Russian literary output, and led a group of writers that came to be called the "Pushkin Pleiad."

He stood at the center of a series of literary changes in the 1820s, one of the most important of which was the unprecedented combination of formal and vernacular Russian to create a

melodic and rich poetic language. With this innovation he came to be looked upon as the founder of modern Russian literature.

Both Pushkin's personality and his literary work have entered Russian mythology. His folktale poems, though their plots were often taken from foreign sources, were quickly blended with Russian folk literature. His fame had declined by the end of his life, but was reestablished after his death and his work has been a point of reference for all major Russian writers of the nineteenth and twentieth centuries.

Both Nikolay Gogol and Michael Lermontov adopted Pushkin's technique of presenting a group of stories as a collection gathered from a number of sources. Gogol called him Russia's national poet. The image of Pushkin as the embodiment of Russian spirit solidified when, in 1880, FYODOR DOSTOYEVSKY delivered his *Discourse on Pushkin* at the unveiling of a monument dedicated to the poet.

Among the writers and intellectuals who have translated and written about Pushkin's work are Vladimir Nabokov, who translated *Eugene Onegin* in 1964, and the poets Anna Akhmatova and Andrei Bely, both of whom wrote important critical works on Pushkin.

Pushkin's work has also been set to music: PETER ILICH TCHAIKOVSKY wrote operas based on *Eugene Onegin*, *Mazeppa*, and *Pikovaya Dama* (*The Queen of Spades*, 1834); IGOR STRAVINSKY on *Domik v Kolomne* (*The Little House at Komna*, 1833); and Cesar Cui on *Kavkazsky Plennik* (*The Captive of the Caucasus*) and *A Feast in Time of Plague*.

Watson

WORLD EVENTS		PUSHKIN'S LIFE
French Revolution begins	1789	
	1799	Aleksandr Pushkin is born
Latin American independence movement begins	1811	
Congress of Vienna reorganizes Europe	1815	
	1820	Pushkin is banished to southern Russia
	1821	Pushkin writes *To Ovid*
	1823	Pushkin begins *Eugene Onegin*
	1826	Pushkin returns to St. Petersburg
	1831	Pushkin publishes *Boris Gudnov*
	1833	Pushkin publishes *Eugene Onegin*
	1837	Pushkin is killed in duel
Revolutions in Austria, France, Germany, and Italy	1848	

For Further Reading

Feinstein, Elaine. *Pushkin*. New York: HarperCollins Publishers, 1999.

Pushkin, Alexander. *Eugene Onegin*. Translated by Vladimir Nabokov. Princeton, N.J.: Princeton University Press, 1990.

Vitale, Serena. *Pushkin's Button*. Translated by Ann Goldstein and Jon Rothschild. New York: Farrar, Straus & Giroux, 1999.

Raphael

(Raffaello Sanzio)

Painter, Architect, and Administrator
1483–1520

Life and Work

Along with MICHELANGELO, LEONARDO DA VINCI, and TITIAN, Raphael was one of the four greatest painters of the Italian High Renaissance.

Raphael (Raffaello Sanzio) was born in 1483 in Urbino, where his father, Giovanni Sanzio, was a court painter. An important center of literature, philosophy and art, the ducal court at Urbino was famous for its elegance and style. Raphael's experience there had a profound effect on his later career.

Giovanni Sanzio died in 1494, when Raphael was only 11. Raphael was sent to Perugia as an apprentice of the prominent painter Pietro Perugino. The young Raphael absorbed his teacher's style so completely that it is sometimes difficult to distinguish between the two artists' works.

Raphael moved to Florence in 1505, and once again found himself in the right place at the right time. The two great heroes of Florentine art, Michelangelo and Leonardo da Vinci, had recently returned to their hometown. Michelangelo had just completed *David* (1501–04), and patriotic enthusiasm for art soared. The young Raphael became an almost instant success, specializing in paintings such as the *Madonna of the Meadow* (1505), which drew on the nascent High Renaissance style being developed by Leonardo.

In 1508 or 1509, Raphael moved again, this time to Rome, where Pope Julius II was assembling the greatest group of artists in Italy in the hope of reestablishing the grandeur of ancient Rome. The prominent architect Donato Bramante had been commissioned to demolish the most sacred church in the city, St. Peter's, and was replacing it with a new, colossal, domed structure. Michelangelo was brought in to paint the ceiling of the Sistine Chapel and to design the Pope's tomb, and Raphael was assigned to paint the papal apartments in the Vatican.

In one of these rooms, the *Stanza della Segnatura*, Raphael painted two of his most famous works: the *School of Athens* (representing Philosophy) and the *Disputa* (or *Disputation Concerning the Blessed Sacrament*, representing Theology), which embodied the essence of Renaissance humanism in its synthesis of Classical and Christian ideals.

Raphael's career soared under Pope Julius II and his successor, Pope Leo IX. In 1514 he was appointed architect of St. Peter's, in effect the official artist of the papal court. He was responsible for overseeing all the projects the court sponsored. At the same time, he continued to produce paintings and even build villas for wealthy private patrons.

Raphael died in 1520 at the age of 37. His burial in the Pantheon, the famous ancient Roman temple converted to a Christian church, can be taken as a symbolic end of the High Renaissance in Rome.

Legacy

Raphael's main contribution to the Renaissance was his establishment of the grand, heroic, larger-than-life style of painting.

Raphael's style directly affected a number of younger artists, including Giulio Romano, Parmigianino, and Antonio Correggio. Indirectly, Raphael's career had a profound effect on Renaissance artists generally. His extraordinary rise from traditional apprentice to valued member of the papal court signaled the rising status of painting as an intellectual enterprise.

In the art academies of Europe in the seventeenth, eighteenth, and nineteenth centuries, Raphael's reputation became even greater than it had been during his lifetime. His works were copied as training exercises. His technique, based on the clear linear definition of forms and geometrically integrated compositions, became standard practice in official art academies throughout Europe. More important, the idealized grandeur of his noble, dignified characters defined what academic artists thought art should be. So infatuated were later artists with Raphael that in 1833 his body was removed from his tomb and his skull was measured to see if it was of normal human dimensions.

Today there is little taste for Raphaelesque idealism. Since the Impressionist movement in the mid-nineteenth century, artists have rebelled against such static academic forms. Raphael's confidence in humanistic ideals, dignity, and grandeur seems quaint and outdated in our world. Nevertheless, even though Raphael is no longer a vital inspiration to contemporary artists, he remains perhaps the best example of an artist at the peak of Renaissance humanism.

McEnroe

WORLD EVENTS		RAPHAEL'S LIFE
Pope Sixtus IV institutes Spanish Inquisition	1478	
	1483	Raphael is born
High Renaissance in Italy	1490–1527	
Columbus sails to Americas	1492	
	1505	Raphael moves to Florence
	1508/09	Raphael moves to Rome
	1514	Raphael is appointed architect of St. Peter's
Protestant Reformation begins	1517	
	1520	Raphael dies
Ottoman dominance of Mediterranean ends	1571	

For Further Reading

Ettlinger, Leopold D., and Helen S. Ettlinger. *Raphael.* Oxford: Phaidon, 1987.

Jones, Roger, and Nicholas Penny. *Raphael.* New Haven, Conn.: Yale University Press, 1983.

Thompson, David. *Raphael: The Life and the Legacy.* London: BBC Books, 1983.

Rauschenberg, Robert

Painter and Multimedia Artist
1925–

Life and Work

R obert Rauschenberg is one of the most important figures in the history of late-twentieth-century art. His reintroduction of

WORLD EVENTS		RAUSCHENBERG'S LIFE
Russian Revolution	1917	
	1925	Robert Rauschenberg is born
Great Depression	1929–39	
World War II	1939–45	
	1947	Rauschenberg enters Kansas City Art Institute
Communist China is established	1949	Rauschenberg moves to New York
Korean War	1950–53	
African independence movement begins	1957	
	1964	Rauschenberg wins grand prize for painting at Venice Biennale
Vietnam War ends	1975	
	1985	Rauschenberg begins Overseas Culture Interchange
Dissolution of the Soviet Union	1991	

representational images, especially from popular culture, helped initiate the transition from Modern to Postmodern art.

Rauschenberg was born October 22 1925, in Port Arthur, Texas, an oil refining town on the Gulf Coast. He drew all during his childhood, but until he was 18, he never realized there was such a thing as being an artist. While serving in the Navy, he visited the Huntington Art Gallery in California and saw original oil paintings for the first time. In 1947, he entered the Kansas City Art Institute and, in 1948, traveled to Paris. While there he read about an experimental art school at Black Mountain, North Carolina, and returned to the United States to take classes there. He also came into contact with two other avant-garde artists, the musician JOHN CAGE and the dancer MERCE CUNNINGHAM; both were important influences on his ideas about art.

Rauschenberg's arrival in New York in 1949 coincided with the recognition of Abstract Expressionism as the most important new art movement of the time. Abstraction was the general trend of modern art and these works were extremely abstract, most without any clear images or subject matter. By the mid-1950s Rauschenberg had reacted against the domination of abstraction and began reintroducing images into his work—postcards, snapshots, fabric, and license plates, which he attached to his canvases. He called the resulting constructions "combines" and explained that they "filled the gap between art and life." At the same time he used more three-dimensional objects to create *assemblages* ("assembled" sculptures), such as *Odalisque* (1955-58).

In the early 1960s, Rauschenberg developed a technique for screenprinting images onto his canvases. Many of these images came from popular visual media, such as newspapers and magazines. Rauschenberg arranged them randomly and painted over parts of them, but they remained quite recognizable. Images of astronauts, TITIAN's nudes, city streets, and John F. Kennedy are juxtaposed. In this way, he captured the power, complexity and chaos of our vibrant modern visual culture. Many of these works, such as *Retroactive* (1964), represented some of the most significant events and personalities of the decade, and function as contemporary history paintings.

In 1964, Rauschenberg won the grand prize for painting at the Venice Biennale, the most prestigious contemporary international art show. His interest then shifted from painting to installation and performance art. Since 1954 he had been working collaboratively, designing costumes, sets, and lighting for the avant-garde dance company of Merce Cunningham. In the 1970s he returned to flat surfaces with works that combined layers of gauzy fabrics, felt, and photographs. In 1985 he began the ambitious Rauschenberg Overseas Culture Interchange, a project that takes him around the world to work collaboratively with artists from many different cultures.

Legacy

T he art that comes after Robert Rauschenberg looks nothing like the art that came before him. His work opened the gates to the great flood of different styles, materials, techniques, and subjects we now call Postmodern.

Rauschenberg's most significant move was to reject the predominant abstract techniques of Modernist art and reintroduce reality into art by using actual found objects in his works. The first to follow his lead were the Pop Artists of the 1960s, including ANDY WARHOL, Claes Oldenburg, and Roy Lichtenstein. In the 1970s, Julian Schnabel and David Salle continued to work with imagery borrowed from other media, which they "combined" in a manner first introduced by Rauschenberg. The enormous posters of Barbara Krueger with their commentary on social issues are also the direct inheritors of Rauschenberg's use of imagery from popular culture. Every artist working today who uses imagery drawn from popular media or ordinary objects found in "real" life is, in some way, beholden to Rauschenberg.

Rauschenberg's predilection for mixing media was also very unmodern, as was his interest in collaboration with other artists . His earliest collaborator was Susan Weil, then his wife. He and Weil combined photography, painting, and printmaking in single images, blurring the boundaries between them. Rauschenberg not only challenged the idea of the artist as a unique creative force, but also the traditional distinctions that defined and separated the different arts. In this way he provided the model for nearly every aspect of Postmodern art-making.

Pokinski

For Further Reading

Forge, Andrew. *Rauschenberg.* New York: Harry N. Abrams, 1969.

Kotz, Mary Lynn. *Rauschenberg Art and Life.* New York: Harry N. Abrams, 1990.

Tomkins, Calvin. *Off the Wall: Robert Rauschenberg and the Art World of Our Time.* New York: Penguin Books, 1981.

Reich, Steve

Composer
1936–

Life and Work

A creator of the popular Minimalist style, Steve Reich found ways to generate large, intricate, shifting musical patterns from the simplest and most repetitive of basic musical materials.

Reich was born in New York on October 3, 1936. His musical education was strongly directed by the percussion lessons he took as a teenager. Reich graduated from Cornell University in 1957 with a degree in philosophy and a wide musical education. He decided to become a composer, and for a time, he supported himself by driving a taxi. His first creative breakthroughs came when he moved west to study at Mills College in Oakland, California. There he worked with the European composers Darius Milhaud and Luciano Berio, and absorbed the non-Western music, especially Indonesian and African, that flourished in the ethnically diverse San Francisco Bay area.

After receiving his masters degree from Mills in 1963, Reich produced his first characteristic compositions: *It's Gonna Rain* and *Come Out,* both from 1965, featured recorded speech fragments played on two tape recorders slightly out of synchronization with each other. He applied this "phase" technique to instrumental music in 1967's *Piano Phase* and *Violin Phase,* and it remained at the core of his increasingly ambitious musical language.

In 1970 Reich went to Ghana to immerse himself in African percussion; the following year he wrote *Drumming,* a vital, florid work for a large group of percussion instruments. *Drumming* was released on record by the prestigious German label Deutsche Grammophon; it made Reich's reputation and has enjoyed continuing popularity. Reich would again synthesize study of non-Western music into a new stylistic advance with *Tehillim,* a 1981 work for voice and orchestra inspired by the composer's study of Jewish liturgical singing. That work and 1983's choral *Desert Music* were large, expressive pieces far removed from Reich's original Minimalist experiments, but his musical personality remained consistent and came across to audiences as genuine. Reich used the taped voices of concentration camp survivors in 1988's *Different Trains,* and in the 1990s, like other Minimalist composers, he contributed to ambitious multimedia works. *The Cave,* an opera-like piece from 1993, explored biblical themes, and the first of *Three Tales* exploring technology's effects had its premiere in 1998.

Legacy

Steve Reich was preceded chronologically in the employment of minimalist ideas by several composers, including Terry Riley and LaMonte Young, but he was in many respects the movement's founding figure.

From the start he understood the connection between Minimalist techniques and the cyclic rhythmic structures of musical cultures around the world, and he inspired a host of young musicians to experiment with the Indonesian *gamelan* percussion orchestra and with African drumming. The creator of colorful, enjoyable music, he was also in some respects Minimalism's intellectual; he was a gifted writer whose essays were translated into French, spreading to Europe his ideas about the communication of pure process in music.

Although other Minimalists moved away from their original spare languages to broader musical palettes, Reich's expansion of his language proved especially influential for the 1990s generation of Minimalist-oriented composers, including John Adams. Reich's rediscovery of his Jewish roots also proved influential in the century's last years, with even

musical radicals like the jazz-classical enfant terrible John Zorn following a similar path.

Beyond the diffusion of any specific stylistic traits, Reich has been known as one of the composers who did the most to bring classical music back within reach of audiences. His works are never simple, corny, or in the least anti-intellectual, but anyone can grasp them quickly and enjoy them. Thus his influence has extended beyond the world of classical music: in the words of musicologist Nicolas Slonimsky, Reich "finds a direct avenue to the hearts, minds, and ears of the young." Creators in popular genres such as techno and electronica, occupied with the textural and perceptual effects of repetition, have repeatedly named Reich as an influence. At the end of the twentieth century, Reich could look back on three decades during which his impact as a composer had steadily broadened.

Manheim

WORLD EVENTS		REICH'S LIFE
Great Depression	1929–39	
	1936	Steve Reich is born
World War II	1939–45	
Communist China is established	1949	
Korean War	1950–53	
African independence movement begins	1957	Reich graduates from Cornell University
	1965	Reich writes *It's Gonna Rain* and *Come Out*
	1967	Reich applies "phase" technique in violin and piano pieces
	1970	Reich studies drumming in Ghana
Vietnam War ends	1975	
	1981	Reich turns to Jewish liturgical singing in *Tehillim*
	1988	Reich writes *Different Trains*
	1993	Reich writes theater piece *The Cave*
Dissolution of Soviet Union	1991	

For Further Reading

Mertens, Wim. *American Minimal Music: LaMonte Young, Terry Riley, Steve Reich, Philip Glass.* New York: A. Broude, 1983.
Reich, Steve. *Writings About Music.* New York: New York University Press, 1974.

Rembrandt (van Rijn)

Painter and Printmaker
1606–1669

Life and Work

Rembrandt van Rijn was born to a working-class family in Amsterdam in 1606. He studied briefly at the University of Leiden before deciding to become a professional painter. He served apprenticeships in Amsterdam and Leiden, and in 1631 returned to Amsterdam to establish a practice with an art dealer named Hendrick van Uylenburg.

World Events		Rembrandt's Life
Ottoman dominance of Mediterranean ends	1571	
	1606	Rembrandt van Rijn is born
Thirty Years' War in Europe	1618–48	
	1631	Rembrandt returns to Amsterdam
	1635	Rembrandt paints *Self Portrait with Saskia in his Lap*
	1642	Rembrandt paints *Nightwatch*
	1662–68	Rembrandt paints *The Prodigal Son*
	1665	Rembrandt declares bankruptcy
	1669	Rembrandt dies
Glorious Revolution in England	1688	

Rembrandt's studio quickly became successful. His religious paintings, mythological scenes, and, especially, portraits were extremely popular among the wealthy Dutch middle class. He oversaw a large, busy workshop and taught many students. His joyous *Self Portrait with Saskia in his Lap* (1635) captures the celebratory enthusiasm of his early career.

Although influenced by the slightly older Flemish painter PETER PAUL RUBENS, Rembrandt quickly established his own deeply emotive style. In portraits and narrative paintings, a warm golden light reveals figures emerging from a dark undefined background.

In *Nightwatch* (1642), for example, Rembrandt turned what could have been a static group portrait into a dramatic narrative by capturing the group's bustling attempt to organize itself into a parade. In numerous anecdotal details, Rembrandt provides human interest that transcends the particular incident. Such paintings established Rembrandt's reputation throughout Europe.

Rembrandt was also a prolific printmaker, specializing in etchings. Even in this fundamentally linear medium, Rembrandt managed to reveal the forms of his figures through dramatic effects of light and dark, rather than harshly defining them with crisp outlines. As a result, prints such as *Christ Preaching* (c. 1652) have the warm, evocative qualities of his paintings.

Despite his fame and success, Rembrandt was frequently in financial trouble, and he declared bankruptcy in 1665. His late works somberly address fundamental human issues. His monumental religious painting, *The Prodigal Son* (c. 1662–68), presents a profoundly moving examination of repentance and forgiveness. Similarly, his late self-portraits convey a penetrating introspection—they are quite different from the confident self-portraits of his youth.

Rembrandt died in Amsterdam on October 4, 1669.

Legacy

Rembrandt van Rijn was one of the most successful painters of his generation. His style was widely imitated by followers and students, many of whom followed his style so closely that even today there are frequent debates over the authorship of paintings that have been attributed to him.

Rembrandt's reputation began to fade shortly after his death. By the late seventeenth century, he was criticized for ignoring the principles and ideals of art laid out by the Italians. His individuality and uncompromising realism did not adhere to conventional notions of idealized beauty.

In the nineteenth century, however, Rembrandt's reputation shifted again; his unorthodoxy was suddenly to his credit. Romantic critics came to admire him as the quintessential artist-genius.

At the same time he came to be regarded by Dutch nationalists as the central figure in the history of Dutch art. When the national Rijksmuseum was opened in 1886, Rembrandt's *Nightwatch* was chosen as its centerpiece. Today, Rembrandt is seen as the epitome of the "Old Master." He is widely esteemed both for the individuality of his style and for the profound humanity of his characterizations.

Rembrandt's paintings continue to excite considerable public interest and controversy. Since 1968, a team of scholars has been engaged on the Rembrandt Project, an ambitious program that will examine, study, and recatalogue all of the paintings that have been attributed to Rembrandt. The team has decided that a number of works formerly attributed to Rembrandt were the works of members of his workshop, followers, or forgers.

McEnroe

For Further Reading

Mee, Charles L. *Rembrandt's Portrait: A Biography.* New York: Simon & Schuster, 1988.

Schwartz, Gary *Rembrandt: His Life, His Paintings: A New Biography.* New York: Viking, 1985.

Von Sonnenburg, Hubert, and Walter Liedtke. *Rembrandt/Not Rembrandt in the Metropolitan Museum of Art.* New York: Harry N. Abrams, 1995.

Renoir, Pierre-Auguste

Painter
1841–1919

Life and Work

Pierre-Auguste Renoir, French painter, print-maker, and sculptor, was one of the leading Impressionist painters from the late 1860s, although he broke with the Impressionist style later in his career.

Renoir was born in Limoges in 1841 and grew up in Paris, the sixth of seven children in a working-class home. At 20, Renoir began to study and copy paintings in the Louvre museum. Among his favorites were the Rococo painters, whose light subject matter influenced his own early work. In 1862, Renoir was admitted to the École des Beaux-Arts, studying with, among others, CLAUDE MONET. He developed a close friendship with Monet, and early works of theirs are considered to be the original and standard-setting statements of the Impressionist style.

Although he had been successful in submitting his pre-Impressionist paintings to the Salon, a series of rejections after 1865 led him to join with fellow artists in the first Impressionist Exhibition in 1874. He was attacked by critics after the second Impressionist Exhibition for his *Study* (*Nude in the Sunlight,* 1875). In 1876, Renoir sent *Le Moulin de la Gallette* to the third Impressionist Exhibition.

Perhaps his most characteristic painting, it celebrates the joys of Parisian middle-class life in a spirited and attractive scene mottled with sunlight and gentle shade. The informally arranged figues suggest more of a snapshot of everyday life than a studio pose, and the viewer is brought directly into the scene by the fact that the painting's space appears to continue beyond its borders. True to the goals of Impressionism, the painting depicts not an idealized, static, carefully representative scene, but a fleeting moment of ordinary life, as actually experienced.

Beginning in 1878, Renoir again began to submit paintings to the official Salon, now with increasing success. Gradually he withdrew from the Impressionist circle. His success at the 1879 Salon with portraits of *Mme Charpentier and Her Children* (1878) and the actress *Jeanne Samary* (1878) made Renoir financially independent. He began to change his style from the Impressionistic concern with fleeting effects of light to an interest in the solid, sculptural forms of the classical tradition.

Travel to Italy in 1881–82 further consolidated the change. There he studied the works of Renaissance masters as well as those of Greek and Roman art. In the 1890s, Renoir continued to assimilate the art of the past, especially the work of RAPHAEL, TITIAN, DIEGO VELÁZQUEZ, and PETER-PAUL RUBENS. In a painting like *La Famille de l'Artiste* (1896) can be seen the turn to more solid forms and somber coloration. By returning to classical forms and subject matter, as in *The Judgment of Paris* (1913–14), Renoir hoped to establish his art as part of the grand academic tradition.

In 1900, Renoir was awarded the Legion of Honor by the French state.

After 1902, Renoir's health began to fail. He completed his first major sculpture in 1913. He moved to the south of France in 1907, and died there in 1919.

Legacy

During his life, Pierre-Auguste Renoir was the most popular of the Impressionists. For many, his brightly dappled scenes of joyful middle-class social life captured the essence of that movement in the history of Modernist art. His withdrawal from the Impressionist group indicated a transitional period for the entire group, many of whom evolved increasingly individual styles.

The early stages of the Impressionist movement had marked the most fundamental change in the history of European art since the Renaissance. By the 1880s, Renoir worked to reconcile Impressionism and more traditional art. His concern with the classical nude had a major impact on the later art of Pierre Bonnard, PABLO PICASSO, and others.

Impressionism spread to the United States in the late nineteenth and early twentieth centuries. The conservative style of Renoir proved highly influential in America, more so than the more radical rendering of insubstantial flickerings of light as painted by Monet and Camille Pissarro.

Recently art historians have begun to reconsider Renoir; art critics have increasingly pointed out the unevenness of his late works. In addition, Renoir's virulent anti-Semitism and the male-centered objectification of women evident in his paintings have spurred some negative reappraisals. Nevertheless, with the general public and the art market, Renoir remains among the most popular artists in European history.

Domenico

WORLD EVENTS		RENOIR'S LIFE
Congress of Vienna reorganizes Europe	1815	
	1841	Pierre-Auguste Renoir is born
Revolutions in Austria, France, Germany, and Italy	1848	
U.S. Civil War	1861–65	
	1862	Renoir enters École des Beaux-Arts
Germany is united	1871	
	1874	Renoir participates in first Impressionist Exhibition
	1876	Renoir submits *Le Moulin de la Gallette* to third Impressionist exhibition
	1878	Renoir paints *Mme Charpentier and Her Children*
Spanish-American War	1898	
	1900	Renoir is awarded Legion of Honor
World War I	1914–18	
Russian Revolution	1917	
	1919	Renoir dies
Great Depression	1929–39	

For Further Reading

Renoir, Jean. *Renoir, My Father.* Translated by Randolph and Dorothy Weaver. Boston: Little, Brown, 1962.
White, Barbara Ehrlich. *Renoir: His Life, Art, and Letters.* New York: Harry N. Abrams, 1984.

Rilke, Rainer Maria

Poet and Novelist
1875–1926

WORLD EVENTS		RILKE'S LIFE
Germany is united	1871	
	1875	Rainer Maria Rilke is born
	1895	Rilke graduates from Charles University
	1896	Rilke publishes *Larenopfer*
Spanish-American War	1898	
	1908	Rilke publishes *New Poems*
	1910	Rilke publishes *The Notebooks of Malte Laurids Brigge*
World War I	1914–18	
Russian Revolution	1917	
	1923	Rilke publishes *The Duino Elegies* and *Sonnets to Orpheus*
	1926	Rilke dies
Great Depression	1929–39	

Life and Work

Rainer Maria Rilke was born in Prague, Czechoslovakia, on December 4, 1875. Raised in an extremely rigid and traditional family, he found emotional release in the poetry that his mother encouraged him to read and write. At the age of 11 he was sent to military school. He graduated from Charles University in Prague in 1895 and then went to Munich, beginning a life of travel that would take him to Russia and throughout Europe.

His first important poetic cycle, *Larenopfer* (1896), was written in the German folk tradition with a Romantic element. He developed a philosophy of existential materialism and considered art to be a religion. In 1897 Rilke met Lou Andreas-Salomé, a writer and psychotherapist, who acted as a mentor to him and was the subject of many of his poems. Rilke's thought and his work were deeply influenced by Andreas-Salomé, and she encouraged him to write in simple and concrete language. His works *Von lieben Gott und Anderes* (*Stories of God,* 1900) and *Das Stunden-Buch* (*The Book of Hours,* 1905) use Christian symbolism to express this philosophy.

Later, while working as AUGUSTE RODIN's secretary, Rilke wrote *Neue Gedichte* (*New Poems,* 1908), in which he attempted to write singularly crafted poems, which he saw as individual works of art comparable to sculptural objects.

His partly autobiographical novel *Die Aufzeichnungen des Malte Laurids Brigge* (*The Notebooks of Malte Laurids Brigge*) was written while he was living in Paris and was published in 1910. Throughout World War I, Rilke isolated himself with his work, although he did serve for six months in the Bureau of War Archives in Vienna before being discharged. Rilke waited more than 10 years to produce his next great work, *Duineser Elegien* (*Duino Elegies,* 1923), an exploration of humanity's relationship to love, nature, death, and language in what he saw as an increasingly inhuman world. Rilke was very concerned with the role of poetry and of the poet in society, and in his work he attempted to confirm the need for poetry despite society's rejection of it.

Late in his life Rilke lived in Switzerland, where he wrote a cycle of 55 poems called *Die*

Sonette au Orpheus (*Sonnets to Orpheus,* 1923). Rilke suffered from leukemia and died in a Swiss sanatorium on December 29, 1926.

Legacy

Ranier Maria Rilke is considered to be one of the greatest lyric poets of German literature.

Rilke's creation of the "object poem," which captured and described abstract ideas in terms of physical objects, was important in the development of modern poetry. He befriended other poets and writers of his day, including Marina Tsvetaeva, André Gide, Paul Valéry, Boris Pasternak, and Stefan Zweig, and his exchange of ideas with these leading figures of literature introduced them to his new form of lyricism.

W. H. Auden was deeply influenced by Rilke's melancholy and occasionally mystical meditations on time and eternity, life and death. Auden said that Rilke was the first poet since WILLIAM BLAKE to find a new way to express abstract ideas in concrete terms, and Rilkean angels appear in Auden's *In Times of War.*

Other important modern poets have been influenced by his work including Sidney Keyes, Stephen Spender, Robert Bly, W. S. Merwin, and John Ashbery. Many of these have credited Rilke with a unique density of poetic observation, presented with a powerful and cold precision.

Watson

For Further Reading

Freedman, Ralph. *Life of a Poet: Rainer Maria Rilke.* New York: Farrar, Straus & Giroux, 1996.

Rilke, Rainer Maria. *The Selected Poetry of Rainer Maria Rilke.* Edited by Erroll McDonald. Translated by Stephen Mitchell. New York: Vintage Books, 1998.

Ringgold, Faith

Painter, Quiltmaker, Teacher,
and Writer
1930–

Life and Work

Faith Ringgold is an extraordinarily versatile artist whose works address the African-American experience with a personal and feminist perspective.

Born Faith Willi Jones in Harlem in 1930, she studied art at City College of New York and taught in New York City public schools from 1955 to 1973.

Ringgold's early career was grounded in the heated atmosphere of the civil rights movement and racial conflicts of the mid-1960s. She addressed those issues directly in works such as *Die* (1967). This 12-foot-long mural, shows a bloody street riot in simplified angular forms reminiscent of the work of JACOB LAWRENCE.

In the 1960s, Ringgold grew increasingly committed to the growing Black Power movement and began experimenting with new styles. Her *Flag for the Moon: Die Nigger* (1969) is at least partly related to Pop art. In it, a flat image of an American flag has been altered by replacing white with black, and spelling out the words "die nigger" within the stars and stripes. Ringgold was responding to the widespread optimism generated by Neil Armstrong's planting a flag on the Moon in July 1969: rather than a "giant step for mankind," here was America's true message to the world.

Beginning in 1970 Ringgold became deeply involved in the feminist movement. Long involved in protesting the racist exclusion of African-American artists from museums and galleries, Ringgold increasingly turned her attention to the equivalent exclusion of women artists. In 1971 she helped to form the group called Where We At to protest the exclusion of women from prominent groups of African-American artists such as Spiral.

In 1972, Ringgold turned to working in textiles, making soft sculptures and quilts. These craft techniques were the traditional media of women, and Ringgold hoped to challenge the boundary between high art and craft. In 1973 Ringgold began to accompany exhibitions of her works with performances.

In the 1980s Ringgold's work became increasingly concerned with personal narrative. In her story quilts she combined painted or photographic images, segments of text and bright printed textiles. *Tar Beach* (1988), for example, records her memory of enjoyable childhood evenings spent with her family on the roof of their Harlem apartment building. In 1991, Ringgold published a modified version of *Tar Beach* as a children's book.

Today Ringgold's work is in the permanent collections of most of those major museums, including the Metropolitan Museum of Art, the Guggenheim Museum, and the Museum of Modern Art, that had earlier excluded African Americans and most women.

Legacy

For more than 30 years, Faith Ringgold has devoted herself and her art to challenging the racial and gender boundaries of the art world.

Ringgold became a professional artist at a time when African-American artists were, for the most part, excluded from galleries, and when African-American women were also excluded from the few galleries run by African-American men. An outsider on both counts, Ringgold confronted these issues in her works and in her political activism. Through groups such as Where We At, Ringgold literally opened the doors of museums and galleries to a new generation of African-American artists.

Ringgold's story quilts were among the very first attempts to create a specifically feminist art.

She turned to traditional women's crafts to make "high art" in media that had traditionally been excluded from consideration as art at all. Soon artists Joyce Kozloff and Miriam Schapiro formalized the use of quilting forms in art in a movement called Pattern and Decoration. Originally regarded as a radical feminist gesture, quilts such as the monumental AIDS quilt have since become respected as mainstream forms of social and personal expression.

Ringgold is a revolutionary artist who challenged many of the major tenets of Western art and helped give voice to people traditionally excluded from the mainstream of the art world. Widely regarded as one of the key artists of the tumultuous 1960s and 1970s, Ringgold created a new visual language to express both her own experience and the experience of a generation.

McEnroe

WORLD EVENTS	RINGGOLD'S LIFE
Great Depression 1929–39	
	1930 Faith Ringgold is born
World War II 1939–45	
Communist China 1949 is established	
Korean War 1950–53	
	1955–73 Ringgold teaches in New York public schools
African independence movement begins 1957	
	1969 Ringgold produces *Flag for the Moon: Die Nigger*
	1970 Ringgold begins involvement with feminist issues
Vietnam War ends 1975	
	1988 Ringgold publishes *Tar Beach*
Dissolution of 1991 Soviet Union	

For Further Reading

Farrington, Lisa E. *Art on Fire: The Politics of Race and Sex in the Paintings of Faith Ringgold.* New York: Millennium Fine Arts, 1999.

Ringgold, Faith. *We Flew Over the Bridge: The Memoirs of Faith Ringgold.* Boston: Little, Brown, 1995.

Rivera, Diego

Painter
1886–1957

Life and Work

One of the principal artists in the Mexican mural movement, Diego Rivera helped initiate a national style based on socialist ideas and indigenous culture.

Born in Guanajuato in 1886, Rivera was a prodigy who was already drawing at age two; at 19 he made his first trip to Europe, and in 1909, he settled in Paris.

The influence of traditional and avant-garde styles, from El Greco to Robert Delaunay, PABLO PICASSO and Juan Gris, can be seen in his early work. In 1917 he began to study early Italian Renaissance painting and the work of PAUL CÉZANNE. In 1919, Rivera was persuaded to return to Mexico to participate in the revolution through his art; in 1920, Rivera went to Italy to study Renaissance murals.

In 1921, Rivera returned to Mexico, and began to intensively study indigenous art and folk culture. In 1922, he began his first government-sponsored mural, *Creation*. Over the next 15 years, he painted a large number of murals, including *The Mine* (1923) and the series *Ballad of the Proletarian Revolution*. In 1929, Rivera became director of the Academia de San Carlos, and in August married the artist FRIDA KAHLO.

In late 1930, Rivera resigned his directorship under duress because of his connection to the recently outlawed Communist Party. During the early 1930s, Rivera was frequently in the United States, where he painted five colossal sets of murals. The *Detroit Industry* frescoes (1932–33), in the Detroit Institute of Arts, was his most important mural project outside of Mexico.

His career in the United States was also affected by his political beliefs. In 1933, Rivera was commissioned to paint a mural in Rockefeller Center, but because it contained an image of Lenin, the Rockefellers dismissed him and had it destroyed. This scandal cost him other commissions as well and forced him to rely on portrait painting to earn a living.

Although he completed several murals upon returning to Mexico, from 1937 to 1942 he received no commissions from the government. During this period, Rivera and Kahlo hosted the exiled Leon Trotsky at their home in Coyoacan.

In his later years, he completed more murals for both public and private buildings in Mexico City. The last of these was a mosaic called *Popular History of Mexico* for the facade of the Teatro de los Insurgentes. He died in 1957.

Legacy

Diego Rivera's career was complicated by his involvement with the Communist Party, most painfully in his forced resignation from the directorship of the Academia de San Carlos.

Nevertheless, Rivera achieved international fame as the greatest mural painter since

MICHELANGELO. His work had a profound influence on muralists around the world. In America, many of the murals funded by the U.S. government closely followed Rivera's use of simplified forms, lively colors, and a narrative, linear style. Rivera's deep commitment to representing the strength and dignity of workers and common people for as broad an audience as possible helped to shape the style of American public art during the Depression. In many towns across the country, banks, post-offices, and other public buildings were painted with Rivera-like murals.

In Mexico, Rivera is regarded as perhaps the greatest artist in Mexican history. Through his abundant work, committed idealism, and forceful personality, he brought Mexican art before the world. The distinctive combination of traditional European style, modern awareness, and socialist motifs embodies the spirit of Mexico in the era of the revolution.

From the 1950s through the 1970s the social-realist style of Rivera's work seemed to critics to have been superseded by Abstract Expressionism. His grand symbolic narratives appeared old-fashioned. That attitude has shifted again over the last couple of decades. The dramatically rising reputation of Rivera's second wife Frida Kahlo has brought new attention to them both. In addition, in the 1980s a new generation of politically active artists, frustrated by the limitations and remoteness of abstract art, began to again work in a style indebted to Rivera's.

Domenico

World Events		Rivera's Life
Germany is united	1871	
	1886	Diego Rivera is born
Spanish-American War	1898	
	1909	Rivera moves to Paris
World War I	1914–18	
Russian Revolution	1917	
	1921	Rivera returns to Mexico
	1922	Rivera begins *Creation*
	1923	Rivera paints *The Mine*
Great Depression	1929–39	
	1930	Rivera is forced to resign as director of Academia de San Carlos
	1932–33	Rivera paints *Detroit Industry* series of frescos in Unites States
World War II	1939–45	
Communist China is established	1949	
Korean War	1950–53	
African independence movement begins	1957	Rivera dies
Vietnam War ends	1975	

For Further Reading

Newman, Cynthia, ed. *Diego Rivera: A Retrospective*. Detroit: Founders Society, Detroit Institute of Arts; London: Hayward Gallery, South Bank Centre, in association with W. W. Norton, 1986.

Wolfe, Bertram D. *The Fabulous Life of Diego Rivera*. New York: Stein and Day, 1963.

Rockwell, Norman

Illustrator

1894–1978

Life and Work

Norman Rockwell presented Americans with idealized images of small-town life on the covers of the *Saturday Evening Post* for nearly 50 years.

Rockwell was born in New York in 1894. At age 16 he began his studies at the Art Students League in New York, planning to become an illustrator in the tradition of Howard Pyle and Howard Chandler Christy. This was a time—before the introduction of television—when magazine illustrators were prominent figures in the rapidly expanding mass media, and Rockwell rose quickly to the top.

At age 19 he landed his first job as art director for *Boys' Life,* the magazine of the Boy Scouts of America, and three years later, in 1916, Rockwell did his first cover for the *Saturday Evening Post.* By 1925, he was a household name. Over a 47-year career, Rockwell would produce more than 300 covers, creating some of the most popular American images ever made.

Rockwell typically showed highly idealized scenes of middle-class people and family life. His gentle humor, relentless optimism, and laborious attention to even the minutest detail remained consistent throughout his career.

Although Rockwell lived through tumultuous times, his pictures showed small-town America as utopia. Even during the Depression, they were intended to provide hope and encouragement. Rockwell avoided the realities that concerned contemporary photographers such as MARGARET BOURKE-WHITE.

During World War II, Rockwell depicted life on the home front, where his characters such as Rosie the Riveter did their part to preserve American freedom. Rockwell reminded his viewers of their wartime blessings in *Freedom from Want* (1943), which shows a joyous family about to enjoy a huge Thanksgiving turkey. It was left to others to show a different side of the war—the horrors of combat, the destruction of cities, the unimaginable cruelty of the Nazi death camps.

The civil rights struggles of the 1960s, however, shook even Rockwell's confidence in the universal goodness of American society. He attempted to address the issue in pictures like *The Problem We All Live With* (1964), showing a little African-American girl being escorted to her newly integrated school by federal marshals.

Rockwell died in 1978 at the age of eighty-four. Many of his paintings are on display at the Norman Rockwell Museum in Stockbridge, Massachusetts, where he had lived since 1953.

Legacy

Norman Rockwell gave Americans the image of themselves that they wanted to see: they were honest, hardworking, pious, down-to-earth, patriotic, and courageous. It was a world of mom, pop, apple pie, Boy Scouts, and the flag.

Along with WALT DISNEY, Rockwell was one of the most popular artists in the country for half a century. People loved him, but critics disdained his shallowness and sentimentality.

Rockwell was a storyteller in an era when museums and galleries were filled with the abstract paintings by artists such as JACKSON POLLOCK, whose works left the public as baffled as the character in Rockwell's *The Connoisseur* (1962), a man in gray suit who stares uncomprehendingly at a Pollock drip painting. While Rockwell had little effect on the art world, his images of America are still common in the mass media. His optimistic, anecdotal images of small-town America lie at the root of many television sitcoms.

Recently, postmodern critics and curators, questioning the boundaries between "high" art and popular culture, have revived interest in Rockwell. A major retrospective of his work was mounted in 1999. Art historians and critics are no longer able to ignore the major impact Rockwell's images have had on shaping the self-image of the United States. Those images framed not only the appearance of an idealized America, but also an ideology. Although some might see the ideology as reactionary and nostalgic, it does reflect an understandable yearning in Americans for a simpler, less mechanized, and more humane world.

McEnroe

WORLD EVENTS		ROCKWELL'S LIFE
Germany is united	1871	
	1894	Norman Rockwell is born
Spanish-American War	1898	
	1910	Rockwell begins studies at Art Students League in New York
	1913	Rockwell is art director for *Boys' Life*
World War I	1914–18	
	1916	Rockwell does his first cover for *Saturday Evening Post*
Russian Revolution	1917	
Great Depression	1929–39	
World War II	1939–45	
	1943	Rockwell finishes *Freedom from Want*
Communist China is established	1949	
Korean War	1950–53	
African independence movement begins	1957	
	1964	Rockwell paints *The Problem We All Live With*
Vietnam War ends	1975	
	1978	Rockwell dies
Dissolution of Soviet Union	1991	

For Further Reading

Hennessey, Maureen Hart. *Norman Rockwell: Pictures for the American People.* Atlanta: High Museum of Art; Stockbridge, Mass.: Norman Rockwell Museum; New York: Harry N. Abrams, 1999.

Meyer, Susan E. *Norman Rockwell's People.* New York: Harry N. Abrams, 1981.

Montgomery, Elizabeth Miles. *Norman Rockwell.* New York: Smithmark Publishers, 1995.

Rodin, Auguste

Sculptor
1840–1917

Life and Work

Auguste Rodin is the most important sculptor of the late nineteenth and early twentieth centuries. He revitalized the sculp-

World Events		Rodin's Life
Congress of Vienna reorganizes Europe	1815	
	1840	Auguste Rodin is born
Revolutions in Austria, France, Germany, and Italy	1848	
U.S. Civil War	1861–65	
Germany is united	1871	
	1876	Rodin travels to Italy
	1877	Rodin completes first major work, *The Age of Bronze*
	1884	Rodin completes *Burghers of Calais*
Spanish-American War	1898	
World War I	1914–18	
Russian Revolution	1917	Rodin dies

tural depiction of the human figure and laid the foundations for the development of modern figurative sculpture.

Rodin was born November 12, 1840, in a working-class area of Paris. Rodin showed enough early talent that his family enrolled him at the Special School of Design and Mathematics; at graduation, he won the first prize in sculpture. After failing the entrance exam to the École des Beaux Arts, he found work as a sculptor's assistant in 1864; the same year his first entry into the annual Salon was rejected. For the next 20 years, Rodin struggled to make a living; from time to time he was able to take classes in life drawing and clay modeling. In 1876 he traveled to Italy, where he was deeply affected by MICHELANGELO's sculpture.

Rodin's debut piece in the Salon was a life-size, standing nude male figure, *L'Âge d'Airain* (*The Age of Bronze*), which he completed in 1877. It was a tremendous success, mostly due to the controversy surrounding it. Because it appeared to be so natural, many assumed it had been made by casting a real man's body. Knowing his skill at clay modeling, other sculptors came to Rodin's defense. Rodin's career was made in 1880, when he received a commission from the government for a set of bronze doors for a planned museum of decorative arts.

Rodin's theme for this work was DANTE's *Inferno*, and he called his composition *La Porte de l'Enfer* (*The Gates of Hell*). From this complex design (which he never finished), he also derived some of his most famous individual sculptures, including *Le Penseur* (*The Thinker*) and *Le Baiser* (*The Kiss*). Prestigious public commissions continued to come his way—in 1884 for *Le Bourgeois de Calais* (*The Burghers of Calais*), and in 1891 for a monument to Balzac. During the 1880s the female figure dominated his work, especially the smaller, more personal compositions. In 1883 he met and fell in love with a young woman sculptor named Claudine Claudel, who worked for a time as his assistant and who became the inspiration for the intense emotion and sensuality expressed in many of his images of women and couples.

By 1900, Rodin was an international celebrity. Exhibitions of his work were seen throughout Europe and the United States. He received honorary degrees from foreign universities and was sought out by royalty, politicians, intellectuals, society figures, and,

especially, young writers and artists. Almost all his twentieth-century works were portraits of statesmen and wealthy patrons.

In 1916 he suffered a severe stroke, and died a year and a half later.

Legacy

In an era when sculpture was dominated by idealized figures based on classical and Renaissance examples, Auguste Rodin introduced something completely new. His works were not based on any previous style, nor were they about literary or historical themes; subjects were complex and enigmatic. His approach laid the foundation for early modern figure sculpture and inspired a generation of twentieth-century sculptors, including Aristide Maillol, Gaston Lachaise, Wilhelm Lembruck, and even PABLO PICASSO, who conceived their figures as metaphors.

Rodin's techniques were also revolutionary. Unlike the smoothly finished surfaces of his contemporaries' work, Rodin's were irregular and when light reflected off them the effect was dynamic. Rodin also reworked and reused parts of his own sculptures, sometimes as separate pieces, sometimes as elements in composite pieces. For example, the Dante figure from *The Gates of Hell* was enlarged and reworked to become *The Thinker*. Rodin's individual sculptures were part of a continuing process; making the creative process visible has become an important element of Modern art and can be seen throughout the century, from Constantin Brancusi to David Smith to Eva Hesse.

Rodin's sculptures were striking not only for their naturalness, but for their expression of complex human psychology and passion. None of Rodin's themes was simple; most of his figures are conflicted by emotions that tear at them, immobilize them, or overwhelm them. This quality became characteristic of modern figurative sculpture, especially in the work of Brancusi, Alberto Giacometti, and HENRY MOORE.

In the middle of World War I, Rodin deeded all his possessions, including his work, his writings, and his art collection, to the French government. His gift became the foundation for the Rodin Museum, today a Paris landmark. Rodin remains the most widely collected sculptor in the world.

Pokinski

For Further Reading
Butler, Ruth, ed. *Rodin in Perspective.* Englewood Cliffs, N.J.: Prentice-Hall, 1980.
Elsen, Albert E., ed. *Rodin Rediscovered.* Washington: National Gallery of Art, 1981.
Grunfeld, Frederic V. *Rodin: A Biography.* New York: Holt, 1987.

Rubens, Peter Paul

Painter and Diplomat
1577–1640

Life and Work

Renowned as a painter, draftsman, and diplomat in the seventeenth century, Peter Paul Rubens signaled a new direction for northern European art with his fusion of Flemish realism and Italian classicism.

Rubens was born in Germany into a prominent Antwerp family in 1577. As a young man growing up in Antwerp, Rubens trained in art and as a courtier, an education that included the mastery of four languages. He became a master painter (member of the guild) in 1598.

In 1600 Rubens became court painter to the duke of Mantua (Italy), a position that set him in a center of Renaissance art and humanistic culture. Rubens remained in Italy for eight years, studying Renaissance painters and classical sculptors, and painting portraits and religious subjects. By 1608, he was working in a style that combined influences of TITIAN, Correggio, and RAPHAEL, and his reputation had been established.

Rubens returned to Antwerp in 1608. His style united the sculptural forms and baroque dynamism of Italian art with his own fervent Roman Catholicism. To complete the huge commissions he was receiving in the early 1620s, Rubens established a studio employing numerous assistants. He was named court painter to Albert and Isabella, the Spanish governors of Flanders, and also painted for Antwerp's prosperous middle class. Among his religious paintings, the *Descent from the Cross* (1610–14) is characterized by such Italian influences as the vivid contrasts of light and dark, after CARAVAGGIO, highly sculptural figures, after MICHELANGELO, and energetic, eloquent poses in the baroque style of GIAN LORENZO BERNINI.

Rubens also treated secular, mythological themes, as can be seen in the *Rape of the Daughters of Leucippus* (1617), which depicts monumental human forms in the act of violent movement. In his later years, Rubens moved to less turbulent depictions of genre scenes, landscapes and portraits, such as *Landscape with the Chateau of Steen* (1636).

In 1626 Rubens took on diplomatic duties for Albert and Isabella; in 1629, acting for Philip IV of Spain, he helped to attain a peace settlement between Spain and England. Rubens's position in the royal courts of Europe helped to further his reputation, making him one of the most sought-after painters of his generation. After achieving enormous success and wealth, Rubens died in 1640.

Legacy

Peter Paul Rubens's prodigious energy and intelligence served him well as both painter and diplomat. He had titles of nobility conferred on him by Philip IV in 1624, was granted a special pension by Isabella in 1628, and was knighted in both Spain and England.

Rubens was regarded as the master of the "painterly" style—a style marked by loose, open brushwork and an emphasis on color. Unlike the "linear" style, which used hard, sharp contour lines to clearly define the edges of objects, the painterly style depends more on suggestion and implication to establish forms.

His influence on contemporary artists was vast, with his students, notably Anthony van Dyck, becoming successful. Even REMBRANDT's dramatic style of the 1630s can be traced to the model of Rubens. Rubens's work was also influential outside his home country. During his mission to Madrid in 1628 he had enormous influence on the Spanish painter DIEGO VELÁZQUEZ. Rubens was not only admired by other painters, but was also celebrated in the writing of contemporary humanists. His reputation remained strong throughout most of the remainder of the seventeenth century.

Rubens's dynamic, twisting forms and painterly approach became the basis for much of the Rococo art of the eighteenth century. In the early nineteenth century, he was regarded as a hero by the French Romantics, and he became a model for such painters as Eugène Delacroix. Later in that century the Impressionist PIERRE-AUGUSTE RENOIR also valued Rubens' painterly approach, using it as a point of departure for his paintings of bathers.

Rubens is now regarded as the most influential artist in northern Europe during the seventeenth century.

Domenico

WORLD EVENTS		RUBENS' LIFE
Ottoman dominance of Mediterranean ends	1571	
	1577	Peter Paul Rubens is born
	1598	Rubens becomes master painter (member of guild)
	1600–08	Rubens is court painter to duke of Mantua
	1610–14	Rubens paints *Descent from the Cross*
Thirty Years' War in Europe	1618–48	
	1626	Rubens begins diplomatic career
	1636	Rubens paints *Landscape with the Chateau of Steen*
	1640	Rubens dies
Glorious Revolution in England	1688	

For Further Reading

Belkin, Kristin Lohse. *Rubens.* London: Phaidon, 1998.

Sutton, P. C., ed. *The Age of Rubens.* Exhibition catalogue. Boston: Museum of Fine Arts; Toledo, Ohio: Museum of Art, 1993.

White, Christopher. *Peter Paul Rubens: Man and Artist.* New Haven, Conn.: Yale University Press, 1987.

Sappho

Poet

c. Sixth Century B.C.E.

Life and Work

Sappho was one of the most accomplished and influential of the Greek poets of her time. She stands out as the greatest female author of the classical world.

Little is certain about Sappho's life. The existing biographical information has been gathered from the writings of Herodotus and from a Greek lexicon called the *Suidas*, compiled at the end of the tenth century C.E. It is fairly certain that Sappho lived during the late seventh and early sixth centuries B.C.E., that she was born at Mytilene or Eresus on the island of Lesbos in Asia Minor, and that she was from an aristocratic family. Lesbos was in a state of political turmoil during her lifetime and she was forced to leave for some time to live in Sicily. After

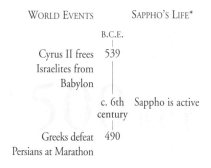

WORLD EVENTS	SAPPHO'S LIFE*
	B.C.E.
Cyrus II frees	539
Israelites from	
Babylon	
	c. 6th Sappho is active
	century
Greeks defeat	490
Persians at Marathon	

Scholars cannot date the specific events in Sappho's life with accuracy.

returning, legend has it that she married and founded a *thiasos*, a school where young girls were taught arts and social graces. The school was also a cult of Aphrodite and Eros, the Greek muses of love and beauty.

How Sappho's work was recorded or passed on during her lifetime is unknown. A substantial body of her work was collected in nine volumes in the third century B.C.E. However, her works twice came under attack for immorality and were burned, first by Bishop Gregory Nazianzus of Constantinople in the 380s C.E. and then by Pope Gregory VII in 1073 C.E. No manuscripts survived these purges and until the nineteenth century only two complete poems and some fragments of her work were known. In 1898 scholars found additional verse fragments on papyrus from the third century B.C.E., and in 1914 coffins were discovered in Egypt wrapped in scraps of paper on which bits of text were written, some of which were attributed to Sappho. The work gathered from these discoveries is primarily in fragments.

From these fragments, it is clear that Sappho wrote primarily in melic or lyric verse and sung to the accompaniment of music. This form is made up of short stanzas, one of which came to be known as Sapphic meter. The great impact of the poems is in their intensely personal tone and the depth of emotion. There is little else in Greek literature to which modern readers can relate on such a personal level.

One version of Sappho's life, recorded by the Roman poet OVID, says that she threw herself off a cliff after being disappointed in love. Other legends say that she lived to old age.

Legacy

Sappho perfected lyric poetry in ancient Greece and her work is some of the most emotionally intimate and personal to have survived.

At the time that she wrote, epic narratives were flourishing in Homer's wake. Sappho brought lyric poetry to prominence with work that was widely read and imitated at the time she produced it. Her work inspired later lyric poets, including Anacreon, Ibycus, and Theocritus.

The marriage songs that Sappho composed and performed raised this form to a high level of art. According to one legend, the great leader Solon of Athens said that he would like to learn a poem of Sappho's and then die, which illus-

trates the importance of her work at the time, as does a couplet attributed to Plato in which Sappho is named as a tenth muse.

Soon after her death, however, Sappho was also regarded as an immoral figure. She was mocked for her supposed promiscuity and lesbianism in many of the burlesque parodies that characterized the middle comedy of the fourth century B.C.E. This controversy has always flourished alongside her poetry. Sappho is as well known for the name of her homeland, which has become synonymous with female homosexuality, as she is for the verse that hints at her own homosexuality.

Her verse is, however, the more intriguing side of her legacy. She was widely read in ancient Rome, and two of the great poets of that era, Horace and Catullus, openly imitated her style, reviving Sapphic meter and drawing on her highly personal diction.

Sappho was virtually unknown in medieval times and for some time after but a new critical interest in her work was sparked by the discovery of the additional fragments in 1898 and 1914. She became the symbol of passion for the Romantic movement of the nineteenth century. Many of the European Romantics translated, imitated, and admired her work, including Algernon Charles Swinburne, Dante Gabriel Rossetti, CHARLES-PIERRE BAUDELAIRE, Madame de Staël, Heinrich von Kleist, and Alfred, Lord Tennyson.

Her emotional directness and the intensity and simplicity of her verse have made Sappho and her poetry a lasting subject for poets, novelists, playwrights, and biographers into the twenty-first century.

Watson

For Further Reading

Barnstone, Willis, ed. *Sappho and the Greek Lyric Poets: Including the Complete Poetry of Sappho.* New York: Schocken Books, 1988.

Greene, Ellen, ed. *Reading Sappho: Contemporary Approaches.* Berkeley: University of California Press, 1999.

Schoenberg, Arnold

Composer

1874–1951

Life and Work

One of twentieth-century classical music's most ingenious composers, Arnold Schoenberg initiated an unprecedented divorce between composers and audiences by his creation of the extraordinarily influential 12-tone method of composition.

The child of a Jewish shoe store owner, Schoenberg was born in Vienna, Austria on September 13, 1874. Even before adolescence he was writing string trios for himself and two classmates. After a period of study with composer Alexander Zemlinsky, Schoenberg emerged as an unusually adventurous explorer of the daring harmonies pioneered by German opera titan RICHARD WAGNER.

Schoenberg's string sextet *Verklärte Nacht* (*Transfigured Night*) of 1899, a richly hued work so radical that it took four years to find its first performance, was followed by the gigantic choral *Gurrelieder* (*Songs of Gurre*), which strained the limits of classical harmony. Between about 1906 and 1912 Schoenberg moved away from the harmonic system entirely. The last movement of 1908's String Quartet No. 2—featuring a vocal part beginning with the (German) text "I feel a breeze from other planets"—was the first piece he wrote without any indication of a harmonic home base. Schoenberg then experimented with new compositional devices, such as sequences of shifting orchestral colors in the Five Orchestral Pieces of 1909, and *Sprechstimme* (*Speech-song*, a novel form of text declamation) in the 1912 song cycle *Pierrot Lunaire* (*Lunar Pierrot*).

Schoenberg struggled during the years around World War I to devise a method of unifying his music in the face of the multiple possibilities that his innovations had opened up. For six years he published nothing new, but in 1923 the 12-tone (or dodecaphonic) method made its debut in Schoenberg's *Suite for Piano*. The essence of the method was that a composition, or an individual movement of one, would be based upon a series or "tone row" consisting of the 12 pitches available in the Western octave, arranged in a fixed order; the row might be reversed or inverted (or both), but not altered. Schoenberg's most ambitious and arguably most successful 12-tone work was the 1932 opera *Moses und Aron*.

In 1933, the rise of Nazism forced Schoenberg to move to the United States, where he continued to compose and gained new followers. He settled in Los Angeles and died there on July 13, 1951.

Legacy

Arnold Schoenberg's 12-tone method and its elaborations dominated university composition curricula in both Europe and the United States for several decades; his earlier works, which toward the end of the century became his most widely performed, proved equally significant.

Schoenberg and his two most famous students, Alban Berg and Anton Webern, became known collectively as the Second Viennese School, a designation whose implied comparison with the Viennese trinity of FRANZ JOSEPH HAYDN, WOLFGANG AMADEUS MOZART, and LUDWIG VAN BEETHOVEN lent it high prestige. The works from the first part of Schoenberg's career had a dark, extreme intensity that seemed to mirror the crisis in European society that culminated in World War I. Berg's opera *Wozzeck*, written between 1917 and 1921, borrowed from Schoenberg the *Sprechstimme* device and many other compositional ideas; based on GEORG BÜCHNER's play, this grim tale of a poor soldier's descent toward madness and suicide is considered by many to be the greatest and most characteristic work of the chaotic period encompassing the war and its aftermath.

Berg's second opera, *Lulu*, followed Schoenberg's 12-tone method, but it was Schoenberg's other major intellectual heir, Webern, who demonstrated the system's profound possibilities. His tiny, concentrated works had a crystalline precision that inspired "serialist" composers (as adherents of the Schoenberg–Webern line were often known) after World War II to awesome heights of compositional complexity.

In the so-called total serialism adopted by the French composer Pierre Boulez and the American Milton Babbitt, not only tones but also other dimensions of music, such as duration, tone color, and dynamics, could be organized into series. The dense concatenations of fixed shapes that resulted made little connection musically with the experiences of ordinary listeners;

indeed, Babbitt likened his colleagues' efforts to those of cutting-edge scholars in the physical scientists whose work might be understood only by a few specialists. It is widely believed, however, that serial music was one of the twentieth century's great intellectual achievements, and that Arnold Schoenberg set it in motion.

Manheim

WORLD EVENTS		SCHOENBERG'S LIFE
Germany is united	1871	
	1874	Arnold Schoenberg is born in Vienna, Austria
Spanish-American War	1898	
	1899	Schoenberg composes string sextet *Verklärte Nacht*
	1908	Schoenberg writes string quartet movement without a harmonic center
	1912	Schoenberg pioneers *Sprechstimme* technique
World War I	1914–18	
Russian Revolution	1917	
	1923	Schoenberg first applies twelve-tone system
Great Depression	1929–39	
	1932	Schoenberg composes twelve-tone opera *Moses und Aron*
	1933	Schoenberg flees Nazism and moves to U.S
World War II	1939–45	
Communist China is established	1949	
Korean War	1950–53	
	1951	Schoenberg dies
African independence movement begins	1957	

For Further Reading

Reich, Willi. *Schoenberg: A Critical Biography.* Translated by L. Black. New York: Praeger, 1971.

Smith, Joan A. *Schoenberg and His Circle: A Viennese Portrait.* New York: Schirmer Books, 1986.

Schumann, Robert

Composer
1810–1856

Life and Work

The ultimate musical Romantic, Robert Schumann was one of the most important European composers of the nineteenth century.

Schumann was born in Zwickau, Germany, on June 8, 1810. During his adolescence he suffered both the death of his father and the suicide of his sister; he himself would be plagued all his life by fears of insanity. His mother urged him to study law, and in 1828 he enrolled at the University of Leipzig with that aim but spent much of his time writing music—his earliest compositions date from this period.

In 1830 Schumann moved into the house of his piano teacher, Friedrich Wieck. His piano skills blossomed, but his habit of passing time in Leipzig's taverns irritated Wieck, whose daughter Clara was herself a promising performer. A hand injury Schumann suffered in 1832 put an end to his performing career; the injury has often been attributed to a mishap with a mechanical device intended to strengthen a pianist's fingers, but his symptoms might have been side effects of venereal disease treatments commonly in use at the time. Depressed over the death of his sister-in-law, Schumann attempted suicide in 1833.

Schumann and Clara Wieck fell in love in 1835; the composer's ways endeared him little to his potential father-in-law, but the romance flourished. Schumann's piano music grew freer and more original as the 1830s progressed; such works as the *Kinderszenen* (*Childhood Scenes*) of 1838 seemed to draw their forms not from pre-existing models but from the spontaneous flow of emotion and ideas. His marriage to Clara in 1840 (the lovers finally had to take Clara's father to court) unleashed a torrent of creativity. That year, he wrote nearly 150 songs, and he soon turned to other genres—symphony, chamber music, dramatic music, and more—with equal intensity.

Schumann became renowned as a composer and critic; his critical writing often relied on two invented characters, Florestan and Eusebius, who represented aspects of Schumann's own personality. Early in 1854 Schumann complained of loud tones ringing in his ears, and soon afterward tried to jump into the Rhine River. Placed in an asylum near Bonn for the rest of his life, he died on July 29, 1856.

Legacy

Robert Schumann's short piano pieces and songs, evanescent but intense moments of mood, are definitive creations of German Romanticism and have long been loved by connoisseurs and amateurs alike.

Indeed, his piano miniatures perfectly exemplify the Romantic association between musical sound and external idea; works such as the *Kinderszenen* are so evocative that they almost seem to be songs without words. In the field of the art song, Schumann was the most

important practitioner after Schubert of the song cycle, a collection of songs depicting emotions and events in the life of a single protagonist, often the poet speaking in the first person. Schumann's song cycles, all written during the hectic year of 1840, employed first-rate texts by Heinrich Heine, Joseph von Eichendorff, and other leading German poets; they did much to establish the art song as a refined dialogue between the musical and verbal realms. As a critic, Schumann contributed to that dialogue in a different way— he is generally regarded as one of the creators of modern musical criticism.

Except for the highly idiomatic piano concerto (completed in 1845), Schumann's works in larger forms today occupy less exalted levels of the classical pantheon than his small pieces. His four symphonies and a few of his chamber works appear moderately frequently on concert programs, but some critics have found them lacking in formal rigor compared to the perfect relation of part to whole found, for example, in LUDWIG VAN BEETHOVEN's works. Nevertheless, these pieces wrestled with the compositional issues of their day, most notably the problem of building large-scale form in an essentially melodic idiom.

In the field of absolute music (music without explicit reference to external narratives or ideas), Schumann's works pointed directly toward those of JOHANNES BRAHMS, who knew Robert Schumann at the end of his life, and later became close to Clara. Schumann's body of work as a whole provides an ideal introduction to the Romantic mind.

Manheim

World Events		Schumann's Life
French Revolution begins	1789	
	1810	Robert Schumann is born in Zwickau, Germany
Latin American independence movement begins	1811	
Congress of Vienna reorganizes Europe	1815	
	1828	Schumann enrolls at University of Leipzig to study law
	1830	Schumann moves into household of Friedrich Wieck
	1833	Schumann attempts suicide
	1835	Schumann and Clara Wieck fall in love
	1838	Schumann writes *Kinderszenen* piano pieces
	1840	Schumann and Clara Wieck marry
Revolutions in Austria, France, Germany, and Italy	1848	
	1854	Schumann attempts to drown himself
	1856	Schumann dies
U.S. Civil War	1861–65	

For Further Reading
Chissell, Joan. *Schumann.* London: Dent, 1977.
Daverio, John. *Robert Schumann: Herald of a "New Poetic Age."* New York: Oxford University Press, 1987.

Sesshū Toyo

Painter and Calligrapher
1420–1506

Life and Work

Sesshū Toyo is widely considered the greatest painter in Japan during the Muromachi Period (1338–1573).

Sesshū was born in 1420 into the Oda family in Bitchu Province. He entered the Buddhist monastery of Mannenji in Kyoto, the capital of Japan, and then went on to study Zen Buddhism in Shokokuji, one of the Gozan, or Five Mountain Temples, in Kyoto. The Ryoan-in, a subtemple of Shokokuji, functioned as an atelier and residence for the monk-painters. It is here that Sesshū came to identify with the painting lineage of Shubun and his predecessor, Josetsu.

In his late thirties Sesshū moved to Suo Province and built his Unkoku studio, where he devoted himself to painting. Sesshū had an opportunity to study Chinese painting when he traveled to China in 1467. He spent two years in China, residing initially in Beijing, capital of the Ming dynasty (1368–1644) before traveling to Hangzhou and Yangzhou.

When Sesshū returned to Japan in 1469, the country was in the middle of the Onin War, a period of tremendous political instability and civil unrest that would last until 1477. At his Unkoku studio, Sesshū immersed himself in his art and began to gain recognition from a wide spectrum of society: the aristocracy, Buddhist monks, and the merchant class.

The civil disturbances eventually forced Sesshū to leave in 1476; he traveled through some of Japan's most beautiful natural scenery, returning to Yamaguchi in 1484, where continued to work until his death in 1506.

One of Sesshū's most famous Zen-inspired paintings is a hanging scroll known as *Haboku Sansui* (*Splashed-Ink Landscape*). Dated 1494, it is painted in the monochrome ink style of the Chinese Chan (Zen) painter Yujian. It deploys a spontaneous and unpremeditated execution of brush strokes and broad washes of ink to capture the immediacy of the *satori*, or enlightenment, experience. This can be seen in the gradual dispersion of landscape forms depicting an experience of the world devolving into the ground of nonarticulation, or "nothingness"—the *yo-haku* or "blank space."

Another side of Sesshū's artistic personality may be seen in *Flowers and Birds of the Four Seasons*, a pair of sixfold screens two of a number of decorative painting attributed to the artist.

Legacy

Sesshū Toyo is known to have studied carefully and made faithful copies of the works of Southern Song and Ming academic painters as well Chan (Zen) Buddhist painters. His brilliance lay in his ability to creatively appropriate and transform these styles in paintings that gave expression to the sensibilities and aesthetic values of Muromachi Japan. For example, *Summer Landscape,* one of a set of four hanging scrolls, is based on *Landscape in the Manner of Guo Xi* by the Ming dynasty court painter Li Zai. The simplicity and clarity of Sesshū's compositional design, however, suggests an intentional interpretation according to the aesthetic ideals of Japanese art.

In keeping with the traditional transmission of Zen teachings from master to disciple, Sesshū identified himself with the artistic lineage of his predecessors at Shokokuji, Shubun, and Josetsu. However, Sesshū is responsible for developing stylistic innovations that became an important model for sixteenth-century painters. This is documented in *Genealogy of the Master's Descendants* composed by the Zen monk Kogetsu Sogen (1574–1643).

Among those who actually studied with the master are the Zen monks Bokusho, Shugetsu, and Shutoku. The decorative screen painters Unkoku Togan (1547–1618) and Hasegawa Tohaku (1539–1610) also made claim to the Sesshū lineage, very likely to gain authority for their own work at a time when the Kano School was in a position of artistic dominance.

Goldberg

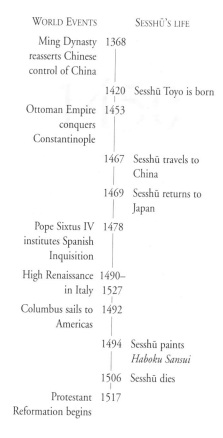

WORLD EVENTS		SESSHŪ'S LIFE
Ming Dynasty reasserts Chinese control of China	1368	
	1420	Sesshū Toyo is born
Ottoman Empire conquers Constantinople	1453	
	1467	Sesshū travels to China
	1469	Sesshū returns to Japan
Pope Sixtus IV institutes Spanish Inquisition	1478	
High Renaissance in Italy	1490–1527	
Columbus sails to Americas	1492	
	1494	Sesshū paints *Haboku Sansui*
	1506	Sesshū dies
Protestant Reformation begins	1517	

For Further Reading

Brinker, Helmut, and Hiroshi Kanazawa. *Zen: Masters of Meditation in Images and Writings.* Translated by Andreas Leisinger. Zurich: Artibus Asiae, 1996.

Mason, Penelope. *History of Japanese Art.* New York: Harry N. Abrams, 1993.

Watanabe, Akiyoshi, Kanazawa Hiroshi, and Paul Varley. *Of Water and Ink: Muromachi Period Paintings from Japan 1392–1568.* Exhibition catalogue. Detroit, Mich.: Founders Society of the Detroit Institute of Arts, 1986.

Shakespeare, William

Dramatist and Poet
1564–1616

WORLD EVENTS		SHAKESPEARE'S LIFE:
Protestant Reformation begins	1517	
	1564	William Shakespeare is born in Stratford-upon-Avon, England
Ottoman dominance of Mediterranean ends	1571	
	1580s	Shakespeare moves to London
	early 1590s	Shakespeare becomes known in theatrical circles
	1599	Shakespeare and associates finance construction of Globe Theatre
	1600	Shakespeare's *Hamlet* is produced
	c. 1610	Shakespeare retires to Stratford-upon-Avon
	1616	Shakespeare dies
Thirty Years' War in Europe	1618–48	

Life and Work

Tradition and contemporary opinion agree in ranking William Shakespeare as the most important writer in the history of the English language.

In an age when art was cultivated largely in aristocratic circles, Shakespeare was a commoner—a fact that has caused some to speculate that someone else might have written the works attributed to him. Shakespeare was baptized on April 26, 1564, in Stratford-upon-Avon, England. His father was a fairly prosperous merchant, and Shakespeare enjoyed what we would call a good high school education. Under circumstances now unknown, in the 1580s he moved to London and embarked on a theatrical career; for much of his life he worked both as an actor and playwright. Three linked plays based on the life of King Henry VI attracted attention around 1590. In the early 1590s a series of romantic comedies, including *The Taming of the Shrew* (1593–94) and *A Midsummer Night's Dream* (1595–96), helped establish his reputation, along with the quintessential romantic tragedy *Romeo and Juliet* (c. 1595–96), and two long narrative poems.

As Shakespeare's popularity grew, he and his associates, the Burbage brothers, constructed the Globe Theater in 1599. Gaining the sponsorship of King James I in 1603, the Lord Chamberlain's Men became the King's Men, and Shakespeare's reach increased. To the following years belong several of Shakespeare's towering tragedies: *Othello* (1604), *King Lear* (1605–06), and *Macbeth* (1606). A collection of 154 sonnets by Shakespeare was published in 1609. By 1610 Shakespeare was able to retire to Stratford; he died there on April 23, 1616.

Shakespeare's 37 plays fall into the broad categories of tragedy, comedy, and historical drama, and several useful subdivisions are apparent. The tragedies include works such as *Julius Caesar* (1599) and *Antony and Cleopatra* (1606–07) that are based on stories of Roman antiquity but update them with contemporary political and moral concerns; these stand in contrast to the almost metaphysical "great" tragedies—*Othello, Lear, Macbeth,* and *Hamlet* (c. 1600). Shakespeare's comedies include sparkling romantic works such as *Twelfth Night* (1601–02), as well as darker, more pointed plays such as *All's Well That Ends Well* (1602–03) and *Measure for Measure* (1604). Difficult to classify are a group of semifantastic works Shakespeare wrote near the end of his career: *Cymbeline* (1609–10), *The Winter's Tale* (1610–11), and *The Tempest* (1611) include both comic and tragic elements.

Legacy

There is no way to delineate the magnitude of William Shakespeare's influence in a few paragraphs, but perhaps a focus upon two contrasting aspects of his legacy will indicate his mastery of both language and material.

Shakespeare enriched the English language to a greater degree than any other writer. Countless sayings, metaphors, and elegant turns of phrase in common use in modern English have their origins in Shakespeare's plays. We may humorously minimize the importance of a law or rule by saying that it is "more honored in the breach than in the observance," without making the connection to *Hamlet,* or sadly remark upon "how sharper than a serpent's tooth it is to have a thankless child" without reflecting upon Lear's harrowing odyssey of exile and return. Even so simple a directive as "let's kill all the lawyers" we owe to Shakespeare, whose words form an elegant lacework within our speech and thought.

Despite the extraordinary richness and brilliance of his language and its consequent familiarity, Shakespeare's plays depend on more than English poetry alone, as the centuries-long Shakespeare tradition outside the English-speaking world demonstrates. Indeed, it was German critics who, in the eighteenth century, first advanced a consideration of Shakespeare beyond the establishment of texts and surface appreciations of his work to a deeper consideration of his outlook. Even outside the Western world Shakespeare is known and appreciated, for the themes of his work—love, power, family—are universal, and the plays take place on a level that is both mythic and mundane. In Shakespeare, literature in English reached its height in a perfect union of form and content.

Manheim

For Further Reading

Andrews, John F. *William Shakespeare: His World, His Work, His Influence.* New York: Charles Scribner's Sons, 1985.
Schoenbaum, S. *Shakespeare's Lives.* Oxford: Oxford University Press, 1991.
Taylor, Gary. *Reinventing Shakespeare: A Cultural History from the Restoration to the Present.* New York: Weidenfeld & Nicolson, 1989.

Shankar, Ravi

Sitarist and Composer
1920–

Life and Work

An indefatigable creative force who introduced the classical music of India to the rest of the world, Ravi Shankar experienced a decade of popular celebrity, largely through his association with the Beatles. His cross-cultural activities, though, have extended far beyond the few collaborations that made him famous.

Shankar was born April 7, 1920, in the Indian holy city of Benares. His older brother Uday was a dancer who took a troupe of Indian musicians and dancers to Paris; Ravi Shankar joined his brother at the age of 10, excelling as a dancer himself and making contact with Western musicians at school. He returned to India in 1938 to study the sitar with the master Ustad Allauddin Khan, submitting himself for more than seven years to a severe practice regimen that would sometimes make his fingers bleed.

Shankar emerged a virtuoso and, after a 1957 tour of the United States, began to seek out Western musical collaborators. At first he worked with classical performers, appearing at a 1958 Paris concert with violinists Yehudi Menuhin and David Oistrakh; he later composed two concertos for sitar and orchestra. In 1962 he released *Ravi Shankar in Concert*, the first in a long string of recordings.

One of those recordings impressed Beatles member George Harrison, who flew to India to study with Shankar for seven weeks in 1966. Harrison's support led to enthusiasm for Shankar's music within the youth culture of the time, which was already awakening to Eastern philosophies and cultures. The two musicians would appear together in 1971 at a pair of massive benefit concerts for Bangladeshi flood victims; thereafter Shankar was a star in his own right. The rigors of popularity took their toll, however, and Shankar became increasingly disillusioned by the drug use that was common among his new fans.

In 1975 a stress-induced breakdown led him to take a two-year break from performing, and when he returned to the stage, he avoided high-profile appearances. But he continued cross-cultural explorations; on his 1979 East Greets East tour he worked with Japanese classical masters, and his score for the 1982 film biography *Gandhi* won wide acclaim.

Shankar remained active as a performer and composer through the 1990s. Among the many indicators of his stature was a 1996 boxed compilation of his recordings, produced by Harrison and entitled *Ravi: In Celebration*.

Legacy

Ravi Shankar not only brought the music of India to the rest of the world, but also inspired a host of later musicians who have pursued various methods of merging Indian and Western styles.

The most famous beneficiaries of Shankar's influence were the Beatles, whose Indian-inflected songs spanned the last five years of their existence as a group. But other Indian–Western fusions of the 1960s and 1970s owed at least something to Shankar's pioneering efforts. The jazz ensemble Shakti, featuring guitarist John McLaughlin and including several Indian performers, explored commonalities in the practice of improvisation between Indian music and jazz. Among Shankar's own later creative partners was the Minimalist composer Philip Glass; the contemplative, repetitive music that came to be called Minimalist took much inspiration from Indian musical thought in general and from the person who had introduced it to America in particular.

In the field of Indian classical music itself, Shankar's influence was also considerable.

Several members of his family became noteworthy performers, and in the late 1990s Shankar devotees closely watched the emergence of his daughter Anoushka as a solo artist in her own right.

Beyond the specific endeavors for which his example was paramount, Shankar must be counted as one of the originators of the category of world music. Expressive elements in film music that drew on Asian sources, displayed, for instance, in the music NUSRAT FATEH ALI KHAN contributed to *Dead Man Walking*, are all traceable to Shankar's cinematic work. The broad success of Indian-based popular music, especially in Britain, where the recordings of vocalist Sheila Chandra gained commercial success, likewise made it hard to remember the time before Shankar, when Indian classical music hardly ever appeared in commercial, popular contexts.

Manheim

WORLD EVENTS		SHANKAR'S LIFE
Russian Revolution	1917	
	1920	Ravi Shankar is born in Benares, India
Great Depression	1929–39	
	1938	After living in Paris, Shankar returns to India for study
World War II	1939–45	
Communist China is established	1949	
Korean War	1950–53	
African independence movement begins	1957	Shankar tours the United States
	1958	Shankar collaborates with Western classical musicians
	1962	Shankar releases *Ravi Shankar in Concert*
	1966	Shankar works with George Harrison
	1971	Shankar and Harrison play benefit concert for Bangladesh flood relief
Vietnam War ends	1975	
	1982	Shankar writes score for film *Gandhi*
Dissolution of Soviet Union	1991	
South Africa dismantles apartheid	1994	
	1996	*Ravi: In Celebration* boxed set of recordings released

For Further Reading

Shankar, Ravi. *My Music, My Life.* Delhi: Vikas Publications, 1969.

Titon, Jeff Todd, ed. W*orlds of Music: An Introduction to the Music of the World's Peoples,* 3rd ed. New York: Schirmer Books, 1996.

Shen Zhou

Painter and Scholar
1427–1509

Life and Work

Shen Zhou was the first great master of the Wu School of literati painting (the art of the *wenren,* or scholar-gentleman) in Ming dynasty of China (1368–1644).

Born in 1427 north of Suzhou, Shen Zhou emulated his wealthy father, uncle, and grandfather—living as a retired scholar, devoting himself to hosting literary and artistic gatherings, visiting the scenic places in and around Suzhou, and dedicating himself to the practice of poetry, painting and calligraphy as means of self-cultivation, gift-giving, and social exchange.

Shen Zhou never took the examinations that would have led to official government service. After the death of his father in 1477, Shen Zhou was known to excuse himself when invited or pressed into official service, claiming that he was obliged to care for his widowed mother. In a gesture of mock humility, he adopted the *zi,* or style name, Shitian ("Field of Stones"), implying his social uselessness.

The tradition of literati painting was sustained during the early Ming by such scholar-artists as Wang Fu (1362–1416), Du Qiong (1369–1474), Yao Shou (1423–95) and Liu Jue (1410–72). All of these artists are known for incorporating into their works stylistic elements derived from earlier Yuan masters. However, with the possible exception of Liu Jue, their work ultimately lacks originality.

Shen Zhou initially studied painting with the little-known artist Chen Mengxian. He benefited most, however, by studying paintings of the Four Masters of the Yuan dynasty in his own collection and the collections of fellow Suzhou literati. Shen Zhou's great contribution was to creatively transform these styles—which originally gave expression to the artists' responses to the alienating conditions created by the Mongol conquest—in ways that enabled him to speak to the radically different conditions of his own world.

For example, he painted *Lofty Mount Lu* in 1467; a visual and metaphorical correlation is drawn between the perfectly erect figure of his teacher, represented in the lower foreground, and the lofty magnificence of Mount Lu, upon which he gazes. In this work, Shen Zhou rendered the mountains and trees in the densely textured, richly inked brushwork and monumental landscape style of the Yuan master Wang Meng (c. 1308–85), to which he brought his own vigorous brush technique and strong sense of structural arrangement. Shen Zhou's incorporation of an earlier master's style in his own self-expression was an assertion of artistic affiliation or identification.

Shen Zhou died in 1509.

Legacy

In the last decades of the Mongol-dominated Yuan dynasty (1279–1368), the city of Suzhou and its surroundings had been a major center of literati painting. During the reign of the first Chinese emperor of the Ming dynasty, there was a purge of scholars from this area for having supported the emperor's rival during the campaigns against the Mongols.

In the middle Ming period, 100 years after the near destruction of Suzhou as a center of literati culture, Shen Zhou was principally responsible for revitalizing the tradition of literati painting, serving as a model for later scholar-painters.

Shen Zhou's most famous disciple was Wen Zhengming (1470–1559). He instructed Wen by having him study the paintings of earlier masters in his private collection. Thus the most profound influence on Wen Zhengming was not Shen Zhou's artistic style, but the values implicit in his stance as a scholar-painter.

Wen, who lived to the age of 89, passed his teacher's legacy to his contemporaries and the younger generation of scholar-painters, defining the general character of sixteenth-century Suzhou painting.

Goldberg

For Further Reading

Cahill, James. *Parting at the Shore: Chinese Painting of the Early and Middle Ming Dynasty, 1368–1580.* New York and Tokyo: Weatherhill, 1978.

Edwards, Richard. *The Field of Stones: A Study of the Art of Shen Chou.* Washington, D.C.: Freer Gallery of Art, 1962.

Fong, Wen, and James C. Y. Watt, et al. *Possessing the Past: Treasures From the National Palace Museum, Taipei.* Exhibition catalogue. New York: Metropolitan Museum of Art, 1996.

Smith, Bessie

Vocalist
1894–1937

Life and Work

Bessie Smith, "The Empress of the Blues," was the most celebrated of the blues singers, mostly female, who brought music from the streets, circuses, and medicine shows of the South to vaudeville stages throughout the nation.

Smith was born into poverty in Chattanooga, Tennessee, on April 15, 1894. During the 1910s she took inspiration from Gertrude "Ma" Rainey, the pioneer of the female vaudeville blues, and by the end of the decade her own headliner gigs on the T.O.B.A. (Theater Owners' Booking Association, or, more colloquially, "Tough on Black Artists") vaudeville circuit came regularly. On stage Smith developed a charisma and down-to-earth power over her audience that for some observers brought to mind the preachers of the black church.

Recordings of the blues, made from 1920 onward, raised the profile of the genre and broadened Smith's reach. Her first recording, 1923's "Down Hearted Blues," sold some 780,000 copies within six months of its release. On recordings, Smith was teamed with such leading jazz instrumentalists of the day as pianist James P. Johnson (who joined her on 1927's "Back Water Blues," her best known recording in her own time), cornetist Joe

Smith, and, most famously, trumpeter LOUIS ARMSTRONG, whose several collaborations with Smith included the famous "St. Louis Blues" of 1925, a masterpiece of measured, stately pessimism. In her encounters with jazz musicians, Smith showed the astonishing technical control and emotional range that became the foundation for the raw power of her performances.

Smith combined vocal mastery with a flamboyant personal style. She and her retinue traveled in a railroad car that she owned herself, and at the height of her career in the 1920s her sold-out shows required considerable crowd control measures. But the Depression dented Smith's popularity, and a parasitic husband and her own abuse of alcohol made things worse. Several key figures in the emerging swing style of the 1930s appreciated her talents, and she seemed to be making a comeback when her life ended in an auto crash in Clarksdale, Mississippi, on September 26, 1937.

Legacy

Bessie Smith possessed a commanding presence and consummate artistry that enthralled audiences of the 1920s and influenced performers long after her death. Like other musicians who brought an existing art form to a high point, Smith in the process gave birth to a new one. Forever identified with the blues, it became clear in retrospect that she had also helped to create the art of the jazz vocal.

Smith was the first African-American woman to become a true star, and as such, her impact in her own time was immense. The extent of her popularity may be gauged not only by her peak weekly earnings of $2,000, but also by the legends that sprang up around her and continued to resonate after her death. It was said that Ma Rainey had kidnapped her to mold her talents and that she died because a whites-only Mississippi hospital refused her admittance after her fatal accident. Neither tale is likely to be true, but they testify to the sheer power that Smith's career held in the imagination of the public that continued to support her even during her descent.

Her popularity stemmed not just from charisma but from vocal versatility, and it was her way of deeply considering what she sang that impressed the jazz singers who came after her. Known best for slow, excruciating blues, Smith could equally well convey the party-time

high spirits of "Gimme a Pigfoot," recorded at her last sessions in 1933; she likewise excelled at rhythmically intelligent interpretations of popular songs of the day, as in her 1927 recording of IRVING BERLIN's "Alexander's Ragtime Band." If the tragic melancholy of BILLIE HOLIDAY is unthinkable without Smith's example, so too are the precise song readings of Ella Fitzgerald and the sharp proto–rock and roll of LaVern Baker. The Empress of the Blues opened whole new domains that later singers explored.

Manheim

WORLD EVENTS		SMITH'S LIFE
Germany is united	1871	
	1894	Bessie Smith is born
Spanish-American War	1898	
	1910s	Smith performs with Ma Rainey
World War I	1914–18	
Russian Revolution	1917	
	1923	Smith makes her first recording, "Down Hearted Blues"
	1925	Smith records "St. Louis Blues" with Louis Armstrong
	1927	Smith records "Back Water Blues" with James P. Johnson
		Smith records Irving Berlin's "Alexander's Ragtime Band"
Great Depression	1929–39	
	1933	Smith's last sessions include "Gimme a Pigfoot"
	1937	Smith dies
World War II	1939–45	

For Further Reading

Albertson, Chris. *Bessie Smith: Empress of the Blues.* New York: Schirmer, 1975.

Harrison, Daphne Duval. *Black Pearls: Blues Queens of the 1920s.* New Brunswick, N.J.: Rutgers University Press, 1988.

Kay, Jackie. *Bessie Smith.* New York: Absolute, 1997.

Sophocles

Playwright

c. 496 B.C.E.–c. 406 B.C.E.

Life and Work

Sophocles was the second of the three great Athenian playwrights (the others were Aeschylus and Euripedes) whose work led to the creation of the theatrical drama.

Sophocles was born in Colonus, near Athens, about 496 B.C.E. He read HOMER and the Greek lyric poets in school, was successful in both music and gymnastics, and studied drama with the great tragic playwright Aeschylus. He took part in the political life of Athens in a variety of roles—serving as the treasurer of the Athenian Empire in c. 443 B.C.E. and on a council of generals in the war against the Samians in 440 B.C.E. He was acquainted with the statesman Pericles and with the historian Herodotus and continued to be active in Athenian political life until his death.

In 468 B.C.E. Sophocles' *Triptolemos*, a play that has been lost, won the prize for the best tragedy at the annual Great Dionysia festival. Sophocles defeated his teacher Aeschylus in the competition and would go on to win the prize more than 20 times.

Of his many plays only seven have survived. The earliest of these is *Ajax*, which was probably written before 446 B.C.E. and tells the story of the Trojan hero destroyed by his own pride. The best known and the most frequently performed of Sophocles' plays make up the Oedipus Cycle. *Oedipus Rex* (c. 430) is the story of King Oedipus, who, despite his attempts to change his preordained fate, kills his father and marries his mother. *Antigone,* probably written around 442 B.C.E., relates the story of Oedipus's daughter, who bravely and defiantly determines to bury her dead brother in spite of an edict forbidding it. The third in the cycle is *Oedipus at Colonus,* which Sophocles wrote late in his life; it was first performed in 401, after Sophocles had died. (In the internal chronology of the Oedipus trilogy, the death of Oedipus [in *Oedipus of Colonus*] precedes that of Antigone [in *Antigone*].)

Between 418 and 410 Sophocles wrote *Electra,* the story of a brother and sister who kill their mother and her lover to avenge their father's death. It was at about this time that he also wrote *Philoctetes*, which won first prize at the festival in 409.

In all of his plays, Sophocles portrays characters with great strengths but also tragic flaws, and he sets them in conflict with destiny. Each character suffers under the weight of responsibility that comes with his or her strengths and is forced to contend with the inevitability of fate. The characters as generalized human types are isolated by their strengths, punished for their weaknesses, and made to conform to the dictates of fate and divine power.

Sophocles died in 406 B.C.E., shortly after leading a public mourning for the death of his rival, Euripides.

Legacy

Sophocles was respected as the greatest Athenian playwright during his lifetime, a reputation that has never diminished. Plutarch (46–119 C.E.) wrote about the plays in an essay called *On Advancement of Virtue.* Aristophanes of Byzantium (257–180 B.C.E.) compiled the first complete edition of Sophocles' plays. They were studied and commented upon by scholars in the years following and in the 300s C.E. were edited by Sallustios.

Sophocles moved away from Aeschylus's tetralogy, a series of four plays depicting consecutive action, and developed the series of three independent tragedies. In these self-contained and complete individual plays, Sophocles used emotional intensity and a clear dramatic structure to bring the story to a powerful end. Aristotle in his *Poetics* used *Oedipus Rex* as an example of a perfectly constructed tragedy, and based his theory of the elements of drama upon it. Sophocles' dramas began with a prologue and an entrance song, followed by four alternating dialogue and choral songs, and ended with a departure song. This structure led to the development of the five-act play of modern classical theater.

Sophocles introduced more elaborate scenes and expressive masks than had been used previously, thus increasing the aesthetic possibilities of theater; he began to use a third actor where traditionally there had been only two, allowing for more complex and intricate dialogue; he used a 15-member chorus instead of 12 and increased the choral role, allowing it to explain and elaborate upon the action of the play.

Sophocles' influence on theater and on thought has remained powerful. Byzantine scholars wrote extensively on his work; the early sixteenth century saw many new editions of his plays; in the seventeenth century the dramatists JOHN MILTON, Pierre Corneille, and Jean Baptiste Racine all showed evidence of his influence in their work; in the eighteenth century John Dryden and Voltaire both wrote versions of *Oedipus Rex;* and in the nineteenth century Gotthold Ephraim Lessing, Georg Wilhelm Friedrich Hegel, Søren Kierkegaard, and Friedrich Wilhelm Nietzsche were among the thinkers who discussed his work, while WILLIAM WORDSWORTH, GEORGE ELIOT, and JOHANN WOLFGANG VON GOETHE wrote about his plays.

The twentieth century saw one of the greatest examples of his importance to Western thought when Sigmund Freud developed his psychological theory of the Oedipus complex based on the story of *Oedipus Rex.*

Watson

World Events	Sophocles' Life
	B.C.E.
Cyrus II frees Israelites from Babylon	539
	c. 496 Sophocles is born
Greeks defeat Persians at Marathon	490
	468 Sophocles wins first prize at Great Dionysia festival with his play *Triptolemos*
	c. 425 Sophocles writes –10 *Electra*
	c. 418 Sophocles writes *Antigone*
	409 Sophocles wins first prize at Great Dionesia festival for *Philoctetes*
	406 Sophocles dies
China's "Warring States" Period begins	403
	401 *Oedipus at Colonus* is first performed
Maurya Empire in India is founded	325

For Further Reading

Sophocles. *The Cure at Troy: A Version of Sophocles' Philoctetes.* Translated by Seamus Heaney. New York: Farrar, Straus & Giroux, 1991.

Sophokles: The Complete Plays. Translated by Carl R. Mueller and Anna Krajewska-Wieczorek. Hanover, N.H.: Smith and Kraus, 2000.

Winnington-Ingram, R. P. *Sophocles: An Interpretation.* Cambridge: Cambridge University Press, 1980.

Stravinsky, Igor

Composer
1882–1971

Life and Work

Igor Stravinsky finds inclusion on any short list of great twentieth-century composers in the classical tradition.

Stravinsky was born in Oranienbaum, near St. Petersburg, Russia, on June 17, 1882. He studied the piano from age nine and began the compositional arts of harmony and counterpoint soon after. In 1901 he enrolled in law school at St. Petersburg University, but his attachment to music was stronger, and the following year he started taking composition lessons from Nikolai Rimsky-Korsakov. From the Russian nationalist music of Rimsky-Korsakov and others, Stravinsky inherited features of his own early style: references to Russian folk music and folklore, colorful orchestration, and a bent toward unorthodox harmonies.

Stravinsky's ballets *The Firebird* and *Petrushka* made his reputation with their Paris premieres in 1910 and 1911, respectively. In 1911, he moved with his family to Switzerland. The 1913 premiere of another ballet, *The Rite of Spring*, precipitated an audience riot with its rhythmic and harmonic daring.

The surprising and sometimes harsh motor rhythms of these ballets, so well suited to dance, grew into a Stravinskian trademark. After World War I, Stravinsky continued to experiment with rhythm, and he absorbed the influence of American jazz in such works as *Ragtime*, of 1918. His works of this period were of a smaller scale than the ballets, and to his recognition of the power of rhythm and ritual he added a characteristic cool precision that could erupt on occasion into sharp musical (and verbal) wit.

Stravinsky moved to France in 1920 and embarked on a new stylistic phase with the dance-and-vocal piece *Pulcinella*, based on the music of the eighteenth-century composer Giovanni Pergolesi. For the next several decades Stravinsky would be identified with a "neo-classicism" that turned to musical models from the past. His works found a ready audience in America, where he moved in 1940; the English-language comic opera *The Rake's Progress* marked his last major neo-classic composition in 1948. Despite his advancing years, Stravinsky sought out new challenges; such works as the *Movements for Piano and Orchestra* of 1959 experimented with the highly structured musical system known as serialism. Stravinsky died in New York on April 6, 1971.

Legacy

In his travels through a multiplicity of styles and in his determination to make his own individual voice heard within them, Igor Stravinsky was perhaps the ideal composer for a stylistically plural century, and few composers since his time have remained untouched by his influence.

The emphasis on rhythm that prevails across a broad spectrum of twentieth-century music is traceable to Stravinsky's music, particularly to the profoundly influential rhythmic intensity of *The Rite of Spring*. Beyond that, each turn that Stravinsky's career took inspired followers. Neo-classicism and the influence of jazz both became dominant trends in French music between the world wars. The iconoclastic expatriate American composer George Antheil extended Stravinsky's rhythmic innovations into a language that evoked the emerging power of technology. Stravinsky's early explorations of folk music as a generator not of nationalistic passions but of fresh rhythmic and harmonic forms influenced Béla Bartók and a host of later composers. Calling four countries home over his long career, Stravinsky helped to shape many of the major styles of the twentieth century.

The ideas he set in motion proved to have deeper ramifications that emerged as time passed. In the century's early years ARNOLD SCHOENBERG and others wrote radical works aimed at connoisseurs, but, with *The Rite of Spring*, Stravinsky confronted the public head-on with genuinely new music. After Stravinsky, the angular, the abrupt, and even the ugly held an equal place with beautiful melody and balance in twentieth-century music.

Yet Stravinsky himself created the opposite number to his own radicalism. "The more art is controlled, limited, worked over, the more it is free," he wrote in his *Poetics of Music*, adding that he felt "terror" at the idea that everything was permissible to him musically. The neo-Romanticism and stylistic eclecticism of classical music in the 1980s and 1990s owed much to Stravinsky, and his ultimate legacy may be his re-imaginations of the musical past.

Manheim

WORLD EVENTS		STRAVINSKY'S LIFE
Germany is united	1871	
	1882	Igor Stravinsky is born near St. Petersburg, Russia
Spanish-American War	1898	
	1901	Stravinsky enrolls in law school, but is drawn to musical composition
	1910	*The Firebird* makes Stravinsky's reputation
	1913	Riots break out at premiere of *The Rite of Spring*
World War I	1914–18	
Russian Revolution	1917	
	1920	Stravinsky moves to France; turns to neo-classic styles
Great Depression	1929–39	
World War II	1939–45	
	1940	Stravinsky moves to the United States
Communist China is established	1949	
Korean War	1950–53	
African independence movement begins	1957	
	1959	Stravinsky writes *Movements for Piano and Orchestra*
	1971	Stravinsky dies
Vietnam War ends	1975	

For Further Reading

Druskin, Mikhail. *Igor Stravinsky: His Life, Works, and Views.* Cambridge: Cambridge University Press, 1983.
Griffiths, Paul. *Stravinsky.* London: J. M. Dent & Sons, 1992.

Swift, Jonathan

Novelist and Political Satirist
1667–1745

Life and Work

Jonathan Swift, one of the leading prose satirists of Augustan literature and an Anglican clergyman, wrote the philosophical travel fiction *Gulliver's Travels.*

Swift was born in Dublin on November 30, 1667. He studied Greek, Latin, metaphysics, and rhetoric at Trinity College, receiving his

WORLD EVENTS	SWIFT'S LIFE
Thirty Years' War 1618–48 in Europe	
	1667 Jonathan Swift is born
	1686 Swift graduates from Trinity College
Glorious Revolution 1688 in England	
	1695 Swift ordained by Anglican Church of England
	1704 Swift writes *A Tale of a Tub*
	1726 Swift publishes *Gulliver's Travels*
	1729 Swift publishes *A Modest Proposal*
	1745 Swift dies in Dublin
United States declares 1776 independence	

bachelor of arts in 1686. He then worked in England as secretary to Sir William Temple, a courtier, statesman, and writer, for some years before being ordained a priest of the Anglican Church of Ireland in 1695.

In 1704 he published his first story, *A Tale of a Tub,* in which he satirically attacked current systems of education and of religion in Ireland. The story was controversial and Swift was accused of blasphemy. The allegorical parody that he would master in *Gulliver's Travels* is first apparent in this early work. In 1713 Swift was appointed dean of St. Patrick's Cathedral in Dublin.

Swift was a vocal proponent of Irish rebellion against the English and his satirical political pamphlets on the subject made him a hero of the movement. In the most famous of these pamphlets, *A Modest Proposal,* written in 1729, he ironically suggested, as a remedy for Irish poverty, that the country's poor children be turned into meat for the rich.

Swift was also an important member of the Scriblerus Club, a group characterized by literary hoaxes and satirical attacks on modern science. He collaborated with other members of the group, including Alexander Pope, John Gay, Thomas Parnell, and Dr. John Arbuthnot, and some of these early satires may have formed the beginnings of *Gulliver's Travels.*

Gulliver's Travels was published as *Travels into Several Remote Nations of the World in Four Parts By Lemuel Gulliver* in 1726. It was based on a form of popular travel narratives, and it presented an allegorical portrait of the relations of the French and English governments of the time. In the humorous story of Gulliver, who, in the book's most well-known episode, finds himself taken captive by a society of tiny people called Lilliputians, Swift denounced human pride, vanity, and immorality while satirizing humankind's assumptions about the superiority of its political and social institutions.

Portions of the book were considered too politically incendiary for publication and were omitted. Nevertheless, controversy accompanied the book, with readers accusing it of blasphemy, subversiveness, and misanthropy.

In 1742 Swift, his health declining, retired from his position at St. Patrick's. He died in Dublin on October 19, 1745.

Legacy

In the golden age of satire, Jonathan Swift's philosophical fiction defined and transformed the genre.

Gulliver's Travels was popular when it was published and was a part of a larger tendency of the time toward satirical writing. In the company of John Dryden, Alexander Pope, Joseph Addison, Oliver Goldsmith, and Richard Steele, Swift helped to develop the style of Augustan literature. These writers imitated the proportion and elegance of such classic writers as VIRGIL, Horace, and OVID. Their attention to the harmony and decorum in their writing style was balanced by searing criticism of the institutions and beliefs of their own era. The movement was not limited to English speakers. In France, for instance, MOLIÈRE had written satirical comedies for the stage in the 1660s and 1670s.

Swift helped to establish the movement, and his works overtly criticized the dominant ideas of the time. *Gulliver's Travels* fit into no established literary genre: it was a travel narrative, a moral guide, and a political allegory. This creative and surprising mixture contributed to the more imaginative writing that followed during the Enlightenment. Voltaire, author of the witty and satirical *Candide* (1759), was heavily influenced by Swift.

The position of the satirist as self-appointed moral guardian of the culture, as promoted by Swift, Thomas Moore, and Juvenal, has been often imitated since. Nineteenth-century Romantic writers, including Lord Byron, Percy Shelley, and JOHN KEATS, drew on Swift's work in their satirical writings as did GUSTAVE FLAUBERT in his satirical work *Bouvard et Pécuchet* (1880), Anatole France, and Samuel Butler. Twentieth-century satirists have included the English writers Evelyn Waugh, Aldous Huxley, and GEORGE ORWELL.

Although *Gulliver's Travels* was read as satire at the time, with readers interested in translating allegory back into the real institutions represented, today the stories have become a part of common cultural knowledge and are often retold as humorous stories—lacking the political impact that they had when they were written.

Watson

For Further Reading

Glendinning, Victoria. *Jonathan Swift: A Portrait.* New York: Henry Holt, 1999.

Greenberg, Robert A., ed. *Gulliver's Travels: An Authoritative Text, the Correspondence of Swift, Pope's Verses on Gulliver's Travels, Critical Essays.* New York: Norton, 1977.

Tagore, Rabindranath

Poet, Novelist, and Philosopher
1861–1941

Life and Work

Rabindranath Tagore has long been revered in India for his lyric poetry and songs. He also played an important part in introducing Indian art and thought to the Western world.

Tagore was born in Calcutta on May 6, 1861, the fourteenth child in a Brahmin (the highest level of the Hindu caste system) Bengali family whose home was a center of creative and intellectual activity. Tagore began to compose poetry at the age of eight. As a child and adolescent, he traveled widely in India with his father, an active religious reformer and Indian nationalist. In 1878 he spent a year studying at University College in London, where he wrote several plays.

In 1883 he published his collection of devotional poems, *Praghat sangit,* considered the first of his great lyrical works, in which he describes the importance of personal communion with God and nature in mystical language.

In 1891 Tagore took charge of his family property in East Bengal (now Bangladesh), where he came into contact with the rural poor who are the subject of many of his best stories. While there he continued to write poetry and songs and became an outspoken advocate for agricultural and educational reform. He also wrote political essays and expressed a belief in the poet's moral duty to society. In 1901 he founded a school, Santiniketan (Abode of Peace) in Bolpur, West Bengal, which in 1921 became Visva-Bharati University.

Tagore wrote the poems that would make up his first internationally known collection of poetry, *Gitanjali* (1910), between 1907 and 1910. Tagore wrote novels as well as poetry. *Naukhadubi* (*The Wreck*, 1906), *Gora* (1910), and *Ghare-bhaire* (*The Home and the World*, 1916) are romantic stories about dilemmas arising from the conflict between traditional and modern Indian life.

In 1912 Tagore toured England and the United States, meeting EZRA POUND, WILLIAM BUTLER YEATS, and George Bernard Shaw. Yeats wrote a preface to the English edition of *Gitanjali* (1912), which contained lyrics from a number of Tagore's books, including the original *Gitanjali,* in prose translations by the author himself. The work brought him recognition throughout Europe and the United States, and in 1913 he became the first Asian writer to receive the Nobel Prize for Literature. In 1915 he was knighted in Britain, an honor that he repudiated in 1919 in protest against the Amritsar Massacre, an incident in which British troops fired on a peaceful political protest, killing hundreds.

In the 1920s and 1930s Tagore traveled throughout the United States, Europe, and the Far East delivering lectures on Indian politics and art, and voicing strong opposition to the rise of fascism. He became known throughout the Western world as the representative of Indian heritage and spirituality. He was a revered literary and nationalist figure within India.

Tagore died on August 7, 1941.

Legacy

Rabindranath Tagore was a prolific writer of poems, songs, plays, novels, stories, essays, and public addresses. He was an important political and cultural figure who spoke frequently against discrimination and fascism and on his concept of the unification of Eastern and Western thought.

Tagore brought new forms and meters to Bengali poetry. He combined the oldest Bengali meters with the commonplace subject matter of daily life; he maintained the personal, emotional tone of the lyric in epic poetry; and he employed colloquial language in place of the formal Sanskrit. With these changes he led the way for other Bengali poets to experiment with language and form. His receipt of the Nobel Prize brought Bengali literature to the attention of the Western world.

The poems in *Gitanjali* in which Tagore discusses divine and human love and the search for peace were profoundly important to many Western writers. Yeats, Pound, and André Gide were all influenced by his work.

Tagore's importance as a cultural representative was equal to his literary influence. In 1930 the *New York Times* published a conversation between Albert Einstein and Tagore in which they discussed the nature of reality. His lectures, held in such venues as Carnegie Hall, were always filled.

Tagore's university attracted the foremost Indian scholars and artists as well as Western thinkers. The filmmaker Satyajit Ray—who later made several classic films based on Tagore's work—was educated there, as was Indira Gandhi.

Tagore has remained a central figure in Bengali literature and culture; two of his songs became the national anthems of India and Bangladesh. New translations of his work in the mid-to-late twentieth century have led to a resurgence of interest in his work.

Watson

WORLD EVENTS		TAGORE'S LIFE
Revolutions in Austria, France, Germany, and Italy	1848	
	1861	Rabindranath Tagore is born
U.S. Civil War	1861–65	
Germany is united	1871	
	1883	Tagore publishes *Praghat sangit*
Spanish-American War	1898	
	1901	Tagore founds his Santiniketan school
	1910	Tagore publishes *Gitanjali*
	1913	Tagore wins Nobel Prize for Literature
World War I	1914–18	
	1915	Tagore is knighted
Russian Revolution	1917	
	1919	Tagore repudiates knighthood
Great Depression	1929–39	
World War II	1939–45	
	1941	Tagore dies
Communist China is established	1949	

For Further Reading

Dutta, Krishna, and Andrew Robinson. *Rabindranath Tagore: The Myriad-Minded Man.* New York: St. Martin's Press, 1995.
Dutta, Krishna, and Andrew Robinson, eds. *Rabindranath Tagore: An Anthology.* New York: St. Martin's Press, 1997.

Tanner, Henry Ossawa

Painter
1859–1937

WORLD EVENTS		TANNER'S LIFE
Revolutions in	1848	
Austria, France,		
Germany, and Italy		
	1859	Henry Ossawa Tanner is born
U.S. Civil War	1861–65	
Germany is united	1871	
	1879	Tanner begins studies at Pennsylvania Academy of Fine Arts
	1891	Tanner moves to France
	1893	Tanner paints *The Banjo Lesson*
	1896	Tanner paints *The Raising of Lazarus*
Spanish-American War	1898	
World War I	1914–18	
Russian Revolution	1917	
	1923	Tanner is named Chevalier of Legion of Honor
Great Depression	1929–39	
	1937	Tanner dies
World War II	1939–45	

Life and Work

Henry Ossawa Tanner was one of the first African-American painters to achieve an international reputation.

The son of an African Methodist Episcopal minister, Tanner was born in Pittsburgh in 1859, and grew up in Philadelphia. He studied art at the Pennsylvania Academy of Fine Arts from 1879 until 1885, where he worked with the prominent American painter and photographer THOMAS EAKINS. After teaching briefly at Clark College in Atlanta, Tanner moved to Paris in 1891 to continue his studies; except for brief visits to America, Tanner spent the rest of his life in Paris.

During a trip to Philadelphia in 1893, Tanner painted one of his most famous works, *The Banjo Lesson*. In this picture Tanner transformed the stereotypical image of the banjo-strumming minstrel into a deeply moving depiction of an old man passing on a tradition to a young child. In many ways the painting is the culmination of Tanner's training. It combined Eakins's interest in American genre, the open brushwork of French Impressionism, and the dramatic lighting that Tanner admired in the works of REMBRANDT.

Tanner returned to Paris later that year and exhibited *The Banjo Lesson* in the Salon of 1894. Over the next few years Tanner moved from American themes to Oriental themes; in the Salon of 1897 his painting, *The Raising of Lazarus* (1896), won a gold medal, a rare honor for an American painter. The painting was done in the dramatic tradition of CARAVAGGIO and Rembrandt. The main figures are bathed in a warm golden light against a shadowy background. A strong diagonal composition focuses the viewer's attention on the interaction between Jesus and Lazarus; in the background, awestruck villagers show their reactions to the miracle.

That picture established Tanner's reputation and encouraged the Philadelphia art patron Rodman Wanamaker to provide the money for Tanner to make extended study trips to the Holy Land. For the rest of his career, Tanner specialized in religious scenes, combining his own deeply held religious convictions with the Orientalism that was then a staple of French academic art.

Tanner was honored with numerous awards both in the United States and in France, culminating in his being named a Chevalier of the Legion of Honor in 1923. He died in Paris in 1937.

Legacy

Henry Ossawa Tanner managed to break the rigid racial barriers of his time and achieved international renown.

Born on the eve of the Civil War and raised in a segregated society, Tanner was immersed in the issues of race in America. In fact, his parents gave him the name "Ossawa" in honor of the abolitionist John Brown, who, along with 40 followers, was attacked in Osawatomie, Kansas, by more than 400 pro-slavery vigilantes in 1856.

For much of his life Tanner associated with famous African-American intellectuals such as W. E. B. Du Bois and Booker T. Washington, and he supported groups such as the National Association for the Advancement of Colored People. Nevertheless, Tanner never returned to genre scenes of African-American life after the 1890s. For most of his career he was more concerned with religious issues than social and racial issues.

In the 1920s a few African-American writers, such as Alain Locke in *The New Negro* (1925), criticized Tanner's attempts to distance himself from racial issues. Succeeding as an academic painter was not enough, Locke insisted; what was needed was a specific African-American aesthetic focusing on African-American subject matter. Tanner was not interested in providing that new aesthetic. For him, art provided a means of escaping social restrictions and transcended the realities of racial discrimination.

Tanner's reputation began to fade after his death largely because of broad changes in the world of modern art. His work belonged to the traditions of nineteenth-century academic art against which the Modernist movement rebelled.

For much of the twentieth century, however, Tanner's success provided a source of inspiration for African-American painters, including Romare Bearden and JACOB LAWRENCE. He regained wider attention later in that century as a part of the growing interest in African-American studies spurred by the civil rights movement. Today, Tanner is generally regarded as one of the most significant African-American painters in history.

McEnroe

For Further Reading

Mathews, Marcia M. *Henry Ossawa Tanner, American Artist*. Chicago: University of Chicago Press, 1969.

Mosby, Dewey F. *Henry Ossawa Tanner*. New York: Rizzoli, 1991.

Tchaikovsky, Peter Ilich

Composer
1840–1893

Life and Work

Composer of some of the most beloved symphonies and ballets in the history of classical music, Peter Ilich Tchaikovsky lived a tragic masquerade. Many observers have concluded that he drew creative inspiration from his confinement within it.

Tchaikovsky was born in Votkinsk, Russia, on April 25, 1840. He was hit hard by his mother's death in 1854, and began composing afterward. He probably recognized his homosexuality while still a young man; his sexual orientation was regarded as a serious crime in late nineteenth-century society. Tchaikovsky became a government law clerk, but grew more and more interested in music, enrolling at the St. Petersburg Conservatory in 1862.

Tchaikovsky's music deepened in the late 1860s under the influence of "The Five," a group of composers who strove toward a distinctively Russian style. His first great successes were the 1869 orchestral overture *Romeo and Juliet*, the spectacular Piano Concerto No. 1 of 1874, and the ballet *Swan Lake* of the following year. In 1877 Tchaikovsky began an opera based on ALEKSANDR PUSHKIN's novel *Eugene Onegin*. As work progressed, Tchaikovsky found himself the object of infatuation on the part of

a young female music student; wracked with guilt over his homosexuality and haunted by the story in which he was immersed, he agreed to marry her. A few months afterward, he tried to commit suicide by wading into a nearly frozen river, and a separation from his wife was arranged.

The rest of Tchaikovsky's life was marked by increasing public success and intensifying private misery, despite his association with a generous patroness whom he never met but to whom he wrote more than 1,000 letters. He conducted his works across Europe and America, and enjoyed considerable success with two more evergreen ballets, 1889's *Sleeping Beauty* and *The Nutcracker* of 1892. The following year, his Sixth Symphony (*Pathétique*) startled audiences with the profound gloom into which its finale descended. Several days after its premiere, on October 25, 1893, Tchaikovsky died. Cholera was given as the cause, but modern scholars speculate that he killed himself to avoid the exposure of a homosexual relationship.

Legacy

Although he has been a popular favorite since his own day, Peter Ilich Tchaikovsky's reputation has suffered for decades at the hands of critics who disdained the unrestrained passion in his works. "The Pathéthique Symphony threads all the foul ditches and sewers of human despair; it is as unclean as music can be," sniffed the Boston *Evening Transcript* in 1898. For much of the twentieth century Tchaikovsky stood as a premier example of the split between popular and "informed" opinion.

Almost without peer as an orchestrator and as a creator of beautiful melodies, Tchaikovsky devised spectacular musical effects that he tended to repeat or to array episodically. Such effects, when complemented by the lush visual creations of nineteenth-century Russia's choreographers, made for unforgettable ballet scores. But when applied to extended units of musical thought, they struck some observers as sentimental or even, when Tchaikovsky indulged his taste for martial, foursquare rhythms, as bombastic. Yet the problem was really that Tchaikovsky, as a melodist and unabashed emotionalist, did not appeal to progressive taste in the twentieth century.

Tchaikovsky's legacy lies really in the hearts and minds of music lovers rather than in the influence he exerted on later composers. His music has never left the American and European symphony concert repertoire, and a performance of *The Nutcracker* is an annual Christmas tradition. Tchaikovsky's exploration of pure sentiment also shaped the art of film music, where romanticism never died.

Although his famous symphonies and ballets were written in a Western-influenced idiom, Tchaikovsky was also an important exponent of musical nationalism, adopting melodic and rhythmic features derived from Russian folk music in his songs and operas. And perhaps twenty-first-century modernity will find new inspiration in Tchaikovsky: the emotion in his works may be seen as a very modern assertion of the self against a hostile external world. Audiences may have been ahead of critics in understanding why Tchaikovsky's music, issuing from the most private of private spheres, has commanded wide public attention.

Manheim

WORLD EVENTS		TCHAIKOVSKY'S LIFE
Congress of Vienna reorganizes Europe	1815	
	1840	Peter Ilich Tchaikovsky is born
Revolutions in Austria, France, Germany, and Italy	1848	
U.S. Civil War	1861–65	
	1862	Tchaikovsky enrolls at St. Petersburg Conservatory
	1869	Tchaikovsky has first great success with *Romeo and Juliet* overture
Germany is united	1871	
	1875	Tchaikovsky writes *Swan Lake* ballet
	1877	Tchaikovsky attempts suicide
	1889	Tchaikovsky composes *Sleeping Beauty*
	1892	Tchaikovsky composes *The Nutcracker*
	1893	Tchaikovsky dies
Spanish-American War	1898	

For Further Reading

Holden, Anthony. *Tchaikovsky: A Biography*. New York: Random House, 1995.

Mundy, Simon. *Tchaikovsky*. London and New York: Omnibus Press, 1998.

Tharp, Twyla

Choreographer and Dancer
1941–

Life and Work

For many dance lovers the early work of Twyla Tharp epitomized the free-spiritedness of American culture in the 1960s. Her later work, though, revealed behind the high spirits a serious attempt to come to grips with great American questions and problems.

WORLD EVENTS	THARP'S LIFE
World War II 1939–45	
	1941 Twyla Tharp is born
Communist China 1949 is established	
Korean War 1950–53	
African independence 1957 movement begins	
	1965 Tharp forms Twyla Tharp and Dancers
	1970 Tharp choreographs *The Fugue*
	1973 Tharp turns to popular music with *Deuce Coupe*
Vietnam War ends 1975	
	1976 Tharp creates *Push Comes to Shove* for Mikhail Baryshnikov
	1979 Tharp contributes choreography to film of musical *Hair*
	1981 Tharp collaborates with musician David Byrne
Dissolution of 1991 Soviet Union	
	1992 Tharp wins MacArthur Fellowship
South Africa 1994 dismantles apartheid	

Tharp was born in Portland, Indiana, on July 1, 1941, the child of a car dealer father and a piano teacher mother who enrolled her in dance classes and arts instruction of every sort from a very young age. The family moved to southern California during Tharp's childhood, and Tharp first attended Pomona College in suburban Los Angeles. Severely disciplined for a romantic tryst in the school's chapel, she transferred to Barnard College in New York City, graduating with an art history degree but going off campus to take dance classes whenever she could. She studied with some of the major figures of modern dance, including MARTHA GRAHAM and MERCE CUNNINGHAM, and formed her own group, Twyla Tharp and Dancers, in 1965.

Some of Tharp's dances of the 1960s and early 1970s were performed outdoors or in other unorthodox spaces such as gymnasiums. Many of them had no music and explored motion in the abstract. Despite the spirit of freedom in her work, Tharp had a rigorous side exemplified by *The Fugue*, a 1970 work that presented a dance analogue for a complex multipart musical texture. Tharp's career reached a new level in 1973 with *Deuce Coupe*, a dance set to music by the Beach Boys.

Tharp continued to use popular and jazz elements in her dances; she worked on the 1979 film version of the rock musical *Hair*, and collaborated with the eclectic musician David Byrne on the stage work *The Catherine Wheel* in 1981. Tharp won a MacArthur Fellowship "genius grant" in 1992 and worked at an undiminished pace through the 1990s, taking a group of young dancers on tour with a group of new works collectively entitled *Tharp!* late in the decade. A spiritual and strong-willed woman whose family was of Shaker background, Tharp has often drawn analogies between the self-sacrifices required in dance and the devotion of religious faith.

Legacy

Twyla Tharp is best known as one of the 1960s and 1970s rebels who opened up the world of dance to groundbreaking new influences.

One of Tharp's most important innovations was the full-fledged incorporation of popular music into the world of serious dance. Jazz had made inroads into dance before Tharp came along, but the use of popular music took dance quite a great distance from its previous position as one of the most elite of the fine arts. In *Deuce Coupe* and other works, Tharp evolved a new choreographic style, filled with allusions to popular dance, to match her unorthodox choice of music.

Further, the popular elements in her work were never deployed to ironic effect, but rather in service of a direct, humanistic language that later in her career could be applied to serious subjects such as family conflict and the American inability to find a sense of community. Tharp's free-spiritedness also influenced younger dancers; one of the dancer-choreographers who captured and extended Tharp's sense of the unexpected was Mark Morris, who was part of her company for a time.

Initially Tharp's own company was all female. Although she claimed that there was no political intent behind the group's composition, Tharp has been known for dances that celebrate female spirituality and sexuality, and she has inspired other choreographers to explore these subjects. Although one of her best-known dances, 1976's *Push Comes to Shove*, was created for Mikhail Baryshnikov, she is credited with fundamentally changing the role of women in dance. Tharp created female roles that replaced the idealized ballerina image of femininity, still prevalent even in many modern styles, with more flexible conceptions that, among other features, sometimes depicted women as openly sexual beings. Twyla Tharp was a 1960s choreographer in the best sense: she broadened the range of choices for artists who came after her.

Manheim

For Further Reading

Siegel, Marcia B. *The Shapes of Change: Images of American Dance*. Boston: Houghton Mifflin, 1979.

Tharp, Twyla. *Push Comes to Shove*. New York: Bantam, 1992.

Titian (Tiziano Vecelli)

Painter

c. 1490–1576

Life and Work

Titian was among the most prominent painters of the Italian High and late Renaissance. He was the leading figure in the Venetian school of painting.

Titian (Tiziano Vecelli) was born about 1490 in the mountain village of Cadore, but lived in Venice after age eight. His most important early instruction came from Giovanni Bellini.

In 1516, upon the death of Bellini, Titian was elevated to official painter of the Republic of Venice. A period of great productivity followed, with Titian producing some of his finest religious and mythological works and portraits. His *Assumption of the Virgin* (c. 1516–18), for the church of the Frari in Venice, is reminiscent of the grandeur of the High Renaissance style of RAPHAEL and MICHELANGELO. *The Madonna of the Pesaro Family* (1519–26) uses strongly diagonal composition to create a monumental effect, and architectural elements to enhance the sense of drama.

Works such as *Sacred and Profane Love* (1516), which deal with mythological themes, are painted on the same grand scale and have comparable emotional power. Titian's paintings of this period feature the vivid color and movement for which he is renowned. His *Venus of Urbino* (1530) is considered one of the greatest portrayals of the goddess of love.

Emperor Charles V called Titian to Augsburg twice as court painter and made him a knight of the Holy Roman Empire, an unprecedented honor for an artist.

In the final 20 years of his life, Titian continued to develop his passionate, dramatic style, using ever freer and more expressive brushwork as light became a more dominant feature. In a late work such as the *Crowning with Thorns* (1570), the violence of Christ's passion is shown through color and expressive brushwork.

Through shrewd investments, by 1531 Titian had enough money to buy a grand residence in Venice, and enjoyed a degree of fame and success achieved by only one other contemporary, Raphael.

Titian died of the plague in 1576.

Legacy

Although he was not the originator of the Venetian school, Titian became its quintessential member through his life-long exploration of new ways of working with the medium of oil paint.

He learned to free his brush from the task of exactly representing details, texture, and volume, instead making it an instrument for conveying the sensation of light through color and the expression of emotion through free and open handling. In addition to open brushwork, Titian perfected a technique of applying colors in glazes, over a reddish ground, that tended both to subdue the colors and to bring forth a deep, rich tone that pervades the work with a strikingly realistic atmosphere. This method of painting, called *colorito*, usually involved working directly on the canvas without preliminary drawings.

An important theoretical debate developed in the sixteenth century between the Florentines, who believed drawing (*disegno*) to be essential for the process of painting, and the Venetians, who practiced *colorito*. This debate pitted those who preferred a more intellectual style of painting with clearly defined forms and orderly composition against those who deliberately pursued an art that was ambiguous and emotional, as expressed through forms revealed by loosely brushed areas of color.

In Venice, Titian's approach won out. He had a profound effect on the style of younger Venetian artists, particularly Paolo Veronese and Tintoretto.

In the seventeenth century, Titian's works were studied and copied by numerous painters, including Annibale Caracci and PETER PAUL RUBENS. In Spain, DIEGO VELÁZQUEZ developed a style inspired by Titian. Through the work of these artists, the method that Titian had initiated became the center of the contentious seventeenth-century debate between the painterly "Rubenistes" and the linear "Poussinistes" (after the French painter Nicolas Poussin), who insisted on the superiority of drawing over expressive application of colors.

This debate continued in art academies through the nineteenth century. For much of that century painting in the linear style dominated the art of the academies, until the rebellion of the painterly Impressionists successfully challenged the academic tradition.

In the twentieth century, Titian once again came to be regarded as one of the central figures in the history of European art. His innovative approach not only shaped the Venetian style, but is seen to have opened up new expressive possibilities for the medium of oil paint.

Domenico

WORLD EVENTS		TITIAN'S LIFE
High Renaissance in Italy	1490–1527	
	c. 1490	Titian is born
Columbus sails to Americas	1492	
Protestant Reformation begins	1517	
	1519–26	Titian works on *The Madonna of the Pesaro Family*
	1530	Titian paints *Venus of Urbino*
Ottoman dominance of Mediterranean ends	1571	
	1576	Titian dies
Thirty Years' War in Europe	1618–48	

For Further Reading

Biadene, Susanna, ed. *Titian, Prince of Painters*. Exhibition catalogue. Munich: Prestel, 1990.

Hope, Charles. *Titian*. New York: Harper & Row, 1980.

Rosand, David. *Painting in Cinquecento Venice*. New Haven, Conn., and London: Yale University Press, 1982.

Tolstoy, Leo

Novelist, Dramatist, and
Short Story Writer
1828–1910

Life and Work

In the course of a life marked by changes in philosophical, religious, and political beliefs, Leo Tolstoy was both a dissolute student and a religious reformer, an aristocrat and a promoter of peasant life, the writer of some of the world's greatest literature and the harshest critic of that work.

Tolstoy was born on August 28, 1828, at Yasnaya Polyana, the Tolstoy family estate south of Moscow, where he lived for most of his life. He studied Asian languages and law at the University of Kazan but abandoned his studies in 1847 and later joined the army to fight in the Crimean War. While in the army, Tolstoy wrote his first novel, the autobiographical *Detstvo* (*Childhood*, 1852). It was soon fol-

lowed by *Sevastapol Stories* (1855–56), which was inspired by his years in the army.

After six years of work, Tolstoy finished *Voyna i mir* (*War and Peace*) in 1869. A portrait of Russia during the Napoleonic age, this epic novel offered an image of a stable and unified society and expressed Tolstoy's own belief that human life is governed not by individual will but by natural law.

After completing the novel, Tolstoy worked on a school for peasant children that he had established on his estate and prepared reading primers that would be used by Russian educators for several generations. He wrote his next great work, *Anna Karenina,* between 1873 and 1877. The novel's strong authorial presence imposes strict moral law on an aristocratic society within which the heroine, living in conflict with social norms, is punished for her adulterous affair. Both of these novels, and most of Tolstoy's other work, are marked by introspective psychological detail and the moral examination of conventional behavior.

Tolstoy's spiritual crisis while completing *Anna Karenina* was first portrayed by the character Levin in that novel. In 1884, *Ispoved* (*My Confession*) presented a complete description of his questioning. Tolstoy's embrace of radical Christianity caused him to repudiate most of the great literature that he had once admired, including his own, and in 1901, to be excommunicated from the Russian Orthodox Church.

During this time, he wrote his great later works—*Smert Ivana Ilicha* (*The Death of Ivan Ilyich*) in 1886, *Kreytserova sonata* (*The Kreutzer Sonata*) in 1891, and *Otets Sergy* (*Father Sergius*) in 1898. He also made important contributions to Russian theater with his plays *Plody prosvescheniya* (*The Fruits of Enlightenment*, 1889) and *Zhivoi trup* (*A Living Corpse*, 1911).

By the end of his life Tolstoy had alienated every member of his extensive family except his daughter, Alexandra. In 1910 he fled Yasnaya Polyana with her, only to develop pneumonia and die in a railroad station.

Legacy

Leo Tolstoy effected profound changes in many intellectual arenas. He provided a firm sense of identity for the Russian intelligentsia; made major contributions to Russian education; brought a new sense of universality, moral clarity, and psychological insight to the

novel; and raised philosophical and theological questions that are discussed to this day.

War and Peace was immediately successful with the reading public but it took some time for the novel to gain critical praise. Leftist critics found the work's patriotic political portrait of the country unpleasantly conservative, while conservative thinkers were offended by the satirical portrayal of aristocratic society. Within several years of its publication, however, the novel's breadth and power were widely recognized and it came to be considered the national epic of Russia.

The genre of the historical novel grew immensely following the publication of *War and Peace*. This was only one of the many ways in which Tolstoy influenced literary history and, indeed, few intellectuals who came after him have not been influenced by his thought. Levin's spiritual crisis in *Anna Karenina,* often read as a description of Tolstoy's own existential and religious struggle of the time, has been analyzed by intellectuals around the world. Tolstoy's later moral and theological tracts, for which he was excommunicated, also gave rise to much religious and philosophical discussion. His treatise of 1898, *Chto takoe iskusstvo?* (*What Is Art?*), in which he repudiated his own work and most works of art by others, began an international discussion on the nature and importance of art.

Tolstoy's work was so influential and his presence so widely felt both in literature and in the cultural life of Russia that for some time after his death, it was necessary for a Russian writer to take a strong position on his ideas.

Watson

World Events		Tolstoy's Life
Congress of Vienna reorganizes Europe	1815	
	1828	Leo Tolstoy is born
Revolutions in Austria, France, Germany, and Italy	1848	
U.S. Civil War	1861–65	
	1869	Tolstoy completes *War and Peace*
Germany is united	1871	
	1877	Tolstoy completes *Anna Karenina*
	1884	Tolstoy writes *My Confession*
	1886	Tolstoy writes *The Death of Ivan Ilyich*
Spanish-American War	1898	
	1901	Tolstoy is excommunicated by Russian Orthodox Church
	1910	Tolstoy dies
World War I	1914–18	

For Further Reading

Berlin, Isaiah. *The Hedgehog and the Fox: An Essay on Tolstoy's View of History.* New York: Simon and Schuster, 1986.
Bloom, Harold, ed. *Leo Tolstoy: Modern Critical Views.* New York: Chelsea House, 1992.

Truffaut, François

Filmmaker and Critic
1932–1984

Life and Work

French film director and critic François Truffaut was the most commercially successful of the French New Wave directors and was an influential proponent of New Wave *auteur* (author) theory.

Born February 6, 1932, in Paris, Truffaut had a troubled and lonely childhood. Unsuccessful in school, he spent a short time in a reformatory and was working in a factory at the age of 14. His one source of comfort during his youth was the cinema. He spent a great deal of time in theaters and even organized film clubs as a teen.

At age 15, Truffaut was befriended by André Bazin, the editor of the avant-garde film magazine *Cahiers du Cinema.* Hired by Bazin as a critic, Truffaut worked with a group of other young critics—Jean-Luc Godard, Claude Chabrol, Jacques Rivette, and Eric Rohmer—who formed the nucleus of the New Wave movement. One of the more acerbic voices in this movement that attacked traditional French cinema, Truffaut was crucial in the development of the *auteur* theory of cinema, the idea that the director is the "author" of a film, giving it its distinctive qualities.

Truffaut's first feature film was *The 400 Blows* (1959), the somewhat autobiographical story of an adolescent delinquent rebelling against a rigid and conformist adult world. The movie, especially popular in England and the United States, won the prize for best direction at the Cannes International Film Festival and the New York Film Critics' Award for Best Foreign Language Film.

Truffaut's third film, *Jules et Jim* (1961), reflected the humanism of film director Jean Renoir. Truffaut's other influences included American B movies, film noir, and the suspenseful films of ALFRED HITCHCOCK, whose style he emulated in such films as *The Bride Wore Black* (1968) and *The Story of Adele H.* (1975).

Truffaut was fascinated with the unique nature of film as an art form and continually explored the relation between cinema and real life. In *Day for Night* (1973), a film about the making of a film, he looks at how the boundary between manufactured images and reality becomes blurred in a world shaped by the visual media. This film won an Oscar for Best Foreign Film in 1973.

In 1979, the American Film Institute and the Los Angeles County Museum of Art honored Truffaut with a 20-year retrospective.

Truffaut died of a brain tumor in 1984.

Legacy

As a critic, François Truffaut not only helped lay the groundwork for the French New Wave movement but also originated the *auteur* theory, which has become the prime analytical tool of modern film criticism. Through his writing and directing, he did more than any other individual to transform the world of filmmaking and challenge the Hollywood studio system.

The generation of directors whose careers took off during the 1970s, including Francis Ford Coppola, Steven Spielberg, and George Lucas, are indebted to Truffaut for the artistic freedom and fame that they have enjoyed. The independent film movement of recent years (as exemplified by the Sundance Festival) is in part a result of Truffaut's efforts, which demonstrated the viability of low-budget, iconoclastic filmmaking.

Truffaut and the other New Wave directors also transformed the cinematic style of film. Their "low-tech" approach to filmmaking, employing hand-held-camera shots, natural lighting, location shooting, unrehearsed dialogue, uneven editing, and jump cutting, introduced an alternative to the polished, impersonal style of mainstream films. Forsaking the artificial verisimilitude of traditional films, the style of New Wave directors reminded viewers that they were watching a film, not a window into reality. These techniques directly influenced documentary film movements, such as cinema verité and America Direct Cinema, which sought to capture unscripted dialogue on film.

The art of cinema has never had a more ardent champion than Truffaut, whose contagious enthusiasm for movies and joyous approach to filmmaking certainly helped to shape the appreciation of film as art.

Domenico

World Events	Truffaut's Life
Great Depression 1929–39	
	1932 François Truffaut is born
World War II 1939–45	
Communist China 1949 is established	
Korean War 1950–53	
African independence 1957 movement begins	
	1959 Truffaut directs *The 400 Blows*
	1961 Truffaut directs *Jules et Jim*
	1973 Truffaut wins an Oscar for *Day for Night*
Vietnam War ends 1975	
	1984 Truffaut dies
Dissolution of 1991 Soviet Union	

For Further Reading

Insdorf, Annette. *François Truffaut.* Rev. ed. Cambridge and New York: Cambridge University Press, 1994.

Petrie, Graham. *The Cinema of François Truffaut.* New York: A. S. Barnes, 1970.

Truffaut, François. *Truffaut par Truffaut.* (*Truffaut by Truffaut*). Texts and documents compiled by Dominique Rabourdin; translated by Robert Erich Wolf. New York: Abrams, 1987.

Ts'ao Hsueh-ch'in

(Cao Xueqin)

Novelist

c. 1715–1763

World Events		Ts'ao's Life
Glorious Revolution in England	1688	
	c. 1715	Ts'ao Hsueh-ch'in is born
	1728	Ts'ao's family is exiled from court
	1763	Ts'ao dies
United States declares independence	1776	
French Revolution begins	1789	
	1792	Kao E's version of *Dream of the Red Chamber* is published
Latin American independence movement begins	1811	

Life and Work

Ts'ao Hsueh-ch'in, or Cao Xueqin, was the author of the *Hong Lou Meng* (variously translated as *Dream of the Red Chamber, A Dream of Red Mansions,* and *The Story of the Stone*), considered one of the greatest novels in Chinese literary history.

Ts'ao was born in approximately 1715. He grew up in Nanjing, a member of a wealthy family whose members held positions in the Ch'ing (Qing) court, the last Chinese imperial dynasty. The family lost its position and fortune in an imperial purge in 1728 when Ts'ao was 13 years old. He and his extended family moved to Beijing, where they depended upon the charity of another branch of the family. This story of the fall of a prominent family to a state of poverty provided the setting for Ts'ao's great novel.

Ts'ao's childhood was a time of great prosperity and artistic productivity in China. Most of the literature that was widely read and respected at the time was written in formal structures and treated Confucian themes of filial duty and the importance of ritual. An alternate strand of literature stemmed from an oral folk tradition of storytelling and poetry that had its roots in the work of the great T'ang dynasty poets, including Tu Fu and Li Po.

Ts'ao wrote the *Dream of the Red Chamber* while living in poverty in Beijing. The novel was circulated in handwritten copies among his friends. He sold paintings to support himself and may also have worked as a private tutor or as a schoolteacher, though this is not certain.

The novel is thought to be somewhat autobiographical in its portrayal of Bao-yu, a young member of the powerful Chia family. The story of his youth is told slowly with a nostalgic idealization of the past that has been compared to Marcel Proust's treatment of his narrator's youth in *A la recherche du temps perdu* (*Remembrance of Things Past*). Ts'ao's novel, like Proust's, is renowned for its psychological insight and its sophisticated humor.

Ts'ao almost certainly wrote the first 80 chapters of the complete 120-chapter novel, while the last 40 chapters were written after his death by Kao E (1740–c.1815), the editor of the 1792 version of the novel.

Ts'ao died on February 12, 1763.

Legacy

The *Dream of the Red Chamber*, a chronicle of the decline of a powerful family, is considered the greatest novel of the Ch'ing dynasty's golden age of literature.

Handwritten copies of Ts'ao Hsueh-ch'in's 80-chapter novel were distributed during his lifetime and following his death. These were often accompanied by commentaries written about the novel and the life of its author by people familiar with his work and close to Ts'ao. The most important of these was the commentary written by Kao E, also known as Red Inkstone, who added 40 chapters to the novel in 1792.

In the late nineteenth century Wang Kuo-ei produced critical work on the novel while others, including the scholar Hu Shih, did historical research on the novel's content. It was not until the beginning of the twentieth century, however, that scholars produced a significant body of critical writing on the novel.

The *Dream of the Red Chamber* brought together the two most important strands of Chinese literature, using elements of the prevailing Confucian literary structure along with a vernacular prose style. The book's conversational dialogue is unprecedented in a serious literary work. The novel is far more sophisticated than the Chinese novels that preceded it. Ts'ao used the mythological elements common to folk tales but rather than making them the focus of the novel, he used them to support the realistic and emotionally complex stories of its characters. This was the first Chinese novel to provide a realistic portrait of family life and corrupt society. It has been valued as much as a historical document as it has as a great work of literature.

The *Dream of the Red Chamber* is an important part of Chinese culture and its characters and stories have often been used in opera and theater. It continues to be studied as a seminal work of Chinese literature.

Watson

For Further Reading

Knoerle, Jeanne. *The Dream of the Red Chamber: A Critical Study.* Bloomington: Indiana University Press, 1976.

Levy, Dore. *Ideal and Actual in the The Story of the Stone.* New York: Columbia University Press, 1999.

Plaks, Andrew H. *Archetype and Allegory in The Dream of the Red Chamber.* Princeton, N.J.: Princeton University Press, 1976.

Tu Fu

Poet

712–770

Life and Work

Considered the greatest of classical Chinese poets, Tu Fu has infused Chinese literature and culture with the rich language and imagery of his poems.

Tu Fu was born to a scholarly Confucian family in Shao-ling in 712, during the T'ang dynasty. He did well in his studies as a young man, and his failure on his official examinations in 736 was a great surprise.

Between 731 and 740 Tu Fu traveled throughout China. Already well known as a poet, he met the older Taoist poet Li Po in 744 and became interested in Taoism, though he eventually returned to Confucianism. Tu Fu was much influenced by Li Po, and wrote a number of poems at this time in the older man's honor. These two poets are often spoken of as the most important in Chinese literary history, though their styles are very different.

In the early part of his career Tu Fu lived under the peaceful reign of the Confucian monarch Hsuan Tsung, who ruled from 713 to 756. Education was vastly improved and the arts flourished. In 756 the An Lu-shan Rebellion ended this period, as Tartar troops occupied the capital, Ch'ang-an. Tu Fu fled with his family but was captured and brought to Ch'ang-an. He escaped in 757, and in the next 13 years produced his best work. In these great poems he chronicled the events of the war and wrote with great compassion about the human suffering that resulted from it.

Tu Fu used many forms, including the popular ballad, the *lu-shih* (a strict form calling for fixed numbers and positions of rhymes), and the *chueh-chu*, another strict form whose use was at its high point during the T'ang dynasty. He wrote poems about his travels; allegorical poems in which he skillfully crafted symbolic systems out of nature imagery; poems about paintings, in which he created ambiguity about the distinction between art and reality that became a tradition in Chinese poetry; and poems honoring friendship.

In 759 Tu Fu retired to a rural area and built a house he called "the thatched hut." He lived a hermit's life for several years and wrote some of his greatest poems. Among these are "The Thatched Hut," in which he recounts the story of the wars, and "Hearing that the Imperial Armies Have Recovered Ho-nan and Ho-pei," a personal response to the events of the day.

Tu Fu spent most of the later years of his life alternately serving in minor government positions and traveling. For a time after the rebellion he was very poor—at least one of his children died of starvation—and these privations eventually affected his health. Tu Fu died in 770.

Legacy

Tu Fu is considered to be China's greatest poet. His work broadened the range of Chinese poetry both technically and in its subject matter, and left a strong imprint on Chinese culture and language.

Tu Fu was extremely erudite and his poetry reveals a deep knowledge of literary history and the technical aspects of poetry. He was a master of the many complex and highly structured forms of Chinese poetry. He changed these by incorporating details of his personal life and public events in an original way, and by using simple language within elaborate forms. He thus imbued common language with a poetic value that was entirely new to Chinese literature. Moreover, by commemorating events such as his son's birthday and times of excess official paperwork, he introduced new subject matter, fostering a tradition of occasional poetry concerned with mundane experience rather than ceremonial occasions.

Tu Fu's work has never been neglected or out of fashion. Many schools of Chinese poetry took their inspiration from his work. Indeed, a critical tradition developed of identifying aspects of Tu Fu from which later poets' work derived. Tu Fu served as a model for poets of the mid- and late T'ang Dynasty, considered a golden age of Chinese poetry; the Kiangsi poets of the twelfth century and those of the Sung period looked to him as the starting point of their work. By the Sung (tenth through thirteenth centuries), Tu Fu was universally acknowledged as the first of China's great poets, a position that has never been challenged. More commentaries have been written about his work than about that of any other Chinese poet.

Among Tu Fu's important poems the "Autumn Meditations" and "Autumn Wilderness" sequences are some of the greatest in the Chinese language. In these works he interweaves his memories of court life with natural description in order to discuss the relationship of time and memory to poetry.

Not only his poems but legends of Tu Fu's life—his brilliance, his Confucian virtue, his poverty, his travels, his thatched hut—have become part of Chinese cultural history.

Watson

WORLD EVENTS		TU FU'S LIFE
Muhammad conquers Mecca	630	
	712	Tu Fu is born
Islamic expansion into northern Europe is halted at Tours	732	
	736	Tu Fu fails official examinations
	756	Tu Fu is taken captive in An Lu-shan Rebellion
	757	Tu Fu escapes from captivity
	759	Tu Fu retires to his thatched hut
	770	Tu Fu dies
Formation of the Holy Roman Empire	800	

For Further Reading

Chou, Eva Shan. *Reconsidering Tu Fu: Literary Greatness and Cultural Context*. Cambridge: Cambridge University Press, 1996.

Hung, William. *Tu Fu: China's Greatest Poet*. Cambridge, Mass.: Harvard University Press, 1952.

Li Po and Tu Fu. *Li Po and Tu Fu: Poems*. Translated by Arthur Cooper. Harmondsworth, England: Penguin Books, 1973.

Twain, Mark

(Samuel Langhorne Clemens)

Novelist, Short Story Writer,
Journalist, and Essayist
1835–1910

Life and Work

Mark Twain drew on the folklore, history, culture, and common language of ordinary Americans in his writing.

Twain was born Samuel Langhorne Clemens in Missouri on November 30, 1835. He grew up on the banks of the Mississippi River, which would later be the setting for some of his most important work. After his father's death in 1847, Clemens left school and began to work. By the time he was 17 he was writing humorous articles and sketches for local newspapers. In 1853 he left home and traveled, working as a printer at newspapers in St. Louis, New York, and Philadelphia, and then spending several years working on a steamboat in the Mississippi.

Clemens adopted the pseudonym of Mark Twain in 1862. In 1865 Twain published *Jim Smiley and His Jumping Frog,* which was reprinted in 1867 in his first book, *The Celebrated Jumping Frog of Calaveras County and Other Sketches.* This wildly funny piece was reprinted around the country, quickly bringing fame to Twain. On a round-the-world cruise in the late 1860s, Twain produced a series of travel letters for American newspapers that cast a new and amusingly irreverent light on venerated customs and institutions of Europe. The letters were reprinted as *The Innocents Abroad or, The New Pilgrim's Progress* in 1869.

Twain published his first novel, *The Gilded Age* in 1874; his next novel, *The Adventures of Tom Sawyer* (1876), was set by the Mississippi River and observed the life of a small town from the perspective of an adventurous boy. In 1884 he published a sequel, *The Adventures of Huckleberry Finn.* This book, framed as a children's story, left the genre behind and became the first novel to express the complexity of American life, addressing subjects of slavery, human cruelty, and intolerance.

Twain returned to humorous narrative with *A Connecticut Yankee in King Arthur's Court,* published in 1889. Twain was also a popular performer, traveling the United States giving lectures in the Yankee character he often wrote about. He moved to Italy in 1903 but returned to the United States after a series of financial and personal losses. He died in 1910.

Legacy

Mark Twain was a wholeheartedly American writer. His subjects and characters sprung

directly from the American experience and contributed to the development of that experience into a literary culture.

Twain broke with the traditions of nineteenth-century literature by embracing American folklore and tradition, using the popular form of the yarn, and having his characters speak in everyday language and dialect. Writing about subjects often considered too crude for literature, and doing so with a sense of humor and strong social and political conviction, he laid the groundwork for American literature.

Huckleberry Finn is one of the most important works of American literature. Banned from public libraries at its publication in 1885, the book continues to be censored to this day. The complaint most often heard is that the novel is racist, an interpretation that disregards the complexity of its treatment of the relationship between a white boy, Huck, and an escaped slave, Jim. Twain commented on the racism and intolerance embedded in common social beliefs with irony and wit, while asking serious questions about the responsibility of the individual to rebel against such conventions.

Many American writers have acknowledged a debt to *Huckleberry Finn.* Ernest Hemingway considered the novel to be the starting point for all American literature and T. S. Eliot called it a masterpiece. WILLIAM FAULKNER referred to Twain as the first truly American writer and gave him credit for contributing to the development of an American culture. Langston Hughes and Kurt Vonnegut are other American writers who have acknowledged Twain's enormous and provocative influence on American literature.

Watson

For Further Reading

Emerson, Everett H. *Mark Twain: A Literary Life.* Philadelphia: University of Pennsylvania Press, 2000.

Hoffman, Andrew. *Inventing Mark Twain: The Lives of Samuel Longhorne Clemens.* New York: William Morrow, 1997.

Tyagaraja

Composer

1767–1847

Life and Work

Prominent among the figures who shaped the tradition of south Indian classical music, which over the last several centuries has diverged from that of the north, is Tyagaraja, often thought of as something of a musician-saint.

Tyagaraja was born on May 4, 1767, in the village of Tiruvaiyaru in what is now the southern Indian state of Tamil Nadu. This area, near the mouth of the Cauvery River, is marked culturally by the absence of Islamic influence; the region might be thought of as a Hindu heartland, its music inextricably linked with religious practice. His family belonged to the Brahmin caste, at the top rung of India's social hierarchy, and his education was a serious one; he studied Sanskrit, the classical language of Hinduism's scriptures. As a child, he suffered a serious illness, but was cured after a visit from a saint. Tyagaraja's parents, it is said, noticed that he stopped suckling when he heard music, and he was trained in music by one of the great court singers of the day. Tyagaraja impressed his teacher and was invited to become a court musician himself, but he declined. Instead, he lived much of his life as a religious mendicant, subsisting on the donations of followers and admirers—much to the dismay of his older brother, who wanted to turn a profit from his musical talents.

Singing is central to south Indian music, and Tyagaraja became famous as a singer, composer of songs, and poet. By the age of 13 he had written his first musical composition, a song in praise of the god Rama. A devotee of Rama, Tyagaraja repeated a mantra in praise of this deity 10 million times over the course of several years and was rewarded with a rapturous vision. Some of his works, including a poem listing 108 separate attributes of Rama, were written in Sanskrit, but the vast majority were in his native language of Telugu.

He was known for his improvisatory techniques within the framework of the Indian raga, a concept that encompasses both particular collections of tones and the melodies or melodic fragments that may be constructed from them. But above all he was famous for his *kirtana*, his devotional songs themselves, which number in the thousands.

Tyagaraja died on January 6, 1847.

Legacy

Sometimes known as "the Beethoven of south India," Tyagaraja occupies a place in south Indian music in some respects comparable to that of LUDWIG VAN BEETHOVEN in the music of western Europe. Not only did he compose music that established an enduring repertoire and remains at its center, but he also defined a new kind of cultural consciousness. Even today, Tyagaraja's songs are thought to represent the best of south India's cultural heritage.

Tyagaraja's music—both his songs themselves and the techniques he used in their performance—spread through south India in the nineteenth century. India's British occupiers permitted some of the region's Hindu kings to remain in place, and highly trained musicians at these courts—some of them disciples of Tyagaraja himself but for the most part simply professionals who closely observed and admired his style—began to elaborate upon the new variation and improvisation techniques embedded in his compositions. In this way, Tyagaraja's art grew into the modern tradition of south Indian, or "Carnatic," classical music.

At the same time, Tyagaraja began to grow in significance as a religious figure. In a process parallel to that by which his music was carried forward, Tyagaraja's life story was first told by an early group of Indian biographers and then embroidered by a second generation that made it into an enduring legend.

"Whenever I go to south India, I hear the songs of Saint Tyagaraja being sung," the Indian independence crusader Mohandas K. Gandhi once recalled. Tyagaraja's songs today form the basis not only for a concert tradition, but also for contemporary cultural observances. An annual festival in Tyagaraja's honor was established around 1900, and is still celebrated on the banks of the Cauvery. The festival is reenacted by Indians abroad, who seek to perpetuate the attitudes embodied in Tyagaraja's songs. "To the community it is more than an event," explains a publication of Tyagaraja's Chicago-area devotees. "It is almost a symbol that stands for the continuity [with] the old culture in the new environment."

Manheim

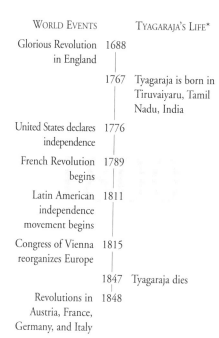

WORLD EVENTS		TYAGARAJA'S LIFE*
Glorious Revolution in England	1688	
	1767	Tyagaraja is born in Tiruvaiyaru, Tamil Nadu, India
United States declares independence	1776	
French Revolution begins	1789	
Latin American independence movement begins	1811	
Congress of Vienna reorganizes Europe	1815	
	1847	Tyagaraja dies
Revolutions in Austria, France, Germany, and Italy	1848	

* Scholars cannot date the specific events of Tyagaraja's life with accuracy.

For Further Reading

Jackson, William J. *Tyagaraja: Life and Lyrics.* Madras: Oxford University Press, 1991.

———. *Tyagaraja and the Renewal of Tradition.* Delhi: Motilal Banarsidass Publishers, 1994.

Van Eyck, Jan

Painter and Manuscript
Illuminator

c. 1370/90–1441

Life and Work

An early master of the art of oil painting, the fifteenth-century Flemish painter Jan van Eyck introduced a fundamentally new style of painting to the art of northern Europe.

Although many details of his life are obscure, van Eyck was born in the late fourteenth century in Maasyck and is said to have

World Events		Van Eyck's Life
Ming Dynasty reasserts Chinese control of China	1368	
	c. 1370 /90	Jan van Eyck is born
	1425	Van Eyck begins work at court of duke of Burgundy
	1425–32	Van Eyck paints *Ghent Altarpiece*
	1434	Van Eyck paints *Arnolfini Wedding*
	1441	Van Eyck dies
Ottoman Empire conquers Constantinople	1453	

been trained by his brother, Hubert. His work also shows influences from the Master of Flemalle and the Gothic International Style, characterized by intricate naturalistic detail and complicated perspective.

Van Eyck spent most of his career, from 1425 until his death, as a court painter for Philip the Good, duke of Burgundy. During his lifetime there were many changes in social structure and the economic climate. With the rapid growth of the middle class, the material world became an appropriate subject for art, but in van Eyck's meticulous rendering of it, the material becomes transparent to the spiritual meaning underlying it.

Van Eyck's most famous work, the *Ghent Altarpiece* (1425–32), is attributed jointly to Jan and his brother Hubert. When closed, the large folding polyptych shows an image of the Annunciation, as well as naturalistic portraits of the donors. When open, it shows images of the entire Christian cycle from the Fall to the Redemption. Using their skill as miniaturists the artists bring out the beauty in the most microscopic details, and create scenes of great concreteness and naturalness, all of which are rich in symbolism.

Van Eyck also painted purely secular portraits such as the *The Man in a Red Turban* (1433). This image, which many believe to be a self-portrait, is clearly of a real person, and is dramatically different in tone from the traditional ethereal quality of medieval representation.

The painting *Arnolfini Wedding* (1434) conveys the inner meaning of a marriage through the same precise attention to the details of the moment and place, revealing through them what cannot be seen. Almost every object in the painting refers symbolically to the holiness of matrimony, from the removed shoes to the faithful dog. The artist himself, witnessing the marriage, can be seen in the mirror on the wall. The painting, perhaps a form of legal witness to the marriage, suggests the mystical vision of van Eyck's contemporary Nicholas of Cusa, who suggested that God is present in the small as well as the large, and that everything is significant because it is seen by God.

The circumstances of van Eyck's death are not known, but records show that he was buried on July 9, 1441

Legacy

Jan van Eyck was the founder of a new style that dominated the art of the Netherlands for several generations and helped to transform art throughout Europe.

With its depiction of material objects selected and arranged to convey symbolic meaning, its glowing atmospheric colors, and its meticulous detailing of architectural interiors and landscapes, van Eyck's style brought a new and striking realism to late medieval art. In addition, van Eyck's appointment to an important position in the court of the duke of Burgundy gave him a social status to which his younger contemporaries aspired.

In Bruges, models from van Eyck's workshop continued to be copied long after his death. Younger artists such as Petrus Christus and Dirk Bouts attempted to imitate his style. The practice of copying his painting continued for the next several generations, culminating in an "Eyckian Revival" at the end of the century. Numerous successful artists, including Gerard David, Quentin Metsys, and Jan Gossart, were commissioned to produce copies of van Eyck's paintings.

Van Eyck's innovative style also had a profound effect outside the Netherlands. His works were imitated as far away as Spain and Switzerland. In Germany, ALBRECHT DÜRER recorded in his diary being taken to see the *Ghent Altarpiece* in 1521. Since 1604, when the first northern European art historian, Karel van Mander, wrote his account of the lives of Dutch and Flemish painters, Jan van Eyck has held a prominent position in all accounts of European painting.

A few years after his death, van Eyck's fame spread to Italy; several of his works made their way into Italian collections, and their highly detailed style was emulated by many Italian artists, including SANDRO BOTTICELLI. Van Eyck's style of portrait became popular among Italian nobility.

Van Eyck remains one of the most highly regarded artists in European history. He is admired both for his painstaking attention to detail and for his ability to translate the traditions of medieval spirituality into the visual language of the emerging bourgeoisie.

Domenico

For Further Reading

Hall, E. C. *The Arnolfini Betrothal.* Berkeley: University of California Press, 1994.

Panofsky, Erwin. *Early Netherlandish Painting.* 2 vols. Cambridge, Mass.: Harvard University Press, 1953.

Seidel, Linda. *Jan Van Eyck's Arnolfini Portrait: Stories of an Icon.* Cambridge and New York: Cambridge University Press, 1993.

Van Gogh, Vincent

Painter
1853–1890

Life and Work

The largely self-taught nineteenth–century Post-Impressionist painter Vincent van Gogh used intense colors and broad vigorous brushwork to express his emotional relationship to the world.

Van Gogh was born in 1853 in Groot-Zundert, the son of a Dutch Protestant pastor. As a young man, van Gogh was an art salesman, a French tutor, and a theological student. Quitting his studies, he worked briefly as a lay preacher to poor miners in Belgium, but was dismissed for taking Christ's teachings too literally, giving away all his possessions. Finally, after a sojourn in northern France in 1879–80, he decided to become a painter of peasants, and pursued his new profession with the same zeal that he had put into his religious work.

From 1880 to 1885, van Gogh studied and painted in Brussels, the Hague, and the rural northern province of Drenthe in the Netherlands. His painting *The Potato Eaters* (1885) reflected his interest in the lives of poor working people. It was a risky subject matter, as art patrons of the day were used to more appealing subjects and a more traditional academic style.

In 1886, he moved to Paris, where he continued traditional instruction in drawing and painting, but of greater importance were such models as the Impressionists CLAUDE MONET and Camille Pissarro, the Pointillist Georges Seurat, and the Japanese woodcuts then popular in France.

In 1888, van Gogh moved to Arles in southern France, where he used color as an expressive vehicle rather than a record of visual sensation. His brushwork moved away from the precise chromatic stippling learned from Seurat to swirling, dynamic strokes. Always prolific, in his 15 months at Arles, he completed 200 paintings.

Increasingly mentally unstable, van Gogh after 1888 was plagued by bouts of insanity. Following a fight with his friend, the painter Paul Gauguin, van Gogh cut off a piece of his own ear. In 1889 he had himself institutionalized at St.-Remy, drawing and painting between attacks. He produced 150 works during his year of institutionalization. *Starry Night* (1889), one of his most famous works, was composed from sketches, rather than directly from nature, his usual method. It is a work of profound psychological and spiritual intensity, like a mystical vision.

He spent the last months of his life in Auvers-sur-Oise, where he continued his prodigious output and had his first small successes. Following a new bout of depression, van Gogh shot himself in July 1890, and died two days later.

Legacy

Although Vincent van Gogh sold only a single painting in his lifetime, *Red Vineyard* (1888), he began to receive recognition after his death. He had a particularly close relationship with his brother, Theo, an art dealer who supported him financially during his years as a painter. His extensive, diary-like correspondence with Theo, as well as with Gauguin and other artists, appeared in print early in the 20th century and had much to do with his later fame.

Van Gogh's deeply personal, emotionally charged style made a powerful impact on the generation of European artists that followed him. An exhibition of his work in Amsterdam in 1905 influenced the young PIET MONDRIAN. In France, the so-called Fauves, a group of artists that included HENRI MATISSE, expanded on van Gogh's bold use of color. In Germany and Austria, Expressionist artists were influenced by van Gogh's introspective, emotionally expressive work. PAULA MODERSOHN-BECKER was also artistically indebted to van Gogh.

Van Gogh has become one of the great icons of modern art. Irving Stone's romantic 1934 novel *Lust for Life* and the 1956 movie of the same name were based upon van Gogh's published correspondence. A popular song of the 1970s, "Starry, Starry Night" by Don McLean, romanticized van Gogh's story for another generation. In 1972 the Rijksmuseum van Gogh opened in Amsterdam. In the 1980s a van Gogh painting set record prices for a European work at auction.

The image of the "Artist" in the popular imagination may owe more to van Gogh than to any other person; he is a lonely hero suffering for the sake of self-expression, straddling the border between genius and madman.

Domenico

WORLD EVENTS		VAN GOGH'S LIFE
Revolutions in Austria, France, Germany, and Italy	1848	
	1853	Vincent van Gogh is born
U.S. Civil War	1861–65	
Germany is united	1871	
	1885	Van Gogh paints *The Potato Eaters*
	1886	Van Gogh moves to Paris
	1888	Van Gogh moves to Arles
	1889	Van Gogh paints *Starry Night*
	1890	Van Gogh commits suicide
Spanish-American War	1898	

For Further Reading

Hulsker, Jan. *The Complete Van Gogh: Paintings, Drawings, Sketches.* New York: Harry N. Abrams, 1977.

Stein, Susan Alyson, ed. *Van Gogh: A Retrospective.* New York: H. L. Levin Associates, 1986.

Sweetman, David. *The Love of Many Things: A Life of Vincent van Gogh.* London: Hodder & Stoughton, 1990.

Varèse, Edgard

Composer
1883–1965

Life and Work

Edgard Varèse's surviving output consists of only a dozen complete compositions; a radical at odds with the musical world that surrounded him, he remained silent as a composer for long periods. Yet Varèse was a pioneer who rethought the nature of musical sound itself, and many composers eagerly picked up the threads of his thinking.

Varèse was born Edgar Varèse in Paris on December 22, 1883. Like so many other musicians he had an aptitude for math, and his father hoped to push him into an engineering career. But he persisted with music, and, in 1903, he began to study composition with Albert Roussel and Charles-Marie Widor, leading composers of the day. In 1907 he went to Berlin to soak up new artistic currents, including the music of the Austrian composer ARNOLD SCHOENBERG. In 1913, Varèse's manuscripts were destroyed in a Berlin fire after he returned to Paris. Discouraged, and with little hope of a permanent job, he headed for America in 1915.

Although the leading edge of European modern music went virtually unheard in America at the time, Varèse made a mark in his adopted country through sheer promotional energy. In 1919 he created a short-lived ensemble of his own, the New Symphony Orchestra, with the intention of introducing contemporary music. Varèse co-founded the International Composers' Guild in New York in 1921; the group's concerts included the premieres of many of Varèse's own groundbreaking compositions, including *Hyperprism* in 1923 and *Intégrales* in 1925. These were typical of the composer's work in their derivation of structure from sequences of textures and sounds rather than from melody, and in their quasi-scientific titles. Some of his pieces incorporated the sounds of urban environments. By 1931 Varèse had created an unprecedented all-percussion work, *Ionisation.*

After World War II Varèse gradually gained renown as a teacher, and his imagination was fired anew by the musical possibilities of electronics and recording tape, technologies that had made great strides during the war. *Déserts,* written between 1950 and 1954, was a pioneering composition that mixed tape sounds with conventional instruments, and the entirely taped *Poème electronique* was written for presentation in the futuristic Le Corbusier pavilion at the Brussels Exposition in 1958. Varèse died in New York on November 6, 1965.

Legacy

Edgard Varèse's compact compositions and his uncompromising commitment to the exploration of sonic frontiers influenced a wide range of later composers.

Even in the culturally fertile 1920s Varèse's "organized sound" (he avoided the term "music") was strikingly original. Varèse, in effect, broke music down to basic sounds and used them to build new kinds of structures. His elevation of instrumental color, register, dynamics, and duration to positions of fundamental formal importance had a tremendous impact after World War II, when composers of the serialist school tried to devise ways of incorporating those musical parameters into their highly structured musical system. Among these composers were the Frenchman Pierre Boulez and the American Milton Babbitt.

Meanwhile Varèse also influenced JOHN CAGE, a composer whose efforts in many ways stood diametrically opposed to those of the serialists. Varèse's openness to new and previously nonmusical sounds, such as sirens, inspired Cage and other postwar experimentalists to break down the boundaries between music and its ambient world.

Even after World War II, when Varèse was in his sixties, he was an influential path breaker. His interest in pure sound had led him naturally to appreciate the potential of musical electronics: Varèse was among the first composers to use taped electronic elements in his music, and the generation that came of age in the 1950s looked to him as an important forebear. Again both Europeans, such as the German electronic composer Karlheinz Stockhausen, and Americans, such as Mario Davidowsky, benefited from Varèse's innovations. The composer's frequent travels across the Atlantic and his energy as a teacher put him in contact with the brightest young musical minds. Varèse was, in sum, one of the twentieth century's most profoundly inventive composers.

Manheim

For Further Reading
Bernard, Jonathan W. *The Music of Edgard Varèse.* New Haven, Conn.: Yale University Press, 1987.
Ouellette, Fernand. *Edgard Varèse.* Translated by Derek Coltman. New York: Da Capo, 1981.

Velázquez, Diego

Painter and Courtier
1599–1660

Life and Work

Diego Velázquez was the most important Spanish painter of the seventeenth century.

Born in 1599 in Seville to a family of minor nobility, Velázquez studied for several months with the painter Francisco de Herrera the elder before entering the studio of Francisco Pacheco in 1613. Velázquez, with the other students, experimented with the naturalism and light-and-dark effects of CARAVAGGIO. His earliest paintings were portraits and conventional religious works.

In 1623, Velázquez, after executing a successful portrait of King Philip IV, was named official painter to the king, a position he never relinquished. Freed from the necessity of taking religious commissions, he produced many somber portraits of the king and the royal family during the late 1620s. Velázquez also studied the royal art collection, in particular the Venetians, and became an admirer of TITIAN.

The great Flemish painter PETER PAUL RUBENS visited Madrid on a diplomatic mission in 1628, and inspired Velázquez to journey to Italy in 1629. During his two years traveling in Italy, Velázquez studied both Renaissance and contemporary artists. Their influence can be seen in the sculptural quality of the figures and the light-and-shadow techniques of *Joseph and His Brothers* (1630). *Venus at Her Mirror* (the *Rokeby Venus*, 1649–51), painted during a second Italian journey, is the first known female nude in Spanish art and one of the great paintings of Venus in Western art, comparable with Titian's *Venus of Urbino*.

Las Meninas, painted in 1656, achieves an experience of reality through its exactness of tone and creation of atmosphere, the precise arrangement of figures, and its forefronting of the disturbing dwarfs in the same plane as the golden-haired princess, Doña Margarita. The painting, Velázquez's major work, is an unusual royal portrait in that the king and queen are shown as reflected images in the mirror on the wall facing the viewer (in effect, the viewer occupies the position of the royal couple). In the foreground of the painting are the Infanta, surrounded by her maids-in-waiting (*las meninas*), her favorite dwarfs, and a large dog. The artist himself appears in the painting's middle ground.

In 1658, through the Pope's intervention, Velázquez was granted the title he had long sought, Knight of Santiago. Two years later, he fell ill and died.

Legacy

Because very few people had access to Diego Velázquez's work (his paintings were all located at the Alcazar, the royal palace in Seville), he had little effect on art for many years after his death. However, his work influenced seventeenth-century portrait painters in Italy.

In the eighteenth century, FRANCISCO GOYA, was deeply influenced by Velázquez. Indeed, his painterly approach derived directly from Velázquez's style.

In the nineteenth century, as Spain opened itself to its European neighbors, Velázquez's work became recognized outside of that country. Beginning in the middle part of the century, Velázquez came to be recognized as one of the great pure painters in European history. His expressive brushwork and bold lighting effects were seen as the Spanish counterpart to the art of Rubens.

In the nineteenth and twentieth centuries, Velázquez's open brushwork, which conveyed an expressive force of its own independent of the objects represented, was seen in a new light by the generation of artists who were experimenting with increasingly abstract forms. The revolutionary works of EDOUARD MANET in the 1860s owed much to Velázquez's influence.

Velázquez's reputation continued to grow in the twentieth century among art historians, critics, and artists. PABLO PICASSO paid homage to his compatriot in a series of works based on *Las Meninas.*

Today Velázquez is regarded as a figure of major international importance. A source of Modernist tradition, he has also become emblematic of the unique tradition of Spanish art.

Domenico

WORLD EVENTS		VELÁZQUEZ'S LIFE
Ottoman dominance of Mediterranean ends	1571	
	1599	Diego Velázquez is born
Thirty Years' War in Europe	1618–48	
	1623	Velázquez is appointed official painter to King Philip IV
	1629	Velázquez makes first trip to Italy
	1656	Velázquez paints *Las Meninas*
	1660	Velázquez dies
Glorious Revolution in England	1688	

For Further Reading

Brown, Christopher. *Velázquez: Painter and Courtier.* New Haven, Conn., and London: Yale University Press, 1986.

Perez Sanchez, Alfonso E., Antonio Dominguez Ortiz, and Julian Gallego. *Velázquez.* Exhibition catalogue. New York: Metropolitan Museum of Art, 1989.

Verdi, Giuseppe

Composer
1813–1901

Life and Work

Since their premiere productions, spread over seven decades of the nineteenth century, the works of Giuseppe Verdi have rarely been absent from the opera houses of Italy and the world.

World Events		Verdi's Life
Latin American independence movement begins	1811	
	1813	Giuseppe Verdi is born
Congress of Vienna reorganizes Europe	1815	
	1839	Oberto premieres
Revolutions in Austria, France, Germany, and Italy	1848	
	1853	La Traviata premieres
U.S. Civil War	1861–65	
Germany is united	1871	Aida premieres
Spanish-American War	1898	
	1901	Verdi dies
World War I	1914–18	

Verdi was born on October 10, 1813, in the village of Roncole, near Busseto, in northern Italy. The child of a bar owner, he grew up in modest circumstances, but took enthusiastically to the spinet, a small keyboard instrument. In 1832 he applied to study music at the Milan Conservatory. He was rejected, but turned to a private teacher and gained a thorough grounding in composition.

In 1834 he went back to Busseto to become the town's music director, although the local bishop, leery of Verdi's big-city education, had tried to squash his appointment. He had already written some small vocal pieces, and turned his eyes toward the prize of a production in one of Italy's great opera houses. Verdi moved to Milan once again, and his first opera, *Oberto*, was produced at the great La Scala theater in 1839.

Successful from the start, Verdi captured the attention of the gradually coalescing nation of Italy with the patriotic chorus "Va pensiero" from his 1842 opera *Nabucco*. Of his stirringly melodic and unfailingly emotion-packed early operas, 1853's *La Traviata* (*The Fallen Woman*), with its tragic story of a woman trying to escape a life of prostitution, has remained among the most popular.

In the middle of his career Verdi worked toward a new gravity, toward ever more sharply etched characters, and toward a freer musical structure that mixed tuneful passages with declamation in such a way to heighten the dramatic ebb and flow. The capstone of several ambitious dramatic and comic works was *Aida*, an 1871 opera given its premiere in Cairo, Egypt. Verdi continued to compose even into old age. His two final operas, written on texts adapted from Shakespeare, were *Otello* and *Falstaff*, from 1887 and 1893, respectively. After these came *Four Sacred Pieces,* choral works premiered in 1898 when Verdi was 85 years old. He died in Milan on January 27, 1901.

Legacy

Giuseppe Verdi's operas towered over those of his Italian contemporaries, and no future opera composer remained untouched by the transformation he wrought in the art.

Most influential of all was the new flexibility Verdi brought to the musical language of opera. Whereas operas prior to Verdi had alternated stretches of dry, half-sung dialogue with set melodic pieces called arias, Verdi freely

combined the two, making his characters appear to speak more naturally but at the same time heightening their dramatic impact. By the time he wrote *Otello*, Verdi had emulated the German opera composer RICHARD WAGNER in replacing a structure divided into musical numbers with a continuous flow of music. This became the norm for Italian opera into the twentieth century, establishing procedures on which composers such as Giacomo Puccini would elaborate. The popular image of an operatic heroine, gradually rising in song from calm to a peak of emotion, was one that Verdi worked out over the course of his career.

Along with Verdi's accuracy of musical representation went a new psychological realism. Verdi sometimes adopted the conventional spectacles of grand opera, but his characters were always flesh and blood, recognizable human figures; though he worked from heavily modified versions of Shakespeare, he had a strong affinity for the work of the great English dramatist. The *verismo*, or realist, movement in Italian opera from the 1890s to the 1920s proceeded from this aspect of Verdi's work. In place of the kings and biblical heroes of operatic tradition, such works as the *Cavalleria Rusticana* of Pietro Mascagni turned to ordinary people and to stories that might be drawn from the streets as easily as from the lives of the nobility. *La Traviata* directly anticipated these works, and other Verdi operas pointed indirectly to them with their vivid characterizations. Above all, Verdi was a great dramatist, and the embrace into which he brought opera and drama continues.

Manheim

For Further Reading

Phillips-Matz, Mary Jane. *Verdi: A Biography.* Oxford and New York: Oxford University Press, 1993.

Walker, Frank. *The Man Verdi.* New York: Knopf, 1962.

Virgil
(Publius Vergilius Maro)

Poet

70 B.C.E.–19 B.C.E.

Life and Work

Virgil was the author of the great national epic of Rome. Appearing during the reign of Augustus after the destruction of the Roman Republic, the *Aeneid* helped to create a national myth that supported and justified the emerging imperial state.

Virgil was born near Mantua in what was then Cisalpine Gaul, in northern Italy, on October 15, 70 B.C.E. He went to school in Mantua and later studied in Cremona, Milan, and Rome. After completing his studies he lived at his parents' farm and wrote, possibly beginning work on the *Eclogues*. Much of his development as a writer took place during the civil wars between 50 and 30 B.C.E. that destroyed the Roman Republic and caused severe social and economic damage on the Italian peninsula.

In 40 B.C.E. Virgil moved to Naples and three years later he finished the *Eclogues*, a cycle of 10 pastoral poems that celebrate the simplicity and harmony of rural life in idealized settings. In 29 B.C.E. he published the *Georgics*, in which he examined the ways and values of farming life, and the disastrous results of the civil wars on the Italian countryside. It was a popular work and the Roman ruler Octavian (emperor in all but name, and soon to rename himself Augustus) honored Virgil with praise and wealth.

Consolidating his rule after the civil wars, Augustus, wishing to foster a national patriotic spirit in support of his new state, commissioned an epic about the founding of Rome. Virgil's poem, the *Aeneid*, introduces the tragic romance of Dido and the Trojan prince Aeneas, and serves as an allegory linking the great civilization of the Greeks to the great new one that was now succeeding it, the Augustan empire. It is rooted in Virgil's sense of relief at the end of the civil ears and in his hope for future peace and prosperity. Modeled on HOMER's *Odyssey*, the *Aeneid* uses material adapted from Greek mythology, religion, poetry, and philosophy as it depicts the progress of Aeneas—whose heroism evokes and honors Augustus—from the end of the Trojan War to the legendary founding of the city of Rome. Virgil shows that Rome was predestined to become the ruler and civilizer of the world. While expressing confidence in the new Augustan regime, Virgil emphasized the human cost of Augustus's victory and the peace that followed it, allowing for greater psychological depth and moral ambiguity than had earlier Roman literature.

In 23 B.C.E. Virgil presented Books II, IV, and VI of the *Aeneid* to Augustus. The work immediately earned the praise of all who read it. When he died of a fever in 19 B.C.E., Virgil was planning to spend three more years revising. On his deathbed he asked friends to burn the book rather than publish it unfinished. They ignored this request, editing the work and publishing the complete twelve books in 17 B.C.E..

Legacy

The *Aeneid* helped to define the spirit of the Roman Empire at its inception and is one of the greatest epic poems of Western literature.

The *Aeneid* was read by every educated Roman during and after Virgil's lifetime. The story of Dido and Aeneas in particular has been invoked and rewritten by a host of later writers, beginning with OVID. Ovid emulated Virgil's artistry while intently subverting its celebration of Augustus's empire. At some level Virgil influenced every poet who followed him.

While his work has been read continuously in the centuries since his death, a particular interest in it arose in the early 800s under the Emperor Charlemagne, when many copies were made and distributed. In 1490 a French version was translated into English by William Caxton. Other famous translators have included the Bishop of Dunkel, Gawin Douglas, in 1553 and Henry Howard, who translated Books II and IV into English in 1557. In 1697 John Dryden translated the *Aeneid* into heroic couplets and in the early nineteenth century JOHN KEATS began a prose translation, now lost, when he was still in school.

The comparison of Virgil to Homer dates from the moment the *Aeneid* was published. While he did base the structure of his epic on the *Odyssey*, Virgil wrote from a far more subjective and compassionate position than Homer. His characters were more complex and their motives and actions more conflicted than those of Homer, and his writing allows for different interpretations of events by different characters.

The *Aeneid* is both a patriotic epic and a personal poem, in which the emotions of the characters are revealed and examined.

Technically, Virgil was notable for his use of dactylic hexameter, a poetic meter he adapted from Greek, and for his clear syntax and rich imagery. Later Latin poets imitated and elaborated upon Virgil, profoundly affecting the development of Western poetry.

There is hardly a poet in the Western world who has not read and admired the *Aeneid*. DANTE was so profoundly affected by the work that he made Virgil his guide through Hell and Purgatory in his *Divine Comedy*. GEOFFREY CHAUCER drew upon it, as did LUÍZ VAZ DE CAMÕES, who wrote the great epic poem of Portugal, *Os Lusiados* (*The Lusiads*, 1572); Torquato Tasso, who wrote *Gerusalemme liberata* (1581); Edmund Spenser, who drew upon it for his great poem *The Faerie Queene* (Books I–III, 1590; Books IV–VI, 1596); and JOHN MILTON, who did the same for his *Paradise Lost*.

In the Middle Ages many Christians saw Virgil as a pre-Christian prophet. The fourth *Eclogue* in particular, which dealt with Virgil's hopes for a peaceful "golden age" after the turmoil of the civil wars, was taken to contain a prediction of the coming of the Christ, the savior (the passage actually referred to a possible child of the recent marriage between Mark Antony and Octavian's sister). Historians have frequently turned to the *Aeneid* for historical details of the Augustan Roman society.

Watson

WORLD EVENTS		VIRGIL'S LIFE
	B.C.E.	
Overland silk trade between Rome and China begins	c. 121	
	70	Virgil is born
Rome's conquest of Gaul completed	50	
	37	Virgil publishes *Eclogues*
	31	Virgil begins *Aeneid*
	29	Virgil publishes *Georgics*
	19	Virgil dies
	17	*Aeneid* is published posthumously
	C.E.	
Jesus is crucified	c. 33	

For Further Reading

Baswell, Christopher. *Virgil in Medieval England*. Cambridge: Cambridge University Press, 1995.

Levi, Peter. *Virgil: His Life and Times*. New York: St. Martin's Press, 1999

Putnam, Michael C. J. *Virgil's Aeneid: Interpretation and Influence*. Chapel Hill: University of North Carolina Press, 1995.

Wagner, Richard

Composer
1813–1883

Life and Work

Richard Wagner was nineteenth-century music's true revolutionary. His monumental operas inhabited a musical and philosophical world that he fabricated virtually alone.

Born Wilhelm Richard Wagner in Leipzig, Germany, on May 22, 1813, Wagner had a colorful career fully consistent with his larger-than-life music, spending considerable time on the run from police, creditors, and ex-lovers. Following study in Leipzig, at the same institution that a century earlier had employed Johann Sebastian Bach, Wagner wrote several operas that adopted prevailing German Romantic styles.

After sneaking away from a conducting job in Latvia to avoid mounting bills, he broke through in 1842 with *Rienzi*, for which, as with all his works, he wrote both music and text. Wagner's

first artistic triumphs were 1843's *The Flying Dutchman*, which clearly anticipated his future work in its seamless integration of music and drama and in its legend-based story, and *Tannhäuser* in 1845. Wagner joined the revolutionary upheavals in Dresden in 1849; he left Germany one step ahead of Prussian troops and would not return for 11 years.

The premiere of *Lohengrin*, with its famous wedding march, was conducted by Wagner's ally Franz Liszt in 1850. Fifteen years elapsed before another major Wagner premiere, but he was absorbed in the creation of vastly original works and of polemical writings, some of which included controversial anti-Semitic elements. Wagner embarked upon a four-opera cycle based on Norse myths, collectively known as *The Ring of the Nibelungs;* its theme, dedicated in the most general terms, was the idea that money is the root of all evil. The four works were linked through Wagner's innovative *leitmotifs*, recurring melodies associated with specific characters and ideas. Wagner's operas, often called "music dramas," worked toward a multimedia fusion of the arts—a notion Wagner referred to as *Gesamtkunstwerk*, or total work of art.

Wagner completed the first two Ring operas, *The Rhine Gold* and *The Valkyries,* in 1854 and 1856, respectively. Breaking off work on the cycle, he finished the harmonically complex *Tristan and Isolde* in 1859 and the comic *The Mastersingers of Nürnberg* in 1867. He had returned to Germany with few prospects, but he was rescued by Ludwig II, king of Bavaria, who offered sumptuous lodgings and urged him to complete the Ring cycle. Wagner finished the third work, *Siegfried,* in 1871, and the fourth and final work, *Twilight of the Gods,* in 1874; the entire cycle was performed at Wagner's newly constructed theater, Bayreuth, in 1876. His last opera was the quasi-religious *Parsifal*, completed in 1882. On February 13, 1883, he died of a heart attack in Venice, allegedly after his wife confronted him about a liaison with a chorus girl.

Legacy

Richard Wagner's importance is revealed in the intensity of feeling exhibited by both his partisans and his detractors. None of his successors could ignore his work.

His harmonic practices marked a major step in the long expansion and eventual dissolution of traditional harmony in European music. *Tristan and Isolde* especially was closely analyzed

by later composers and theorists, who puzzled over the implications of a highly dissonant chord that recurred at key points in the work. The composers of the early twentieth century, who would eventually eliminate classical harmony from their works, began their careers as committed Wagnerians; such works as Arnold Schoenberg's string sextet *Transfigured Night* of 1899 took the expanded harmonic palette of *Tristan* and *Parsifal* as a point of departure for further experiment.

In the sheer scope of his music, too, Wagner was influential; the vast plans of his operas inspired gigantic instrumental works by Richard Strauss, Gustav Mahler, and Anton Bruckner, who when he met Wagner went down on one knee, kissed Wagner's hand, and exclaimed, "O Master, I worship you!"

The spiritual leaders of the anti-Wagnerian camp were the Viennese critic Eduard Hanslick, whom Wagner satirized with the character of Beckmesser in *The Mastersingers of Nürnberg,* and the composer Johannes Brahms, whose abstract instrumental-music aesthetic was diametrically opposed to Wagner's. Tension between musical radicals and conservatives, to be sure, was ages old, but Wagner's overwhelming art and personality brought it to new levels.

Encompassing intricate webs of musical and textual symbols and a wide-reaching philosophy with aspects of socialism, Christianity, Eastern religion, and German cultural nationalism, Wagner's operas may fairly be called whole worlds in themselves. His ambitious, totalizing spirit shaped fundamentally the future of classical music.

Manheim

WORLD EVENTS	WAGNER'S LIFE	
	1813	Richard Wagner is born in Leipzig, Germany
	1842	Wagner has first major success with *Rienzi*
Revolutions in Austria, France, Germany, and Italy	1848	
	1849	Wagner flees Dresden during period of unrest
	1859	Wagner completes *Tristan and Isolde*
U.S. Civil War	1861–65	
	1867	Wagner completes *The Mastersingers of Nürnberg*
Germany is united	1871	
	1874	Final Ring cycle opera, *Twilight of the Gods*
	1876	Wagner completes theater at Bayreuth
	1882	Wagner completes *Parsifal*
	1883	Wagner dies
Spanish-American War	1898	

For Further Reading
Deathridge, John, and Carl Dahlhaus. *The New Grove Wagner.* New York: W. W. Norton, 1984.
Millington, Barry. *Wagner.* Princeton, N.J.: Princeton University Press, 1992.

Warhol, Andy

Painter, Printmaker, and
Filmmaker
1928–1987

Life and Work

Remembered as the best-known practitioner of Pop Art during the 1960s, and an icon of fashion and celebrity in the 1970s and 1980s, Andy Warhol was a painter, printmaker, sculptor, illustrator, draftsman, filmmaker, writer, and collector.

Andrew Warhola was born in 1928 in Pittsburgh, one of three children in a working-class Roman Catholic family. He studied art at the Carnegie Institute of Technology from 1945 to 1949, and then moved to New York. He was successful as a commercial artist and illustrator during the 1950s.

Warhol turned to painting in 1960, inspired by the work of young artists like Jasper Johns and ROBERT RAUSCHENBERG. His first paintings, among the earliest examples of American Pop Art, were of images taken from comic strips and advertisements. He also exploited images of familiar commercial products, such as Coca-Cola bottles and Campbell's Soup cans, as well as contemporary celebrities such as ELVIS PRESLEY, Elizabeth Taylor, and Marilyn Monroe.

Warhol's works, deliberately impersonal, often were made using the commercial processes of stenciling and silk-screening. His

large troupe of assistants, working in what Warhol called the Factory, were the actual producers. Such art was thus philosophically the opposite of the deeply personal and original Abstract Expressionist work that then dominated the art scene. Pop Art's largely mechanically reproduced images of mass consumer culture conveyed the condition of being an uninvolved spectator in a society flooded with information and media-generated images, both fascinating and affectless at the same time.

Warhol experimented with a variety of media. He began making films in 1963, including *Empire* (1964), a seven-hour film showing the Empire State Building continuously from one vantage point. He also produced multimedia events combining the live music of the band Velvet Underground with projections of film and light by his company the Exploding Plastic Inevitable. He launched the magazine *Interview*, which quickly achieved cult status.

His later life, as a central figure in the New York social world, was filled with the sort of lurid-banal events that were the stuff of his beloved tabloid press. In 1968, he survived an assassination attempt by a demented would-be playwright. He became a celebrity, the human equivalent of a commercial product, a status he also conferred on the subjects of his many commissioned portraits of the 1970s. Warhol's work became more experimental in the 1980s when he collaborated with Francesco Clemente and JEAN-MICHEL BASQUIAT. This later work included paintings on religious themes such as *Last Supper* (1986).

In 1987, Warhol died from complications after routine surgery.

Legacy

In many ways, Andy Warhol's greatest creation was Andy Warhol; his own highly stylized image, with pasty complexion and disheveled white wig, was an icon of the age. Surrounded by an entourage of druggies, drag queens, and hangers-on, he was the embodiment of 1960s camp sensibility, as well as a creator and exemplar of the culture of celebrity that transformed the American art world, and much else, in the 1970s and 1980s.

Warhol, although a great promoter of the Pop sensibility, was not the inventor of Pop Art. British artists such as Richard Hamilton had

been exploiting similar material since the mid-1950s, and in America Rauschenberg and Johns, while never Pop artists, had laid the groundwork by the time Warhol began to make his earliest Pop images. Nevertheless Warhol became the best known of the Pop artists, and the most closely connected with the style.

By blurring the lines between "high" art and commercial imagery, Warhol had a profound effect on late twentieth-century art. While Abstract Expressionism had received critical acclaim, it did not, at first, sell. But Pop Art did sell, leading to an explosion in the number of galleries, a corresponding rise in art prices, and a reinforcement of New York's position as the center of the art world.

As an influential art world figure, Warhol supported numerous young artists, and his sensibility also had a profound effect on performance art, music, and dance. His work with younger artists such as Jean-Michel Basquiat helped carry his influence into the next generation.

Warhol's reputation has continued to grow. He has been the subject of numerous books and articles and even two popular films. The Warhol Museum, which houses the largest collection in the United States devoted to a single artist's work, opened in Pittsburgh in 1994. The Warhol Foundation provides an important source of funding for the arts.

Domenico

WORLD EVENTS		WARHOL'S LIFE
Russian Revolution	1917	
	1928	Andy Warhol is born
Great Depression	1929–39	
World War II	1939–45	
	1945–49	Warhol studies at Carnegie Institute of Technology
Communist China is established	1949	
Korean War	1950–53	
African independence movement begins	1957	
	1960	Warhol produces his early Pop paintings
Vietnam War ends	1975	
	1987	Warhol dies
Dissolution of Soviet Union	1991	

For Further Reading

Bockris, Victor. *The Life and Death of Andy Warhol.* New York: Bantam Books, 1989.

McShine, Kynaston, ed. *Andy Warhol: A Retrospective.* Exhibition catalogue. New York: Museum of Modern Art, 1989.

Warhol, Andy. *The Philosophy of Andy Warhol: From A to B and Back Again.* New York: Harcourt Brace Jovanovich, 1977.

Welles, Orson

Actor and Filmmaker
1915–1985

Life and Work

The multitalented but egomaniacal Orson Welles excelled in film acting and directing, while also breaking ground in theater and radio. His masterpiece was the film *Citizen Kane* (1941), which is regarded by many as among the most important, influential, and greatest films in the history of cinema.

Welles was born in Kenosha, Wisconsin, in 1915. His father was a wealthy inventor and his mother a concert pianist. Growing up in Chicago, Welles showed early talent in the arts. After graduating from high school in 1931, he studied art briefly and then went on a sketching tour of Ireland; there he managed to get a part in a play at the Gate Theater in Dublin, and remained in Ireland for another year, followed by travel in Morocco and Spain.

Returning to the United States, Welles joined Katherine Cornell's theatrical company

WORLD EVENTS	WELLES' LIFE
World War I 1914–18	
	1915 Orson Welles is born
Russian Revolution 1917	
Great Depression 1929–39	
	1938 Welles broadcasts *War of the Worlds*
World War II 1939–45	
	1941 Welles directs *Citizen Kane*
	1942 Wells directs *The Magnificent Ambersons*
	1947 Wells directs *The Lady from Shanghai*
Communist China 1949 is established	
Korean War 1950–53	
African independence 1957 movement begins	
Vietnam War ends 1975	
	1985 Welles dies
Dissolution of 1991 Soviet Union	

and made his New York debut as Tybalt in *Romeo and Juliet*. In 1937, together with John Houseman, Welles formed the innovative Mercury Theater, where he became known as an actor and director. In 1938 the Mercury Theater moved into radio with a series of dramas based on literary sources. The most famous was the October 30, 1938 broadcast of H. G. Wells's *War of the Worlds*. Using the format of a simulated news broadcast, an attack on New Jersey by Martian invaders was dramatized; although the performance was bracketed by announcements that it was a fictional presentation, many listeners thought it was real and were terrified. The scandal resulted in intense criticism of—and publicity for—Welles.

Courted by several Hollywood studios, the "boy wonder" at age 24 signed a precedent-setting contract with RKO that gave him complete artistic control over his films. In 1941, working with a script he had developed with Herman J. Mankiewicz, Welles made *Citizen Kane*. On a relatively small budget, he produced a landmark film whose innovative narrative structure, cinematography and sound revolutionized American and ultimately world cinema.

The initial commercial failure of *Citizen Kane*, led to significant studio interference in Welles's next film, *The Magnificent Ambersons* (1942), based on Booth Tarkington's novel. Evoking nostalgia for the past, it told the story of the decline of a turn-of-the-century family. RKO forced Welles to cut the film from 148 to 88 minutes before its release. This film, too, was both box-office failure and critical success. It is also seen as prophetic, predicting the destruction of the quality of American life by urbanization and the automobile.

Welles also acted in other people's films—including a noteworthy performance in *The Third Man* (1939), and he directed several more, including *The Lady from Shanghai* (1947). Welles's reputation as a difficult and profligate director gained steam over the years, a situation that was not improved by the financial failure of most of his projects. In order to continue working, Welles moved to Europe after 1948, where he made such films as *Othello* (1952), and *The Trial* (1962), based on the work by FRANZ KAFKA. He returned briefly to Hollywood to make *Touch of Evil* (1958), considered by critics to be another masterpiece.

His last film, *F for Fake* (1975), was based on the exploits of a real-life art forger and is a reflection on the relation between art and reality. Returning to the United States after nearly 30 years of voluntary exile, Welles received the American Film Institute's Life Achievement Award (1975). Until his death in 1985, Welles appeared frequently on television shows and commercials and occasionally in film.

Legacy

Arguably the most influential movie in film history and widely regarded as the greatest film ever made, *Citizen Kane* is certainly the heart of Orson Welles's legacy. In his debut feature film, Welles clearly produced a work that was years ahead of its time and one that has shaped the face of serious cinema to this day.

Beginning with its complex, multileveled, fragmented, Modernist narrative structure, *Kane* was revolutionary in nearly every aspect of its production. Its cinematography (by Gregg Toland), which featured deep-focus shots, unconventional camera angles, and swooping camera movements, changed the way films were shot. The sound techniques, including overlapping sound montage, which sought to emulate the actual experience of hearing, were similarly innovative. Many of these techniques anticipated the approaches of French New Wave films and cinema verite.

The financial failure of *Citizen Kane* marked the beginning of Welles's declining career and a longstanding antagonism between Welles and those in charge of the American film industry. This antagonism reached a peak after his first three film failures, when he was pulled off a project being filmed in Brazil called *It's All True,* and much of the film's negative was destroyed.

Citizen Kane was withdrawn from circulation until the 1950s; nevertheless it became an art-house favorite and acquired a sophisticated audience.

Welles's career continues to be reevaluated; five of his films are now considered masterpieces: *Citizen Kane, The Magnificent Ambersons, The Lady from Shanghai, Touch of Evil,* and *Chimes at Midnight* (1966).

Domenico

For Further Reading

Callow, Simon. *Orson Welles.* New York: Viking, 1996.

Thomson, David. *Rosebud: The Story of Orson Welles.* New York: Alfred A. Knopf, 1996.

Welles, Orson, and Peter Bogdanovich. *This Is Orson Welles.* Edited by Jonathan Rosenbaum. New York: HarperCollins, 1992.

Whitman, Walt

Poet

1819–1892

Life and Work

"I celebrate myself and sing myself," wrote Walt Whitman in one of his most famous poems. But, he added, "every atom belonging to me as good as belongs to you." Whitman was the poetic spokesman at once for American individualism and American democracy.

Whitman was born on Long Island, New York, on May 31, 1819; his father was a house builder and real estate speculator, and carpentry would pay Whitman's own bills at several low points in his career. The family moved to Brooklyn, and Whitman's schooling ended at 12 with his apprenticeship to a printer. He worked as a schoolteacher between 1836 and 1841, but drifted back into the publishing world and flourished as a writer with a keen eye for New York life and an ear for music of all kinds. Whitman wrote a novel, *Franklin Evans* (1842), and several short stories cast in common forms of the day, and by 1848 he was the editor of the *Brooklyn Daily Eagle.*

Losing that post in a political dispute with the newspaper's publishers, Whitman traveled to New Orleans, and then returned to New York and tried to make a living as a freelance lecturer. In the early 1850s, Whitman began to experiment with poetry in which he frankly expressed his own experiences and beliefs in a rhapsodic free verse and in a direct American vernacular. The fruit of his efforts, a volume called *Leaves of Grass,* appeared in 1855. Whitman spent much of the rest of his life expanding and revising this book, his principal work. It went through nine editions before his death but found few readers at first; some condemned its openly sensual passages as indecent. Influential praise came from the great Transcendentalist essayist and philosopher Ralph Waldo Emerson, to whom Whitman had sent a copy of the privately printed work. *Leaves of Grass* exalted equality, the poet's own feelings and his desire to express them, and the fecundity of nature—the blades of grass of its title he memorably describes as "the beautiful uncut hair of graves."

Whitman worked as a nurse during the Civil War and wrote two volumes of poetry (later incorporated into *Leaves of Grass*) about the conflict; one of them contained a lament for the murdered Abraham Lincoln, "When Lilacs Last in the Dooryard Bloom'd" (1865), that is among his finest works. Censorship attempts gave subsequent editions of *Leaves of Grass* valuable publicity, and Whitman eventually achieved financial stability and he bought a home in Camden, New Jersey. He wrote poetry until his death there on March 26, 1892.

Legacy

Virtually without models, Walt Whitman created a distinctive style revolutionary enough that it could, with its essentials little altered, serve the needs of poetic radicals a century later.

Whitman essentially invented free verse—unrhymed poetry in free rhythm—for the modern era; his chant-like, repetitive cadences differed entirely from every other work of his time. During his own lifetime Whitman attracted no school of followers; he was admired in later life in England, but in his homeland was regarded mostly as an odd patriot of sorts. Whitman's treatment of love as a sexual thing was so far removed from Victorian mores that no other poet would follow him. Modern analysts have pursued interpretations of his entire body of work based on historical evidence that he was a homosexual.

In the twentieth century Whitman's reputation followed a steady upward curve. Free verse was favored by many poets with widely divergent outlooks; all of them owe something to Whitman, as do the countless amateur poets who set down their thoughts without the encumbrances of meter and rhyme. Poets as diverse as the coolly Modernist T. S. Eliot and the Beat avatar Allen Ginsberg admired Whitman, and he remains among the most widely read American poets. Ginsberg's style, with its long, irregular lines that gather in enthusiasm as they proceed, is especially reminiscent of Whitman's, and the 1960s counterculture, too, found the free-spirited Whitman inspiring. Walt Whitman was American poetry's great nonconformist.

Manheim

WORLD EVENTS		WHITMAN'S LIFE:
Congress of Vienna reorganizes Europe	1815	
	1819	Walt Whitman is born
	1836	Whitman takes job as schoolteacher
Revolutions in Austria, France, Germany, and Italy	1848	
	1855	Whitman publishes first edition of *Leaves of Grass*
U.S. Civil War	1861–65	
	1865	Whitman writes "When Lilacs Last in the Dooryard Bloom'd"
Germany is united	1871	
	1892	Whitman dies
Spanish-American War	1898	

For Further Reading

Kaplan, Justin. *Whitman: A Life.* New York: Simon & Schuster, 1980.

Reynolds, David S. *Walt Whitman's America: A Cultural Biography.* New York: Vintage Books, 1996.

Zweig, Paul. *Walt Whitman: The Making of the Poet.* New York: Basic Books, 1984.

Williams, Hank

Vocalist and Songwriter
1923–1953

Life and Work

Equally brilliant and equally tortured as a vocalist and as a songwriter, Hank Williams is the single most important figure in the history of country music.

Williams was born Hiram King Williams in the tiny community of Mount Olive, Alabama, on September 17, 1923. He suffered from spina bifida, which later in his life caused him chronic pain that played a role in his substance-abuse troubles. Williams sang in a Baptist church and learned to play guitar from a black street musician named Tee-tot. He won a talent show in Montgomery, Alabama, in 1937, singing a song called the "WPA Blues," and soon put together a band that performed on radio station WSFA there.

During World War II, Williams worked at a shipyard in Mobile, Alabama, performing on the side in tough honky-tonk bars he called "blood buckets." Williams made a trip to Nashville in 1946 and played some songs for Fred Rose, a publisher and songwriter who had recently moved from Hollywood with a vision of expanding the country music business. Rose immediately signed Williams to a songwriting contract.

Rose also paved the way for Williams to record, first on the Sterling label and then on nationally distributed MGM in 1947. His first big hit, "Move It On Over," came in the fall of that year; it was a cocky, upbeat blues piece that pointed forward to rock and roll . Williams joined the cast of the *Louisiana Hayride* radio program in Shreveport, Louisiana, in 1948. On the *Hayride*, he noticed that audiences responded wildly to a decades-old yodel number called "Lovesick Blues," and recorded the song in 1949. The song propelled Williams to national stardom and to a spot on Nashville's *Grand Ole Opry*, the most prominent country radio show.

From then until then end of his life, Williams feverishly wrote and recorded an astonishing string of country hits, some of them based emotionally in his deteriorating relationship with his wife, Audrey. The phrase "instant classic" applies to such Williams songs as "Your Cheatin' Heart," "Hey Good Lookin'," and "I Can't Help It If I'm Still in Love with You." Williams's drinking intensified, and he was fired from the *Opry* in August of 1952. En route to a show in Canton, Ohio, he died in his sleep in West Virginia on January 1, 1953.

Legacy

The songs of Hank Williams, elemental cries of emotional distress shaped with some help from Fred Rose into clear, unforgettable, classically elegant country songs, shaped the history of the country genre definitively.

Williams spawned a host of close followers during and immediately after his brief career. While a few distinctive country stylists of the early 1950s, such as Lefty Frizzell and Webb Pierce, forged independent vocal personalities, most other singers of the time imitated Williams for some period of their careers. Some of the singers who followed directly in the Williams mold were Carl Smith, Faron Young, and Ray Price, who began his career with Williams's Drifting Cowboys band. Unlike most country singers, Williams also had a strong impact on pop music, with Tony Bennett's version of "Cold Cold Heart" numbering among the most famous of the many "cover" versions pop artists made of Williams's songs.

Even when country music turned away from the raw emotion Williams exemplified toward rockabilly-influenced music in the late 1950s and toward lush, orchestral "country-politan" music in the 1960s and beyond, Williams's influence hardly abated. Through the 1990s artists continued to record versions of his songs, and it became clear that his impact had gone deeper than simply the creation of a new style of singing or songwriting.

Although he had forebears in Roy Acuff and Ernest Tubb, Williams changed the nature of country music itself. The country song, from Williams until the advent of fundamental influence from rock and popular dance musics in the 1990s, dealt with the emotional experience of a single individual, frequently with romantic loss. Whether dressed up with string-orchestra backing, as in the music of Patsy Cline, or presented plainly in the fervent stylings of George Jones, whose vocal intensity matched Williams's own, country songs followed patterns Williams created. The genre's preeminent figure, Williams was also one of country music's most fundamental expressive architects.

Manheim

For Further Reading

Escott, Colin. *Hank Williams: The Biography.* Boston: Little, Brown, 1994.

Williams, Roger M. *Sing a Sad Song: The Life of Hank Williams.* Urbana: University of Illinois Press, 1981.

Williams, Tennessee

Playwright
1911–1983

Life and Work

Tennessee Williams helped to create the modern American theater, bringing a dark portrait of the South and of human frailty to the stage.

Williams was born Thomas Lanier Williams in Columbus, Mississippi, on March 26, 1911. He attended the University of Missouri and Washington University, where he began writing drama. Working through the Depression in a shoe factory, he continued to write, and small theaters staged his work. He earned his bachelor's degree from the University of Iowa in dramatic writing in 1938.

In 1939 his collection of one-act plays, *American Blues,* won a Group Theatre award, and Williams began to gain recognition as a playwright. Williams continued to work odd jobs until 1944, when his play *The Glass Menagerie* was widely acclaimed after it was staged. The story of the relationships between a domineering mother, her fragile daughter, and her cynical son won a New York Drama Critics Circle Award for the 1944–45 year.

It was the staging of *A Streetcar Named Desire* in 1947 that truly brought Williams into his own as a playwright. This play and the later work *Cat on a Hot Tin Roof* (1955) both won Pulitzer Prizes and New York Drama Critics Circle Awards in the years they were written. The two plays deeply explored alienated and unhappy characters that also populate his later work.

Williams's plays are steeped in a southern gothic sensibility, where sex and violence take on symbolic proportions and wreak havoc with characters' lives. His characters exhibit a mixture of strength and fragility, and the plays blend the harshness of reality and the pleasures of escapist fantasy.

Williams also wrote essays, fiction, and poetry. *Where I Live: Selected Essays* was published in 1978 and his *Collected Stories* was published posthumously in 1985. Both received critical praise. He published two novels: *The Roman Spring of Mrs. Stone* in 1950 and *Moise and the World of Reason* in 1975.

Williams's health was poor for much of his adult life and was made worse by his alcoholism and addiction to sleeping pills. He died in New York City on February 25, 1983.

Legacy

Tennessee Williams was one of the key figures in American theater, and he was one of the first to use American English as a poetic language.

Williams's plays revolted against the traditional morality and classical structure of drama still prevalent at the beginning of the twentieth century. Along with his contemporary, Arthur Miller, Williams wrote plays about Americans that were set in the United States and intended for American audiences.

He brought issues of sexuality—Williams himself was gay—to the stage and wrote passionate and violent plays about the harshness of middle- and lower-class American life. The desperation and sexual depravity of the characters that populate his Gothic stories were unprecedented in their vividness and provided a new impetus for American theater.

Watson

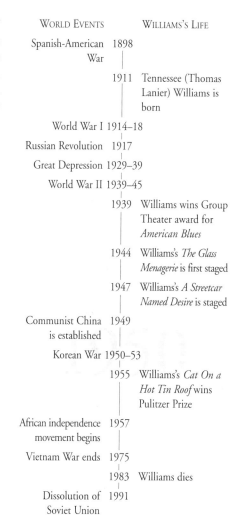

WORLD EVENTS		WILLIAMS'S LIFE
Spanish-American War	1898	
	1911	Tennessee (Thomas Lanier) Williams is born
World War I	1914–18	
Russian Revolution	1917	
Great Depression	1929–39	
World War II	1939–45	
	1939	Williams wins Group Theater award for *American Blues*
	1944	Williams's *The Glass Menagerie* is first staged
	1947	Williams's *A Streetcar Named Desire* is staged
Communist China is established	1949	
Korean War	1950–53	
	1955	Williams's *Cat On a Hot Tin Roof* wins Pulitzer Prize
African independence movement begins	1957	
Vietnam War ends	1975	
	1983	Williams dies
Dissolution of Soviet Union	1991	

For Further Reading

Roudane, Matthew C., ed. *Williams.* Cambridge Companions to Literature. New York: Cambridge University Press, 1998.

Spoto, Donald. *The Kindness of Strangers: The Life of Tennessee Williams.* New York: Da Capo Press, 1997.

Woolf, Virginia

Novelist and Essayist
1882–1941

Life and Work

Virginia Woolf was one of the earliest to experiment with stream-of-consciousness prose, using rich interior monologue to depict psychologically fragmented plots and relationships. Her essays about women's position in society placed feminism at the center of literary consciousness.

Adeline Virginia Stephen was born in London on January 25, 1882. Her father, Sir Leslie Stephen, was a well-known literary figure. Artists, writers, and intellectuals—including Ralph Waldo Emerson and Henry James—visited the Stephen family home. Woolf was educated at home by her parents (largely through access to her father's library).

Both her writing and the emotional instability that would haunt Woolf until her death began when she was young. She suffered mental breakdowns in 1895, when her mother died, and in 1904, after her father died. On the latter occasion she attempted suicide. During the rest period that followed, she wrote her first published work, a description of her father's rela-

tionship with his children to be included in his biography. She also began reviewing books on a regular basis for the *Times Literary Supplement.*

Soon after her father's death, she and her sister, the painter Vanessa Bell, moved to the Bloomsbury area of central London, where they hosted the gatherings of artists, writers, and philosophers that formed what became known as the Bloomsbury Group. G. E. Moore, E. M. Forster, Lytton Strachey, Clive Bell, Duncan Grant, Roger Fry, and John Maynard Keynes were all members, and others, including Bertrand Russell, Aldous Huxley, and T. S. Eliot, took part in their lively discussions.

In 1912 Virginia Stephen married Leonard Woolf. Shortly after her marriage she suffered another breakdown; during the period of recovery, she completed her first novel, *The Voyage Out* (1915). In 1917 she and Leonard founded the Hogarth Press, which published Woolf's own work as well as those of Forster, FYODOR DOSTOYEVSKY, Katherine Mansfield, Eliot, Sigmund Freud, and Maxim Gorky. Woolf's early novels *The Voyage Out* and *Night and Day* (1919) were her most conventional. *Jacob's Room* (1922) was a literary portrait of her brother Thoby, who had died in 1906, in which she used the story of a young man's education to illustrate the illusory nature of life and personality.

In her more experimental works, *Mrs. Dalloway* (1922), *To The Lighthouse* (1927), and *The Waves* (1931), Woolf depicted characters and events through the characters' consciousnesses rather than narrative description. The character of Mrs. Ramsay, the central figure in *To the Lighthouse,* for example, is rendered cumulatively by others in the book through their perceptions of her at particular moments, their impressions built upon memory, association, and emotion.

During the 1920s, Woolf became romantically involved with the poet Vita Sackville-West, a relationship she celebrated in her novel *Orlando* (1928). The novel follows a beautiful aristocrat of ambiguous gender through different periods of history, exploring themes of sexual liberation and experimentation.

In 1941, not long after completing her final novel, *Between the Acts,* Woolf drowned herself near her home in Sussex.

Legacy

Virginia Woolf wrote at a time of great social and cultural disruption, and its emotional and psychological import was registered in her work through the sensitive formal innovations of her prose.

In the early twentieth century, World War I had ravaged a generation and destroyed the social and political order of Europe. Woolf was among the Modernist writers and artists, including JAMES JOYCE, Eliot, WILLIAM FAULKNER and D. H. Lawrence, who experimented with new ways of expressing this understanding of an unstable world. Her stream-of-consciousness prose registered this experience on a personal level. Her narrative techniques made a sharp break with the linear narrative of the nineteenth-century novel, finding new ways of writing the experience of consciousness in time. Her formal innovations were part of the radical changes introduced into literature by the Modernist movement.

A Room of One's Own (1929) has become one of the founding texts of contemporary feminist literary criticism. Woolf's persuasive description of the social forces that work against a woman's attempt to write is required reading for the most basic study of feminist theory today.

The 1960s saw the beginnings of a revival of interest in Woolf's work. Her letters, diaries, and new autobiographical material were all published in the 1970s, and in the 1980s new collections of reviews and essays were brought to light. There have been numerous biographies of Woolf and biographical and critical works about others in the Bloomsbury Group. The interest in Woolf's work today is partly based on the interest in Modernist art and in the origins of feminist theory, and partly on the sharp beauty of Woolf's perceptions and the language she used to describe them.

Watson

WORLD EVENTS		WOOLF'S LIFE
Germany is united	1871	
	1882	Adeline Virginia Stephen is born
Spanish-American War	1898	
	1912	Virginia Stephen marries Leonard Woolf
World War I	1914–18	
	1915	Woolf publishes *The Voyage Out*
Russian Revolution	1917	The Woolfs found Hogarth Press
	1927	Woolf publishes *To the Lighthouse*
	1928	Woolf publishes *Orlando*
	1929	Woolf publishes *A Room of One's Own*
Great Depression	1929–39	
World War II	1939–45	
	1941	Woolf drowns herself
Communist China is established	1949	

For Further Reading
Gorsky, Susan Rubinow. *Virginia Woolf.* Boston: Twayne Publishers, 1978.
Bloom, Harold, ed. *Modern Critical Views: Virginia Woolf.* New York: Chelsea House, 1986.

Wordsworth, William

Poet
1770–1850

Life and Work

William Wordsworth was the first of the great English Romantic poets. He introduced new attitudes toward nature and the self into English literature, writing in a powerful, revolutionary plain style.

Wordsworth was born in Cockermouth, England, on April 7, 1770. His parents both died when he was young and he spent much of his youth at boarding school. There he read Edmund Spenser, WILLIAM SHAKESPEARE, JOHN MILTON, Henry Fielding, and MIGUEL DE CERVANTES in the rural setting of England's Lake District.

He attended Cambridge from 1787 to 1791. In 1793 he published his first two books of poetry, *Descriptive Sketches* and *An Evening Walk: An Epistle in Verse*, both of which were fairly traditional in form and content. In 1795 he moved to Racedown with his sister Dorothy. There he met the poet Samuel Taylor Coleridge. The two became philosophical and poetic partners, with Coleridge encouraging Wordsworth to broaden the philosophical base of his poetry. Together in 1798 they anonymously published a book of experimental poetry, *Lyrical Ballads*. The collection included short lyrical poems by Wordsworth as well as his longer poem, "Tintern Abbey," and the "Preface" in which he set down many of the precepts of the Romantic movement. Coleridge's "The Rime of the Ancient Mariner" was also included in the book. In these poems Wordsworth attempted to speak in the language of common people in order to reveal truths of nature and human nature in a simple and direct style.

In 1798 Wordsworth, his sister, and Coleridge went to Germany to study. Dorothy Wordsworth was deeply involved intellectually with the two men and modern critics have emphasized the importance of her thought to Wordsworth's, as well as the freedom she allowed him by making it possible for him to concentrate solely on his poetry. In Germany, Wordsworth began "The Prelude," the long autobiographical poem that would occupy him for much of his life. The poem emphasized the supremacy of the imagination in life.

Both Wordsworth's life and his work changed profoundly after 1805. He accepted a well-paying government position as distributor of stamps, and became politically conservative, more strictly religious, and less experimental in his writing. It was at this time that he became estranged from Coleridge and from Percy Bysshe Shelley, another Romantic poet who was a great admirer of his early work. In 1843 he was named Poet Laureate of England. He died on April 23, 1850.

The Prelude, or *Growth of a Poet's Mind*, which he had revised several times, was published in 1850 after his death. It is generally regarded as Wordsworth's greatest poem. In epic form, it combines his autobiography with history while glorifying the transcendent power of the imagination and the experience of childhood.

Legacy

Beginning with the poems and "Preface" from *Lyrical Ballads*, William Wordsworth introduced into English poetry an unprecedented formal freedom while bringing personal emotion to the heart of the tradition.

At the dawn of the Industrial Revolution Wordsworth and Coleridge together brought radical changes to English poetry. Emphasizing the direct relationship between humanity and nature, Wordsworth presented the power of nature and the imagination as a means of transcending the limitations of daily life. His use of simple direct language was particularly shocking in a Neoclassical poetic culture in which poets worked under strict limitations of form and subject matter, and often wrote in ornamented classical verse.

Lyrical Ballads was the starting point of the Romantic movement in English poetry. In Wordsworth's work and in the work of those who followed, emphasis was placed on the subjective, on intensely personal emotion rather than on dispassionate observation of external objects or activities. Poets who were directly influenced by Wordsworth include Lord Byron, Shelley, and JOHN KEATS. Other European writers who show an affinity to Wordsworth include Novalis and Johann-Christian Friedrich Hölderlin in Germany; Viscount de Chateaubriand and Madame de Staël in France; and ALEKSANDR PUSHKIN and Michael Lermontov in Russia, among others.

Interest in Wordsworth's poetry continued to grow after his death. In 1874 the novelist and critic Walter Pater wrote an essay closely examining the relationship between nature and emotion in the poems. In 1879 Matthew Arnold published an anthology of Wordsworth's poems and wrote that he ranked with Milton and Shakespeare. The anthology established Wordsworth's position as a major English poet.

The twentieth century also saw a great deal of critical and creative interest in his work. WALT WHITMAN's emphasis on simplicity and direct, honest language can be traced to Wordsworth, while the free-flowing verse that he used to express the unique nature of every situation had a profound influence on French poets, including CHARLES-PIERRE BAUDELAIRE, Arthur Rimbaud, Stéphane Mallarmé, and Paul Valéry, who created a tradition of free verse in French poetry.

Watson

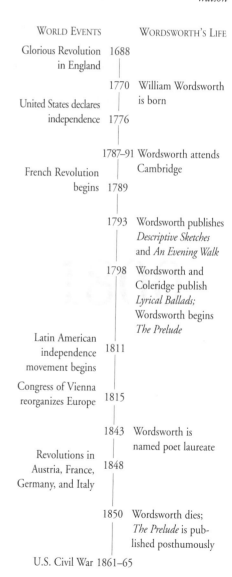

WORLD EVENTS		WORDSWORTH'S LIFE
Glorious Revolution in England	1688	
	1770	William Wordsworth is born
United States declares independence	1776	
	1787–91	Wordsworth attends Cambridge
French Revolution begins	1789	
	1793	Wordsworth publishes *Descriptive Sketches* and *An Evening Walk*
	1798	Wordsworth and Coleridge publish *Lyrical Ballads*; Wordsworth begins *The Prelude*
Latin American independence movement begins	1811	
Congress of Vienna reorganizes Europe	1815	
	1843	Wordsworth is named poet laureate
Revolutions in Austria, France, Germany, and Italy	1848	
	1850	Wordsworth dies; *The Prelude* is published posthumously
U.S. Civil War	1861–65	

For Further Reading

Bromwich, David. *Disowned by Memory: Wordsworth's Poetry of the 1790s.* Chicago: University of Chicago Press, 1998.
Johnston, Kenneth R. *The Hidden Wordsworth: Poet, Lover, Rebel, Spy.* New York: W. W. Norton, 1998.
Williams, John, ed. *Wordsworth.* New York: St. Martin's Press, 1993.

Wright, Frank Lloyd

Architect, Designer, Educator
1867–1959

Life and Work

Frank Lloyd Wright achieved worldwide fame for his revolutionary architecture during a nearly seven-decade career.

Born in 1867 in Richland Center, Wisconsin, Wright was one of three children born to his father's second wife, Anna Lloyd Jones. After studying engineering at the University of Wisconsin for two quarters, Wright went to Chicago in 1887 to pursue a career in architecture.

WORLD EVENTS	WRIGHT'S LIFE
U.S. Civil War 1861–65	
	1867 Frank Lloyd Wright is born
Germany is united 1871	
	1887 Wright moves to Chicago
	1893– Wright develops 1909 "prairie style"
Spanish-American 1898 War	
	1909 Wright designs Robie House
World War I 1914–18	
Russian Revolution 1917	
Great Depression 1929–39	
	1935 Wright designs Fallingwater
World War II 1939–45	
Communist China 1949 is established	
Korean War 1950–53	
African independence 1957 movement begins	
	1959 Wright designs Guggenheim Museum
	Wright dies
Vietnam War ends 1975	

During this early period, Wright became interested in complex interior spaces, and learned to appreciate the rough beauty of abstract masses. At the same time, Wright also developed an interest in Japanese architecture. These three sources combined to form what Wright called "organic" design—each building should relate harmoniously to its setting and a structure should embody a dynamic line with flowing, open interior spaces.

From 1893 to 1909 Wright developed what he called the "prairie" style, and was the leader of the "Prairie School" of architecture. The Wards Willetts house (1900–02), the design for which was inspired by the Japanese exhibition hall at the 1893 Chicago Exposition, epitomized the prairie style house, with its low pitched roofs and predominantly horizontal lines extending into the landscape, its beams and walls held in visual tension by contrasting vertical stripping on the facade.

The masterpiece of the prairie style house was the Robie House (1909) in Chicago, for which Wright also designed furniture and geometrically patterned art-glass windows. The largest and most significant examples of Wright's nonresidential architecture were the Larkin Building (1904) in Buffalo, New York, and Unity Temple (1905–08) in Oak Park, Illinois.

Wright became increasingly concerned with the education of architects. In 1932, he established the Taliesin Fellowship, a school for architects where students learned by working with building materials and solving problems of design and construction. He wrote several books, including *The Disappearing City* (1932) and *The Natural House* (1954).

After 1935, Wright was immensely productive. In 1935 he built Fallingwater, near Pittsburgh, a multilevel reinforced structure cantilevered over a waterfall. The house is regarded as one of his most successful designs. He also developed "Usonian" (a term he preferred to "American") homes intended to be affordable houses for middle-class Americans. His innovative use of the circle and the spiral can be seen most famously in the Guggenheim Museum (1959) in New York.

Frank Lloyd Wright died in 1959.

Legacy

Frank Lloyd Wright was probably America's most famous architect, and through his

architectural work, his teaching, his writing, and lectures attained a worldwide reputation.

Wright broke with the traditions of European and American architecture. His organic architecture moved from the inside out, like a plant growing from the ground up. It began with the material and subjective requirements of the building, rather than with a preconceived idea of its exterior form.

For many of his houses, such as the Robie House and the Martin House, Wright designed the furniture and interiors to achieve integrated works of art. He also designed the office furniture and filing cabinets for the Larkin Building. Wright provided a link between the nineteenth-century Arts and Crafts movement and twentieth-century Modernism.

Despite his fame, Wright had relatively little immediate effect on the course of architecture in the United States. It is likely that a portfolio of drawings and photographs of his work published in Europe in 1911 influenced Modern movement architects like Le Corbusier, Walter Gropius, and LUDWIG MIES VAN DER ROHE. In the United States, Mies's austere Modernism set the standard for the International Style, rather than Wright's "organic" style.

Wright's style was so distinctive that few architects have directly imitated it. His legacy can best be seen in some of the most original and famous buildings in the country, as well as in the many homes designed on a more open architectural plan, traceable to Wright's prairie style.

Domenico

For Further Reading

Brooks, H. Allen. *Frank Lloyd Wright and the Prairie School.* New York: Braziller, in association with the Cooper-Hewitt Museum, 1984.

Storrer, William Allin. *The Frank Lloyd Wright Companion.* Chicago: University of Chicago Press, 1993.

Yeats, William Butler

Poet and Playwright
1865–1939

Life and Work

William Butler Yeats is regarded as Ireland's greatest poet, and one of the greatest poets writing in English in the twentieth century.

The man who contributed much to Irish nationalism was born a Protestant in Dublin (although he grew up largely in England) on June 13, 1865, the son of a painter father and a mother from western Ireland who was steeped in the folklore of the area. An erratic student in high school, he found a more congenial atmosphere at Dublin's Metropolitan School of Art, where he enrolled in 1884. There Yeats became interested in the occult, in Irish history and mythology, in the ancient world, and in the belief systems of Theosophy, Spiritualism, and Rosicrucianism, among others. In the mid-1880s he warmed to the cause of Irish independence, and in 1889 he met Maude Gonne, an Irish political activist of whom he later wrote, in the poem "The Circus Animals' Desertion," "I thought my dear must her own soul destroy,/So did fanaticism and hate enslave it." He wrote love poems and a play for her, and though he unsuccessfully proposed marriage both to her and, later, to her

daughter, he found inspiration in his acquaintance with her. Gonne was imprisoned after the 1916 Easter Uprising, which presaged Irish independence. Yeats served for six years in the new Irish Senate in the 1920s.

Yeats published his first book of poetry, *The Wanderings of Oisin, and Other Poems,* in 1889, and had several more published in the 1890s. In 1899 he helped establish the Irish Literary Theatre (later the Abbey Theatre), and in 1904 became its director. In the first decade of the twentieth century he wrote a series of plays on Irish themes. Yeats employed the American poet EZRA POUND as a secretary in 1913, and was influenced both by the precision of Pound's poetry and by the minimalist Japanese Noh dramas that Pound was translating at the time. When nearly 50 years old, Yeats entered a remarkable period of late-life creativity; the poems and plays he wrote between World War I and the end of his life are considered his best—complex and noble in tone, yet deeply personal, they draw the reader in with striking imagery and then offer many layers of meaning to discover with repeated readings. In 1923 Yeats was awarded the Nobel Prize for Literature.

He died in Roquebrune, France, on January 28, 1939.

Legacy

The chief qualities of William Butler Yeats's poetry—a visionary streak, an exaltation of nature and myth that was not far from Romantic, an unorthodox but essentially traditional use of rhyme—placed him outside the progressive mainstream of his day, which generally favored technical experimentation and a dispassionate outlook. Yeats's legacy is to be defined less in terms of influence on his immediate successors and more in terms of the broad appeal of his work.

The occult beliefs of Yeats's youth matured into an outlook that may broadly be called spiritual. His poetic world returned again and again to certain personal touchstones: familiar scenery, Greek myths, images of himself as a blind man or beggar, real and mythical animals, astronomical bodies. The spiritual geography he described seemed to be ornamented with wellsprings of joy, and his works are always infused with a fervent quality. In a bleak century where two world wars drained life of meaning and the modern arts offered lit-

tle in the way of faith, Yeats provided a kind of inspiration. His poetry is never simple, but it is almost always deeply positive.

Yeats influenced some of his contemporaries, including the Anglo-American poet W. H. Auden (who considered Yeats the rescuer of English poetry) and the novelist JAMES JOYCE. With the so-called High Modernists Yeats's relationships were chilly, but later in the century his influence was renewed. Adrienne Rich and Philip Larkin were two prominent poets among the many whose works showed his influence. With Modernism in decline and poetry forming for some a cornerstone of a new spirituality, Yeats seemed an avatar of a poetry that was less about formal concerns and more about embracing life.

Manheim

WORLD EVENTS	YEATS'S LIFE
U.S. Civil War 1861–65	
	1865 William Butler Yeats is born in Dublin
Germany is united 1871	
	1884 Yeats enrolls at Metropolitan School of Art
	1889 Yeats publishes *The Wanderings of Oisin*
Spanish-American War 1898	
	1904 Yeats becomes director of Abbey Theatre
	1913 Yeats works with Ezra Pound
World War I 1914–18	
Russian Revolution 1917	
	1923 Yeats wins Nobel Prize for Literature
Great Depression 1929–39	
	1939 Yeats dies
World War II 1939–45	

For Further Reading

Archibald, Douglas. *Yeats.* Syracuse, N.Y.: Syracuse University Press, 1983.

Bloom, Harold. *Yeats.* Oxford: Oxford University Press, 1970.

Jeffares, A. Norman. *W. B. Yeats: A New Biography.* New York: Farrar, Straus & Giroux, 1989.

Zeami Motokiyo

Founder of Noh Drama
1363–1443

Life and Work

With his father Kanami Kiyotsugo, Zeami Motokiyo founded the Noh drama, a characteristic Japanese art form whose otherworldly, evocave qualities have fascinated Eastern and Western audiences.

Zeami (often known by that name alone, or as Kanze Motokiyo) was born near Kyoto, Japan, in 1363. In the work of his father, a Buddhist temple priest, the Noh genre began to take shape, coalescing from earlier forms of courtly and folk entertainment. Noh, which means "ability" or "performance," is sometimes described as ritualistic; slow-moving and evocative rather than action-oriented, a Noh drama features elaborate costumes, masks, and make-up. Its measured, sung dialogue is accompanied by precise choreography and by a small group of flute and drum players. Kanami became the leader of the Kanze school, a performance troupe that flourished and developed in sophistication under the protection of the shogun Yoshimitsu Ashikaga. In 1384, upon the death of his father, Zeami assumed leadership of the Kanze school. Both a performer and a highly prolific creator of new works, Zeami gained renown.

Zeami wrote a series of books that put in place the basic principles of Noh, defining it as an art form. These treatises included both theoretical and practical elements and were intended to help pass Zeami's style on to his students, specifically to his son, Motomasa.

The most famous of these treatises, *Fushi kaden* (*The Transmission of the Flower of Acting Style,* 1400–18), described the three basic roles that a performer should master: warrior, woman (Noh dramas are performed by all-male casts), and old person—together with appropriate musical style and dance movements for each. These three roles expanded into the five basic types of classical Noh drama: the god play, the warrior play, the woman or "wig" play, plays in which the dead return to Earth, and plays featuring supernatural figures. Zeami became a Zen monk in 1422, turning the Kanze troupe over to Motomasa.

The ascendancy of the next shogun in 1428 dealt another blow to the fortunes of Zeami and his circle: Motomasa was denied the right to perform, for the ruler's favor rested on Zeami's nephew. The death of Motomasa in 1432 caused Zeami profound grief, and shortly thereafter the rivalry between the two performing lineages led to Zeami's exile to the island of Sado. His poems of exile are famous works in their own right. Zeami returned to Kyoto at the end of his life, dying there in 1443.

Legacy

Noh is an art form not easily classifiable as theater, music, or dance in Western terms; it incorporates aspects of all three. Noh music has exerted influence upon both theatrical and nontheatrical genres, including the music of Kabuki theater and the repertoire of the *koto* zither; it features singing from a chorus as well as from individual characters and differs in its fundamental tonal make-up from other types of Japanese music. Noh also spawned a system of musical notation, one of the few to have developed outside the West.

Zeami's theoretical treatises codified the Noh drama so accurately that more than six centuries later it retains many of its ancient characteristics. Zeami's spirit of codification and prescription continued to influence the form—as more and more rules accrued, performances grew longer. A performance of one of Zeami's dramas might take three times as long today as it did in his time. Noh is a living art; maintained by Japanese rulers and noble families for centuries, it is now supported by the Japanese public as an emblem of national culture.

Zeami's works themselves are his greatest legacy. Of the approximately 230 Noh dramas that are still regularly performed (of a total repertoire of around 2,000 surviving manuscripts), Zeami is the author of nearly ninety, including many of the most famous. Although some of his works were written in a realistic style, many feature the delicate shading of present into past, of natural into supernatural, that has influenced such Western playwrights as WILLIAM BUTLER YEATS and Maurice Maeterlinck. Both in Japan and in the West, Zeami's exquisite creations continue to inspire makers of contemporary theater; Robert Wilson is among the figures of the Western theatrical avant-garde who have experimented with Noh elements. Such is Zeami's prominence within the history of Noh that he has been called "the Shakespeare of Japan."

Manheim

For Further Reading

Hare, Thomas Blenman. *Zeami's Style: The Noh Plays of Zeami Motokiyo.* Palo Alto, Calif.: Stanford University Press, 1986.

Smethurst, Mae J. *The Artistry of Aeschylus and Zeami: A Comparative Study of Greek Tragedy and Noh.* Princeton, N.J.: Princeton University Press, 1989.

Appendices,
Bibliography, and Index

APPENDIX ONE:
Highlights in the History of Art, Literature, and Music

c. 800   Scholars believe Homer writes his two great epic poems, *Iliad* and *Odyssey*, Western culture's first works of literature and inspiration for all the others that followed.

c. 500   Sappho, the greatest female author of the classical world, founds a *thiasos*, a school where young girls were taught arts and social graces.

c. 450–430   Sophocles writes three famous plays: *Ajax, Antigone,* and *Oedipus Rex,* leading to the creation of theatrical drama; he is considered the greatest Athenian playwright during his lifetime.

31   Virgil begins writing *Aeneid,* the national epic of Rome, which will help to create a national myth that supported and justified the emerging imperial state.

C.E.

590   Pope Gregory I accepts election to the papacy, where he will, under supposed divine inspiration, compose the body of unison musical church song that is called Gregorian chant.

759   Tu Fu retires to the Chinese countryside and begins to write some of his greatest poems on his travels, nature, paintings, and friendship, among other subjects; he is considered to be the greatest of classical Chinese poets.

c. 1001–04   Murasaki Shikibu writes much of *The Tale of Genji,* often referred to as the greatest work in the Japanese literary canon, it has influenced all subsequent Japanese literature and art.

1072   Guo Xi completes his monumental hanging scroll *Early Spring,* defining him as the leading landscape painter in the Imperial Painting Academy at the court of the Northern Song Dynasty (960–1127) in the second half of the eleventh century.

1328   After the death of an older brother, Ni Zan becomes heir to the family fortune and erects a library to house his literati paintings and written works; later in his life he will be considered the ideal embodiment of the scholar-artist.

1384   Upon the death of his father, Zeami Motokiyo assumes leadership of the Kanze school of Noh drama; Zeami will gain renown as a prolific writer and performer of this art form.

1387   Geoffrey Chaucer begins work on *The Canterbury Tales,* his greatest work; a poet, government official, and diplomat, Chaucer is widely regarded as the founder of English literature.

1425–32   Jan van Eyck paints his most famous work, the *Ghent Altarpiece,* founding a new style that will dominate the art of the Netherlands for several generations.

1435   Leon Battista Alberti publishes *De Pictura,* providing the first theoretical descriptions of the new Renaissance style and the first organized explanation of the revolutionary developments in the works of contemporary Florentine artists.

1467   Shen Zhou, the first great master of the Wu School of literati painting, paints *Lofty Mount Lu,* now famous for its vigorous brush technique and strong sense of structural arrangement.

1480–1506   Leonardo da Vinci paints many pictures for the Duke of Milan, two of which will become the most recognized in the world: *Last Supper* (c. 1495) and *Mona Lisa* (1503–06).

1482–85   Sandro Botticelli paints *Primavera* and *The Birth of Venus,* which reflect his fusing of the humanist interest in ancient mythology with Christian faith.

1484   Josquin des Prez is hired as a musician by Cardinal Ascanio Sforza, who was based in Milan and Rome; he will later become a member of the Papal Choir, write 20 masses and many secular songs (*chansons*), all of which reflect the mixture of expression and compositional skill that is at the heart of his music.

1494   Sesshū Toyo paints *Splashed-Ink Landscape,* a classic example of his stylistic innovations; it will become an important model for sixteenth-century Japanese painters.

1498   Michelangelo is commissioned to do his first important work, the *Pietá;* after completing his subsequent works, he will come to be revered as a genius whose creativity paralleled that of God.

1505–10   Hieronymus Bosch paints *The Garden of Earthly Delights,* the apex of Bosch's fantastic, imaginative, and personal works; his artistic creations reflect the pessimistic, fear-filled time in which he lived, yet serve as a forerunner to modern comic book artists.

1514   Raphael is appointed official artist of the papal court at St. Peter's; his main contribution to the Renaissance is his establishment of the grand, heroic, larger-than-life style of painting.

1516   Titian becomes official painter of the Republic of Venice and engages in a period of great artistic productivity, slowly becoming the leader of the Venetian school through his life-long exploration of new ways of working with oil paint.

1523–26   Renaissance artist Albrecht Dürer paints a series of Lutheran-themed works that will mark him as the first great Protestant painter; he is widely regarded as the greatest artist in German history.

1537–80   Palladio builds a series of villas in the Veneto, the countryside around Venice; the Palladian villa style will change the lifestyle of the wealthy and make Palladio the most influential architect in European history.

1551   The greatest musical representative of the Counter-Reformation, Giovanni Pierluigi da Palestrina, is appointed choir director at St. Peter's church, where his rise will be rapid; he will be successful in reconciling the Roman Catholic church's new demands for simplicity with complex Renaissance music.

1559   Sofonisba Anguissola is invited to Madrid to become the painting instructor for Philip II's new young queen, Isabel of Valois; Anguissola will produce scores of paintings in Madrid and become one of the first highly successful women artists.

1572   Luíz Vaz de Camões publishes Portugal's great epic poem, *The Lusiads*, the story of Vasco de Gama's discovery of the sea route to India and a celebration of Portugal at the height of its expansionist empire.

c. 1590   Kōetsu, founder of the Rimpa school of decorative Japanese art, produces a number of poem scrolls and some of the most profound examples of *rakuware* (pottery); he will become one of the important calligraphers of the Edo period.

1597–98   Caravaggio paints *The Calling of St. Matthew* for the Church of San Luigi dei Francesi; his style, filled with realism, simplicity, and piety, suited the taste of the Roman Catholic authorities who commissioned him to produce religious scenes and contributed to his large following.

1599   As William Shakespeare's popularity as a playwright grows, he and his associates construct the Globe Theater; Shakespeare, considered to be the most important writer in English, enriched the English language to a greater degree than any other writer.

1605   Miguel de Cervantes publishes the first part of *Don Quixote* and is immediately successful; the book will become known internationally, exerting its comedic influence on world literature, including that of Spanish America.

1607   Claudio Monteverdi puts opera on the map with *Orfeo*, a retelling of the Greek legend of Orpheus and Eurydice, thereby becoming one of Western music's crucial innovators.

1611–12   Artemisia Gentileschi paints *Judith Decapitating Holofernes*, typical of her depictions of heroic women from history and the Bible; she will be the first woman artist to become a successful painter of important large-scale figure compositions.

1629   Gian Lorenzo Bernini is appointed architect of St. Peter's Basilica at the Vatican; greatly esteemed by the popes, artists, and prominent men of his time, Bernini will be considered a universal genius because of his talents as a painter, architect, and sculptor.

As a diplomat and a famous artist, Peter Paul Rubens helps negotiate a peace settlement between Spain and England, furthering his reputation and making him one of the most sought-after painters of his generation.

1642   Rembrandt paints *Nightwatch* in his characteristically emotive style, establishing his reputation throughout Europe as a painter of individuality and uncompromising realism who did not adhere to conventional notions of idealized beauty.

1643   Molière, whose works relied on ridicule and satire, forms the theater troupe Illustre Théâtre, with whom he will write, direct, and act in many successful plays.

1656   Diego Velázquez paints his most famous work, *Las Meninas*, using characteristic expressive brushwork and bold lighting effects; his work is seen as the Spanish counterpart to the art of Peter Paul Rubens.

1667   John Milton publishes his masterwork, *Paradise Lost*, an essential contribution to both Christian thought and English literature.

1680   Bashō takes his literary name, and through the publication of several poetry anthologies and travel journals, he will give lasting poetic life to the haiku. His works also develop the theme of human spiritual identification with nature that would come to characterize Japanese poetry.

Sor Juana Inés de la Cruz writes *The Divine Narcissus*; Cruz is one of the earliest examples of a prominent female intellectual and is considered to be the "first feminist of the Americas."

1708   Johann Sebastian Bach assumes directorship of the ducal chapel in Weimar, Germany, where he will write some of his greatest organ music and establish himself as one of the towering geniuses of Western musical culture.

1726   In the golden age of satire, Jonathan Swift's book of philosophical fiction, *Gulliver's Travels*, defines and transforms the genre.

c. 1740   Ts'ao Hsüeh-ch'in writes *Dream of the Red Chamber*, a chronicle of the decline of a powerful family and the greatest novel of the Ch'ing Dynasty's golden age of literature; it continues to be studied as a seminal work of Chinese literature.

1742   George Frideric Handel writes the most famous of his many brilliant oratorios, *Messiah*, which remains one of the most widely performed pieces in the entire classical repertoire.

1780   Tyagaraja, often thought of as something of a musician-saint and already a famous singer, writes his first musical composition by the age of 13, a song in praise of the god Rama.

1786–87   Wolfgang Amadeus Mozart, a genius since childhood, reaches his operatic high point and his ability to please a crowd with *The Marriage of Figaro* and *Don Giovanni*; his universally popular works are unexcelled for sheer lyrical beauty.

1788   William Blake, engraver and poet, prints his first two books and establishes himself as a unique and innovative artist as well as a radical thinker and one of the greatest English Romantics.

1790   Johann Wolfgang von Goethe publishes the first version of *Faust*, today considered one of the greatest monuments of nineteenth-century Romanticism. The book set a course for many of the Romantic writers who followed.

1790–94   Franz Joseph Haydn, master of musical humor, makes two trips to London, where he will write 12 symphonies whose form he becomes famous for standardizing and bringing to prominence in European music.

1803–08   Ludwig van Beethoven breaks vast new musical ground with a series of symphonies, piano sonatas, and string quartets, most of which seemed to communicate intense conflict and triumphant resolution.

1811–14   Jane Austen publishes three of her six novels; Austen's writing contributes a combination of perceptive wit and acute emotional and historical observation of everyday life to English literature.

1814   Francisco Goya paints his best known work, *The Third of May, 1808*, expressing his individualistic style and deeply emotional approach that was ill suited to the more conservative world of Spanish court painting; his work will be appreciated by the coming Romantic movement.

1820   John Keats publishes his final collection of poetry, *Lamia, Isabella, The Eve of St. Agnes, and Other Poems*, exemplary of his characteristic combination of technical perfection with deeply sensual imagery.

1821   Living in exile, Aleksandr Pushkin writes *To Ovid*, a model of poetic craftsmanship that will eventually make him the leading figure of the Russian Romantic movement.

1831   Fryderyk Chopin settles in Paris, the center of Continental Romanticism, where he will create intense musical miniatures, sweeping quasi-improvisatory essays, and stirring pieces with a flavor of Polish nationalism, becoming a giant among nineteenth-century piano composers.

Victor-Marie Hugo publishes *The Hunchback of Notre Dame*; the novel achieves immediate international acclaim. Hugo will become a national hero in his lifetime; his poems, novels, and plays have all inspired musical and theatrical works.

1833–34   With the publication of the series *Fifty-three Stations of the Tokaido*, Hiroshige emerges as the most famous and popular printmaker of the Tokugawa period in Japan.

1836   Georg Büchner writes *Woyzeck*, the last of three plays that will leave a permanent impression on Western literature and European theater.

Charles Dickens publishes his first book, *Sketches by Boz*, which rewarded him with celebrity status unprecedented for an author; his appeal will come from his comedic genius and the power of his indictments of social evils, as well as from his skill at creating fantastically unique characters.

1840   Inspired by marriage, Robert Schumann, already an established composer, writes nearly 150 songs—symphonies, chamber music, dramatic music, and more; he will become known as the ultimate musical Romantic and one of the most important European composers of the nineteenth century.

1843   Richard Wagner's first artistic triumph, *The Flying Dutchman*, is performed; it clearly anticipates his future work in its seamless integration of music and drama and in its legend-based story; his harmonic practices will mark a major step in the long expansion and eventual dissolution of traditional harmony in European music.

1847   Charlotte Brönte publishes one of her most famous works, *Jane Eyre*, which will make her one of the first novelists to depict the psychological and social reality of a woman's struggle for power.

Jāmi writes *The Precious Pearl*, a poetic discussion on the positions of theologians, philosophers, and Sufis; he is considered to be the last of the "seven masters" in Persian literature.

1850   *The Prelude, or Growth of a Poet's Mind*, generally regarded as William Wordsworth's greatest poem, is published after his death; he is responsible for introducing an unprecedented formal freedom into English poetry while bringing personal emotion to the heart of the tradition.

1851   Herman Melville publishes *Moby Dick*—what many consider to be the supreme American novel; although not appreciated by Victorian audiences, his work will receive international acclaim after his death.

1853   Nadar sets up a photography studio for his younger brother, only to take it over a few years later and quickly became one of the most successful and innovative practitioners in the new medium, specializing in portraits of intellectuals and celebrities.

1854   Franz Liszt, the foremost piano virtuoso of the nineteenth century, dazzles audiences throughout Europe with his *Faust* Symphony and goes on to become the first true musical superstar.

1857   Charles-Pierre Baudelaire publishes his first collection of poetry, *Les Fleurs du Mal*, an evocative analysis of urban life and decay and erotic love, that uses suggestion rather than traditional description; he goes on to establish the foundation on which Symbolist poetry will be built.

Madame Bovary, Gustave Flaubert's most celebrated work, will at first result in his prosecution for blasphemy and immorality; later he will be hailed as the father of the Realist movement that developed soon after its publication.

1862   Claude Monet and a group of fellow painters who share Monet's interest in landscape painting develop the style that will come to be known as Impressionism; this style will stand at the very beginning of the Modernist movement in art and will spread throughout Europe and the United States.

1863–65   Edouard Manet scandalizes the art world with his paintings *Luncheon on the Grass* and *Olympia*; with their sexual content and innovative style, the two works exemplify Manet's attempt to create a form of art appropriate for the modern world.

1868   Johannes Brahms composes his breakthrough mass, *German Requiem*; this mass for the dead will reach beyond the music of Brahms's own time, incorporating the rich multipart choral textures of the religious music of the seventeenth and eighteenth centuries.

1868   American painter Mary Cassatt gains international recognition when *The Mandolin Player* is included in one of the Paris Salon exhibitions; Cassatt will be one of the first painters to depict modern women as a primary subject.

1869   After six years of work, Leo Tolstoy finishes his novel *War and Peace*; within several years of its publication, the novel's breadth and power will be widely recognized and it will come to be considered the national epic of Russia.

1871   Giuseppe Verdi's capstone opera *Aida* premieres in Cairo; his operas tower over those of his Italian contemporaries, and no future opera composer will remain untouched by the transformation he wrought in the art.

1871–72   George Eliot writes *Middlemarch*, her most ambitious novel; her novels are especially insightful in their treatment of women and will make her one of the most influential British novelists of the nineteenth century.

1872   Paul Cézanne, studying painting under Camille Pissaro and other Impressionists, begins to concentrate on the purely optical effects in painting and will eventually develop his own style that is the precursor of radical art styles of the early twentieth century.

1873   Winslow Homer's career blossoms when he takes up watercolor painting, which will become his signature medium; today he is regarded as a uniquely American painter who helped nineteenth-century American painting emerge from the shadows of French art.

1874   A group of Impressionist painters, including Edgar Degas, organize their own independent exhibition in Paris; subsequently Degas will become one of the key figures associated with that artistic movement, which revolutionized art in the late nineteenth century.

1877–82   Henrik Ibsen publishes four realistic social plays that catch the public's attention: *The Pillars of Society* (1877), *A Doll's House* (1879), *Ghosts* (1881), and *An Enemy of the People* (1882); he will use the theater as a socially relevant forum in which to explore the problems and fears of a people.

1879–80   Fyodor Dostoyevsky writes *The Brothers Karamazov*, which is widely considered to be his greatest work and which made him a visionary, an existentialist, and a proto-Freudian thinker; his books continue to be studied and analyzed, with new dimensions constantly being revealed.

1880   Auguste Rodin's career is made when he receives a commission from the government for a set of bronze doors for a planned museum of decorative arts; he is selected for his incredible skill in sculpting and his revolutionary technique that made sculptures life-like and dynamic.

1882   Thomas Eakins, a teacher at the Pennsylvania Academy of Fine Arts, becomes director of instruction there, instituting a curriculum that places the study of the human figure at its core; he will become known as the leading American Realist of the late nineteenth century.

1884   Mark Twain publishes *The Adventures of Huckleberry Finn*, the first novel to express the complexity of American life, addressing slavery, human cruelty, and intolerance.

1886   After her death, Emily Dickinson's poems are discovered. Some are published by her sister in a collection *Poems by Emily Dickinson* (1890); her experiments with rhyme, assonance, consonance, and tonal harmony will defy poetic conventions of the time.

1888   Vincent van Gogh moves to Arles, France, where he begins using color as an expressive vehicle and changes his brushwork to swirling, dynamic strokes; in his 15 months at Arles, he will complete 200 paintings and develop a unique style that expresses his emotional relationship to the world.

1889–92   Peter Ilich Tchaikovsky enjoys considerable success with two ballets, *Sleeping Beauty* (1889) and *The Nutcracker* (1892); his music has never left the American and European symphony concert repertoire.

1893–1909   Frank Lloyd Wright develops his "prairie" style of architecture; in so doing, he creates a style so distinctive that few architects have directly imitated it.

1894   Claude Debussy writes his first master musical composition, *Prelude to the Afternoon of a Faun*; his free-style, yet subtle works, many of which represent the natural world, will find favor with audiences even as they break new musical ground, and he will gradually become an icon of French modern music.

1897   Henry Ossawa Tanner, one of the first African-American painters to achieve an international reputation, wins a gold medal at the Salon, Paris, for his painting *The Raising of Lazarus* (1896); the picture will establish Tanner's reputation and inspire future African-American painters.

1898   Anton Chekhov's most famous play, *The Sea Gull*, is performed by the newly formed Moscow Art Theater to much acclaim; Chekhov, one of the great innovators in the short-story form, will give new direction to Russian drama and bring it to an international audience.

1899   Scott Joplin's most famous song, "Maple Leaf Rag," is published, beginning the twentieth century's first great musical craze; Joplin, with that composition and others, will define the ragtime genre.

1899–1907   Joseph Conrad writes a series of novels based on his travels as a merchant ship's officer and captain; Conrad will become one of British literature's leading novelists of the early twentieth century.

1900   Pierre-Auguste Renoir is awarded the Legion of Honor by the French state for his prolific work as an Impressionist painter; his brightly dappled scenes of joyful middle-class social life capture the essence of that movement in the history of modern art.

1901   Rabindranath Tagore, a prolific writer of poems, songs, plays, novels, stories, and essays, founds a school, Santiniketan (Abode of Peace) in West Bengal, India, which will become Visva-Bharati University in 1921; an important political and cultural figure, he frequently speaks against discrimination and fascism and about the unification of Eastern and Western thought.

1904   The creator of modern dance, Isadora Duncan, becomes well enough established to give a performance at the Bayreuth

Festival, the seat of power for the followers of the influential nineteenth-century composer Richard Wagner.

1907   Paula Modersohn-Becker, one of the first artists to take a distinctly feminist approach to the depiction of the female nude, paints *Kneeling Mother and Child*; she will be the first German artist to incorporate the innovations of French Post-Impressionist art into her own unique style.

1908   Rainer Maria Rilke writes *New Poems*, in which he presents the "object poem," which captures and describes abstract ideas in terms of physical objects; this will be very important in the development of modern poetry and consequently make Rilke one of the greatest of lyric poets.

1909   Serge Diaghilev forms the Ballets Russes (Russian Ballet), the daring Russian dance company that will take Paris and the rest of the world by storm in the early twentieth century.

Henri Matisse paints *Dance*, one of his most famous paintings; in the Fauvist style, it expresses emotion through the use of bold colors.

1911–15   One of the most naturally talented individuals who shaped American entertainment in the early years of the twentieth century, Irving Berlin writes more than 180 songs, both music and lyrics, and goes on to play a unique role in the development of the modern popular song.

1912   Marcel Duchamp paints *Nude Descending a Staircase No. 2*, his best-known work; it was almost immediately considered inappropriate for Cubism because of its nontraditional subject; Duchamp gained international celebrity because of the his consistent defiance of established standards and practices in art.

1913   Marcel Proust publishes *Swann's Way*, the first volume of his opus, *Remembrance of Things Past*; on the basis of his single monumental novel, Proust is considered to be the most significant French novelist of the twentieth century.

The Rite of Spring, Igor Stravinsky's ballet, precipitates an audience riot with its rhythmic and harmonic daring; the ideal composer for a stylistically plural century, Stravinsky will influence many future composers.

1914   Franz Kafka writes *The Metamorphosis*, one of the great short stories of the twentieth century; his fiction will give literary voice to social ills that will come to typify that century.

1915   D. W. Griffith's first major film, *The Birth of a Nation*, opens and soon becomes one of the most controversial films ever made. Griffith will become a key figure in establishing Hollywood as the movie-making capital of the world.

Piet Mondrian paints *Composition No. 10*, aiming to reduce painting to its essence as expressed by harmonious compositions of vertical and horizontal lines and primary colors; his work will be important for the founding of geometric abstraction during World War I.

1916   American Modernist painter Georgia O'Keeffe has her first major exhibition at Gallery 291; she is now regarded as one of the genuinely unique figures in the Modernist movement.

1921   Edgard Varèse co-founds the International Composers' Guild in New York to house and perform his radical compositions; his compact pieces and uncompromising commitment to the

exploration of sonic frontiers will influence a wide range of later composers.

Diego Rivera begins painting his first mural, *Creation*; during his lifetime, Rivera will achieve international fame as the greatest mural painter since Michelangelo.

1922   James Joyce publishes his novel *Ulysses*, in which he pushes the English language to its limit, and in so doing he will become the prime exponent of Modernist experimentation in the novel.

1923   Bertolt Brecht produces his first play, *Baal*, in Bavaria, Germany, and gains public recognition when he receives the prestigious Kleist Prize; this event will mark the beginning of his prolific career as an international playwright, poet, and theatrical reformer.

William Butler Yeats, regarded as Ireland's greatest poet and one of the greatest poets writing in English in the twentieth century, is awarded the Nobel Prize for Literature for his enormous body of work, which favored technical experimentation and a passionate outlook on life.

1923–42   American poet Robert Frost wins the Pulitzer Prize four times for his collections of poetry; his work will earn the love of a wide public as well as the ongoing scrutiny of critics and scholars fascinated by his craftmanship.

1924   Pablo Neruda publishes his first collection of poetry, *Twenty Love Poems and a Song of Despair*, bringing Latin America's poetry to international attention with his recurring themes of love, nature, and justice.

1925   Bessie Smith, the most celebrated of the blues singers, and trumpeter Louis Armstrong collaborate on the famous "St. Louis Blues," a masterpiece of measured, stately pessimism; her popularity will bring blues to a high point.

1925–28   Louis Armstrong organizes a group, the Hot Five, in Chicago, with whom he will record many songs that are considered milestones in jazz history; Armstrong also pioneers the scat technique of vocally imitating an instrument, forever affecting the styles of future vocalists.

1927   *Show Boat*, Jerome Kern's greatest musical, opens, proving that his innovations defined the musical as a substantial art form; no subsequent composer of musicals has remained untouched by Kern's work.

1928   Salvador Dalí achieves international renown when three of his paintings are included in the third annual Carnegie International exhibition; in the following years he will paint, illustrate, sculpt, and make films mostly associated with the Surrealist movement.

Walt Disney and his brother, Roy, produce a cartoon, *Steamboat Willie*, featuring their new character Mickey Mouse and the innovative technology that was adding sound to motion pictures; his style will set the benchmark for other leading animators.

Gospel composer Thomas A. Dorsey teams with guitarist Hudson Whitaker to form Georgia Tom and Tampa Red; the duo's "hokum" blues recordings feature sexually suggestive lyrics that will make Dorsey an important figure in the history of the blues.

1929   Virginia Woolf publishes *A Room of One's Own*, one of the founding texts of contemporary feminist literary criticism; her book will help to place feminism at the center of literary consciousness.

While recuperating from a serious bus accident, Frida Kahlo shows her paintings to her future husband, Diego Rivera; during her lifetime she will become a celebrity, partly because of her romantic associations, but mostly because she used art as a way of analyzing and thinking about issues that are both profoundly personal and universally human.

Thomas Mann is awarded the Nobel Prize for Literature before he even writes what many consider to be his greatest work, *Dr. Faustus* (1947); his combining of intellectual fiction with political and cultural commentary is continued by writers today.

1930   Ezra Pound completes *A Draft of XXX Cantos*, the first version of his major work, *The Cantos*; his legacy is sometimes thought to reside as much in his energetic promotion of Modernist trends in the arts as in his politically controversial life.

Ludwig Mies van der Rohe is appointed the director of the Bauhaus, the prestigious Weimar-era school of art and design; his influence at Bauhaus will set the direction for the next generation of American architects and change the face of American cities.

1931   Famed jazz composer and bandleader Duke Ellington begins touring the United States with his band, creating and performing innovative jazz pieces; during his lifetime he will integrate improvised jazz solos into composed pieces, combine individual instruments to form unique orchestral colors, and broaden the jazz form to include large, abstract structures.

1932   Arnold Schoenberg writes his most ambitious and arguably most successful 12-tone work, the opera *Moses und Aron*; his 12-tone method and its elaborations will dominate university composition curricula in both Europe and the United States for several decades.

1933–36   Already a prolific poet, Federico García Lorca reaches enthusiastic Spanish audiences with three famous tragedies about women: *Blood Wedding* (1933), *Yerma* (1934), and *The House of Bernardo Alba* (1936); he will broaden the focus of Spanish poetry and theater and raise the traditional arts of Spain to the level of avant-garde art.

1935   George Gershwin writes his masterpiece for opera, *Porgy and Bess*, drawing on the composer's long familiarity with black music; he is known primarily for crossing other musical boundaries and for creating a series of works that bridged the divides between popular music, classical music, and jazz.

1936   Margaret Bourke-White joins *Life* magazine as a photojournalist; the medium allows Bourke-White to be recognized around the world as the quintessential photographer-adventurer who would go to almost any extreme to capture her story.

Robert Johnson records 16 songs for the ARC record label, his most famous being "Terraplane Blues"; during his lifetime he will transform the blues from a shared folk music into an individualistic art form.

1937   Octavio Paz attends the Writers' Congress Paris, where he is profoundly affected by his exposure to Parisian Surrealism; Paz will subsequently become one of the main introducers of Surrealism to Mexico. Paz will be the first Mexican writer to be awarded the Nobel Prize for Literature (1990).

Pablo Picasso, celebrated during his lifetime, is commissioned by the Spanish government to create a painting for the Spanish Pavilion at the World's Fair; *Guernica* embodies his Cubist influence and his far-reaching vision as a modern artist.

1938–44   Aaron Copland composes several ballet scores, including *Billy the Kid* (1938) and *Appalachian Spring* (1944) that draw on American folk music and that will make him one of the most loved American composers.

1939   Marian Anderson sings at the Lincoln Memorial, Washington, D.C., before an audience of 75,000, bringing her long, quiet struggle against racial discrimination to the media forefront and paving the way for African-American operatic singers for years to come.

Never a runaway popular success, Billy Holiday performs "Strange Fruit" and gains favor with progressive audiences, especially in New York City; she will eventually be widely recognized as jazz's greatest vocalist.

1940   The "golden age" of Umm Kalthum's musical career begins; she will become one of the first musicians from the Third World to cross national borders through the power of radio and film (and eventually television, on which she made her debut in 1960).

1940–41   Jacob Lawrence paints the *Migration Series*, making him one of the first artists to self-consciously address the African-American experience in order to develop a uniquely African-American style of art.

1941   The multitalented Orson Welles produces his masterpiece film, *Citizen Kane*, which is regarded by many as among the most important, influential, and greatest films in the history of cinema.

1943   During World War II and at the height of his popularity, Norman Rockwell paints *Freedom from Want*, depicting American ideology through images Americans wanted to see of themselves.

1943–44   Charlie Parker and fellow jazz musician Dizzy Gillespie perform in a series of New York clubs, where they take giant steps forward stylistically, defining the musical language of bebop, which, in turn, will become the foundation of modern jazz.

1944   Martha Graham choreographs a dance to Aaron Copland's *Appalachian Spring*, which will became one of her most famous pieces. Graham pioneers the concept of dance as a basic form of expression, and not just as an accompaniment to music or any other art.

1944–49   Jorge Luis Borges, acclaimed for creating a new fictional world for Latin American literature that addressed and challenged the experience and tradition of Latin American life, publishes two collections of short stories: *Fictions* (1944) and *The Aleph* (1949).

1945–49 George Orwell publishes two of the most famous satirical novels of the twentieth century, *Animal Farm* and *Nineteen Eighty-Four*; a serious political thinker and a craftsman of language, Orwell's works embody moral integrity and independence.

1946 Mahalia Jackson's career takes off with a recording on the Apollo label, "Move On Up a Little Higher," spreading her fame as the greatest black gospel vocalist far and wide in black churches and eventually throughout the United States via television.

Edith Piaf rises to international stardom, thanks partly to the strong sales of her hit "La Vie en Rose" ("Life in the Color Rose"); she will enjoy considerable success in the notoriously monolingual United States, despite singing mostly in French.

Jackson Pollock begins to develop the "drip" paintings for which he is best known, creating a unique form of Abstract Expressionism and making him a key figure in the surge of interest in avant-garde art in post–World War II America.

Aimé-Fernand Césaire, one of the founding poets of *negritude*, publishes his long poem, *Notebook of a Return to the Native Land*, which is widely considered to be his greatest work.

1947 The staging of *A Streetcar Named Desire* will bring Tennessee Williams into his own as a playwright; he will be one of the key figures in American theater and he will be one of the first to use American English as a poetic language.

1948 George Balanchine founds (with Lincoln Kirstein) the New York City Ballet, shaping ballet in the United States and establishing a dance tradition where only fragments of one had existed previously.

1949 William Faulkner is awarded the Nobel Prize for Literature for his prolific writing; technical innovations and complex characterization make his work some of the most innovative and difficult of American twentieth-century writing.

Hank Williams records his version of the yodel number called "Lovesick Blues," which propels him to national stardom and to a spot on Nashville's *Grand Ole Opry*; he will become the most important figure in the history of country music.

1950 Akira Kurosawa's famous film *Rashomon* wins the top prize at the Venice Film Festival, bringing Kurosawa into the international spotlight as Japan's best film director.

1952 Composer John Cage writes *4'33"*, the most famous of his avant-garde musical repertoire that pushed the boundaries of experimental music to the limit.

1953 James Baldwin completes his first novel, *Go Tell It On the Mountain*, setting a precedent for the literary activists of the 1960s and beyond with his insistent and tolerant treatment of racial and sexual difference.

Merce Cunningham forms his own dance group, the Merce Cunningham Dance Company, with musicians John Cage and David Tudor; one of the truly groundbreaking choreographers of the twentieth century, Cunningham will use experimental ideas derived from music and visual art.

1955 Miles Davis recovers temporarily from a heroin addiction to form the New Miles Davis Quintet, with saxophonist John Coltrane; his musical vision will be so compelling that even the musicians who only passed through his bands will become jazz all-stars.

1955–57 Diane Arbus studies photography with Lisette Model, under whom she will develop her personal artistic style, capturing images of people living on the margins of society; she will challenge the limitations of what is considered artistically tasteful or acceptable.

1958 Chinua Achebe publishes his first and best-known novel, *Things Fall Apart*, establishing himself as a founder of a new Nigerian literature movement in the 1950s.

Alvin Ailey founds the Alvin Ailey American Dance Theater to celebrate concert dance and African-American artistic expression.

Leonard Bernstein becomes the first native-born American to assume the conductorship of the New York Philharmonic Orchestra, arguably the nation's flagship symphonic orchestra.

Gaining fluency as a songwriter, Antonio Carlos Jobim collaborates with guitarist and singer João Gilberto in the creation of the bossa nova musical style.

1959 Marguerite Duras gains international recognition with the script she writes for the film *Hiroshima, Mon Amour*, a film that employs many of the techniques characteristic of the French Nouveau Roman (New Novel), while maintaining her own distinct and impassioned writing style.

Miriam Makeba launches her American singing career; she will bring the evils of South African apartheid to public consciousness and find success with her American releases.

1960 Andy Warhol produces his early Pop paintings; he will became the best known of the Pop artists and the most closely connected with the style.

Alfred Hitchcock releases his most famous and most frightening film, *Psycho*, a masterpiece by the inventor of the thriller genre.

1962 Loretta Lynn reaches the country music top ten chart with her hit "Success." She gains celebrity for giving a voice to the histories and emotional lives of American women of many different backgrounds

Bob Dylan records his first album, *Bob Dylan*, now a rock and blues standard; he will be celebrated as one of the first "singer–songwriters" whose fans would come to value his honest representation of personal experience as much as his powerful lyrics.

1963 James Brown's *Live at the Apollo* album spreads the word about his manic and compelling live performances, his musical innovations will inspire the funk style of the late 1970s and then the hip-hop revolution of the 1980s and 1990s.

John Coltrane, bouncing back from his addictions to drugs and alcohol, records the album *A Love Supreme* with the Miles Davis Quintet; his musical style will change both the sound and the spirit of jazz, and he will emerge as a major influence on the music of the 1960s and beyond.

Several members of the Irish musical group Ceoltóirí Cualann join Paddy Moloney to form the Chieftains; Moloney will serve as the producer and as the main musical arranger for the Chieftains' many albums.

Nam June Paik has his first one-person show, *Exposition of Music—Electronic Music*; this event is often regarded as the first work of video art, hence Paik is widely regarded as the father of video art.

1963–65 Henry Moore sculpts *Bronze Reclining Figure* for Lincoln Center, New York; his work as a modern artist will draw inspiration from natural objects and will eventually make him the most important sculptor of the twentieth century.

1964 The group the Beatles, led by John Lennon and Paul McCartney, rises to international fame with an appearance on U.S. television's *Ed Sullivan Show* and a simultaneous conquest of the five top spots on U.S. pop charts; the Beatles will stand at the creative summit of rock music for years to come, primarily because of the range of styles their music encompassed.

Robert Rauschenberg wins the grand prize for painting at the Venice Biennale, the most prestigious contemporary international art show; his avant-garde vision opened the gates to the great flood of different styles, materials, techniques, and subjects now called Postmodern.

1966 Soul music's best female vocalist, Aretha Franklin, has her major creative breakthrough when she signs with Atlantic and produces a string of magnificent recordings that will bring her gospel piano to the fore and set the tone for a string of hits over the next five years

1967 Bob Marley and the Wailers begin writing songs expressing aspects of the Rastafarian faith and laying the groundwork for a new style, later known as reggae, that featured complex rhythmic patterns over a foundation of heavy, hypnotic bass guitar; Marley will become the chief musical ambassador of this style.

Gabriel García Márquez publishes *One Hundred Years of Solitude*, a major contribution to the literary movement known as magical realism; he will be awarded the Nobel Prize for Literature in 1982.

1968 Astor Piazzolla wins over tango traditionalists and becomes an Argentine hero with his stage work *Maria de Buenos Aires: A Tango-Operita*.

Rock legend Elvis Presley, after over a decade of success, stages a televised return to the stage in which he seems to recapture his rock-and-roll roots.

1969 Samuel Beckett is awarded the Nobel Prize for Literature in acknowledgment of his profound influence on twentieth-century theater and literature; he is best known for exploring fundamental questions of existence, absurdist sensibility, and Minimalism.

Jimi Hendrix, widely considered to be the greatest instrumentalist in the history of rock music, indelibly ingrains his musical stylings into the popular consciousness with his performance of the American national anthem at the Woodstock festival.

1970 Maya Angelou publishes *I Know Why the Caged Bird Sings* to immediate acclaim; its the first book by an African-American woman to reach the *New York Times* bestseller list.

American composer Steve Reich goes to Ghana to immerse himself in African percussion, and a year later he will write *Drumming*, which will make Reich's reputation as a Minimalist composer.

1970–72 African-American artist Faith Ringgold becomes deeply involved in the feminist movement, working in textiles and making soft sculptures and quilts, crafts that are traditionally made by women; her work will continually challenge the boundary between high art and craft.

1971 Ravi Shankar and former Beatle George Harrison appear together at a pair of massive benefit concerts for Bangladeshi flood victims, promoting Shankar to international superstardom as a performer of classical Indian music as well as an innovator who merged Eastern and Western musical styles.

1973 Twyla Tharp produces *Deuce Coupe*, a dance set to music of the Beach Boys that would epitomize her free-spiritedness and groundbreaking dance style.

1975 Celia Cruz contributes to the Fania All Stars' *Live at Yankee Stadium* album, which captures the excitement of her performances and spreads her fame as a salsa vocalist beyond the Latin community.

1977 In protest of the Nigerian government's dictatorship and the murder of his mother, antiauthoritarian musician and vocalist Fela travels to the ruling party's headquarters and places his mother's coffin on the steps of the building; Fela attracts a massive political and musical following with a mix of Western and African elements in his music.

1978 *Village Voice* article features Jean-Michel Basquiat's art, exposing him as a pioneer of the underground New York graffiti art movement and as an individual capable of merging the traditions of street life and clubs, graffiti and fine art.

1979 The American Film Institute and the Los Angeles County Museum of Art honor François Truffaut with a 20-year retrospective of his films; he will both lay the groundwork for the French New Wave movement and originate the auteur theory, the prime analytical tool of modern film criticism.

1981 Maya Lin is awarded the commission for the Vietnam Veterans Memorial; her profoundly moving public sculptures currently commemorate many important episodes in American history.

1985 Nusrat Fateh Ali Khan of Pakistan, the foremost modern exponent of *qawwali*, performs his vocal stylings for the first time in Europe, reasserting the vitality of that centuries-old tradition and establishing the precedent for "world music."

1993 Toni Morrison is awarded the Nobel Prize for Literature for her lyrically innovative novels that discuss the conflict inherent in the lives of African Americans who inhabit white culture.

Appendix Two:
Geographic Listing of Biographies

The listing below classifies the individuals in the book according to the country in which they produced important work. In most instances, this is the person's place of birth. In other cases, however, individuals left their country of origin to study and work in a different place. In these instances, we have noted the birthplace and/or additional place of work parenthetically. We have also noted ethnic and/or ancestral origins of minorities in the United States parenthetically.

Argentina

Borges, Jorge Luis
   Short Story Writer, Poet, and Essayist   1899–1986

Piazzolla, Astor (also worked in the United States)
   Composer   1921–1992

Austria

Beethoven, Ludwig van (born and also worked in Germany)
   Composer   1770–1827

Brahms, Johannes (born and also worked in Germany)
   Composer   1833–1897

Haydn, Franz Joseph (also worked in Hungary)
   Composer   1732–1809

Mozart, Wolfgang Amadeus
   Composer   1756–1791

Schoenberg, Arnold (also worked in the United States)
   Composer   1874–1951

Bangladesh

Tagore, Rabindranath (born and also worked in India)
   Poet, Novelist, and Philosopher   1861–1941

Belgium (formerly part of Flanders)

Rubens, Peter Paul
   Painter and Diplomat   1577–1640

Brazil

Jobim, Antonio Carlos (worked in the United States)
   Musician   1927–1994

Chile

Neruda, Pablo
   Poet   1904–1973

China

Guo Xi
   Painter and Theoretician   c. 1000–c. 1090

Ni Zan
   Painter and Scholar   1301–1374

Shen Zhou
   Painter and Scholar   1427–1509

Ts'ao Hsüeh-ch'in
   Novelist   c. 1715–1763

Tu Fu
   Poet   712–770

Colombia

García Márquez, Gabriel (also worked in Mexico)
   Novelist and Journalist   1928–

Cuba

Cruz, Celia (also worked in the United States)
   Vocalist   1924–

Czech Republic
(formerly part of Czechoslovakia and Austria-Hungary)

Kafka, Franz
   Novelist and Short Story Writer   1883–1924

Rilke, Rainer Maria (also worked in Germany)
   Poet and Novelist   1875–1926

Egypt

Kalthum, Umm
   Vocalist   c. 1904–1975

England

Austen, Jane
   Novelist   1775–1817

Blake, William
   Poet   1757–1827

Brontë, Charlotte
   Novelist   1816–1855

Chaucer, Geoffrey
   Poet   c. 1340–1400

Conrad, Joseph (born in Berdichev, present-day Ukraine)
   Novelist   1857–1924

Dickens, Charles
   Novelist   1812–1870

Eliot, George
   Novelist   1819–1880

Handel, George Frideric (born and also worked in Germany)
   Composer   1685–1759

Hitchcock, Alfred (also worked in the United States)	
Filmmaker	1899–1980
Keats, John	
Poet	1795–1821
Lennon, John (also worked in United States)	
Songwriter and Vocalist	1940–1980
McCartney, Paul	
Songwriter and Vocalist	1942–
Milton, John	
Poet and Essayist	1608–1674
Moore, Henry	
Sculptor	1898–1986
Orwell, George (born in India)	
Journalist, Novelist, and Essayist	1903–1950
Pound, Ezra (born in the United States; also worked in Italy)	
Poet	1885–1972
Shakespeare, William	
Dramatist and Poet	1564–1616
Swift, Jonathan (born and also worked in Ireland)	
Novelist and Political Satirist	1667–1745
Woolf, Virginia	
Novelist and Essayist	1882–1941
Wordsworth, William	
Poet	1770–1850

France

Baldwin, James (African American; also worked in United States)	
Novelist and Dramatist	1924–1987
Balanchine, George (born and also worked in Russia; also worked in the United States)	
Choreographer and Dancer	1904–1983
Baudelaire, Charles-Pierre	
Poet	1821–1867
Beckett, Samuel (born and also worked in Ireland)	
Playwright, Poet, and Novelist	1906–1989
Büchner, Georg (born and also worked in Germany)	
Playwright	1813–1837
Cassatt, Mary (born and also worked in the United States)	
Painter and Printmaker	1844–1926
Césaire, Aimé-Fernand (born and also worked in Martinique, formerly a French colony)	
Poet, Dramatist, and Essayist	1913–
Cézanne, Paul	
Painter	1839–1906
Chopin, Fryderyk (born and also worked in Poland)	
Composer	1810–1849
Debussy, Claude	
Composer	1862–1918
Degas, Edgar	
Painter	1834–1917
Diaghilev, Serge (born and also worked in Russia)	
Dance Impresario	1872–1929

Duchamp, Marcel (also worked in the United States)	
Artist	1887–1968
Duncan, Isadora (born in the United States)	
Dance Pioneer	1878–1927
Duras, Marguerite (born and also worked in former French colony of Indochina, now Vietnam)	
Novelist, Dramatist, Filmmaker, Short Story Writer, and Journalist	1914–1996
Flaubert, Gustave	
Novelist and Short Story Writer	1821–1880
Hugo, Victor-Marie	
Novelist, Poet, Dramatist, and Critic	1801–1885
Josquin des Prez (also worked in Italy)	
Composer	c. 1455–1521
Joyce, James (born and also worked in Ireland)	
Novelist	1882–1941
Manet, Edouard	
Painter and Printmaker	1832–1883
Matisse, Henri	
Painter and Sculptor	1869–1954
Molière	
Playwright, Actor, and Director	1622–1673
Monet, Claude	
Painter	1840–1926
Nadar	
Caricaturist and Photographer	1820–1910
Piaf, Edith	
Vocalist	1915–1963
Picasso, Pablo (born and also worked in Spain)	
Painter and Sculptor	1881–1973
Proust, Marcel	
Novelist	1871–1922
Renoir, Pierre-Auguste	
Painter	1841–1919
Rodin, Auguste	
Sculptor	1840–1917
Stravinsky, Igor (born and also worked in Russia; also worked in the United States)	
Composer	1882–1971
Tanner, Henry Ossawa (African American; born and also worked in the United States)	
Painter	1859–1937
Truffaut, François	
Filmmaker and Critic	1932–1984
Van Gogh, Vincent (born and also worked in Netherlands)	
Painter	1853–1890
Varèse, Edgard (also worked in the United States)	
Composer	1883–1965

Germany

Bach, Johann Sebastian	
Composer	1685–1750

Beethoven, Ludwig van (also worked in Austria)
Composer 1770–1827

Brahms, Johannes (also worked in Austria)
Composer 1833–1897

Brecht, Bertolt (also worked in the United States)
Playwright and Director 1898–1956

Büchner, Georg (also worked in France)
Playwright 1813–1837

Dürer, Albrecht
Painter, Printmaker, and Theoretician 1471–1528

Goethe, Johann Wolfgang von
Poet, Novelist, and Dramatist 1749–1832

Handel, George Frideric (also worked in England)
Composer 1685–1759

Ibsen, Henrik (born in Norway; also worked in Italy)
Playwright and Poet 1828–1906

Liszt, Franz (born in Hungary)
Composer, Pianist, and Conductor 1811–1886

Mann, Thomas (also worked in the United States)
Novelist 1875–1955

Mies van der Rohe, Ludwig (also worked in the United States)
Architect and Educator 1886–1969

Modersohn-Becker, Paula
Painter 1876–1907

Rilke, Rainer Maria (born and also worked in Prague, now capital of Czech Republic)
Poet and Novelist 1875–1926

Schumann, Robert
Composer 1810–1856

Wagner, Richard
Composer 1813–1883

Greek and Roman Empires

Homer (Greece, under Greek rule)
Poet c. 8th Century B.C.E.

Ovid (Rome and Tomis, present-day Romania, under Roman rule)
Poet 43 B.C.E.–18 C.E.

Sappho (Asia Minor, under Greek rule)
Poet c. Sixth Century B.C.E.

Sophocles (Athens, Greece, under Greek rule)
Playwright c. 496 B.C.E.

Virgil (Rome, under Roman rule)
Poet 70 B.C.E.–19 B.C.E.

Hungary

Haydn, Franz Joseph (born and also worked in Austria)
Composer 1732–1809

Liszt, Franz (worked in Germany)
Composer, Pianist, and Conductor 1811–1886

India

Camões, Luíz Vaz de (born and also worked in Portugal)
Poet c. 1524–1580

Shankar, Ravi
Sitarist and Composer 1920–

Tagore, Rabindranath (also worked in Bangladesh)
Poet, Novelist, and Philosopher 1861–1941

Tyagaraja
Composer 1767–1847

Iran

Jāmi
Poet 1414–1492

Ireland

Beckett, Samuel (also worked in France)
Playwright, Poet, and Novelist 1906–1989

Joyce, James (also worked in France)
Novelist 1882–1941

Moloney, Paddy
Musician 1938–

Swift, Jonathan (also worked in England)
Novelist and Political Satirist 1667–1745

Yeats, William Butler
Poet and Playwright 1865–1939

Italy

Alberti, Leon Battista
Architect, Sculptor, and Theoretician 1404–1472

Anguissola, Sofonisba (also worked in Spain)
Painter c. 1535–1625

Bernini, Gian Lorenzo
Sculptor, Architect, and Painter 1598–1680

Botticelli, Sandro
Painter 1445–1510

Caravaggio
Painter 1571–1610

Dante
Poet 1265–1321

Gentileschi, Artemisia
Painter 1593–1652

Giotto
Painter c. 1267–1337

Gregory I, Pope
Musically Influential Church Leader c. 540–604

Ibsen, Henrik (born in Norway; also worked in Germany)
Playwright and Poet 1828–1906

Josquin des Prez (born and also worked in France)
Composer c. 1455–1521

Leonardo da Vinci
Painter, Sculptor, and Scientist 1452–1519

Michelangelo
Sculptor, Painter, Architect, and Poet 1475–1567

Monteverdi, Claudio
Composer 1567–1643

Palestrina, Giovanni Pierluigi da
    Composer   1525 or 1526–1594

Palladio
    Architect and Theoretician   1508–1580

Pound, Ezra (born in the United States; also worked in England)
    Poet   1885–1972

Raphael
    Painter, Architect, and Administrator   1438–1520

Titian
    Painter   c. 1490–1576

Verdi, Giuseppe
    Composer   1813–1901

Jamaica

Marley, Bob
    Musician and Bandleader   1945–1981

Japan

Bashō
    Poet   1644–1694

Hiroshige
    Printmaker   1797–1858

Kōetsu
    Calligrapher and Potter   1558–1637

Kurosawa, Akira
    Filmmaker   1910–1998

Murasaki Shikibu
    Novelist   c. 978–1014

Sesshū
    Painter and Calligrapher   1420–1506

Zeami Motokiyo
    Founder of Noh Drama   1363–1443

Korea

Paik, Nam June (also worked in the United States)
    Musician, Sculptor, and Performance and Video Artist   1932–

Martinique (formerly a French colony)

Césaire, Aimé-Fernand (also worked in France)
    Poet, Dramatist, and Essayist   1913–

Mexico

Cruz, Sor Juana Inés de la
    Poet   1651–1695

García Márquez, Gabriel (born and also worked in Colombia)
    Novelist and Journalist   1928–

Kahlo, Frida
    Painter   1907–1954

Paz, Octavio
    Poet, Essayist, and Journalist   1914–1998

Rivera, Diego
    Painter   1886–1957

Netherlands

Bosch, Hieronymus (born in Flanders, present-day Netherlands)
    Painter   1453–1517

Mondrian, Piet
    Painter and Theorist   1872–1944

Rembrandt
    Painter and Printmaker   1606–1669

Van Eyck, Jan (born in Flanders, present-day Netherlands)
    Painter and Manuscript Illuminator   c. 1370/90–1441

Van Gogh, Vincent (also worked in France)
    Painter   1853–1890

Nigeria

Achebe, Chinua
    Novelist   1930–

Fela
    Songwriter and Vocalist   1938–1997

Norway

Ibsen, Henrik (also worked in Germany and Italy)
    Playwright and Poet   1828–1906

Pakistan

Khan, Nusrat Fateh Ali
    Vocalist   1948–1997

Poland

Chopin, Fryderyk (also worked in France)
    Composer   1810–1849

Portugal

Camões, Luíz Vaz de (also worked in India)
    Poet   c. 1524–1580

Russia

Balanchine, George (also worked in France and the United States)
    Choreographer and Dancer   1904–1983

Chekhov, Anton
    Short Story Writer and Dramatist   1860–1904

Diaghilev, Serge (also worked in France)
    Dance Impresario   1872–1929

Dostoyevsky, Fyodor
    Novelist   1821–1881

Pushkin, Aleksandr
    Poet, Novelist, and Critic   1799–1837

Stravinsky, Igor (also worked in France and the United States)
    Composer   1882–1971

Tchaikovsky, Peter Ilich
    Composer   1840–1893

Tolstoy, Leo
    Novelist, Dramatist, and Short Story Writer   1828–1910

South Africa

Makeba, Miriam (also worked in the United States)
Vocalist — 1932–

Spain

Anguissola, Sofonisba (born and also worked in Italy)
Painter — c. 1535–1625

Cervantes, Miguel de
Poet and Novelist — 1547–1616

Dalí, Salvador (also worked in the United States)
Artist — 1904–1989

Goya, Francisco
Painter — 1746–1828

Lorca, Federico García
Poet and Playwright — 1898–1936

Picasso, Pablo (also worked in France)
Painter and Sculptor — 1881–1973

Velázquez, Diego
Painter and Courtier — 1599–1660

United States

Ailey, Alvin (African American)
Dance Pioneer — 1931–1989

Anderson, Marian (African American)
Vocalist — 1897–1993

Angelou, Maya (African American)
Poet and Autobiographer — 1928–

Arbus, Diane
Photographer — 1923–1971

Armstrong, Louis (African American)
Trumpeter — 1901–1971

Baldwin, James (African American; also worked in France)
Novelist and Dramatist — 1924–1987

Balanchine, George (born and also worked in Russia; also worked in France)
Choreographer and Dancer — 1904–1983

Basquiat, Jean-Michel (Afro-Carribean American)
Painter and Graffiti Artist — 1960–1988

Berlin, Irving (born in Russia)
Songwriter — 1888–1989

Bernstein, Leonard
Composer and Conductor — 1918–1990

Bourke-White, Margaret
Photojournalist — 1904–1971

Brecht, Bertolt (born and also worked in Germany)
Playwright and Director — 1898–1956

Brown, James (African American)
Vocalist — c. 1933–

Cage, John
Composer — 1912–1992

Cassatt, Mary (also worked in France)
Painter and Printmaker — 1844–1926

Coltrane, John (African American)
Saxophonist — 1926–1967

Copland, Aaron
Composer — 1900–1990

Cruz, Celia (born and also worked in Cuba)
Vocalist — 1924–

Cunningham, Merce
Choreographer — 1919–

Dalí, Salvador (born and also worked in Spain)
Artist — 1904–1989

Davis, Miles (African American)
Trumpeter — 1926–1991

Dickinson, Emily
Poet — 1830–1886

Disney, Walt
Cartoonist, Filmmaker, and Entrepreneur — 1901–1966

Dorsey, Thomas A. (African American)
Composer — 1899–1993

Duchamp, Marcel (born and also worked in France)
Artist — 1887–1968

Duncan, Isadora (also worked in France)
Dance Pioneer — 1878–1927

Dylan, Bob
Singer-Songwriter — 1941–

Eakins, Thomas
Painter and Photographer — 1844–1916

Ellington, Duke (African American)
Composer and Bandleader — 1899–1974

Faulkner, William
Novelist — 1897–1962

Franklin, Aretha (African American)
Vocalist — 1942–

Frost, Robert
Poet — 1874–1963

Gershwin, George
Songwriter and Composer — 1898–1937

Graham, Martha
Choreographer — 1894–1991

Griffith, D. W.
Filmmaker — 1875–1948

Hendrix, Jimi (African American)
Guitarist — 1942–1970

Hitchcock, Alfred (born and also worked in England)
Filmmaker — 1899–1980

Holiday, Billie (African American)
Vocalist — 1915–1959

Homer, Winslow
Painter, Printmaker, and Illustrator — 1836–1910

Jackson, Mahalia (African American)
Vocalist — 1911–1972

Jobim, Antonio Carlos (born and also worked in Brazil)
Musician   1927–1994

Johnson, Robert (African American)
Guitarist   1911–1938

Joplin, Scott (African American)
Pianist and Composer   1868–1917

Kern, Jerome
Composer   1885–1945

Lawrence, Jacob (African American)
Painter   1917–2000

Lennon, John (born and also worked in England)
Songwriter and Vocalist   1940–1980

Lin, Maya (Chinese-American)
Sculptor and Architect   1959–

Lynn, Loretta
Vocalist and Songwriter   1935–

Makeba, Miriam (born and also worked in the South Africa)
Vocalist   1932–

Mann, Thomas (born and also worked in Germany)
Novelist   1875–1955

Melville, Herman
Novelist, Short Story Writer, and Poet   1819–1891

Mies van der Rohe, Ludwig (born and also worked in Germany)
Architect and Educator   1886–1969

Morrison, Toni (African American)
Novelist and Critic   1931–

O'Keeffe, Georgia
Painter   1887–1986

Paik, Nam June (born and also worked in Korea)
Musician, Sculptor, and Performance and Video Artist   1932–

Parker, Charlie (African American)
Saxophonist   1920–1950

Piazzolla, Astor (born and also worked in Argentina)
Composer   1921–1992

Pollock, Jackson
Painter   1912–1956

Pound, Ezra (also worked in Italy and England)
Poet   1885–1972

Presley, Elvis
Vocalist   1935–1977

Rauschenberg, Robert
Painter and Multimedia Artist   1925–

Reich, Steve
Minimalist Composer   1936–

Ringgold, Faith (African American)
Painter, Quiltmaker, Teacher, and Writer   1930–

Rockwell, Norman
Illustrator   1894–1978

Schoenberg, Arnold (born and also worked in Austria)
Composer   1874–1951

Smith, Bessie (African American)
Vocalist   1894–1937

Stravinsky, Igor (born and also worked in Russia; also worked in France)
Composer   1882–1971

Tanner, Henry Ossawa (African American; also worked in France)
Painter   1859–1937

Tharp, Twyla
Choreographer and Dancer   1941–

Twain, Mark
Novelist, Short Story Writer, Journalist, and Essayist 1835–1910

Varèse, Edgard (born and also worked in France)
Composer   1883–1965

Warhol, Andy
Painter, Printmaker, and Filmmaker   1928–1987

Welles, Orson
Actor and Filmmaker   1915–1985

Whitman, Walt
Poet   1819–1892

Williams, Hank
Vocalist and Songwriter   1923–1953

Williams, Tennessee
Playwright   1911–1983

Wright, Frank Lloyd
Architect, Designer, Educator   1867–1959

Vietnam (formerly French colony of Indochina)

Duras, Marguerite (also worked in France)
Novelist, Dramatist, Filmmaker, Short Story Writer,
and Journalist   1914–1996

APPENDIX THREE:
Listing of Biographies by Discipline

The listing below classifies the individuals in the book according to the artistic discipline in which they worked. As many individuals frequently worked in several disciplines, some are listed here more than once.

Dance

Ailey, Alvin
Dance Pioneer   1931–1989

Balanchine, George
Choreographer and Dancer   1904–1983

Cunningham, Merce
Choreographer   1919–

Diaghilev, Serge
Dance Impresario   1872–1929

Duncan, Isadora
Dance Pioneer   1878–1927

Graham, Martha
Choreographer   1894–1991

Tharp, Twyla
Choreographer and Dancer   1941–

Film

Disney, Walt
Cartoonist, Filmmaker, and Entrepreneur   1901–1966

Griffith, D. W.
Filmmaker   1875–1948

Hitchcock, Alfred
Filmmaker   1899–1980

Kurosawa, Akira
Filmmaker   1910–1998

Truffaut, François
Filmmaker and Critic   1932–1984

Warhol, Andy
Painter, Printmaker, and Filmmaker   1928–1987

Welles, Orson
Actor and Filmmaker   1915–1985

Literature

Achebe, Chinua
Novelist   1930–

Angelou, Maya
Poet and Autobiographer   1928–

Austen, Jane
Novelist   1775–1817

Baldwin, James
Novelist and Dramatist   1924–1987

Bashō
Poet   1644–1694

Baudelaire, Charles-Pierre
Poet   1821–1867

Beckett, Samuel
Playwright, Poet, and Novelist   1906–1989

Blake, William
Poet   1757–1827

Borges, Jorge Luis
Short Story Writer, Poet, and Essayist   1899–1986

Brecht, Bertolt
Playwright and Director   1898–1956

Brontë, Charlotte
Novelist   1816–1855

Büchner, Georg
Playwright   1813–1837

Camões, Luíz Vaz de
Poet   c. 1524–1580

Cervantes, Miguel de
Poet and Novelist   1547–1616

Césaire, Aimé-Fernand
Poet, Dramatist, and Essayist   1913–

Chaucer, Geoffrey
Poet   c. 1340–1400

Chekhov, Anton
Short Story Writer and Dramatist   1860–1904

Conrad, Joseph
Novelist   1857–1924

Cruz, Sor Juana Inés de la
Poet   1651–1695

Dante
Poet   1265–1321

Dickens, Charles
Novelist   1812–1870

Dickinson, Emily
Poet   1830–1886

Dostoyevsky, Fyodor
Novelist   1821–1881

Duras, Marguerite
Novelist, Dramatist, Filmmaker, Short Story Writer,
and Journalist   1914–1996

Eliot, George
Novelist   1819–1880

Faulkner, William
Novelist   1897–1962

Flaubert, Gustave
Novelist and Short Story Writer   1821–1880

Frost, Robert
Poet   1874–1963

García Márquez, Gabriel
Novelist and Journalist   1928–

Goethe, Johann Wolfgang von
Poet, Novelist, and Dramatist   1749–1832

Homer
Poet   c. Eighth Century B.C.E.

Hugo, Victor-Marie
Novelist, Poet, Dramatist, and Critic   1801–1885

Ibsen, Henrik
Playwright and Poet   1828–1906

Jāmi
Poet   1414–1492

Joyce, James
Novelist   1882–1941

Kafka, Franz
Novelist and Short Story Writer   1883–1924

Keats, John
Poet   1795–1821

Lorca, Federico García
Poet and Playwright   1898–1936

Mann, Thomas
Novelist   1875–1955

Melville, Herman
Novelist, Short Story Writer, and Poet   1819–1891

Milton, John
Poet and Essayist   1608–1674

Molière
Playwright, Actor, and Director   1622–1673

Morrison, Toni
Novelist and Critic   1931–

Murasaki Shikibu
Novelist   c. 978–1014

Neruda, Pablo
Poet   1904–1973

Orwell, George
Journalist, Novelist, and Essayist   1903–1950

Ovid
Poet   43 B.C.E.–18 C.E.

Paz, Octavio
Poet, Essayist, and Journalist   1914–1998

Pound, Ezra
Poet   1885–1972

Proust, Marcel
Novelist   1871–1922

Pushkin, Aleksandr
Poet, Novelist, and Critic   1799–1837

Rilke, Rainer Maria
Poet and Novelist   1875–1926

Sappho
Poet   c. Sixth Century B.C.E.

Shakespeare, William
Dramatist and Poet   1564–1616

Swift, Jonathan
Novelist and Political Satirist   1667–1745

Tagore, Rabindranath
Poet, Novelist, and Philosopher   1861–1941

Tolstoy, Leo
Novelist, Dramatist, and Short Story Writer 1828–1910

Ts'ao Hsüeh-ch'in
Novelist   c. 1715–1763

Tu Fu
Poet   712–770

Twain, Mark
Novelist, Short Story Writer, Journalist, and Essayist 1835–1910

Virgil
Poet   70 B.C.E–19 B.C.E

Whitman, Walt
Poet   1819–1892

Williams, Tennessee
Playwright   1911–1983

Woolf, Virginia
Novelist and Essayist   1882–1941

Wordsworth, William
Poet   1770–1850

Yeats, William Butler
Poet and Playwright   1865–1939

Music

Anderson, Marian
Vocalist   1897–1993

Armstrong, Louis
Trumpeter   1901–1971

Bach, Johann Sebastian
Composer   1685–1750

Beethoven, Ludwig van
Composer   1770–1827

Berlin, Irving
Songwriter   1888–1989

Bernstein, Leonard
Composer and Conductor   1918–1990

Brahms, Johannes
Composer   1833–1897

Brown, James Vocalist	c. 1933–
Cage, John Composer	1912–1992
Chopin, Fryderyk Composer	1810–1849
Coltrane, John Saxophonist	1926–1967
Copland, Aaron Composer	1900–1990
Cruz, Celia Vocalist	1924–
Davis, Miles Trumpeter	1926–1991
Debussy, Claude Composer	1862–1918
Dorsey, Thomas A. Composer	1899–1993
Dylan, Bob Singer-Songwriter	1941–
Ellington, Duke Composer and Bandleader	1899–1974
Fela Songwriter and Vocalist	1938–1997
Franklin, Aretha Vocalist	1942–
Gershwin, George Songwriter and Composer	1898–1937
Gregory I, Pope Musically Influential Church Leader	c. 540–604
Handel, George Frideric Composer	1685–1759
Haydn, Franz Joseph Composer	1732–1809
Hendrix, Jimi Guitarist	1942–1970
Holiday, Billie Vocalist	1915–1959
Jackson, Mahalia Vocalist	1911–1972
Jobim, Antonio Carlos Musician	1927–1994
Johnson, Robert Guitarist	1911–1938
Joplin, Scott Pianist and Composer	1868–1917
Josquin des Prez Composer	c. 1455–1521
Kalthum, Umm Vocalist	c. 1904–1975

Kern, Jerome Composer	1885–1945
Khan, Nusrat Fateh Ali Vocalist	1948–1997
Lennon, John; Paul McCartney Songwriters and Vocalists	1940–1980; 1942–
Liszt, Franz Composer, Pianist, and Conductor	1811–1886
Lynn, Loretta Vocalist and Songwriter	1935–
Makeba, Miriam Vocalist	1932–
Marley, Bob Musician and Bandleader	1945–1981
Moloney, Paddy Musician	1938–
Monteverdi, Claudio Composer	1567–1643
Mozart, Wolfgang Amadeus Composer	1756–1791
Paik, Nam June Musician, Sculptor, and Performance and Video Artist	1932–
Palestrina, Giovanni Pierluigi da Composer	1525 or 1526–1594
Parker, Charlie Saxophonist	1920–1950
Piaf, Edith Vocalist	1915–1963
Piazzolla, Astor Composer	1921–1992
Presley, Elvis Vocalist	1935–1977
Reich, Steve Composer	1936–
Schoenberg, Arnold Composer	1874–1951
Schumann, Robert Composer	1810–1856
Shankar, Ravi Sitarist and Composer	1920–
Smith, Bessie Vocalist	1894–1937
Stravinsky, Igor Composer	1882–1971
Tchaikovsky, Peter Ilich Composer	1840–1893
Tyagaraja Composer	1767–1847
Varèse, Edgar Composer	1883–1965

Verdi, Giuseppe
Composer 1813–1901

Wagner, Richard
Composer 1813–1883

Williams, Hank
Vocalist and Songwriter 1923–1953

Theater

Baldwin, James
Novelist and Dramatist 1924–1987

Beckett, Samuel
Playwright, Poet, and Novelist 1906–1989

Brecht, Bertolt
Playwright and Director 1898–1956

Büchner, Georg
Playwright 1813–1837

Césaire, Aimé-Fernand
Poet, Dramatist, and Essayist 1913–

Chekhov, Anton
Short Story Writer and Dramatist 1860–1904

Duras, Marguerite
Novelist, Dramatist, Filmmaker, Short Story Writer,
and Journalist 1914–1996

Goethe, Johann Wolfgang von
Poet, Novelist, and Dramatist 1749–1832

Hugo, Victor-Marie
Novelist, Poet, Dramatist, and Critic 1801–1885

Ibsen, Henrik
Playwright and Poet 1828–1906

Kern, Jerome
Composer 1885–1945

Lorca, Federico García
Poet and Playwright 1898–1936

Molière
Playwright, Actor, and Director 1622–1673

Shakespeare, William
Dramatist and Poet 1564–1616

Sophocles
Playwright c. 496 B.C.E.

Tolstoy, Leo
Novelist, Dramatist, and Short Story Writer 1828–1910

Williams, Tennessee
Playwright 1911–1983

Yeats, William Butler
Poet and Playwright 1865–1939

Zeami Motokiyo
Founder of Noh Drama 1363–1443

Visual Arts

Alberti, Leon Battista
Architect, Sculptor, and Theoretician 1404–1472

Anguissola, Sofonisba
Painter c. 1535–1625

Arbus, Diane
Photographer 1923–1971

Basquiat, Jean-Michel
Painter and Graffiti Artist 1960–1988

Bernini, Gian Lorenzo
Sculptor, Architect, and Painter 1598–1680

Bosch, Hieronymus
Painter 1453–1517

Botticelli, Sandro
Painter 1445–1510

Bourke-White, Margaret
Photojournalist 1904–1971

Caravaggio
Painter 1571–1610

Cassatt, Mary
Painter and Printmaker 1844–1926

Cézanne, Paul
Painter 1839–1906

Dalí, Salvador
Artist 1904–1989

Degas, Edgar
Painter 1834–1917

Duchamp, Marcel
Artist 1887–1968

Dürer, Albrecht
Painter, Printmaker, and Theoretician 1471–1528

Eakins, Thomas
Painter and Photographer 1844–1916

Gentileschi, Artemisia
Painter 1593–1652

Giotto
Painter c. 1267–1337

Goya, Francisco
Painter 1746–1828

Guo Xi
Painter and Theoretician c. 1000–c. 1090

Hiroshige
Printmaker 1797–1858

Homer, Winslow
Painter, Printmaker, and Illustrator 1836–1910

Kahlo, Frida
Painter 1907–1954

Kōetsu
Calligrapher and Potter 1558–1637

Lawrence, Jacob
Painter 1917–2000

Leonardo da Vinci
Painter, Sculptor, and Scientist 1452–1519

Lin, Maya
    Sculptor and Architect   1959–

Manet, Edouard
    Painter and Printmaker   1832–1883

Matisse, Henri
    Painter and Sculptor   1869–1954

Michelangelo
    Sculptor, Painter, Architect, and Poet   1475–1567

Mies van der Rohe, Ludwig
    Architect and Educator   1886–1969

Modersohn-Becker, Paula
    Painter   1876–1907

Mondrian, Piet
    Painter and Theorist   1872–1944

Monet, Claude
    Painter   1840–1926

Moore, Henri
    Sculptor   1898–1986

Nadar
    Caricaturist and Photographer   1820–1910

Ni Zan
    Painter and Scholar   1301–1374

O'Keeffe, Georgia
    Painter   1887–1986

Paik, Nam June
    Musician, Sculptor, and Performance and Video Artist   1932–

Palladio
    Architect and Theoretician   1508–1580

Picasso, Pablo
    Painter and Sculptor   1881–1973

Pollock, Jackson
    Painter   1912–1956

Raphael
    Painter, Architect, and Administrator   1438–1520

Rauschenberg, Robert
    Painter and Multimedia Artist   1925–

Rembrandt
    Painter and Printmaker   1606–1669

Renoir, Pierre-Auguste
    Painter   1841–1919

Ringgold, Faith
    Painter, Quiltmaker, Teacher, and Writer   1930–

Rivera, Diego
    Painter   1886–1957

Rockwell, Norman
    Illustrator   1894–1978

Rodin, Auguste
    Sculptor   1840–1917

Rubens, Peter Paul
    Painter and Diplomat   1577–1640

Sesshū
    Painter and Calligrapher   1420–1506

Shen Zhou
    Painter and Scholar   1427–1509

Tanner, Henry Ossawa
    Painter   1859–1937

Titian
    Painter   c. 1490–1576

Van Eyck, Jan
    Painter and Manuscript Illuminator   c. 1370/90–1441

Van Gogh, Vincent
    Painter   1853–1890

Velázquez, Diego
    Painter and Courtier   1599–1660

Warhol, Andy
    Painter, Printmaker, and Filmmaker   1928–1987

Wright, Frank Lloyd
    Architect, Designer, Educator   1867–1959

Bibliography

VISUAL ART

Art Reference Books

Chipp, Herschel B. *Theories of Modern Art: A Sourcebook by Artists and Critics.* Berkeley: University of California Press, 1984.

Encyclopedia of World Art. 16 vols. New York: McGraw-Hill, 1972–83.

Hall, James. *Dictionary of Subjects and Symbols in Art.* Rev. ed. New York: Harper & Row, 1979.

Holt, Elizabeth Gilmore. *A Documentary History of Art.* 3 vols. Princeton, N.J.: Princeton University Press, 1986.

Jones, Lois Swan. *Art Information. Research Methods and Resources.* Dubuque, Iowa: Kendall/Hunt Publishing, 1990.

———. *Art Information and the Internet: How To Find It, How To Use It.* Phoenix, Ariz: Oryx Press, 1999.

Turner, Jane, ed. *Dictionary of Art.* 34 vols. New York: Grove's Dictionaries, 1996.

General Art History Surveys

Chadwick, Witney. *Women, Art, and Society.* 2d ed. New York: Thames and Hudson, 1997.

Janson, H. W. *History of Art.* 5th ed. Revised and expanded by Anthony F. Janson. New York: Harry N. Abrams, 1997.

Kostof, Spiro. *A History of Architecture: Settings and Rituals.* 2d ed. New York: Oxford University Press, 1995.

McEnroe, John C., and Deborah F. Pokinski, eds. *Critical Perspectives on Art History.* Upper Saddle River, N.J.: Prentice Hall, forthcoming.

Stokstad, Marilyn. *Art History.* Rev. ed. New York: Harry N. Abrams, 1999.

Trachtenberg, Marvin, and Isabelle Hyman. *Architecture, from Prehistory to Postmodernism.* New York: Harry N. Abrams, 1986.

Wilkins, David G., Bernard Schultz, and Katheryn M. Linduff. *Art Past/Art Present.* 4th ed. Upper Saddle River, N.J.: Prentice Hall, 2000.

Asian Art

Brend, Barbara. *Islamic Art.* Cambridge, Mass.: Harvard University Press, 1991.

Collon, Dominique. *Ancient Near Eastern Art.* Berkeley: University of California Press, 1995.

Craven, Roy. *Indian Art: A Concise History.* New York: Thames and Hudson, 1997.

Fisher, Robert E. *Buddhist Art and Architecture.* New York: Thames and Hudson, 1993.

Lee, Sherman E. *A History of Far Eastern Art.* 5th ed. New York: Harry N. Abrams, 1994.

Mason, Penelope. *History of Japanese Art.* New York: Harry N. Abrams, 1993.

African Art

Eyo, Ekpo, and Frank Willett. *Treasures of Ancient Nigeria.* New York: Knopf, 1980.

Sieber, Roy, and Roslyn Adele Walker. *African Art in the Cycle of Life.* Washington, D.C.: National Museum of African Art, Smithsonian Institution, 1987.

Smith, W. Stevenson. *The Art and Architecture of Ancient Egypt.* Rev. ed. New Haven, Conn.: Yale University Press, 1998.

Vogel, Susan. *Africa Explores: Twentieth Century African Art.* New York: Center for African Art, 1991.

Willett, Frank. *African Art: An Introduction.* Rev. ed. New York: Thames and Hudson, 1993.

American Art

Baigell, Matthew. *A Concise History of American Painting and Sculpture.* New York: Icon Editions, 1996.

Bjelajac, David. *American Art: A Cultural History.* New York: Harry N. Abrams, 2001.

Craven, Wayne. *American Art: History and Culture.* New York: Harry N. Abrams, 1994.

Lewis, Samella. *African American Art and Artists.* 2d ed. Berkeley: University of California Press, 1990.

Ancient Art

Boardman, John, ed. *The Oxford History of Classical Art.* Oxford: Oxford University Press, 1997.

Preziosi, Donald, and Louise A. Hitchcock. *Aegean Art and Architecture.* Oxford: Oxford University Press, 1999.

Ramage, Nancy H., and Andrew Ramage. *Roman Art: Romulus to Constantine.* 2d ed. Englewood Cliffs, N.J.: Prentice Hall, 1996.

Spivey, Nigel. *Understanding Greek Sculpture: Ancient Meanings, Modern Readings.* New York: Thames and Hudson, 1996.

Medieval Art

Camille, Michael. *Image on the Edge: The Margins of Medieval Art.* Cambridge, Mass.: Harvard University Press, 1992.

Rodley, Lyn. *Byzantine Art and Architecture.* Cambridge: Cambridge University Press, 1994.

Snyder, James. *Medieval Art: Painting, Sculpture, Architecture.* New York: Harry N. Abrams, 1989.

Stokstad, Marilyn. *Medieval Art.* New York: Harper & Row, 1986.

Renaissance Art

Hartt, Frederick. *History of Italian Renaissance Art: Painting, Sculpture, and Architecture.* 4th ed. New York: Harry N. Abrams, 1994.

Paoletti, John T., and Gary M. Radke. *Art in Renaissance Italy.* Upper Saddle River, N.J.: Prentice Hall, 1997.

Snyder, James. *Northern Renaissance Art: Painting, Sculpture and the Graphic Arts from 1350 to 1575.* New York: Harry N. Abrams, 1985.

Tinagli, Paola. *Women in Italian Renaissance Art.* Manchester and New York: Manchester University Press, 1997.

Baroque Art

Brown, Jonathan. *The Golden Age of Painting in Spain.* New Haven, Conn.: Yale University Press, 1991.

Haak, Bob. *The Golden Age: Dutch Painters of the Seventeenth Century.* Translated and edited by Elizabeth Willems Treeman. New York: Harry N. Abrams, 1984.

Levey, Michael. *Painting and Sculpture in France, 1700–1789.* New Haven, Conn.: Yale University Press, 1993.

Wittkower, Rudolf. *Art and Architecture in Italy, 1600–1750.* 5th ed. New Haven, Conn.: Yale University Press, 1982.

Nineteenth Century Art

Eisenman, Stephen F. *Nineteenth Century Art: A Critical History.* London: Thames and Hudson, 1994

Eitner, Lorenz. *An Outline of Nineteenth Century European Painting from David to Cezanne.* 2 vols. New York: Harper & Row, 1987.

Herbert, Robert. *Impressionism.* New Haven, Conn.: Yale University Press, 1991.

Rosenblum, Robert, and H. W. Janson. *Nineteenth Century Art.* New York: Harry N. Abrams, 1984.

Twentieth Century Art

Hughes, Robert. *Shock of the New.* Rev. ed. New York: Knopf, 1991.

Hunter, Sam, John Jacobus, and Daniel Wheeler. *Modern Art: Painting, Sculpture, Architecture.* 3d rev. ed. Upper Saddle River, N.J.: Prentice Hall, 2000.

Sandler, Irving. *Art of the Postmodern Era: From the Late 1960s to the Early 1990s.* New York: Icon Editions, 1996.

Wheeler, Daniel. *Art Since Mid-Century: 1945 to Present.* New York: Vendome Press, 1991.

Film and Photography

Fell, John. *Film and the Narrative Tradition.* Norman: University of Oklahoma Press, 1974.

Kaminsky, Stuart M. *American Film Genres.* 2d ed. Chicago: Nelson-Hall, 1985.

Newhall, Beaumont. *The History of Photography from 1839 to the Present.* Rev. ed. New York: Museum of Modern Art, 1982.

Rosenblum, Naomi. *A World History of Photography.* 3d ed. New York: Abbeville, 1997.

Sontag, Susan. *On Photography.* New York: Farrar, Straus & Giroux, 1977.

Szarkowski, John. *Photography until Now.* New York: Museum of Modern Art, 1989.

MUSIC

Music Reference Books

Arnold, Denis. *The New Oxford Companion to Music.* Oxford and New York: Oxford University Press, 1983.

Clarke, Donald, ed. *The Penguin Encyclopedia of Popular Music.* 2d ed. London and New York: Penguin, 1998.

Nectoux, Jean M., et al. *The New Grove Twentieth-Century Masters.* New York: Norton, 1986.

Randel, Don Michael. *The Harvard Biographical Dictionary of Music.* Cambridge, Mass.: Belknap Press of Harvard University Press, 1996.

Sadie, Stanley, and John Tyrrell, eds. *The New Grove Dictionary of Music and Musicians.* New York: Grove's Dictionaries, 2001.

Western Classical Music

Atlas, Allan W. *Renaissance Music: Music in Western Europe, 1400–1600.* New York: Norton, 1998.

Austin, William W. *Music in the 20th Century, from Debussy through Stravinsky.* New York: W. W. Norton, 1966.

Grout, Donald Jay, and Claude V. Palisca. *A History of Western Music.* 5th ed. New York: W. W. Norton, 1996.

Mertens, Wim. *American Minimal Music: La Monte Young, Terry Riley, Steve Reich, Philip Glass.* New York: A. Broude, 1983.

Nectoux, Jean M., et al. *The New Grove Twentieth-Century Masters.* New York: W. W. Norton, 1986.

Rosen, Charles. *The Classical Style: Haydn, Mozart, Beethoven.* New York: W. W. Norton, 1997.

———. *The Romantic Generation.* Cambridge, Mass.: Harvard University Press, 1995.

Sadie, Stanley, ed. *The New Grove Dictionary of Opera.* New York: Grove's Dictionaries, 1992.

Schulenberg, David. *Music of the Baroque.* New York: Oxford University Press, 2001.

Strunk, W. Oliver. *Source Readings in Music History.* Rev. ed. New York: W. W. Norton, 1998.

Jazz and Blues

Davis, Francis. *The History of the Blues.* New York: Hyperion, 1995.

Guralnick, Peter. *Sweet Soul Music: Rhythm and Blues and the Southern Dream of Freedom.* Boston: Little, Brown, 1999.

Harris, Michael W. *The Rise of Gospel Blues: The Music of Thomas Andrew Dorsey in the Urban Church.* New York: Oxford University Press, 1992.

Harrison, Daphne Duval. *Black Pearls: Blues Queens of the 1920s.* New Brunswick, N.J.: Rutgers University Press, 1990.

Heilbut, Anthony. *The Gospel Sound: Good News and Bad Times.* 5th ed. New York: Limelight Editions, 1997.

Kernfeld, Barry, ed. *The New Grove Dictionary of Jazz.* New York: St. Martin's Press, 1994.

Kirchner, Bill, ed. *The Oxford Companion to Jazz.* Oxford and New York: Oxford University Press, 2000.

Oliver, Paul, Max Harrison, and William Bolcom. *The New Grove Gospel, Blues, and Jazz, with Spirituals and Ragtime.* New York: W. W. Norton, 1986.

Ward, Geoffrey C. *Jazz: A History of America's Music.* New York: Knopf, 2000.

Country & Western

Bufwack, Mary A. *Finding Her Voice: The Illustrated History of Women in Country Music.* New York: Henry Holt, 1995.

Encyclopedia of Country Music. New York: Oxford University Press. 1998.

Feiler, Bruce S. *Dreaming Out Loud: Garth Brooks, Wynonna Judd, Wade Hayes, and the Changing Face of Nashville.* New York: Avon Books, 1998.

Kingsbury, Paul. *The Grand Ole Opry History of Country Music: 70 Years of the Songs, the Stars, and the Stories.* New York: Villard Books, 1995.

Kingsbury, Paul, et al., eds. *The Encyclopedia of Country Music: The Ultimate Guide to the Music.* New York: Oxford University Press, 1998.

Oermann, Robert K. *A Century of Country: An Illustrated History of Country Music.* New York: TV Books, 1999.

Stambler, Irwin. *Country Music: The Encyclopedia.* 3d ed. New York: St. Martin's Press, 1997.

Rock, Pop, and Folk

Clarke, Donald, ed. *Penguin Encyclopedia of Popular Music.* New York: Penguin, 1998.

McKeen, William, ed. *Rock and Roll Is Here To Stay: An Anthology.* New York: W. W. Norton, 2000.

Romanowski, Patricia, Holly George-Warren, and Jon Pareles, eds. *The New Rolling Stone Encyclopedia of Rock and Roll.* Rev. ed. New York: Fireside, 1995.

Stambler, Irwin. *Folk and Blues: The Encyclopedia.* New York: St. Martin's Press, 2001.

Ward, Ed, Geoffrey Stokes, and Ken Tucker. *Rock of Ages: The Rolling Stone History of Rock & Roll.* New York: Rolling Stone Press, 1986.

World Music

Broughton, Simon, Mark Ellingham, David Muddyman, and Richard Trillo, eds. *World Music: The Rough Guide.* New York: Penguin, 1999.

Curtis, P. J. *Notes from the Heart: A Celebration of Irish Traditional Music.* Dublin: Torc, 1994.

Danielson, Virginia Louise. *"The Voice of Egypt": Umm Kalthum, Arabic Song, and Egyptian Society in the Twentieth Century.* Chicago: University of Chicago Press, 1997.

Garland Encyclopedia of World Music. Bruno Nettl and Ruth M. Stone, advisory eds.; James Porter and Timothy Rice, founding eds. New York: Garland, 1998.

Gwangwa, Jonas, and E. John Miller, Jr., eds., and Miriam Makeba, comp. *The World of African Song.* Chicago: Quadrangle Books, 1971.

Jackson, William. *Tyagaraja and the Renewal of Tradition.* Delhi: Motilal Banarsidass Publishers, 1994.

McGowan, Chris, and Ricardo Pessanha. *The Brazilian Sound: Samba, Bossa Nova, and the Popular Music of Brazil.* Philadelphia: Temple University Press, 1998.

Muñoz, Isabel. *Tango.* New York: Stewart, Tabori, and Chang, 1997.

Qureshi, Regula. *Sufi Music of India and Pakistan: Sound, Context and Meaning in Qawwali.* Chicago: University of Chicago Press, 1995.

Schnabel, Tom. *Rhythm Planet: The Great World Music Makers.* New York: Universe Publishing, 1998.

Titon, Jeff Todd, ed. *Worlds of Music: An Introduction to the Music of the World's Peoples,* 3d ed. New York: Schirmer Books, 1996.

Dance

Anderson, Jack. *Art Without Boundaries: The World of Modern Dance.* Iowa City: University of Iowa Press, 1997.

Au, Susan. *Ballet and Modern Dance.* New York: Thames and Hudson, 1988.

Cohen, Selma Jeanne. *Dance As a Theatre Art: Source Readings in Dance History from 1581 to the Present.* 2d ed, revised by Kathy Matheson. Princeton, N.J.: Princeton Book Co., 1992.

Cunningham, Merce, et al., eds. *Art Performs Life: Merce Cunningham, Meredith Monk, Bill T. Jones.* Minneapolis, Minn.: Walker Arts Center; New York: Distributed Art Publishers, 1998.

Greskovic, Robert. *Ballet 101: A Complete Guide to Learning and Loving the Ballet.* New York: Hyperion, 1998.

Highwater, Jamake. *Dance: Rituals of Experience.* 3d ed. New York: Oxford University Press, 1996.

LITERATURE

Literature Reference Books

Altick, Richard D., and John J. Fenstermaker. *The Art of Literary Research.* 4th ed. New York: W. W. Norton, 1993.

Baker, Nancy L., and Nancy Huling. *A Research Guide for Undergraduate Students: English and American Literature.* 5th ed. New York: Modern Language Association of America, 2000.

Finnegan, Ruth. *Oral Traditions and the Verbal Arts: A Guide to Research Practices.* New York: Routledge, 1992.

Harner, James L. *Literary Research Guide: An Annotated Listing of Reference Sources in English Literary Studies and Related Topics.* 3d ed. New York: Modern Language Association of America, 1998.

Magill, Frank N., and A. J. Sobczak, eds. *Cyclopedia of Literary Characters.* Rev. ed. Pasadena, Calif.: Salem Press, 1998.

MLA International Bibliography of Books and Articles on the Modern Languages and Literatures. New York: Modern Language Association, 1921–.

Comparative Literature

Bassnett, Susan. *Comparative Literature: A Critical Introduction.* Oxford: Blackwell Publishers, 1993.

Brunel, Pierre, ed. *Companion to Literary Myths, Heroes and Archetypes.* London: Routledge, 1992.

Elkhadem, Saad. *The York Companion to Themes and Motifs of World Literature: Mythology, History and Folklore.* Fredericton, Neb.: York Press, 1981.

Guillén, Claudio. *The Challenge of Comparative Literature.* Cambridge, Mass.: Harvard University Press, 1993.

Kirby, John T., ed. *The Comparative Reader: A Handlist of Basic Reading in Comparative Literature.* New Haven, Conn.: Chancery Press, 1998.

Thompson, George A., Jr. *Key Sources in Comparative and World Literature: An Annotated Guide to Reference Materials.* New York: Ungar, 1982.

Literary Theory and Critical Methods

Abrams, M. H. *A Glossary of Literary Terms.* 7th ed. Fort Worth, Tex.: Harcourt Brace College Publishers, 1999.

Baker, Mona, ed. *Routledge Encyclopedia of Translation Studies.* New York: Routledge, 1998.

Cambridge History of Literary Criticism. 9 vols. New York: Cambridge University Press, 1989–.

Eagleton, Terry. *Literary Theory: An Introduction.* Minneapolis: University of Minnesota Press, 1983.

Groden, Michael, and Martin Kreiswirth, eds. *Johns Hopkins Guide to Literary Theory and Criticism.* Baltimore, Md.: Johns Hopkins University Press, 1994.

Harmon, William, and C. Hugh Holman. *A Handbook to Literature.* 8th ed. Upper Saddle River, N.J.: Prentice Hall, 2000.

Harris, Wendell V., and Glenda A. Hudson. *Dictionary of Concepts in Literary Criticism and Theory.* New York: Greenwood Press, 1992.

Hawthorn, Jeremy. *A Concise Glossary of Contemporary Literary Theory.* New York: Oxford University Press, 1998.

Makaryk, Irene R., ed. *Encyclopedia of Contemporary Literary Theory: Approaches, Scholars, Terms.* Toronto: University of Toronto, 1993.

Ong, Walter J. *Orality and Literacy: The Technologizing of the Word.* London: Methuen, 1982.

Selden, Raman, Peter Widdowson, and Peter Brooker. *A Reader's Guide to Contemporary Literary Criticism.* 4th ed. London and New York: Prentice Hall/Harvester Wheatsheaf, 1997.

Wellek, René, and Austin Warren. *Theory of Literature.* 3d. ed. New York: Harcourt, Brace & World, 1964.

Narrative

Booth, Wayne C. *The Rhetoric of Fiction.* 2nd ed. Chicago: University of Chicago Press, 1983.

Magill, Frank N., ed. *Critical Survey of Long Fiction: English Language Series.* 8 vols. Englewood Cliffs, N.J.: Salem Press, 1983.

———. *Critical Survey of Long Fiction: Foreign Language Series.* 5 vols. Englewood Cliffs, N.J.: Salem Press, 1984.

———. *Critical Survey of Long Fiction: Supplement.* Englewood Cliffs, N.J.: Salem Press, 1984.

———. *Critical Survey of Short Fiction.* Rev. ed. 7 vols. Pasedena, Calif.: Salem Press, 1993.

Ousby. Ian. *Cambridge Guide to Fiction in English.* New York: Cambridge University Press, 1998.

Scholes, Robert, and Robert Kellogg. *The Nature of Narrative.* New York: Oxford University Press, 1966.

Seymour-Smith, Martin, ed. *Novels and Novelists: A Guide to the World of Fiction.* London: Windward, 1980.

Poetry

Brogan, T. V. F. *Verseform: A Comparative Bibliography.* Baltimore, Md.: Johns Hopkins University Press, 1989.

Hoffman, Herbert H. *Hoffman's Index to Poetry: European and Latin American Poetry in Anthologies.* Metuchen, N.J.: Scarecrow, 1985.

Lennard, John. *The Poetry Handbook: A Guide to Reading Poetry for Pleasure and Practical Criticism.* New York: Oxford University Press, 1996.

Magill, Frank N., ed. *Critical Survey of Poetry: English Language Series.* 2d rev. ed. 8 vols. Pasadena, Calif.: Salem Press, 1992.

———. *Critical Survey of Poetry: Foreign Language Series.* 5 vols. Englewood Cliffs, N.J.: Salem Press, 1984.

———. *Critical Survey of Poetry: Supplement.* Englewood Cliffs, N.J.: Salem Press, 1987.

Preminger, Alex, and V. T. F. Brogan, eds. *The New Princeton Encyclopedia of Poetry and Poetics.* Rev. ed. Princeton, N.J.: Princeton University Press, 1993.

Theater

Banham, Martin, ed. *The Cambridge Guide to Theatre.* Rev. ed. New York: Cambridge University Press, 1995.

Gassner, John, and Edward Quinn, eds. *The Reader's Encyclopedia of World Drama.* New York: Crowell, 1969.

Hawkins-Dady, Mark, ed. *International Dictionary of Theater.* 3 vols. Chicago: St. James Press, 1992–95.

Hochman, Stanley, ed. *McGraw-Hill Encyclopedia of World Drama.* 2d ed. 5 vols. New York: McGraw-Hill, 1984.

Magill, Frank N., ed. *Critical Survey of Drama.* Rev. ed. Pasadena, Calif.: Salem Press, 1994.

Pavis, Patrice, ed. *Dictionary of the Theatre: Terms, Concepts, and Analysis.* Toronto: University of Toronto Press, 1998.

Shipley, Joseph T. *The Crown Guide to the World's Great Plays: From Ancient Greece to Modern Times.* Rev. ed. New York: Crown Publishers, 1984.

World Literature

Benson, Eugene, and L. W. Conolly, eds. *Encyclopedia of Post-Colonial Literatures in English.* New York: Routledge, 1994.

Buchanan-Brown, J., ed. *Cassell's Encyclopedia of World Literature.* 3 vols. New York: William Morrow, 1973.

Chevalier, Tracy, ed. *Contemporary World Writers.* 2d ed. Detroit, Mich.: St. James Press, 1993.

Goring, Rosemary, ed.. *Larousse Dictionary of Writers.* Edinburgh: Larousse, 1994.

Henderson, Lesley, ed. *Reference Guide to World Literature.* 2d ed. London: St. James Press, 1995.

Klein, Leonard S., ed. *Encyclopedia of World Literature in the 20th Century.* Rev. ed. 5 vols. New York: Ungar, 1981–84.

Magill, Frank N., ed. *Cyclopedia of World Authors.* 3d ed. 5 vols. Englewood Cliffs, N.J.: Salem Press, 1997.

Ousby, Ian. *The Cambridge Guide to Literature in English.* Rev. ed. New York: Cambridge University Press, 1993.

Parks, George B., and Ruth Z. Temple, eds. *The Literatures of the World in English Translation: A Bibliography.* 4 vols. New York: Ungar, 1967–70.

African Literatures

Belcher, Stephen. *Epic Traditions of Africa.* Bloomington: Indiana University Press, 1999.

Cox, C. Brian, ed. *African Writers.* 2 vols. New York: Scribner's, 1997.

Gérard, Albert S., ed. *European-Language Writing in Sub-Saharan Africa.* Budapest: Akadémiai Kiadó, 1986.

Ibnlfassi, Laïla, and Nicki Hitchcott, eds. *African Francophone Writing: A Critical Introduction.* Oxford: Berg, 1996.

Limb, Peter, and Jean-Marie Volet. *Bibliography of African Literatures.* Lanham, Md.: Scarecrow Press, 1996.

Moser, Gerald, and Manuel Ferreira, eds. *A New Bibliography of the Lusophone Literatures of Africa.* 2d ed. London: H. Zell, 1993.

Okpewho, Isidore. *African Oral Literature: Backgrounds, Character, and Continuity.* Bloomington: Indiana University Press, 1992.

Owomoyela, Oyekan, ed. *A History of Twentieth-Century African Literatures.* Lincoln: University of Nebraska Press, 1993.

Parekh, Pushpa Naidu, and Siga Fatima, eds. *Postcolonial African Writers: A Bio-Bibliographical Critical Sourcebook.* Westport, Conn.: Greenwood Press, 1998.

Literatures of the Americas

Dance, Darkly Camber, ed. *Fifty Caribbean Writers: A Bio-Bibliographical Critical Sourcebook.* New York: Greenwood Press, 1986.

Flores, Angel. *Spanish American Authors: The Twentieth Century.* New York: Wilson, 1992.

Foster, David William, comp. *Handbook of Latin American Literature.* New York: Garland, 1992.

Hart, James D. *The Oxford Companion to American Literature.* 6th ed. New York: Oxford, 1995.

Hart, Stephen M. *A Companion to Spanish-American Literature.* Rochester, N.Y.: Tamesis, 1999.

Herzberg, Max J. *The Reader's Encyclopedia of American Literature.* New York: Crowell, 1962.

Perkins, George, Barbara Perkins, and Phillip Leininger, eds. *Benét's Reader's Encyclopedia of American Literature.* New York: HarperCollins, 1991.

Rela, Walter. *A Bibliographical Guide to Spanish American Literature: Twentieth-Century Sources.* New York: Greenwood Press, 1988.

Salzman, Jack. *The Cambridge Handbook of American Literature.* New York: Cambridge, 1986

Smith, Verity, ed. *Encyclopedia of Latin American Literature.* Chicago: Fitzroy Dearborn, 1997.

Spiller, Robert E., ed. *Literary History of the United States.* 4th ed. 2 vols. New York: Macmillan, 1974.

Unger, Leonard, ed. *American Writers: A Collection of Literary Biographies.* 10 vols. New York: Scribner's, 1974–.

Asian Literatures

Allen, Roger, comp. and ed. *Modern Arabic Literature.* New York: Ungar, 1987.

Datta, Amaresh, ed. *Encyclopaedia of Indian Literature.* 6 vols. New Delhi: Sahitya Akademi, 1987–94.

Idema, Wilt, and Lloyd Haft. *A Guide to Chinese Literature.* Ann Arbor: Center for Chinese Studies, University of Michigan, 1997.

Lang, David M., ed. *A Guide to Eastern Literatures.* New York: Praeger, 1971.

Meisami, Julie Scott, and Paul Starkey, eds. *Encyclopedia of Arabic Literature.* New York: Routledge, 1998.

Miller, Barbara Stoler, ed. *Masterworks of Asian Literature in Comparative Perspective: A Guide for Teaching.* Armonk, N.Y.: M. E. Sharpe, 1994.

Mukherjee, Sujit. *A Dictionary of Indian Literature.* New Delhi: Orient Longman, 1999.

Prusek. Jaroslav, ed. *Dictionary of Oriental Literatures.* 3 vols. New York: Basic, 1974.

Rimer, J. Thomas. *A Reader's Guide to Japanese Literature.* 2d ed. Tokyo: Kodansha International, 1999.

Williams, Mark. *Post-Colonial Literatures in English: Southeast Asia, New Zealand, and the Pacific, 1970–1992.* New York: G. K. Hall, 1996.

European Literatures

Bédé, Jean-Albert, and William B. Edgerton, eds. *Columbia Dictionary of Modern European Literature.* 2d ed. New York: Columbia University Press, 1980.

Bloom, Harold. *The Western Canon: The Books and School of the Ages.* New York: Harcourt Brace, 1994.

Conrad, Peter. *The Everyman History of English Literature.* London: Dent, 1987.

Daemmrich, Horst S., and Ingrid Daemmrich. *Themes and Motifs in Western Literature: A Handbook.* Tübingen, Germany: Francke, 1987.

Drabble, Margaret, ed. *The Oxford Companion to English Literature.* 6th ed. New York: Oxford University Press, 2000.

France, Peter, ed. *The New Oxford Companion to Literature in French.* New York: Oxford University Press, 1995.

Garland, Henry, and Mary Garland. *The Oxford Companion to German Literature.* 2d ed. Oxford: Oxford University Press, 1986.

Harvey, Paul, ed. *The Oxford Companion to Classical Literature.* New York: Oxford University Press, 1984.

Hollier, Denis, ed. *A New History of French Literature.* Cambridge, Mass.: Harvard University Press, 1989.

Jackson, William T. H., and George Stade, eds. *European Writers.* 14 vols. New York: Scribner's, 1983–91.

Kunitz, Stanley J., and Vineta Colby, eds. *European Authors 1000–1900: A Biographical Dictionary of European Literature.* New York: Wilson, 1967.

Lambdin, Robert Thomas, and Laura Crooner Lambdin, eds. *Encyclopedia of Medieval Literature.* Westport, Conn.: Greenwood Press, 2000.

Lord, Robert. *Russian Literature: An Introduction.* 2d ed. London: Kahn and Averill, 1980.

Luce, T. James, ed. *Ancient Writers: Greece and Rome.* 2 vols. New York: Scribner's, 1982.

Pynsent, Robert B. with S. I. Kanikova. *Reader's Encyclopedia of Eastern European Literature.* New York: HarperCollins, 1993.

Stapleton, Michael. *The Cambridge Guide to English Literature.* New York: Cambridge University Press, 1983.

Terras, Viktor, ed. *Handbook of Russian Literature.* New Haven, Conn.: Yale University Press, 1985.

Vinson, James, ed. *Great Writers of the English Language.* 3 vols. New York: St. Martin's Press, 1979.

Ward, Philip, ed. *The Oxford Companion to Spanish Literature.* New York: Oxford University Press, 1978.

Watson, George, ed. *The New Cambridge Bibliography of English Literature.* 5 vols. London: Cambridge University Press, 1969–77.

Index

Note: Page numbers in **boldface** indicate subjects of articles.

feminist movement (*continued*)
  "first of the Americas," 47
  on *Jane Eyre*, 30
  Kahlo reputation and, 101
  Modersohn-Becker's reputation and, 124
  O'Keeffe reputation and, 137
  Woolf's essays, 198
Fernández de Avellaneda, Alonso, 37
Fervor de Buenos Aires (Borges), 24
Festivals (Ovid), 139
Feydeau, Georges, 125
F for Fake (Welles film), 194
Fictions (Borges), 24
Fielding, Henry, 37, 199
Fifty-three Stations of Tokaido (Hiroshige prints), 86
figure drawing, 65
films
  animated, 57
  antiapartheid, 115
  anti-films, 140
  of Austen novels, 11
  auteur theory, 181
  on Caravaggio, 35
  choreography, 13, 178
  Dalí and, 49
  early Hollywood, 81
  experimental, 62
  French New Wave, 181, 194
  gospel music, 93
  of Hugo's works, 91
  Japanese, 107
  on Liszt, 112
  of Lynn autobiography, 114
  Moby Dick versions, 120
  musicals, 20
  on Pollock, 148
  salsa, 46
  on Sor Cruz, 47
  soundtrack scores, 45, 105, 126, 169
  Surrealist, 49
  suspense thrillers, 87
  of Tagore's works, 175
  tango, 146
  on van Gogh, 187
  Warhol experimental, 193
  Welles projects, 194
Finnegans Wake (Joyce), 18, 99
Firebird, The (Stravinsky ballet), 173
Fire Next Time, The (Baldwin), 14
First Dream (Cruz), 47
First Impressions (Austen), 11
Fistful of Dollars, A (film), 107
Fitzgerald, Ella, 46, 95, 171
"Five, The" (Russian composers), 177
Five Mountain Temples (Kyoto), 167
Five O'Clock Tea (Cassatt painting), 36
Five Orchestral Pieces (Schoenberg), 165
Five Tango Sensations (Piazzolla composition), 146
Flag for the Moon: Die Nigger (Ringgold artwork), 159
Flames (group), 31
Flaubert, Gustave, 37, **70**, 100, 131, 174
Fletcher Henderson Orchestra, 10
Fleurs du mal, Les (Baudelaire), 16, 91
Flexible (Basquiat artwork), 16
Flood From the Muses' Springs (Cruz), 47
Florence, Italy, 5, 26, 74, 76, 110, 121, 153
flower pictures (O'Keeffe), 137
Flowers and Birds of the Four Seasons (Sesshū painting), 167
Flowers and Plants of the Four Seasons (calligraphic scroll), 106
Flowers and Trees (Disney film), 57
Flowers of Evil, The (Baudelaire), 17
Fluxus, 140
Flying Dutchman, The (Wagner opera), 192
Fog Warning, The (Homer watercolor), 90
Fokine, Michel, 54

Foley, Red, 58
folk blues, 96
folk culture
  as muralist influence, 160
  Russian literary influence, 152
  Sturm und Drang, 77
  Twain's use of, 184
folk music, 42, 45, 64
  Irish traditional, 126
  Russian influences, 177
  as Stravinsky influence, 173
folk-rock genre, 64, 85
Fontana, Lavinia, 8
Fontana Mix (Cage composition), 33
Ford, Gerald, 8
Forest Moon (Paz), 144
Formentor Prize, 24
Forster, E. M., 198
Fortune (magazine), 27
found object artwork, 60, 154
Fountain (Duchamp artwork), 60
Four Apostles (Dürer painting), 63
Four Books on Architecture, The (Palladio), 142
Four Books on Human Proportion (Dürer), 63
400 Blows, The (Truffaut film), 181
Four Masters (Yuan dynasty), 136, 170
Four-Piece Composition: Reclining Figure (Moore sculpture), 130
Four Sacred Pieces (Verdi composition), 190
4'33" (Cage composition), 33
Four Zoas, The (Blake), 23
France
  anticolonial literature, 38, 62
  auteur theory, 87, 181
  avant-garde, 60, 78, 119
  Caravaggism, 35
  comedic theater, 125
  Existentialism, 32
  Fauves, 39, 119, 187
  Impressionism, 36, 39, 53, 86, 90, 116, 128, 157
  modern music, 52
  New Wave, 181, 194
  nineteenth-century intelligentsia, 134
  Nouveau Roman, 62
  novel, 62, 70, 151
  Orphism, 147
  photography, 134
  poetry, 139, 199
  Post-Impressionism, 39, 124, 128, 147
  Romanticism, 42, 164, 199
  sculpture, 162
  Surrealism, 38, 49, 60, 144
  Symbolist poets, 17, 59, 91
  torch singer, 145
  troubadours, 139
  See also Paris
France, Anatole, 70, 174
Francesca da Rimini (Tchaikovsky composition), 50
Francis I, King of France, 110
Francis Albert Sinatra and Antonio Carlos Jobim (album), 95
Franco, Francisco, 113, 147
Frankenthaler, Helen, 137
Franklin, Aretha, 58, **71**, 93
Franklin, C. L., 71
Franklin Evans (Whitman), 195
Frederick the Great, 12
Freedom from Want (Rockwell illustration), 161
free jazz, 43, 143
Freemasons, 132
free verse, 195, 199
free will, 123
French Impressionists. *See* Impressionism
French Resistance, 18, 62
French Revolution, 23, 32, 55
frescoes, 76

Freud, Sigmund, 49, 59, 172, 198
Frida Kahlo Museum, 101
Frizzell, Lefty, 196
From the Depths I Cried to Thee (Josquin composition), 98
Frontier (Graham dance), 79
Frost, Robert, **72**, 149
Fruits of Enlightenment, The (Tolstoy), 180
Fry, Northrop, 23
Fry, Roger, 198
Fuentes, Carlos, 24, 68, 73
Fugard, Athol, 18
fugues, 12
Fugue, The (Tharp choreography), 178
Fujiwara family, 106, 133
Fujiwara no Nobutaka, 133
Fuller, Jesse, 64
Fuller, Loïe, 61
Funkadelic (group), 31
furniture design, 122, 127, 200
Further Range, A (Frost), 72
Fushi kaden (Zeami), 202
fusion music, 51, 115, 146, 169
Futurism, 60, 147
Fux, Johann Joseph, 141

G

Gabriel, Peter, 69, 105
Gaddi, Taddeo, 76
Galatea, La (Cervantes), 37
Galway, James, 126
Gama, Vasco da, 34
gamelan, 52, 155
Game of Croquet (Homer painting), 90
Gandhi (film), 169
Gandhi, Indira, 175
Gandhi, Mohandas K., 185
García Lorca, Federico. *See* Lorca, Federico García
García Márquez, Gabriel, 24, 68, **73**, 131, 144
Gardel, Calos, 146
Garden of Earthly Delights, The (Bosch painting), 25
Garland, Judy, 145
Gaskell, Elizabeth (Mrs. Gaskell), 30
Gates of Hell, The (Rodin sculpture), 162
Gauguin, Paul, 86, 119, 124, 147, 187
Gay, John, 29, 174
Genealogy of the Master's Descendants (Sogen), 167
General in His Labyrinth, The (García Márquez), 73
Generation of 1927, 113, 135
Genji: A Small Mirror (plot summary), 133
Genji Monogotari (Murasaki), 133
genre painting, 90, 163, 176
Gentileschi, Artemisia, 8, 35, 74
Gentileschi, Domenichino, 35
Gentileschi, Orazio, 74
Geometric Abstraction, 127
George I, King of Great Britain, 83
George IV, king of England, 11
George, Stefan, 50
Georgia, Georgia (Angelou screenplay), 7
Georgia O'Keeffe Museum (Santa Fe), 137
Georgia Tom and Tampa Red (duo), 58
Georgics (Virgil), 191
German culture, 77, 117
German Pavilion (Barcelona Exposition), 121
German Requiem (Brahms), 28
Germany
  age of Goethe, 77
  Bauhaus, 122
  church music, 12
  Expressionism, 32
  French Post-Impressionist art, 124
  literature, 77, 117
  lyric poetry, 158
  music, 12, 19, 28, 83, 192
  radical theater, 29, 32

Renaissance art, 63
Romanticism, 37, 77, 112, 166, 199
Wagnerian opera, 192
See also Nazis
Gérome, Jean-Leon, 65
Gershwin, George, 13, 51, 75, 104, 146
  Jobim comparison, 95
Gershwin, Ira, 75
Gerusalemme liberata (Tasso), 191
Gesamkuntswerk (Wagnerian term), 192
Getz, Stan, 95
Ghafur al-Lari, Abd al-, 94
Ghana, 7, 155
ghazals, 94
Ghent Altarpiece (Van Eyck polyptych), 186
Ghibellines, 50
Ghirlandaio, Domenico, 121
Ghosts (Ibsen), 92
Giacometti, Alberto, 130, 162
Gide, André, 70, 158, 175
"Gift Outright, The" (Frost), 72
Gilberto, Astrud, 95
Gilberto, João, 95
Gilchrist, Alexander, 23
Gilded Age, The (Twain), 184
Gillespie, Dizzy, 95, 143
"Gimme a Pigfoot" (Smith record), 171
Ginsberg, Allen, 23, 33, 195
Giocondo, Francesco del, 110
Giorgione, 116
Giotto, 76, 130
Giovanni's Room (Baldwin), 14
Girl Before a Mirror (Picasso painting), 119
Girl Crazy (Gershwin musical), 75
"Girl from Ipanema, The" (Jobim song), 95
Gitanjali (Tagore), 175
Giulio Cesare (Handel opera), 80
Given: 1 The Waterfall: 2 The Iluminating Glass (Duchamp artwork), 60
"Gladiolus Rag" (Joplin composition), 97
Glass, Philip, 169
Glass Menagerie, The (Williams), 197
Gleizes, Albert, 60
Gleyre, Charles, 128
Globe Theatre, 168
Godard, Jean-Luc, 181
"God Bless America" (Berlin song), 20
"God Bless the Child" (Holiday song), 88
Go Down, Moses (Faulkner), 68
Goethe, Johann Wolfgang von, 77, 117, 172
Gogol, Nikolay, 125, 152
Going to Meet the Man (Baldwin), 14
Gold Eagle Award, 7
Goldsmith, Oliver, 174
Goldwyn Follies, The (film), 13
Golliwog's Cakewalk (Debussy composition), 52
Gonne, Maude, 201
Gonzaga family, 129
Gonzales, Eva, 116
González Videla, Gabriel, 135
Goodman, Benny, 10, 67, 88
Good Woman of Setzuan, The (Brecht), 29
Goofy (Disney character), 57
Gora (Tagore), 175
Gorky, Arshile, 147
Gorky, Maksim, 41, 148
gospel music, 14, 58, 71, 93, 150
Gospel Starlighters, 31
Gossart, Jan, 186
Go Tell It on the Mountain (Baldwin), 14
Gothic International Style, 186
Gothic stories, 30, 197
"Goulante de Pauvre Jean, La" (Piaf song), 145
Gower, John, 139
Goya, Francisco, 37, **78**, 116, 189